Fifth Edition

SUBSTANCE ABUSE COUNSELING

THEORY AND PRACTICE

Patricia Stevens

Adjunct Faculty, Practitioner, and Consultant, Boulder, CO

Robert L. Smith

Professor & Department Chair,
Counseling & Educational Psychology
Texas A&M University, Corpus Christi, TX

PEARSON

Boston Columbus Indianapolis New York San Francisco Upper Saddle River
Amsterdam Cape Town Dubai London Madrid Milan Munich Paris Montreal Toronto
Delhi Mexico City São Paulo Sydney Hong Kong Seoul Singapore Taipei Tokyo

Vice President and Editorial Director: Jeffery W. Johnston
Senior Acquisitions Editor: Meredith D. Fossel
Editorial Assistant: Andrea Hall
Vice President, Director of Marketing: Margaret Waples
Senior Marketing Manager: Christopher Barry
Senior Managing Editor: Pamela D. Bennett
Project Manager: Kerry Rubadue
Senior Operations Supervisor: Matthew Ottenweller
Senior Art Director: Diane Lorenzo

Text Designer: S4Carlisle Publishing Services
Cover Designer: Jayne Conte
Cover Art: Fotalia
Media Project Manager: Rebecca Norsic
Full-Service Project Management: S4Carlisle Publishing Services
Composition: S4Carlisle Publishing Services
Printer/Binder: STP/RRD/Harrisonburg
Cover Printer: STP/RRD/Harrisonburg
Text Font: 10/12 Meridien LT Std Roman

Credits and acknowledgments borrowed from other sources and reproduced, with permission, in this textbook appear on appropriate page within text.

Every effort has been made to provide accurate and current Internet information in this book. However, the Internet and information posted on it are constantly changing, so it is inevitable that some of the Internet addresses listed in this textbook will change.

Library of Congress Cataloging-in-Publication Data
Stevens, Patricia
Substance abuse counseling : theory and practice / Patricia Stevens, Robert L. Smith.—5th ed.
    p. ; cm.
Includes bibliographical references.
ISBN-13: 978-0-13-261564-8
ISBN-10: 0-13-261564-9
I. Smith, Robert L. (Robert Leonard)   II. Title.
    [DNLM: 1. Substance-Related Disorders—therapy.   2. Counseling—methods. WM 270]
LC Classification not assigned
362.29—dc23

                                                                2011047683

10 9 8 7 6 5

PEARSON

ISBN 10:   0-13-261564-9
ISBN 13: 978-0-13-261564-8

Dedication

This book is for all the dedicated students and practitioners who strive to make a difference in the lives of their clients and in the quality of life for all. May they continue to find this text to be helpful for them in their personal journey and in their professional career.

—Patricia Stevens

This text is dedicated to the many brave individuals and family members experiencing problems and challenges related to addictions, and to the many professionals devoted to working and conducting research in the field of addictions.

—Robert Smith

ABOUT THE AUTHORS

Patricia Stevens Ph.D., NCC, CFI, is a retired Counselor Educator. She is currently in private practice in Louisville, Colorado, and consults in a variety of venues. Dr. Stevens has published and presented at the local, state, regional, national, and international level in the areas of substance abuse, gender implications in counseling, training counselors, and ethical and legal issues in counseling. She is a Fulbright Scholar and a Mental Health Disaster Relief volunteer for Red Cross. She has been honored by her professional organizations and by her university for her teaching, scholarship, service, and mentoring of students and staff. Her professional career in substance abuse issues has included clinical practice as well as research and publications.

Robert L. Smith, Ph.D., FPPR, is Professor & Chair of the Counseling and Educational Psychology Department, as well as the Doctoral Program Coordinator at Texas A&M University–Corpus Christi. He completed his Ph.D. at the University of Michigan. As a licensed psychologist, he has worked as a private practitioner in addition to serving as the chair of three counselor education programs. He is the author of several books and more than 80 professional articles. He serves as the Executive Director and co-founder of the International Association of Marriage and Family Counselors. He is also the founder of the National Credentialing Academy for Family Therapists. His research interests include the efficacy of treatment modalities in individual psychotherapy, family therapy, and substance abuse counseling. He is a Diplomate-Fellow in Psychopharmacology with the International College of Prescribing Psychologists and consultant with the Substance Abuse Program in the U. S. Navy. Dr. Smith as an international lecturer is currently involved in the development and implementation of graduate programs in counseling and psychology in Latin America.

Linda L. Chamberlain, Psy.D., is a licensed psychologist and Coordinator of the Center for Addiction and Substance Abuse (CASA) at the Counseling Center for Human Development, the University of South Florida in Tampa, Florida. She has worked in the addictions field since 1980 as both a clinician and educator with a focus on individual and family recovery from substance abuse and the treatment of problem gambling. Dr. Chamberlain coauthored a book on the treatment of problem gambling entitled *Best Possible Odds* and has written numerous articles and contributed to several books on the dynamics and treatment of addictions and family therapy. Dr. Chamberlain has presented workshops and counselor training through the American Counseling Association and the American Psychological Association, and has been an invited speaker at local, national, and international conferences on addictions.

Robert A. Dobmeier, Ph.D., LMHC, CRC is an Assistant Professor of Counselor Education at the College at Brockport, State University of New York. He earned his doctorate in Counselor Education with a concentration in rehabilitation counseling at the University of Buffalo. He has master's degrees in social work and theology, and has practiced as a mental health counselor, supervisor, and administrator. He has worked in New York

State Office of Mental Health and Office of Alcoholism and Substance Abuse Services, licensed agencies in western New York, and has taught in counselor education and education programs at Canisius College and Buffalo State College. Dr. Dobmeier is a Licensed Mental Health Counselor and has been an advocate for recognition of diagnosis in the scope of practice for mental health counselors along with the New York Mental Health Counseling Association. He is a member of the American Counseling Association and five of its divisions and has presented at national, regional, and state conferences. Dr. Dobmeier has conducted research on coexisting disorders and spirituality in the counselor education curriculum and as a resource in counseling; he teaches a course on spirituality in counseling and is interested in the expression of spirituality among diverse groups. He has published on risk factors for mental health problems, including substance abuse, on college campuses. Committed to the unity of the counseling profession, he has participated on research teams investigating counselor educators' views of counseling as a single profession and the need for school counselors in elementary schools.

Cynthia A. Faulkner, Ph.D., LCSW, is Associate Professor of Social Work at Morehead State University in Kentucky. She received her bachelor of science degree in social work from Kansas State University in 1984, a master's in social work from the University of Kansas in 1989, and her PhD from the University of Texas at Arlington in 2001. Dr. Faulkner has practiced social work for over 20 years in multiple settings and is a Licensed Clinical Social Worker in both Kentucky and Texas with an expertise in mental health and substance abuse counseling. Dr. Faulkner's research interests are in substance abuse and institutional abuse. Her book *Research Methods for Social Workers: A Practice-Based Approach* (2009), co-authored with Dr. Samuel Faulkner, is available through Lyceum Books (lyceumbooks.org).

Elda E. Garcia, Ph.D., M.S., LCDC, SWA, is a consultant for Data Analysis, Monitoring, and Evaluation of at-risk programs for the Corpus Christi Independent School District's Office of Research, Testing, and Evaluation and a research assistant at Texas A&M University–Corpus Christi. She is actively involved in counseling at-risk youth for substance abuse agencies across the state. Dr. Garcia is a licensed Chemical Dependency Counselor and a licensed Social Worker Associate. In addition to her work with at-risk youth, she has worked with terminally ill children, adults, women, families, and the elderly. She is well-versed in the areas of criminal justice, residential treatment, and medical social work.

Margaret Sherrill Luther, Ph.D., LPC, LMFT, CCDS, is licensed and certified as a Licensed Professional Counselor, Licensed Marriage and Family Therapist, and Certified Chemical Dependency Specialist in Texas. She is also a Licensed Supervisor for LPC and LMFT. Pitcairn currently has a broad-based practice for individual, family, and couple counseling and has worked as Adjunct and Visiting Assistant Professor in the Department of Counseling and Educational Psychology at Texas A&M University–Corpus Christi. She has many years of professional and clinical experience in private practice, foster care, and program development and implementation in a community nonprofit setting. Pitcairn has published and presents for professional training, as well as general education programs for the community, on a variety of topics associated with mental health, substance abuse, professional development, and life skills acquisition, on local, state, and national levels. Pitcairn completed her Ph.D. in Counselor Education at Texas A&M University–Corpus Christi in May 2006, and her research interests include family interventions; substance abuse and treatment; violence and victimization (including physical abuse/assault, sexual abuse/assault, neglect, domestic violence, and witnessing maltreatment); resilience and prevention; Latino culture; at-risk youth, foster care, and juvenile justice; program development; community and personal supportive resources; and ethics.

Davina A. Moss-King, Ph.D., CRC, NCC, CASAC, is a Certified Rehabilitation Counselor, a National Certified Counselor, and a Credentialed Alcohol and Substance Abuse Counselor in New York State and has 18 years of experience in the area of addiction counseling. Dr. Moss-King is an adjunct professor in the Department of Counseling and Human Services at Canisius College and works full-time as a vocational rehabilitation counselor at the New York State Education Department, the Office of Adult Career and Continuing Educational Services–Vocational Rehabilitation for the past 7 years. She received her master's degree in deafness rehabilitation from New York University in 1998 and her doctorate in counselor education from the State University of New York at Buffalo in 2005. Dr. Moss-King authored a book on heroin recovery, *Unresolved Grief and Loss Issues Related to Heroin Recovery: Grief and Loss with Heroin Recovery*. Her research interest is heroin addiction and she has presented her research on acupuncture and opiate detoxification at the National Acupuncture Detoxification Association Conference and the Society for Acupuncture Research Conference.

John Joseph Peregoy, Ph.D., (Confederated Salish and Kootenai Tribes of Montana) received his doctorate from Syracuse University in 1990. There he studied counselor education with a specialty in multicultural counseling. Dr. Peregoy has taught master's and doctorate-level students for 15 years. He has conducted funded research on resiliency training and family strengthening as protective factors for Native American children against ATOD. He is currently in private practice with Awareness Dynamics in Louisville, Colorado.

Summer M. Reiner, Ph.D., LMHC, NCC, is an assistant professor in the Department of Counselor Education, the College at Brockport, State University of New York in Brockport. She served on the executive board of the Association for Adult Development and Aging (AADA) for eight years, serving in many capacities as president, secretary, and webmaster. After serving as the webmaster of the North Atlantic Region Association for Counselor Education and Supervision (NARACES) for five years, she was elected president (2012–2013). She is a National Certified Counselor, a Licensed Mental Health Counselor in New York, and a permanently certified school counselor in New York. She teaches courses in career, school counseling, practicum, internship, and human development, and provides clinical supervision to students.

Dr. Reiner has authored journal articles on spirituality issues and school counseling issues. In 2010, she received a research grant from the Council for Accreditation of Counseling and Related Educational Programs (CACREP).

Stephen Southern, Ed.D., is Professor and Chair in the Department of Psychology and Counseling at Mississippi College. Dr. Southern previously taught at Texas A & M University–Corpus Christi, University of Southern Mississippi, University of North Texas, and Temple University. During 32 years of professional experience, Dr. Southern integrated roles of clinician, supervisor, consultant, administrator, and educator. As a clinical consultant to several hospitals and residential treatment centers, Southern designed, implemented, and evaluated group treatment programs for individuals and families recovering from addiction. He is a member of the editorial board of the *Journal of Addictions & Offender Counseling* and co-editor of The *Family Journal: Counseling and Therapy for Couples and Families.*

Connie Tait, Ph.D., is Professor and Chair at Central Connecticut State University in the Department of Counseling and Family Therapy. Her responsibilities include coordinating the School Counseling Program, teaching master's level courses, and advising students. Her doctorate, from Syracuse University, is in counselor education with a concentration in multicultural counseling. Dr. Tait's master's degree is also from Syracuse University in secondary school counseling and her bachelor's is from Kent State University in elementary education. Dr. Tait has worked extensively with schools doing consulting, training, research, and coordination of programs. Her research interests are youth in at-risk environments and resiliency.

PREFACE

The fifth edition has been revised to address changing substance abuse problems in our nation and across the globe. The population demographics that counselors work with have shifted as the drugs used and abused have changed. There are drugs available and used regularly today that were unknown when the first edition of this book was published. We continue to have "naturally" manufactured drugs; however, designer drugs—synthetic drugs—are becoming more frequently abused. We see prescription drug use among adolescents skyrocketing. Meth production is at a pandemic level. Ethical, moral, and legal boundaries are being broken as we witness drugs being given to unsuspecting victims who are then often violated. Suffice it to say, the misuse and abuse of drugs worldwide continues to be a significant problem and a multibillion dollar business.

NEW TO THIS EDITION

The authors of this fifth edition have significantly updated its content and references. In some cases, references have been eliminated to provide the reader with the most current citations. Changes have been made to keep text material current and useful to both students and practitioners. Authors have attempted to keep up with changes in substance abuse counseling practices and the settings in which they are performed. Examples of these changes include the use of neuroscience research, and substance abuse rehabilitation and prevention in branches of the military. New cases in each chapter provide the student with critical thinking exercises related to the chapter topic. MyCounselingLab videos and questions have also been added. Other changes include the following:

- Moved coverage of Ethical and Legal issues to Chapter 2, providing guiding principles for students prior to working with clients. Chapter 2 also includes a new section on client criminal activity.
- Chapter 3 has been completely updated and is nearly 100% new.
- Chapter 3 emphasizes the importance and potential use of the latest neuroscience research, including findings from 2010 to the present.
- Chapter 4 includes a new table on Genetic Risks and Protective Factors for ATOD Dependency.
- Chapter 5, in addition to 70% of the references updated, provides greater emphasis on how to prepare clinicians for the assessment process.
- Chapter 6, with 95% of the references changed or updated, places greater emphasis on the Minnesota Model of Treatment and covers treatment settings in the military.
- Chapter 7 has lengthened the sections on Motivational Interviewing and Harm Reduction to provide current information on treatment options.
- Chapter 7 also includes a discussion of the use of medications (suboxone, methadone, buprenorphine, and disulfiram) in treatment.
- Chapter 7 has added Vocational Readiness (prevocational counseling) and its impact on treatment and recovery.

- Chapter 8 includes seminal citations related to group approaches in substance abuse counseling and updated references.
- Chapter 9 includes new information on evidence-based family therapy programs as researched through SAMHSA.
- Chapter 10 includes an expanded section on spirituality.
- Chapter 10 examines findings of outcome studies on the effectiveness of AA and other self-help groups.
- Chapter 10 contains a new section on the growing prevalence of co-occuring substance abuse and mental health disorders.
- Chapter 11 contains updated population demographics and added new treatment protocols with selected populations.
- Chapter 12 has expanded demographics to address the growing minority population and added an examination of health disparities related to substance abuse among minorities.
- Chapter 13 focuses more on the evaluation of prevention programs, including current research and conclusions when critiquing well-known models.
- Chapter 13 presents an expanded emphasis on professional development and training, which has implications for counseling in the future.

In the first edition the stated goal was to develop a text that would be helpful to the general clinician as well as for students enrolled in beginning substance abuse courses. That goal remains the same. This text is to be used as the major resource in substance abuse courses as it provides information specific to the substance abuse field. The text can also be used as an adjunct, not a replacment, for a number of core counseling courses: counseling theory, techniques of counseling, counseling strategies, and school counseling.

As we originally intended, the book is designed to increase ones' knowledge base about alcohol, tobacco, and other drugs (ATOD) and to help professionals more clearly understand the process of working with clients who are misusing or abusing these drugs. The chapters generally build on each other as they take one through the process of understanding substance abuse counseling, both theory and practice. To assist in the development of a skill set with potential clients, the authors have included case studies with critical thinking questions that are utilized across chapters. In addition, the MyCounselingLab˝ videos and exercises provide opportunities to examine and discuss a variety of cases.

We hope that you find the text an enjoyable, informative, and practical read. If so, we have met our goal.

MyCounselingLab™

Help your students bridge the gap between theory and practice with MyCounselingLab˝. MyCounselingLab˝ connects your course content to video- and case-based real-world scenarios, and provides:

- *Building Counseling Skills* Exercises that offer opportunities for students to develop and practice skills critical to their success as professional helpers. Hints and feedback provide scaffolding and reinforce key concepts.

- *Assignments & Activities* assess students' understanding of key concepts and skill development. Suggested responses are available to instructors, making grading easy.
- *Multiple-Choice Quizzes* help students gauge their understanding of important topics and prepare for success on licensure examinations.

Access to MyCounselingLab™ can be packaged with this textbook or purchased stand-alone. To find out how to package student access to this website and gain access as an instructor, go to www.MyCounselingLab.com, email us at counseling@pearson.com, or contact your Pearson sales representative.

ACKNOWLEDGEMENTS

We wish to thank, first and foremost, the professors who choose this text and the students who purchase the book—some of whom have let us know how valuable the book has been for them. We appreciate the time and energy the reviewers invested in the reviews for this edition. Their insightful comments assist us in publishing a better text.

Thanks to Meredith Fossel for her outstanding editorial ability and for keeping us on task. Her support, kindness, and gentle promptings were invaluable. It would not have happened without you, Meredith!

Thanks to Nancy Holstein for always having the answers to the questions we ask! She is indeed a treasure chest of information.

Thanks to Jean Ives for her careful reading of this edition and her always-on-target questions and comments. We continue to owe you so much for your input and time.

We wish to thank our authors. They have all worked diligently to provide a state-of-the-art textbook for training students and clinicians. New contributors have added knowledge and skills to the text and a new perspective that aligns with the changing field. In addition, we thank the reviewers of the fifth edition: John J. Benshoff, Southern Illinois University, Carbondale; Deborah J. Ebener, Florida State University; Cynthia Glidden-Tracey, Arizona State University; Virginia Magnus, University of Tennessee at Chattanooga; and Mark S. Parrish, University of West Georgia.

And, again and again, we are grateful to our family and friends who continue to be supportive each time we revise this text.

BRIEF CONTENTS

CONTENTS

1

Introduction to Substance Abuse Counseling

PATRICIA STEVENS, PH.D.

MyCounselingLab™

Visit the MyCounselingLab™ site for *Substance Abuse Counseling,* Fifth Edition to enhance your understanding of chapter concepts. You'll have the opportunity to practice your skills through video- and case-based Assignments and Activities as well as Building Counseling Skills units, and to prepare for your certification exam with Practice for Certification quizzes.

A*lcohol, tobacco, caffeine, prescription drugs, illegal drugs*—all are commonplace words today. Alcohol, tobacco, and other drugs (ATOD) are used for celebrations, for mourning, for religious rituals, for pain relief, and recreationally. We read about them in the newspaper daily, we hear about them on the radio and television, and we can find just about anything, from what they are to how to make them, about any substance use and abuse on the Internet. We see children abusing at younger ages and elders abusing. Drugs are misused to forget, to feel better or not feel at all, to be friendly, to disinhibit, and because of peer pressure. Tobacco and alcohol, legal drugs, are used and abused with social sanction and are easily available. If we don't use them, we probably have a user/abuser in the family or a close friend who has abused, or know someone who uses alcohol or other drugs inappropriately.

Consequences of use and abuse of legalized substances continue to be minimized in a variety of settings. Until the mid-1990s, the tobacco industry denied addiction while people were dying from lung cancer and others continued to smoke. After multiple suits against the companies, they tried to settle, paying out $10 billion per year in perpetuity and placing in the public domain over 35 million pages of internal documents on the effects of smoking.

In 2009, an estimated 69.7 million Americans aged 12 or older were current (past month) users of a tobacco product. This represents 27.7% of the population in that age range. In addition, 58.7 million persons (23.3% of the population) were current cigarette smokers; 13.3 million (5.3%) smoked cigars; 8.6 million (3.4%) used smokeless tobacco; and 2.1 million (0.8%) smoked tobacco in pipes (Substance Abuse and Mental Health Services Administration [SAMHSA], 2010c).

Slightly more than half of Americans aged 12 or older reported being current drinkers of alcohol in the 2009 SAMHSA survey (51.9%). Nearly one quarter (23.7%) of persons aged 12 or older participated in binge drinking. Heavy drinking was reported by 6.8% of the population aged 12 or older, or 17.1 million people. The rate of current alcohol use among youths aged 12 to 17 was 14.7%. Among persons aged 12 to 20, past month alcohol use rates were 16.1% among Asians, 20.4% among Blacks, 22.0% among American Indians or Alaska Natives, 25.1% among Hispanics, 27.5% among those reporting two or more races, and 30.4% among Whites. An estimated 12.0% of persons aged 12 or older drove under the influence of alcohol at least once in the past year (SAMHSA, 2010d).

Alcohol also plays a significant role in acts of violence. While the exact correlation between alcohol and violence, particularly intimate partner violence, continues to be debated, there are sufficient data to indicate a correlation between heavy drinking and a higher number of domestic violence events whether the perpetrator is actively drinking or dry. According to the survey of violence against women in Canada, for example, women who lived with heavy drinkers were five times more likely to be assaulted by their partners than those who lived with non-drinkers (World Health Organization, 2005).

The research is very clear about the relationship between alcohol and criminal behavior: In 2004, 17% of U.S. state prisoners and 18% of federal inmates said they committed their current offense to obtain money for drugs. Reports state that about 73% of felonies are alcohol related. One survey shows that in about 67% of child-beating cases, 41% of forcible rape cases, 80% of wife-battering, 72% of stabbings, and 83% of homicides, either the attacker or the victim or both had been drinking (SAMHSA, 2010b; Yacoubian, 2003).

Further, an average of one alcohol-impaired-driving fatality occurred every 48 minutes in 2009 (U.S. Department of Transportation, 2009). The United States has spent billions of dollars on ad campaigns combined with drug busts to try to rid the country of both the local seller and the international drug lords who are importing drugs into this country. While some impact may be felt from this combined effort, the use and abuse of both legal and illegal drugs continue to be a considerable crisis in the United States. At any given time in the United States, substance abuse is either directly or indirectly related to emergency room (ER) admissions, psychiatric emergencies, suicide attempts, psychiatric conditions in adolescents, domestic violence cases, homicides, and ischemic stroke in adults. In 2006, hospitals in the United States delivered a total of 113 million emergency room visits. DAWN, the Drug Awareness Warning Network (SAMHSA, 2010a) estimates that 1,742,887 ER visits were associated with drug misuse or abuse.

This estimate included the following statistics:

- 958,164 ER visits involved illicit drugs alone or in combination with other drugs.
- 577,521 ER visits involved the use of alcohol alone or in combination with other drugs.

- 860,108 ER visits were associated with nonmedical use of pharmaceuticals alone or in combination with other drugs.

The analysts found that of the 1.7 million drug abuse visits, about two thirds (66%) were associated with a single drug type. ER visits involving nonmedical use of pharmaceuticals alone accounted for another 28%. About 34% of the visits involved some combination of illicit drugs, alcohol, and/or nonmedical use of pharmaceuticals. No significant changes were shown from the 2008 report (Drug Awareness Warning Network, 2009).

In 2009, an estimated 21.8 million Americans aged 12 or older were current (past month) illicit drug users, meaning they had used an illicit drug during the month prior to the survey interview. This estimate represents 8.7% of the population aged 12 or older. Illicit drugs include marijuana/hashish, cocaine (including crack), heroin, hallucinogens, inhalants, or prescription-type psychotherapeutics used nonmedically.

Marijuana was the most commonly used illicit drug. There were 16.7 million past-month users. There were 1.6 million current cocaine users aged 12 or older, comprising 0.7% of the population. Hallucinogens were used in the past month by 1.3 million persons (0.5%) aged 12 or older in 2009, including 760,000 (0.3%) who had used ecstasy. In 2009, there were 7.0 million (2.8%) persons aged 12 or older who used prescription type psychotherapeutic drugs nonmedically in the past month. Among youths aged 12 to 17, the current illicit drug use rate increased from 2008 (9.3%) to 2009 (10.0%).

From 2002 to 2009, there was an increase among young adults aged 18 to 25 in the rate of current nonmedical use of prescription-type drugs (from 5.5% to 6.3%), driven primarily by an increase in pain reliever misuse (from 4.1% to 4.8%). Among persons aged 12 or older in 2008–2009 who used pain relievers nonmedically in the past 12 months, 55.3% got the drug they most recently used from a friend or relative for free.

These data were collected by the Substance Abuse and Mental Health Services Association, which is part of the Department of Health and Human Services, one of the premier research organizations in the world. And yet, we still must ask questions about research in the field, due to the very nature of the field. For example, how many of the "current users" are abusing their drug of choice? How many of them concern recreational use or no use at all? How many of them are physiologically or psychologically addicted to the drug? How do we define *use, abuse,* and *dependency*? Does this difference in definition lead to problems when comparing data collected? Another problem is an outgrowth of the first: the question of how to collect data. Not only do definitions differ, but substance abuse lends itself to isolation and minimization of the facts about the problem.

These issues leave us without a clear idea of the actual number of recreational users and those with more serious problems. In the United States we have waged a "war on drugs" for over a century. In spite of the billions of dollars spent on these efforts in everything from media campaigns to criminal enforcement in an effort to eliminate drug use, virtually every drug that has ever been discovered is available to recreational chemical users in the United States (Doweiko, 2011). In addition, the authors would note, alcohol and tobacco (legal drugs) are easily accessible in this country no matter your age.

THE HISTORY OF SUBSTANCE: NO WONDER WE USE

Wonder how long humans have been using mind-altering drugs? Did they even realize they were mind altering before we had the technology to ascertain the brain and physiological changes? Or did it just feel good? Humankind has used mind- or mood-altering drugs at least since the beginning of recorded history and maybe before. The use of substances goes back to prehistoric times. Over the centuries, drugs have been used medicinally, religiously, and socially. In tribal societies, mind-altering drugs were commonly used in healing practices and religious ceremonies. Alcohol consumption was recorded as early as the Paleolithic times of the Stone Age culture with the discovery that drinking the juice of fermented berries created a pleasant feeling. Alcohol, cocaine, marijuana, opium, and caffeine have all been used for medical purposes through the years.

An overview of the historical perspective of humankind's use of substances for both analgesic and mind-altering purposes and the multidimensional functions that drugs have played throughout history may provide a context for understanding today's substance abuse issues and ensuing ramifications. History may also provide some rationale for the treatment methods used with substance abusers over the past 50 years.

A perusal of some of the early legends that relate to the discovery of substances as well as the development of other drugs may add a perspective to the current view of drug use in our Western society. A complete history would be impossible to provide here, so we endeavor to provide you with the most entertaining and educational summary of the early use of ATOD.

Alcohol

It has been documented that early cave dwellers drank the juices of mashed berries that had been exposed to airborne yeast. The discovery of late Stone Age beer jugs has established the fact that intentionally fermented beverages existed at least as early as the Neolithic period (ca. 10,000 B.C.). When they found that the juice produced pleasant feelings and reduced discomfort, they began to intentionally produce an alcoholic drink.

Beer was the major beverage among the Babylonians, and as early as 2,700 B.C. they worshipped a wine goddess and other wine deities. Oral tradition recorded in the Old Testament (Genesis 9:20) asserts that Noah planted a vineyard on Mount Ararat in what is now eastern Turkey. In fact, Noah was perhaps the first recorded inebriate. Egyptian records give testimony to beer production. They believed that the god Osiris, who was worshipped throughout the entire country, invented beer, a beverage that was considered a necessity of life and was brewed in the home on a regular basis.

Homer's *Iliad* and *Odyssey* both discuss drinking wine, and Egypt and Rome had gods or goddesses of wine. The first alcoholic beverage to obtain widespread popularity in what is now Greece was mead, a fermented beverage made from honey and water. However, by 1700 B.C., wine making was commonplace, and during the next thousand years, wine drinking assumed the same function so commonly found around the world: It was incorporated into religious rituals, it became important in hospitality, it was used for medicinal purposes, and it became an integral part of daily meals. As a beverage, it was drunk in many ways: warm and chilled, pure and mixed with water, plain and spiced.

A 4,000-year-old Persian legend tells the story of the discovery of wine. A king had vats of grapes stored, some of which developed a sour liquid at the bottom. The king labeled these vats as poison but kept them for future use. One lady of the court was prone to severe headaches that no one could remedy. Her pain was so severe that she decided to kill herself. She knew of the poisoned grape juice, went to the storage area, and drank the poison. Needless to say, the lady didn't die but in fact found relief. Over the next few days, she continued to drink the "poison" and only later confessed to the king that she had been in the vats. In the 10th century, an Arabian physician, Phazes, who was looking to release the "spirit of the wine," discovered the process of distillation.

By the Middle Ages, alcohol was used in ceremonies for births, deaths, marriages, treaty signings, diplomatic exchanges, and religious celebrations. Monasteries offered wine to weary travelers who stopped for rest and safety. In Europe, it was known as the "water of life" and considered the basic medicine for all human ailments. Water pollution is far from new; to the contrary, supplies have generally been either unhealthful or questionable at best. Ancient writers rarely wrote about water, except as a warning. Travelers crossing what is now Zaire in 1648 reported having to drink water that resembled horse's urine. In the late 18th century, most Parisians drank water from a very muddy and often chemically polluted Seine. Certainly we can see why wine was the beverage of choice during this time period.

In addition to being used in rituals and for its convivial effect, alcohol was one of the few chemicals consistently available for physicians to use to induce sleep and reduce pain. Alcohol has been used as an antiseptic, an anesthetic, and in combinations of salves and tonics. As early as A.D. 1000, Italian winegrowers were distilling wine for medicinal purposes.

When European settlers brought alcoholic beverages in the form of wine, rum, and beer to the Americas, native cultures were already producing homegrown alcoholic beverages. The *Mayflower*'s log reports, "We could not take time for further search or consideration, our victuals having been much spent, especially our bere." Spanish missionaries brought grapevines, and the Dutch opened the first distillery in 1640. American settlers tested the strength of their brews by saturating gunpowder with alcohol. If it ignited, it was too strong; if it sputtered, too weak.

A 1790 federal law provided that each soldier receive one-fourth pint of brandy, rum, or whiskey. In the Civil War, army regulations prohibited the purchase of alcohol by enlisted men, and soldiers who violated the rule were punished, but men on both sides found ways around it. Members of a Mississippi company got a half gallon of whiskey past the camp guards by concealing it in a hollowed-out watermelon; they then buried the melon beneath the floor of their tent and drank from it with a long straw. If they could not buy liquor, they made it. One Union recipe called for bark juice, tar water, turpentine, brown sugar, lamp oil, and alcohol.

World War I, which took place primarily in Europe between 1914 and 1918, saw foot soldiers as well as commanders imbibing when in Europe. With the advent of Prohibition (1920–1933), when the U.S. Constitution outlawed the manufacture, transport, and sale of alcoholic beverages, many returning soldiers were none too happy. The Eighteenth Amendment prohibited the sale of alcoholic beverages, but the federal Volstead Act, which became law during the Prohibition era, enforced the amendment.

During this time there was also a strong temperance movement against all alcoholic consumption (Goode, 2007).

During Prohibition, alcohol continued to be made and used (sometimes called bathtub gin because it was made in bathtubs). After Prohibition was repealed, alcohol became legal again, and its use and abuse continues today.

It is of interest to note the remarks of the founding director of the NIAAA: "Alcohol has existed longer than all human memory. It has outlived generations, nations, epochs and ages. It is a part of us, and that is fortunate indeed. For although alcohol will always be the master of some, for most of us it will continue to be the servant of man" (Chafetz, 1965, p. 223).

This brief history provides context of the use of alcoholic beverages throughout time. It is at our peril that we ignore the impact of alcohol on societies throughout history.

Cocaine

Like alcohol, coca has been around for thousands of years. South American Indians have used cocaine as it occurs in the leaves of *Erythroxylon coca* for at least 5,000 years. In traditional Indian cultures, Mama Coca was considered a benevolent deity. She was regarded as a sacred goddess who could bless humans with her power. Before the coca harvest, the harvester would sleep with a woman to ensure Mama Coca would be in a favorable mood. Typically, a decoction of coca and saliva was rubbed onto the male organ to prolong erotic ecstasy. Traditionally, the leaves have been chewed for social, mystical, medicinal, and religious purposes. Coca has even been used to provide a measure of time and distance. Native travelers sometimes described a journey in terms of the number of mouthfuls of coca typically chewed in making the trip.

The active ingredient in cocaine was not isolated until 1860 by Albert Neiman. Cocaine was then added to wine and tonics in the mid-19th century as well as to snuff, and advertised as a cure for asthma and hay fever. Sigmund Freud experimented with cocaine as a cure for depression and digestive disorders, hysteria, and syphilis. He also recommended cocaine to alleviate withdrawal from alcohol and morphine addiction. He and his friends experimented with every method of introducing cocaine into the body. Freud himself used cocaine daily for a considerable period of time.

During this time, the mid- to late-1800s, the medical profession was blissfully ignorant of the addictive qualities of cocaine. So, not surprisingly, by the late 1800s, more than half the scientific and medical community had developed healthy coke habits. One notable example was William Halstead, a founding father of the Johns Hopkins Hospital in Baltimore. As more was learned about cocaine's addiction, these individuals discontinued their own use and also stopped prescribing it to patients to alleviate all types of medical problems. An American named John Stith Pemberton brought out his own version of a European drink that included extract of coca leaves and kola nuts. He advertised this product as an "intellectual beverage" or "brain tonic." This product, later known as Coca-Cola, contained about 60 milligrams of cocaine in an 8-ounce serving. It was only a moderate hit, and after the cocaine and alcohol ingredients were banned in Atlanta, Georgia, Pemberton sold the company to Asa Griggs Candler for a paltry $2,300.

In the 20th century, cocaine grew in popularity as it decreased in cost. However, as people began to see the rise of violence among abusers of the drug in the lower socioeconomic stratum and a rise in the awareness of cocaine's harmful physical effects, anticocaine legislation began. The first federal legislation regarding cocaine was the 1906 Pure Food and Drug Act that required manufacturers to precisely label product contents. In 1914, the U.S. Congress passed the Harrison Narcotics Act, which imposed taxes on products containing cocaine. Soon, drug enforcement officials transformed the law to prohibit all recreational use of cocaine. By the 1930s, synthetic amphetamines were available and began to take the place of the now-illegal cocaine. By the early 1980s, the use of freebase cocaine became popular again among those searching for the "highest" high. Freebase is a form of cocaine produced when the user takes cocaine hydrochloride and mixes it with a liquid base such as baking soda or ammonia to remove the hydrochloric acid and then dissolves the resultant alkaloidal cocaine in a solvent, such as ether, and heats it to evaporate the liquid. The result is pure, smokable cocaine. The conversion process in freebasing was dangerous and time-consuming and was not suitable for mass production. The danger and volatility of the process led to drug dealers developing a more potent, less volatile form of cocaine. This was when crack became the option. In the conversion process of crack, the drug is similarly cooked down to a smokable substance, but the risky process of removing the impurities and hydrochloric acid is taken out. Thus, all that is required is baking soda, water, and a heat source, often a home oven. As this process allowed people essentially to get more bang out of their buck, by delivering the drug more efficiently, cocaine became available to the lower socioeconomic stratum. This development gave rise to the "crack epidemic," and all classes from low to high became affected by the scourge of cocaine use spreading across the United States (Karch, 2005).

Heroin

Heroin, the hydrochloride of diacetylmorphine, was discovered by acetylation of morphine. In pharmacological studies, heroin proved to be more effective than morphine or codeine. The Bayer Company started the production of heroin in 1898 on a commercial scale. The first clinical results were so promising that heroin was considered a wonder drug. Indeed, heroin was more effective than codeine in respiratory diseases. It turned out, however, that repeated administration of heroin resulted in the development of tolerance and the patients soon became heroin addicts. In the early 1910s, morphine addicts "discovered" the euphorizing properties of heroin, and this effect was enhanced by intravenous administration. Heroin became a narcotic drug, and its abuse began to spread quickly. Restrictions on its production, use, and distribution were regulated by international treaties (Fernandez, 2011).

Marijuana

Marijuana (or cannabis) has been used recreationally and medicinally for centuries. The earliest account of its use is in China in 2737 B.C. (Scaros, Westra, & Barone, 1990). In Egypt, in the 20th century B.C., cannabis was used to treat sore eyes. From the 10th century B.C. up to 1945 (and even to the present time), cannabis has been used in India to treat a wide variety of human maladies. In ancient Greece, cannabis was used as a remedy for earache, edema, and inflammation.

   In Europe in the mid-19th century, cannabis was used extensively by members of the French romantic literary movement, and through their writings, American writers became aware of the euphoric effects attributed to the drug. Use of marijuana, medicinally or otherwise, has always been controversial.

In colonial times, hemp, the plant from which marijuana is derived, was an important crop. Our forefathers used it to produce paper, clothing, and rope. It was so important in those early days of America that Virginia introduced legislation in 1762 that exacted penalties on farms that did not produce it. In 1793, the invention of the cotton gin made the separation of cotton fiber from the hull easier and far less expensive than it had been previously. Hemp, however, remained a cash crop until well after the Civil War because of its availability and the ease with which it could be made into clothing. Eventually, the price dropped until it was no longer profitable, and many hemp growers switched to tobacco.

In 1850, the *United States Pharmacopeaia* (*USP*) recognized marijuana (hemp) for its medicinal value. It was used to treat lack of appetite, gout, migraines, pain, hysteria, depression, rheumatism, and many other illnesses. Nothing is mentioned about the "high" that marijuana is famous for in the early reports on the herb, but that omission seems appropriate in contexts where its medicinal aspect is stressed. Dosage problems due to different plant strengths kept it from being continued as a "legitimate" drug, and it has been removed from the *USP*, but adherents still point to marijuana's medicinal value as a major point for legalization.

The continued primary interest in this drug has been for its euphoric effects. In November 1883, *A Hashish-House in New York* by H. H. Kane was published in *Harper's Monthly*. He carefully describes the wonders of the hashish (a cannabis derivative) house and writes a vivid description of his trip to "Hashishdom." He enjoys the experience but is grateful for the sights and sounds of the "normal" world upon exiting the house of dreams.

With the beginning of Prohibition, individual use of marijuana increased in the 1920s as a substitute for alcohol. After Prohibition, its use declined until the 1960s, when it gained significant popularity along with LSD and "speed." It has been used as an analgesic, a hypnotic, an anticonvulsant, and recently an antinausea drug for individuals undergoing chemotherapy for cancer treatment. Advocates of marijuana for medicinal use cite it as a treatment for asthma, depression, drug withdrawal, epilepsy in children, glaucoma, and as an antibiotic.

On October 27, 1970, the Comprehensive Drug Abuse Prevention and Control Act was passed. Part II of this act is the Controlled Substance Act (CSA), which defines a scheduling system for drugs and places most of the known hallucinogens (LSD, psilocybin, psilocin, mescaline, peyote, cannabis) in Schedule I. Through all the years of conflict about whether marijuana was medicinal or not and the history of its medicinal use, in 1988 administrative law judge Francis Young of the Drug Enforcement Agency (DEA) found after thorough hearings that marijuana has clearly established medical use and should be reclassified, as a prescriptive drug (Booth, 2005).

Even in the 16 states (AK, AZ, CA, CO, DE, HI, ME, MI, MT, NV, NJ, NM, OR, RI, VT, WA) and Washington, DC where marijuana has been legalized, the controversy continues about the value of the drug as a viable medication for certain conditions, as well as the financial implications of legalization and abuse of that legalization.

Opioids

Opium is a derivative of the poppy plant, and early humans learned that by splitting the top of the *Papaver somniferum* (poppy) plant, they could extract a thick resin.

Later it was discovered that the dried resin could be swallowed to control pain. By the Neolithic Age, there is evidence that the plant was being cultivated (Doweiko, 2011).

As long ago as 3400 B.C. the opium poppy was cultivated in lower Mesopotamia. The Sumerians refer to it as *Hul Gil*, the "joy plant." Hippocrates, "the father of medicine," in 460 B.C. dismissed the magical attributes of opium but acknowledged its usefulness as a narcotic and styptic in treating internal diseases, diseases of women, and epidemics. In A.D. 129–199, there are reports of opium cakes being sold in the streets of Rome. Ships chartered by Queen Elizabeth I in 1601 were instructed to purchase the finest Indian opium and transport it back to England. In 1729, China found it necessary to outlaw opium smoking because of the increasing number of opium addicts.

Friedrich Sertürner of Paderborn, Germany, made a startling discovery in 1806. He found the active ingredient of opium by dissolving it in acid and then neutralizing it with ammonia. The result: alkaloids—*Principium somniferum,* or morphine. Physicians believe that opium had finally been perfected and tamed. Morphine was lauded as "God's own medicine" for its reliability, long-lasting effects, and safety. Morphine was freely used in the Civil War and in other wars both for pain as well as for dysentery. The resulting addiction was known as "soldier's disease."

When Dr. Alexander Wood of Edinburgh in 1843 discovered a new technique of administering morphine, injection with a syringe, he also found that the effects of morphine on his patients were instantaneous and three times more potent. To add to its success, in 1895, Heinrich Dreser, who worked for the Bayer Company in Elberfeld, Germany, found that diluting morphine with acetyls produces a drug without the common morphine side effects. Bayer began production of diacetylmorphine and coined the name "heroin." Heroin would not be introduced commercially for another three years. So from 1895 until 1914, opium, morphine, and heroin were available without a prescription. However, on December 17, 1914, the Harrison Narcotics Act, which aimed to curb drug abuse (especially of cocaine, as discussed earlier, but also of heroin) and addiction, was passed. It required doctors, pharmacists, and others who prescribed narcotics to register and pay a tax. This one law created a significant change in the use and availability of opioids.

Heroin, illegally available on the street, is usually diluted to a purity of only 2% to 5%, being mixed with baking soda, quinine, milk sugar, or other substances. The unwitting injection of relatively pure heroin is a major cause of heroin overdose, the main symptoms of which are extreme respiratory depression, deepening into coma and then into death. Aside from this danger, heroin addicts are prone to hepatitis and other infections owing to their use of dirty or contaminated syringes. Scarring of the surfaces of the arms or legs is another common injury, because of repeated needle injections and subsequent inflammations of the surface veins.

Another drug, oxycodone, is a semisynthetic opioid agonist derived from thebaine, a constituent of opium. Oxycodone will test positive for an opiate in the available field test kits. Pharmacology of oxycodone is essentially similar to that of morphine in all respects, including its abuse and dependence liabilities. Pharmacological effects include analgesia, euphoria, feelings of relaxation, respiratory depression, constipation, papillary constriction, and cough suppression. Oxycodone abuse has been a continuing problem in the United States since the early 1960s. It is abused either as intact tablets or by crushing or chewing the tablet and then swallowing, snorting, or injecting the drug (Chouvy, 2010).

Amphetamines

Amphetamines were discovered in 1887 and used in World War II by U.S., British, German, and Japanese soldiers for energy, alertness, and stamina. In the late 1920s, they were seriously investigated as a cure or treatment for a variety of illnesses and maladies, including epilepsy, schizophrenia, alcoholism, opiate addiction, migraine, head injuries, and irradiation sickness, among many others.

Amphetamines were also prescribed for depression, weight loss, and heightened capacity for work. Soon it was realized that these capsules could be broken open and their contents injected into the body with a needle, heightening the effect of the drug. Amphetamines also replaced high-priced cocaine. Amphetamine was appealing to cocaine users because the high it produced was much like that of cocaine. Street amphetamine is 5% to 15% pure. The remainder is either a less powerful stimulant, such as caffeine, or inert, such as glucose. Occasionally it is cut with chalk or talcum powder. It will not deliver quite the same peak, but its effects last longer. The current street cost ranges between $12 and $18 per gram, still below the cost of cocaine. More significantly, this form is cheap, readily available, and legal as it is usually made with over-the-counter amphetamines, no prescription necessary.

Methamphetamines, more potent and easy to make, were discovered in Japan in 1919. The crystalline powder was soluble in water, making it a perfect candidate for injection. In Japan, intravenous methamphetamine abuse reached epidemic proportions immediately after World War II, when supplies stored for military use became available to the public.

In the United States in the 1950s, legally manufactured tablets of both dextroamphetamine (Dexedrine) and methamphetamine (Methedrine or meth) became readily available and were used nonmedically by college students, truck drivers, and athletes.

Meth is produced as pills, powders, or chunky crystals called *ice*. The crystal form, nicknamed *crystal meth*, is a popular drug, especially with young adults and those who frequently go out to dance clubs and parties. Swallowed or snorted (also called *bumping*), methamphetamines give the user an intense high. Injections create a quick but strong, intense high, called a *rush* or a *flash*. Methamphetamines, like regular amphetamines, also take away appetite.

Meth labs are becoming an increasing problem across the country—in every type of neighborhood, rich and poor. Meth labs turn up in houses, barns, apartments, trailers, campers, cabins, and motel rooms—even the back of pickups. The equipment for a meth lab can be as small as to fit in a duffel bag, a cardboard box, or the trunk of a car. It is important to be alert about the possibility of a lab near your home, as the fumes from the product are lethal (Harris, 2004; Weisheit & White, 2010).

Hallucinogens

Hallucinogens have been around for about 3,500 years. Central American Indian cultures used hallucinogenic mushrooms in their religious ceremonies. When the New World was discovered, Spanish priests, in an effort to "civilize" the Indians, tried to eliminate the use of the "sacred mushrooms." This continued until the American Indian Religious Freedom Act in 1978 and its amendment in 1994 provided natives with the right to use peyote in religious services.

In 1938, the active ingredient that caused hallucinations was isolated for the first time by a Swiss chemist, Albert Hofman. He was studying a particular fungus in bread that appeared to create hallucinations. The substance he synthesized during this research was LSD (lysergic acid diethylamide). Between 1950 and the mid-1970s, LSD was well researched by the U.S. government in the hope that it could be used to understand the psychotic mind and to view the subconscious. LSD was used in the treatment of alcoholism, cancer, and schizophrenia. It was also one of the drugs of choice during the drug epidemic that began in the 1960s.

One of the newer hallucinogens is a drug called MDMA (methylenedioxymethamphetamine). MDMA, or ecstasy, was first synthesized in 1912. It was patented in Germany by the Merck Company in 1914 after Merck stumbled across MDMA when trying to synthesize another drug. MDMA was an unplanned by-product of this synthesis. It may have been tested by Merck and also by the U.S. government over the next years to treat a variety of symptoms. However, it was never found to be effective.

Hallucinogens were a primary drug in the 1960s drug culture and have been used nonmedically at an ever-increasing rate since that time (Williams, 2004).

Tobacco

Tobacco was being used by the Indians in the New World over 2,000 years ago. Sailors who had visited that land and taken up the habit carried it home across the Atlantic. Smoking became quite popular in Europe and Asia, but it faced harsh opposition from the church and government. Public smoking was punishable by death in Germany, China, and Turkey and by castration in Russia. Despite this early response, people continued to smoke and eventually were at least moderately accepted into society.

With the Industrial Age came the invention of machinery to make the cigarette a smaller, less expensive, neater way to smoke, making the price affordable to almost everyone. Laws were passed that allowed the decrease in price, and after 1910, public health officials began to campaign *against* chewing tobacco and *for* smoking tobacco. Smokers also realized that, unlike cigars, cigarette smoke could be inhaled, entering the lungs and the bloodstream.

Nicotine is one of the most addictive drugs on the market. A few hours of smoking are all that is needed for tolerance to begin to develop. The body immediately begins to adapt to protect itself from the toxins found in tobacco. As this process begins, it creates a rapid physiological development that requires smoking again to return to a normal feeling.

Over time the opinions about smoking have varied greatly. Early in its use, tobacco was seen as medicinal. In the 1940s and 50s, smoking was seen as sophisticated. Currently, the view of tobacco use has shifted. The highly addictive nature of nicotine was acknowledged as a health hazard by the surgeon general of the United States in his 1964 report on tobacco. In his report, the surgeon general outlined the various problems that could be related to, or caused by, smoking tobacco. Since then, the relationship between smoking and cancer has continued to be researched and substantiated.

This information has required individuals to rethink their position on cigarette smoking. Many cities and states now ban smoking in public buildings and in the whole city (Norton, 2010).

Caffeine

The legend of initial caffeine use lies with a goatherd in Arabia about 1,000 years ago, who observed the energetic behavior of his goats and wondered what was happening. He noticed that this started after they ate the berries of a particular bush. So he tried the berries himself and liked the effect. Usage spread from Arabia to China and to Europe. As more easily ingested versions became available, such as liquid coffee, usage increased.

Tea was first mentioned in writing in A.D. 3560 but is believed to have been available in China as early as 2700 B.C. Tea came to Europe in A.D. 1600. The kola nut was found in common use in West Africa and was later introduced into cola drinks as a source of caffeine. The cacao tree was found in Mexico, the West Indies, and much of Central and South America. Chocolate from this tree was the favorite beverage of the Emperor Montezuma; it was said that 50 pitchers a day were prepared for his use. This drink was soon popular throughout the world.

The ilex plant, source of the caffeine drink known as *mate,* was found in Brazil and elsewhere in the American tropics; this tea is still drunk in the United States as Yerba mate, and in parts of South America it rivals coffee and tea in popularity.

Cassina, also known as the North American tea plant, was found in common use as the source of a caffeine beverage among Indians from Virginia to Florida and west along the Gulf Coast to the Rio Grande. It was reported at the time that only the "great Men and Captains" of the Indian tribes were allowed to use this beverage.

White settlers in these regions prepared a tea known as the "black tea" or "black drought" from the same plant; they also let the leaves ferment to produce a drink containing both alcohol and caffeine.

During the Civil War, when the South was under blockade so that supplies of coffee and tea were cut off, cassina again became a popular beverage in the Confederacy. During and after World War I, when coffee prices soared, Congress and the United States Department of Agriculture launched projects to popularize cassina as a substitute source of caffeine; cassina-flavored ice cream and cassina soft drinks as well as cassina teas were marketed.

Both tea and coffee have had their advocates and detractors throughout history, with debates about usage. Whether caffeine should be categorized as a "drug" comparable to alcohol and opioids continues to be discussed. Caffeine intoxication is listed in the *Diagnostic and Statistical Manual of Mental Disorders,* fourth edition (*DSM-IV*-TR) (American Psychological Association [APA], 2001) as well as caffeine-induced anxiety disorder and sleep disorder.

In low doses, caffeine is a mild stimulant that dissipates drowsiness or fatigue, speeds up the heart rate, raises blood pressure, and irritates the stomach. Tolerance and withdrawal are associated with long-term use.

Some researchers report overdose and lethality at 1 gram. An average cup of coffee contains 85 to 100 milligrams of caffeine; an average cola beverage contains about 10 to 50 milligrams of caffeine per serving. By contrast, energy drinks such as Red Bull contain as much as 80 milligrams of caffeine per serving. Chocolate has about 25 milligrams per ounce (Weinberg & Beale, 2002).

While this has been a brief description of many of the most popular drugs available, it is easy to see the context in which these drugs have existed through history, often back to prehistoric times. It is no wonder that we seek altered states of consciousness through the use of these plants. However, the problem becomes the overuse or dependence on these drugs over a period of time in order to obtain a "content" lifestyle.

SOCIETAL COSTS OF ATOD USE, ABUSE, AND DEPENDENCY

The total cost of ATOD use, abuse, and dependency is estimated to be anywhere from $180 billion to approximately $484 billion (see Table 1.1). The largest proportion of costs is from lost potential productivity, followed by nonhealth, "other" costs, and health-related costs. This major source of societal costs totals $69 billion. Deaths attributable to illicit drugs were 25,493, a significant factor in the nation's death rate statistics. Of these deaths, the rate of mortality has accelerated because of AIDS among injection drug users, which added 10,737 deaths in the same year. Another 3,600 injection drug users died from hepatitis B and C. See Table 1.2 for a summary of health-related issues, some of which are due to substance abuse.

Drug abuse and dependency also reduce the capacity of individuals to work productively in their workplaces and homes. One source of loss is the shortfall in wages and employment among drug abusers, which accounts for $14.2 billion.

The final major component of costs came to $36.4 billion in 2002. The largest detailed component of these costs is for state and federal corrections at $14.2 billion, which is primarily for the operation of prisons. Another $9.8 billion was spent on state and local police protection, followed by $6.2 billion for federal supply reduction initiatives.

The impact of drug abuse on the quality of life of the family, neighbors, and victims of drug abusers or on the drug abuser cannot be estimated. Economic valuation studies increasingly endeavor to incorporate such quality-of-life impacts and costs, and the resulting cost estimates are typically several times greater than the productivity losses.

In addition to the cost of treatment, multitudes of other costs are associated with chemical use. These include the losses to society from premature deaths and fetal alcohol syndrome; costs involving the criminal justice system, social welfare administration, and property losses from alcohol-related motor vehicle crashes; and costs related to hepatitis C and HIV/AIDS (see Table 1.3).

TABLE 1.1 Estimated societal cost of drug abuse, 1992–2002 overall costs (in billions of dollars)

Cost Category	1992	1993	1994	1995	1996	1997	1998	1999	2000	2001	2002
Health care	$10.7	$11.8	$12.1	$11.9	$11.5	$11.8	$12.5	$13.0	$13.5	$14.6	$15.8
Productivity losses	$77.4	$79.3	$83.9	$89.2	$93.4	$95.5	$99.3	$107.3	$113.4	$120.0	$128.6
Other costs	$19.4	$19.8	$21.3	$23.8	$24.7	$26.7	$28.4	$31.1	$33.8	$34.6	$36.4
Total	$107.5	$110.9	$117.3	$124.9	$129.6	$133.9	$140.1	$151.4	$160.7	$169.2	$180.8

Note: The Lewin Group, 2004 (latest available figures).

TABLE 1.2 Comparison of costs of major health problems in the United States (costs in billions of estimate-year dollars)

Health Problem	Total	Direct	Indirect	Year of Estimate
Drug abuse	$180	$52	$129	2002
Alcohol abuse	$185	$50	$134	1998
Alzheimer's	$100	$15	$85	1997
Arthritis	$65	$15	$50	1992
Cancer	$96	$27	$69	1990
Diabetes	$98	$44	$54	1997
Eye diseases	$38	$22	$16	1991
Heart disease	$183	$102	$81	1999
HIV/AIDS	$29	$13	$16	1999
Homicide	$34	$10	$23	1989
Kidney	$40	$26	$14	1985
Mental illness	$161	$67	$94	1992
Obesity	$99	$52	$46	1995
Pain, chronic	$79	$45	$34	1986
Smoking	$138	$80	$58	1995
Stroke	$43	$28	$15	1998

Source: National Institute of Health, Office of Policy and Analysis (http://ospp.od.nih.gov/ecostudies/COIreportweb.htm).

SUBSTANCE-RELATED DISEASES

Hepatitis

Although hepatitis may take multiple forms, we will discuss only two here.

Both hepatitis B (HBV) and hepatitis C (HCV) are liver-damaging viruses that are spread through exposure to contaminated blood and body fluids. Hepatitis B is the most common cause of liver disease in the world. HBV is blood-borne and can be transmitted through any sharing of blood. HBV is also found in the semen of infected males, and transmission through sexual contact is likely. Is it estimated that 17%, or 13,000 of the 73,000 new cases of hepatitis B that occurred in 2000, occurred among intravenous drug users (IDU) (CDC, 2006).

Hepatitis C, the most common blood-borne infection in the United States, is a viral disease that destroys liver cells. Hepatitis C is now at epidemic proportions in the United States. According to the CDC (2006), approximately 2.7 million persons are chronically infected. Some say that the numbers are higher than those with HIV/AIDS. It is mostly transmitted through the sharing of needles, and sexual transmission is low. Acquisition of hepatitis C infection is very rapid among new drug injectors, with 50% to 80% infected within 6 to 12 months (National Institute of Drug Abuse [NIDA], 2000). Approximately 36,000 new cases of acute hepatitis C infection occur each year in the United States, according to the CDC (2006). People with newly acquired HCV are

TABLE 1.3 Estimated societal cost of drug abuse, 1992–2002 health care costs (in millions of dollars)

Cost Components	1992	1993	1994	1995	1996	1997	1998	1999	2000	2001	2002
Community-based specialty treatment	$3,770	$4,188	$4,425	$4,569	$4,930	$5,091	$5,369	$5,257	$5,159	$5,563	$5,997
Federally Provided Specialty Treatment											
Department of Defense	$14	$9	$5	$5	$5	$5	$5	$7	$7	$7	$8
Indian Health Services	$26	$33	$31	$51	$33	$31	$32	$41	$42	$52	$54
Bureau of Prisons	$17	$17	$17	$18	$19	$20	$21	$32	$34	$38	$39
Department of Veterans Affairs	$113	$127	$153	$169	$152	$135	$119	$108	$109	$119	$116
Support											
Federal Prevention	$616	$623	$639	$624	$560	$657	$725	$934	$1,024	$1,075	$1,203
State and Local Prevention	$89	$93	$91	$101	$81	$85	$118	$141	$143	$145	$148
Training	$49	$51	$53	$55	$57	$59	$60	$62	$65	$67	$69
Prevention Research	$158	$164	$175	$180	$212	$231	$250	$286	$317	$353	$402
Treatment Research	$195	$242	$254	$261	$283	$313	$328	$382	$417	$497	$564
Insurance Administration	$268	$302	$329	$335	$344	$333	$333	$349	$365	$413	$476
Medical Consequences											
Hospital and Ambulatory Care Costs	$518	$657	$796	$843	$879	$1,000	$1,103	$1,172	$1,239	$1,341	$1,454
Special Disease Costs											
Drug-Exposed Infants	$407	$424	$439	$453	$468	$480	$503	$525	$558	$579	$605
Tuberculosis	$30	$29	$29	$28	$27	$25	$22	$20	$20	$20	$19
HIV/AIDS	$3,489	$3,894	$3,694	$3,221	$2,592	$2,484	$2,603	$2,853	$3,158	$3,461	$3,755
Hepatitis B and C	$462	$399	$419	$457	$394	$439	$434	$371	$376	$340	$312
Crime Victim Health Care Costs	$92	$142	$148	$139	$136	$132	$127	$118	$111	$109	$110
Health Insurance Administration	$340	$383	$392	$360	$301	$287	$308	$347	$397	$448	$513
Total	$10,652	$11,776	$12,087	$11,854	$11,474	$11,806	$12,461	$13,004	$13,522	$14,628	$15,843

Source: Analysis by The Lewin Group, 2004. *SAMHSA,* 2005.

either asymptomatic or have a mild clinical illness. HCV RNA can be detected in blood within 1 to 3 weeks after exposure. Acute HCV infection may exhibit such symptoms as jaundice, abdominal pain, loss of appetite, nausea, and diarrhea. However, most infected people exhibit mild or no symptoms. No vaccine for hepatitis C is available, and prophylaxis with immune globulin is not effective in preventing HCV infection after exposure.

About 85% of people with acute hepatitis C develop a chronic infection. Chronic hepatitis is an insidious disease whose barely discernible symptoms can mask progressive injury to liver cells over two to four decades. An estimated 4 million Americans are infected with chronic hepatitis C (CDC, 2006).

Chronic hepatitis C often leads to cirrhosis of the liver and liver cancer and causes between 8,000 and 10,000 deaths a year in the United States. It is now the leading cause of liver cancer in this country and results in more liver transplants than any other disease (NIDA, 2000).

HIV/AIDS

An estimated 33.3 million people are living with HIV or AIDS worldwide in 2009 with more than 2.2 million being newly infected that year. More than 3 million die every year from AIDS-related illnesses. Since the beginning of the epidemic (considered to be 1983), an estimated 617,025 people with AIDS have died in the U.S. (CDC, July, 2010). In 2005, there were 100,000 deaths in the United States and dependent areas from AIDS (CDC, 2007). Also in 2005, the World Health Organization (WHO) reported that the United States had 1.2 million people living with HIV/AIDS (WHO, 2005).

African Americans are at higher risk, with Whites next and then Hispanics. Co-infection is another risk factor with HIV and hepatitis C being common among IDUs. It is estimated that 60% to 90% of IDUs are co-infected. Women account for an increasing proportion of people with HIV and AIDS. At the end of 2005, according to the WHO, 17.5 million women worldwide were infected with HIV. AIDS cases in the United States increased 10% among females and 7% among males. In 2004, women accounted for 27% of the 44,615 newly reported AIDS cases among adults and adolescents. The adult and adolescent female numbers represent less than 25% of all U.S. women, yet they account for more than 79% of AIDS cases in women. Documentation of this comes from a variety of research, but all one has to do is watch the nightly news or a television special to know the horror of AIDS in Africa and other third world countries. In the United States, the most common means by which HIV-1 is transmitted is by sharing of contaminated needles (CDC, 2007). Further infection comes from sexual relations with an infected partner. Worldwide, more than 90% of all adolescent and adult HIV infections have resulted from heterosexual intercourse. Women are particularly vulnerable to heterosexual transmission of HIV due to substantial mucosal exposure to seminal fluids. This biological fact amplifies the risk of HIV transmission when coupled with the high prevalence of nonconsensual sex, sex without condom use, and the unknown and/or high-risk behaviors of their partners (U.S. Department of Health and Human Services, 2006).

We would be remiss not to discuss these diseases along with the other horrific secondary costs of the primary abuse and dependence on ATOD. At best this information is frightening; in reality, it is terrifying. The cost of addiction and diseases related to addiction, in addition to the monetary and societal costs, is, in many cases, a human life. Many times the life of a person abusing ATOD ends in pain and suffering, alone in an unimaginable place.

It is imperative that all counselors have the knowledge to make connections about ATOD use with their clients' problems. It is not unusual for clients to "forget" to let the counselor know about their use and abuse, yet this is often the root of the problem they are presenting. Ethical codes now give us direction in handling cases of infectious diseases with clients. Read and understand your responsibility to your client, their partners, and yourself. Without thorough knowledge and understanding of the complete context of the client's life, you cannot serve the client ethically or effectively.

THE IMPORTANCE OF TERMINOLOGY IN SUBSTANCE ABUSE COUNSELING

As indicated, substance misuse, abuse, and addiction are multifaceted problems that vary across cultures and families as well as with individuals. It is an issue that affects everyone, and the costs are staggering. The complexity of the problem has resulted in no single treatment method evolving as *most* effective for health-distressed individuals experiencing the consequences of substance abuse. However, current research does find that some approaches are more effective than others and that family treatment approaches for substance abusers and their families may be one of those approaches.

All counselors, whether they work in the field of substance abuse counseling or in the general field of psychotherapy, will encounter issues of substance abuse with many of their clients. Considering the economic costs and the price in human suffering of substance use and abuse, it seems imperative that counselors be trained in all aspects of substance abuse intervention and prevention. It is essential that all mental health professionals understand the process of abuse and addiction, the etiology of addiction, the individual, family, and societal costs, and available treatment modalities. The professional must also be aware of the psychological and physiological effects of drugs on the human brain and thereby on human behavior. *Substance Abuse Counseling* has been written to guide mental health professionals in their recognition, assessment, and treatment of substance abuse or dependency in their clients.

For consistency throughout this book, we have used the terms *substance abuse* and *substance dependency* when describing the client's use pattern. These terms coincide with the *DSM-IV*-TR (APA, 2001) definitions and criteria. Being consistent with the *DSM-IV*-TR allows for a measurable and consensually defined diagnosis. The *DSM-IV*-TR, the primary diagnostic tool for the profession, defines *substance abuse* and *dependency* with varying criteria for each of these categories. It is of interest to note that the *DSM-IV*-TR further divides dependence as being "with physiological dependence" or "without physiological dependence." This distinction is an addition to the criteria for dependence. Many designer drugs show psychological dependence but may, in fact, cause little or no physical dependence.

Two components separate the diagnostic categories of "abuse" from "dependence": tolerance and withdrawal. *Tolerance* means that a higher dosage of the drug is needed to produce the same level of effect over a period of time. The length of time may be influenced by the amount and frequency at which the drug is administered. (NOTE: The criteria for some substance abuse disorders may change in the DSM-V (fifth edition) which is in review at the time of this text's publication.)

We have used the term *ATOD* to include, as is our philosophy, alcohol, tobacco, and other drugs, indicating our belief that alcohol and tobacco, though legal, are still drugs. We are aware that a variety of terms are used in the field, including *chemical addiction, chemical dependency, drug abuse,* and *addiction.* Our choice of *substance abuse* and *dependency* is in no way intended to imply that other terms do not have validity but is merely a way to develop consistency of terminology and meaning throughout the text.

We also have used the term *substance* or *chemical* to include alcohol, nicotine, caffeine, prescription drugs, and illegal drugs. We may, however, at times refer to alcohol and other drugs when the distinction is necessary to maintain clarity or when the majority of the research has focused on alcohol. It is, of course, relevant to acknowledge that alcohol, nicotine, and caffeine are legal and societally accepted drugs. This fact lends a different dynamic to the use, abuse, and even dependency issues related to these substances that do not exist for illegal drugs. It is imperative, however, to acknowledge that these drugs represent a major threat to a person's biological, psychosocial, and familial health.

The definition of *drug* is one that changes with fluctuations in social mores as well as with shifts in the law. Cultures also differ considerably on classification of substances such as foods, poisons, beverages, medicines, and herbs.

In this text, *drug* will be defined as any nonfood substance whose chemical or physical nature significantly alters structure, function, or perception (vision, taste, hearing, touch, and smell) in the living organism. Legality of a substance has no bearing on whether it is defined as a drug. Alcohol, nicotine, and caffeine are legal but considered drugs in the same way as are marijuana, hallucinogens, and narcotics. A *drug user* or *substance abuser* is a person who intentionally takes legal or illegal drugs to alter his or her functioning or state of consciousness. A drug might be instrumental but still abused. Instrumental drugs are used to reduce anxiety, induce sleep, stay awake, and so on. However, instrumental drugs are often abused and serve as an entry to other drugs.

A term that is closely associated with drug use is *drug of choice*. A person's drug of choice is just that: Of all the possible drugs available—of all the drugs a person may have used over the years—what specific drug(s) would this person use if given the choice (Doweiko, 2011)? This concept is of particular importance as the number of polydrug users increases. In assessment, diagnosis, and treatment, drug of choice may play an important role.

Drug use, misuse, and *abuse* are also somewhat difficult to define. In this text, *drug use* refers to the intake of a chemical substance and does not distinguish whether the drug is used therapeutically, legally, or illegally. *Abuse* is defined by Merriam-Webster (2011) as improper use, or use that injures or damages. Therefore, we might say that *substance abuse* would be the use of a drug without medical justification that would injure or do damage. Further defined, *to abuse* is seen as "to will to injure or damage"—all phrases and language that are easily understood. Whereas *misuse* is using a substance in a manner that causes detrimental effects in some area of the person's life, *abuse* is more specifically defined as the continued use of a psychoactive drug despite the occurrence of major detrimental effects associated with its use, such as social, vocational, health, scholastic, or economic difficulties.

Tolerance is an interesting concept that differentiates in the *DSM-IV-*TR between abuse and dependency. There appear to be at least two types of tolerance: (a) metabolic tolerance and (b) pharmacodynamic tolerance. *Metabolic tolerance* refers to liver function. Drugs are a foreign substance to the body, and the liver will assign chemicals to break down or metabolize these chemicals. If the liver is continuously exposed to the chemical, then more cells are assigned the task of metabolizing this chemical. The result is that the chemical is metabolized faster and therefore eliminated from the body more rapidly. *Pharmacodynamic tolerance* is the central nervous system's increasing insensitivity to a chemical. As the nerve is bombarded with a continuous amount of a chemical, the nerve makes minute changes in its structure to continue normal functioning. The nerve becomes less sensitive to the chemical's effect, creating the need for an increased dosage to achieve the same effect (Doweiko, 2011).

Withdrawal refers to a specific set of symptoms that occur when use of the drug is discontinued—that is, withdrawn from the central nervous system (CNS). The particular nature of the withdrawal is contingent on the class or type of drug being taken, the length of time taken, the amount of the chemical taken, and the health of the individual.

Each class or type of drugs produces certain physical withdrawal symptoms. As the nerves endeavor to readapt to their original state of functioning and the body learns to function again without the chemical, the person experiences the physical symptoms of withdrawal. This *withdrawal syndrome*, also with criteria in the *DSM-IV*-TR, is strong evidence of dependence or addiction.

It is important to see drug use, misuse, abuse, and addiction as a continuum of behavior. Although this approach will make assessment and diagnosis more difficult, it will also result in more effective treatment for the individual. An either/or diagnosis may lead to a generalized treatment plan that may be ineffective and usually meets the needs of only the most chronic substance abusers (Lewis, Dana, & Blevins, 2011).

A continuum model does not imply progression of drug use. It *does* imply that some users may progress but that others may fixate at a particular position on the continuum. This position may, in fact, be problematic for the client but not at a level that could be clinically diagnosed as "abuse" or "dependence."

Looking at substance use on a continuum allows the counselor to design individualized treatment plans. An adolescent who begins to use drugs may need only facilitation in good decision-making skills. An adult who is abusing a substance to cope with a recent loss may need facilitation in improvement of coping skills as well as support in a new life stage. These individuals need significantly different clinical intervention than do longtime, daily users who have developed a tolerance to a particular drug.

THE PROFESSION IN THE 21st CENTURY

The field of substance abuse counseling is changing dramatically. Where once confrontation was the norm, now a collaborative approach that fits the client's life is being utilized. Research-based programs are being adopted that show more efficacy than previous programs based in "opinion and ideology" (Miller & Carroll, 2006).

SAMHSA's Evidence-Based Program and Practices site (nrepp.samhsa.gov/) shows the commitment to research-based treatment that is the standard for today's treatment world. Evidence-based practices "have been subjected to randomized clinical trials and other experimental research designs and have been found to be more effective than 'treatment as usual'" (Eliason, 2007, p. 310).

The use of motivational interviewing (MI) is another example of new collaborative and positive treatment skills. Motivational interviewing is a process to elicit change in the client through skillful questioning. Further, MI recognizes that change comes from within the client and that the client-counselor interaction is the most powerful aspect of the treatment process (Hettema, Steele, & Miller, 2005).

AN OVERVIEW OF THIS BOOK

The authors of this book endeavored to thoughtfully bring you the process of working with clients in this field. We have tried to make this book mimic that process from the beginning of your work with the client in out- or in-patient treatment to ending with relapse planning for continued recovery. It is our hope that this progression will assist you in understanding how to work effectively with your clients—and also how to care for yourself in the process.

MyCounselingLab™

Go to Topic 1: *Introduction to Substance Abuse Counseling*, on the MyCounselingLab™ site (www.MyCounselingLab.com) for *Substance Abuse Counseling*, Fifth Edition, where you can:

- Find learning outcomes for *Introduction to Substance Abuse Counseling* along with the national standards that connect to these outcomes.
- Complete Assignments and Activities that can help you more deeply understand the chapter content.
- Apply and practice your understanding of the core skills identified in the chapter with the Building Counseling Skills unit.
- Prepare yourself for professional certification with a Practice for Certification quiz.
- Connect to videos through the Video and Resource Library.

CONCLUSION

We have endeavored to organize the material in this text in a manner that presents a logical progression of knowledge about substance abuse and counseling. As a supplement to the knowledge base, we have incorporated the following three brief cases throughout the book to illustrate concepts discussed in each clinical chapter. The cases assist in understanding the process of assessment and diagnosis, treatment, and relapse prevention planning. Since a "live" case was not an option, the written cases will allow you to integrate the many concepts presented in the text. Authors have also developed and presented cases in each chapter as appropriate.

CASE 1
Sandy and Pam

Presenting Problem

Sandy, a White female, age 52, and Pam, her biracial daughter, age 29, came into counseling to examine their relationship with each other as well as their relationships with men. They have noticed patterns in their interactions that are similar and create conflict between them and with partners that they choose. When asked to rate their problem on a scale of 1 to 10 (with 10 being the best), Sandy stated it was a 1 while Pam chose 4.

Family History

Sandy (mother) was the child of two alcoholic parents. Her parents divorced when Sandy was 10 years old, and her father basically "was never seen again." Her mother dated throughout her adolescence and finally married Harry when Sandy was 17. Harry was a heavy drinker, and Sandy is sure that he "ran around on her mother" until he died. Sandy is the oldest child and has a younger brother and sister. She reports feeling like she had to take care of her siblings throughout her life. However, she took on the role of the rebellious child from an early age, drinking, sneaking out of the house, and finally getting pregnant at 18. Sandy's mother died in an automobile accident while drinking when Sandy was 30 years old.

Sandy married Jim, an African American and Pam's father, who was an alcoholic and abusive to both Sandy and Pam. Sandy had two children with Jim: Pam and Albert. Albert is two years younger than Pam. When Pam was 7 years of age, her parents separated. Pam has had a distant and often disappointing relationship with her father. Her relationship with her mother has been close but conflictual.

Sandy admits to continuing to abuse alcohol. She remembers leaving Pam and her brother at home when she thought they were asleep so that she could go to bars. After her separation, she brought home numerous men and would be sexual with them. Pam remembers hearing her mother in the bedroom with strangers and feeling frightened and alone. Sandy stopped drinking two months ago and has been trying to make amends to Pam. Pam stated, "There is nothing to forgive. Mother was doing the best she could do." Pam admits to "following in her mother's footsteps"—sneaking out of the house when she was younger, using alcohol, and "downers" from her mother's medicine cabinet. She also admits having sex with many partners since she was 12 or 13.

Pam states she drinks "too much" but "not as much as a couple of years ago." She was living with a cocaine abuser, Sam, who abuses alcohol and is emotionally and verbally abusive to her. She has used cocaine on "several occasions" with him but says she prefers to drink alcohol. She has not been using "downers" as much since living with Sam. Pam says she is tempted to "sleep around to get even" with Sam.

Pam recently moved out of Sam's house and back in with her mother. She is attempting to stay away from him, but he is pursuing her. She states that she "feels drawn to him and wants to make it work." She believes he will not be abusive if they both stop using alcohol and cocaine.

Education/Work History

Sandy did not complete high school, nor does she have any technical training. She has worked various jobs throughout her life as well as being on welfare for the past five years. Pam is a bright young woman with a high school degree and two years of study at a community college. Her career counseling indicated that her best fit was in a people-oriented position, but she has been uninspired by any job she has held. Like her mother, her job history is sporadic, with Pam holding jobs for an average of about three months as a waitress, receptionist, and bank teller. She then quits her job because she "hates it" and usually drinks and uses drugs heavily for several weeks before "getting it together" and finding another job. She is currently employed as a cashier in a convenience store and works the night shift.

Pam believes her problem is her inability to commit to anything. Sandy says that this issue is her problem also, so Pam must have "learned it from me." Pam has recently begun to experience anxiety attacks that she attributes to her fear of being alone. She has been prescribed an anti-anxiety drug but still drinks alcohol along with it.

Medical Information

Sandy is on Medicare and Social Security Disability for back problems that prevent her from working. She has been disabled for the past five years. Sandy reports that she has been in pain for over 10 years. The pain level varies but she takes prescribed narcotics for the pain. She says that "sometimes" she mixes the drugs with alcohol when the pain is "really bad."

Pam is in fairly good health but was prescribed an antidepressant and an antianxiety medication about six months ago.

Support Systems

Sandy and Pam have both been in Alcoholics Anonymous (AA) but only occasionally. They both state that they don't really know anyone who doesn't drink or use drugs.

Counseling Goal(s)

Both women admit that they drink and use drugs to "help them with life's stresses" but would like to learn other ways of handling life. Sandy appears to be less willing to abstain but seems to be willing to "drink in moderation." They also want to understand why they continue to seek out bad relationships that "just get them back into using again."

CASE 2
The Martinez Family

Presenting Problem

Jose and Juanita are in their mid-40s, with a daughter from Juanita's first marriage, Sarita, age 15, and their birth daughter, Karen, age 4. The family comes into therapy due to conflict between Jose and Sarita. The parents described the chaos and hatred that ensues when Sarita blows-up at Jose, using Sarita's phrase that Jose "is not my real father." When asked to describe the problem on a scale from 1 to 10 (scale of 1 being worst to 10 being best), Jose and Juanita chose 3 and 4 respectively, while Sarita chose 1.

Family History

Juanita and her family came to the United States from Mexico when she was 5 years old. Her father was not able to find steady employment and was very bitter about being away from his home in Mexico and the disappointment of his life in the United States. Juanita states that "I only wanted to be like the other children in my school. I resented my father for his continued use of Spanish, his rigid rules, and his drinking." Her mother died when Juanita was only 5 months old. She has a brother, Alberto, who is seven years older than Juanita. She left home at age 14 and was placed in a foster home with an American family that was loving and supportive. Juanita states that she is grateful for the four years she had in the foster home. She states that she has made peace with her father and forgiven her brother, both of whom she continues to have a relationship with as an adult.

At age 19, she married Hector, a traditional Hispanic male. She was married for less than two years and reports he was just like her father and "that it was too difficult to be what he wanted me to be." Sarita is the child of this marriage, and her father is still involved in her life, according to Sarita, "as much as Mother will allow." Hector drinks only socially and does not use drugs. Juanita states that he is "very concerned about Sarita." Juanita divorced Hector when Sarita was 10 and married Jose shortly thereafter, having met him at the bar where she worked.

Jose is the oldest of five children and had to parent the younger children from about age 10. Both parents drank "a lot," but Jose does not see them as alcoholics. Jose's parents came from Ecuador before he was born. They acclimated well to their life in the States, and Jose and his siblings were raised as "Americans" with no sense of their own culture or heritage. Jose also left home at an early age but has had no relationship with his parents or siblings as an adult. He chooses to share no other information regarding his family of origin.

Sarita has been raised with the conflicting values and messages from the Spanish culture that her mother knows and her birth father supports, and the American culture that is her stepfather's. She is beginning to act out both at home and in the classroom. Her grades are dropping, and she is sneaking out of the house at night. She admits to yelling and screaming at Jose and turning up the stereo too loud "just to bug him." She also says he drinks too much, and when he is drunk, he tells her how much he loves her and how he hates that they fight all the time. Sarita says he then yells at her, tells her to get out of his face, and calls her friends "dummies." Jose's response to Sarita's acting out behavior when he is sober is to tighten the rules.

Karen, the younger daughter, is not present at the session. Juanita reports that she is "visibly sad." She is "quiet and withdrawn" from the family fights. She spends lots of time in her room playing with her stuffed toys.

Trauma, Domestic Violence, Substance Abuse

Juanita reports a traumatic childhood with an alcoholic and abusive father. She recalls being sexually abused by Alberto, her older brother, beginning at around age 9 or 10 and going on until she left the house.

Both have abused alcohol for approximately 20 years. Juanita stopped drinking five years ago for health reasons and remained sober for one year before beginning to drink beer and then wine again. She states that she drinks only after the children are in bed and does not think that Sarita or Karen have ever seen her drunk. She states that she uses cocaine only at work—never at home. Jose drinks mostly beer every evening after work, many times with his friends, and smokes some "pot" on the weekends. He admits to drinking in front of the girls but not smoking pot until they are in bed or not around.

Both Jose and Juanita admit that quitting the use of drugs and alcohol would be difficult but express a desire to stop. Juanita particularly believes this is a problem in the family. The longest they have been able to stop (except for Juanita's one year) was 14 days. When they started again, both drank alcohol and used drugs to intoxication. Juanita is somewhat reluctant to give up her "uppers." She says she feels more socially upbeat when she "does a line or two" and, since she gets it for free and has "no ill effects," sees no reason to abstain. She states it really helps at work.

Jose does not like that she gets drugs from "friends" at the bar, and he says he would like to stop using pot and for Juanita to stop using cocaine completely. Both admit that their use may be part of the problem with Sarita—and with Karen—but are not sure what to do about the problem. They believe that Sarita "just needs a stronger hand" and that she is "just acting her age and will get over it soon."

Medical Information

None reported.

Education/Work History

Juanita currently works as a bartender and receives free cocaine from her patrons. Jose worked as a bartender at the same place for almost two years but has changed professions. He is currently working as a contractor and is fairly successful. Both state a sporadic work history with many different jobs as they moved quite frequently before marriage. Neither has kept a job more than two years. Jose was incarcerated as a teenager for theft and illegal drug possession.

Sarita works after school at a local shop. She reports that she really likes it and loves to be out of the house.

Support Systems

Both parents share mutual couple friends (Jane and Marta; Fernando and Marie), whom they describe "as close to the family, like uncles and aunts." These are friends who live in the same neighborhood as the family does. Jose talks loosely about his friends that he hangs out with after work but does not identify a significant male friend outside of the neighborhood. Jose reports no close ties to church or cultural organizations. Juanita attends church with Karen and Sarita "when she will go." Sarita says that her aunts are her support and also her friends at school.

Counseling Goals

Both parents report that they would like to learn different parenting skills. Their goals for alcohol and drug use is to continue use on a moderate basis. Jose, Juanita, and Sarita would like a better relationship among themselves but differ in how to achieve this. Juanita has indicated that the girls might be interested in learning more about their culture. She thinks this might help Sarita to understand herself in a deeper way.

CASE 3

Leigh

Presenting Problem

Leigh, age 16, has been referred because of problems at school and a shoplifting charge. Leigh and her mother moved to this area about eight months ago. She is currently in 11th grade and is attending a new school this year. She is dressed in black with pierced ears, nose, eyebrow, and lip. Her appearance is disheveled and her hygiene poor. She appears to be overly thin. She has previously admitted to "smoking some dope" every now and then and having a drink or two with her friends. When asked to rate her problem on a scale of 1 to 10 (with 10 being no problem), Leigh replied "9" but said her mom's problem was a –5. Leigh says the shoplifting charge is a mistake; that she intended to pay for the makeup and just forgot it was in her purse. She doesn't understand why everyone is making such a "big deal out of it."

When directly asked about her drug and alcohol use, Leigh admits that she has been smoking, drinking, and using ecstasy, cocaine, and pot at parties for the past four months. She also implies that some of her friends have a meth connection and she has "tried meth" on a couple of occasions but denies steady use. She says "maybe" she raids her mother's medicine cabinet "like all the other kids." She also admits to multiple sex partners at these parties. She states that she sees nothing wrong with any of this and that she is "tired of everyone trying to tell her what to do." She says that running away with her friends seems to be the best solution for her.

When asked about why she believes running away is the best solution, she describes a series of losses that she has had over the past 10 years. Leigh's parents divorced when she was 5 years old. When she was a young child she had a close relationship with her brother, who is two years older, but now they do not speak. Both children lived with their mother after the divorce. Until eight months ago they lived in the same town as their father. Leigh and her brother saw him frequently, although she says he was "always busy with work" and she could never talk to him about much of anything. Leigh states that her mother was also busy but would "sometimes" stop and listen. She reports that her mother has a temper and is stressed all the time about money and work. She also reports that her mom and dad still fight about money and "us kids." She feels like she is in the middle and is always being asked to choose.

Family History

Leigh's father and brother have "disappeared from her life." Although her brother is attending college about one hour from their new home, he infrequently comes to visit. He is moody and withdrawn and either goes out to "party" or sleeps most of the time. Her father now lives about four hours away, and she has not seen him since they moved, although he calls her on occasion.

Leigh's mother is working as a real estate salesperson at a new office and dating Hank, whom she met in their old town and who moved to be close to her in the new town. Leigh says that Hank is "OK" but that she misses her father and never sees her mother now that she is dating as well as working all the time.

In addition to the changes in her family life, she reports missing her old school and friends. At her previous school she received excellent grades and good conduct reports. She was involved in several extracurricular activities and had many friends. Her grades have dropped significantly this year, and her new friends are "different" from her old friends but "accept her for what she is." Leigh states that her new friends are more fun than her old friends but that she sometimes misses her old school and friends.

Medical Information

Leigh recently went to the doctor for her school physical and reports that the doctor said she was in good health. She is underweight and her menses have not been regular. She denies any eating disorder but some of her comments reflect that behavior. She discusses her mother's struggle with weight and how she never wants to be "fat." She also says she "knows different ways to zone out besides drugs and sex when she needs to do that." Further, she is taking an antidepressant prescribed by the new doctor two months ago.

Leigh reports that her mother is diabetic and she has lots of mood swings. Sometimes she gets really angry and manic. Leigh is worried about her mother's health and states that she drinks alcohol with Hank every night. The mother is on an anti-anxiety drug as she is "very stressed" at her new job according to Leigh. Her blood pressure is high and she is "on some drug" for that problem. Leigh expresses worry about where she would live if something happened to her mother.

Trauma, Domestic Violence, Substance Abuse

Leigh says the divorce and moving was a very big trauma and that she did not want to move and that now she never sees her father. When they lived in the previous town, at least she saw him sometimes. She also reports that Mom and Hank fight a lot when they are drinking.

Support Systems

Leigh's only current support system is her new friends. She does stay in touch (text, email) with one of her best friends from her old school, Kathy. She says Kathy is worried about her but that is "crazy; I'm doing fine." She wants Kathy to visit. When asked about her mother as a support system, she states "No way!"

Counseling Goals

Leigh states that her goal is just to "get this done." We did agree that she will attend at least five more sessions and that we would discuss her grades as well as her drug use.

2

Ethical and Legal Issues in Substance Abuse Counseling

SUMMER M. REINER, PH.D.

MyCounselingLab™

Visit the MyCounselingLab™ site for *Substance Abuse Counseling*, Fifth Edition to enhance your understanding of chapter concepts. You'll have the opportunity to practice your skills through video- and case-based Assignments and Activities as well as Building Counseling Skills units, and to prepare for your certification exam with Practice for Certification quizzes.

Ethical and legal issues facing substance abuse counselors stem from many sources. Substance abuse counselors are recruited from a variety of health and mental health professions. Each profession has its own representative organizations and licensing and certification requirements; these representative, certifying, and/ or licensing entities offer their own distinctive ethical codes. In addition, there are conflicting federal and state laws, as well as agency regulations, that influence ethical decision making. This chapter briefly reviews the legal and ethical issues that impact the substance abuse counselor.

Due to the variety of professions that offer substance abuse counseling and space constraints, this chapter will be presented from the perspective of a substance abuse counselor from a counseling background. The narrowed scope will exemplify the conflicting laws and ethical issues within the substance abuse counseling field, bringing to light the issues that substance abuse professionals in general may face despite their background. It is imperative that substance abuse professionals are aware of the federal, state, and local laws, regulations, and code of ethics that apply to them and their profession.

It should be noted that entire books are devoted to reviewing the ethical and legal issues that affect substance abuse counselors; this chapter is meant to provide an introduction and awareness of the complexity of legal and ethical issues in substance abuse counseling. The complexity of legal and ethical issues will be illustrated by the review of laws and standards of this decade. Laws, standards, requirements, and ethical codes continually change in response to societal needs. It is the responsibility of the substance abuse counselor to be aware of the current federal and state laws, workplace regulations, and ethical codes governing his or her profession.

EDUCATION AND TRAINING OF SUBSTANCE ABUSE COUNSELORS

The substance abuse counseling field comprises counselors with an array of educational and experiential differences. Historically, the substance abuse counseling community embraced the counselor who had experienced the substance abuse and recovery process, accepting successful recovery rather than education as a qualifier for professional counselor status (Smith & Capps, 2005). Recovering counselors are believed to be able to empathize with and assist their clients simply through personal experiences and the ability to relate (Kaplan, 2005). Today personal experience is not considered adequate enough to prepare substance abuse counselors as most states and organizations require some coursework in substance abuse counseling for those who will be working in the clinical field. In addition, there is still a discrepancy in academic requirements between substance abuse counselors and mental health counselors. Mental health counselors typically need to complete a master's degree to be credentialed, whereas substance abuse counselors can be recognized after a few specialized courses.

As described earlier, state licensing boards contribute to the confusion as states vary on formal education and supervised experience requirements for addictions counselors (Kerwin, Walker-Smith, & Kirby, 2006; Substance Abuse and Mental Health Services Administration [SAMHSA], 2005). A 2006 study of 31 of the 50 states and the District of Columbia revealed that only 9.68% ($n = 3$) required that substance abuse counselors hold a master's degree, whereas, 97.92% ($n = 47$) required mental health counselors to hold a master's degree (Kerwin et al., 2006). These findings support the claims that state standards for substance abuse counselors are less stringent than for mental health counselors. In regard to the difference in supervised work experience, 90.32% ($n = 28$) of states required substance abuse counselors to have a supervised work experience, compared with 97.92% ($n = 47$) of states that required mental health counselors to have a supervised work experience (Kerwin et al., 2006). Kerwin et al. also reported that 93.6% of states required substance abuse counselors and 100% of mental health counselors to pass an examination. It is important to note that the discrepancy of education requirements persists today. In 2009, all 50 states required mental health counselors to hold a master's degree and to pass an examination for license eligibility (American Counseling Association [ACA], 2010). In some states (i.e., Alabama, New York), a high school diploma or GED and experience are the criteria for earning addictions professional credentials (National Addiction Technology Transfer Center, 2010).

In response to the inconsistency of educational and experiential requirements, the National Board for Certified Counselors (NBCC), an organization affiliated with ACA, in conjunction with the International Association of Addictions and Offenders Counselors (IAAOC), developed a *Master's of Addiction Counseling* (MAC) certification (NBCC, 2011; Smith & Capps, 2005). To earn an NBCC MAC certification, counselors must complete a master's degree; earn 12 credits of graduate-level course work in addictions counseling or 500 continuing education hours in substance abuse issues, which may include 6 credits in group and/or family counseling; pass the *Examination for Master Addictions Counselors* (EMAC); and complete 3 years (36 months, 24 of which must occur after earning a master's degree) of experience in substance abuse counseling under the supervision of a master-degreed counselor, psychologist, psychiatrist, marriage and family therapist, or clinical social worker (NBCC, 2011). *Nationally Certified Counselors* (NCC) who hold the MAC credential are eligible to seek *Substance Abuse Professional* status through the U.S. Department of Transportation (USDOT). The content of the EMAC includes questions on assessment, counseling practices, treatment process, treatment planning and implementation, and prevention specific to addictions.

The *National Association of Alcoholism and Drug Abuse Counselors* (NAADAC) also developed a Master Addiction Counselor (MAC) credential. The criteria for the NAADAC MAC includes holding a master's degree in a "healing art" or related field with an emphasis in addictions counseling; having a current state license in your profession or certification as a substance abuse counselor; having 3 years (6,000 hours) of supervised substance abuse counseling; documenting 500 clock hours of education in alcoholism and drug abuse counseling matters, with at least 6 hours of HIV/AIDS training and 6 hours of ethics training; signing the NAADAC ethical statement; and passing the written Master Addiction Counselor examination. The content of the exam focuses on pharmacology and psychoactive substances, counseling practices, and professional issues. NAADAC also offers certifications to professionals with less than a master's degree (see Table 2.1).

The U.S. Department of Health and Human Services even expressed concern about the inconsistent educational and experiential requirements of substance abuse counselors (Broderick, 2007). In 1999, the Workforce Issues Panel recommended that the SAMHSA address workforce issues, develop and strengthen the addictions profession to attract and maintain a representative workforce, and improve workforce competency. SAMHSA identified five needs, one of which focused on the educational standards and credentialing of the substance abuse professionals. In a report to Congress, it called for a national set of core competencies for all substance abuse professionals (physicians, nurses, counselors, social workers, psychologist, etc.), an adoption of a

TABLE 2.1 NAADAC addiction counselor certification

Title	License/ Certificate Requirement	Education Contact Hours			Supervised Experience	Degree Requirement
		Substance Abuse Counseling	Ethics	HIV/AIDS		
National Certified Addictions Counselor, Level I (NCAC I)	Substance abuse counselor	270	6	6	3 years/ 6,000 hours	None
National Certified Addictions Counselor, Level II (NCAC II)	In your profession	450	6	6	5 years/ 10,000 hours	Bachelor's
Master Addictions Counselor	In your profession	500	6	6	3 years/ 6,000 hours	Master's

national accreditation for addictions education programs, and an increase in salaries for individuals who work in the substance abuse field.

Clearly there are different avenues for entering the substance abuse counseling profession. Despite how substance abuse counselors enter the profession, they must adhere to professional ethical codes, laws, and work site regulations. Knowing and understanding these codes, laws, and regulations is necessary for the professional substance abuse counselor. Furthermore, it is paramount that counselors understand how these codes, laws, and regulations interact, as they can impact the substance abuse counselor's ethical decisions.

ETHICS

As previously mentioned, ethical codes are maintained by most mental health organizations. Ethical codes are intended to be the minimum standard that counselors are to abide by when working with clients. The purpose of the ACA *Code of Ethics*, for example, is

> (1) to enable the association to clarify to current and future members, and to those served by members, the nature of ethical responsibilities held in common by its members; (2) to support the mission of the association; (3) to establish principles that define ethical behavior and best practices; (4) to serve as an ethical guide designed to assist members in constructing a professional course of action that best serves those utilizing counseling services and best promotes the values of the counseling profession; and (5) to serve as the basis for procession of ethical complaints and inquiries initiated against members of the association. (Glosoff & Kocet, 2006)

Many ethical codes of mental health organizations are based on moral principles (see Table 2.2) such as: autonomy, nonmaleficence, beneficence, justice, fidelity, and veracity (Remley & Herlihy, 2010).

Upon reviewing ethical codes of a handful of mental health organizations including ACA, the American Mental Health Counseling Association (AMHCA), NAADAC, and NBCC, it is clear that despite the fact that the ethical codes offer differing principles and focus on varied ethical issues, they also have many similarities (see Table 2.3). The commonalities between the ethical codes embrace principles aimed at protecting client

TABLE 2.2 Moral principles and definitions

Moral Principles	Definition
Justice	Fair, equitable, and nondiscrimination.
Beneficence	Promote mental health and wellness.
Nonmaleficence	Do no harm.
Autonomy	Foster self-determination.
Fidelity	Fulfilling the responsibility of trust.
Veracity	Truthfulness and honesty.

Source: T. Remley and B. Herlihy, *Ethical, legal, and professional issues in counseling* (3rd ed.), 2010, Upper Saddle River, NJ: Pearson Education.

TABLE 2.3 Organizational ethical codes' content

ACA Code of Ethics 2005, Sections A–H

A. The Counseling Relationship

B. Confidentiality, Privileged Communication, and Privacy

C. Professional Responsibility

D. Relationships with Other Professionals

E. Evaluation, Assessment, and Interpretation

F. Supervision, Training, and Teaching

G. Research and Publication

H. Resolving Ethical Issues

NAADAC Code of Ethics 2008, Principles 1–9

1. Non-Discrimination

2. Client Welfare

3. Client Relationship

4. Trustworthiness

5. Compliance with the Law

6. Rights and Duties

7. Dual Relationships

8. Preventing Harm

9. Duty of Care

NBCC Code of Ethics 2005, Sections A–G

A. General

B. Counseling Relationship

C. Counselor Supervision

D. Measurement and Evaluation

E. Research and Publication

F. Consulting

G. Private Practice

AMHCA Code of Ethics 2010, Principles 1–6

1. Commitment to Clients

2. Commitment to Other Professionals

3. Commitment to Students, Supervisees, and Employee Relationships

4. Commitment to the Profession

5. Commitment to the Public

6. Resolution of Ethical Problems

welfare; avoiding harm and imposing personal values; professional qualifications and competence, and knowledge of standards; consultation and counselor supervision with other counseling professionals; competence to administer, use, or interpret assessment instruments; and knowledge of and adherence to the laws and ethical codes (ACA, 2005; AMHCA, 2010; International Association of Marriage and Family Counselors

[IAMFC], 2005; NAADAC, 2008; NBCC, 2005). One important commonality that exists in all five of the highlighted ethical codes is the emphasis on confidentiality and client rights. As shown in the Table (2.3) for the NBCC and NAADAC ethical codes, confidentiality is actually embedded in the NBCC "*Counseling Relationship*" section and the NAADAC "*Client Welfare* principle." The following sections will focus on confidentiality standards regarding counselors in general and as they apply to substance abuse counseling, as well as group settings and working with minors.

CONFIDENTIALITY

Clients seeking counseling often reveal information and emotions that are potentially embarrassing or damaging to the reputation; they do so with an understanding that the counselor will maintain confidentiality. Confidentiality is considered the core value of mental health professionals and is intended to reduce stigma, foster trust, protect privacy, and allow clients to discuss their issues without fear of future repercussions (Remley & Herlihy, 2010). It is the counselor's responsibility to protect client confidential information. It is important to note that the right or privilege of confidentiality belongs to the client, even the deceased client (ACA, 2005), not the counselor. Confidentiality is not only an ethical principle; law often protects it. In fact, clients receiving substance abuse treatment have their confidentiality strictly protected by federal laws—specifically, the laws 42 CFR Part 2 and HIPAA, which will be discussed later.

Because the privilege of confidentiality belongs to the client, the client has the right to waive confidentiality and/or consent to the transmission of confidential information (Remley & Herlihy, 2010). Typical client consents include information being shared with third party payers, other health or mental health professionals, and family or loved ones. The counselor should involve the client in the disclosure decision-making process and obtain written consent to release confidential information (ACA, 2005). Counselors should only release the essential information that was discussed with the client. It is also the counselor's responsibility to ensure information that is transmitted via fax, email, telephone, or another method maintains the client's right to confidentiality (ACA, 2005; AMHCA, 2010), because technology can often lead to unintended breaches of confidentiality and to an increase in the number of people with access to information (Remley & Herlihy, 2010).

Confidentiality cannot be entirely protected, and it is the counselor's responsibility to inform the client of the limits of confidentiality at the onset of the counseling relationship. In general, counselors may be ethically or legally obligated to break confidentiality, without client consent, in limited situations (see Table 2.4).

Some of the limits to confidentiality are a result of the *Tarasoff v. The Regents of the University of California* court decision in 1976. This case imposed a *legal* duty onto therapists to warn people who may become victims of a violent act by a client, and the phrase "duty to warn" was set in motion (Herbert & Young, 2002). The case was redecided in 1976, changing the language to "duty to protect"; the language change reflects the therapist's responsibility to protect or lessen the threat by contacting either authorities or the targeted person, not necessarily both. Although this case technically applies only in California, other states' laws and ethical codes were adopted to reflect

TABLE 2.4 Common limits to confidentiality

If client intends to:
- Harm self
- Harm an identifiable third party
- Transmit a communicable, life-threatening disease to an identifiable third party

If client is the victim or perpetrator of:
- Child abuse/neglect
- Elder abuse/neglect or domestic abuse (depending on state law)
- If client receives a valid court order
- Any emergency situation in which information would be necessary

the *Tarasoff* decision. *Lipari v. Sears, Roebuck & Co.* was a federal case that further extended the duty of counselors to warn *and* protect unknown *and* identifiable victims (Remley & Herlihy, 2010).

The *Tarasoff* decision also contributed to the legal and ethical obligations of counselors to notify a third party if the third party is at high risk for contracting a communicable disease from the client (ACA, 2005; American School Counselor Association [ASCA], 2010). With that being said, however, not all states legally allow this information to be shared; therefore, it is important to refer to the valid state laws and consult with an attorney. Finally, the *Tarasoff* decision influenced the requirement of counselors to break confidentiality in the event that a client intends to commit suicide (ACA, 2005; AMHCA, 2010). Another situation that may constitute a counselor sharing confidential information is in the event that the counselor is presented a valid court order (ACA, 2005; AMHCA, 2010). In the event that a counselor is court ordered to release confidential information, counselors should first attempt to obtain the client's written consent to share information, but they must obey the court order.

Many ethical codes and state laws also indicate that counselors are responsible for reporting indications of abuse or neglect of children, the elderly, and/or persons not competent to care for themselves. Substance abuse counselors need to be aware of their state laws regarding the reporting of abuse; as indicated in earlier chapters, there is a higher incidence of child and/or domestic abuse in substance abuse families (Chamberlain & Jew, 2005; Stevens, 2005). States differ slightly, on which forms of abuse and the minimum age of victims required to be reported.

It is important to note that counselors may discuss client cases with treatment team members; however, the counselor must inform the client of the type of information that will be shared with the team, as well as describe the purpose for sharing information. Counselors may also consult with other counselors and supervisors about clients, as counselor supervision and consultation is necessary for counselors to monitor their effectiveness and to receive guidance with ethical issues; counselors receiving supervision or consultation, however, must protect the identity of the client (ACA, 2005).

Code of Federal Regulations 42, Part 2

The previous section discussed common confidentiality issues pertaining to counselors in general. Counselors providing substance abuse screening or treatment services are legally bound to additional confidential restrictions under the federal law known as *Code of Federal Regulations* (*CFR*) 42, Part 2. *CFR* 42 strictly protects the confidentiality of "records of the identity, diagnosis, prognosis, or treatment of any patient" that are maintained by a program that provides screening or treatment of drug or alcohol abuse and receives funds (directly or indirectly) from the federal government (*CFR* 42, Part 2). The purpose of *CFR* 42 is to encourage substance abusers to seek treatment without fear of discrimination, legal ramifications, or fear of losing one's job. The information shared in this section is only a summary of the federal regulation; substance abuse counselors need to review and follow the *entire* law.

According to *CFR* 42, Part 2, confidential client and former client information can be disclosed in only a few instances: (a) to medical professionals in the event of an emergency; (b) to qualified individuals for the purpose of conducting research, audits, and program evaluations—but such personnel may not directly or indirectly identify any individual patient; (c) with an appropriate court order indicating the extent of the necessary disclosure; and (d) with client consent. The federal confidential regulations, however, do *not* apply in the following circumstances: (a) members or veterans of the armed forces under the care of military facilities, (b) communications within a program, (c) qualified service organizations (e.g., blood work laboratories conducting drug testing), (d) crimes on program premises or against program personnel, and (e) reports of suspected child abuse and neglect. The law *does not* permit the disclosure of information in the event of preventing imminent danger to a third party, preventing the transmission of communicable diseases, or reporting elder abuse or domestic violence. It is important to note that CFR 42, Part 2 supercedes state laws regarding reporting abuse of adults or warning a third party about imminent danger.

The most common disclosure of information under *CFR* 42, Part 2 is as a result of client consent. Clients consenting to a disclosure of information must do so in writing. A written consent must contain the following elements:

- The name of the person or program permitted to make the disclosure
- The name of the person or program receiving the disclosed information
- Patient name
- The purpose of the disclosure
- How much and nature of information
- Patient or authorized person's signature
- Date of consent
- A statement indicating that consent can be revoked at any time, including through verbal indication
- The date, event, or condition on which the consent will expire

In addition to the written consent of disclosure, a written statement, indicating that further disclosure of information is prohibited and that confidential information cannot be used to investigate or prosecute any alcohol or drug patient, must also accompany each disclosure. Any person who violates the *CFR* 42 shall be fined no more than $500 for the first offense and up to $5,000 in each subsequent case.

Confidentiality of Alcohol and Drug Abuse Patient Records

The confidentiality of alcohol and drug abuse patient records maintained by this program is protected by Federal law and regulations. Generally, the program employees may not say to a person outside the program that a patient attends the program, or disclose any information identifying a patient as an alcohol or drug abuser unless:

1. The patient consents in writing. or;
2. The disclosure is allowed by a court order; or,
3. The disclosure is made to medical personnel in a medical emergency or to a qualified personnel for research, audit, or program evaluation. Violation of the Federal law and regulations by a program is a crime. Suspected violations may be reported to appropriate authorities in accordance with Federal regulations. Federal law and regulations do not protect any information about a crime committed by a patient either at the program or against any person who works for the program or about any threat to commit such a crime. Federal laws and regulations do not protect any information about suspected child abuse or neglect from being reported under State law to appropriate State or local authorities.

CFR 42 stipulates that clients be made aware of the federal confidentiality requirements "at time of admission or when patient is capable of rational communication." A sample notice is as follows (*CFR* 42; 2.22 [d]):

Health Insurance Portability and Accountability Act of 1996 (HIPAA)

As with most federal regulations, the Health Insurance Portability and Accountability Act of 1996 (HIPAA) is complex and can only be summarized in this chapter; service providers need to read and adhere to the entire rule. The information shared in this section is not a thorough explanation of HIPAA but is rather outlined with the intent to illustrate how HIPAA and *CFR* 42 often conflict. The purpose of HIPAA is to protect individually identifiable health information while increasing the flow of information between health care providers, health plans, and health care clearinghouses. *Health care providers* are defined as any provider, or third party on behalf of the provider, who electronically transmits health information for the purpose of claims submissions, inquires about patient eligibility benefits, and authorizing referrals. *Health plans* refer to health insurance companies, HMOs, Medicare, Medicaid, and other health carriers. Health care clearinghouses often refer to billing services, community health management information systems, and other processing systems.

The individually identifiable health information that is protected by HIPAA includes demographic data regarding an individual's past, present, or future physical or mental health condition and payment for the health care provided to the individual. It also protects information related to the provision of health care to the individual. HIPAA does not apply to health information contained in employer records or in educational records. Personally identifiable health information may only be disclosed to a covered entity as the privacy rule permits or at the discretion of the client (or personal representative who is legally authorized to make health care decisions on behalf of the client), which must be consented to in writing. A covered entity must disclose information when requested by the client or in compliance investigations conducted by the

U.S. Department of Health and Human Services. The privacy rule permits, but does not require, covered entities to disclose protected health information without client authorization in the following circumstances: (a) to the individual; (b) to treatment, payment, and health care operations; (c) as part of an opportunity to agree or object (informal permission or in instances where the client is incapacitated, or in emergency situations); (d) incident to an otherwise permitted use and disclosure; (e) for public interest and benefit activities (e.g., reporting communicable diseases or keeping employers informed in the event of a work-related injury); and (f) as part of limited data sets for research activities related to public health or health care operations. It should be noted that private information disclosures must be limited to necessary information.

Permitted disclosures of protected health information, without client consent, under the *public interest and benefit activities* circumstance also includes the reporting of abuse, neglect, and domestic violence of victims; the release of information with a court order; the release of information for law enforcement purposes; health oversight activities; in the event of the death of the client to funeral directors and medical examiners; and to facilitate organ, eye, or tissue donation. Personal health information may also be disclosed if there is a serious threat to health or safety to the client or other persons. Finally, information may be disclosed without client permission for "assuring proper execution of a military mission, conducting intelligence and national securities activities that are authorized by law, providing protective services to the President, making medical suitability determinations for US State Department employees, protecting the health and safety of inmates or employees in a correctional institution, and determining eligibility for conducting enrollment in certain government benefit programs" (Office for Civil Rights [OCR], 2003, p. 8).

Health care providers must furnish a privacy practices notice to clients no later than the first service encounter, and they should make every attempt to obtain a written acknowledgment from the client. Covered entities must also supply the notice to anyone on request. Health plans must inform members of the privacy notice to all new enrollees at enrollment, and they must send reminder notifications every three years.

The previous two sections described federal laws protecting confidentiality; they also delineated the limits to confidentiality related to these laws. The next two sections will focus on confidentiality issues in specific settings or with specific populations, particularly group settings and school settings, and working with minors and diverse clients.

Confidentiality in Group Counseling or 12-Step Groups

Group counseling and 12-step-type groups are popular treatment/support options for clients in recovery from drug or alcohol abuse. Despite the legal and ethical regulations that apply to professional counselors, confidentiality cannot be assured in group settings. In group counseling, the leader may be a certified/licensed professional who is bound by confidentiality, but the group members are not legally bound to confidentiality, even if they signed an agreement at the onset of the group experience (Coleman, 2005). Confidentiality and privileged communication laws do not protect 12-step-type groups that are not run by licensed, credentialed professionals. In fact, group members can actually be forced to testify against another group member (Coleman, 2005). Such an instance occurred in the *Cox v. Miller* appellate case when Paul Cox admitted to killing two people while under the influence (Coleman, 2005). Group members were subpoenaed and forced to testify against Cox by divulging the information that he revealed during group. On the other end of the spectrum, the District of Columbia imposes civil and criminal penalties for group members who disclose confidential information shared in a group counseling setting (Coleman, 2005). Clearly the disparity between these policies highlights the importance of substance abuse counselors having an awareness and understanding of federal regulations and their state regulations.

The limits to confidentiality in group settings seriously undermine the substance abuse recovery process. Substance abuse clients need to be assured of and are legally entitled to confidentiality when disclosing personal information—or at least when working with a substance abuse professional. It is therefore important that when a client is referred to group therapy or 12-step groups that they be made aware of their rights and the limits to confidentiality and privileged information prior to attending group support. Unfortunately, many insurance companies require clients to attend a 12-step group for eligibility of substance abuse treatments. Professional counselors must consider that not all clients are appropriate for group counseling settings, as many clients have coinciding mental health conditions (Coleman, 2005). Counselors are obligated to screen clients for group appropriateness for the safety and benefit of all clients. If group counseling is an inappropriate course of treatment for the client, it is the counselor's responsibility to communicate this with the insurance company.

Confidentiality of Minors

Understanding the privilege and limits of confidentiality of minors can be difficult, particularly because there are several conflicting laws that govern confidential information of minors, including *CFR* 42, HIPAA, the Family Educational Rights and Privacy Act of 1974 (FERPA), the Individuals with Disabilities Education Act of 1997 (IDEA), and the 1994 Protection of Pupil Rights Amendment Act (PPRA). Generally, parents have legal authority over their minor children with few exceptions. FERPA, IDEA, and PPRA ensure parental authority, whereas *CFR* 42 and HIPAA restrict information that can be shared with parents.

This section will discuss the confidentiality issues that both substance abuse counselors and school counselors may face when working with minors. School counselors will usually not be providing substance abuse counseling to students; however, they may become aware of a student's substance abuse and will be responsible for providing appropriate referrals and support. In addition, there has been a push for school-based drug and alcohol prevention, in which students are identified and referred to, in-school or contracted staff, substance abuse counselors (Burrow-Sanchez, Jenson, & Clark, 2009). Substance abuse counselors working in a school assistance program, or under contract of a school district, would be responsible for understanding the education laws such as FERPA, IDEA, and PPRA that regulate the confidentiality of minors and parental rights. Furthermore, community substance abuse counselors working with minors may utilize the school counselor as a resource for information and as a support for preventing relapse. Having an awareness of the education laws governing school counselors may be useful to the substance abuse counselor partnering with a school counselor; as the substance abuse counselor will have an understanding of the laws that school counselors need to follow and how the laws conflict with *CFR* 42, Part 2. Substance abuse counselors may also need to educate school counselors about *CFR* 42, Part 2, as some school counselors will be unaware of the regulations and may unintentionally break the law and be subject to litigation.

According to the ASCA *Code of Ethics* (2010), the professional school counselor has a primary obligation to the student and is knowledgeable of laws, regulations, and policies aimed at protecting students' rights. These laws, regulations, and policies impact the confidentiality that can be assured to the student. Confidential information gained through the counseling relationship should not be revealed to others without the informed consent/assent of the student. The exceptions include applicable limits to confidentiality based on federal and state laws, written policies, and ethical standards. Unfortunately, counselors working with minors are faced at the onset with the issue of informed consent; *informed consent* refers to the legal and ethical requirement of counselors to inform the client of the potential risks and benefits of counseling. Although the primary client is the minor, minors often do not have the legal right to give consent; only their parents have this right (Glosoff & Pate, 2002). Typically school counselors do not need the consent of the parents to work with students, simply the minors' assent (Remley & Herlihy, 2010); some scholars, however, recommend that school counselors seek both minor assent and parental consent if working with a particular student for more than three sessions.

Minor clients must also be informed of the limits of confidentiality in understandable language. Typical limits to confidentiality reflect the same limits imposed on adult clients, including consulting with other professionals, preventing imminent danger to the client or others, court orders, and preventing a third party from contracting a communicable disease from the student/client. In the event that the counselor must disclose confidential information it is recommended that the counselor inform the student before disclosing the information and remind the student of the limits of confidentiality that were outlined at the onset of the relationship. The counselor should also describe the purpose for disclosing and the type of information that will be shared.

In regard to the school counselor's obligation to the parent, the ASCA Ethical Code (2010) states that although the counselor's primary obligation is to the student, counselors "recognize that working with minors in a school setting requires school counselors to collaborate with students' parents/guardians to the extent possible" (B.2.b). The ethical code also indicates that it is the counselor's responsibility to inform parents of the counselor's role and the confidential nature of a counseling relationship that is afforded to the student. Students should be informed that the school counselor would contact the parent(s) or guardian(s) in the event that the student indicates a clear and imminent danger to oneself or others. *Imminent danger* refers to an immediate serious threat but is often the counselor's values and beliefs that influence the perception of danger (Glosoff & Pate, 2002). Finally, although school counselors are ethically bound to keep student information confidential, possibly from parents, school counselors must adhere to Family Educational Rights and Privacy Act (FERPA)/ Buckley Amendment, IDEA, and PPRA utilizing any exceptions to those laws that serve confidentiality.

FAMILY EDUCATIONAL RIGHTS AND PRIVACY ACT OF 1974 (FERPA)   FERPA gives parents the right to inspect school records; when the student reaches the age of majority or attends an educational institution beyond high school, the right is transferred to the student (Remley & Herlihy, 2010; U.S. Department of Education, 2009). Parents and eligible students may also request corrections to inaccurate records. Student records can only be disclosed with written parental permission or under the following conditions: (a) to school employees with legitimate educational interests; (b) to a school to which the student is transferring; (c) in connection with financial aid for the student; (d) to organizations conducting studies on behalf of the school; (e) in health and safety emergencies; (f) to comply with a judicial order; (g) to appropriate authorities in connection with the juvenile justice system in accordance to state laws. Schools may also make directory information available without parental consent, provided the school informs and offers an opportunity for the parent/student to request that directory information not be disclosed. It is the school's responsibility to inform parents and students at the age of majority of their rights protected under FERPA.

A parent or eligible student may request any and all school records, including digital data contained on computer servers and email. Often this raises the question as to whether the counselor's personal counseling notes are considered school records. Personal counseling notes would be considered a school record the moment anyone other than the counselor knows of their existence, including students, parents, other counselors, or any other person. Due to the accessibility afforded to parents, school counselors should be careful about what information is placed or retained in a school record, keeping in mind that student confidentiality needs to be protected (ASCA, 2002).

INDIVIDUALS WITH DISABILITIES EDUCATION ACT OF 2004 (IDEA) IDEA was intended to ensure that students with disabilities receive a Free Appropriate Public Education (FAPE) with accommodations in the Least Restrictive Environment (LRE). In 2008, it was expanded to ensure that students with disabilities enrolled in private schools would have access to accommodations and be placed in the LRE. Essentially an Individual Education Plan (IEP) is developed for every child with an identified disability that would qualify the student for special education services (U.S. Department of Education, 2009). Fortunately, educational records and the disclosure of confidential information of special education students fall under FERPA regulations, effectively eliminating conflicts between the two federal regulations. School districts need to inform parents when the district intends to destroy student records. Parents may decide and are entitled to keep their child's records, as they may need the records for other purposes, such as to file for Social Security benefits.

PROTECTION OF PUPIL RIGHTS AMENDMENT OF 1994 (PPRA) PPRA has been referred to as the Hatch Amendment, the Grassley Amendment, and the Tiahrt Amendment after authors of the amendments to the Goals 2000: Educate America Act. It was further revised in 2001, by the No Child Left Behind Act (Illinois State Board of Education, n.d.). Essentially, PPRA states that information collected from students through surveys, analyses, or evaluations funded by the U.S. Department of Education must be available for parental inspection (PPRA, 1994). PPRA also requires state and local entities to obtain consent from parents prior to collecting information from students concerning the following items: (a) political affiliation; (b) mental and psychological problems; (c) sexual behavior and attitudes; (d) illegal or self-incriminating behavior; (e) clinical assessments of other individuals or family members; (f) privileged information shared with lawyers, physicians, or ministers; (g) religious practices, affiliations, or beliefs; and (h) income, other than what is required by law for program eligibility.

Obviously this regulation could complicate screening, referral, and treatment of minors seeking substance abuse counseling without parental consent.

HIPAA   Although HIPAA was discussed earlier, there are regulations that are specific to minors and parental access to confidential information. This section is particularly targeted for substance abuse counselors who are considered "covered entities." HIPAA states that parents can access medical records on behalf of their child, except in cases where the parent is not considered the personal representative; in this case, the privacy rule defers to the state and local laws to determine parental access to the minors' records. If state and local laws do not address this issue, a covered entity (licensed health care professional) has the discretion to deny parental access to the minor's records if the professional determines that the access is not in the minor's best interest. In states where the minor can consent to treatment, and there are no other laws that state otherwise, the minor can decide whether the parents are entitled to confidential information.

CFR 42, PART 2   *CFR* 42, Part 2 warrants a special discussion in regard to minors as it contributes to the complexity of working with minors. According to the federal regulation, counselors must maintain the client's confidentiality, with few exceptions. In fact the counselor may not be able to share information with the parents of a minor. The entire *CFR* 42, Part 2, law applies to any person, regardless of age. The law protects any information about a minor who has received any substance abuse–related services or referrals from a program that receives any federal funding. This would include public schools. Information may be shared with parents if the minor provides written consent (Schwartz & Smith, 2003). The written consent must have all of the elements that *CFR* 42 requires (as described earlier in the chapter), including the minor's signature. The minor may verbally revoke this consent at any time. The exception is if the counselor believes that the minor lacks the capacity to disclose or if there is a substantial threat to the minor's life or well-being.

When a minor seeks treatment for substance abuse, a counselor is faced with a confusing situation. On one hand, the student's confidentiality must be maintained; on the other hand, some state laws restrict the minor from entering a treatment program without parental permission. It is imperative that the counselor knows the appropriate legal age in his/her state for which a minor can seek treatment without parental consent. Fortunately the Internet provides quick and easy access to the current state and federal laws.

Some recommendations are available to counselors working with minors, both in and out of school settings. Glosoff and Pate (2002, p. 27) suggested when working with minors in school settings, counselors should

- apply the applicable ethical code,
- apply the applicable laws,
- apply school and district policies and procedures,
- participate in continuing education workshops to keep abreast of new laws and ethical codes,
- practice prevention through education of stakeholders,
- educate stakeholders on the counseling process, and
- consult.

Lawrence and Robinson Kurpius (2000, p. 135) suggested that when working with minors in a nonschool setting, counselors should

- provide counseling only within areas of competence;
- know the laws regarding privilege and minors;
- at the onset of the therapeutic relationship, state the policies regarding confidentiality, and have both the parent and minor sign an agreement;
- if working with a minor without parental consent, ask the minor to assent in writing;
- keep accurate and objective records of counseling sessions;
- maintain professional liability insurance; and
- consult with colleagues or legal counsel.

MULTICULTURALISM, DIVERSITY, AND ETHICS

In addition to confidentiality, many ethical codes embody the values that counselors need to be competent in diversity and multicultural issues (ACA, 2005; AMHCA, 2010; IAMFC, 2005; NAADAC, 2008; NBCC, 2005). Furthermore, the various codes emphasize that ethical counselors do not discriminate based on age, race, ethnicity, culture, disability, gender, gender identity, sexual orientation, religion, socioeconomic status, or any other bias that would impact the person or the counseling relationship negatively. Clearly, clients are diverse; counselors need to serve the needs of their clients while also ensuring that values are not imposed on clients (Henricksen & Trusty, 2005). Unfortunately, counselors may inadvertently impose their own values onto clients when they lack knowledge about their clients' worldview. In an effort to ensure that counselors will be able to meet the needs of a diverse clientele, the ACA adopted and embraced the *Multicultural Counseling Competencies* (Arredondo et al., 1996). The *Competencies*, influenced by Sue and Sue (1990) and Sue, Arredondo, and McDavis (1992) indicate that culturally competent counselors examine their attitudes, knowledge, and skills in three areas: (a) awareness of own cultural values and biases; (b) awareness of client's worldview; and (c) use of culturally appropriate intervention strategies.

Previously, many ethical codes were value laden and conflicted with cultural values (Toriello & Benshoff, 2003); however, some organizations have taken measures to correct value imposition and pathologizing of misunderstood cultural norms. In 2005, the ACA *Code of Ethics* was updated with an emphasis on multicultural and diversity issues, compelling counselors to keep in mind the cultural context when counseling (Henricksen & Trusty, 2005). For example, ACA's *Code* asserts that counselors need to be aware of how historical and social prejudices have often led to misdiagnosis and pathological labeling of individuals. It also directs counselors to use instruments that have the proper psychometric properties for the client population.

Multicultural counseling competence is particularly relevant to substance abuse counseling. For example, as described in Chapter 11, several naturally occurring drugs/herbs and alcohol are used in conjunction with religious ceremonies. Lack of awareness of the worldview of the client from such a culture could lead to misdiagnosis and inappropriate treatments. The client's worldview is influenced by cultural values but is also individually unique; counselors should not presume that because a client is from a particular ethnic background that he or she subscribes to all of the beliefs of the culture.

The recommendations for working with people from diverse backgrounds is not a prescription of how to work with culturally different people, but rather reveals that what may be viewed as pathological in mainstream culture may in fact be culturally appropriate in other cultures. It is also important to recognize that acculturation impacts personal values as well. In addition, culturally appropriate strategies and treatments may conflict with other laws or ethical guidelines, also complicating decision making on the part of the substance abuse counselor. For example, many cultural groups rely on family for support and expect the family to be included in the decision-making and goal-setting processes of treatment. Despite how effective family inclusion might be for treating the client, unless the client provides the specific written consent, as described earlier, *CFR* 42, Part 2 strictly forbids the sharing of confidential information (without written consent) with family, even in the case of minors.

ETHICAL CONFLICTS SPECIFIC TO SUBSTANCE ABUSE COUNSELORS

Dual Relationships

Counselors in smaller communities, particularly recovered substance abuse counselors (Kaplan, 2005), are at risk for developing dual relationships (Schank, Helbok, Haldeman, & Gallardo, 2010). Small communities create opportunities for increased interactions between individuals. Picture a small town; the only pharmacist in town comes to the only counselor for substance abuse treatment. They likely know each other well. Clearly, the counselor is faced with an ethical dilemma: if the counselor treats the pharmacist, they will have a dual relationship, if the counselor refuses treatment and refers the pharmacist, the pharmacist may not find appropriate treatment. In addition to the dual relationship, there may also be a power differential, since the pharmacist could know personal information about the counselor. Also as described earlier in this chapter, many substance abuse counselors entered the profession through recovery. For many substance abuse counselors, abstinence from drugs or alcohol is attributed to ongoing support such as 12-step groups. However, substance abuse counselors are at risk for developing dual relationships if the recovered counselor participates in the local meetings and former, current, or future clients also attend the meetings (Kaplan, 2005).

Situations like this complicate the counseling relationship and quite possibly detract from the effectiveness of the 12-step-support meeting. First, the counselor is faced with a dilemma as to whether to acknowledge the client/former client. Acknowledging the client creates legal and ethical problems, as it suggests that the individual was or is in treatment, which threatens the confidentiality of the client. However, not acknowledging the client/former client may damage rapport. In regard to the content of the meeting, the counselor may feel compelled to guard the information that he or she shares in order to protect him/herself, the client, or both. The self-imposed restrictions placed on the counselor may make the ongoing support less effective for all, including the counselor, perhaps increasing the chance of relapse. In the event that the counselor does relapse and shares this information with the group, it may impact the former client, perhaps increasing the likelihood that he or she will also relapse. Furthermore, this situation may create a power differential, as the client may gain personal information about the counselor that changes the client's view of the counselor; or, in the case of the former client, the counselor may exploit the lingering power differential that was created during the counseling relationship (Kaplan, 2005). White (2008) also raised concerns about therapist counter-transference, and impairment should the therapist relapse. Clearly, the recovering substance abuse counselor is faced with a myriad of ethical decisions.

Substance abuse counselors who are faced with dual relationships are encouraged to seek supervision, find alternate support for ongoing recovery, look for support from recovery designed for substance abuse professionals, review ethical codes, and use common sense when engaging in situations that create dual relationships (Kaplan, 2005). A recent study revealed that recovered substance abuse counselors under supervision were more ethically aware than those who were not receiving supervision (Kenney Hollander, Bauer, Herlihy, & McCollum, 2006).

Clients and Criminal Activity

Substance abuse counselors are often faced with a dilemma when their clients have or are currently engaged in criminal activities. Aside from the legal and ethical issues that may arise from knowledge of criminal activities, counselors may be torn by their moral values. Due to the nature of the confidential relationship between a counselor and a client, some clients will reveal past criminal acts such as rape and murder. Most ethical codes that apply to counselors only indicate that it is ethical to breech confidentiality if an individual is presently in danger, with the exception of child abuse. Given that the victim has already been victimized, the counselor would not be able to breech confidentiality, as a third-party is not currently in danger. Despite state and local laws, or moral obligations, according to *CFR* 42, Part 2, counselors providing substance abuse counseling are not permitted to report these past crimes. The exception, as previously stated, is when it becomes clear that a client has engaged in activities that are considered child abuse. Counselors are ethically and legally mandated to report child abuse.

When clients are currently engaged in criminal activities substance abuse counselors may be concerned that there is a duty to warn a third party about the client's current or planned acts. Clients dealing illegal drugs are potentially placing others at risk for death. According to the ethical codes and state laws presented earlier, if a third party is in imminent danger, it is the counselor's duty to protect that individual. Also as described earlier, imminent danger is often perceived through the counselor's values and beliefs. Some counselors may believe that the people purchasing the illegal substances are in danger and may feel as though this activity should be reported. Some counselors may feel the need to report based on the illegality of the activity itself. Counselors may also feel like they are faced with a dilemma if a client admits to "lacing" the drugs with toxic substances, either to increase their customers' addiction or to thin out the product to increase the amount that can be sold. In this instance, the counselor may believe that the purchasers are in imminent danger and feel compelled to report the client. However, if the substance abuse counselor works in a setting that is covered under *CFR* 42, Part 2, the counselor may not be able to report this crime or danger. In fact, the regulation states that the information gained through substance abuse counseling cannot be used to convict a person of a crime. There are, however, a few instances in which the counselor may be able to report this danger. If the drugs are being sold to identifiable children, this activity could constitute child abuse. Drugs sold on the school premises are a reportable crime as well. This is especially important to recognize in school settings; students who are receiving substance abuse counseling in a school setting, who also sell drugs to their peers on school grounds, could be reported for committing a crime on the premises.

Conflicting Laws

There are many conflicting federal and state laws that leave counselors in legal and ethical dilemmas. It is the counselor's responsibility to be aware of all the laws and to follow the most stringent law, whether it is a federal or state law. For example, *CFR* 42, Part 2 conflicts with state laws and ethical codes that indicate that counselors have a duty to warn a third party of foreseeable or imminent harm. *CFR* 42 has very strict guidelines for breaking confidentiality; warning a third party is not one of the permissible reasons for breaking confidentiality. A counselor in this situation has four options: (a) obtain a federally sanctioned court order allowing the disclosure, (b) make a disclosure that does not identify the client, (c) make a limited report to medical personnel, or (d) obtain written informed consent from the client (Schwartz & Smith, 2003).

Ethical Code Conflicts

Differences among ethical codes can be problematic because some counselors are actually responsible for knowing and adhering to several codes simultaneously. For example, a substance abuse counselor may belong to ACA and AMHCA and be MAC certified. In this instance, the substance abuse counselor must follow all three ethical codes associated with these organizations. Although all of these codes are similar, they do vary as well, and therefore the counselor must follow the most restrictive statements across all ethical codes. For example, the ACA *Code of Ethics* (2005) requires that at least 5 years must pass since the termination of counseling services before a counselor can engage in a sexual or romantic relationship with a former client, whereas the NAADAC *Code of Ethics*, states that it is never ethical to enter into a sexual or romantic relationship with a former client (NAADAC, 2008).

ETHICAL DECISION MAKING

Toriello and Benshoff (2003) indicated that most ethical decisions are related to confidentiality, dual relationships, informed consent, business practices, competence, sensitivity to differences, and appropriate interventions. A number of ethical decision-making models are available, but counselors must first determine if they are actually faced with an ethical dilemma. Rubin, Wilson, Fisher, and Vaughn (1992) identified the four characteristics of an ethical dilemma: (a) a choice between two courses of action must be made, (b) there are significant consequences for selecting either course of action, (c) each decision is supported by ethical principles, and (d) the ethical principle of the non-selected action will be compromised.

The ACA endorsed *A Practitioner's Guide to Ethical Decision Making* (Forester-Miller & Davis, 1996). This decision-making model has seven steps to assist the practitioner in making ethical decisions:

1. Identify the problem.
2. Apply the ACA *Code of Ethics*.
3. Determine the nature and dimensions of the dilemma.
4. Generate a potential course of action.

5. Consider potential consequences for all options, and choose a course of action.
6. Evaluate the selected course of action.
7. Implement the course of action.

For substance abuse counselors working in conjunction with a school district, the ASCA ethical code (ASCA, 2010) offers an ethical decision-making model Solutions to Ethical Problems in Schools (STEPS; Stone, 2001):

1. Define the problem emotionally and intellectually.
2. Apply the ASCA Ethical Standards and the law.
3. Consider the students' chronological and developmental levels.
4. Consider the setting, parental rights and minors' rights.
5. Apply the moral principles.
6. Determine your potential courses of action and their consequences.
7. Evaluate the selected action.
8. Consult.
9. Implement the course of action.

The decision-making models described here can be slightly altered to assist the substance abuse counselor with decision making; for example, we will use the ACA *Code of Ethics* decision-making model. Step 1 involves determining if the problem is legal, ethical, professional, or clinical. The second step is to apply to the ACA *Code of Ethics;* however, it might be better termed to consult the applicable laws, applicable ethical codes, and/or seek supervision. Often, reviewing the applicable laws and/or ethical codes will reveal a proper course of action. Step 3 involves applying the moral principles of autonomy, nonmaleficence, beneficence, justice, veracity, and fidelity; it also calls for reviewing relevant professional literature and seeking supervision. Step 4 involves brainstorming courses of action with at least one colleague. Step 5 involves reviewing the potential consequences for the generated courses of action and eliminating less useful and/or negative options. Step 6 involves evaluating the selected course of action for ethical or legal dilemmas. Step 7, the final step, is to actually implement the course of action. Using a decision-making model and seeking supervision will ensure that the counselor has considered the legal and ethical issues related to the situation, the best interests of the client, and provide a justification for his or her course of action.

Case Discussions

This section highlights the ethical and/or legal issues facing the counselor with each of the three case studies. At the onset of the counseling session, the counselor should have described the client's right to and the limits of confidentiality. The counselor should also be aware of the state laws, federal laws, and ethical codes that are applicable to the counseling relationship. Each time we encounter an ethical dilemma, using the criteria described earlier, we will use the seven-step decision-making model. To determine whether the ethical concerns are in fact an ethical dilemma, the counselor must answer four questions:

1. Is there a choice between two courses of action?

(Continued)

(*Continued*)

2. Are there significant consequences for selecting either course of action?
3. Can each decision be supported by ethical principles?
4. Will the ethical principles of the non-selected action be compromised?

Case 1 (Sandy and Pam). Possible ethical concerns:

- Pam is emotionally abused by her boyfriend Sam.
- Pam is biracial.

Ethical concern dilemma test:

1. Yes, there is a choice between two courses of action: the counselor could report the emotional abuse or not report the emotional abuse.
2. Yes, if the abuse is reported, Pam may endure more emotional abuse, as she feels "drawn" to Sam and already endures the abuse; if the abuse is not reported, Pam's self-esteem could suffer further, complicating her abuse of drugs and alcohol.
3. Yes, reporting may support beneficence, or doing what is in the best interest of the client; not reporting respects client autonomy.
4. Yes, both beneficence and autonomy are important moral principles at the heart of the counseling profession, but there may have to be a trade-off in this instance.

Now that we have determined that we are faced with an ethical dilemma, we can apply the steps of ethical decision making.

1. Identify the problem: Pam is being emotionally abused by her boyfriend.
2. Apply the applicable ethical codes, state and federal laws to the question:
   Does the emotional abuse require mandatory reporting or allow the reporting? This question can only be thoroughly answered through a series of questions. Before asking the questions, it is important to note that although Sandy and Pam entered into counseling to repair their relationship with each other and with men, they actually received at least a drug/alcohol abuse screening, possibly protecting their confidentiality under *CFR* 42, Part 2. The first question in this case is, does the counselor work for an entity that is covered under HIPAA or *CFR* 42, Part 2? If so, it is unlikely that the emotional abuse could be reported without Pam's express written consent. If the answer is no, then is emotional abuse considered abuse under state law? If the answer is no, then the emotional abuse does not have to be reported. If the answer is yes, then the counselor will want to remind the client of the limits of confidentiality and inform Pam that the abuse must be reported. The counselor should clearly state the process and how much information will be revealed. However, if the counselor determined at the onset that this information could not be disclosed to the authorities, due to *CFR* 42 or HIPAA, the dilemma is resolved. The options are limited to (a) not reporting the abuse or (b) obtaining Pam's written consent to report the abuse. If the counselor determines that the client is not covered under *CFR* 42 or HIPAA, the decision needs further review, as follows:

3. Determine nature and dimensions of the dilemma. This matter was actually already addressed in question 3 of our ethical dilemma test. In this situation, the counselor is faced with the choice to protect client autonomy or beneficence.
4. Generate potential courses of action:
   - Report Sam with client consent.
   - Report Sam without client consent.
   - Do not report Sam.

5. Consider potential consequences for all options, and select a course of action.
   • If the counselor reports Sam with client consent, the counselor will need to provide support to Pam and be aware that the abuse could get worse.
   • If the counselor reports Sam without client consent, the counselor risks losing Pam's trust, and the counselor will need to provide support to Pam and be aware that the abuse could get worse.
   • If the counselor does not report Sam, Pam's self-esteem could suffer further, possibly increasing her use of drugs/alcohol.
6. Evaluate the selected course of action.
7. Implement the course of action.

Clearly, this is a complex series of questions. Due to the limits of this chapter, we will assume that each ethical concern described from here on meets the ethical dilemma test.

The other ethical concern for the counselor working with Sandy and Pam is whether the counselor is competent to work with them. Multicultural counseling competence will be ethically necessary to work most effectively with Sandy and Pam, as Pam is a biracial client—her father is African American, and her mother, Sandy, is White. It will be important for the counselor to have an understanding of the values that both Sandy and Pam have regarding counseling, substance use, and treatment.

Case 2 (Jose and Juanita). Possible ethical concerns:

   • Multicultural issues: Juanita is Mexican, Sarita is Mexican and Hispanic, Jose is Ecuadorian but was raised with American values, and Karen is Mexican and Ecuadorian. Sarita complains of receiving mixed cultural messages.
   • Sarita, age 15, and Karen, age 4, are minors.
   • When Jose is drunk, he tells Sarita he loves her and is upset that they fight so much. When sober, he yells at her and calls her friends dummies.
   • Jose and Juanita think that Sarita needs a stronger hand.
   • Karen is visibly sad and withdrawn.
   • Jose and Juanita drink alcohol or use drugs when they believe the kids are sleeping.

Based on these ethical concerns, it will be necessary for the counselor to be multiculturally competent. Also, ethically, the counselor will have to follow up on whether Jose is sexually, physically, or emotionally abusing Sarita or Karen. If so, this activity will likely have to be reported. If the counselor is planning to report the abuse, he or she should remind Jose of the limits of confidentiality, and what exactly will be reported, in an effort to maintain the trust of the clients and the counseling relationship. The counselor would also want to explore whether Jose or Juanita become intoxicated when the girls are "sleeping." If they were intoxicated, they would likely be unable to appropriately respond to an emergency situation (e.g., fire), and therefore may be reported for child neglect of their 4-year-old daughter.

Case 3 (Leigh). Possible ethical concerns:

   • Leigh is a minor, age 16.
   • Mom has a temper.
   • Leigh is considering running away.

In this situation, it will be important for the counselor to determine whether *CFR* 42 or HIPAA are factors. Because Leigh is a minor, her parents could be entitled to her personal information under HIPAA regulations, but they would not be privy to information

(Continued)

(Continued)

under *CFR* 42, without Leigh's written consent. Determining what may or may not be disclosed to the parents will be particularly important if Leigh runs away, as the counselor may know her whereabouts but would be unable to tell her parents. The counselor will also want to explore what Leigh means by Mom having a temper. If Leigh were being abused, this would have to be reported to authorities.

Case Study

Jamaal

Jamaal, a 19-year-old college student and Division 1 athlete, scheduled an appointment with a counselor in the College Counseling Center. His intake form reveals that he grew up in a single-family home in an inner-city environment. He describes himself as multiracial. He begins the session by reporting that he is experiencing some anxiety. He describes that he has had a really successful football season thus far, and that his coach has stated that professional football team scouts are expected to be attending some of his upcoming games. Jamaal indicates that he is really excited about the prospect of playing for a professional football team, as that has always been his dream. His excitement, however, is diminished by fears of not performing well enough to be drafted by a professional football team.

He tells the counselor that he has been working out for additional hours each day and is watching his diet carefully, but is concerned that his actions are still not sufficiently preparing him for impressing the team scouts. As he becomes more comfortable with his counselor, he states "on the down-low" that his coach has been supplying him with "something to enhance his performance." Jamaal indicates that he is concerned that if he does not use the "performance enhancers" that he will not be at the top of his game. On the other hand, he is concerned that if he is caught using the performance enhancers,

his professional sports career will be over before it even begins. He further explains that he feels pressured by the coach to use performance enhancement drugs. He does not want to let the coach down and states that the coach probably knows what is in Jamaal's best interest. At times Jamaal wonders if the coach is really looking out for him, or if he is looking to gain team wins to improve his coaching status. After sharing his concerns, Jamaal indicates that his thoughts are consumed with these worries and that he just wants to learn how to not worry.

As the counselor probes Jamaal further, Jamaal reveals that if he does not take the provided performance-enhancing drugs, his coach has suggested that Jamaal will not be "fit enough" to be a starter for all of the games. Jamaal is concerned that if he does not get sufficient field time, he will not be able to impress the scouts. He reports feeling stuck between knowing that it is unacceptable to use performance-enhancing drugs in collegiate and professional football, and being able to perform at the top of his game, and wanting to keep his coach satisfied. He has considered telling someone "in power" that he feels coerced by the coach to use performance-enhancing drugs, but is terrified that he will lose his opportunity for a professional football career. He does not want to lose field time, and does not want his drug use to be revealed. He is also concerned that if he reported the coach, it would be his word against the coach's word, and that he would have to admit to using performance-enhancing drugs. Furthermore, he believes that his teammates would never forgive him and would consider him a snitch. Finally, he is concerned that he would lose his athletic scholarship and that he would need to drop out of college and return home, to a place where he feels as though he has a bleak future.

Critical Thinking Questions

1. What are the possible legal issues in this situation?
2. What are the possible ethical issues in this situation?
3. What impact does *CFR* 42 have on the counselor's obligations to the client?
4. What are the personal implications that the counselor may face in this situation?
5. Using the ethical decision-making model, how could this case be resolved?

MyCounselingLab™

Go to Topic 13: *Ethical and Legal Issues in Substance Abuse Counseling*, on the MyCounselingLab™ site (www.MyCounselingLab.com) for *Substance Abuse Counseling*, Fifth Edition, where you can:

- Find learning outcomes for *Ethical and Legal Issues in Substance Abuse Counseling* along with the national standards that connect to these outcomes.
- Complete Assignments and Activities that can help you more deeply understand the chapter content.
- Apply and practice your understanding of the core skills identified in the chapter with the Building Counseling Skills unit.
- Prepare yourself for professional certification with a Practice for Certification quiz.
- Connect to videos through the Video and Resource Library.

MyCounselingLab™ Exercises

Go to the Video and Resource Library on the MyCounselingLab™ site for your text and search for the following clips:

A Counselor Is Caught in the Middle

1. Assuming that the husband was seeking substance abuse counseling, and he asked for his wife to join his counseling sessions, how do you suppose the counselor will proceed?
2. Now assume that it was the wife who was seeking substance abuse counseling, and asked her husband to join her counseling sessions; how do you suppose the counselor will proceed?

(Continued)

(*Continued*)

A Helpful Receptionist

1. Assume that the client is seeking substance abuse treatment; did the receptionist violate any laws or ethical codes? If so, what laws or codes did she specifically violate?
2. If the receptionist works for a private practitioner, how could the receptionist's actions legally or ethically impact the counselor?

A Sexual Attraction

1. Ethically, when would it be okay for a sexual relationship to develop between the therapist and a former client?
2. Legally, when would it be okay for a sexual relationship to develop between the therapist and a former client?

An Ethical Decision to Make

Assume the counselor is the only substance abuse counselor within a 75 mile radius; how should the counselor proceed with this client? What are the ethical issues of referring the client? What are the ethical issues of *not* referring the client?

CONCLUSION

Clearly the substance abuse counselor is faced with a number of legal and ethical issues. Although many of the codes and laws are similar and support analogous principles, there are important differences, even conflicts. Substance abuse counselors should be aware of applicable laws, codes, and regulations, as they are all designed to protect the client. Lack of awareness can potentially lead to infringement of client rights, harm of the client, or malpractice lawsuits. Ethical decision-making models, such as the ones presented, offer a methodical structure for reasoning through dilemmas. Using a decision-making model ensures that all options are reviewed, that the counselor consults with other counselors, and that all applicable laws and ethical principles are considered.

Finally, it is important that the substance abuse professional remain abreast of contemporary laws and ethical codes, as they reflect the current needs of society. Doing so can often be accomplished through participation in continuing education opportunities and organizational affiliations.

3

The Major Substances of Abuse and the Body

ROBERT L. SMITH, PH.D., NCC, CFT, FPPR

Drugs are chemicals that affect the brain and the processing of information. When drugs enter the brain they disrupt its normal processing and change how mechanisms within the brain work. These changes can lead to addiction. As the result of scientific research, neuroscience, it is realized that addiction is a disease that affects both the brain and behavior. The cause or causes of substance use, abuse, and addiction, however, are complex, as indicated in the cases of Leigh, the Martinez Family, and Sandy and Pam. However, we do know that the long-term abuse of alcohol and illicit drugs does affect the brain and most parts of the body with many cases leading to an early death.

Research (Licata & Renshaw, 2010) demonstrated that drug abuse affects neuronal health, energy, metabolism and maintenance, inflammatory processes, cell membrane turnover, and neurotransmission. These changes are believed to be the neuropathology that illicit the cognitive and behavioral impairments related to drug addiction. Despite evidence of the effects of illicit drug and alcohol abuse on the brain and the body, the overall attraction to these chemicals remains strong.

Changes in the drugs that are abused as well as how they are used are consistent themes in the study of addictions. As an example, there continues to be a tendency to inhale rather than to inject drugs such as heroin. Drug users seek out the easiest access to their system whether it be an inhalant, an injection, smoking, or in pill form.

First time use, social abuse, and creative manufacturing of drugs continue, particularly with the club drugs ecstasy, rohypnol, and methamphetamine. Over-the-counter drug abuse and illegal access and abuse of prescription drugs continue to be at the forefront.

All drugs have an effect on the body and brain. This chapter explores some of the physical factors in addiction—the chemical makeup of the commonly abused substances, their effects on the body and brain, addictive factors, and symptoms of withdrawal and overdose. Neuroscience research findings are beginning to provide us with more defined information on the damage caused to the brain as the result of illicit drug abuse.

THE BRAIN

The human brain is the command center of one's body. Evolving over hundreds of millions of years, the brain possesses different centers or systems that process different kinds of information. The complexity of the brain and its interactions with other systems of the body (e.g., endocrine, muscular, vascular) continue to challenge researchers as they attempt to find causes and more effective treatments for substance use, abuse, and addiction. Neuroscience, the branch of biology that focuses on the body's nervous system including the brain, attempts to shed light on the effects of drug abuse on the brain and how brain chemistry is changed (Campbell, 2010). The NIDA Neuroscience Consortium, through its research efforts has established that addiction is a brain-based disease. Research findings have focused on identifying the brain mechanisms that underlie drug cravings and reward systems, vulnerabilities to addiction, and the consequences of abusing drugs (Buckholtz et al., 2010).

Neuroscience Research

Neuroscience research findings continue to provide evidence of how the brain works and how drugs affect the brain (NIDA, 2009b). Technological advances using modern imaging findings on CT, MR imaging, and conventional angiography have allowed researchers to identify the damage to the brain when drug abuse is present (Geibprasert, Gallucci, & Krings, 2009). The consequences of persistent drug abuse and addiction have become evident and convincing as the result of neuroscience research. Leading the charge in researching drug use and abuse is the National Institute on Drug Abuse with its establishment of the Neuroscience Consortium. The consortium provides the forum to facilitate the development of neuroscience research programs to understand, prevent, and treat drug addiction (NIDA, 2009a). The goals in basic neuroscience of the NIDA Neuroscience Consortium include:

- Continue and expand molecular structure-function studies to improve definition of molecular sites of abused drug action and possible therapeutic targets.
- Determine neurobiological events underlying vulnerability factors in drug taking (environmental, physiological/genetic, and cognitive).
- Determine the neurobiological bases of addiction as a possible manifestation of learning or memory.
- Extend the mapping of the neuroanatomy and neurochemistry of the brain reward system as it relates to reward, dysphoria, withdrawal and craving.
- Determine the effects of drug abuse on neuro-endocrine, immune, and autonomic systems.

The goals in Clinical Neuroscience include:

- Expand research on the effects of drugs of abuse and addiction on the structure and function of the human brain.
- Determine the effects upon the human brain of pharmacological, non-pharmacological, and behavioral treatments for drug abuse and addiction.
- Elucidate the pharmacokinetics and pharmacodynamics of drugs of abuse and therapeutic drugs in the human brain.
- Determine the neurobiological, etiologic, and mechanistic relationships of drug abuse and mental disorders.
- Determine the effects of drugs of abuse on cognitive processes as well as the role of cognitive processes in drug-seeking behavior (NIDA, 2009b).

Throughout this chapter the most recent neuroscience research findings are cited providing the reader with an update on the effects of drug abuse and how they have changed the makeup of the brain. Neuroscience research provides us with an understanding of how drugs affect the brain structure, but more importantly the parts of the brain that have shown the ability to repair themselves following the abstinence of substance abuse.

The Structure of the Brain

The brain itself is a 3-pound mass of gray and white matter, divided into two sections called *hemispheres*. The body of the corpus callosum forms the fissure dividing them and connects them with fibers. The corpus callosum serves as the communication vehicle between the left and right sides of the brain. The left hemisphere controls the right side of the body and is basically concerned with thinking and intellectual functions. It is the site of logic and verbal ability, producing and understanding language. The right hemisphere controls the left side of the body and is considered to be the creative side involving intuitive and creative processes. The right hemisphere is involved with temporal and spatial relationships, analysis of nonverbal information, and communicating emotion. It uses pictures, while the left hemisphere uses words. The sex of an individual, which is determined hormonally in the brain before birth, influences the development, organization, and basic shape of the brain (Scholz et al., 2006).

The brain consists of three basic parts: the *hindbrain,* which contains the cerebellum and lower brain stem; the *midbrain,* which houses relay areas from the upper brain stem; and the *forebrain* (see Figures 3.1 and 3.2) (Ormrod, 2008). Although substance use affects the brain overall, the forebrain houses the mechanisms that most often interact with substances that can cross the blood–brain barrier. The forebrain includes the cerebral hemisphere and the rind or outer covering (about 2 millimeters thick) called the *cortex.* Higher state of consciousness activities take place in the cortex, including thought, perception, motor function, sensory data processing, and vision. Neuroscience research (Xue et al., 2009) used magnetic resonance imaging (MRI) to investigate functional specificity in the medial prefrontal cortex regarding decision making. Results demonstrated that the relative strengths of signals in the brain indicate the behavioral decisions one makes involving risk and uncertainty. The brain also includes the *limbic system* and the structures of the *diencephalon,* which contains the *thalamus* and the *hypothalamus.* The limbic system lies just below and interconnects with

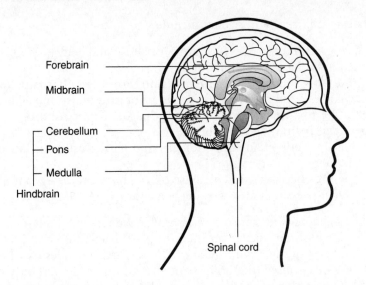

FIGURE 3.1   The human brain.

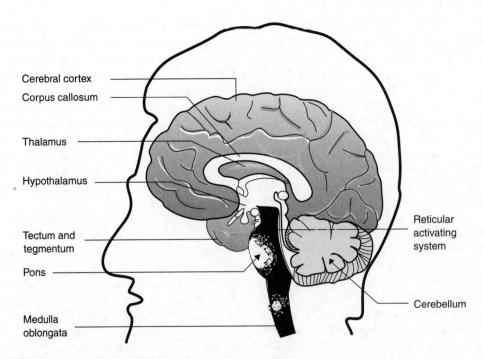

FIGURE 3.2   Cross section of the brain.

Source: From *Abnormal and Clinical Psychology, Series II* (Transparencies) by David Steele, 1996, Upper Saddle River, NJ: Prentice Hall.

the cortical area. It is involved in emotional behavior and long-term memory, while the hypothalamus regulates more basic, autonomic (primitive) functions such as hormonal activity, thirst, hunger, temperature, sex drive, and sleep. The complexities of the brain's structural and functional systems are becoming more understood through brain imaging and graph theoretical analysis (Bullmore & Sporns, 2009).

The brain interfaces with all of these systems in a space about the size of a grapefruit. It accomplishes this through *neuronai* (nerve cell) networking. The brain is composed of an estimated 100 billion neurons (see Figure 3.3), with an astounding amount of structural variations and functional diversity found in brain cells that in complex ways are important to cognition, behavior, and psychopathology (NIDA, 2010a). Unlike most other cells, it has been believed that neurons cannot regrow after damage (except neurons from the hippocampus). This belief is now being challenged (Lau, Yau, & So, 2011). About 1/10 of these neurons are nerve cells that have actual or potential links with tens of thousands of others. Signals are processed by groups of neurons called nuclei areas (Johnson & Kenny, 2010). These groups are cellular clusters that form highly specialized centers. These centers are interconnected by bundles of nerve fibers called *tracts,* which link up the different switchboards of the brain.

The tracts all conduct information in much the same way. Chemical messengers (molecules) called *neurotransmitters* are released by electrical impulses (action potentials) that reach the presynaptic membrane of a given synapse. These pathways can send thousands of electrochemical messages per second and yet work in harmony, because each cell in a tract responds like a complex, megamicroscopic information processor (NIDA, 2010a). It is this process of electrical "blipping" and chemical "dripping" that allows the brain to communicate. Newly sensed experiences (*imprints*) are

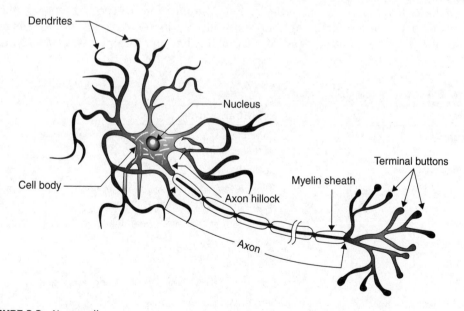

FIGURE 3.3 Nerve cell.

Source: From *Abnormal and Clinical Psychology, Series II* (Transparencies) by David Steele, 1996, Upper Saddle River, NJ: Prentice Hall.

sifted, rejected, or passed onto appropriate pathways. These imprints are matched to ones already encoded in the data banks directing conscious and unconscious feelings, thoughts, and actions. A bulk of this encoding is stored at an unconscious level.

Each neuron has a central body, from which wispy tendrils called *dendrites* appear to sprout at one end, and a long slender thread called an *axon* at the other. When stimulated, the axon and dendritic branches generate electrical impulses by the exchange of electrically charged sodium and potassium atoms through ionic channels in the cellular membrane. This creates a reversed polarity that allows the impulse to zoom down the axon at speeds up to 300 miles per hour.

A neuron's cell membrane can reverse its polarity from negative to positive and back again in one-thousandth of a second. A strongly stimulated neuron can easily fire 1,000 times per second. When the impulse reaches the button (*terminal*) at the end of the axon, it causes tiny sacs (*vesicles*) to fuse with the membrane (via calcium release) and discharge chemical molecules called (neuro-) *transmitters* and *peptides* (see Figure 3.3).

It is believed that most neurons contain multiple transmitters. The chief chemical messenger may be a neurotransmitter (amine/amino acid), but it acts in conjunction with a neuropeptide to modulate the transmission and/or a neurohormone to prolong the transmission. There are several main neurotransmitters: *acetylcholine* (Ach), *dopamine* (DA), *norepinephrine* (NE), *epinephrine* (E), *serotonin* (5-HT), *histamine* (H), and *gamma-amino-butyric acid* (GABA) (see Table 3.1). These neurotransmitters discharge from the terminal of one neuron (presynaptic), cross a small gap called the *synapse*, and find their way into "receptor" sites on the adjoining neuron (postsynaptic) (see Figure 3.4). Each neurotransmitter or hormone has a particular shape that allows it to fit into the appropriate receptor site, much like a key fitting into a lock. If the key fits the lock, it will turn on a message in the adjoining neuron. The receptors exhibit a self-regulatory capacity, changing their sensitivity during excessive or infrequent use. The classic neurotransmitters tend to have more than one receptor. *Glycine*, a simple

TABLE 3.1 Drugs related to neurotransmitters

Drug	Neurotransmitter
Alcohol	Gamma-aminobutyric acid (GABA), serotonin, metenkephalin
Marijuana	Acetylcholine
Cocaine/amphetamines	Epinephrine (adrenaline), norepinephrine (noradrenaline), serotonin, dopamine, acetylcholine
Heroin	Endorphin, enkephalin, dopamine
Benzodiazepines	GABA, glycine
LSD	Acetylcholine
PCP	Dopamine, acetylcholine, alpha-endopsychosine
MDMA (ecstasy)	Serotonin, dopamine, adrenaline
Nicotine	Adrenaline, endorphin, acetylcholine
Caffeine	Dopamine, norepinephrine

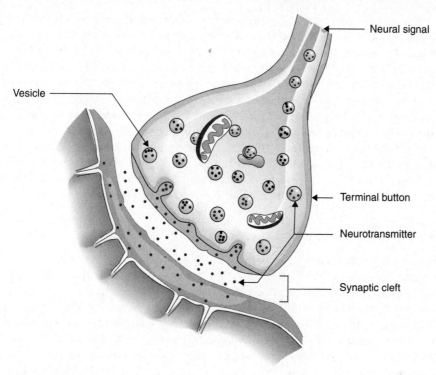

FIGURE 3.4 Synapse.

Source: From *Abnormal and Clinical Psychology, Series II* (Transparencies) by David Steele, 1996, Upper Saddle River, NJ: Prentice Hall.

amino acid, is unique in that it is only found as a transmitter in vertebrates (NIDA, 2010a). Another amino acid, *glutamate,* is present in high concentration in the brain and is a powerful stimulant of neuronal activity. *Adenosine* and *peptides* also influence neuronal activity, but their actions are much more mysterious, in that their activity is widespread (i.e., they can be released presynaptically or postsynaptically). In addition, adenosine, found at virtually every synapse, can inhibit release of presynaptic transmitters or increasing postsynaptic response in some cases.

The neurotransmitter interaction functions for the well-being of the individual, ensuring the basic survival of that organism. Survival is accomplished by the recall of memory imprints that have been stored in the neocortex of the brain. These survival skills become more sophisticated as the organism develops and uses them repeatedly in day-to-day functions.

The human brain has many abilities. One of these is the ability to conceptualize and formulate future possibilities, including dangers. In early childhood, the brain forms pathways based on the raw data it receives from the environment. The mind wires up these pathways quickly so that it can avoid or survive potential dangers. For instance, if a child is repeatedly exposed to "fight or flight" situations, whether real or perceived, the association to this stimuli will cause the mind to strengthen developing excitatory pathways. This allows the organism to be more vigilant and foster its survival.

The feeling of pleasure is considered one of the most important emotions connected to survival. Closely connected to this feeling is the brain's reward system, found to be highly associated with drug abuse (SAMHSA, 2010). It is produced and regulated by a circuit of specialized nerve cells in a limbic structure called the *nucleus accumbens*. Dopamine-containing neurons relay pleasure messages through this part of the brain via a circuit that spans the brain stem, the limbic system, and the cerebral cortex. Scientists consider this feeling of pleasure or reward to be a strong biological force. If something elicits strong pleasure within the brain, it is wired so that its owner will develop behaviors that will reinforce this good feeling. Basic drives such as eating, sexual activity, and the need for power are activities that evoke rewards in the brain. We learn quickly to reproduce events that bring us pleasure, and such rewards become one of the brain's most powerful learning mechanisms (NIDA, 2010a).

Psychoactive Substances and the Brain

For centuries, the brain has been the recipient of psychoactive substances, often allowing human beings to cope with both internal and external stressors. Substances have offered the user a variety of effects, including pain relief, pleasure, mystical insight, escape, relaxation, stimulation, and ecstasy, as well as a sense of social and spiritual connectedness. It has been proposed that the pursuit of intoxication is as powerful a drive in human beings (and many animal species) as the innate survival drives of hunger, thirst, and sex. A "barrier," known as the blood–brain barrier acts to keep certain substances in the blood away from brain cells. Although not well understood, a factor in the barrier is the nonpermeability of capillaries in the brain. Brain capillaries have no pores, preventing water-soluble molecules from passing through capillary walls. Only lipid-soluble substances can pass through the lipid capillary wall. The blood–brain barrier is not completely developed in humans until age 1 to 2 and can be damaged by head trauma or cerebral infection.

Substances are considered psychoactive when they can cross the blood–brain barrier and create changes in the brain and, therefore, in the mind and behavior. The primary use of psychoactive substances is to change the neurochemistry of the brain and alter one's consciousness. Substances accomplish this by exciting, quieting, or distorting the chemical and electrical state. Substance addiction can include intoxicating substances such as ethanol (ethyl alcohol), marijuana, crack cocaine, heroin, and caffeine, which produce rapid neurochemical shifts (8 seconds to 20 minutes), or nonintoxicating substances such as nicotine, and refined carbohydrates.

Specific sites in the brain demonstrate a possible neurochemical basis for the ongoing use of substances. These sites include the *medial forebrain bundle* (MFB), the *ventral tegmental area* (VTA), the *nucleus accumbens*, the *hypothalamus*, and the *locus coeruleus* (LC).

The hypothalamus houses multiple nerve centers that are necessary for the maintenance of life. Among them is the "pleasure center" that converges with the MFB as well as the nucleus accumbens and the VTA. There is a profuse convergence of cell bodies, axons, and synaptic terminals among these systems. The MFB region has been associated with the positive reinforcement associated with drugs of abuse by the release of dopamine (DA). Likewise, it has been found that several categories of abusable substances have a *synergistic*, or an enhancing effect on the brain stimulation reward thresholds that involve the DA system. This includes all major drugs of abuse except some of the hallucinogenics.

Neuroscience studies have clearly shown that abnormalities in the brain are produced by drug abuse. As an example, Tobias et al. (2010) found microstructural abnormalities in white matter underlying and interconnecting prefrontal cortices and hippocampal formation as the result of methamphetamine abuse.

Of particular interest is the effect of drugs of abuse on *plasticity*. Plasticity is the ability of brain cells to remember. It is thought, for example, that repeatedly stimulated synapses are changed in function (i.e., they learn). The changes seem to be maintained for extended periods of time. This phenomenon is known as *long-term potentiation* (LTP). N-methyl-D-aspartate (NMDA) receptors are thought to be pivotal in LTP, plasticity, and long-term depression. Repeated exposure to drugs create a condition called *excitotoxicity,* which damages and eventually kills NMDA neurons, thus altering plasticity, especially in the developing brain of children and adolescents. With the findings regarding drug damage to the brain we are also beginning to unlock the secrets of its adaptability or "plasticity" with implications for reversing damage as the result of drugs and other phenomenon (Doidge, 2007).

CONTROLLED SUBSTANCES SCHEDULES

In an effort to control the growing consumption of both the types and quantity of drugs that were being abused in the 1960s, the U.S. Congress passed the Comprehensive Drug Abuse Prevention and Control Act in 1970, establishing the Drug Enforcement Agency (DEA) within the Department of Justice in order to enforce drug policy. Another provision of the act established a schedule of controlled substances that, by federal law, regulates the sale of certain drugs. They vary from low potential for abuse, with currently accepted medical use (Schedule V), to those with a high potential for abuse and no currently acceptable medical use (Schedule I). Schedule V drugs include some over-the-counter medications, while Schedule I drugs are prohibited from medical and most research uses.

The remainder of the chapter discusses specific classifications of abused substances. Substances in each classification with their properties, effects of the substance, and withdrawal symptoms are presented.

DEPRESSANTS

Depressants of the central nervous system (CNS) include *ethanol, barbiturates, methaqualone* (a prescription depressant that is no longer legal in the United States), *meprobamate* (Librium, sometimes used in alcohol detoxification and a forerunner of Valium), and all *benzodiazepines* (e.g., Valium and Xanax). At usual doses, depressants dampen CNS activity while displaying a weak analgesic effect. CNS depressants such as ethanol are sometimes referred to as "top-down" CNS depressants, because their action begins in the cerebral cortex and works its way "down" to the core or reptilian brain. This action explains why the course of intoxication starts with disinhibition and impaired judgment, moves on to emotional liability and loss of motor skills, and, in cases of severe intoxication referred to as *alcohol poisoning,* ends with coma or death. In the latter case, virtually the entire CNS has been put to sleep by the drug, so breathing and heartbeat simply cease.

All drugs in this class can become physically addictive, can be lethal in overdose, and demonstrate a cross-tolerance and potentiation of one another. *Cross-tolerance* refers to the ability of one classification of drugs to produce a tolerance to the effects of another pharmacological classification, and *potentiation* to the ability of the combined action of some drugs used together to be greater than the sum of the effects of each drug being used alone. Potentiation is sometimes referred to as *synergistic effect.* Depressants also have the ability to induce severe depression as well as promote extreme anxiety during withdrawal.

Alcohol

Ethyl alcohol (ethanol) is a clear liquid with a bitter taste. It can be used as an anesthetic, a poison, a foodstuff, an antiseptic, or a surface blood vessel dilator. It is an unstable CNS depressant that produces euphoria and disinhibition. These well-known side effects, together with the fact that its use is legal for most adults, undoubtedly account for alcohol's popularity. Without question, alcohol is the most used psychoactive drug in existence.

INCIDENCE The National Survey on Drug Use and Health (NSDUH) estimates the prevalence of alcohol use by reporting on participation at three levels. The NSDUH report defines a "drink" as a can or bottle of beer, a glass of wine or a wine cooler, a shot of liquor, or a mixed drink with liquor in it.

PSYCHOACTIVE EFFECTS Ethanol is a small organic molecule consisting of only two carbon atoms surrounded by hydrogen atoms, with a hydroxyl group attached to one of the carbons (CH_3-CH_2-OH). This molecular arrangement provides ethanol with water-soluble properties as well as lipid- (fat-) soluble properties. As it passes the blood–brain barrier after ingestion and affects the cerebral cortex, most people feel their inhibitions quickly disappear and sense a more relaxed social attitude concerning their interactions with others. Contrary to the belief of some, alcohol does not improve mental or physical capabilities. Individuals who continue to drink for an extended period of time (two to three drinks per hour for several hours) often disregard their own pain, exhibit poor judgment, and endanger their own or others' safety.

As a depressant, alcohol has a relaxing effect, but also clouds one's inhibitions and judgment. Many people erroneously assume that alcohol is a powerful aphrodisiac and a sexual stimulant. The assumption is based on observing people who appear to have a heightened sexual response when drinking. This reaction is due to the disinhibiting factor of ethyl alcohol and its immediate influence on the frontal lobes of the brain where the neurochemical mechanisms for exercising judgment are located.

Early thinking was that the primary action of alcohol in the brain included the activation of the endorphin reward system. More recently it has been demonstrated that ethanol has a more complex mechanism.

One issue is the report by many that alcohol stimulates them. This could be caused by the *biphasic* action of ethanol, whereby some neurons are activated by low levels of the drug. This notion is consistent with reports that the stimulation of the drinker occurs in the beginning of the drinking cycle. At higher levels of ETOH concentration, the effect on the same nerve cells is reversed. However, biphasic action is only one theory of alcohol mechanism. The evidence points to the reality that we are beginning to understand the effects of alcohol on brain functioning. Neuroscience research has begun to help us better understand the effects of alcohol, particularly with reward and pleasure channeling.

Of particular interest is alcohol's effect on two amino acid neurotransmitters, glutamate (Glu), an excitatory transmitter, and gamma-amino butyric acid (GABA). GABA is the major inhibitory transmitter in the brain. The amino acid transmitters are thought to be the major transmitters in the mammalian CNS, but others—serotonin, dopamine, and noreprinephrine have received more attention. Recently, however, the importance of alcohol's effect on Glu and on GABA has been demonstrated. These advances have led to the discovery that alcohol increases the inhibitory activity of GABA and decreases the excitatory activity of Glu receptors, two major ways of suppressing brain activity. The increase in GABA is likely to be a major factor in the general sedation characteristic of alcohol.

Alcohol's effect on glutamate may impair the formation of new memories by suppressing activity at NMDA receptor sites. It is responsible as well for impairing complex thought and judgment while intoxicated. Suppression at NMDA sites may explain alcohol-related memory deficits.

EFFECTS ON THE BODY   A standard drink contains approximately 0.5 ounce of ethyl alcohol. It makes no difference whether that drink is served in a 12-ounce can of beer, a 4- or 5-ounce glass of wine, or a single shot (about 1.25 ounces) of distilled spirits. A standard drink is the measure used to compute blood alcohol levels.

Blood alcohol level (BAL) or blood alcohol concentration (BAC) is measured in milligrams per 100 milliliters of blood (e.g., 80 mg/100 ml), but it is more often expressed as a percentage of blood ethanol (0.08 BAC). Either of the foregoing examples represents the level of legal intoxication in most states and requires the consumption of roughly three standard drinks within 1 hour to achieve this status.

One ounce of pure ethyl alcohol contains about 210 calories that can convert to energy at the cellular level, but it contains no nutrients to nourish the cell. It can pass through every tissue cluster in the brain and body if enough is consumed. Immediately after drinking, the mouth and esophagus begins to absorb small amounts via the mucous membranes. The stomach will rapidly assimilate about one-quarter of a dose, followed by complete absorption through the walls of the small intestine within 20 to 30 minutes.

The cardiovascular system is affected by low doses of alcohol through the dilation of peripheral blood vessels, while severe alcohol intoxication will create a depression of the entire cardiovascular system. Alcohol irritates the gastrointestinal tract through direct contact, as well as by stimulating the secretion of stomach acid and pepsin, which can cause gastritis and injury to the mucous membranes of the stomach lining. The presence of food can modify these effects to some extent and also slows the absorption rate of alcohol. Because alcohol is a diuretic, it overstimulates the production of urine in the kidneys.

The liver, the body's largest glandular organ, is associated with dozens of processes of body chemistry and metabolism. It is the primary organ of alcohol detoxification.

This 3-pound organ is the central filter for the blood and is the site of 90% of alcohol metabolism. The major pathway for such conversion involves the enzyme *alcohol dehydrogenises* and occurs in two phases in the liver. The first phase produces the metabolite *acetaldehyde,* and the second converts acetaldehyde to *acetic acid*. With continued heavy intake of alcohol, the liver cells begin to accumulate fatty deposits that destroy the cells and produce scarring called *cirrhosis*. This disease occurs in, and is fatal to, about 10% of chronic alcoholic patients.

Nearly every organ in the body is affected by heavy use of alcohol. Gastritis, diarrhea, and gastric ulcers are commonly associated with heavy drinking. A single heavy drinking episode can cause the pancreas to hemorrhage. The consumption of large amounts of alcohol can depress the respiratory center in the medulla, causing death. Alcohol can be deadly for individuals with epilepsy because it can promote convulsive seizures due to a hyperexcitable rebound condition in the brain after drinking has ceased.

Strong evidence indicates links between alcohol and cancers that occur in the upper digestive tract, respiratory system, mouth, pharynx, larynx, esophagus, and liver. There is a possible link between alcohol and cancer of the pancreas, stomach, large intestine, rectum, and breast. Alcohol ingested with cocarcinogens such as tobacco is believed to account for some of the cancer deaths that occur in the United States (American Cancer Society, 2010).

Besides liver damage (cirrhosis), alcoholics may develop pathology of the nervous system due to vitamin deficiencies, as well as experience neurological complications such as the Wernicke-Korsakoff syndrome. This chronic brain syndrome is the result of thiamin deficiency from poor absorption, metabolism, and storage of the vitamin in the prolonged presence of alcohol, as well as poor diet while drinking. It has as its most striking feature a dementia characterized by permanent short-term memory loss coupled with filling in the blanks of memory with exaggerated stories.

TOLERANCE AND DEPENDENCE   In the presence of repeated drinking, tolerance to the effects of alcohol begins as the body adapts to try to maintain its normal functioning in the continual presence of a foreign chemical. The liver becomes more efficient in detoxifying alcohol, the cells of the brain become less and less sensitive to the intoxicating effects of the chemical, and the chronic drinker exhibits fewer of the behavioral effects of intoxication. In addition, while brain cells may be less sensitive, damage continues unabated to the brain and organs such as the liver.

Risk of dependence on alcohol, both physically and psychologically, is moderate to high. The etiology is complicated and appears to be affected by such factors as genetics, biological changes, brain reward systems, and stress relief mechanisms. It is suggested that the younger the onset of drinking, the greater the chance of that person developing a clinically defined alcohol disorder.

WITHDRAWAL   The acute withdrawal syndrome generally appears within 12 to 72 hours after drinking has ceased. The earliest signs of withdrawal are associated with *hyperarousal* and can include anxiety, irritability, insomnia, loss of appetite, tachycardia (rapid heartbeat), and tremulousness. An "eye-opener" (i.e., a drink first thing in the morning) is a common solution to hyperarousal for the problem drinker. Hence, alcohol abuse interviews commonly include a question concerning morning drinking.

Alcoholic hallucinosis occurs in about 25% of withdrawal episodes, usually within the first 24 hours. It includes true auditory and visual hallucinations, illusions, and misperception of real environmental stimuli.

Convulsive seizures, or "rum fits," can occur with acute alcohol withdrawal. These seizures are most often of the grand mal variety, in which the eyes roll back in the head; body muscles contract, relax, and extend rhythmically and violently; and loss of consciousness occurs. About a third of alcoholics who have seizures in withdrawal develop delirium tremens.

Delirium tremens, or DTs, is the most serious form of withdrawal. Without medical intervention, mortality rates are as high as 20%. With medical help, there still remains a 1% to 2% death rate.

Benzodiazepines have worked as a prophylactic for DTs. In addition, these medications can mitigate the anxiety and irritability of hyperarousal. However, because of the potential of cross-addiction, they must be prescribed judiciously. Chlordiazepoxide (Librium), which was the prototype for benzodiazepines, has been used to manage acute withdrawal, because it has a lower potential for abuse than other drugs of its type.

TOXIC AND LETHAL EFFECTS   Comas can occur at BALs of 0.40%. Alcohol becomes lethal in higher concentrations by depressing the respiratory center in the medulla.

GENDER DIFFERENCES   Early studies on the effects of alcohol had only men as subjects, assuming that their findings could be generalized to women. However, it has been found that, under standard conditions, BALs in women can reach higher levels, for several reasons. First, men have a greater average body water content (65% ± 2%) than women (51% ± 2%). Since alcohol is absorbed into total body water, a standard dose of alcohol will be therefore more concentrated in women. Second, women have a lower level of gastric alcohol dehydrogenase (ADH), thus metabolizing significantly less than men under standard conditions. Women develop alcohol-related disorders such as brain damage, cirrhosis, and cancers at lower levels of drinking than men.

FETAL ALCOHOL SYNDROME   Alcohol ingested during pregnancy easily passes through the placental barrier and can result in fetal alcohol syndrome (FAS). Doctors first recognized and reported FAS in 1973 as a pattern of birth defects emerged in children born to alcoholic mothers. Since that time, numerous studies have established ethanol as a *teratogenic* agent, producing defects in utero. FAS is characterized by distinct symptoms that can generally be observed in the newborn. The child will exhibit fetal growth retardation and is at risk to suffer craniofacial deformities, incur central nervous system damage, and have major organ malformations. A high percent, 80% to 90%, will exhibit mental retardation. The symptoms can range from gross *morphological* defects (defects to the structure or form of the body) to more subtle cognitive–behavioral problems. FAS is one of the leading causes of mental retardation in newborns, resulting in a significant cost of hundreds of millions of dollars annually in the United States.

Fetal alcohol effects (FAE) have been associated with moderate prenatal drinking. The typical symptoms of hyperactivity, distractibility, impulsiveness, and short attention spans are similar to attention deficit hyperactivity disorder (ADHD). However, children with FAS or FAE are more intellectually impaired than ADHD-diagnosed children. Technology continues to improve to help identify and assess children with Fetal Alcohol Spectrum Disorder (FASD) (Drake, 2009).

Benzodiazepines: Prescription and Over-the-Counter Medications

Benzodiazepines such as diazepam (Valium), chlordiazepoxide HCI (Librium), and alprazolam (Xanax), are the most widely prescribed group of drugs in the treatment of anxiety, acute stress reactions, and panic attacks. Unfortunately, these prescription drugs, over-the-counter medications, are abused and often lead to an addiction (NIDA, 2009e). Sedating benzodiazepines, such as triazolam (Halcion) and estazolam (Pro-Som) are prescribed for short-term treatment of sleep disorders. Although commonly prescribed and considered less lethal than the barbiturates, they are supposed to be used only for brief periods of time. Many are capable of achieving a daytime anxiolytic response without excessive drowsiness. However, drugs from the benzodiazepine family can interfere with the normal sleep cycle, and upon withdrawal after prolonged use, the patient may experience rapid eye movement (REM) rebound, with a greatly increased need for REM sleep, often accompanied by vivid, frightening dreams.

Xanax, as a central nervous system (CNS) depressant remains popular as a prescription drug that ends up being abused by children and adolescents. *Xanbars, french fries,* and *footballs* are terms used to describe individual doses of Xanax by youthful users who favor the drug because of its portability, ease of access, concealment, and its euphoric effect. Xanax has been a prescribed drug that has been easy for youngsters to obtain.

INCIDENCE   The incidence of benzodiazepine abuse depends partly on the definition of substance abuse. If the criterion is any nonmedical use, then benzodiazepine abuse is common.

The 2005 NSDUH data on benzodiazepine use was partially obscured by the way drugs of this type are defined. The NSDUH reported that 2.5 million persons aged 12 or older used psychotherapeutics nonmedically for the first time within the past year. Of those, 2.2 million indicated they used pain relievers, 1.3 million mentioned tranquilizers, and 247,000 named sedatives. Methodological problems prevented an accurate data set for indicating the incidence of benzodiazepine abuse. However, it is known that taking these drugs beyond how they are prescribed can affect the body and brain. Neuroscience research has demonstrated the effects on the brain through altering the reward system and thus increasing a craving for over-the-counter drugs (NIDA, 2009e).

PSYCHOACTIVE EFFECTS   There are more than a dozen varieties of benzodiazepines. The most notorious and controversial are diazepam (Valium), chlordiazepoxide (Librium), and triazolam (Halcion). Benzodiazepines, however, have been prescribed for a number of reasons. Alprazolam (Xanax) has been found effective in the treatment of panic attacks. Benzodiazepines are considered effective in the short-term treatment of anxiety, regardless of the cause. Short-term effects can include a "sleepy" and uncoordinated feeling during the first few days, as the body becomes accustomed to the drug. Long-term use has the potential for tolerance, physical dependence, withdrawal, and/ or addiction (DEA/OD/ODE, 2010). Since benzodiazepines are often used to get high as a buffer to stimulants, it is not unusual to see a dose of diazepam or temazepam at 20 to 30 times greater than the manufacturer's recommended maximum.

A very potent benzodiazepine, flunitrazepam (Rohypnol), manufactured by Hoffman La Roche, which also manufactures Librium and Valium, has a rapid onset. Although not approved for sale in the United States, flunitrazepam looks like a legal prescription because it is typically distributed in the manufacturer's bubble pack. A 2-milligram standard dose of Rohypnol is approximately equivalent to 20 milligrams of Valium. It produces a dreamy stupor. A characteristic of Rohypnol is that it can be added to a drink without affecting the taste, but compounding the effect of alcohol and producing a comatose state of anterograde amnesia. Rohypnol quickly gained the reputation as a "date rape" drug.

EFFECTS ON THE BODY   Gamma-aminobutyric acid (GABA) is considered the most important inhibitory neurotransmitter in the brain. CNS depressants slow brain activity through actions on the GABA system and, therefore, produce a calming effect. Benzodiazapines produce CNS depression by enhancing the effects of gamma-aminobutyric acid, and thus decreasing brain activity (DEA/OD/ODE, 2010). Receptor sites become more sensitive to GABA. This inhibitory action produces anxiolytic, anticonvulsant, and sedative effects, useful in treating seizures, short-term insomnia, preoperative sedation and anesthesia, and anxiety disorders.

Benzodiazepines are lipid-soluble and absorbed into the gastrointestinal tract after oral ingestion. They can also pass the blood–brain barrier and the placental barrier. Peak effects from use occur within 2 to 4 hours. By virtue of their specific recognition sites, the benzodiazepines act by potentiating the action of GABA, which increases neural inhibition (DEA/OD/ODE, 2010).

The half-life of benzodiazepines can vary from 1.5 to 5.5 hours (Halcion) to 18 to 30 hours (Klonipin). Faster-acting compounds tend to promote psychological dependence by positively reinforcing through the rapid onset of the effect, while a shorter half-life contributes to physiological dependence by negatively reinforcing avoidance of withdrawal (NIDA, 2009h). Benzodiazepines are classified by their duration of action that ranges from less than 6 hours to more than 24 hours. Some of the benzodiazepines have active metabolites that can prolong their effects (DEA/OD/ODE, 2010).

TOLERANCE AND DEPENDENCE   Benzodiazepines, like alcohol and barbiturates, are CNS depressants. Frequent chronic use can cause physiological dependence (tolerance and withdrawal syndromes) as well as psychological dependence. Yet, benzodiazepines are not as reinforcing as many other drugs; that is, they do not produce the euphoric effect that is the main attraction of drug abuse for most people. A history of alcohol dependence increases risk for benzodiazepine dependence. Benzodiazepines are often misused along with alcohol abuse.

GENDER DIFFERENCES   A growing number of individuals aged 12 to 25 of both genders are using benzodiazepines. However, the profile of the typical long-term user has been a female over 50 years of age with multiple, chronic health problems.

WITHDRAWAL   Withdrawal symptoms from low dosages of benzodiazepines can allow symptom reemergence (a return of the symptoms such as anxiety or panic attacks, for which the benzodiazepines were originally prescribed). For others, including those on higher doses, withdrawal symptoms may include anxiety, mood instability, sleep disturbance, agitated depression, seizures, or schizophrenia (Choy, 2007). It is important for treatment to differentiate between symptom reemergence and withdrawal symptoms. Over time, withdrawal symptoms gradually subside. Despite the half life of some of these drugs withdrawal symptoms may persist for weeks. In addition, chronic consumers of high doses of benzodiazepines may be at risk for severe, perhaps life-threatening, withdrawal symptoms.

Although benzodiazepines are most commonly used for reduction of anxiety or sleep induction, on the street, they are often self-administered by drug addicts to reduce symptoms of withdrawal from heroin, alcohol, and other drugs or to lessen the side effects of cocaine or methamphetamine intoxication. Addicts also use benzodiazepines to enhance the effects of heroin, alcohol, or marijuana.

Barbiturates

"Street people" first viewed barbiturates as drugs of abuse. However, benzodiazepines (e.g., Halcion, Librium, Valium, Xanax, Rohypnol) have largely replaced short-acting barbiturates in therapeutic medicine, as well as on the streets. Furthermore, controls have been placed on the availability of barbiturates, listing them as II, III, or IV on the DEA Controlled Substances Schedule. They are still present in today's society, however, and deserve a cursory look.

INCIDENCE   From 1950 to 1970, barbiturates were second only to alcohol as drugs of abuse. Although abuse of barbiturates has decreased significantly since then as benzodiazepines have largely replaced them in medical use for insomnia and anxiety, certain populations continue to abuse them. Among individuals 40 and older, subgroups became addicted when they were younger, sometimes on prescribed barbiturates.

PSYCHOACTIVE EFFECTS   Barbiturates are used medically for their anesthetic, sedative, hypnotic, and anticonvulsant effects. They are short-acting sedative-hypnotics that can be administered as recreational drugs orally or by injection to produce intoxication similar to that of alcohol. This intoxicated state produces "disinhibition," elevated mood, a reduction of negative feelings and negative self-concept, and an increase in energy and confidence. The euphoric mood can shift quite suddenly to sadness. Someone who is intoxicated on barbiturates may possess an unsteady gait, slurred speech, and eye twitching and may exercise poor judgment.

The most commonly used barbiturates include thiopental (sodium pentothal), amobarbital (Amytal), pentobarbital (Nembutal), secobarbital (Seconal), amobarbital in combination with secobarbital (Tuinal), butabarbital (Butisol), and phenobarbital (Luminal). On the street, the drug may be assigned a name that correlates with the color of the capsule, such as *yellow jackets* (Nembutal), *red birds* (Seconal), or *rainbows* (Tuinal).

Barbiturates are a lipid-soluble compound, which allows them to pass the blood–brain barrier. They are also capable of passing the placental barrier and affecting the fetus. Barbiturates depress the CNS and inhibit neuronal activity, ranging from anxiety reduction to coma. This depressant action is achieved by potentiation of GABA-ergic transmission, which creates a diminished calcium ionic channel action resulting in a decreased state of neurotransmitters. Barbiturates also reverse the action of glutamate, which induces depolarization and adds to the CNS depression. Barbiturates and any of the other CNS depressants, such as narcotic-based analgesics, benzodiazepines, or alcohol, potentiate the effects of each other, causing dangerous combinations or even death. In potentiation, each drug interferes with the biotransformation of the other chemical by the liver, allowing for the toxic effects of each drug to be at a higher level than expected from each drug alone.

As cited earlier, barbiturates, being replaced by sedative-hypnotics benzodiazepines, have declined in use. Research on barbiturates abuse has waned over time, with studies examining side effects of other medications containing this drug. Some studies have found that a number of medications containing barbiturates or narcotics used to relieve migraine headaches actually made migraines worse, particularly when there is an overdose (Staff, 2009).

NONBARBITURATE SEDATIVE-HYPNOTICS   Other sedative-hypnotics that have an abuse potential similar to barbiturates include Quaalude, chloral hydrate, and meprobamate. Methaqualone (Quaalude) is chemically distinct from the barbiturates but is an example of a drug approved by the Food and Drug Administration (FDA) that became a severe social hazard. Through its depression of the CNS, a dramatic reduction in heart rate, respiration, and muscular coordination may result from its use.

TOLERANCE AND DEPENDENCE   Like all sedative-hypnotic drugs, barbiturates can create tolerance in the user with a single dose. Although tolerance to barbiturates builds quickly, it is not uniform to all of its actions. For example, those taking a barbiturate for control of epileptic seizures may develop tolerance to its sedative effects but not to the anticonvulsant effect. Risk of both physical and psychological dependence on barbiturates is high to moderate.

WITHDRAWAL   Withdrawal symptoms generally begin 12 to 24 hours after the last dose and peak in intensity between 24 and 72 hours. These symptoms include anxiety, tremors, nightmares, insomnia, anorexia, nausea, vomiting, delirium, and seizures. Death from overdose can occur through respiratory arrest when centers of the brain that control oxygen intake are severely depressed.

GHB (Identified as a Club Drug)

GHB (gamma-hydroxybutyrate) is a metabolite of GABA, an inhibitory neurotransmitter, and a naturally occurring depressant. Dr. Henri Labroit, a French researcher, synthesized GHB in 1960. With the ability to rapidly produce a deep coma, GHB became popular in Europe as an over-the-counter sleep aid. However, GHB seemed to cause neurological problems. That, coupled with its failure to alleviate pain, prevented GHB from being marketed for its original intended use as a surgical anesthesia. GHB acts on at least two sites in the brain: the GABAB receptor and a specific GHB binding site (NIDA, 2010d).

GHB can be produced in clear liquid, white powder, tablet, and capsule forms. It is typically marketed as a liquid in a small, sometimes brightly colored plastic bottle. The cap is used for dosing. GHB has over 80 street names. Some of the more popular are *liquid ecstasy, easy lay, grievous bodily harm, soap, salty water,* and *Georgia home boy.*

Other names associated with GHB include: *Bedtime Scoop* and *Cherry Meth.* Analogs, such as GBL (gamma-butyrolactone), are marketed as blue nitro, gamma-G, renewtrient, or reviverent. GHB has been increasingly involved in poisonings, overdoses, date rapes, and fatalities.

INCIDENCE   GHB has been used predominantly by adolescents and young adults, along with other abusing party drugs like Ecstasy and Ketamine, when attending nightclubs and raves. It is often manufactured in homes with recipes and ingredients found and purchased on the Internet. Because of its rapid resolution in the body and limited testing capabilities, along with its sedative effect accompanied by anterograde amnesia, GHB use is believed to be underreported. However, GHB and its analogs, GBL and BD (1, 4-butanediol), have gained popularity as a club drug. The typical user is an 18- to 25-year-old white (94%) male (79%) and either a bodybuilder or someone attending a rave or party. GHB in 2009 was reported at 1.0 percent, an increase from 0.5 percent of the U.S. population in 2008 (NIDA, 2010d).

PSYCHOACTIVE EFFECTS   GHB is a precursor of the neurotransmitter gamma amino-butyric acid (GABA) that acts on the dopaminergic system. Some individuals are synthesizing GHB in home laboratories. GBL and BD, ingredients in GHB, can also be converted by the body into GHB. These ingredients are found in a number of dietary supplements available in health food stores and gymnasiums to induce sleep, build muscles, and enhance sexual performance. GBL is widely available as an organic solvent used for cleaning circuit boards, stripping paint, or flavoring soy products.

GHB is a central nervous system depressant. Intoxication, increased energy, happiness, talking, desire to socialize, feeling affectionate and playful, mild disinhibition, sensuality, and enhanced sexual experience are reported effects at low doses. At higher doses it can slow breathing and heart rate to dangerous levels. GHB's intoxicating effects begin 10 to 20 minutes after the drug is taken. The effects typically last up to 4 hours, depending on the dosage.

EFFECTS ON THE BODY   GHB is unpredictable and dose-sensitive. At lower doses, GHB can relieve anxiety and produce relaxation. It can also produce blurred vision, stumbling, dizziness, and loss of gag reflex. As the dose increases, the sedative effects may result in unconsciousness within 15 minutes and coma within 30 to 40 minutes. Severe cases present a triad of symptoms: coma, bradycardia (slowing of the heart rate), and myoclonus (brief, involuntary twitching of a muscle or a group of muscles). Anterograde amnesia is common, thus making GHB a dangerous date rape drug along with Rohypnol and Ketamine.

TOLERANCE, DEPENDENCE, AND WITHDRAWAL   GHB is difficult to detect and is often taken with other drugs that produce similar symptoms. It has a strong risk for dependence. One can develop a tolerance where individuals need more of the drug to produce the desired high. Withdrawal as profuse diaphoresis (sweating), anxiety attacks, dangerously elevated blood pressure, and rapid pulse have been reported. Often, these symptoms subside after 3 days or in response to medical treatment. Hallucinations and an altered mental state may be delayed until day 4 or 5, often after a seemingly well patient has been released from medical care.

TOXIC AND LETHAL EFFECTS   Other effects of GHB include nausea and vomiting. These can be especially dangerous when the user is comatose, as the gag reflex is also depressed. Adverse effects are potentiated by alcohol, ketamine, and benzodiazepines. Methamphetamine use increases the risk of seizure. Overdose can result in death by itself or as a complication of a number of factors.

Opiates (Prescription Drugs Often Abused)

Opium is derived from the poppy flower (*Papaver sominiferum*). It possesses a variety of pharmacological activities that have been studied by scientists for years. The main active ingredient is *morphine alkaloid,* which is widely used because it is the most effective and most powerful painkiller (analgesic) available. Other effects and signs of usage include euphoria, drowsiness, constricted pupils, nausea, possible respiratory distress, coma, and death. Other derivatives include heroin, codeine, hydromorphone (Dilaudid), hydrocodone (Hycodan), oxymorphone (Numorphan), and Oxycodone (Percodan), as well as a number of synthetic medical compounds, including mesiridine (Demerol), methadone (Dolophine), fetanyl (Sublimaze), and propoxyphene (Darvon). At least 20 drugs are available in the United States that have opioid actions that may differ in the way they are absorbed, metabolized, and eliminated from the body. The most abused opioid substance is heroin. However, an extended release version of Oxycodone (OxyContin) has recently been widely publicized due to its growing popularity among abused drugs.

INCIDENCE   In 2009 there were 180,000 persons who used heroin for the first time within the past year (SAMHSA, 2010). This was significantly higher than the average annual number fom previous years. In 2005, the National Survey on Drug Use and Health showed there were 108,000 persons, 12 years and older, who had abused heroin for the first time within the last year (NIDA, 2010f). Heroin appears to be gaining in popularity again, especially among the young, who may be lured by inexpensive, high-purity heroin that can be sniffed or smoked instead of injected, and among the affluent. OxyContin, an opioid prescribed for pain, use among adolescents is a concern because of its addictive presence. In 2009 the number of new nonmedical users of OxyContin aged 12 or older was 584,000 with an average age of first use at 22.3 years. These estimates are slightly up from 2008 that reported estimated use at 478,000 (SAMHSA, 2010).

PSYCHOACTIVE EFFECTS   Injection continues to be the predominant method of heroin use, with intravenous injection providing the greatest intensity and most rapid onset of euphoria (7 to 8 seconds). Taking heroin via a needle revealed a small, but statistically significant increase in 2010 (Johnston et al., 2011). Intramuscular injection produces euphoria in 5 to 8 minutes; while sniffing or smoking requires 10 to 15 minutes for peak effects to occur. Although nasal ingestion does not produce as intense or as rapid a rush, all forms of heroin administration are addictive.

Recent scientific demonstration of receptors in the central nervous systems of both animals and humans, followed by the discovery that the body makes its own opiate-like substances, has greatly enhanced the understanding of the action of opioids. Administered opioids are thought to act at the neuronal synapses, either by acting as a neurotransmitter decreasing the transynaptic potential or by modulating the release of a neurotransmitter postsynaptically. This appears to be the basis of their analgesic effect and may be similar to the action of the body's endogenous opioids.

EFFECTS ON THE BODY   It is believed that chronic morphine use produces marked structural changes in the dopamine neurons in the brain's ventral tegmental area (VTA). In research studies with mice, the size of mesolimbic dopamine neurons originating in the VTA showed a dramatic decrease, and the shape of the neurons also changed. No changes were observed in nondopaminergic neurons. Thus, the opioids affected exactly those brain cells implicated in continuing drug use.

TOLERANCE AND DEPENDENCE   The risk of dependence of opioids, both physical and psychological, is high. Physiological tolerance and dependence results from brain changes after prolonged use, while psychological tolerance and dependence are a result of linking learned associations between drug effects and environmental cues. These phenomena of tolerance to and physical dependence (neuroadaption) on opioids appear to be receptor site-specific. Endogenous molecules have been identified with opioid activity and at least 12 peptides have been discovered, including the beta-endorphins and dynorphines. These long-chain peptides are believed to bind to their own specific opioid receptors. Stimulation of opioid receptors located in critical cells, such as those located in the locus coeruleus, produce a decrease in cell firing, ultimately causing the cells to become hyperexcitable. Markers for potential dependence have been recently investigated. *Naloxone 'Reboots' Opioid Pain-Relief System* (2010) identified self-reported craving as a potential marker for individuals at risk for opioid medication misuse.

Tolerance to opioids can develop quite rapidly in frequent users, and experiments have verified that a clinical dose of morphine (60 milligrams a day) in an individual can be increased to 500 milligrams per day in as little as 10 days. Over time, the brain substitutes administered chemical opiates for natural endorphins, causing effects such as euphoria to become less intense. As the body accommodates to the presence of chemical opioids, long-term usage produces a "threshold effect," after which time the chronic opioid user will use the drug just to function in a normal state, no longer getting high.

WITHDRAWAL   The symptoms of withdrawal from opioids include feelings of dysphoria, nausea, repeated yawning, sweating, tearing, and a runny nose. It is during this period that subjects experience craving or "drug hunger" for repeated exposure to the drug. The symptoms of opiate withdrawal are the result of interactions between the opioid and other neurotransmitter systems.

OVERDOSE   Mortality figures indicate that death by overdose on heroin/morphine is highly prevalent throughout the nation. This phenomenon occurs because an important effect of narcotics is to depress the respiratory centers response to blood levels of carbon dioxide. In addition, this effect is additive with alcohol or other sedative-hypnotics, which increases the danger of fatal overdose.

Naloxone (Narcan), a narcotic antagonist, is administered for emergency medical treatment of overdose. Overdose on narcotics may be diagnosed by observation of the *narcotic triad:* coma, depressed respiration, and pinpoint pupils. In addition, the number of users of opioid analgesics increased 96.6% from 1997 to 2002 with Oxycodone increasing 727.8% (Paulozzi, 2006). The increased availability of this pain medication is correlated with an increase in its abuse. The number of opioid detoxification admissions, particularly Oxycodone at medical centers has increased over the past several years with physician prescriptions identified as the main source for obtaining this opioid (Sproule, 2009). The comorbid pain, psychiatric symptoms, and use of other drugs complicate the treatment of abusers of Oxycodone. This schedule II compound produces effects similar to morphine. Researchers Zacny and Gutierrez (2003) state that excessive use can produce cognitive and psychomotor impairment. Hassan et al. (2010) studied the gene expression in brain tissues of rats treated with high doses of Oxycodone. Based upon their findings they believe that global changes in gene expression in the brain may be possible with the excessive use of this opioid by humans.

STIMULANTS

This section focuses on drugs of arousal, which include all forms of cocaine, amphetamine, prescription weight-reducing products, amphetamine-like drugs such as methylphenidate (Ritalin), some over-the-counter (OTC) weight-reducing drugs, and the minor stimulant drugs, nicotine and caffeine. The potential difficulties with frequent use of these drugs include possible overdoses, physical addiction, psychoses, severe depressions, and all anxiety syndromes, including panic attacks and obsessions. Stimulants were historically used to treat asthma (respiratory problems), obesity, and neurological disorders, increase alertness, attention, and energy. They also elevate blood pressure and increase heart rate and respiration. Stimulants, such as Dexedrine, Adderall, and Ritalin that are often prescribed have been frequently abused.

Minor psychoactive stimulants include caffeine and nicotine. These substances are considered minor because they can induce and exacerbate anxiety but usually are not capable of producing the more intense psychiatric syndromes such as psychosis and major depression.

Cocaine

Cocaine is an alkaloid drug compound that creates intense CNS arousal. It is a powerfully addictive stimulant that is processed from an organic source, the coca leaf. The natural source for the leaf (*Erythroxylon coca*) comes from two varieties of flowering coca shrubs, the *huanuco* and *truxillo*, which can exist only in the fertile soil of South America. They are grown and cultivated in the mountainous regions of Peru, Bolivia, Ecuador, and Colombia. Over time new plantations have been developed in Venezuela and Brazil as a result of the huge demand for cocaine in the United States and Europe (NIDA, 2010i).

To convert the coca leaf into a substance that can be used psychoactively, various chemical processes involving mixtures of alcohol, benzol, sulfuric acid, sodium carbonate, and kerosene or gasoline baths combined with several shaking and cooling segments convert the coca leaf into a paste. The final product is a precipitate of crude cocaine called *bazooko*. With the addition of acetone, potassium permanganate, and hydrochloric acid, this pasty sulfate becomes powdery flakes or rocks of nearly pure *cocaine hydrochloride*. At this point it is a white, odorless, crystalline powder that is a member of the tropane family. Most bazooko is converted into cocaine hydrochloride in the jungle laboratories around Colombia and then smuggled out through the networks of organized crime to various destinations including the United States, Europe, and Asia. While en route, it is diluted several times ("stepped on") with various additives such as lactose or dextrose (sugar), inositol (vitamin B), mannitol (baby laxative), and even cornstarch, talcum powder, and flour to stretch the quantity. This "stretching" process increases profits as the now-diluted cocaine finds its way onto the streets of major cities throughout the world (NIDA, 2010i).

Drug dealers have developed new marketing strategies by processing cocaine hydrochloride (powder) into a potentiated form of prefabricated, freebase cocaine called *crack*. Crack, cocaine that has been neutralized by an acid to make the hydrochloride salt now comes in a rock crystal that can be heated and its vapors smoked. The term *crack* refers to the crackling sound made when the substance is heated. This inexpensive method of psychoactive stimulant conversion can be accomplished in one's own kitchen by applying heat to cocaine cooked in a mixture of water, ammonia, baking soda, or liquid drain opener. Crack intensifies the biochemical experience in the brain but also increases the toxic effect on neurological tissue that is involved with cocaine stimulation (NIDA, 2010e). Cocaine is listed as a Schedule II drug on the DEA Controlled Substance Schedule.

INCIDENCE Cocaine use in the United States peaked in 1985 at 5.7 million (3% of the population 12 or older). Since that time use among eighth, 10th, and 12th graders has declined (Johnston et al., 2011). SAMHSA (2010) reported that the number of past-year cocaine initiates declined from 1.0 million in 2002 to 617,000 in 2009. Although crack cocaine is still considered a serious problem, the number of initiates has declined from 337,000 in 2002 to 94,000 in 2009.

PSYCHOACTIVE EFFECTS The quality of the cocaine experience depends on a number of variables, such as the strength of the drug, the setting, the circumstances under which it is taken, the user's attitude, emotional state, drug-taking history, and expectation of what the drug should produce. Most users will experience at least a mild euphoria, an increased heartbeat, and a subtle sense of excitement. Some may get little or no reaction from using the drug. This occurs most frequently as tolerance builds and cocaine is required to maintain the body in a relatively normal state.

Cocaine is a tremendous mood elevator, filling the user with a sense of exhilaration and well-being. It melts away feelings of inferiority while loosening inhibitions and evaporating tensions. It relieves fatigue and imparts the illusion of limitless power and energy. Many compulsive users "treat" themselves for obesity, lack of energy, depression, shyness, and low self-esteem. High doses may be associated with rambling speech, headache, tinnitus, paranoid ideation, aggressive behavior, disturbances in attention and concentration, auditory hallucinations, and tactile hallucinations (coke bugs). Users of cocaine have reported feelings of restlessness, irritability, and anxiety. The use of cocaine in a binge, at which time the drug is taken repeatedly at increased dosage levels, can result in a period of full-blown paranoid psychosis, with the user losing touch with reality and experiencing auditory hallucinations.

Cocaine can be ingested through inhalation through the nose, commonly called *snorting* or *tooting,* injection under the skin into a muscle or a vein, and smoking freebase or crack. Death can and has occurred with the use of all forms of cocaine ingestion.

Cocaine usage may also indirectly lead to the user's premature death through suicide resulting from cocaine-induced depression or aggressive or risk-taking behaviors. Cocaine-related deaths reported in 2005 were greater than 100 in the following Community Epidemiology Work Group (CEWG) areas that cite local mortality data: Philadelphia (423); Detroit/Wayne County (325); Miami-Dade County (162); Broward County, Florida (136); Newark/Essix County (135); and St. Louis (103) (NIDA, 2011).

When cocaine is snorted, the moist nasal membranes quickly dissolve the powder into microscopic molecules that flood the circulatory system within 1 to 2 minutes. These molecules encounter and pass through the protective blood–brain barrier, penetrating the cortical tissue that surrounds the deeper layers of the brain. The molecules find their way into stimulatory pathways in the limbic system, which regulate emotion and connect to primitive pain/pleasure centers deep within the brain. These pathways are normally indirectly activated by pleasurable activities such as eating, drinking, and sex. So powerful is the reward/pleasure stimulus by cocaine that responsibilities, family, job, morality, sleep, and safety may be ignored in its pursuit.

EFFECTS ON THE BODY   Cocaine acts directly on the heart muscle, causing the heart to beat inefficiently and its vessels to narrow, restricting the oxygen needed for peak performance. The heart has to work harder to keep up with the restricted blood flow in the rest of the body. Heavy use can cause angina, irregular heartbeat, and even a heart attack. As cocaine constricts blood flow, it can injure cerebral arteries. The acute hypertension brought on by cocaine use has been known to burst weakened blood vessels or produce strokes in young people.

It is not uncommon for chronic users to experience seizures that result in a constant tingling sensation of the jaw and neck region. The seizures are a result of neurons firing in bursts, creating uncontrollable electrical storms in the brain. They can cause a general diminution of alertness and mental functioning and can induce epilepsy, even in those with no previous signs of it. Chronic cocaine users exhibit loss of laterality of motor–cortical recruitment (Hanlon et al., 2010; Hanlon et al., 2009). In other words, chronic cocaine abusers have alterations in brain chemistry that affect their movement.

Many other potential difficulties may ensue with the chronic use of cocaine, both physical and psychological. Physical dangers include possible overdose and physical addiction; psychological effects may manifest themselves as severe depression, paranoid psychosis, and anxiety syndromes including panic attacks and obsessions. The most common causes of death from cocaine are heart attacks, strokes, respiratory failure, paralysis, heart rhythm disturbances, and repeated convulsions, usually from massive overdoses or at the end of a binge.

TOLERANCE AND DEPENDENCE   Physical dependence on cocaine is possible, while the risk of psychological dependence is high. Smoking cocaine as coca paste, freebase, or crack has the highest addictive potential. An intense high, described by some as a "full-body orgasm," occurs within 8 to 10 seconds after inhaling the smoke. Effects of the drug only last 5 to 10 minutes and the symptoms of withdrawal (anxiety, depression, and paranoia) are in proportion to the high obtained, leading to intense craving. The intense high occurs when cocaine blocks the reuptake of dopamine, greatly increasing the availability of the neurotransmitter. This flooding allows dopamine to stimulate the receptors more intensely, acting directly on the reward pathways of the brain. The pattern of rapid onset of intense euphoria, followed in a few minutes by intense dysphoria that can be quickly relieved by another self-administered dose of more cocaine, establishes a highly addictive cycle. This neurochemical response creates a rapid tolerance and dependence (drug hunger) for almost anyone who uses this drug. Each time the effects of cocaine wear off, dopamine levels drop, sending the user into a serious state of withdrawal. Normally, the brain replenishes dopamine from proteins in food, but in cocaine addicts, dopamine is quickly depleted, partly because of poor diet and partly because cocaine blocks the mechanism that recycles the neurotransmitter for future use. Chronic cocaine use can deplete the normal stores of dopamine in the brain, causing serious depression, not infrequently leading to suicide. Many individuals depress the action of the central nervous system with alcohol or benzodiazepines to temporarily counter the loss of the brain's dopamine supply. In the long run, this only heightens the need for more cocaine. Neuroscience studies have demonstrated that individuals addicted to cocaine have different responses to cholinergic probes in areas of the brain relevant to craving, learning, and memory (Adinoff et al., 2010).

EFFECTS ON THE FETUS   A sizeable number of children born at inner-city hospitals, 10% to 20%, are believed to have been exposed to cocaine in utero. However, of the abnormalities that have been identified in the offspring of pregnant cocaine users, including low birthweight, are more probably related to the lifestyle of the drug user rather than to the pharmacological effects of cocaine. There is no doubt, however, that the drug constricts the blood vessels of the placenta, reducing the supply of blood and oxygen that reaches the fetus. Cocaine is also thought to contribute to premature and stillborn births, because of both vasoconstrictive effects on the developing fetus and its ability to induce intrauterine contractions. Babies born to cocaine-using women may have persistently elevated cocaine levels for days, and the possibility exists that the enzymatic pathway for conversion of cocaine into metabolites may not be fully developed in the newborn. Predictions were made that the 1980s would produce a generation of crack babies. Currently it is believed that many of the effects of prenatal crack use appears to be largely the result of poor nutrition related to the lifestyle of the mother, polydrug use, lack of prenatal care, and premature birth. The exact nature of cocaine itself on the developing fetus is still unknown (Meyer & Zhang, 2009).

Amphetamines

Amphetamines are psychomotor stimulants that were first proposed as a treatment for asthma. Their actions on the CNS were not reported until 1933, followed by reports of amphetamine abuse. The most commonly prescribed amphetamines include Adderall, a mix of amphetamine salts, and methylphenidates Ritalin and Concerta. Although these medications were first prescribed for the treatment of hyperactive (attention deficit disordered) children they are currently frequently abused. Amphetamines can be orally ingested, intravenously injected, snorted, or smoked, creating intense CNS arousal and a rapid increase of dopamine (NIDA, 2010b).

Amphetamines and methamphetamines have a similar but slightly different molecular structure. Methamphetamine has been making inroads into the United States from the Pacific Basin and is considered the most hypercharged analog of this family of drugs.

During the last three decades, "speed" epidemics have been reported in Japan, Sweden, and the United States. In the United States, this situation led to a change in laws when amphetamines were restricted to medical use by the Controlled Substances Act of 1970. They are listed as Schedule II drugs on the Controlled Substances Schedule, and their use is strictly enforced by the DEA. In recreational use, amphetamines can be "snorted," smoked, administered by injection, or taken orally. In recent years, the explosive use of methamphetamines by bisexual and homosexual men is of grave concern, as the disinhibiting and sexual stimulating effects of the drug place homosexual male users at even higher risk for HIV infection.

The underground production of amphetamines in North America is largely accomplished through small, clandestine laboratories. They produce more than $3 billion worth of illegal amphetamines per year with a huge profit margin. Law enforcement officials believe these "speed labs" are often financed by motorcycle gangs who distribute the final product mainly in Australia (Amphetamine Epidemics, 2011).

Methamphetamine is the most potent form of amphetamine. As a Schedule II stimulant it has a high potential for abuse. Illicit forms of methamphetamine sold on the street may be called *ice, crystal (meth), crank, Btu, slate,* or *glass* (NIDA, 2010h). Ice is an odorless, colorless form of crystal methamphetamine, up to 100% pure, resembling a chip of ice or clear rock candy. Methamphetamines are often made in small, illegal laboratories. It is taken orally, intravenously (snorting the powder), or by needle injection. Neuroscience research has demonstrated the effects of long-term use of methamphetamine on the brain, particularly with white/gray matter distortions (Tobias et al., 2010).

INCIDENCE Amphetamine abuse in the United States peaked in the late 1960s or early 1970s, and then declined to a low in the late 1980s or early 1990s. NIDA (2009g) reported past-year nonmedical use of Ritalin at 1.6% for eighth-graders, 2.9 for 10th-graders and 3.4% for 12th-graders. Amphetamines as a group ranked third among 12th-graders for past-year illicit drug use, with Adderall the drug being mainly abused.

Methamphetamine spread from Japan to Hawaii after World War II and has remained endemic there. Methamphetamine has long been the dominant drug problem in the San Diego, California, area and has spread to other sections of the West and Southwest, as well as to both rural and urban sections of the South and Midwest. As it has spread from the traditionally blue-collar user to a more diverse user population, SAMHSA (2010) reported that methamphetamine users decreased between 2006 and 2008, but then increased in 2009. The numbers were 731,000 (0.3%) in 2006, 529,000 (0.2%) in 2007, 314,000 (0.1%) in 2008, and 502,000 (0.2%) in 2009.

EFFECTS ON THE BODY Amphetamines cross the blood–brain barrier easily after oral ingestion. Once the amphetamine molecules pass through the stomach, they absorb into the blood via the intestines where they are able to reach peak levels within 1 hour. After absorption, the lipid-soluble molecules are distributed into the brain, lung, and kidneys. Brain levels reach about 10 times the blood levels, which accounts for the intense CNS effect. Some of the metabolites are active and, if present in sufficient quantity, can cause high blood pressure and hallucinations.

In the CNS, amphetamines mimic cocaine, acting on the neurotransmitters, dopamine, and norepinephrine. They cause a tremendous release of newly synthesized dopamine from the presynaptic neuron to bind and stimulate the postsynaptic neurons

(NIDA, 2010b). The nerve endings (terminals) of dopamine and serotonin-containing neurons are damaged and new growth is limited. According to NIDA (2010g), heavy use of methamphetamine produces alterations in the activity of the dopamine system, reduced motor speed, impaired verbal learning and possible structural and functional changes in the brain affecting emotion and memory. Amphetamines also inhibit the action of monoamine oxidase (MAO), the enzyme that ends the action of these neurotransmitters, allowing them to remain active in the synapse for a longer time. They act on the sympathetic nervous system (SNS) through the stimulation and release of norepinephrine while blocking the reuptake of norepinephrine back into the presynaptic terminal. This action elicits a "fight or flight" response. Thus, the psychostimulants are called *sympathomimetic* drugs and have been said to mimic the action of the SNS. These drugs are identified as sympathomimetic since they produce physiological effects resembling those caused by the sympathetic nervous system. They can increase cardio action and blood pressure. High doses of amphetamines have a direct effect on serotonergic receptors. Electroencephalogram (EEG) recordings have shown that amphetamine accelerates and desynchronizes neuronal firing rates in the brain, a possible explanation for some of the behavioral effects of amphetamines (NIDA, 2010g).

With large doses of amphetamines, extreme symptoms may occur, including rapid heartbeat, hypertension, headache, profuse sweating, and severe chest pain. This generally occurs when dosages exceed 50 to 100 milligrams per day on a continuous basis, and the user may appear psychotic or schizophrenic. Severe intoxication also can produce delirium, panic, paranoia, and hallucinations. Murders and other violent offenses have been attributed to amphetamine intoxication, and early studies have shown increased aggression in humans after ingestion of amphetamines.

TOLERANCE AND DEPENDENCE   Tolerance develops to specific actions of amphetamines including euphoria, appetite suppression, wakefulness, hyperactivity, and heart and blood pressure effects. The risk of physical dependence on amphetamines is possible, and the risk of psychological dependence is high.

WITHDRAWAL   During withdrawal, there is a reduction of available neurotransmitters due to depletion and reduced reuptake, causing a period of depression, fatigue, increased appetite, and prolonged sleep accompanied by REM (dream sleep) following the cessation of use. Death occurs from extreme heat elevation, convulsions, and circulatory collapse.

Minor Stimulant: Nicotine

Nicotine is not listed as a controlled substance on the DEA's Controlled Substances Schedule. However, nicotine has had its share of controversy. It has come to light that cigarette manufacturers have long known that the psychoactive agent in cigarettes is nicotine and that they have often viewed cigarettes as little more than a single-dose container of nicotine. Lawsuits won by several states have held tobacco manufacturers liable for health problems caused by tobacco use because of their awareness of the addictive nature of nicotine and the effects of smoking on the nonsmoker (FDA, 2009).

INCIDENCE   Tobacco smoking has been prevalent for thousands of years. Modern use in the United States peaked in the mid-1960s, when 52% of adult males and 32% of adult females were cigarette smokers. Following the surgeon general's report on the health hazards of smoking, published in 1964, the incidence of smoking in the United States began to drop. SAMHSA (2010) estimated in 2009 that 69.7 million Americans aged 12 or older were current (past-month users) of a tobacco product. This represented 27.7% of the population over 12 years old. It was estimated that 58.7 million persons (23.3%) were current cigarette smokers; 13.3 million (5.3%) smoke cigars; 8.6 million (3.4%) used smokeless tobacco; and 2.1 million (0.8%) smoked tobacco in pipes. Between 2002 and 2009, past-month use of any tobacco product decreased from 30.4% to 27.7% with cigarette use declining from 26.0% to 23.3%. The Centers for Disease Control and Prevention (CDC) (2005) indicated that tobacco use is the leading preventable cause of death in the United States.

PSYCHOACTIVE EFFECTS   Nicotine is both a stimulant and a sedative to the central nervous system. The absorption of nicotine is followed almost immediately by a "kick" because it causes a discharge of epinephrine from the adrenal cortex. This, in turn, stimulates the CNS and other endocrine glands, producing a sudden release of glucose. As the effects of the sudden release of epinephrine and glucose wear off, depression and fatigue follow, leading the abuser to seek more nicotine. Research (NIDA, 2010b) has also shown that nicotine, like cocaine, heroin, and marijuana, increases the level of the neurotransmitter dopamine, affecting the brain pathways that control reward and pleasure.

EFFECTS ON THE BODY   Nicotine is readily absorbed in the body from every site with which it comes into contact, including the skin. It is both water- and lipid-soluble, allowing it to cross over the blood–brain barrier quickly to reach the brain and virtually every other blood-rich tissue in the body. Inhaled nicotine reaches the brain within 7 to 19 seconds of puffing. Once in the bloodstream, a portion is carried to the liver, where it is metabolized into cotinine (90%) and nicotine-N-oxide (10%). It has a wide range of effects on the peripheral and CNS, including increased blood pressure and heart rate, cardiac output, coronary blood flow, and cutaneous vasoconstriction. Women who smoke tend to have an earlier menopause, and those who use oral contraceptives, particularly those older than 30, are more prone to cardiovascular and cerebrovascular diseases than are other smokers (Sherman, 2006; Buttigieg et al., 2008).

Cigarette smoking is a profound contributor to mortality. Cigarette smoking and smokeless tobacco use claim thousands of lives every year in the United States. Tobacco-related health problems include cardiovascular disease, cancer, chronic obstructive lung disease, and complications during pregnancy. Nonsmokers exposed to environmental tobacco smoke (passive smokers) also are at an increased risk for the same diseases as smokers. They breathe in a mixture of chemicals including formaldehyde, cyanide, carbon monoxide, ammonia, and nicotine. These carcinogens increase the risk of developing heart disease by 25% to 30% and lung cancer by 20% to 30% (NIDA, 2010c).

TOLERANCE AND DEPENDENCE   Tolerance is believed to occur as the body becomes accustomed to the presence of nicotine which appears to be linked to the number of binding sites. Nicotine accumulates in the body, and regular use causes it to remain in body tissues 24 hours a day. Nicotine is high in potential for both physical and psychological dependency.

WITHDRAWAL   When chronic smokers are deprived of cigarettes for 24 hours, they experience increased anger, hostility, aggression, and loss of social cooperation. They take longer to regain emotional equilibrium following stress. During periods of craving or abstinence, smokers experience impairment across a wide range of cognitive and psychomotor functioning. Neuroscience research, through the use of PET ligand imaging, demonstrated nicotine receptor changes during acute and prolonged cigarette abstinence, concluding that these changes may contribute to difficulties with tobacco cessation (Cosgrove et al., 2009).

Minor Stimulant: Caffeine

Caffeine belongs to a chemical class of alkaloids known as *xanthine derivatives,* and it was chemically isolated more than 170 years ago. It is found in coffee, tea, cocoa, chocolate, and a number of soft drinks, as well as hundreds of prescription and OTC drugs. Caffeine is not listed as a controlled substance on the Controlled Substances Schedule.

INCIDENCE   Caffeine is the most widely consumed psychoactive agent in the world. About 80% of the adults in the United States use caffeine regularly, a per capita intake of 220 to 240 milligrams per day. The chronic overuse of this substance is called *caffeinism.* Clinical and epidemiological data show that its overuse induces an intoxication of the CNS that includes habituation, tolerance, and a withdrawal syndrome.

EFFECTS ON THE BODY   Caffeine is rapidly absorbed into the gastrointestinal tract, and peak plasma levels occur within 30 to 45 minutes after ingestion. It crosses the blood–brain barrier very quickly and concentrates in brain plasma relative to the amount that is ingested.

Caffeine and other xanthines block the brain's receptors for adenosine, a neuromodulator. Adenosine has sedative, anxiolytic, and anticonvulsant actions. When caffeine occupies adenosine-binding sites, these actions cannot occur and there is a stimulating or anxiogenic effect. Two hundred milligrams of caffeine (the equivalent of two cups of coffee) will activate the cortex of the brain, showing an arousal pattern on an EEG. At this level, caffeine acts directly on the vascular muscles, causing dilation of the blood vessels. The CNS stimulation is also responsible for "coffee jitters" and increases the time it takes to fall asleep.

At higher dose levels (500 milligrams and above), autonomic centers of the brain are stimulated, causing increased heart rate and respiration and constriction of the blood vessels in the brain. Caffeine increases heart rate and contraction, physiologically creating arrhythmias and mild tachycardia. It increases gastric acidity and is contraindicated for patients with ulcers. Caffeine directly acts on the kidneys to increase urine output and also increases salivary flow.

Caffeine is generally not considered a toxic drug. Approximately 15% of circulating caffeine is metabolized an hour, with a half-life of 3.5 to 5 hours. A lethal dose for an average adult male would be 5 to 10 grams, the equivalent of 50 to 100 cups of regular coffee, probably necessitating ingestion in a non-beverage form.

TOLERANCE AND DEPENDENCE   The key reinforcing factor for caffeine may be its effects on the pleasure and reward centers found in the hypothalamus and the median forebrain bundle. Stimulation of the brain's reward center might be the most powerful reason that people move from a controlled phase of caffeine ingestion to the stage of caffeine dependency, or caffeinism.

Children do not seem to possess an innate craving for caffeine, and most people in our society seem to be exposed to it gradually as their intake eventually progresses to a pattern of frequent or daily use. Moreover, there appears to be an age-related rate of metabolism of caffeine, leaving newborns, infants, and small children more vulnerable to its effects.

The potential for both physical and psychological dependence on caffeine is small. However, a large number of variables make it difficult for researchers to determine users' responses to varying doses of caffeine intake. These include a subject's age, body mass, other psychoactive substances in use, amount of stress, level of fatigue, sleep disorders, and varying degrees of sensitivity to the drug. Furthermore, the acute use of caffeine produces very different biological consequences when compared with chronic use.

WITHDRAWAL   Caffeine withdrawal may precipitate such symptoms as craving for caffeine, headache, fatigue, nausea or vomiting, or marked anxiety or depression. There have been a number of reports on caffeine withdrawal. The most rigorous demonstration of physiological effects of caffeine withdrawal was reported by Sigmon, Herning, Better, Cadet, & Griffiths (2009). Chronic caffeine effects were demonstrated on measures of EEG beta 2 power, and acute caffeine abstinence produced changes in cerebral blood flow velocity, EEG, and subjective effects. Yet, most reports conclude that symptoms of withdrawal are not significant enough to include caffeine as a disorder in the DSM. However, based upon the severity of symptoms and functional impairment it has been argued that caffeine could find a place in DSM revisions (Rogers et al., 2010; Sigmon et al., 2009; Hsu, Chen, Wang, & Chiu, 2009).

Cannabis

Marijuana is the most widely abused illicit drug in the United States. Marijuana is also the illicit drug with the highest level of dependence or abuse. In 2009 there were 16.7 million past month users of marijuana among individual 12 years of age and older (SAMHSA, 2010). The percent of users in 2009 (6.6%) was higher than the rate in 2008 (6.1%). The increase in youth drug use, particularly marijuana, is disturbing when considering the results of the 2010 Monitoring the Future Survey (MTF). The MTF survey found that marijuana use in 2010 increased among eighth-graders, and daily use significantly increased among eighth, 10th, and 12th graders. The rates in 2010 were 6.1% for high school seniors, 3.3% for 10th graders, and 1.2% for eighth graders. The daily use of marijuana increased at all three levels when compared to 2009 findings. Most disturbing is the fact that high rates of marijuana use during teen and preteen years as the brain continues to develop, places users at risk to addiction.

Marijuana and hashish are produced from the hemp plant, cannabis. As a psychoactive agent, it is used primarily to produce euphoria followed by relaxation. Cannabis is known by many names—*Indian hemp, marijuana, hash, pot, herb, weed, grass, widow, ganja,* or *dope*—and is a controversial drug in U.S. society (NIDA, 2010b). Cannabis is usually smoked as cigarettes (joint, nail) or in a pipe (bong). The strength of the end product that comes from the hemp plant vary, owing to the climate and soil in which it is grown and the method of cultivation and preparation. Its potency and quality depend mainly on the type of plant that is grown. Experienced growers identify potency by grading the plant with East Indian names. *Bhang* is identified as the least potent and cheapest and is made from the cut tops of uncultivated plants that contain low-resin content. *Ganja* is derived from the flowering tops and leaves of selected plants that have been carefully cultivated having a high content of resin and, therefore, being more potentiated to the user. *Charas* is the highest grade and is produced from the resin itself, obtained from fully mature plants. This highly potentiated source is generally referred to as *hashish*.

The potency of marijuana, a Schedule I substance on the Controlled Substances Schedule, has drastically increased in the United States as California growers have successfully cultivated an unpollinated plant known as *sinsemilla*. Imported products from Thailand, Hawaii, and the Netherlands have also been tested with incredibly high amounts of tetrahydrocannabinol (THC), the active ingredient in marijuana. Additionally, clandestine laboratories have developed a method of producing a liquid called "hash oil," which has been found to have more than 60% THC content compared with an average 30% in regular hashish and 7% to 15% in sinsemilla and neiterweit at 27%.

INCIDENCE As indicated earlier in this chapter, marijuana is the most frequently used illicit drug in the United States; 16.7 million past month users 12 and older, or 6.6% of the population (SAMHSA, 2010). Marijuana was thought to have reached its peak in the 1970s. However, marijuana use began rising, particularly among teens from 2008 on. Marijuana use in 2010 increased for all prevalence periods studied (lifetime, past year, past 30 days, and daily in the past 30 days). Reports indicate that about one in sixteen 12th graders in 2010 used marijuana on a daily or near-daily basis. One explanation is that over the past several years the perceived risk and disapproval rate has declined among the teenage population. In 2009 it was estimated that marijuana had 2.4 million initiates, users of the drug for the first time. In the same year, the average of an initiate was 17 years, significantly lower than the average age of 17.8 in 2008. These trends of incidence again are disturbing, particularly as we learn more about the habitual use of this drug as the result of neuroscience research findings.

PSYCHOACTIVE EFFECTS Smoking of cannabis can produce relaxation following euphoria, loss of appetite, impaired memory, loss of concentration and knowledge retention, loss of coordination, as well as a more vivid sense of taste, sight, smell, and hearing. Stronger doses cause fluctuation of emotions, fragmentary thoughts, disoriented behavior, and psychosis. It may also cause irritation to the lungs and respiratory system and cancer. The short-term effects of marijuana include problems with memory and learning, distorted perception, difficulty in thinking and problem solving, loss of coordination, and increased heart rate (Hester, Nestor, & Garavan, 2009). Long-term marijuana abuse indicates some changes in the brain similar to those seen after long-term abuse of other major drugs (Quickfall & Crockford, 2006; Rais et al., 2008).

EFFECTS ON THE BODY In the United States, cannabis is generally smoked in a cigarette called a *joint* or a *doobie*. A marijuana cigarette contains 421 chemicals before ignition. There are 61 cannabanoids, including delta-1 tetrahydrocannabinol, which is the psychoactive agent. Neuroscience research findings have indicated the effects of this psychoactive agent on the modulation of mediotemporal and ventrostraital functions of the brain (Bhattacharyya et al., 2009). There are also 50 different waxy hydrocarbons, 103 terpines, 12 fatty acids, 11 steroids, 20 nitrogen compounds, as well as carbon monoxide, ammonia, acetone, benzene, benzathracene, and benzoprene. When ignited, these chemicals convert into more than 2,000 other chemicals. As these are metabolized by the body, they convert to about 600 chemical metabolites. Cannabinoids have a half-life of 72 hours in the human body. When ingested, effects appear to be dose-dependent. Cannabinoids are lipid-soluble and store at megamicroscopic levels for indefinite periods of time in the body (Bhattacharyya et al., 2009).

Early research findings on cannabis have been mixed. However, more recent neuroscience research using structural imaging findings on CT or MR imaging, and conventional angiography clearly indicates that excessive use of cannabis leads to functional or structural impairment of the central nervous system (Geibprasert et al., 2009). Chemicals found in marijuana and hashish are believed to interfere with the cell's ability to manufacture pivotal molecules, which grossly affects the substances necessary for cell division including DNA, RNA, and proteins. This causes an "aging process" in particular clusters of cells found in the brain, liver, lungs, spleen, lymphoid tissues, and sex organs. Findings of long-term damage have been based upon laboratory work with animal models.

Many of the early studies on the effects of long-term use of cannabis were conducted at a time when the THC content of cannabis was extremely low (0.05% to 4%). With some strains of the drug reportedly now reaching THC content that extends into the teens (sinsemilla, 14%) and even the 20s (neiterweit, 27%), there is evidence that cannabis is doing more damage than previously realized.

One well-confirmed danger of heavy, long-term use is its ability to damage the lungs due to the fact that it burns 16 times "hotter" than tobacco and produces twice as many mutagens (agents that cause permanent changes in genetic material). Biopsies have confirmed that cannabis smokers may be at an extremely high risk for the development of lung diseases including bronchitis, emphysema, and cancer. NIDA (2010f) reports a study of 450 individuals that found that people who smoke marijuana frequently, but do not smoke tobacco, have more health problems and miss more days of work than nonsmokers. Another study comparing 173 cancer patients and 176 healthy individuals produced evidence that marijuana smoking doubled or tripled the risk of these cancers. It is believed that some of marijuana's adverse health effects may occur because THC impairs the immune system's ability to fight disease. There is a prevalence of studies supporting the biological association of marijuana smoking with lung cancer (Mehra, Moore, Crothers, Tetrault, & Fiellin, 2006).

It is believed that long-term marijuana use causes mental or emotional deterioration. Amotivational syndrome, which includes symptoms of passivity, aimlessness, apathy, uncommunicativeness, and lack of ambition, has been attributed to prolonged marijuana use (Bartholomew, Holroyd, & Heffernan, 2010). Marijuana has the potential to cause problems in daily life or make a person's existing problems worse with depression, anxiety, and personality disturbances exacerbated with chronic marijuana use. One still needs to ask whether these symptoms result from the use of marijuana, the personality characteristics of heavy drug users—bored, anxious, depressed, listless, cynical, and rebellious or a combination.

Marijuana has also been looked on as the "gateway drug," or precursor to use of other, more dangerous drugs. Anyone who uses one drug may be interested in others, for the same reasons. Users of one drug often find themselves in the company of users of other drugs, and therefore making them readily available.

TOLERANCE AND DEPENDENCE   It remains difficult to distinguish between marijuana use as a cause of problems or as the consequence of problems. Many individuals who develop a dependency on marijuana are susceptible to other dependencies because of anxiety, depression, or feelings of inadequacy. In general, there appears to be both a psychological and physical potential for dependency.

Signs of possible misuse of marijuana include animated behavior and loud talking, followed by sleepiness, dilated pupils and bloodshot eyes, distortions in perception, hallucinations, distortions in depth and time perception, and loss of coordination. An overdose of marijuana can cause fatigue, lack of coordination, paranoia, and psychosis. Withdrawal can cause insomnia, irritability, anxiety, and a decrease in appetite.

WITHDRAWAL   Studies since the 1970s have suggested a marijuana withdrawal syndrome, characterized by insomnia, restlessness, loss of appetite, and irritability. A 1999 study conducted at Harvard Medical School confirmed higher levels of aggression in marijuana users during withdrawal when compared with the infrequent or former marijuana user (Bartholomew et al., 2010). Research also reported by Bartholomew et al. (2010) indicated that cannabinoid (THC or synthetic forms of THC) withdrawal in chronically exposed animals leads to an increase in the activation of the stress-response system and changes in the activity of nerve cells containing dopamine. It should be noted that dopamine neurons are involved in the regulation of motivation and reward, and are directly or indirectly affected by all drugs of abuse including cannabis.

MEDICAL USE   Cannabis use for treatment of some medical ailments has held the interest for several years, particularly in obtaining relief from glaucoma and asthma, as well as from the side effects of chemotherapy used in the treatment for some types of cancer. Some have experimented with its usefulness in treating the physical wasting that can occur with advanced AIDS. Its effectiveness over other methods of treatment remains controversial, partly because of legal complications involved in doing such research.

Although some states have legalized marijuana for medicinal purposes, there continues to be political discussion to legalize marijuana, particularly for medical use. However, the medical community, as a whole, remains skeptical of its medical value over other drugs, and research supporting each position is scarce. Recent neurological research findings have provided evidence that long-term use of cannabis creates structural abnormalities in the hippocampus and amygdale, and is associated with brain abnormalities and later risk of psychosis (Yucel et al., 2008; Welch et al., 2010).

HALLUCINOGENS

Hallucinogens, as the name implies, cause hallucinations and profound distortions in a person's perception of reality. When using hallucinogens, individuals report seeing images, hearing sounds, and feeling sensations that seem real but do not exist. Some users report emotional mood swings. Hallucinogenic compounds from plants and mushrooms have been used for centuries. Most hallucinogens contain nitrogen and have chemical structures similar to those of natural neurotransmitters such as serotonin (NIDA, 2009e). Hallucinogenic substances include the *indoles,* which include (a) lysergic acid derivatives and (b) substituted tryptamines such as dimethyltryptamine (DMT), psilocybin, and psilocin. All the indole-type hallucinogens have a structure similar to the neurotransmitter serotonin, while the substituted phenylethylamine-type hallucinogens are structurally related to the neurotransmitter norepinephrine. It is believed that the mechanism of action occurring in the indole-type hallucinogens involves the alteration of serotonergic neurotransmission (NIDA, 2009d). It should be noted that the serotonin system is involved in the control of behavioral, perceptual, and regulatory systems, including mood, hunger, body temperature, sexual behavior, muscle control, and sensory perception. The four most common types of hallucinogens include: LSD (d-lysergic acid diethylamide, manufactured from lysergic acid), peyote (a small cactus with an active ingredient of mescaline), psilocybin (a mushroom containing psilocybin), and PCP (phencyclidine, manufactured for anesthetic use).

Lysergic acid diethylamide (LSD) is probably the best known of the indole-type hallucinogens and has been most abused by white males between the ages of 10 and 29 years. LSD is also often viewed as a club drug. A few of the indole-type hallucinogens such as psilocybin and psilocin are found in nature, while mescaline is a naturally occurring hallucinogen derived from the peyote cactus.

The overall effects of many of the hallucinogens are similar, although there is a multitude of variability involving the rate of onset, duration of action, and the intensity of the drug experience. This is due to the wide range of potency available and the amount of the drug that is ingested relative to its specific dose–response characteristics. Because the goal of this text is to give an overview of the topic of substance abuse, a discussion of LSD and PCP (phencyclidine) will represent the hallucinogenic substances used for recreation.

Lysergic Acid Diethylamide (LSD)

LSD is between 100 and 1,000 times more powerful than natural hallucinogens but weaker than synthetic chemicals such as DOM and STP (NIDA, 2009d). Confiscated street samples of LSD can range from 10 to 300 micrograms in a single dose. LSD is listed as a Schedule I substance on the Controlled Substances Schedule.

INCIDENCE   In 2007 more than 22.7 million individuals aged 12 or older reported they had used LSD in their lifetime (9.1%) (NIDA, 2009d). There was no change reported between 2006 and 2007 in the number of new initiates of LSD. The Monitoring the Future Survey reported no significant changes in LSD use from eighth, 10th, and 12th graders. However, when questioning the past-month use of LSD a significant increase among 12th graders was reported (NIDA, 2009c).

PSYCHOACTIVE EFFECTS   LSD triggers behavioral responses in some individuals after doses as low as 20 micrograms. Psychological and behavioral effects begin about an hour after oral ingestion and generally peak between 2 and 4 hours. There is a gradual return to the predrug state within 6 to 8 hours. The subjective effects can be somatic with symptoms of dizziness, weakness, and tremor, followed by perceptual changes of altered vision and intensified hearing, which gradually change into visual distortions, dreamlike imagery, and synesthesia that includes "seeing" smells and "hearing" colors. LSD is metabolized mainly at the site of the liver to various transformation products, and very little is eliminated as an unchanged product.

TOLERANCE AND DEPENDENCY   There appears to be no potential for physical dependence on LSD as it does not lead to compulsive drug-seeking behavior. Yet, LSD does affect tolerance with regular users needing to take progressively higher doses to achieve the sought after affect of the drug.

Phencyclidine (PCP)

Phencyclidine (PCP, "angel dust") is considered a hallucinogenic drug. It was originally developed as a general anesthetic for human application but was found to be unstable. It was then offered as an anesthetic for veterinary applications but was soon placed in the classification of Schedule I drugs under the Anti–Drug Abuse Act. Currently there are extreme penalties for trafficking PCP or manufacturing PCP.

In its pure form, PCP is a lipid-soluble white powder. It is often adulterated or misrepresented as a variety of other drugs, including THC, cannabinol, mescaline, psilocybin, LSD, amphetamine, or cocaine. On the street, it can be found in powder, tablet, and liquid form. A typical street dose (one pill, joint, or line) is about 5 milligrams, but confiscated street samples have revealed that purity can run from 5% to 100% depending on the form. This wide variance can create a tremendous risk to the user (NIDA, 2009h).

INCIDENCE   PCP use peaked, reaching epidemic proportions, between 1973 and 1979, and again between 1981 and 1984. In 1979, 14.5% of 18- to 25-year-olds had ever used PCP, compared with 9.5% in 1976. In 2007, 6.1 million individuals 12 and older reported using PCP in their lifetime which was a decrease from previous years (NIDA, 2009h). In 2008, 99,000 Americans age 12 and older had abused PCP at least once in the past year (SAMHSA, 2010). Whites are more likely to use PCP than other groups, followed by Hispanics and African Americans.

PSYCHOACTIVE EFFECTS   PCP can be ingested orally, smoked, snorted, intravenously injected, and even inserted vaginally. The mode of administration can drastically alter the onset of effects. Smoking and injection create a rapid onset of effects that usually peak within 30 minutes. The highs last from 4 to 6 hours. For typical chronic users, PCP is generally the primary drug of choice, whereas users of other substances may occasionally combine PCP with other substances they are using. Staying high on PCP may last 2 to 3 days, during which time the user remains sleepless. Chronic users may also exhibit persistent cognitive memory problems, speech difficulties, mood disorders, weight loss, and decrease in purposeful behavior for up to a year after cessation of use. Coma can occur at any time during intoxication. When used in this fashion, many of these chronic users may need emergency room treatment to overcome the residual effects of the drug.

PCP is a potent compound and extremely lipid-soluble. Its psychological/behavioral effects are dose-dependent. The dose range for PCP effect on brain stimulation reward enhancement is relatively narrow. At low doses, it produces reward enhancement or a "good trip"; at high doses, it inhibits the brain reward system and may produce a "bad trip." It is believed that PCP binds to specific sites in the human brain and blocks the reuptake of several major neurotransmitter systems. It also disrupts electrophysiological activity by blocking the ionic exchange of sodium and potassium. These serious actions on major brain systems probably account for PCP's symptoms of dissociative anesthesia and its ability to create coma and lethal complications. Currently, there is no PCP antagonist available to block its effects, and treatment for overdose must address the symptoms of toxicity. Close observation of the PCP-toxic patient must continue for days, as PCP levels may continue unevenly for hours or days.

TOLERANCE AND DEPENDENCE   PCP is addictive as repeated abuse can lead to craving and compulsive PCP-seeking behavior (NIDA, 2009h). There exists a high potential for psychological dependency.

Ketamine (Targeted as a Club Drug)

Ketamine is known on the street as *special K, vitamin K, cat valium, super K, ketalar, green,* or simply *K.* It has become a favorite of young people at raves, dance parties and nightclubs. Ketamine was approved for human and veterinary medicine (Veterinary Practice News, 2010).

INCIDENCE   Ketamine is usually taken with other drugs, making data on incidence of use difficult to verify. According to the Drug Abuse Warning Network data on ketamine has been too imprecise to predict accurately. It is popular due to its hallucinogenic effect, its availability over the Internet and from legal purchase in many countries, including Mexico. In the United States, ketamine is a Schedule III drug used in veterinary medicine. Break-ins at veterinary practices have increased, serving as a source for obtaining illegal use of ketamine. Ketamine was a major drug of choice in Russia for teenagers. Ketamine was used by 0.9% of eighth graders, 1.0% of 10th graders, and 1.4% of 12th graders in the United States in 2006 (NIDA, 2010d). Similar to a number of other illicit drugs, the use of ketamine has remained relatively unchanged in 2010 (Johnston et al., 2011).

PSYCHOACTIVE EFFECTS   Ketamine is a dissociative anesthetic with effects similar to PCP's but less potent. It is available in liquid and powder forms. As a liquid, it is ingested orally and has a bitter taste. It is most frequently insufflated (snorted) as a powder. An insufflated dose is known as a *bump*. When a user experiences the desired hallucinations and visual distortions, he or she is said to be in *K-land*. At high doses, dissociation is at a level of producing a sensation of near-death, known as the *K-hole*.

EFFECTS ON THE BODY   Tachycardia, hypertension, impaired motor function, and respiratory depression are all physiological consequences of ketamine ingestion. Dissociation, depression, recurrent flashbacks, delirium, and amnesia are psychological consequences. There is an added risk of unintentional injury because a person under the influence of ketamine feels little or no pain. Long-term effects in humans are unknown, but long-term brain damage has been noted in animal studies (NIDA, 2010d).

A FURTHER LOOK AT CLUB DRUGS

The term *club drug* refers to one of a variety of psychoactive drugs that are grouped not by effect but by the milieu in which they are typically used (e.g., raves, dance parties, and nightclubs). They include amphetamine and methamphetamine, MDMA (most commonly known as *ecstasy*), LSD, PCP, ketamine, GHB, and benzodiazepines flunitrazepam (Rohypnol) and alprazolam (Xanax).

Many club drugs were introduced in response to the scheduling of controlled substances. Black market chemists began manufacturing *designer drugs*, which are essentially synthetic substances that are used for their psychoactive properties. MDMA (ecstasy), MDEA (Eve), and several others either surfaced or gained in popularity between 1970 and 1986, when the Controlled Substances Analogues Enforcement Act was passed. The act placed onto Schedule I or II those synthetic substances "substantially similar" to the chemical structure of a substance already listed under those categories in the Controlled Substances Act.

Club drugs have gained in popularity during the past decades because of their ease of manufacture, availability of precursors of the final chemical compound, and ease of sale. New club drugs have continued to surface. A form of methamphetamine was introduced from Southeast Asia called *ya ba*, which means "crazy drug." Gas chromatography analyses have determined that the methamphetamine pills were adulterated with a variety of substances, ranging from caffeine to morphine, making the effects unpredictable and dangerous.

Many, if not most, club drugs are anything but pure. Drugs are nearly always adulterated, sometimes with extremely unhealthy substances, making dance floor pharmacology a very risky business. Many are analogs of the drug that customers believe they are buying. MDA, MDEA, GHB, and other drugs are often substituted for the most popular club drug, ecstasy.

The use of club drugs in conjunction with alcohol, cocaine, and marijuana— which is highly likely—is even more dangerous, due to potentiation. In an attempt to minimize adverse reactions, club drug users frequently use a quasi-scientific approach to dose administration during a drug-using episode. Partygoers, with the aid of information gained often from the Internet, measure doses with crude devices such as teaspoons or bottle caps. Often, a companion will monitor the drug use of a raver or club hopper. These attempts at safe drug use frequently end in a trip to the emergency room or, for the most unfortunate, to the morgue.

MDMA (Ecstasy)

Ecstasy (3, 4-methlenedioxymethamphetamine, or MDMA), is a unique club drug, possessing aspects of amphetamine and of a mild hallucinogen. But the effect of MDMA that makes it unique and the one every consumer of the drug desires is called *empathogenesis*, the ability to open up, feel affection and connectedness to everyone around them. MDMA was first known as ADAM on the street, ostensibly because the rearrangement of letters made it easier to pronounce and perhaps because of the hint of biblical mysticism, both of which probably helped marketing efforts. When it was outlawed in 1986, black market entrepreneurs changed its name to ecstasy (NIDA, 2009d).

INCIDENCE Popularity of MDMA spread from the United States to England in the 1980s and rapidly through Europe, becoming a feature at rave dance parties. After 1994, the use of ecstasy skyrocketed. In 2008, 2.1 million Americans age 12 and older had abused MDMA at least once in the past year (NIDA, 2009d). A drop in the use of ecstasy of high school students appeared from 2001 to 2004, as its use began to be perceived as a high risk. However, a rebound has taken place in 2010 with ecstasy use increasing for eighth, 10th, and 12th graders, with significant increases for eighth and 10th graders (Johnston et al., 2011).

PSYCHOACTIVE EFFECTS MDMA has both stimulant and hallucinogenic effects. It is a synthetic, psychoactive drug chemically similar to the stimulant methamphetamine and the hallucinogen mescaline (NIDA, 2009d). Studies in which animals were trained to recognize amphetamines also recognized ecstasy.

When MDMA is first used, the primary effects are elevated mood, euphoria, and a feeling of closeness with others. At lower doses (40 to 80 mg), MDMA also produces high self-esteem, intensified senses of touch and taste, intensified colors, and a feeling of insight into one's self. Doses of 120 milligrams produce panic, depression, confusion, and anxiety.

The behavioral and psychological effects of MDMA use appear to be an acute, depletion of serotonin in the brain. Animal studies have suggested that damage to the serotonergic system may be reversible in rats. However, studies with primates are not as encouraging.

Neuroscience research has identified that dopamine systems can be affected by MDMA abuse. Although low doses produce few side effects, larger doses, particularly when taken with alcohol or other drugs, have produced fatalities. Cardiovascular events (heart attacks) have occurred, as have cerebrovascular accidents (strokes). Liver disease, hyperthermia, panic disorder, paranoid psychosis, and depression have been reported to be precipitated by MDMA use (NIDA, 2009d).

Some evidence indicates that people who take MDMA, even just a few times, may be risking permanent problems with learning and memory. Animal studies found that serotonin neurons in some parts of the brain, specifically those that use the chemical serotonin to communicate with other neurons, were permanently damaged (Rio, 2011). Areas particularly affected were the neocortex (the outer part of the brain where conscious thought occurs) and the hippocampus (which plays a key role in forming long-term memories).

Research (Raj et al., 2009) has linked MDMA use to long-term damage to those parts of the brain critical to thought, verbal memory, and pleasure. All indications are that MDMA is toxic to the brain. R. Cowan and colleagues at Vanderbilt University (2006) revealed altered activation in motor system brain regions by Ecstasy users. Their research findings were consistent with MDMA-induced alterations in basal ganglia-thalamocortical circuit neurophysiology demonstrated by earlier studies.

EFFECTS ON THE BODY MDMA is readily absorbed, and effects can be noticed in approximately 30 minutes after ingestion. Peak effects are noticed in 1 to 5 hours. Consumers take a dose or "roll" at designated intervals to prolong peak effects. MDMA is metabolized in the liver and eliminated by the kidneys as an active metabolite in about 24 hours.

Short-term side effects include dizziness, nystagmus, jaw clenching, and hallucinations. More severe effects include dehydration, hyperthermia, hyponatremia, seizures, and arrhythmia. With prolonged use, euphoria and empathy effects are diminished and replaced by a jittery amphetamine-like experience. Long-term effects include dysphoric mood and cognitive dulling.

MDMA has implications for sexual activity. It has been reported to cause impotence in men. At the same time, some men have reported sustained erection but an inability to achieve an orgasm. MDMA users report decreased sexual interest when intoxication effects are highest, followed by a rapid switch to intensified sexual desire. When effects of disinhibition and social openness are factored in, it is very likely that unsafe sex practices are increased.

VOLATILE SUBSTANCES OR INHALANTS

This group contains several chemicals that can be "sniffed," "snorted," "huffed," "bagged," or inhaled. Current use includes volatile organic solvents, such as those found in paint and fuel, aerosols, such as hair sprays, spray paints, and deodorants; volatile nitrites (amyl nitrite and butyl nitrite); and general anesthetic agents, such as nitrous oxide (NIDA, 2010j). Volatile substances, as ordinary household or medical items, are not listed on the DEA Controlled Substances Schedule.

INCIDENCE Abuse of inhalants is a much larger problem than most people realize. The National Survey on Drug Use and Health reported in 2008 that 2 million Americans age 12 and older had abused inhalants (SAMHSA, 2010). The NIDA 2008 Monitoring the Future Study revealed that 8.9% of eighth graders, 5.9% of 10th graders, and 3.8% of 12th graders had abused inhalants at least once in the past year. However, fortunately this does not represent a rise in the use of inhalants in recent years (Johnston et al., 2011).

PSYCHOACTIVE EFFECTS Inhalants are widely available, readily accessible, inexpensive, and legally obtained, making them attractive to adolescents. The toxic vapors make users forget their problems as they obtain a quick high with a minimal hangover. Short-term effects are similar to those of anesthetics. Disruptive and antisocial behavior as well as self-directed aggression is associated with individuals who abuse inhalants. However, it is not clear whether there is a cause-and-effect relationship—that is, whether inhalant use promotes antisocial and self-destructive tendencies or, conversely, whether those youths who have antisocial or self-destructive tendencies tend to use inhalants.

EFFECTS ON THE BODY Acute symptoms associated with the use of inhalants include excitation turning to drowsiness, disinhibition, lightheadedness, and agitation. With increasing intoxication, the user may develop ataxia, dizziness, and disorientation. Extreme intoxication may create signs of sleeplessness, general muscle weakness, nystagmus, hallucinations, and disruptive behavior. After the high wears off, the user may sleep, appear lethargic, and experience headaches. Chronic abusers may experience continued weight loss, muscle weakness, general disorientation, inattentiveness, and lack of coordination. These physical conditions can be complicated by the use of other drugs (mainly alcohol, cigarettes, and marijuana), malnutrition, and respiratory illness.

TOXICITY Neurotoxicity is predominantly related to the type of substance inhaled and the dose and duration of exposure. Acute, high-level exposure to solvents will induce short-term effects on brain functioning, but appear to be reversible. Chronic, high-level exposure over a longer time slowly produces irreversible neurological syndromes. Severe damage to the brain and nervous system can occur, and prolonged use can cause death by starving the body of oxygen or forcing the heart to beat more rapidly and erratically. There is a concern over the number of deaths caused by the direct toxic effects of inhalants, particularly in young people. Harmful irreversible effects including loss of hearing, central nervous system damage, peripheral neuropathies, and bone marrow damage can be caused by spray paints, glues, dewaxers, dry-cleaning chemicals, correction fluids, and gasoline inhalation (Volkow, 2005).

ANABOLIC-ANDROGENIC STEROIDS

Anabolic-androgenic steroids (AASs), although strictly not psychoactive or mood-altering drugs, are included in this chapter because of their incidence of abuse and their effects on the body. The use of AASs to enhance athletic performance and muscular appearance has been widespread both in world-class athletes and nonathletes, such as adolescents, law enforcement and corrections officers, and physical fitness devotees. They are listed as Schedule III drugs on the DEA Controlled Substances Schedule. AASs are man-made substances related to male sex hormones. Steroids refers to a class of drugs that are legal only by prescription (NIDA, 2009f). The abuse of anabolic steroids can lead to serious health problems including risk of liver and heart disease, stroke, hepatitis and infections from contaminated needles (Volkow, 2006).

INCIDENCE Use of AASs has been viewed as a silent epidemic. A SAMHSA report in 1995 showed 1,084,000 Americans as having used AASs, with 312,000 (29%) using in the previous year, compared with a lifetime heroin use of 2,083,000 Americans and 281,000 (13%) having used in the previous year. However, steroid use among all three grades assessed remained unchanged from 2005 to 2006 for both males and females. There has been little change in steroid abuse from 2008 to 2010. It has been reported that use of steroids in 2010 was only 0.5%, 1.0%, and 1.5% for grades 8, 10, and 12 (Johnston et al., 2011).

Factors that have contributed to AAS use include: increased muscular strength, improved physique, improvement in athletic performance, and increased self-confidence. Some coaches and parents of young athletes exert pressure to use AASs to become more competitive. In addition, certain groups, or personality types seem more associated with AAS use. It has been suggested that histrionic, narcissistic, antisocial, and borderline personality disorder groups have a higher incidence of use, as do those with dissatisfaction of body image (NIDA, 2009f).

EFFECTS ON THE BODY *Anabolic* describes the action of this category of drugs to increase the speed of growth of body tissues, while *steroids* refers to their chemical structure. Anabolic-androgenic steroids are only one in the classification of steroids, produced naturally in the body. Testosterone and similar altered steroids are androgenic, having masculinizing effects on the body, increasing muscle mass, aggression, and self-confidence. Testosterone has the disadvantage of having a brief elimination half-life, making it available to the body only for short periods of time.

Administration of AASs is oral or, more commonly, by injection, typically in cycles of weeks or months (referred to as "cycling"). Dosing is usually done with a pyramid-dosing schedule, in which a cyclic building to a peak followed by a gradual reduction in dosage is maintained. Cycles typically run 4 to 18 weeks on AASs, with 1 month to 1 year off the drugs. Alternatively, the intermittent use of up to eight AASs concurrently may be used.

AASs affect many body systems. Unwanted effects may include cardiovascular conditions, such as myocardial infarction, myocarditis, cardiac arrest with enlargement of the heart and death of heart cells, cerebrovascular accident (stroke), and severe restriction of blood flow to the lower limbs of the body. Liver changes may also occur. Testosterone and other AASs are metabolized in part by estrogen antagonists, such as estradiol. The estrogen antagonists can cause breast pain in men and gynecomastia (enlargement and development of breast tissue) requiring medical or surgical intervention. Testicular atrophy in men is common, as is voice deepening, clitoral hypertrophy, shrinking of breasts, menstrual irregularities, and excessive growth of hair in women. These changes are largely irreversible in females, while the sexual side effects in males are often reversible. The masculinizing effects of testosterone are achieved by its binding to intracellular receptors in target cells. This forms an androgen-receptor complex that binds to chromosomes, leading to increases in proteins and RNAs within the chromosome (NIDA, 2009f). Mood disturbances of hypomania, mania, irritability, depressed mood, major depression, elation, recklessness, feelings of power and invincibility, and both increased and decreased libido have been reported during use of AASs.

The first reports of psychological dependence on AASs emerged in the late 1980s. Loss of control and interference with other activities has been reported during use. Withdrawal symptoms include the desire to take more AASs, fatigue, dissatisfaction with body image, depressed mood, restlessness, anorexia, insomnia, decreased libido, and headache. Suicidal thoughts have been reported after cessation of use.

Case Study

The background of this client follows: He is a 63-year-old Caucasian male. He is currently financially stable with an income exceeding $250,000 annually. He has worked for 30 years in the oil and gas industry. He has been married for 35 years and has two married children, five grandchildren, ages 5 to 17 years old. He has provided minimal information regarding his family of origin.

The presenting issue of this client is polysubstance abuse. He is physiologically dependent on opiates as a result of taking medication as originally prescribed by his medical doctor for pain management. Prescriptions include hydrocodone, Oxycodone, and fentanyl. Along with abusing these meds daily for 13 years, the client has been a regular user of cocaine. In fact his cocaine habit at times affected his family's economic stability. He was referred by his employer for treatment with the goal of total abstinence as a condition for continued employment.

Topics that immediately need to be explored include his use/abuse of cocaine, use of narcotics, the ethics of misusing drugs prescribed for pain management, withdrawal issues, brain damage, and treatment strategies.

Other pertinent information includes level of responsibility, degree of denial, attitude toward treatment, family support, methods of treatment, and severity of brain damage.

Critical Thinking Questions

1. What additional information would you need from this client in order to properly assess damage potentially caused by the long-term abuse of drugs?
2. What would you expect to find through neuroscience brain imaging considering cocaine and prescription drug abuse?
3. Is it possible for the brain to repair itself under the above circumstances of long term polysubstance abuse?

MyCounselingLab

Go to Topic 2: *The Major Substances of Abuse and the Body,* on the MyCounselingLab site (www.MyCounselingLab.com) for *Substance Abuse Counseling*, Fifth Edition, where you can:

- Find learning outcomes for *The Major Substances of Abuse and the Body* along with the national standards that connect to these outcomes.
- Complete Assignments and Activities that can help you more deeply understand the chapter content.
- Apply and practice your understanding of the core skills identified in the chapter with the Building Counseling Skills unit.
- Prepare yourself for professional certification with a Practice for Certification quiz.
- Connect to videos through the Video and Resource Library.

MyCounselingLab Exercises

Go to the Video and Resource Library on the MyCounselingLab site for your text and search for the following clip: *Assessing the Negative Impact of Substance Abuse.*

After reviewing the video, answer the following questions:

1. For this client, what do you think are the effects of heroin abuse on the brain?
2. What does neuroscience research say about the long-term effects of heroin abuse and brain damage?
3. What are some other problems that result from heroin abuse? Consider physiology as well as behavior.

CONCLUSION

The human brain is the major site for all psychoactive drug interactions. All psycho-active substances manipulate the biochemistry of the brain and change the neuron's process of communication within its existing structural framework. Drugs affect the brain's communication system and interfere with the way nerve cells normally send, receive, and process information. These changes alter the user's perceptions, emotions, thoughts, and behaviors over time. In addition, drugs have effects on many other body organs. (Table 3.2 summarizes the characteristics of various drugs.) Neuroscience research is making significant strides in determining the biological actions that make people reliant on drugs and how over time they affect the makeup of the brain. Research involving the neurosciences, psychopharmacology, and new therapeutic strategies with chemically dependent populations is producing new insights to successfully identify the effects of illicit drug abuse on the CNS, particularly the brain, and strategies to repair some of the damage. Several recent findings of neuroscience research have been reported in this chapter.

TABLE 3.2 Summary of characteristics of drugs

| Classification | Trade or Other Names | Dependence | | Possible Effects | Effects of Overdose | Withdrawal Syndrome |
		Physical	Psycho-logical			
Depressants						
Ethanol	Alcohol (beer, wine, liquor, etc.)	Low–moderate	Moderate–high	Tolerance, diminishment of inhibitions, Fetal Alcohol Syndrome, poor judgment, staggering, slurred speech, blackouts	Severe CNS depression, coma, death. Prolonged use: damage to all organs of body, Wernicki-Korsakoff syndrome	Shakes, irritability, diaphoresis, anxiety, nausea, diarrhea, hallucinations, general disorientation. In severe cases, seizures, delirium tremens, cardiovas-cular collapse, death
Barbiturates	Sodium Pentothal, Amytal, Nembutal (yellow jackets), Seconal (red birds), Tuinal (rainbows), Butisol, phenobarbital, Quaalude (ludes), chloral hydrate, meprobamate	High–moderate	High–moderate	CNS depression, disinhibition, elevated mood, increased self-concept, increased energy and confidence, decreased anxiety	Unsteady gait, slurred speech, nystagmus, vomiting, poor judgment, coma	CNS hyperactivity, hand tremor, insomnia, nausea, hallucinations, illusions, rebound anxiety, panic attacks, delirium, psychosis, mania, paranoia, psychomotor agitation
Benzodiazepines	Diazepam (Valium), Librium, Halcion, Xanax, Buspar, Klonopin, Rohypnol	Low	Moderate–high	Anticonvulsant, anxiety reduction, muscle relaxant. Reduces adverse effects of cocaine, methamphetamine, heroin, and alcohol	Similar to barbiturates	Anxiety, tremors, nightmares, insomnia, anorexia, nausea, vomiting, delirium, seizures, respiratory arrest, death

(Continued)

TABLE 3.2 (*Continued*)

| Classification | Trade or Other Names | Dependence | | Possible Effects | Effects of Overdose | Withdrawal Syndrome |
		Physical	Psycho-logical			
Opiates	Opium, morphine, heroin (horse, smack), Dilaudid, Demerol, Hycodan, Numorphan, Percodan, Darvon, Dolo-phine, Sublimaze, black tar	High	High	Analgesia, rapid tolerance, euphoria, drowsiness, respiratory distress, constricted pupils, nausea	Slow and shallow breathing, clammy skin, convulsions, runny nose, possible coma, death	Dysphoria, nausea, repeated yawning, sweating, tearing, craving, "drug hunger"
Stimulants						
Cocaine	Coke, crack, snow, blow	Possible	High	Psychological: Intense CNS arousal—tremendous mood elevation, exhilaration, feeling of well-being, decreased inhibitions, relief of limitless power and energy, impaired judgment. Physiological: increased or decreased pulse and blood pressure, insomnia, pupillary dilation, nausea or vomiting, weight loss, muscular weakness, respiratory depression, chest pain, cardiac arrhythmias, confusion, seizures	Acute hypertension, angina, irregular heartbeat, heart attack, injury to cerebral arteries, seizures, coma, possible death	Dysphoria, seizures, hypotension, depression, anxiety, panic attacks, insomnia or hypersomnia, obsessions

Drug	Source			Effects	Long-term effects	
Nicotine	Cigars, cigarettes, chewing tobacco, snuff	High	High	Euphoria, cardiac acceleration	Long-term effects: lung disease, cardiac disease, linked to several cancers	Weight gain, negative emotions, interpersonal conflicts, depression, insomnia, irritability, frustration or anger, anxiety, difficulty concentrating
Caffeine	Ingredient in tea, coffee, cocoa, chocolate, many soft drinks, and many OTC drugs	Low	Low	Alertness, sleeplessness, specific blood vessel construction, increase in heart rate and contraction, rapid heartbeat, psychomotor agitation, diuresis, insomnia, nervousness, gastrointestinal complaints	Anxiety, sleep disturbances, mood changes, respiratory failure, death	
Amphetamines	Speed, crystal (meth), crank, batu, slate, glass, ice, ya ba	Possible	High	Intense CNS arousal, rapid heartbeat, excitation, insomnia, loss of appetite, teeth grinding, muscle tension	Rapid heartbeat, hypertension, headache, profuse sweating, severe chest pain, delirium, panic, paranoia, hallucinations	Depression, fatigue, increased appetite, prolonged sleep with REM; death due to extreme heat elevation, convulsions, circulatory collapse

(Continued)

TABLE 3.2 *(Continued)*

		Dependence				
Classification	Trade or Other Names	Physical	Psycho-logical	Possible Effects	Effects of Overdose	Withdrawal Syndrome
Cannabis	Indian hemp, marijuana, hashish (hash), pot, grass, dope, Mary Jane, weed	Unknown	Moderate	Psychological: euphoria, grandiosity, impairment of short-term memory, impaired judgment, distorted sensory perceptions, impaired motor performance, impaired perception of time Physiological: increased appetite, conjunctival injection, dry mouth, rapid heartbeat	Intoxication, delirium, hallucinations, delusions, anxiety, psychosis	
Hallucinogens	LSD, acid, ecstasy, mescaline, psilocybin, psilocyn, PCP, angel dust, TCP, peyote, ketamine	LSD, mescaline, peyote, psilocybin, psilocyn: none Others: unknown	PCP, angel dust, TCP: high Others: unknown	Dizziness, weakness, tremor, intensified hearing, visual distortions, dreamlike imagery, synesthesia, sleeplessness, poor perception of time and distance, marked anxiety or depression, pupillary dilation, rapid heartbeat, palpitations, sweating, blurred vision, tremors, incoordination	Dissociative anesthesia, coma, psychosis, possible death	Not reported (Long-term, heavy LSD users have been reported to have schizophrenia symptoms for several months following cessation of drug.)

Volatile Substances or Inhalants	Solvents, glue, gasoline, thinners, aerosols, correction fluid, cleaning fluids, refrigerant gases (fluorocarbons), anesthetics, whipped cream propellants, organic nitrites, cooking or lighter gases	None. Neurotoxicity is related to type and dose of inhalant. Neurotoxicity of short-term high dosage appears to be reversible; chronic, high dose use produces irreversible neurological syndromes	Unknown	Excitation, drowsiness, disinhibition, agitation, lightheadedness, dizziness, disorientation, slurred speech, unsteady gait, tremor, depressed reflexes, blurred vision. Chronic use: weight loss, muscle weakness, general disorientation, inattentiveness, incoordination	Sleeplessness, general muscle weakness, headaches, joint pain, nystagmus, hallucinations, disruptive behavior; damage to kidneys, liver, lungs, heart, and blood	Lethargy, sleep, headaches
Anabolic-Androgenic Steroids	Andro	Low	Low	Increased muscular strength, aggression, self-confidence, euphoria	Cardiovascular conditions, masculinizing effects on women, depression, psychotic conditions	Depression, appetite and sleep disturbances

4

Etiology of Substance Abuse: Why People Use

CYNTHIA A. FAULKNER, PH.D., LCSW

MyCounselingLab™

Visit the **MyCounselingLab**™ site for *Substance Abuse Counseling*, Fifth Edition to enhance your understanding of chapter concepts. You'll have the opportunity to practice your skills through video- and case-based Assignments and Activities as well as Building Counseling Skills units, and to prepare for your certification exam with Practice for Certification quizzes.

Theories about what causes addiction are varied and highly controversial. For instance, does a weak moral character cause substance abuse or is it a disease? Is substance abuse a learned behavior? Or, is substance abuse a result of heredity or caused by environmental factors? This chapter will address these questions by examining theories used to explain why individuals begin and continue to use alcohol, tobacco, and other drugs (ATOD). Understanding the theoretical foundation of use may be important when developing a treatment plan for individuals and their families. While some theories are no longer believed to be valid by professionals, they provide the reader with an understanding of the progression and advancements in the field.

UNDERSTANDING THEORY

In common usage, people often use the word *theory* to express an opinion or a speculation. In this usage, a theory is not necessarily based on facts and is not required to provide true descriptions of reality. However, in research, Faulkner & Faulkner (2009) define a *theory* as a "statement or set of statements designed to explain a phenomenon based upon observations and experiments and often agreed upon by most experts in a particular field" (p. 9). Therefore, in research, the terms *theory* and *fact* do not necessarily stand in opposition. For example, it is a fact that an apple dropped from a tree can be observed to fall toward the earth, and the theory used to explain this phenomenon is the theory of gravitation.

This chapter addresses the question of why people abuse drugs by examining each major theory within the following aspects: (1) why people begin to use drugs—*initiation,* (2) why they continue to use or abuse drugs—*continuation,* (3) why some people escalate to dependence on drugs and others do not—*addiction,* (4) why some people quit using drugs and others do not—*recovery,* and (5) why some people remain clean and/or sober and others do not—*relapse.*

OVERVIEW OF *ATOD* THEORIES

Moral Theory

For centuries, alcohol consumption was considered a natural part of daily living. It was used at mealtimes, celebration times, mourning times, for pleasure, and for controlling pain. Only at certain periods in time, did alcohol addiction create problems in societies. For example, during the early industrial revolution in England, gin was so cheap that alcohol consumption became problematic among both adults and young children. But at the same time, in the United States the consumption of alcohol was largely considered to be a personal choice, and those who could not "hold" their liquor were considered to have a lack of willpower and, in some cases, were judged to be morally corrupt. This attitude, with its roots in a Puritan belief system, prevailed through much of the 18th and 19th centuries. During the Civil War, the temperance movement began to gain some momentum. The growing sentiment among many people was that alcohol and the uncontrolled ingestion of alcohol (alcoholism) was a sin. Any individual who took to drink and who could not control his or her drinking was morally corrupt. This attitude prevailed and gained momentum until it reached its apex with the passage of the Eighteenth Amendment to the United States Constitution: *Prohibition of Intoxicating Liquors* (National Prohibition Act, 1919). This amendment made the sale, manufacture, or transportation of alcoholic beverages illegal. The Eighteenth Amendment was repealed in 1933, and once again alcohol could be bought and sold legally in the United States.

It is of note that some prohibitionist themes continue even today, including both user and supplier defined as "fiends" and drug use viewed as "contagious" (an epidemic) (White, 2009, p.18). But perhaps the best evidence of the populous-held beliefs that moralizes addiction is with the cultural "stigma" attached to it (Corrigan, Watson, & Miller, 2006; Room, 2005; White, Evans, & Lamb, 2009). This includes drug users being stigmatized by outsiders as well as stigmatizing other drug users for having less "control" of their drug use and prevention and educational campaigns that still portray the drug user as ". . . physically diseased, morally depraved, and criminally dangerous . . ." (White, 2009, p. 20).

Aspects of Use Addressed by the Moral Theory

INITIATION Le Moal and Koob (2007) state that drug use begins with social influences and an acute reinforcement, such as relief from a negative emotional state. Therefore, personal needs or *moral deficiencies* under this theory include a "means to cope with painful and threatening emotions" (Le Moal & Koob, 2007, p. 380); childhood factors such as disrupted families, lack of parental supervision, behavioral problems, and drug-using parents (Hayatbakhsh, Mamun, Najim, O'Callihan, Bor, & Alati, 2008), and peer substance use (Urberg, Goldstein, & Toro, 2005; Park, Kim, & Kim, 2009). Le Moal and Koob (2007) report that self-regulation (either underregulation or misregulation) can lead to addiction. Underregulation is manifested in either failure to establish standards of behavior or conflicts in standards. Misregulation is misdirected attempts to self-regulate behavior.

CONTINUATION   The perceived rewards perpetuate the continued use of the drug. Rewards can be as simple as the increase in energy or fatigue reduction after using caffeine. Rewards can be the reduction of physical pain through the use of narcotics, using stimulants to increase alertness or performance, or using barbiturates to reduce anxiety. Becoming dependent on the benefit or reward leads to addiction. In addition, to mimic the same benefit, continued use of the drug must increase in quantity. Further, it masks the underlying physical or emotional problems.

ADDICTION   Criteria for evaluating addiction can start with the initial motivation as listed in the initiation phase. For instance, if the drug is used to reduce or eliminate pain, anxiety, or problems, then its use will tend to be addictive. Users are unable to derive any pleasure from the use because they are relying on the drug to avoid unpleasantness as opposed to seeking pleasure. The sign of the addiction is the absence of choice the user has over the drug use. Finally, the user's identity and functioning are so connected with the drug use that it becomes impossible for the addict to envision life without the drug.

RECOVERY   To cease the addiction, the user must develop alternative rewards to replace the gratification of the drug experience. This can be accomplished many ways, including identifying better coping mechanisms using pain management, stress management for anxiety, and cognitive therapy for working through feelings. Frequently, an artificial setting, such as an in-patient hospital or halfway house, is necessary during this transition period to remove the user from the addictive pattern of use. Finally, the process of "maturing out" has been found to be related to psychological maturation that occurs between the ages of 18 and 35, particularly in the areas of impulsivity and neuroticism (Littlefield, Sher, & Wood, 2009).

RELAPSE   Relapse occurs when the needs and the lifestyle of the addict are not addressed when the drug use is ceased. When the addict is reintroduced to the stressors that led to the use to begin with, there is no alternative coping other than going back to the drug use. Certain addictions are dependent on a setting or level of stress. For instance, an adolescent who is developmentally immature, or someone repeatedly exposed to stressful situations such as police officers may be more prone to relapse. Conversely, users exposed to a one-time life crisis such as soldiers at war may use and abuse but not be addicted when they leave the stressful environment.

Conclusion.   A renewed interest in the moral theory (Eskapa, 2008; Husak, 2004; Peele, 2004) has placed emphasis on the intersection of personal choice, values, motivation, and intentions. Through this lens, alcoholism is viewed as an accumulation of choices that include the definition of self and willingness to accept responsibilities. In addition, problem drinkers do not become alcoholic overnight but will increase drinking as problems increase over the years. Additionally, the moral theory purports that addiction can be "cured" (Ameisen, 2008; Eskapa, 2008; Prentiss, 2005). With this point in mind, a major pitfall of this theory is that it focuses exclusively on individual ability (willpower) and characteristics to control or quit drug use and ignores the compounding factors of genetics and environment.

DISEASE THEORY

In 1935 an organization was founded known as Alcoholics Anonymous (AA). AA shifted responsibility away from the alcoholic as morally deficient with the concept that the alcoholics suffer from an illness. AA retained some elements of the moral model, believing that the help of a Higher Power is needed to achieve and maintain sobriety and individuals are responsible for seeking their own recovery. However, AA was a shift in philosophy from the moral model in that the individual was no longer held responsible for "having the disease" of alcoholism, only for seeking help to arrest the disease. This shift toward the disease model gained validity when the American Medical Association recognized alcoholism as a disease in a 1966 policy statement (American Medical Association, 1966). It is this shift in paradigms that allowed alcoholism and other substance abuse to be scientifically studied. These research studies precipitated the development of new theoretical models for causality and treatment.

It was a physician, Dr. E. M. Jellinek (1946), who provided an understanding of the progression of alcoholism as a disease utilizing the Jellinek curve, or the v-chart. On this chart, the disease progresses downward on the left side and recovery progresses upward on the right side of the chart (Figure 4.1). In his book titled *The Disease Concept of Alcoholism* (1960) he described five types of drinking behaviors identified by the first five letters of the Greek alphabet—alpha, beta, gamma, delta, and epsilon. This information suggested that there were distinct signs and symptoms of alcoholism, a criterion important if it is to be termed a disease. These symptoms were clustered into stages of alcoholism: early, middle, and late.

(A caveat: It is important to keep in mind that the Disease Theory was initially developed to address alcohol consumption exclusively and only with male alcoholics. Therefore, the Jellinek chart may or may not represent the progression of other drug use or differences in progression by gender. However, this theory has been applied universally to all populations, and the Jellinek chart modified to accommodate other drug use, in 12-step recovery groups, such as Narcotic Anonymous, and in treatment programs.)

Aspects of Use Addressed by the Disease Theory

INITIATION The disease theory does not specifically address "why" an individual chooses to take the first drink of alcohol. However, Jellinek's (1960) Pre-Alcoholic

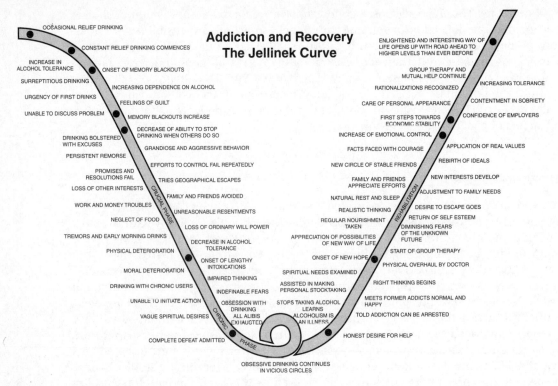

FIGURE 4.1   Jellinek curve.

Source: Retrieved from http://www.in.gov/judiciary/ijlap/jellinek.pdf

Phase describes use as being socially motivated. In fact, it is postulated that individuals with the disease of addiction do not know they have it until they start using. In other words, the disease will lie dormant until the first use. Therefore, abstinence as prevention (and treatment) is strongly recommended within this theory.

CONTINUATION   According to Jellinek (1960) in the next phase in the progression, the Prodromal Phase, the individual uses alcohol early in the disease to relieve pain, whether physical pain, emotional pain, tension from job or family, or other stress. Driving while intoxicated and memory blackouts can occur during this phase. However, the user will continue the alcohol use despite negative consequences. As the disease progresses to the Crucial Phase more visible changes occur, such as job or family problems, absenteeism, financial problems, or changes in moral behavior. Internal changes are also taking place throughout these phases, including a variety of physical and mental health problems. As physical tolerance increases, more must be consumed to provide the minimum level of "comfort" afforded by the drug. If allowed to progress into the last phase, deterioration of the body or brain may make effective treatment impossible.

ADDICTION   Jellinek's (1960) Chronic Phase (the final phase) describes the drinking as a total loss of control and the loss of a choice to drink. In 1970, Davis and Walsh published experimental research on the brain stem of rats that found evidence of a specific effect on an alkaloid type neurotoxin called THP (tetrahydro-papaveroline) when introduced to alcohol. When ethanol and its metabolites acetaldehyde interact with THP, the conversion creates morphine-like alkaloids in the brain stem of rats creating a preference for alcohol. Davis and Walsh (1970) state "These data support the concept that alcoholism is a true addiction which may involve specific biochemical events leading to the formation of the morphine-type alkaloids" (p. 1006).

(A caveat: There are variations of an elaborate story about the discovery of THIQs in alcoholic brains that is repeated on multiple Internet sites and in the treatment community. The story purports that Virginia Davis was a physician [even a medical examiner] and was doing cancer [or other] research using the brains of recently deceased homeless "winos" in Houston (or San Antonio), Texas. During these brain autopsies she discovered the connection between alcohol and a substance normally found in heroin users, namely THIQ. However, there is no empirical evidence that supports these claims. In fact, the findings from Davis's research with Michael Walsh [1970] were through her work with rat brain stems.)

THP is one of a variety of THIQs (tetrahydroisoquinolines) that have been studied because they are chemically related to opiates and it was thought that this might explain the difference between alcoholic drinkers and normal drinkers. In 1983, Sjoquist, Perdahl, and Winblad published autopsy results on the brains of two groups of alcoholics (those with alcohol levels in the body and those without) that seemed to confirm the presence of THIQs but also confirmed that THIQs were present (at lower levels) in the brains of the nonalcoholic control group. Also in 1983, D. L. Ohlms expressed a popular theory of alcohol addiction in his book, *The Disease Concept of Alcoholism*, that proposed that alcoholics produce a highly addictive substance called THIQs during the metabolism of alcohol in the body. THIQs are supposedly not metabolized by nonalcoholics when they drink. According to Ohlms, a small amount of THIQs injected into the brains of rats produced alcoholic rats and THIQs remained in the brain long after an animal had been injected. Therefore, the theory is that alcoholics are genetically predisposed to produce THIQs in response to alcohol, that the THIQs creates a craving for alcohol, and that the THIQs remains in the brain of the alcoholic long after the use of alcohol is discontinued. More recently, Quertemont and Didone (2006) note that measuring the presence and quantities of THIQs in the brain is not an easy task and that more sophisticated measures are needed. Therefore, it is not as simple as stating that those with THIQs in their brains are predisposed to become alcoholics and those without THIQs are not.

RECOVERY In the disease theory, an alcoholic or addict is never considered cured, only "in remission," "recovering," or a "nonpracticing" alcoholic or addict. One Alcoholics Anonymous–approved brochure (1976) titled *Is There an Alcoholic in Your Life?* states:

> The alcoholic is a sick person suffering from a disease for which there is no known cure; that is, no cure in the sense that he or she will ever be able to drink moderately, like a nonalcoholic, for any sustained period. Because it is an illness—a physical compulsion combined with a mental obsession to drink—the alcoholic must learn to stay away from alcohol completely in order to lead a normal life.

Recovery is, therefore, focused on abstinence. After abstinence, AA believes that relieving the guilt and shame felt by addicts experiencing the consequences of their disease through the Twelve Step process might make them more amenable to treatment. A rigorous review of AA studies indicated that 12-step programs are at least as helpful in recovery as other intervention approaches (Kelly, Magill, & Stout, 2009).

Initial detoxification, if necessary, is followed by cognitive-behavioral treatment to make lifestyle changes that eliminate being around the drug(s) of choice and "using" friends. Sayings such as "If you don't want to get shot, don't go where the shooting is" reinforce behavioral changes to eliminate exposure to temptation. Twelve-step programs are a major part of many professional treatment plans, and treatment staff often recommend that clients attend "90 meetings in 90 days." A 12-step "home group" is identified by the addict, and a recovering "sponsor" is attained to provide ongoing social support for sobriety.

However, by claiming to have a disease, some addicts believe they can deny responsibility for change, especially since denial is a primary symptom of substance abuse. Some may refuse treatment with the attitude of "What do you expect from a person with a disease?"

RELAPSE   In the disease model, relapse is seen as "failure" on the part of the individual who is working a recovery program. But, it is also viewed as part of the recovery process. Once sober, the addict may begin to feel confident that he or she can now be in control of the use. But before long, the addict's usage is as frequent and tolerance is as high as before recovery. The research on THIQ would provide a physiological explanation for the fact that recovering alcoholics who relapse quickly return to their previous use patterns. In addition, underlying or confounding problems may be ignored during recovery.

While Jellinek's theory referred only to alcoholism, in today's treatment world, alcoholism and other substance abuse are many times treated in the same way. When this occurs there is minimal recognition of the complex factors that accompany other drugs or polydrug use.

Generalities from Jellinek's theory should be used with caution because of limitations in the sample population used for his study. The sample was small (98) and homogeneous; male, late-stage, and gamma alcoholics (Jellinek, 1946). Females were included only as the control group. A more recent study conducted by Moss, Chen, and Yi (2007) using a sample of 1,484 U.S. residents (mean age 32, 68% men, 71% Caucasian) identified five subtypes of alcohol dependence (AD): (1) Young Adult Subtype; (2) Functional Subtype; (3) Intermediate Familial Subtype; (4) Young Antisocial Subtypes; and (5) Chronic Severe Subtype. Nevertheless, Jellinek's contribution in conceptualizing alcoholism as other than a moral problem is an important foundation for other theories.

Conclusion.   Viewing alcohol dependence as a disease caused a major paradigm shift in social perception and treatment approaches of addiction in this country. The belief that there is no cure for alcoholism but that it can be brought into remission through sobriety is one of the strengths of the disease theory. Alcoholics were no longer blamed for their disease (much as one would not blame someone for having cancer or diabetes). Having a disease also removed some of the social stigma of being an alcoholic, thus making it easier and more palatable for someone to seek treatment. Categorizing an addiction as a disease created opportunities for scientific research and the study of genetic influences, as discussed in the next section.

A limitation of the disease theory is that it does not address the individuals who seek to reduce their alcohol consumption as opposed to abstaining. Newer recovery groups, such as Moderation Management (MM), which was founded in 1994, is a harm-reduction, self-help organization that is designed to help problem drinkers moderate their consumption rather than require that they abstain from alcohol (Klaw, Horst, & Humphreys, 2006). In fact, some argue that the disease concept disables an individual into being "sick" and with no control over their own actions (Larkin, Wood, & Griffiths, 2006) and that the "ill" person is disempowered (Graham, Young, Valach, & Wood, 2008). Regardless of this debate, the disease theory remains the prominent etiology for diagnosing substance disorders.

A final note of consideration in the therapeutic community is that a recovering counselor is viewed as an asset because addicts are more likely to believe recovery is possible from someone who has "been there." "Recovering" alcoholics and addicts commonly work as paraprofessional staff members or peer mentors in treatment programs. This is reinforced by the 12th step of *The Twelve Steps of Alcoholics Anonymous*: "Having had a spiritual awakening as the result of these steps, we tried to carry this message to alcoholics, and to practice these principles in all our affairs" (Alcoholics Anonymous, 2002). While personal experiences are empowering for clients, additional professional training and/or education in treatment techniques and skills strengthen the possibility of client recovery. In fact, Culbreth's findings (as cited in Crabb & Linton, 2007) of a review of 16 studies concluded that clients' perceptions regarding the effectiveness of treatment were not related to the recovery status of a counselor.

GENETIC THEORIES

Research involving intergenerational studies, twin studies, adoption studies, biological research, and a search for genetic markers of alcohol and substance dependence are currently being utilized in an attempt to further explain alcohol and drug dependency. In addition to Jellinek's five phases of addiction, other topologies have emerged. Research on subtypes consists of single domain (e.g., age of onset) and multi-dimensional classification schemes (Babor & Caetano, 2006). For instance, Windle and Scheidt (2004) conducted a cluster analysis to determine if two subtypes was enough and identified four subtypes: mild course, polydrug, negative affect, and chronic/antisocial. Another study conducted by Lynskey et al. (2005) on 6,265 young (median age 30 years) Australian twins revealed four classifications of alcohol-related problems related to women and an additional fifth classification for men. These were (1) no/few problems, (2) heavy drinking, (3) moderate dependence, (4) severe dependence, and (5) abuse (men only).

However, researchers have consistently identified two basic subtypes of alcoholics, or binary topologies (Babor & Caetano, 2006). In a cluster study consisting of 321 male and female alcoholics, Babor et al. (1992) found two typologies of alcoholics and labeled them Type A and Type B. Type A alcoholics are characterized by later onset, fewer childhood risk factors, less severe dependence, fewer alcohol-related problems, and less psychopathological dysfunction. Type B alcoholics are characterized by childhood risk factors, familial alcoholism, early onset of alcohol-related problems, greater severity of dependence, polydrug use, a more chronic treatment history, greater psychopathological dysfunction, and more life stress. Although scientists have not been able to identify specific genes responsible for addiction to alcohol, studies have demonstrated that these findings, again, lends more credence to the possibility of a genetic component to addiction.

Another binary topology was discovered as the result of studying the behavior of a large birth cohort of children born in Stockholm that had been separated from their biological parents at birth and reared in adopted homes. Cloninger, Bohman, and Sigvardsson (1981) collected extensive data about the genetic background of the adoptees' biological parents including about alcohol abuse, criminality, and physical and mental complaints to physicians. Information was also measured about their rearing environment by their adoptive parents and home environment. This allowed several contributions of the genetic and environmental backgrounds to be studied independently and in combination in a sample of thousands of adoptees. This research distinguished two subtypes of alcoholism: Type 1 and Type II. Type I alcoholics, it is believed, transmit cross-gender (from mothers to sons or grandfathers to granddaughters). Type II alcoholics transmit the disease to the same gender (fathers to sons or grandmothers to granddaughters). Type I alcoholics tend to have less criminal behavior, have less dependent personality traits, be less violent when they drink, and have a later onset of the disease (most often after age 25). Type II alcoholics, on the other hand, tend to exhibit more violent behaviors when they drink, have signs of compulsive drinking (blackouts for example), and have more dependent personality traits. What was once considered to be a normal part of the alcoholic drinking pattern (fighting and argumentative behavior) is now seen as germane to Type II alcoholics. These original findings were later confirmed by the same researchers in a replication study using the same methods (Sigvardsson, Bohman, & Cloninger, 1996). These adoption studies provided strong evidence for the contribution of both genetic and environmental influences on vulnerability to alcoholism, somatization, criminality, anxiety, and depressive disorders.

Studies on families, adoption, and twins conclusively demonstrated that genetic factors contributed between 50% and 60% of the variance of risk for alcoholism (Foroud, Edenberg, & Crabbe, 2010). Dependence on illicit drugs has recently been studied in twins, and heritability estimates range from 45% to 79% (Dick & Agrawal, 2008). Family studies look at both alcoholic and nonalcoholic members and have provided convincing evidence of the genetic influence for the risk of alcohol dependence (Gelernter & Kranzler, 2009; Prescott et al., 2006; Prescott et al., 2005).

Adoption studies have examined the influence of genetics and environment that addresses the ongoing debate of nature versus nurture (genetics vs. environment). Adoption studies compare the disease status of adoptees with their birth parents and their adoptive parents with whom they have no genetic relationship. If addiction were influenced by genetic factors, then we would expect to find a high rate of ATOD dependence in children of parents who were addicted regardless of whether they were raised by their substance-abusing parents or someone else (King et al., 2009; Philibert et al., 2009).

Twin studies compare the rates of addiction for monozygotic twins (twins developing from one egg and one sperm)—what are commonly referred to as identical twins. If a disease (such as alcoholism) is genetically transmitted, then monozygotic twins should both exhibit that disease (because they are genetically identical) (Agrawal et al., 2008; Agrawal & Lynskey, 2008; Goldman, Oroszi, & Ducci, 2006).

Aspects of Use Addressed by Genetic Theories

INITIATION There are many factors that influence the motivation to engage in drinking behavior (Vengeliene, Bilbao, Molander, & Spanagel, 2008; Weiss, 2005). Initiation of alcohol use generally starts early in life (preadolescence or early adolescence) and may be quite different from those that influence misuse, abuse, and addiction. Initiation is more likely to be environmental (King et al., 2009; Duff, 2007) and to co-occur with tobacco use (Burrow-Sanchez, 2006; Schlaepfer, Hoft, & Ehringer, 2008) and marijuana (Burrow-Sanchez, 2006; Tu, Ratner, & Johnson, 2008). Therefore, initiation of use increases with exposure to environmental influences and social forces such as peer-related events where drugs are used and a high level of sensitivity to peer pressure exists (Becker, 2008). A history of parental drinking, smoking, or drug use, and the degree of life stability are also important factors for initiation of use (Burrow-Sanchez, 2006; Park, Kim, & Kim, 2009). With the use of other drugs (such as heroin, cocaine, methamphetamines, etc.) genetically influenced factors such as personality types (e.g., antisocial personality) were linked with alcohol and drug dependence (Kendler, Prescott, Myers, & Neale, 2003; Krueger et al., 2002) and other individual factors such as coping strategies (Feil & Hasking, 2008).

More recently, personality traits have been reexamined (i.e., neuroticism, extraversion, agreeableness, conscientiousness, openness) using a five-factor model (FFM) and are considered in identifying risk factors for drug use and dependency (Kornør & Nordvik, 2007; Harakeh, Scholte, de Vries, & Engels, 2006; Hopwood et al., 2007; Luo, Kranzler, Zuo, Wang, & Gelernter, 2007; Terracciano, Löckenhoff, Crum, Bienvenu, & Cosa Jr., 2008). Based on the FFM or "Big Five," the NEO Personality Inventory was developed by Costa & McCrae (1985) and revised in 1992 as the NEO PI-R to include additional characteristics (six characteristics under each factor for a total of 30 characteristics). One factor, Neuroticism measures anxiety, hostility, depression, self-consciousness, impulsiveness and vulnerability, all of which could be risk factors for ATOD use.

CONTINUATION The decision to continue using a drug may involve a combination of social and biological factors, with social factors playing a larger role. Genetically influenced factors may be important in how the effects are experienced. For instance, the individual's personality, level of anxiety, rate of metabolism, and the nervous system's sensitivity to the drug (e.g., coughing, nausea, and vomiting) may all contribute to the final balance between a positive and negative experience of the first ingestion of a drug that will influence the individual's decision to try again. Social and psychological factors that interact with biological reactions—including peer pressure, the desire to assume an adult role, the need to copy parental models, and society's general attitude about the drug may induce an individual to repeat the drug use despite a negative effect.

Antisocial behavior is also linked with substance abuse, although the causality is unclear. Possibilities include (a) antisocial behavior and substance abuse may share risk factors, (b) antisocial behavior may be caused by substance abuse, or (c) substance abuse may result from antisocial behavior disorder (Moos, 2007). Further research is needed to determine any link to cause and effect or association by risk factors.

Research on the genetics of tolerance has found a new gene (*Hangover*) that has contributed to the development of rapid tolerance to alcohol in fruit flies and then was correlated with alcohol dependence in Irish populations (Pietrzykowski & Treistman, 2008; Riley, Kalsi, Kuo, Vladimirov, Thiselton, & Kendler, 2006). When Scholz, Franz, and Heberlein (2005) announced the discovery of the *hangover* gene in August 2005, the press had a field day. The researchers claim to have isolated a mutant strain of flies (AE10) that lacks the ability to acquire ethanol tolerance. Even when exposed to ethanol 4 hours prior, AE10 flies, referred to as *hang*, require the same amount of ethanol to become intoxicated as in the instances when they were not previously exposed to ethanol vapors. Thus, this particular mutant strain apparently fails to produce the protein product (the P-element inserted into gene CG32575) called *hangover*. Scholz et al. (2005) cite their previous work that demonstrates that when normal flies are exposed to ethanol 4 hours prior to a second exposure, the flies require more ethanol in repeated ethanol exposures to reach the same effects as compared to the first event (Scholz, Ramond, Singh, & Heberlein, 2000). In other words, just like humans, fruit flies have the capacity to develop tolerance to alcohol when repeatedly exposed to the drug.

ADDICTION   The greatest impact of genetics might hypothetically occur in the transition between use and abuse (Chastain, 2006). In this theoretical framework, a variety of genetically influenced factors create a predisposition toward alcoholism (see Table 4.1). Based on family and twin studies, multiple genes are involved (i.e., a polygenic inheritance) or one major gene that acts differently in different circumstances (i.e., incomplete penetrance). This genetic predisposition, or "inheritability" has the greatest impact in explaining why most individuals between their mid-20s to 30s decrease their drinking while others maintain or increase their use (Agrawal & Lynskey, 2008; Agrawal & Lynskey, 2006; Dick & Agrawal, 2008; Foroud et al., 2010; Nurnberger, Jr. & Bierut, 2007; Schlaepfer et al., 2008).

Affected individuals may use substances as a way to cope with these conditions. Genetic factors continue to play a role in the transition from use to abuse and addiction. In Dick and Agrawal's (2008) paper reviewing the genetics of addiction, genetic variables could be *protective factors,* such as the gene encoding protein ALDH resulting in an acute reaction to alcohol that leads to facial flushing. Or, they could be *risk factors,* such as a high tolerance leading to more ingestion of the drug to obtain the pleasant effects related to the gene encoding protein (ADH) that affect how alcohol is metabolized.

These genetic factors interact with the social and psychological environment. This gene–environment interaction is critical for determining the risk for abuse and dependency is challenging (i.e., how to define environment and lifespan considerations) and is underresearched (Sher, Dick, Crabbe, Hutchinson, O'Malley, & Heath, 2010; van der Zwaluw & Engels, 2009; Foroud et al., 2010).

RECOVERY   Addiction is a process. Therefore, alcoholics generally do not get drunk and stay drunk until they die. Whatever the causes of the addiction in the first place, the course of the problem includes temporary periods of abstinence or remission alternating with periods of exacerbation of problems.

TABLE 4.1 Genetic risks and protective factors for ATOD dependency

Gene	Location	Encoded protein	Function	Gene variant effect	Linked to other traits or disorders
ADH 4	Chromosome 4	Alcohol dehydrogenase	Alcohol-metabolizing enzyme	Increased risk (certain variants)	None
ALDH1	Chromosome 4	Aldehyde dehydrogenase	Alcohol-metabolizing enzyme	Protective	None
CHRM2	Chromosome 7	Muscarinic acetylcholine receptor M2	Regulates neural signaling	Muscarinic acetylcholine	Major depression; delta- and theta-frequency EEG variations
*DRD2	Chromosome 11	Dopamine D2 receptor	Regulates reward reinforcement	Increased risk	Habitual smoking
GABRG3	Chromosome 15	GABAA receptor g3 subunit	Regulates neural signaling	Increased risk	None
GABRA2	Chromosome 4	GABAA receptor g2 subunit	Regulates neural signaling	Increased risk	Drug dependence; conduct disorders; beta-frequency EEG variations
HTAS2R16	Chromosome 7	hTAS2R16 receptor	Contributes to bitter taste sensitivity	Increased risk	None
OPRK1 PDYN	Chromosome 8 Chromosome 20	Kappa opioid receptor and prodynorphin, the peptide to which the receptor binds	Both participate in regulating aversion and reward	Increased risk	Stress response; may play a role in heroin and cocaine habituation

Note: *To date, evidence for DRD2 is contradictory. Further investigation is needed to confirm this gene's role in alcohol or nicotine dependence.

Source: Information from Nurnberger & Bierut (2007)

Genetic factors may play a role in temporary remission as metabolism or tolerance changes over time or organ damage leads to an illness that motivates the user to take a "break" from using. A thorough physical examination and family history are important parts of the assessment protocol to identify genetic predisposition. Genetic factors also interact with environmental influences that may encourage the addict to stop (at least temporarily) to salvage a marriage, job, or avoid legal prosecution. Crisis situations are sometimes referred to as "hitting bottom" and include any compromised ability to maintain adequate personal health or self-care and may prompt the user to seek treatment.

RELAPSE Relapse may be defined as the consumption or use of a drug after a prolonged period of abstinence. As stated previously, genetic research continues to build evidence of heritability and molecular changes in individuals that lead to dependence, withdrawal, and relapse. This includes multiple neuronal pathways in the brain such as systems related to dopamine and serotonin and opiate receptors (Schlaepfer et al., 2008). While the primary focus of research has been on the risk for and development of abuse and dependency, Clapp, Bhave, and Hoffman (2008) report that reinstatement of alcohol drinking can be induced by antagonists such as stress, environmental cues, and by the use of alcohol. They further report that excessive glutamate activity, especially in the hippocampus, play a role in "memory" of alcohol cues that can lead to relapse. Other studies found that excessive craving as a result of deficits in serotonin may lead to a loss of control over drinking, thus resulting in habitual or automatic drinking behavior (Addolorato, Leggio, Abenavoli, & Gasbarrini, 2005; Kalivas & O'Brien, 2008).

Substance abuse has a high comorbidity rate with other psychiatric diagnoses (Carbaugh & Sias, 2010; Demetrovics, 2009; Hasin et al., 2006) and polydrug use (Le Moal & Koob, 2007). This vulnerability to comorbid conditions may be from a common genetic liability that has been conceptualized as a general predisposition (Dick & Agrawal, 2008). Therefore, as with any disease or pathology, multiple and co-existing conditions may create more complexity in the stabilization and recovery process.

In fact, concurrent use of alcohol with other substances is commonly found to be a part of relapse. Doweiko (2011) cites correlations to be 74% between tobacco and alcohol-dependent persons, 77% with cocaine-dependent persons, and 85% with those dependent on heroin. The high incidence of concurrent multiple drug usage may be a result of addictive-like patterns of behavior (e.g., reaching for a cigarette and/or an alcoholic drink when under stress) or may be the result of the effects of one drug on another (Hasin et al., 2006).

Conclusion.   A review of the literature reveals a consensus that children of alcoholics run a higher risk of developing alcoholism than children in the general population. The results of several studies suggest a genetic predisposition to alcoholism. Others point to environmental dynamics of the family in predicting the intergenerational transmission of alcohol and drug abuse and addiction. Recent studies point to the possibility that there may be several distinct types of genetic conditions, each with its own pattern of heritability and susceptibility that increase the risk of dependency. Further, recent studies examine the interaction between the genetic conditions and environmental conditions that relate to abuse and dependency. The finding of associations between genetically determined personality traits and disorders and substance use may shed more light on the risk factors involved in determining which individuals may be more vulnerable to the development of alcoholism and other substance abuse.

BEHAVIORAL THEORIES

Behavioral theories have their beginnings in psychology with behavioral psychologists such as Pavlov, Thorndyke, Watson, and Skinner (Maultsby & Wirga, 1998). They postulated that all behavior is learned thus lending credence to an environmental perspective. Yin (2008) states that studies identify three modes of behavioral control which are important for understanding alcohol addiction: Pavlovian approach (e.g., approaching environmental stimuli associated with reward), goal-directed action (repeat of stimulation that leads to increased activity), and habit (continued behavior regardless of consequences).

Aspects of Use Addressed by the Behavioral Theory

INITIATION In social learning theory, substance use is a function of positive norms, expectations, and modeling from family members and peers who engage in obtaining and using them (Moos, 2007). A study conducted by King et al. (2009) compared the effects of alcoholism history on offspring in 409 adoptive and 208 nonadoptive families. The results showed an association between exposure to parental alcoholism as a risk factor for a child using alcohol.

However, the drug of preference is more likely to be a function of availability and affordability (e.g., caffeine, alcohol, nicotine). Drug experimentation might be viewed by behaviorists as a function of undesirable behaviors caused by weak or absent social controls such as deviant friends or lack of supervision (Moos, 2007). For instance, a rebellious child takes a puff of a cigarette even though he or she has been told never to smoke. In addition, individuals might try a drug to succumb to the perceived rewards of drug use—for example, a teenager who drinks alcohol for the first time as an initiation to be a part of a peer group.

Social Learning Theory, published by Albert Bandura (1977), also forms a part of the behavioral theory about substance abuse. Cognitive, genetic, and sociocultural factors are thought to predispose or influence the experimentation with alcohol or drugs as well as subsequent usage. Therefore, initial use of a drug may occur when an individual's coping abilities, through the interaction of personality sets, learned responses, and current circumstances, are overwhelmed.

CONTINUATION While continued use is generally seen as dependent on a positive experience or other reward (such as group inclusion or relief from anxiety), researchers are beginning to examine whether the chemicals themselves act to reinforce the continued use of the drug. For example, a review of the literature on addiction and dose response by Calabrese (2008) suggests that psychomotor stimulation (the arousal or acceleration of physical activity), based upon Skinnerian operant reinforcement theory, is a predictor of whether a drug will be reinforcing (i.e., addictive). Considerable support for this conclusion was found in caffeine, nicotine, alcohol, and pentobarbital (a short-active barbiturate).

Hyman (2007) summarized the effects of dopamine research as a positive reinforcement for drugs (especially opiates) that have the ability to increase dopamine in synapses made in various parts of the brain. The individual uses a particular drug and receives a positive reaction from the drug, the brain creates dopamine (a substance associated with enjoyment and feeling good), and a reinforcing loop is created. This works on several levels, not just within the brain but socially as well. For example, if an individual is naturally shy and withdrawn and then becomes talkative and outgoing after using a particular chemical, it is a natural occurrence that this person will continue to use that chemical to achieve mastery over shyness.

ADDICTION A characteristic of positive reinforcement is when an individual would continue to engage in a behavior long after negative consequences are experienced—simply because of the rewarding characteristics. In other words, the alcoholic will continue to drink even though it is clearly causing problems (legal, familial, problems with work, etc.). A characteristic of social learning is when the addict is engaging in compulsive behavior because it is a "habit" that has become a part of daily functioning, sometimes tied to certain times of the day (e.g., first thing in the morning or after 5:00), events (e.g., clubbing or entertaining), or rituals (while cooking or talking on the phone). However, Yin and Knowlton (2005) point out that habit formation resembles addiction but that enhanced habits are not the same as addictive habits. Several studies (Jedynak, Uslaner, Esteban, & Robinson, 2007; Nelson & Killcross, 2006; Porrino, Lyons, Smith, Daunais, & Nader, 2004) show exposure to drugs (i.e., cocaine, amphetamines) and to alcohol (Yin, Park, Adermark, & Lovinger, 2007) can accelerate use from action to habit.

Addictive behavior is maintained by reinforcement (i.e., the rewarding aspects of drug consumption and the social setting). Several principles of reinforcement are active in behavior formation and maintenance, including addictive behavior. Some examples are as follows:

1. The more rewarding or positive an experience is, the greater the likelihood that the behavior leading to that experience will be repeated. Thus, an individual who is depressed and becomes "the life of the party" after using cocaine will want to re-create that experience by using again.

2. The greater the frequency of obtaining positive experiences through drug consumption, the more likely that drugs will be consumed again.

3. The more closely in time that the behavior (drug consumption) and consequences of the behavior are experienced, the more likely the behavior will be repeated. Conversely, the further in time a consequence of the behavior is experienced, the less the likelihood that the consequence will affect future behavior. For example, a lonely man who finds companionship in the bar drinking with others is likely to remember the camaraderie associated with the drinking, and the hangover the next day is more easily attributed to "overdrinking" than to drinking with certain friends. It is this reinforcing association of the two events that increase the likelihood of his drinking when feeling lonely or isolated.

RECOVERY Recovery involves a behavior change to break the cyclical pattern of substance abuse and may include replacing the rewards gained by continued use. One way to break a habit is to present the drug (stimulus) to the individual until a negative effect results or aversive conditioning. An example would be giving an individual a cigar (stimulus) to smoke until he or she becomes ill (negative response). However, this would be a dangerous approach to use in ATOD treatment and could lead to multiple physical problems or death.

A second way to break a habit is to introduce the drug (stimulus) selectively until the addict learns over time not to respond in a habitual manner. There is much controversy over the use of "controlled drinking" as a form of therapy and no longitudinal studies that this approach works. However, some treatment approaches have included introducing the drug in the presence of the addict to *desensitize* the effect. An example of this would be watching drug-related television programs or commercials over time until the "urge to use" subsides.

Finally, the last way to break a habit is to replace it with a new habit. "Switching addictions" is commonly reported by individuals in recovery and may include overeating, a relationship dependency, sexual compulsions, or even use of another drug.

In this case, treatment would focus on searching for rewards that are nondestructive, such as hobbies, exercise, education, support groups, and spirituality.

RELAPSE   The drug user's whole life is dominated by drug-related activities: planning the use, talking about using, and being with other users. Therefore, it is not surprising that treatment is difficult. Personality, motivation, and habit are particularly important in bringing about a relapse to drug usage. There is a spontaneous recovery of behaviors learned in the past when motivation to abstain is no longer stronger than the motivation to use drugs.

Results of heroin-induced brain changes, such as disturbances and problems with bladder control, require months to reverse themselves, whereas it takes only a few minutes to get a high. Unable to feel good without drugs for months during withdrawal, an individual gets immediate reinforcement from drug-taking behavior.

Situational antecedents, such as time of day of drinking, place of drinking, and association with certain people or emotional states, are all important when analyzing the cause of the behavior. For example, drinking with friends at the local bar three to four times a week to blow off steam, snorting cocaine at parties with friends once a week, and shooting heroin alone would be evaluated for behavioral and situational antecedents, associations, and situational settings. Each of these factors is analyzed so that the maladaptive behavioral sequences can be restructured and changed.

Cognitive behavior processes involved in substance abuse originate with the interaction between the person and his or her environment. Anticipating the desired effects of the drug, remembering past pleasant associations with the behavior, and modeling the behavior by others are all important as reinforcements of substance use (Burrow-Sanchez, 2006).

According to Becker (2008), events that can trigger relapse fall into three categories: drinking small amount of alcohol; exposure to alcohol-related (conditioned) cues; and stress. Studies show that alcoholics are more sensitive to the effects of these three categories of stimuli which elicit craving and other negative effects that can increase the risk of relapse (Fox, Bergquist, Hong, & Sinha, 2007; Sinha, Fox, Hong, Bergquist, Bhagwagar, & Siedlarz, 2009).

Conclusion.   Behaviorists approach substance abuse as they approach all behavior—as the product of learning. Recent theories add cognitive factors and brain reward mechanisms as mediating variables to the learning patterns believed responsible for addictions. Addiction and substance abuse are seen as the result of learning patterns, and antecedent actions and situational factors are analyzed to determine the sequence of these patterns. In treatment, goals are easily formulated because behaviors are easily observed and measured.

A major disadvantage of the behavioral approach is that the intergenerational, family, and biological factors are not directly addressed. Critics would claim that, although present behavior of the individual might be changed, long-lasting change requires a shift in family patterns and attention to the biological changes involved in addiction, as well as the genetic differences in addicts. Behavioral approaches may not have the total answer to causal factors in abuse of alcohol and other substances, but they do have certain advantages. Relationships between antecedent actions and addictive behavior can be clearly viewed and measured, as can social conditions associated with that behavior.

SOCIOCULTURAL THEORIES

Just as with the debate that exists about behavior (is it shaped strictly by environment or strictly by genetics?), these theories look at social and cultural factors that can lead to substance abuse. Environmental support for heavy drinking is an important sociological variable contributing to alcoholism. Attitudes toward alcohol consumption and abuse vary from culture to culture and greatly affect the amount and context of alcohol consumption. In general, solitary, addictive, pathological drinking is more associated with urbanized, industrial societies than with societies that remain largely rural and traditional. However, recent findings show differences in illicit drug use by race/ethnicity when looking at urban (metropolitan) and rural (nonmetropolitan) counties. For instance, marijuana use among Blacks, Hispanics, Whites, and American Indian/Native Americans are lower in nonmetropolitan (rural) counties than in small or large metropolitan counties (urban) while the converse is true for Asians (i.e., marijuana rates are higher for Asians in rural areas than urban areas) (Substance Abuse and Mental Health Services Administration, 2007a).

Additionally, socially disruptive use of alcohol tends to occur almost exclusively in social settings; however, drunken behavior is seldom seen when alcohol is used in a religious context (protective factor). Moos (2007) states that "According to social control theory, strong bonds with family, friends, work, religion, and other aspects of traditional society motivate individuals to engage in responsible behavior and refrain from substance abuse" (p. 2).

As women are beginning to be included in alcohol studies, researchers have identified risk factors for women that differ from those of men. The National Institute of Health and the National Institute on Alcohol Abuse and Alcoholism (U.S. Department of Health and Human Services, 2008) compiled a collaborative summary of research on women and alcohol. Findings include the following: women and adolescents being more vulnerable to being a victim of sexual violence; drinking over a long term causing more health problems than for men even if the amount is less; individual risk factors including stress, childhood sexual abuse, and depression; and social risk factors such as biological relatives with drinking problems and a partner who drinks heavily.

However, the gap between gender differences in alcohol use, abuse, and dependency has decreased over the past 80 years (Keyes, Grant, & Hasin, 2008). Subgroups of women with elevated rates of heavy drinking include younger women, those lacking social roles or occupying unwanted social status; women in nontraditional jobs; cohabiting women; and ethnic minority women experiencing rapid acculturation (Schuckit, Smith, & Danko, 2007). Interestingly, most of these factors are associated with the rapidly changing societal conditions for women in this country.

The socialization and cultural environment of the adolescent creates factors that influence drug and alcohol experimentation and abuse that may differ from those of adults. Peer groups' practices, such as fraternities, have a great influence on whether an adolescent within that group will or will not use drugs. It may be "cool" to experiment with or abuse drugs, or it may be considered "in" to abstain. Moreover, the peer group can facilitate substance use by providing the social structure within which use is part of the culture, as well as providing the substances to use. Club drugs such as ecstasy are a good example. Developmentally, adolescents not only feel omnipotent and invulnerable to life's tragedies but also are attracted to risk-taking behaviors. They often feel a rise in self-esteem when accepted by a group who approves of drug usage.

Researchers recently examined another group, older men, and alcohol dependence (Jacob, Blonigen, Koenig, Wachsmuth, & Price, 2010; Jacob, Bucholz, Sartor, Howell, & Wood, 2005; Jacob, Koenig, Howell, Wood, & Haber, 2009; Jacob, Seilhamer, Bargiel, & Howell, 2006). They have identified four distinct groups of alcoholics: severe nonchronic alcoholics, severe chronic alcoholics, young-adult alcoholics, and late-onset alcoholics. These findings are similar to the alcohol dependence subtypes found in the five-cluster model drawn from a nationally representative sample (Moss et al., 2007). These subtypes are: (1) Young Adult; (2) Functional; (3) Intermediate Familial; (4) Young Antisocial; and (5) Chronic Severe and are recognized by the National Institute on Alcohol Abuse and Alcoholism (Moss et al., 2007).

Racial/ethnic differences have been found as sociocultural considerations as well with Asians demonstrating the lowest rates of substance abuse, followed by Blacks and Hispanics, and with the highest rates among Whites and Native Americans (Akins et al., 2010; Johnston et al., 2011; Substance Abuse and Mental Health Services Administration, 2007a). One study found that multiracial adolescents are at an even greater risk for substance use (Jackson & LeCroy, 2009).

Finally, social inequality is a strong predictor of alcohol and drug use, especially related to lower social class (Room, 2005). For instance, when looking at race/ethnicity in the existing literature, alcohol use increased with income for White men, but for Black men alcohol use decreased with income (Akins et al., 2010). While looking at the relationship between socioeconomic status (SES) and drug use, the literature has shown that adolescents with lower SES are more likely to engage in substance abuse, as are adults with high SES (Humensky, 2010).

Aspects of Use Addressed by Sociocultural Theories

INITIATION   Social factors can contribute to the introduction of the first use of a drug. Factors that appear to protect youngsters from initiating substance use and progressing toward abuse include bonding, goal-direction, and monitoring from family, peers, religion, and other societal processes; participating in rewarding activities and prosocial behaviors; selecting and emulating individuals who model temperance or shun substance use; and increased self-confidence and coping skills (Moss, 2007).

A cultural trend is that newly introduced drugs may influence the rise in the use and abuse of chemicals. Key findings from Johnston et al. (2011) state that "generational forgetting" involves the fading use of current drugs and reintroduction of older drugs. This then increases the risk of initiation because ". . . word of the supposed benefits of using a drug usually spreads faster than information about the adverse effects" (p. 6).

Cultural beliefs may be attributed to the use of alcohol. Some protective factors, such as Hispanic communities' strong cultural prohibitions among women, and Confucian and Taoist philosophies, may contribute to the low consumption rate among Hispanic women and Asians. Risk factors influenced by culture include drinking as a business practice among Chinese and Japanese men, and experiences of oppression and discrimination among Native American groups (National Institute on Alcohol

Abuse and Alcoholism, 2005). There is also a wide variety of literature on Hispanics that finds that acculturation is a key predictor of substance use (Akins et al., 2010).

Family factors, such as cultural attitudes, which were previously discussed, and customs of the family involving alcohol and other substances, tolerance toward public intoxication and drug use, and childhood exposure to alcohol and drug use models, form a background for adolescent attitudes toward substance usage. Additionally, several types of parenting have been associated with an increase in substance abuse in offspring. Three common types used in research are Authoritative parenting (clear and direct parenting with a high degree of warmth); Permissive parenting (warm but free of discipline or structure); and, Authoritarian parenting (lacks warmth but demands unquestionable obedience). Authoritative was related to lower alcohol use and greater control of drinking resulting in less alcohol related problems, whereas, the Permissive and Authoritarian parenting styles had the opposite effects (Patock-Peckman & Morgan-Lopez, 2009). In addition, parental monitoring and supervision were found to be protective factors for drinking control (White et al., 2006; Veal & Ross, 2006).

CONTINUATION   General sociological studies give expected conclusions: Those who continue drug use report having a positive initial experience. However, a positive reaction to a drug does not always occur with the first use. The circumstances or inadequacies that drove a person the first time may encourage him or her to try again, hoping to capture the desired psychological effect or social acceptance. Existence of a drug-using peer group appears important to the continuing use of drugs. If the initial experience is with pro-drug peers, these peers would encourage a positive interpretation of the experience and encourage further drug use.

Pressure can be great to conform and to "fit in." Peers and parents show how and where to drink. In fact, having friends who use drugs is predictive of alcohol abuse for Whites, Blacks, and Hispanics; however, having parents with substance abuse problems is not a predictor among Blacks. This indicates that pathways to alcohol use are different among racial/ethnic groups (Akins et al., 2010), and these findings may have application for prevention and intervention in Black communities. To refuse to comply with cultural expectations to drink heavily or continue drug use may mean turning away from friends and changing relationships with one's family. Another concern is the growing evidence that adolescents with high SES are at risk for substance abuse (Humensky, 2010). For instance, higher parental education is associated with higher rates of binge drinking, and marijuana and cocaine use in early adulthood, and higher parental income is associated with higher rates of binge drinking and marijuana use.

Substance abuse can also be seen as being both system maintained and system maintaining. For instance, reactive changes in family dynamics usually occur when substance abuse is introduced into the family. Once the family assimilates these changes and reorganizes around the substance abuse, these changes actually support the addiction or substance abuse (Saatcioglu, Erim, & Cakmak, 2006). For example, if a 10-year-old child begins to watch over a 3-year-old sibling because their mother is high on crack, family function is preserved, if imperfectly. However, this assumption of parental roles by the child also makes it easier for the mother to continue with her crack use, causing a circular pattern of reinforcement. When a family attempts to reorganize itself in the face of a prolonged crisis such as alcoholism, changes in roles, rules, and boundaries of the family occur in an effort to stabilize the system. Behavior of family members within the family system, observed from the outside, can appear strange or abnormal, whereas, when viewed within the context of the addictive family, they can be seen as being adaptive or an integral part of maintenance of family *homeostasis*. This often places children in these families at greater risk for addiction (Doweiko, 2011).

ADDICTION   Sociocultural theories suggest that a confluence of sociological and cultural factors contribute to the proliferation of addiction. One only has to look as far as a cursory examination of two or three different cultures to gain support for this argument. For example, cultures where alcohol has been present for several centuries and is an accepted part of daily life tend to have a lower rate of alcoholism than cultures where alcohol is a fairly recent phenomenon. This is particularly evident among northern European cultures where alcohol has been an accepted part of daily life for over 2,000 years. The French and Italian peoples regularly drink wine with their meals and even serve a watered-down version to their children.

On the other hand, Indigenous peoples have been exposed to alcohol for less than 500 years. Over the past 30 years, drug use among American Indian youth remains at a higher level than any other culture (Beauvais, Jumper-Thurman, & Burnside, 2008). In fact, alcohol and illicit drug use disorders were more likely among American Indians and Alaska Natives than other racial groups (Substance Abuse and Mental Health Services Administration, 2007b). These higher incidences of drug use disorders could be due to a variety of factors, including physiology, poverty, and a lack of cultural norms about drinking and intoxication.

Diagnosis of an alcohol disorder shows some variation in pathways between other racial/ethnic groups. When looking at age, marital status, gender, level of strain, and emotional status, age is a predictor for Whites and Blacks (younger) but not for Hispanics; negative emotions are a predictor for Whites and Hispanics but not for Blacks; marital status is a predictor for Whites and Hispanics (unmarried) but not for Blacks; and, rural status was a predictor for Hispanics but not for Whites and Blacks. Common predictor's across all three races were high levels of strain and being male (Akins et al., 2010). Being culturally sensitive during all aspects of prevention, assessment, and treatment is critical for treatment providers.

RECOVERY   Drug subculture theory was first developed based on a framework of deviant acts. However, drug use trends indicate that in today's society the widespread recreational drug use across ethnicity, gender, and social class suggests that the behavior is being accommodated into the larger society (Gourley, 2004). These "cohort effects" are observed when usage rates, along with attitudes and beliefs about various drugs, increase and decrease over time (Johnston et al., 2011). Therefore, while replacing pro-drug socialized peer activities with non-using peers is an important goal in recovery, social and cultural tolerance may be a limiting factor to maintaining recovery.

RELAPSE   Within the sociocultural model, if the broader systems of the individual are not addressed or changed, the chances of relapse are increased. Therefore, relapse occurs because users return to familiar patterns within a group, family, job, or other social, cultural, or environmental setting. An addict who ceased drug use due to an involuntary intervention may never have truly left the drug subculture and will revert back quickly to old drug-using patterns upon completion of treatment.

Conclusion. Several components of culture and the environment affect the likelihood that an individual will become involved with substance abuse (see example illustrated in Figure 4.2). The expansion of the urban ghetto has encouraged the growth of substance abuse as an industry. A decline in labor-intensive jobs has caused unskilled laborers to sink further into poverty. At the same time, the increased cost of adequate housing has created a sizable population who have inadequate or no housing. The proportion of families headed by single mothers, particularly among minorities, has increased dramatically. Such families are also likely to have inadequate housing or live with relatives in crowded conditions. Inner-city youths are less likely to finish high school or to have marketable skills. Child abuse and neglect have increased, and homicide continues to be a leading killer of young Black men. As households experience severe crises concurrently, many are socialized into deviant behavior, such as antisocial acts, child abuse or neglect, or criminal activity. In such settings, families may also experience learned helplessness and feel disenfranchised from society as a whole (Moos, 2007).

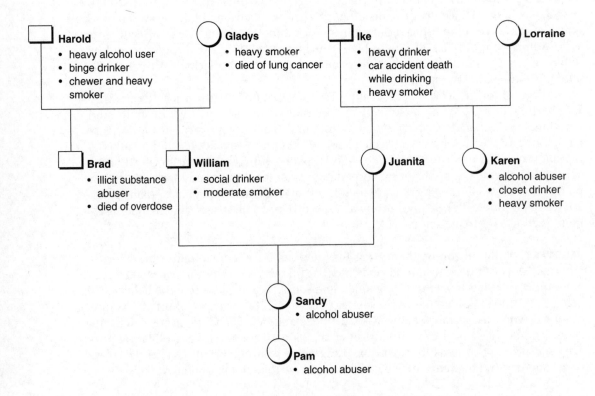

As indicated above, the genogram of Pam and Sandy reveals that alcohol and other substances have been abused for four generations, causing family problems and death throughout the family's history.

FIGURE 4.2 Genogram: Pam and Sandy.

Treatment that changes an individual also affects that person's interpersonal system. Therefore, in order for drug abuse treatment to be successful, the social and cultural context of the abuser must be considered. For instance, finding family environment patterns that predispose children for alcoholism and other substance abuse may enable counselors to prevent these conditions in children considered to be at risk. Dysfunctional family patterns can be changed through family therapy and parent training. In general, environmental forces, cultural context, and peer and family relationships that influence the development and maintenance of addiction should be considered under this theory.

AN INTEGRATED APPROACH

New research and schools of thought are moving toward an integrated theoretical approach (Graham et al., 2008; West, 2006; Young, Valach, & Domene, 2005). Researchers are beginning to view addiction as more than a one-dimensional process that can be explained by one single theory. New ways of viewing addiction are beginning to synthesize several of the models listed earlier. For instance, researchers are beginning to postulate a model that is an amalgamation of genetics, environment, and learned behavior.

Current research cites many factors contributing to, or having an effect on, substance abuse: genetics, family environment and structure, and brain changes from addiction expressed in behavioral ways and within a social context (Bryson & Silverstein, 2008). An integrated theory, taking all of these factors into consideration, conceptualizes behavior as a function of mutual determination and reciprocal effects of an individual, the environment, and behavior. It assumes that many influences combine to create the conditions under which an individual will abuse, or not abuse, alcohol or other substances. Integrated rather than eclectic, it weaves all of the influences and components of substance abuse into holistic concepts with contributing parts, rather than being a collection of ideas and concepts. This approach also accounts for differences in substance use and abuse, based on individual differences in genetics, personality, family, and social environment. For example, identical twins, raised in the same family, have identical predispositions toward alcohol abuse based on their liver enzyme production. One of the twins begins drinking at an early age, experiencing a heightened sense of reinforcement. The other twin becomes successfully engaged in sports and school activities, avoiding the use of alcohol. Thus, they have identical genes but a different addiction profile.

One such blending of perspectives is an integral quadrant model that divides the Interior: Individual (individual-level factors), Exterior: Individual (genetic factors), Interior: Collective (socio-cultural factors), and Exterior: Collective (geopolitical formations and material circumstances) (Eliason & Amodia, 2007). This model purports differences from a 12-step model in the following ways: it is based on empowerment as opposed to powerlessness; it identifies uniqueness of individuals as opposed to similarities among addicts; it is based on cross-cultural themes as opposed to a White, middle-class, heterosexual, male model; it is based on cross-cultural spirituality as opposed to Christianity; and it practices harm reduction as opposed to abstinence. One commonality is that it includes the disease model plus individual, sociocultural, and societal influences.

Case Study

Tom

Tom is a 28-year-old male born to Japanese immigrants. His parents immigrated to the United States after World War II and are proud to be American. They, however, have held on to many traditional customs and beliefs (such as the value that the family is all important, and to act in ways that brings shame on the family disgraces the entire family). Recently, Tom attended a party with friends (the party was hosted by friends of friends and he did not know the people well). While at the party, Tom admits to smoking marijuana. Later that night, he was arrested for acting strangely in a local supermarket. Tom was approached by the police when the manager saw him wandering up and down the aisles aimlessly taking items off of the shelves. Tom was arrested for public intoxication and spent the night in jail. The judge sent him to you for an evaluation. When questioned, Tom admits to trying marijuana in the past, but never with these results. He also admits to occasional use of other drugs (such as alcohol and cocaine). He reports that he is not particularly fond of the drugs he uses, but he only partakes to fit in with his friends who seem to enjoy getting high. Tom is very embarrassed by his arrest and the shame it has brought on his family and seems eager to comply with your recommendations.

Critical Thinking Questions

1. How would you apply the moral theory to this case? And which aspects of use does he fit under (initiation, continuation, addiction, recovery, relapse)?

2. How would you apply the disease theory to this case? And which aspects of use does he fit under (initiation, continuation, addiction, recovery, relapse)?

3. How would you apply the behavioral theory? And which aspects of use does he fit under (initiation, continuation, addiction, recovery, relapse)?

4. How would you apply the sociocultural theory? And which aspects of use does he fit under (initiation, continuation, addiction, recovery, relapse)?

MyCounselingLab™

Go to Topic 3: *Etiological Theories of Substance Abuse*, on the MyCounselingLab™ site (www.MyCounselingLab.com) for *Substance Abuse Counseling*, Fifth Edition where you can:

- Find learning outcomes for *Etiological Theories of Substance Abuse* along with the national standards that connect to these outcomes.
- Complete Assignments and Activities that can help you more deeply understand the chapter content.
- Apply and practice your understanding of the core skills identified in the chapter with the Building Counseling Skills unit.
- Prepare yourself for professional certification with a Practice for Certification quiz.
- Connect to videos through the Video and Resource Library.

CONCLUSION

There has been a progression of theories of addiction starting with a view that alcoholism is a result of personal choice to an integration of several possible factors that contribute to initiation, continuation, addiction, recovery, and relapse. Viewing addiction as a progressive disease led to the epidemiology of alcohol abuse and alcohol dependence published in the American Psychiatric Association's publication of the *Diagnostic and Statistical Manual of Mental Disorders* (*DSM*). A review of the history of the *DSM* by the National Institute on Alcohol Abuse and Alcoholism (1995) reveals that the *DSM-I* and *DSM-II* categorized Alcoholism as a subset of personality disorders, homosexuality, and neuroses. However, the evolution of diagnostic criteria for behavioral disorders involving alcohol reached a turning point in 1980 with the publication of the *DSM-III*. For the first time, the term "alcoholism" was dropped in favor of two distinct categories labeled "alcohol abuse" and "alcohol dependence." These criteria have continued through several revisions and editions including the current *DSM-IV*-TR. However, the proposed *DSM-V* edition will combine abuse and dependence into a single disorder called Substance-Use Disorder (e.g., Alcohol-Use Disorder, Nicotine-Use Disorder, Cannabis-Use Disorder, Amphetamine-Use Disorder, etc.) (American Psychiatric Association, 2010).

Sociocultural influences appear to offer mitigating factors in the development of alcohol abuse. It is uncertain whether these sociocultural differences are due to genetic predispositions, socioeconomic conditions, or cultural attitudes toward drinking, but the overall effect remains clear: some ethnic groups have more problems concerning alcohol consumption than others (Moore, Montaine-Jaime, Carr, & Ehlers, 2007; Scott & Taylor, 2007). Psychological factors that may interact with a genetic or biological predisposition and sociocultural factors include the effects of growing up in an alcoholic home, learned or conditioned drinking behavior, and cognitive deficiencies.

All of the preceding factors—personal choice, medical epidemiology, sociocultural factors, and psychological/behavioral factors—may be present, yet an individual may not become addicted to alcohol or other substances. Therefore, perhaps the most promising research is identifying genetic pathways that can help explain why some people develop an addiction but not others. Genetic research is expanding rapidly and becoming more specific in identifying variances in an array of characteristics. For instance, researchers have found a sex-specific gene (ADCY7) that is associated with alcohol dependence in women but not men (Desrivières et al., 2011).

5

Assessment and Diagnosis

LINDA L. CHAMBERLAIN, PSY.D.

MyCounselingLab™

Visit the MyCounselingLab™ site for *Substance Abuse Counseling*, Fifth Edition to enhance your understanding of chapter concepts. You'll have the opportunity to practice your skills through video- and case-based Assignments and Activities as well as Building Counseling Skills units, and to prepare for your certification exam with Practice for Certification quizzes.

Accurate assessment and diagnosis in the treatment of alcohol, tobacco, and other drug abuse are crucial for adequate treatment planning and delivery of services. Improper assessment and faulty diagnosis can lead counselors to create ineffective treatment plans, have inappropriate expectations for therapy and instill an overall sense of frustration in both the client and the therapist. You cannot treat what you do not recognize or understand. As with other diseases and disorders, the earlier a therapist diagnoses a substance abuse problem, the better the prognosis for the client.

This chapter will present a theoretical and practical framework for assessment and acquaint clinicians with several methods and tools that can aid in the diagnosis of substance abuse or dependence, or Substance-Use Disorder according to the *DSM-IV-TR*. Guidelines for conducting an assessment interview and obtaining a reliable history are provided. Several major assessment instruments generally available to clinicians will be reviewed. The issue of diagnosis and the problems related to differential and dual diagnosis will be explored. It is the intent of this chapter to give counselors a pragmatic orientation to making an accurate diagnosis of a substance abuse problem.

ISSUES IN ASSESSMENT

It may be helpful to note at the onset that the assessment and diagnosis of substance abuse are not exact sciences. Currently, there is no single medical or psychological test that can determine with absolute certainty that a person is drug or alcohol dependent. Also, the inconsistency in social attitudes about alcohol and drug use, and the imprecise standards that define what constitutes a drinking or drug problem, often complicates a clinician's awareness and attitudes about a client's substance use. The stigma associated with alcoholism or drug addiction often leads to denial by the user, their family, and many health professionals. "Many people are influenced, often unwittingly, by social stigma, and are predisposed to dislike or distrust those in deviant, stigmatized categories. Helpers must also honestly confront their own stigmatizing attitudes toward people with addictions" (Myers & Salt, 2007, p. 65).

The beginning therapist must be aware of several problems that may interfere with the diagnostic process. First, the therapist may have developed some biases about substance abuse clients. Beliefs that substance abusers are uncaring, irresponsible, untrustworthy, dangerous, or untreatable are concepts that are certain to interfere with a clinician's ability to conduct an accurate and sensitive diagnostic interview. As Lewis, Dana, and Blevins point out (2011), "It is vital that clinicians avoid preconceived notions about the client and that they make treatment determinations based only on data collected during the initial evaluation" (p. 81). Second, the client's attitude about alcohol or drugs and his or her sense of shame in seeking help from a mental health professional may create a barrier to accurate assessment. It is not unusual for clients to seek help from clinicians for problems such as depression, anxiety, or behavioral problems that may be secondary to their drug use or drinking. The stigma of being labeled a "drunk" or "addict" is still a powerful deterrent to disclosing a pattern of substance use for many people, especially women.

In large part, a clinician's awareness of common factors and problems related to substance abuse is of great importance. An understanding of the dynamics of denial, tolerance, loss of control, and the diverse medical consequences associated with different drugs of abuse is an essential prerequisite for accurate diagnosis. A familiarity with common medical, behavioral, cognitive, social, and emotional symptoms associated with alcohol and drug abuse can help guide the clinician in the assessment process (American Psychiatric Association, 2010). Materials that delineate the progression of symptoms for alcohol and other drugs of abuse can help guide the clinician in the assessment process. Later in this chapter, the behavioral and social characteristics associated with substance abuse will be described in greater detail. Previous chapters have acquainted you with some of the symptoms, effects, and dynamics that should serve as "red flags" for pursuing more formal diagnostic procedures. Assessment, however, is still somewhat a process of "skunk identification," meaning that if it looks, smells, and walks like a skunk, it's probably a skunk. Any one or two symptoms of abuse or dependence don't necessarily constitute a clear diagnosis. An isolated or occasional experience of intoxication, a single DUI or other legal problem, or any other symptom that is out of character or unusual for an individual does not constitute a diagnosis of abuse or dependence. Just as we suggest moderation in substance use, we encourage moderation in assessment and diagnoses as well. It is important to be thorough, ask all the necessary questions, know the symptoms and patterns of problematic substance use, and don't jump to conclusions without evidence of a pattern of problematic use. Not everyone who uses cocaine, alcohol, heroin, or any other drug is dependent or addicted.

The process of conducting an assessment and diagnosing substance abuse problems is perhaps most relentlessly complicated by the phenomena of denial. Denial and minimization of the severity of a drug abuse problem are often an essential part of how substance abusers learn to function in their world. For the drug abuser, denial is a coping mechanism, albeit one with a negative outcome, that protects them from facing the increasing consequences of their behavior. As a result of denial, the substance abuser is often the last to acknowledge that they have a problem. Without the mechanism of denial, the user could not continue the pattern of substance abuse. Although not all substance abusers exhibit patterns of denial, most minimize or avoid facing the consequences of their use on both themselves and others. Denial or minimization serves to keep reality at arm's length and allows the dependent person to believe that no one is aware of the excessive drug use and the negative impact it is having on his or her life. Denial has been viewed as a selective perceptional process about the past and present. The use of denial to delude oneself and others tremendously complicates the assessment process. Establishing some standardized format for assessment and diagnosis is essential in helping clinicians maintain consistency in providing appropriate detection and treatment for their clients. Importantly, counselors must be cautious of developing an aggressive or combative reaction to obvious denial or minimization when assessing clients. Typically, the "more a confrontational counselor insists a client admit to being an addict, the more a denying client resists anything the counselor says" (Myers & Salt, 2007, p. 245).

A critical part of beginning an assessment with substance users is to encourage them to be honest and forthright in their responses and interactions with the evaluator or counselor. It may be helpful to assure them that the assessment process is primarily for their benefit, to help them in making decisions about whether they have a problem and, if so, what actions they might take. Even with clients who are mandated for assessment through the courts or brought in by family members, it is important to focus the diagnostic interview and assessment on addressing the needs of the substance user.

THE DIAGNOSTIC INTERVIEW

The most important aspect of any assessment of substance abuse is the diagnostic interview. A carefully planned and conducted interview is the cornerstone of the diagnostic process. The initial contact with someone for the assessment of substance abuse may occur within the context of individual, family, group, or marital counseling. The clinician may be aware of the possible problem by the nature of the referral, or it may be discovered within the context of a family or marital problem. Referrals from physicians, other clinicians, or the legal system may be clearly defined as a referral for the purpose of assessing a drug or alcohol problem. Many assessments, however, will initially be undertaken as a part of the clinicians' normal interviewing procedure. It is striking how many mental health professionals do not include at least some questions about a client's drug and alcohol use history in their standard interview format. A routine clinical interview should include questions about clients' habits of using both prescription and/or illicit drugs, alcohol, tobacco, and caffeine (Nace & Tinsley, 2007). Clinical training programs are often lacking in course work or opportunities for practical experience that expose medical and mental health professionals to the dynamics and treatment of addictions.

Given the prevalence of denial on the part of substance abusers, if there is any suspicion about a possible substance use problem, it is important in the first interview to request permission to involve family members, friends, coworkers, and others who may be able to provide more objective information about the client's pattern of substance use and related behaviors. Collateral interviews often help to give a more complete picture of both the user and the impact they are having on others in their environment. Partners and family members of alcoholics and drug addicts often want to be helpful in the user's treatment (Nace & Tinsley, 2007).

An important part of the diagnostic interview is an assessment of the client's readiness for change. The transtheoretical model (Prochaska and DiClemente, 1983) offers clinicians very useful guidelines and information to assist in evaluating where the client is in the process of change. This model describes a series of six stages people experience in making changes, whether the changes are in therapy or not: precontemplation, contemplation, determination, action, maintenance, and relapse. By determining the stage that the client is in, therapists can focus treatment on helping that client proceed through the various stages of change.

The transtheoretical model has been incorporated into the principles of motivational interviewing with substance abuse clients. It elaborates on targeting specific questions and responses to the stages of change, which can be enormously helpful in the process of diagnostic interviewing. A clinical interview that incorporates motivational interviewing techniques sets the stage for a successful counseling relationship and helps with treatment planning. Therapists who plan to work with substance abuse clients benefit greatly from familiarity with the model and techniques of interviewing. Given the frequency of denial and minimization encountered with clients who are experiencing substance abuse problems, having a supportive, respectful, effective strategy for interviewing is essential.

Initially, it is still important to ask the client directly about his or her use of drugs or alcohol. A useful question is "Do you believe that your use of alcohol or other drugs has caused problems in your life?" Many clinicians find it helpful to assure the client that they are not asking questions about substance use in order to make judgments. Often, people will respond less defensively if they are reassured that "I'm not here to tell you that you are or aren't an addict. I simply need to understand as much about the problem as I can and to help you (and your family) determine whether your drug and/ or alcohol use may be playing a role in the current situation." Also ask significant others in the client's life about his or her use in order to get information on whether they view the client's problems as related to substance abuse. If either a substance user or family member is describing examples of domestic violence, legal problems, financial problems, medical complications, or other issues that are often related to substance abuse, it can be helpful to ask if they believe the problem would have occurred if alcohol or drugs were not a factor. Questions for family members include, "Does the user's personality change while using?, Has anyone been concerned or embarrassed about the use?, Have you or others been uncomfortable about your safety in circumstances such as riding in a car when the user has been driving after having a drink?" (Nace & Tinsley, 2007, p. 57).

An interview format that gathers information specific to substance abuse should be a standard part of the assessment process. An example of a structured interview format is the Substance Use History Questionnaire (Appendix A: Substance Use History Questionnaire, at the end of this chapter). It may be given to the client to complete, or the questions can be asked during the interview. The information from this procedure will help in determining what additional assessment instruments to use. Information regarding work habits, social and professional relationships, medical history, and previous psychiatric history are also necessary for the assessment. Questions related to each of these areas should be included as a part of the standard intake interview.

It is important to note that family members and significant others may be unaware of or reluctant to divulge information about the client's substance use patterns. Like the client, they are often experiencing denial or avoiding a confrontation with the user. Common misinformation about substance abuse may divert the focus of the problem to other factors that are then presented as the primary problem. For example, a spouse may describe the partner as using alcohol to relieve feelings of depression rather than identifying the substance use as a causal or maintaining factor in the partner's emotional turmoil. Due to the shame and embarrassment that frequently accompany the admission of substance abuse, the clinician may need to reassure everyone involved in the assessment that appropriate help can only be made available if an understanding of the problem is accurate and complete.

DSM-IV-TR DIAGNOSIS

One of the primary difficulties encountered in diagnosing alcohol and drug problems may lie in the inadequate definitions commonly used. In an attempt to provide more comprehensive, specific, symptom-related criteria for diagnosis, the American Psychiatric Association (2010) developed categories for "Substance-Use Disorders" in the *Diagnostic and Statistic Manual*, fourth edition (*DSM-IV*-TR). The term *substance* refers to a drug of abuse, a medication, or a toxin that is used in a manner incongruent with medical treatment. It is not the substance itself but the manner in which it is employed that provides the critical information for a diagnosis of substance abuse or dependence. Substances are grouped into 11 classes: alcohol; amphetamines; caffeine; cannabis; cocaine; hallucinogens; inhalants; nicotine; opioids; phencyclidine (PCP); and sedatives, hypnotics, or anxiolytics (anti-anxiety drugs). The substance-related disorders have been traditionally divided into two basic groups: the Substance Use Disorders (Substance Dependence and Substance Abuse) and the Substance-Induced Disorders (including Substance Intoxication and Substance Withdrawal).

Criteria for Substance Dependence

A maladaptive pattern of substance use, leading to clinically significant impairment or distress, as manifested by three (or more) of the following, occurring at any time in the same 12-month period:

1. Tolerance, as defined by either of the following:
   a. a need for markedly increased amounts of the substance to achieve intoxication or desired effect
   b. markedly diminished effect with continued use of the same amount of the substance
2. Withdrawal, as manifested by either of the following:
   a. the characteristic withdrawal syndrome for the substance
   b. the same (or a closely related) substance is taken to relieve or avoid withdrawal symptoms
3. The substance is often taken in larger amounts or over a longer period than was intended

4. There is a persistent desire or unsuccessful effort to cut down or control substance use

5. A great deal of time is spent in activities necessary to obtain the substance (e.g., visiting multiple doctors or driving long distances), use the substance (e.g., chain smoking), or recover from its effects

6. Important social, occupational, or recreational activities are given up or reduced because of substance use

7. The substance use is continued despite knowledge of having a persistent or recurrent physical or psychological problem that is likely to have been caused or exacerbated by the substance (e.g., current cocaine use despite recognition of cocaine-induced depression, or continued drinking despite recognition that an ulcer was made worse by alcohol consumption)

Criteria for Substance Abuse

A maladaptive pattern of substance use leading to clinically significant impairment or distress, as manifested by one (or more) of the following, occurring within a 12-month period:

1. Recurrent substance use resulting in a failure to fulfill major role obligations at work, school, or home (e.g., repeated absences or poor work performance related to substance use; substance-related absences, suspensions, or expulsions from school; neglect of children or household)

2. Recurrent substance use in situations in which it is physically hazardous (e.g., driving an automobile or operating a machine when impaired by substance use)

3. Recurrent substance-related legal problems (e.g., arrests for substance-related disorderly conduct)

4. Continued substance use despite having persistent or recurrent social or interpersonal problems caused or exacerbated by the effects of the substance (e.g., arguments with spouse about consequences of intoxication, physical fights)

The symptoms have never met the criteria for Substance Dependence for this class of substance.

The category of Substance Dependence is the more severe diagnosis and is the *DSM-IV*-TR's description of what may otherwise be defined as addiction. The *DSM-IV*-TR also lists several criteria for rating the severity of the dependence. Clinicians should be acquainted with the physiological and psychological manifestations of both acute drug or alcohol intoxication and withdrawal symptoms as outlined in the *DSM-IV*-TR. Certain drugs, such as barbiturates, can have serious medical complications associated with withdrawal and clients must be under a physician's care in order to assure they will safely complete the detoxification period.

BEHAVIORAL CHARACTERISTICS

Substance abuse almost always occurs within the context of other problems. Common presenting problems related to substance abuse are marital and family conflict, child abuse or neglect, unemployment, financial problems, multiple medical problems, anxiety, depression, suicide, and problems with aggression and violence. In assessing the role of substance abuse within the context of other problems, the clinician needs to understand the dynamics of other behavioral problems and how they may be exacerbated by substance abuse. It is estimated that most domestic violence occurs during periods when one or both parties are abusing some substance and that as many as two-thirds of homicides and serious assaults involve alcohol (Hart & Ksir, 2011). Criminal behavior such as child abuse or sexual molestation may be committed when the perpetrator is under the influence of a drug or alcohol. It is estimated that alcohol is implicated in two-thirds of all cases of family violence (Kinney, 2006). Although there is some disagreement about the exact nature of the relationship between substance abuse and violence, clearly a strong correlation exists between the two.

An important question for the clinician during a first interview is "Did all or any of these problems [the presenting problems] occur while you were drinking or using any other type of drug?" If the answer is yes, one can then begin to gather information to determine if a pattern of use is causing or contributing to the client's behavioral symptoms. Again, given the nature of denial, this query should also be made with significant others who are participating in the assessment.

As a general rule, a drug or alcohol problem exists and requires treatment if the use of the substance continues despite significant interference in any one of the six major areas of a person's life:

- Job or school
- Relationships with family
- Social relationships
- Legal problems
- Financial problems
- Medical problems

Behaviorally, substance abuse can be considered any use of a psychoactive substance that causes damage to the individual, family, and/or society.

Chemical dependency involves interactions between biological, psychological, and social factors. Becoming dependent on any substance is a process that occurs over differing periods of time for different individuals and varies with the use of different substances. A dependence on alcohol may take several decades to develop, whereas an addiction to cocaine, especially crack cocaine, may occur almost immediately. There are, however, certain phases that individuals are likely to pass through as their dependence on a substance increases. An old proverb regarding alcoholism outlines the progression of addiction: "The person takes a drink, the drink takes a drink, and the drink takes the person." The journey from controlled use to being controlled by the use is the nature of addiction. No one begins using alcohol or other drugs with the goal of becoming addicted. A more in-depth, definitive review of the behavioral symptoms will provide a basis for recognizing the path that many substance abusers travel.

Phase 1: The Prodomal Phase

The first phase of chemical addiction can be labeled the prodomal phase. In the prodomal phase, casual or social use of a substance begins to change and the first signs of dependence can be charted. In this early phase, the following behavioral changes generally occur:

- Increase of tolerance
- First blackout or loss of significant time to drug use
- Sneaking drinks or drugs
- Preoccupation with drinking or drug use
- Gulping drinks or hurried ingestion of chemicals
- Avoiding reference to drinking or drug use

The first symptom noted in the prodomal phase is an increase in tolerance. Tolerance can be defined as the "decreasing effects of a drug on the body, due to repeated ingestion and habituation, resulting in the need to greatly increase the amounts of the drug to achieve intoxication" (Coombs & Howatt, 2005, p. 378). Physiologically, the brain and central nervous system adapt over time to the effects of almost any psychoactive substance. Therefore, the user must increase over time the amount of the substance or the frequency of use in order to achieve the sought-after effect. Counselors should ask about any changes in the amount or frequency of drug use in order to establish the symptom of tolerance.

The second symptom in this phase is the onset of blackouts or loss of significant amounts of time to drug use. Not all substances cause blackouts; it is primarily a symptom associated with central nervous system depressants like alcohol, benzodiazepines, barbiturates, and narcotics. A blackout isn't unconsciousness; the user remains awake and active but later doesn't remember what was said or done while he or she was using. It is an indication that the user was able to ingest enough of the substance to "anesthetize" the part of the brain that processes short-term memory. Blackouts are a prominent feature of alcohol abuse, particularly with binge drinkers.

The third behavioral symptom is sneaking drinks or drugs. This often means that the user will "pre-use" by drinking or using before a social gathering in order to assure that she has enough. It also means that the user is "stockpiling" drugs or hiding them from others who might share them. The user typically experiences discomfort or irritability with others who are not keeping up with his rate of drinking or using drugs.

The fourth symptom involves a cognitive change in which the user becomes more preoccupied with time spent using. Behavior is manifested by making social plans that increasingly focus on the opportunity to drink, leaving work early in order to have extra time to drink, becoming irritable if there is any interruption in the time set aside to get high, and spending an increased amount of time and effort in assuring that the user has plenty of alcohol or drugs available.

The fifth symptom, a more hurried ingestion of drugs or alcohol, is an extension of the development of tolerance. Users become concerned that they won't have enough of the substance to relax or "get a buzz" and use more quickly in order to get a higher level in their system. Nearly all of the behaviors in the first stage are summarized by describing the user who might develop a serious problem as the one who must have a drink (or drug), and have it fast.

The final symptom in the prodomal phase sets the stage for denial. The user begins to feel uncomfortable with others' comments or questions about the changes in his pattern of drug or alcohol use and avoids confrontation. The user begins to become estranged from others who might express concern about his/her use and avoids questioning himself about the changed relationship with the substance.

Phase 2: The Crucial Phase

In the middle or crucial phase, the substance abuser experiences some of the more obvious and pronounced behavioral changes associated with addiction. This phase is labeled "crucial" because it offers the most hope for an intervention in the growing physical and psychological dependence before some of the more severe medical and social consequences enter the picture. It is also during this phase that family and significant others usually become more aware of the user's growing dependence on drugs or alcohol. In this second phase, the following behavioral symptoms generally occur:

- Loss of control of substance use
- Denial and minimization of use
- Confrontation by others
- Behavioral loss of control
- Guilt and remorse
- Periodic abstinence or change in patterns of use
- Losses
- Medical and psychological interventions
- Growing alienation and resentment
- More frequent substance use

The first symptom, loss of control of the substance, is often misunderstood and poorly defined. In the dynamics of addiction, loss of control can be thought of as a loss of predictability. For example, an individual who is abusing alcohol begins to experience times when she drinks more than she intends. On one night, she may have only the three beers she planned to drink after work. On the following night, the same plan falls apart, and the person drinks until she passes out. The user cannot predict with any certainty when she will be able to stick to the plan and when she will use more than intended.

The next set of behavioral symptoms (Denial and Minimization through Loss) will be considered together since they usually occur as part of a pattern of confrontation and denial. At this point, changes in the user's behavior related to drugs or alcohol is generally more obvious. While intoxicated or recovering from a binge, the user is more likely to become aggressive, impulsive, extravagant, or otherwise unpredictable in her behavior. If confronted, the user is likely to insist that she can control it and stop any time. In fact, the user may quit for a brief period of time to "prove" she has control. Guilt feelings may begin when the user is confronted with the result of some harmful behavior that occurred while intoxicated (e.g., missing a child's birthday because the user was drinking with buddies at the bar instead of picking up the birthday cake and going home as promised). Fear sets in, followed by flashes of remorse and sometimes aggressiveness or isolation to keep others at a distance. The consequences of the user's actions while using are increasingly difficult to minimize, rationalize, or deny and have a more pronounced impact on their relationships.

The final group of symptoms in the crucial phase outlines some of the more overt consequences that users experience as the addiction progresses. These include loss of friends, divorce, loss of a job or financial setbacks, loss of other interests such as hobbies or leisure pursuits, and loss of a normal, daily routine that does not revolve around substance use. Other, less clearly observable losses include a loss of ordinary willpower, loss of self-respect, and an abandonment of moral or spiritual values. Often during this phase, the user experiences some acute medical consequences related to their use and will seek medical intervention for specific symptoms (problems that are secondary to the drug or alcohol use). For example, a cocaine user may experience periodic heart arrhythmias (irregular heartbeat) and seek a doctor's advice for the heart problem, but not for the cocaine use that is causing the difficulty (the primary problem). Denial creates and perpetuates a vicious circle. Because the user denies that he has a problem, he can't go to anyone else to talk about it and so may use more to overcome the guilt or anxiety that results from the loss of control of his behavior. As the user becomes further trapped in the cycle of remorse, resentment and blame help externalize the fears, but lead to increased alienation.

Phase 3: The Chronic Phase

The final or chronic phase of addiction is typified by a more profound loss of behavioral control and by the physical manifestations that accompany chronic drug or alcohol abuse. In the last phase, the following symptoms appear and often continue in a vicious circle until the user either dies or finds help. The general symptoms are as follows:

1. Continuous use of the substance for longer periods
2. Indefinable fears and vague spiritual desires
3. Impaired judgment and irrational thinking
4. Tremors, malnutrition, overdoses, decreased tolerance, and/or other physiological problems associated with the drug
5. Obsessive use of the substance until recovery or death

Binges, benders, daily use, and the inability to stop without help are characteristic of this phase. The user engages in prolonged, continuous use and is unable to function without using his drug of choice on some regular basis. The addict neglects daily needs to the point of not eating or caring for himself or others. Attempts to control usage are abandoned as the periods of intoxication and recovery encompass most of the user's time.

Symptoms 2 and 3 reflect the loss of ability to function that accompanies brain deterioration associated with prolonged use of psychoactive drugs and alcohol. The user can't think clearly and will make outlandish claims that are obviously irrational. The addict, for example, will claim and believe that someone broke into the house and took all the cocaine while she was asleep. As the fears increase, the addict may experience a vague yearning for some miracle or "divine intervention" to stop the continuation of the downward spiral that is the course of addiction.

The final two symptoms comprise the absolute deterioration of the addict prior to death. Especially with alcohol dependence, the addict may experience a "reverse tolerance" in which he once again becomes very intoxicated by a smaller dose of alcohol. This is an indication that the user's system has essentially been saturated with alcohol and cannot process the alcohol quickly enough to remove it from the body. Obsessive use, if unbroken, ultimately leads to death by suicide, homicide, accident, or medical complications. Here, the drug truly "takes the person" by becoming the solitary focus of life. The addict becomes obsessed with using not to get high but to feel normal and avoid the consequences of withdrawal.

ASSESSING THE BEHAVIORAL SYMPTOMS

The following questions are suggested for helping the clinician evaluate the behavioral symptoms of addiction. In Figure 5.1 they are classified under the headings Preoccupation, Increased Tolerance, Rapid Intake, Using Alone, Use as a Panacea (Cure-all), Protecting the Supply, Nonpremeditated Use, and Blackouts (for Alcohol).

The more yes answers a client gives, the more indications there are of serious abuse or dependence on substances. In assessing the behavioral components of a client's substance use, it is important to remember that each individual will experience some diversity in the pattern of addiction. Some individuals who are addicted to cocaine will experience periods of profound depression following a binge, and some will not. Not all alcoholics will experience a reverse tolerance even in the chronic stage of the addiction. The symptoms certainly overlap and occur in a variety of different orders depending on the individual situation. The description of the behavioral characteristics and questions about behavioral changes are meant to serve as guidelines and directions for further exploration with the client.

Social Characteristics

It is through the investigation of a client's social and family life that evidence of substance abuse is often initially detected. As the user continues to become more heavily involved in abuse or dependence on a drug, the primary relationship in life eventually becomes the relationship with the substance. As the use becomes increasingly important and central to the person's life, it is inevitable that other social relationships will suffer.

Abusers develop clear patterns over time of focusing their life on social activities that afford them opportunities to indulge in substance use. Especially with the use of illegal substances, in order to protect themselves from detection, they become increasingly involved in socializing with others who use similar drugs in a similar manner. Users prefer to use with others who use like them. Family members or friends who are sober and do not use become excluded from a significant part of the user's life. As a person's "affair" with a substance grows and the barrier of denial is fortified, the chasm in important relationships with family and friends deepens. Increasing family conflict related to their substance use, a very constricted social life, lack of involvement in activities that do not afford an opportunity to use, and general withdrawal from sober friends are signals that the affair with a substance is well under way. The more advanced the dependence on the substance, the more alienated the user becomes from others who don't indulge with him or her.

Patterns of behaviors that are found in families of abusers are well established (Lewis et al., 2011). The strength of the dependence on the substance is easily evidenced when users fail to make attempts to prevent family breakups or isolation from significant others in order to maintain their substance use. Intimate relationships that endure a user's increasing dependence on a substance become distorted through the denial or "enabling" behaviors exhibited by the user's family.

Family Characteristics

Family members, like the user, progress through different phases in their journey with the addict. Addiction is often classified as a "family illness" because the effects

1. Preoccupation

Yes	No	
_____	_____	Do you find yourself looking forward to the end of a day's work so you can have a couple drinks or your drug of choice and relax?
_____	_____	Do you look forward to the end of the week so you can have some fun getting high?
_____	_____	Does the thought of using sometimes enter your mind when you should be thinking of something else?
_____	_____	Do you sometimes feel the need to have a drink or "hit" at a particular time of the day?

2. Increased Tolerance

Yes	No	
_____	_____	Do you find that you can sometimes use more than others and not show it too much?
_____	_____	Have friends ever commented on your ability to "hold your alcohol or drugs"?
_____	_____	Have you ever experienced an increased capacity to drink or use drugs and felt proud of this ability?

3. Rapid Intake

Yes	No	
_____	_____	Do you usually order a double or like to drink your first two or three drinks fairly fast, or use your drug of choice in a way it works the fastest to get you high?
_____	_____	Do you usually have a couple of drinks before going to a party or out to dinner or use a drug before going out in order to "get a head start"?

4. Using Alone

Yes	No	
_____	_____	Do you routinely stop in a bar alone and have a couple of drinks or go home and get high by yourself?
_____	_____	Do you sometimes use alone when no one else with you is using?
_____	_____	Do you usually have an extra drink by yourself when mixing drinks for others or have extra drugs of your own when using with others?

5. Use as a Panacea (Cure-all)

Yes	No	
_____	_____	Do you fairly routinely drink or get high to calm your nerves or reduce tension or stress?
_____	_____	Do you find it difficult to enjoy a party or social gathering if there is nothing to drink or use?
_____	_____	Do you often think of relief or escape as associated with your use?
_____	_____	When encountering any physical or emotional problems, is your first thought to use?
_____	_____	Does life seem easier knowing your drug of choice will help you out?

FIGURE 5.1 Questions for assessing behavioral symptoms. *(Continued)*

6. Protecting the Supply

Yes	No	
_____	_____	Do you sometimes store a bottle or drug away around the house in the event you may "need" to use or do you fear you may run out?
_____	_____	Do you ever keep a bottle or substance in the trunk of your car or office desk or stashed in the house "just in case" you might need it?

7. Nonpremeditated Use

Yes	No	
_____	_____	Do you sometimes start to have a drink or two or use just a little and have several more drinks or hits than you had planned?
_____	_____	Do you sometimes find yourself starting to use when you had planned to go straight home or do something else?
_____	_____	Do you sometimes use more than you think you should?
_____	_____	Is your use sometimes different from what you would like it to be?

8. Blackouts (for Alcohol)

Yes	No	
_____	_____	In the morning following an evening of drinking, have you ever had the experience of not being able to remember everything that happened the night before?
_____	_____	The morning after a night of drinking, have you ever had difficulty recalling how you got home or who you were with and what you did?

FIGURE 5.1   *(Continued)*

of the addiction on those who are in a close relationship with the abuser also experience symptoms that, while different, are frequently as serious as those suffered by the addict. Essentially, everyone in the addict's family and social system suffers. Some evidence-based treatment approaches have emphasized that the addict's behavior cannot be viewed in isolation from the family (Substance Abuse and Mental Health Services Administration, 2009).

Four Stages in the Family System of the Addict Stages or Phases (Lewis et al., 2011) can delineate the dynamics that are often seen in families with substance-dependent members. Although these stages represent common patterns of family interaction with substance users, not all families can be defined or described using these criteria. These are not discrete stages; it is likely that there will be some overlap or that several stages will be in evidence simultaneously. Also, not every family will experience the same intensity or exact set of responses in each stage. Some families may stay in a prolonged state of denial, even to the point of the addict's death. The description of the stages, however, can provide some guidelines for assessing the dynamics in the user's family and provide a basis for treatment planning with both the addict and other family members.

1. *Denial*   In this stage, family members deny that there is a substance abuse problem. They try to hide the substance abuse both from each other and from those outside the family. Excuses are made, members "cover" and make excuses for the addict's behavior, other explanations are offered, and the family begins to isolate from others who might suspect "something is wrong."

2. *Home Treatment* Family members try to get the addict to stop using. Hiding drugs or bottles, nagging, threatening, persuasion, and sympathy are attempted. Home treatment, or the family's effort to stop the addict from using without seeking outside help, may fail because the focus is on controlling the behavior of someone else. The roles in the family often change significantly, usually with deleterious effects. Children may try to care for a parent, coalitions among family members are formed, and family members ignore or minimize their own problems by keeping the focus on the addict.

3. *Chaos* The problem becomes so critical that it can no longer be denied or kept secret from those outside the family. Neighbors and friends become aware of the addiction. Conflicts and confrontations escalate without resolution. The consequences for family members become more pronounced and a child or partner of the addict may experience serious emotional or physical problems. Threats of divorce, separation, or withdrawal of family support are often made but not acted on. There may be domestic violence or abuse or neglect of children in the family that must be carefully assessed in order to intervene if needed.

4. *Control* A spouse or family member attempts to take complete control of and responsibility for the user. If still living within the family, the addict becomes an emotional invalid who exists outside the "normal" functioning of the family. Control is often exercised through divorce, separation, or a total emotional alienation from the family. The family, like the addict, exists in a state of suspended animation, trapped in a cycle of helplessness and futile attempts to control the addict's behavior.

ASSESSING THE SOCIAL AND FAMILY-RELATED SYMPTOMS

As previously noted, it is important to have access to family members, friends, and/ or important others in the addict's life in order to adequately assess a substance abuse problem. If an addict has somehow entered the mental health system, through a doctor's referral or employer's recommendation, it is highly likely that the situation has become unmanageable enough for significant others in the addict's life to break the barrier of denial. Many clients report that their "entrance into treatment was the result of an intervention" (Lewis et al., 2011, p. 172). As with the addict, it is critically important to undertake the assessment in a supportive, caring, nonjudgmental manner. Many family members experience a high degree of guilt or shame about the addict's behavior and feel that the continuation of the addiction is somehow their fault. They may feel that they have not been a good enough spouse, child, or parent or that they have created so much stress in the addict's life that they have promoted the addiction.

The following questionnaire (Figure 5.2) can be given to family members or friends in order to gain important information about the user's pattern of substance use.

Information gathered from others can be compared with the responses given by the client in order to assess the degree of minimization or denial that may be present. A yes response to any of the preceding questions indicates some possibility of substance abuse; a yes response to four or more indicates a substance abuse problem.

In addition to gathering information from others who are familiar with the addict, counselors must be alert to some of the common social consequences that

---

Questionnaire: Do You Have a Spouse, Friend, or Loved One Who Has a Drinking or Drug Abuse Problem?

1. Do you worry about how much they use drugs or drink?
2. Do you complain about how often they drink or use?
3. Do you criticize them for the amount they spend on drugs or alcohol?
4. Have you ever been hurt or embarrassed by their behavior when they are drinking or using?
5. Are holidays in your home unpleasant because of their drinking or drugging?
6. Do they ever lie about their drinking or drug use?
7. Do they deny that drinking or drugs affect their behavior?
8. Do they say or do things and later deny having said or done them?
9. Do you sometimes feel that drinking or drug use is more important to them than you are?
10. Do they get angry if you criticize their substance use or their drinking or drug using companions?
11. Is drinking or drug use involved in almost all your social activities?
12. Does your family spend almost as much on alcohol or drugs as it does on food or other necessities?
13. Are you having any financial difficulties because of their use?
14. Does their substance use keep them away from home a good deal?
15. Have you ever threatened to end your relationship because of their drinking or drug use?
16. Have you ever lied for them because of their drug use or drinking?
17. Do you find yourself urging them to eat instead of drink or use drugs at parties?
18. Have they ever stopped drinking or using drugs completely for a period of time and then started using again?
19. Have you ever thought about calling the police because of their behavior while drunk or high?
20. Do you think that alcohol or drugs create problems for them?

FIGURE 5.2   Questions to determine patterns of substance abuse.

frequently appear in an addict's life. Frequent job loss, a driving under the influence (DUI) arrest or other legal problem (particularly domestic violence), the breakup of important relationships, a series of moves (also called "the geographic cure"), a history of psychological or medical problems that are unresolved, and a lack of interest in activities that were once important to the individual are all indicators of addiction. Several of the assessment devices discussed in the next part of the chapter will assist the clinician in gathering information related to the symptoms and social characteristics of substance abuse.

SCREENING AND ASSESSMENT INSTRUMENTS

To assist in the diagnosis and assessment of substance abuse, psychometric instruments are often very helpful. It is estimated that there are at least 100 different screening tests for substance abuse. The primary benefit of assessment is to accurately and efficiently determine the treatment needs of the client. Assessment can be defined as the "act of determining the nature and causes of a client's problem" (Lewis et al., 2011, p. 81). A variety of specific psychometric instruments are generally available to counselors. Material from the initial interview should help the clinician select appropriate measures that will enhance understanding of the exact nature, dynamics, severity, and effects of the client's substance use. For example, several tools are focused on alcohol abuse only, while others include abuse of additional or other substances.

Numerous assessment tools are available to counselors. One resource that counselors are strongly encouraged to take advantage of is the National Institute on Alcohol Abuse and Alcoholism (NIAAA) publication Assessing Alcohol Problems: A Guide for Clinicians and Researchers, 2003. For a nominal charge, the NIAAA will provide a manual that includes articles about the use of alcohol abuse measurements and samples of instruments used with both adults and adolescents. A copy of the material can be requested by contacting the NIAAA at 6000 Executive Boulevard, Bethesda, MD 20892-7003, and requesting NIH Publication No. 03-3745.

The assessment measures reviewed in this text are only a sample of those available to counselors. They were chosen based on their widespread use and availability, ease of administration and scoring, and reliability and validity. The assessment devices that are included in this segment include the Michigan Alcoholism Screening Test (MAST) and the Short Michigan Alcoholism Screening Test (SMAST), the Drug Abuse Screening Test (DAST-20), the CAGE Questionnaire, the Alcohol Use Inventory (AUI), the Substance Abuse Subtle Screening Inventory-2 (SASSI-2), and the Addiction Severity Index (ASI), and the Adolescent Diagnostic Interview (ADI). In addition, those who are trained to use the Millon Clinical Multiaxial Inventory (MCMI-II) and/or the Minnesota Multiphasic Personality Inventory (MMPI-2) may use information from those tests to help with diagnostic and treatment considerations. Some information on using these tests in the assessment of substance abuse will be reviewed.

The Michigan Alcoholism Screening Test (MAST)

The most researched diagnostic instrument is the self-administered Michigan Alcoholism Screening Test (MAST), which was created in 1971 by M. L. Selzer. The 25-item MAST correctly identifies up to 95% of alcoholics, and the SMAST, an even shorter 10-question form of the MAST has also been shown to identify over 90% of the alcoholics entering general psychiatric hospitals. The MAST was originally validated with treatment-seeking alcoholics. Numerous studies have used it to assess both adolescent and adult populations in a variety of settings. The MAST may realistically and effectively be used with virtually any population.

The MAST is simple to administer; clients are instructed to answer all questions either yes or no. After clients complete the test, the points assigned to each question are totaled. The MAST text indicates a number of points assigned for each question. A total of 4 points is presumptive evidence of alcoholism and a total of 5 or more points makes it extremely unlikely that the individual is not an alcoholic. In addition, given the scoring values, a positive (yes) response to three test items; 10, 23, or 24 are enough to diagnose alcohol addiction. Three questions from the MAST that quickly diagnose potential alcohol problems are:

1. Has your family ever objected to your drinking?
2. Did you ever think you drank too much in general?
3. Have others said you drink too much for your own good?

These three questions can be easily incorporated into the interview process to serve as indicators for a more thorough evaluation. They may also be adapted to use with clients who are abusing other substances by substituting "using [their drug of choice]" for "drinking."

The Short Michigan Alcoholism Screening Test (SMAST)

The Short Michigan Alcoholism Test (SMAST) can be administered in the same manner as the MAST, or it can be given verbally. It consists of 13 of 25 questions taken from the MAST.

The SMAST is very easy to score. One point is given for each of the following answers: no on questions 1, 4, and 5; yes on all other questions (2, 3, and 6–13). A score of 0–1 indicates a low probability of alcoholism, a score of 2 points indicates the client is possibly alcoholic, and a score of 3 or more points indicates a strong probability of alcoholism.

The Drug Abuse Screening Test (DAST-20)

The DAST-20 (Appendix B) is a 20-item self-report inventory designed to measure aspects of drug use behavior, not including alcohol. It was derived from the Michigan Alcoholism Screening Test (MAST) and reflects similar content. DAST-20 scores are computed by summing all items positively endorsed for drug use. Higher scores indicate a greater likelihood of drug dependency. The DAST-20 is designed for use with adult male and female drug users.

The DAST-20 is a useful tool for helping to differentiate between several categories of drug users. In clinical trials, the DAST-20 scores demonstrated significant differences between the alcohol, drug, and poly-substance abuse groups. DAST-20 scores were also found to correlate highly with other drug use indices.

The CAGE Questionnaire

The CAGE is a four-item questionnaire that includes questions related to a history of attempting to cut down on alcohol intake (C), annoyance over criticism about alcohol (A), guilt about drinking behavior (G), and drinking in the morning to relieve withdrawal anxiety, sometimes known as an "eye-opener" (E). Most questionnaires duplicate information by using different phrases or words to detect similar patterns of behavior. The CAGE condenses the essential diagnostic questions into a brief but powerful tool for assessing alcohol dependency. This is also an extremely useful questionnaire to use with family members or others who are participating in the assessment.

The CAGE was originally developed and used with adult alcoholics presenting for treatment. Like the MAST, the CAGE may be used to screen for alcoholism in a variety of health care settings. Use of the CAGE questions effectively discriminates alcoholics from nonalcoholics at or above the 90% range.

The CAGE is generally administered verbally as part of the diagnostic interview. Instructions for administering the CAGE include observing the client's attitude in responding to the questions. The counselor should ask her to explain any yes answer and watch for signs of rationalization, denial, projection of blame, and minimization. The first question deals with the alcoholic's common problem of repeatedly trying to get the drinking under control only to lose control again and again once she resumes drinking. The next detects sensitivity to criticism of her drinking behavior. The third question taps into the personal sense of guilt, and the fourth looks at the tendency to use morning drinking as a remedy for excessive drinking the night before.

To administer the CAGE, the client is asked to answer yes or no to four questions.

CAGE Questionnaire for Alcoholism

1. Have you ever tried to cut down on your drinking?
2. Are you annoyed when people ask you about your drinking?
3. Do you ever feel guilty about your drinking?
4. Do you ever take a morning eye-opener?

Only yes responses are scored on the CAGE. One yes response indicates a possibility of alcoholism, two or three yes responses indicate a high alcoholism suspicion index, and four yes responses indicate an alcoholism diagnosis is highly likely. As with the SMAST, the CAGE questions can be adapted as an assessment tool for other substances.

A variation of the CAGE Questionnaire that offers alternative questions to assess abuse of substances other than or in addition to alcohol is also available (Appendix C). Several follow-up inquiries are noted on this form that can assist the clinician in getting more detailed information if the client answers yes to any of the four questions. Also, a version of the CAGE for Youth and Adolescents is helpful in assessing substance abuse problems with clients in this age range.

The Substance Abuse Subtle Screening Inventory (SASSI-3 and SASSI-A2)

The Substance Abuse Subtle Screening Inventory-3 (SASSI-3) for adults and the Adolescent SASSI-A2 for adolescents (Miller, 1997) are single-page, paper-and-pencil questionnaires. On one side are 52 true/false questions that generally appear unrelated to chemical abuse; on the other side are 26 items that allow clients to self-report the negative effects of any alcohol and drug use. Clients can complete the SASSI in approximately 10–15 minutes, it is easily scored, and training is available in interpretation and use of the SASSI as a screening tool for identifying substance abuse. The SASSI is available only to therapists who have met certain criteria and completed some training in its use. Information, training, and materials are available through the SASSI Institute, P.O. Box 5069, Bloomington, IN 47407.

The primary strength of the SASSI is in identifying abuse patterns that are hidden by the more subtle forms of denial common to substance abusers. Items on the SASSI touch on a broad spectrum of topics seemingly unrelated to chemical abuse (e.g., "I think there is something wrong with my memory" and "I am often resentful"). The questions are designed to be nonthreatening to abusers to avoid triggering the client's defenses and denial. The SASSI is resistant to faking and defeats efforts to "second-guess" the "right" answer. As a result, the SASSI is effective in identifying clients who are minimizing or in denial about their substance abuse. It is also effective in identifying substance abuse regardless of the drug of choice. Both of the SASSIs are adapted for either male or female clients.

The data from research with the SASSI indicate approximately 90% accuracy in identifying substance abuse patterns in clients. Thousands of test items were designed or considered, then given to samples of alcoholics, other drug abusers, and controls (non-substance-abusing people). The inventory was tested over a period of 16 years and is still being adapted and updated. In 1997, the Adult SASSI-3 replaced the adult SASSI-2. Two scales from the original test were dropped and three new scales were added. Counselors have used the SASSI as a screening tool for court-ordered substance abuse programs, employee assistance programs, and in general mental health settings.

The Alcohol Use Inventory (AUI)

The Alcohol Use Inventory (AUI) is a hierarchically organized set of self-report scales that provides a basis for diagnosing different problems associated with the use of alcohol. The AUI is based on the hypothesis that alcoholism should be diagnosed from a multiple-syndrome model, and the AUI scales are designed to provide an operational definition of the multiple manifestations of alcohol-related problems. It should be used to provide a more thorough diagnostic picture if there are clear indications from the MAST or CAGE that an alcohol problem is probable. Like the SASSI, the AUI is a protected test. Information and materials for the AUI are available by contacting the publisher at pearsonassessments@pearson.com.

The AUI consists of 228 multiple-choice items (expanded from 147 in the original test), and is used with people 16 years or older. The specific areas of assessment that are the focus of the AUI are motivation for treatment, physical health, anger and aggression management, risk-taking behavior, social relationships, employment and/or educational situation, family situation, leisure-time activities, religious/spiritual activities, and legal status. The AUI is a very simple test to administer and can generally be given to the client with little additional instruction. The client should be told that it is important he respond as honestly as possible to all questions and not to skip questions or give more than one response per question. Both hand- and computer-scored versions of the AUI are available.

The Addiction Severity Index (ASI)

The Addiction Severity Index (ASI) provides basic information that is useful both for the clinician and the clients. The ASI manual gives clear instructions for administering, scoring, and using the data in planning treatment strategies. The current ASI is designed for use with adults, but variations for use with adolescents are being developed. A particular strength of the ASI is its utility with dual diagnosis populations. For treatment planning purposes, the ASI is especially helpful in determining the severity of the client's drug use and the need for additional or extended treatment.

The ASI is administered as a structured interview with specific questions that cover several basic areas of treatment needs, including medical, employment/support, drug/alcohol use, legal, family/social relationships, and psychiatric. The drug/alcohol subscale includes an extensive history of all drug and alcohol abuse, the longest period of abstinence, and previous drug treatment history. Administration of the ASI relies on fairly basic clinical interviewing skills. Counselors can adjust questions to use terms that are familiar to the client and fit with his or her level of education and "sophistication." In some treatment settings, the ASI questions can also be given as writing projects for the client to further examine their history of drug/alcohol use and the impact it has had.

The client uses a 0- to 4-point scale to rate how "bothered" he has been in the past 30 days by problems in the different areas of assessment. This serves to give a clearer picture from the client's perspective of how he rates the severity of his problem and gives some indication of the desire for treatment. These ratings are then compared with the counselor's ratings on the same scales. With the influence of denial or minimization on the client's perceptions, it is common for the interviewer to perceive a higher severity of problems than the client.

A final benefit of the ASI is its usefulness as a training tool for counselors. It can greatly facilitate training in substance abuse and dual diagnosis work, particularly when clients are somewhat resistant or evasive. The structured format of the ASI gives the counselor some place to go when clients are not forthcoming.

The Adolescent Diagnostic Interview (ADI)

The Adolescent Diagnostic Interview (ADI) assesses substance use disorders in 12- to 18-year-olds. The ADI is a structured interview format that evaluates psychosocial stressors, school and interpersonal functioning, and cognitive impairment. The ADI also screens for behavioral problems commonly associated with substance abuse in adolescents. It is designed to help professionals identify, refer, and plan for treatment of adolescents with substance abuse problems.

The ADI can be ordered through Ken Winters, Ph.D., University of Minnesota, Department of Psychiatry, 420 Delaware Street, SE, Box 393 Minneapolis, MN 55455.

The Millon Clinical Multiaxial Inventory (MCMI-II) and Minnesota Multiphasic Personality Inventory (MMPI-2)

Although both the MCMI-II and the MMPI-2 are primarily designed for the assessment of personality, they are often used to assess a full range of psychopathology, including substance abuse. Both are copyrighted, protected evaluation instruments that require additional training to administer, score, and interpret. Both have elaborate computer-scoring programs available through the resources that sell the tests. Incorporated into both the MMPI-2 and MCMI-II are validity scales that may help to identify clients who are "attempting to look good" or answering randomly.

It is not in the scope of this text to provide the reader with an in-depth understanding of either of these instruments. As noted, additional training is required to use these tests. There is, however, some information that can be used in a basic assessment.

The MCMI-II is useful in identifying several aspects of personality functioning: clinical syndromes (e.g., depression, anxiety), changing symptoms, and personality styles or disorders. It is certainly a useful addition to any evaluation in which there is a question of dual diagnosis. It is a simple, true/false, 173-question self-report regarding the client's behavior and experience. Given the difficulty of hand scoring, it is generally scored by a computer program.

The symptom scales on the MCMI-II are useful in corroborating a clinical impression of the types or patterns of symptoms experienced by the client. The personality scales may help a clinician understand the relationship between the client's substance use and his typical pattern of managing his experience and relationships. For example, someone with a score indicating a Narcissistic Personality style may use drugs to establish or maintain a particular image. Understanding a client's basic personality can be very useful in planning treatment to address specific character traits that may either support or undermine his recovery.

Like the MCMI-II, the Minnesota Multiphasic Personality Inventory-2 (MMPI-2) is useful in identifying behavioral and personality patterns and clinical symptoms. These tests are generally used as part of a comprehensive personality or behavioral assessment. The MMPI-2 is a self-report questionnaire that consists of 567 true/false questions. There is also a version of the MMPI-2 for adolescent populations, the Minnesota Multiphasic Personality Inventory—Adolescent (MMPI-A).

The MMPI has been used extensively for over 20 years in the evaluation of alcoholics. There is a common pattern in MMPI scores among alcoholics. Elevations on scales 2, 4, and 7 represent a combination of personality characteristics commonly found in male alcoholics. These scores reflect depressive, sociopathic, and obsessive-compulsive features. They also reported symptoms of anxiety, marital discord, financial problems, insomnia, and tension that were reflected in the MMPI profiles of alcoholics.

In addition to the basic clinical scales, both the MMPI-2 and MMPI-A contain items that indicate the possibility of substance abuse problems. A subscale of both tests, the MacAndrew Alcoholism Scale—Revised (MAC-R), was developed using items from the original MMPI and became widely used as a method of screening for substance abuse problems. The revised MAC (MAC-R) deleted several questions and added others to further refine the content of the scale. The MAC-R has been an effective tool for identifying substance abuse problems in both adults and adolescents.

Two other subscales on both MMPIs are the Addiction Acknowledgement Scale (AAS) and the Addiction Potential Scale (APS). Persons who obtain a high score on the AAS are usually acknowledging a substance abuse problem, and additional assessment of the nature of their substance use would be indicated. The APS may help discriminate between persons who abuse substances and those who do not. Both the APS and AAS are still in the process of being validated and evaluated for their reliability in assessing substance abuse problems. Particularly with the APS, high scores on this scale should be corroborated with other data and information.

The ASAM Criteria for Patient Placement

The American Society for Addiction Medicine (ASAM) provided specific criteria as a multidimensional approach to determine the biopsychosocial severity of a client's condition and provide guidance for placement through assigning one of the four levels of care. In clinical settings for substance abuse, the ASAM guidelines were the most widely used criteria to define intensity of medical necessity and associated evaluation of level of required services and structure, ranging from standard outpatient care to intensive inpatient facilities for those with more severe problems (Shepard et al., 2005).

The four levels of care, reflective of the strength of services needed by a client, include (a) outpatient treatment; (b) intensive outpatient/partial hospitalization; (c) medically monitored intensive inpatient, such as residential treatment; and (d) medically managed intensive inpatient treatment, seen in hospitalization. The particular level would be identified along biopsychosocial assessment dimensions: (a) acute intoxication and/or withdrawal potential, (b) biomedical conditions and complications, (c) emotional/behavioral conditions and complications, (d) treatment acceptance/resistance, (e) relapse potential, and (f) recovery environment (National Institute on Drug Abuse, 2009).

Further clarification was offered when the American Society of Addiction Medicine (ASAM) (2007) published a revised second edition of the guidelines, ASAM

PPC-2R, with two sets of criteria, one for adults and another for adolescents. Also in the updated criteria for both client groups, there was the addition of a new level to precede the original four, "0.5 early prevention."

DIAGNOSIS

Professionals who have to make decisions about the presence or absence of substance abuse or dependence for their clients must make a series of complex judgments. An adequate conceptualization of substance abuse and addiction emphasizes the interaction among the individual user, the physiological effects, and the social context in which the user functions. The simple diagnostic definition that addiction exists when drug or alcohol use is associated with impairment of health and social functioning is a useful general thesis. The technical definitions are found in the *DSM-IV*-TR using the category of Substance-Use Disorder and the levels of *moderate* and *severe*.

Inconsistent attitudes and imprecise standards for what constitutes an "addiction" have always complicated the diagnosis of substance abuse. Inadequate definitions of chemical dependence have often been cited as the primary reason for a lack of success in developing adequate epidemiological, diagnostic, and prognostic assessment tools. With many medical illnesses, the etiology, prognosis, and treatment are known, and no biases, mis-information or stigma interfere with the identification of the disease. This is certainly not the case with the diagnosis of substance abuse. Here, much of the information needed to establish a diagnosis is based on self-reports from an often unreliable population given the preponderance of denial and minimization and possible cognitive impairment. Long-standing prejudices and moral attitudes further complicate making an adequate diagnosis. Although the *DSM-IV*-TR offers seemingly clear, behavioral descriptions of symptoms that constitute Substance-Use Disorders, exceptions to the rule are always a possibility.

Differential Diagnosis

It is frequently the case that one of the most challenging aspects of diagnosing substance abuse is the interplay of addiction and other mental disorders. Counselors who effectively treat individuals with a primary diagnosis of substance abuse may be faced with treating additional psychological disorders. Other diagnostic categories such as personality disorders, post-traumatic stress disorder, mood disorders, and thought disorders are common differential or coexisting diagnoses. Symptoms related to other disorders may be accentuated or mollified by a client's substance abuse.

It is important that clinicians working with substance abusers be trained in diagnosing other mental disorders as well as substance abuse. Many symptoms of intoxication or withdrawal from certain substances mimic the behaviors seen in psychiatric disorders. Clinicians who are untrained in the recognition of such problems as depression, mania, psychosis, and dementias may risk misdiagnosing a client. For example, if a client arrives in the counselor's office with symptoms of slurred speech, difficulty with coordination, and difficulty focusing his attention, the counselor might assume that these behaviors are evidence of a substance abuse problem. These symptoms, however, are also associated with certain neurological diseases such as multiple sclerosis or medical disorders such as diabetes. Differentiating between a bipolar or manic-depressive disorder and the highs and lows experienced by substance abusers is often a complicated diagnostic process.

Generally, a longitudinal approach is useful in differentiating between psychiatric and substance abuse–related symptoms. Many symptoms of substance intoxication and withdrawal improve or are alleviated within days or weeks. It is not unusual for substance abusers to appear far more disturbed when initially assessed than they will after a period of abstinence. Family or others who can be consulted regarding a client's behavioral history prior to the onset of abusing substances can also be invaluable in accurately diagnosing and planning for treatment.

A standard rule of practice for counselors working with substance abusers is to refer clients for a thorough physical as an early part of the assessment process. Establishing a good working relationship with a physician who is familiar with drug and alcohol abuse is a mandatory step in providing appropriate and adequate services. Also, a psychologist who is trained in differential diagnostic techniques for assessing addiction and other psychological and neuropsychological problems should be a part of the counselor's assessment referral network. Licensed psychologists have a broader range of standardized evaluation techniques that they can administer to help differentiate among emotional, characterological, or psychological disorders and alcohol- or drug-related problems.

Dual Diagnosis

Many individuals diagnosed with substance abuse problems also meet the criteria for other psychological disorders. It is important to discover whether symptoms of a psychological problem either preceded the onset of the abuse problems or persist after the substance abuse has been treated and a period of abstinence has been maintained for several months. For example, alcoholics typically exhibit a high rate of depressive symptoms due to the depressant effects of their chronic use of alcohol. Sleep and appetite disturbances, feelings of helplessness and hopelessness, and loss of pleasure and motivation are symptoms of depression and also part of the pattern of addiction to alcohol. The deterioration of an alcoholic's lifestyle and health, the loss of significant relationships, and other problems related to excessive drinking along with the basic chemical effects of alcohol make it nearly inevitable that an alcohol addicted client will appear depressed while actively drinking. However, this depression is usually reactive and should decrease significantly with abstinence and efforts to resolve life problems that accumulated during the period of addiction. In alcoholics with a primary depression, the symptoms either preceded the onset of alcohol abuse or became more pronounced during periods of abstinence.

Some clients may have begun using drugs to alleviate symptoms of anxiety or depression. Psychoactive drugs may initially offer some relief to individuals who suffer from mood disorders. It is helpful for clinicians to question clients carefully about their psychological history prior to using drugs or alcohol and to seek information regarding a family history of psychological problems. The learning theory of chemical dependency in fact proposes that the concept of anxiety reduction related to drug or alcohol use is the basis for many addictions (Lewis et al., 2011).

Research addressing the question of whether substance abusers are more likely to exhibit personality and other psychiatric disorders has produced mixed results. In some of the research studies, the link between substance abuse and passive-dependent, antisocial, or narcissistic personality types indicate the presence of co-occurrence is about 50%. One obvious difficulty with diagnosing a personality disorder is that if a person is involved in using an illegal substance such as cocaine, some aspects of the user's lifestyle of necessity engender the symptoms of an antisocial or paranoid personality. It is a matter of self-preservation for the user to become suspicious, secretive, alienated from others who do not use, and, by definition of the cocaine use, involved in illegal pursuits. However, these behaviors may be secondary to the dependence on cocaine and should diminish when the person maintains abstinence.

It is believed that one-third of the substance-abusing population meet the criteria for one of the psychiatric diagnoses. Among those with the diagnosis of alcoholism, almost half have a second psychiatric diagnosis. Phobias were particularly common among males, followed by depression, schizophrenia, panic, and mania. For alcoholic women in this study, phobias and depression, followed by antisocial personality, panic, schizophrenia, and mania, were the most prevalent.

Other social and familial factors appear more frequently in substance-abusing groups. Genetic factors clearly play a role as a predisposing factor for the development of alcohol addiction. A lack of family cohesiveness, which involved such factors as an early death or divorce or separation of parents, appears to be associated with an increase in alcohol-related problems for offspring of these families. Adolescents who later became substance abusers are more likely to

- identify with others who share alcohol and drugs
- exhibit impulsive behavior
- display signs of rebelliousness and/or nonconformity.

Additionally, substance abusers tend to be less likely to learn from experience and less conservative or reserved behaviorally than their peers.

There is also a frequent relationship between substance abuse and suicide (Doweiko, 2011). Estimates are that approximately 25% of substance abusers entering treatment have made a suicide attempt at some point in the past. The incidence of completed suicide is thought to be three to four times higher than that found in the general population. As previously noted, these clients may be using alcohol or other drugs to treat the symptoms of depression. In these clients, it is essential to provide an accurate diagnosis and initiate treatment for the depression as soon as possible. Involvement of a qualified psychologist and/or physician to assist in diagnosing and providing treatment for these clients at an early stage is critical.

Case Discussions

Case 1 (Sandy and Pam).

Effective assessment and diagnosis in the case of Sandy and Pam would begin with the diagnostic interview. Using the Substance Use History Questionnaire (see Appendix A), information would be gathered regarding each of their histories of substance use and abuse. Significant factors to consider about Sandy's substance use are as follows:

- She has a history of alcohol use dating back to junior high.
- By self-report, Sandy admitted to continuing to abuse alcohol into adulthood.

(Continued)

(Continued)

In assessing Sandy's substance use, it is apparent that her alcohol use has affected her family life and social relationships. She reports that she had married Joe, a violent alcoholic, and that during her drinking days, she left the children at home so she could go to bars and pick up numerous men. This behavior would clearly indicate that Sandy's alcohol abuse affected her judgment and ability to care for herself and her children.

With the information from the Substance Use History Questionnaire, it is possible to assess the phase of abuse/dependence that Sandy is experiencing. The crucial phase is characterized by obvious and pronounced behavioral changes. Sandy reported behavioral loss of control coupled with guilt and remorse about her actions while using alcohol.

In diagnosing Sandy's substance abuse, additional information is needed. The MAST and the CAGE Questionnaire would be useful in differentiating whether Sandy meets the criteria 257 for substance abuse or substance dependence in the *DSM-IV-TR*, or a *severe* category of substance use disorder on the *DSM-5*. Sandy's childhood history is indicative of the potential for a personality or mood disorder. Her marriage to Joe may indicate that she has suffered some type of physical or emotional abuse. Posttraumatic stress disorder is also a diagnostic possibility. Differential or dual diagnoses must be considered when evaluating Sandy's substance abuse. After a period of sobriety, additional psychological testing would be indicated to assess whether Sandy needed treatment for other disorders.

Pam's history of substance use included cocaine and alcohol. In assessing Pam's substance use, the significant factors are her

- employment history,
- unstable relationships, and
- report of anxiety symptoms.

In addition to the diagnostic interview using the Substance Use History Questionnaire, use of the Substance Abuse Subtle Screening Inventory-3 (SASSI-3) would be useful in identifying treatment issues and potential diagnoses. Clearly, Pam's substance abuse has also affected her judgment regarding relationships. The history with her live-in boyfriend seems to indicate intense conflict resulting in potential negative outcomes. Pam's history of unsuccessful employment indicates that she may be in the crucial phase of the progression of substance abuse/dependence. This pattern of substance abuse after a loss is a clear indicator of the overt consequences of the progression.

Other factors that need to be explored are the periodic abstinence or changes in Pam's pattern of substance use. The information from the SASSI-3 may be helpful in distinguishing between the diagnosis of substance abuse or substance dependence with a focus on polydrug use. Pam's childhood and recent conflicts with her boyfriend may indicate a possible personality disorder or mood disorder. Pam's statement regarding her boyfriend—that she "feels drawn to him" and wants to "make it work"—may indicate a dependent personality style. Pam's increasing anxiety could be indicative of either periodic withdrawal from the substances or an underlying anxiety disorder.

In summary, additional information gathered through an assessment would be needed in both cases in order to make accurate diagnoses and assist in planning treatment. Contacting other family members or significant others to gather information would be useful. Once each woman had established abstinence of at least 2 months, further assessment would help with answering questions about dual diagnoses.

Case 2 (Jose and Juanita).

In this case, Jose and Juanita's substance abuse is of primary importance and must be addressed. It is important to note that Juanita and Jose admit to abusing alcohol for 23 years and to recent use of cocaine. Both continue to have ample access to both substances through contacts at work.

In assessing substance abuse/ dependence, some psychometric instruments may be valuable in gaining more information. Using the Substance Use History Questionnaire and the Drug Abuse Screening Test (DAST-20) helps in evaluating the degree of substance abuse. It is extremely useful to distinguish between substance abuse and substance dependence to plan appropriate treatment. In addition, the questionnaire for families should be given to Sarita and Karen along with the interview. This would provide further information regarding the parents' substance use and its impact on the family.

In assessing Juanita's substance use, some significant factors are her

- attempt to stop drinking for health reasons;
- reluctance to give up drugs completely; and
- traumatic childhood history with an alcoholic/abusive mother, sexual abuse by a brother, foster home placement, and cultural assimilation issues.

Juanita's substance use indicates that she is in the crucial to chronic phase of substance abuse/dependence evidenced by her denial and minimization of her cocaine use and her 5-year periodic attempts at abstinence from alcohol. Juanita's traumatic childhood history needs to be evaluated as to the impact that these factors have in her substance use.

Diagnostically, Juanita would meet the criteria of *severe* for a substance use disorder on the *DSM-V* and substance dependence in the *DSM-IV*-TR. Her history may indicate other diagnoses such as a personality disorder, depression, and posttraumatic stress disorders are likely.

In assessing Jose's substance use, the significant factors are his

- frequent substance use,
- family history, cultural messages, and assimilation issues, and
- increasing conflict with Sarita over his drinking.

Jose's history of alcohol use every day, marijuana use on the weekend, and his behavioral changes when drinking are indicative of the crucial phase of substance abuse/ dependence. It is clear that when Jose drinks, he loses control and acts inappropriately toward Sarita. In addition, Jose's longest period of abstinence was 9 days, and after that, he drank to the point of intoxication. This pattern indicates a tolerance for alcohol, as well as minimization and denial.

Diagnostically, Jose would meet the criteria of *severe* substance use disorder on the *DSM-5* and substance dependence in the *DSM-IV*-TR. In addition, diagnoses of depression and personality disorder need to be investigated. Additional information about Jose's childhood experiences should be gathered.

In summary, it is clear that Juanita and Jose's substance use is a major factor to be considered in treatment of this family. Sarita's increasing and escalating behavioral problems could be indicative of her response to her parents' drinking and drug use. Sarita may also be at risk for abusing substances. The patterns of both children should be evaluated using information about typical coping styles or roles adopted by children in response to substance abuse problems in the parents.

Case 3 (Leigh).

Leigh's substance use needs to be evaluated in the context of her developmental stage. Coupled with her reported substance use, other factors such as problems at school, shoplifting, parental conflict, parental divorce, and

(Continued)

(Continued)

relocation to a new area are issues that need to be examined.

During the diagnostic interview the adolescent version of the Substance Abuse Subtle Screening Inventory (SASSI-A2) and the Adolescent Diagnostic Interview (ADI) can be administered, along with other instruments to determine a general level of functioning. More information from parent interviews and school assessment needs to be gathered.

In assessing Leigh's substance use, the significant factors include

- her development stage (adolescence),
- loss of parental support,
- increased conflict with her mother, and
- ambivalent feelings toward the conflict between her mother and father.

Leigh's acting-out behavior may be indicative of substance abuse or the substance use may be an "outlet" for her problems. This possibility needs to be evaluated before treatment interventions can be implemented. It is clear that Leigh's behavior at school and in the community must be addressed. Her appearance of being "overly thin" must be investigated so that a possible eating disorder can be assessed. Referral to a physician for a thorough physical would be indicated. In order to diagnose substance abuse/dependence with Leigh, more information needs to be gathered. Family members should be interviewed to assist in obtaining this information. Family conflict and Leigh's feelings of isolation must be addressed. Parent–child conflict, adjustment disorder, and eating disorder are potential dual diagnoses.

In summary, Leigh may be experiencing some prodomal phase symptoms related to her substance abuse. It will be important, however, to more carefully evaluate her previous functioning to determine whether her substance use is a temporary, reactive response to conflict and changes in the family.

Case Study

Tania

Tania is a 19-year-old single female, sent for assessment and diagnosis of a possible substance abuse disorder by her college counseling center. She was arrested by campus police for resisting arrest approximately 1 month prior to the time of the assessment. Tania reported that she and three friends were celebrating the end of the college semester by partying for three straight days. Tania used cocaine continuously; she did not sleep through the entire binge. On the third day of use, Tania began to experience thoughts that she was a vampire, that others identified her as such, and that they meant to do her harm. She was running through the campus when spotted by the police. In an attempt to escape, she ran into the college bookstore, frightened some of the customers, and the police apprehended her. She resisted arrest and the police report indicated that Tania was speaking incoherently and was clearly "out of touch with reality."

In the interview, Tania reported a history of cocaine use starting at 16 years of age. She uses cocaine by snorting, usually only on the weekends. The incident leading to the arrest was the only time she used in a binge manner. Tania began using alcohol at age 14, getting intoxicated nearly every weekend. She does not use alcohol much except to help her sleep after using cocaine. Tania smokes one to two packs of cigarettes per day. She is in college with a B to C average, but feels she could do better if she tried. She reported no previous psychiatric treatment and no prior symptoms like those experienced on the day of the arrest. There was no reported history of family substance abuse or psychiatric treatment.

Tania did not present with any bizarre or unusual behavior and was completely free of psychotic or other psychiatric symptoms since a day or so after the arrest. She does not feel that she is an "addict," but does appear distressed by the arrest and subsequent problems related to her education (her college was notified about the arrest since it occurred on campus and she was placed on probation) and her family (her parents were also notified about the arrest since she is underage).

Critical Thinking Questions

1. Identify the primary problem areas and issues that need to be assessed. Which assessment tools/methods might you use to get more information?
2. Do you believe that there might be a dual diagnosis? What mental health diagnosis is possible with Tania?
3. Would you consider a diagnosis of Substance Abuse or Dependence? Why? To which drugs?

MyCounselingLab™

Go to Topic 4: *Assessment and Diagnosis* on the MyCounselingLab™ site (www .MyCounselingLab.com) for *Substance Abuse Counseling,* Fifth Edition where you can:

- Find learning outcomes for *Assessment and Diagnosis* along with the national standards that connect to these outcomes.
- Complete Assignments and Activities that can help you more deeply understand the chapter content.
- Apply and practice your understanding of the core skills identified in the chapter with the Building Counseling Skills unit.
- Prepare yourself for professional certification with a Practice for Certification quiz.
- Connect to videos through the Video and Resource Library.

APPENDIX A
SUBSTANCE USE HISTORY QUESTIONNAIRE

1. What substances do you currently use? (Check all that apply.)

   _____ alcohol   _____ amphetamines (uppers)

   _____ cocaine   _____ barbiturates (downers)

   _____ marijuana   _____ nicotine (cigarettes)

   _____ other (specify) _____

2. What are your present substance use habits?

   _____ daily use   _____ social use (with friends or at parties)

   _____ weekend use only   _____ occasional heavy use (to point of intoxication)

   _____ occasional light use (not to point of intoxication)

3. How many days ago did you last take a drug or drink? _____ days

4. Have you used daily in the past 2 months? _____ yes _____ no

5. Do you find it almost impossible to live without your drugs or alcohol? _____ yes _____ no

6. Are you always able to stop using when you want to? _____ yes _____ no

7. Where do you do most of your drinking or drug use? (Check all that apply.)

   _____ home

   _____ friends

   _____ bars, restaurants, or other public places

   _____ parties or social gatherings

   _____ other

8. Do you drink or use during your work day? _____ yes _____ no

9. Do most of your friends use like you do? _____ yes _____ no

10. With whom do you use or drink? (Check all that apply.)

    _____ alone _____ neighbors

    _____ family _____ coworkers

    _____ friends _____ strangers

11. Do you consider yourself to be a

    _____ very light user _____ fairly heavy user

    _____ moderate user _____ heavy user

    _____ nonuser

12. Do friends or family think you use more than other people? _____ yes _____ no

13. Have any family or friends complained to you about your drug or alcohol use? _____ yes _____ no

14. Do you feel you use more or less than other people who use? _____ yes _____ no

15. Were your drug use or drinking habits ever different from what they are now? _____ yes _____ no
   If yes, please explain why the habits changed:

16. Has your drinking or drug use ever caused you to (check all that apply):
   _____ lose a job or have job problems
   _____ have legal problems (DUI, arrest for possession)
   _____ have medical problems related to your use
   _____ have family problems or relationship problems
   _____ be aggressive or violent

17. Have you ever neglected your obligations, family, or work for 2 or more days in a row because you were drinking or using drugs? _____ yes _____ no

18. Because of your alcohol or drug use, have you felt (check all that apply):

	Often	Sometimes	Seldom	Never
Tense or nervous	_____	_____	_____	_____
Suspicious or jealous	_____	_____	_____	_____
Worried	_____	_____	_____	_____
Lonely	_____	_____	_____	_____
Angry or violent	_____	_____	_____	_____
Depressed	_____	_____	_____	_____
Suicidal	_____	_____	_____	_____

19. Do you ever feel bad about things you have done while using? _____ yes _____ no
   If yes, please specify:

20. People use alcohol and/or drugs for different reasons. How important would you say that each of the following is to you?

	Very	Somewhat	Not at all
It helps me relax.	_____	_____	_____
It helps me be more sociable.	_____	_____	_____
I like the effect.	_____	_____	_____
People I know use drugs or drink.	_____	_____	_____
I use when I get upset or angry.	_____	_____	_____
I want to forget or escape.	_____	_____	_____
It helps cheer me up.	_____	_____	_____
It makes me less tense or nervous.	_____	_____	_____
It makes me less sad or depressed.	_____	_____	_____
It helps me function better.	_____	_____	_____
I use to celebrate special occasions.	_____	_____	_____

(Continued)

Are there other reasons you use drugs or alcohol? Please specify:

21. Have you tried to stop using drugs or alcohol in the last 2 months? _____ yes _____ no
    If yes, did you experience any medical or physical problems when you stopped? Please explain:

22. Have you ever gone to anyone for help about your drinking or drug use? _____ yes _____ no
    If yes, please explain:

23. Have you ever attended a meeting of Alcoholics Anonymous (AA), or any other self-help group be-
    cause of your drug or alcohol use? _____ yes _____ no

24. Do you feel that you have an addiction to alcohol or drugs? _____ yes _____ no

25. Do you want help with a drug or alcohol problem at this time? _____ yes _____ no

APPENDIX B
DRUG USE QUESTIONNAIRE (DAST-20)

Name:_____   Date:_____

The following questions concern information about your potential involvement with drugs *not including* alcoholic beverages during the past 12 months. Carefully read each statement and decide if your answer is "Yes" or "No." Then, circle the appropriate response beside the question.

In the statements drug abuse refers to (1) the use of prescribed or over the counter drugs in excess of the directions and (2) any nonmedical use of drugs. The various classes of drugs may include: cannabis (e.g., marijuana, hash), solvents, tranquilizers (e.g., Valium), barbiturates, cocaine, stimulants (e.g., speed), hallucinogens (e.g., LSD), or narcotics (e.g., heroin). Remember that the questions do not include alcoholic beverages.

Please answer every question. If you have difficulty with a statement, then choose the response that is mostly right.

These questions refer to the past 12 months	*Circle your response*	
1. Have you used drugs other than those required for medical reasons?	Yes	No
2. Have you abused prescription drugs?	Yes	No
3. Do you abuse more than one drug at a time?	Yes	No
4. Can you get through the week without using drugs?	Yes	No
5. Are you always able to stop using drugs when you want to?	Yes	No
6. Have you had "blackouts" or "flashbacks" as a result of drug use?	Yes	No
7. Do you ever feel bad or guilty about your drug use?	Yes	No
8. Does your spouse (or parents) ever complain about your involvement with drugs?	Yes	No
9. Has drug abuse created problems between you and your spouse or your parents?	Yes	No
10. Have you lost friends because of your use of drugs?	Yes	No
11. Have you neglected your family because of your use of drugs?	Yes	No
12. Have you been in trouble at work because of drug abuse?	Yes	No
13. Have you lost a job because of drug abuse?	Yes	No
14. Have you gotten into fights when under the influence of drugs?	Yes	No
15. Have you engaged in illegal activities in order to obtain drugs?	Yes	No
16. Have you been arrested for possession of illegal drugs?	Yes	No
17. Have you ever experienced withdrawal symptoms (felt sick) when you stopped taking drugs?	Yes	No
18. Have you had medical problems as a result of your drug use (e.g., memory loss, hepatitis, convulsions, bleeding, etc.)?	Yes	No
19. Have you gone to anyone for help for a drug problem?	Yes	No
20. Have you been involved in a treatment program specifically related to drug use?	Yes	No

Source: © 1982 by the Centre for Addiction and Mental Health. Author: Harvey A. Skinner, Ph.D. For information on the DAST-20, contact the Education and Publishing Department, CAMH, 33 Russell St., Toronto, Ontario, Canada, M5S 2S1.

APPENDIX C
ADULT CAGE QUESTIONNAIRE

C. Have you ever felt a need to CUT DOWN on your drinking/drug use? (This includes prescription drugs.)

Alternative Questions:

Have you ever tried to cut down on your usage? Were you successful? What was it like? Why did you decide to cut down or go on the wagon? Are you able to drink as much now as you could a year ago? Five or ten years ago? How do you feel about your drinking or drug use now? Has anyone ever commented on how much you are able to consume?

A. Have you ever been ANNOYED at criticism of your drinking/drug use?

Alternative Questions:

Have you ever been concerned about your usage? Has anyone else been concerned about your drinking or use of drugs? What caused the concern or worry? Do you get irritated by their concern? Have you ever limited how much you use in order to please someone?

G. Have you ever felt GUILTY about something you've done when you've been drinking/high from drugs?

Alternative Questions:

Do you feel that you are a different person when you are high? How would you compare yourself when you are using and when you are not? Have you ever been bothered by anything you have said or done while you have been high/drunk? Has anyone else been bothered by your usage?

E. Have you ever had a morning EYE OPENER—taken a drink/drugs to get going or treat withdrawal symptoms?

Alternative Questions:

Do you ever get a hangover? How often? Have you ever felt shaky after a night of heavy drinking? Have you ever had a drink to relieve the hangover or the shakiness? Have you ever had trouble sleeping after a heavy night of drinking or getting high? Do you ever have difficulty remembering what happened while you were high? How many times has this occurred?

Source: "Detecting Alcoholism: The CAGE Questionnaire" by J. A. Ewing, 1984, *Journal of the American Medical Association,* 252, 1905–1907. Used by permission.

6

Treatment Setting and Treatment Planning

ROBERT L. SMITH, PH.D., NCC, CFT, FPPR
ELDA E. GARCIA, PH.D., M.S., LCDC, BSW

Methods for developing accurate assessments and diagnoses for substance abusers and dependents are described elsewhere in this text. The proposed *DSM5* will be used to identify a category or level (*moderate* or *severe*) of individuals diagnosed with a substance use disorder. This essential first step provides the theoretical and practical base for making future decisions about how to develop and organize an effective treatment experience for clients.

We continue the study of substance abuse by presenting the next step in organizing treatment. By building on the concepts of accurate assessment and diagnosis, this chapter introduces the reader to the basic terms and processes of treatment settings and treatment planning. Each element is defined, described, and illustrated, providing a strong base by which to understand topics from subsequent chapters, including treatment modalities, working with special populations, and relapse prevention. In this chapter, it is assumed that case examples received adequate and reliable assessment and diagnosis, which paved the way for the treatment considerations of setting and planning.

WHAT IS A TREATMENT SETTING?

A *treatment setting* is the place or environment where substance abuse treatment services are provided. These environments may look very different to the outside observer and range from most restrictive to least restrictive. *Restrictive* refers to the degree of physical and social structure provided by the professional staff for the recovering substance abuser. For example, a highly restrictive environment would be considered a locked, inpatient hospital setting where clients are encouraged to live and receive their treatment. The *DSM*5 descriptor category of *severe* would be used for individuals in restrictive settings that have been classified with a *substance use disorder*. In contrast, a weekly voluntary outpatient substance abuse treatment program would be considered a setting of less restriction where clients generally reside in their homes and attend scheduled meetings with professionals at designated agencies, offices, churches, and/or treatment facilities. A *moderate* category would be used in these cases.

As mentioned in the previous chapter, clients fall within a range of diagnoses and severity of illness. In general, the more severe the substance use disorder diagnosis (*moderate, severe*), the more restricted the environment or setting that is recommended. This rationale suggests that clients need settings that match their diagnosis and descriptor category for treatment to be effective. Selection of a treatment setting is similar to the manner in which physicians prescribe different medications, medication strengths, and dosing schedules for patients. Settings, like medications, should fit the diagnosis, meeting the needs of the client and presenting problems.

Clients can move between settings depending on their progress in treatment and the recommendations of treatment staff. The goal is always to provide the least restrictive environment that offers the optimal types of services that match client needs. This approach ensures a respect for the client's autonomy and ability to move away from an unhealthy dependency. It embraces the client's self-determination skills, which are essential in initiating and maintaining substance abuse/dependency recovery.

This chapter provides examples of seven of the most common treatment settings. It is not an exhaustive list but will provide a working knowledge of traditional treatment settings, ranging from most restrictive to least restrictive. In addition treatment settings in the military are described at the conclusion of this chapter following the case of Andrew.

- Medical detoxification and stabilization
- Dual-diagnosis hospital inpatient
- Free-standing rehabilitation and residential programs
- Partial hospitalization
- Temporary recovery or halfway homes
- Intensive outpatient
- Outpatient DUI/DWAI/DUID programs

Important distinctions among the settings exist even though similar services may be offered such as prevention, counseling, education, and/or self-help. Clients involved in any one setting can be either voluntary or involuntary participants. This means that within any one setting, some participants may be court ordered or mandated, while others enter treatment without legal requirements.

Settings do not consistently reflect the client's voluntary or involuntary status. An exception to this rule would be prison-based drug treatment facilities and DUI diversion programs. Otherwise, many substance abuse treatment professionals argue that most "voluntary" clients entering treatment have an "involuntary" element to their decision to enter treatment. These "voluntary" clients can often feel pressured by coworkers, family members, and/or physicians. Fisher and Roget (2009) support that coerced treatment, although popular and successful for some, may have little benefit, adding that self-motivation is essential for long-term success. Important considerations determining the client's success or failure include quality and effectiveness of the treatment program.

Case Discussion

Case 3 (Leigh).

To illustrate the concept of treatment settings, let us extend Case 3 and imagine Leigh, a 16-year-old marijuana and alcohol user who has run into trouble with her substance use. Her problems intensified one evening when she and her friends were brought into custody for questioning by police. Leigh was partying with some new friends in a wooded area close to the high school she attends. Police, responding to a complaint initiated by neighbors in the area, confronted the adolescents and found alcohol and marijuana. Officials were concerned about the underage drinking, illegal use of marijuana, and in particular Leigh's emotional state, which was hostile, disoriented, and apparently intoxicated.

Police contacted Leigh's mother and discussed the possibility of charging Leigh with possession of marijuana and disorderly conduct. After several unsuccessful attempts by police to persuade Leigh to seek immediate medical care, she was evaluated to be at risk to herself and was involuntarily admitted to medical detoxification. She spent several days in detoxification and getting "clear headed," and then she voluntarily agreed to attend a rehabilitation program. When she had 28 days of successful treatment, her counselors recommended an intensive outpatient program to continue her recovery.

This scenario illustrates that treatment settings are not stagnant environments but integrative opportunities to move clients toward recovery and health. The reverse is also possible. Leigh might have a relapse (or slip) and need a temporary, more restrictive setting to regain her hard-won progress.

Moving up and down this continuum of care provides a multitude of treatment services designed to fit the client's unique needs. The effectiveness of treatment settings comes from their flexibility, adaptability, and responsiveness to the client's current recovery needs.

TYPES OF TREATMENT SETTINGS

Medical Detoxification and Stabilization

Detoxification is the safe and complete physical withdrawal of incapacitating substances such as alcohol, barbiturates, hallucinogens, and heroin. Detoxification units can be within hospitals or freestanding units.

Research published by the U.S. Department of Health and Human Services, Substance Abuse and Mental Health Services Administration (SAMHSA) Center for Substance Abuse Treatment (2009) describes a medical and social model of detoxification (*Detoxification and Substance Abuse Treatment Training Manual*). The medical model utilizes medical staff, including doctors and nurses, to administer medication to safely assist people through withdrawal. The social model, on the other hand, rejects the use of medication and relies on a supportive, non-hospital setting to help the client through withdrawals (Fisher & Roget, 2009). Admittedly, there is no "pure" model for detoxification treatment; as both models utilize each others concepts in their respective programs with notable success.

Medical models establish medical necessity before admission and refer to the risk of medical problems (e.g., seizures) or psychiatric difficulties (e.g., suicidal ideation) the client exhibits. In drug and alcohol detoxification facilities, doctors use medication to lessen the often uncomfortable and sometimes brutal side effects of drug withdrawal, while preparing the client for the counseling and addiction treatment (Grohsman, 2009). This process includes gradual tapering of the drug(s) over a period of several days or weeks. For example, heroin can be weaned from an individual and substituted with a longer-acting opioid such as methadone. Other medications may be administered to lessen physical and psychological symptoms associated with withdrawal.

The length of stay is usually less than two weeks. Detoxification should be considered only the beginning of treatment. Although medical detoxification is an effective method of treatment, it alone is rarely sufficient to help clients achieve long-term sobriety (Grohsman, 2009). It is important to establish a treatment plan that will outline the client's intervention and goals well past the point of detoxification. Treatment planning, including discharge plans and long-term goals should begin upon client admission into a service and/or program and the discharge plan should continue to be updated during the course of the client's treatment (Baron, Erlenbusch, Moran, O'Conner, Rice, & Rodriguez, 2008).

Detoxification settings provide:

- screening for presence of withdrawal symptoms and/or psychiatric conditions,
- on-site medical and psychiatric care that promotes safe and complete withdrawal,
- staff who structure and nurture the environment,
- staff who protect clients from self-harm or harm to others, and
- staff who educate and counsel clients about substance abuse and dependency.

Dual-Diagnosis Hospital Inpatient

Usually based in psychiatric hospitals, dual-diagnosis programs are designed to treat clients with the presence of both serious psychiatric illness and substance abuse/dependency. Services are provided to diagnose and treat substance dependency as well as symptoms attributable to psychiatric illness. Each condition must be assessed independently and in relation to the other presenting conditions or symptoms. This is done to withdraw the affected client safely from substances, stabilize the client emotionally and physically, and identify and treat the concomitant disorders.

The personnel's expertise is helping dually diagnosed clients stop abusing substances and maintain their psychiatric treatment regimens, which may include prescribed psychotropic medication (e.g., antidepressants, antipsychotics, antianxiety drugs). Specialized training in dual diagnosis requires staff and counselors to understand how concomitant disorders can interact and manifest in the clients' lives. Individuals may reside in these hospital units from several days to several weeks. Programs are designed for either adult or youth treatment.

Dual-diagnosis hospital inpatient settings provide:

- on-site medical and psychiatric care that includes 24-hour nursing and milieu supervision and locked units with limited access to family and friends;
- personnel with specialized knowledge in dual diagnosis;
- 7-, 14-, or 28-day stays in a protective, restricted environment;
- psychiatric and substance abuse crisis stabilization;
- more intensive assessment and diagnostic services; and
- daily intensive group contact with other clients and staff.

Figure 6.1 defines some common staffing patterns for inpatient and partial hospital treatment settings.

Free-Standing Rehabilitation and Residential Programs

REHABILITATION PROGRAMS   Rehabilitation programs are usually free-standing, non-hospital-based facilities. Doweiko (2011) maintains that the well-recognized Minnesota Model of addiction treatment has been the dominant model for rehabilitation programs in the United States since its inception. Fisher and Roget (2009) add that it is the leading model for addiction treatment today for many alcohol and other drug treatment centers in the United States and worldwide. Despite revisions in its basic model due to changes in insurance program reimbursement policies, it still remains a strong influence on both inpatient and outpatient rehabilitation programs. Hazelden, an inpatient and outpatient treatment facility dedicated to treating alcoholics, is considered to be one of the major contributors to the Minnesota Model (Stinchfield & Owen, 1998). Founded in 1949, Hazelden pioneered the 28-day rehabilitation program for alcoholics.

Today, the Minnesota model is known as the Hazelden model for its continuation of the legacy of the original model through ongoing evaluation of research and the enhancement of the model with newer and more effective techniques (Fisher & Roget, 2009). Two long-term treatment goals of the Minnesota Model are total abstinence from all mood-altering substances and an improved quality of life. Consistent with the philosophy of AA, the objectives for the individual are to grow in transcendental, spiritual awareness, to recognize personal choice and responsibility, and to develop peer relationships. The resources for recovery, then, lie primarily within the client with treatment providing the opportunity to discover and utilize those resources and the therapeutic atmosphere conducive to change (client-centered approach) (Derry, 2009).

Patricia Owen, director of the Butler Center for Research and Learning for the Hazelden Foundation, describes the Minnesota Model Counseling Approach in her work published in the National Institutes of Health (Owen, 2000). She describes the Minnesota Model's concept by stating "chemical addiction is seen as a primary, chronic, and progressive disease" (p. 117). It is a disease that is treated largely in group sessions. By engaging with counselors and members of the peer group, the client is encouraged to develop meaningful relationship experiences and clarify feelings and definitions of reality. Success of the process is characterized by relief, peace, increased sense of self-worth, acceptance by self and the group, and the existential restoration of meaning to life (Derry, 2009). Examples of the type of therapy offered by group treatment include: focusing on a broader reality; overcoming denial and gaining greater acceptance of personal responsibility and hope for change; learning about the disease and related

Attending Physician or Provider

In a medical/hospital setting, the physician, psychologist, or other approved mental health professional who "attends" the patient's stay is responsible for approving the course and methods of treatment and will assume dispensing or monitoring of correct medications; credentialed by the hospital medical staff.

Medical Director

Typically, an addictions-trained physician who oversees the delivery of services in the unit; not necessarily a direct provider of patient care; assumes general supervision of the nursing staff; occasionally directly involved with addictions counselors directly assigned to patient care.

Nursing Staff

Generally responsible for day-to-day patient care; often 24 hours per day on site or directly supervising nonmedical unit staff members; will help determine program procedures, patient care, treatment, and discharge planning.

Social Worker

Will provide required transition, discharge, or placement planning; will assure all record documentation meets standards; often has a portion of his or her time allocated from the social services department to the chemical dependency (CD) unit; not required to be addictions certified. Will conduct assessments and make treatment recommendations. This person often will not be the primary counselor or assigned therapist.

Mental Health Workers

Mental health professionals trained in the delivery of general mental health and counseling services; not typically the primary provider or attending practitioner; assist in treatment planning, conducting education portions of the IP milieu, cofacilitating, activity, therapy, or skill-building groups; on dual diagnosis units, need not be certified in addictions treatment.

Certified Substance Abuse or Addictions Specialists; or Primary Care Counselors

In a medical facility, a member of the treatment team under the direction of the attending practitioner; certified by the state as a trained counselor in the field of addictive disorders. In residential, nonmedical setting, often the primary counselor/therapist directly responsible for clinical care, treatment plans, education sessions, group treatment, and after-care planning. In residential, free-standing units, may be a recovering individual with no primary or advanced degrees, but with technical, approved training in the field of substance abuse treatment.

Clinical Director

Generally a trained, advanced-degree mental health professional who is a certified or licensed addictions specialist; oversees the delivery of clinical care to patient and significant others; may directly provide group and specialty services, such as CD education, couples' group therapy, multifamily therapy, supervises primary counseling staff, and other professionals.

FIGURE 6.1   Inpatient and partial hospital modalities: Common staffing patterns.

factors; orienting to 12-step philosophy and groups (e.g., Alcoholics Anonymous [AA], Narcotics Anonymous [NA], or Cocaine Anonymous [CA]); looking at special-issue groups; focusing on topics specific to clients who have special characteristics (e.g., women, elderly persons, those with dual disorders, incest survivors); and participating in recreation groups, meditation groups, work task groups, groups for individuals to tell their stories and receive feedback, and groups where members review their behavioral homework assignments. Individual sessions are used for reviewing progress and addressing issues that may be too sensitive or complex to be dealt with routinely in a group setting (Dombeck, 2005).

Individualized treatment plans (which will be described in detail later in this chapter) are used to guide treatment. These plans identify behavioral problems and develop goals and strategies for their resolution. Common problem areas are maintaining abstinence, family relations, career decisions, and social interactions. Often a "level system" for privileges and benefits is used to encourage clients to participate successfully in the program.

Derry (2009) reflects on McElrath's 1997 description of the Minnesota Model as being "inextricably interwoven with the program, practice and philosophy of Alcoholics Anonymous (AA)." He maintains that the success of the Minnesota Model is largely due to the fact that it addresses the fundamental and core issues of addiction. Its foundation consists of an existential philosophy that allows for a caring, nurturing, client-centered environment where the 12 steps provide direction and patients suffering from addiction can find healing.

Doweiko (2011) describes the strength of the Minnesota Model of treatment as its redundancy and its multi-member concept, which prevents the chemical dependency counselor from having to be a "jack of all trades, master of none." The model emphasizes a diverse professional staff that directs and controls the planning process and its implementation (e.g., enforces and maintains facility rules, provide treatment recommendations and evaluations, educate clients about substance abuse). This approach helped make the Minnesota Model one of the dominant treatment program models for more than 40 years. The Hazelden program describes the ideal counselor as an active program of recovery from a chemical addiction. Understanding and practicing the 12-step philosophy (e.g., self-help group attendance, AA/NA, Al-Anon, CA) in personal life are essential. All counselors must demonstrate good chemical health. Non-recovering counselors can also do quite well. The counselors assume the role of educator and coach. The client-counselor relationship appears to be most effective when a client perceives the counselor as an ally in the work toward recovery and sees her as an important resource. Ideal personal characteristics of a counselor include being tolerant and nonjudgmental of client diversity; collaborative when working with clients and able to elicit and use input from other professionals; flexible in accepting job responsibilities; having good verbal and written communication skills; having personal integrity; and conveying compassion to clients (Owen, 2000).

The Minnesota Model denotes an effective and frequently used philosophy and methodology of delivering treatment. It incorporates medical, social, and self-help approaches. The importance of self-help and peer support are the foundation of the Minnesota Model of addiction treatment. Moore, Rothwell, & Segrott (2010) address the social and self-help approaches in their recent work. They describes the 12 steps of social support in the Minnesota Model as so important to the ongoing recovery of chemically dependent persons that behavioral health professionals developed a series of parallel therapeutic approaches that maintained consistency with the steps themselves. This consistency allowed clients to transition from treatment to social support relatively easily. The Minnesota Model allows for a consistent service model that transfers to the national 12 step programs, recovery clubs, and connected recreational or social events. Involvement in self-help groups (AA, NA, and CA) is considered critical for long-term abstinence (Owen, 2000). The social/self-help elements of the Minnesota Model encourage clients to be responsible for developing their own recovery. Self-help groups have become an important part of the system of care for substance use clients; some studies have found correlation between clients who participate in self-help groups and lower relapse rates (Timko, Billow, & DeBenedetti, 2006). Humphreys and Wing (2004) maintain that self-help organizations are a key resource for addicted individuals. Additionally, potential strategies, including the encouragement of self-help group involvement, hold significant promise of helping more individuals recover from drug and alcohol problems (Humphrey & Wing, 2004).

For most rehabilitation programs, psychiatric evaluations are usually done off site, but some may staff their own psychiatrists. This obviously depends on the site, personnel, and available resources.

Currently, Hazelden provides treatment based on "levels of care," which include inpatient, outpatient, residential, hospital-based, and partial hospitalization. In inpatient, stays are typically 21 to 28 days and provide health care services. In inpatient treatment, the client stays overnight at an inpatient facility, typically a hospital. On an outpatient basis, the typical length of treatment is 5 to 6 weeks of intensive therapy (3 to 4 nights a week, 3 to 4 hours a session) followed by 10 or more weeks of weekly aftercare sessions.

RESIDENTIAL PROGRAMS   Residential programs are often used as a bridge between the more restrictive dual-diagnosis inpatient and rehabilitation programs and the less restrictive outpatient programs. Many use a level system similar to the Minnesota Model but are designed for long-term treatment stays. Sometimes, with lower-income clients, residential programs are used as an alternative to outpatient programs because of their housing resources.

In residential treatment, the client stays in a residential setting that is not hospital based but is, rather, a freestanding facility. Residential programs are intermediate-care facilities that allow individuals to live within a residential setting, be employed during the day, and receive comprehensive treatment, including individual, group, and family therapy as well as education and relapse prevention services. Average stays can range from 4 months up to a year. Rehabilitation and residential programs are designed for either adult or adolescent/youth treatment.

Youth services offer rehabilitative and residential programs specially designed to meet the needs of children and adolescents. Ybrandt's (2010) research revealed that the general risk factors for alcohol use were leisure and peer problems, problems associated with family background and relationships, and criminal behavior for those aged between 12 and 18 years. These results suggest that drug abuse treatment planning should focus on altering the predisposing factors that exist in these areas. This study also found that alcohol and drug use–related crimes also appear to be problem areas. This is evidenced by the high numbers of these cases being processed in juvenile courts. Ruiz, Stevens, Fuhriman, Bogart, and Korchmaros (2009) maintain that the implementation of juvenile drug courts is being utilized as an approach for addressing substance related issues. Youth participation in the drug court indicates a positive change in substance-related issues, delinquency and juvenile justice involvement, and sexual risk behaviors. Youth involvement in the use/abuse of substance is well documented by recent research (National Institute on Drug Abuse, 2010; Johnston, O'Malley, Bachman, & Schulenberg, 2010). A study conducted by Bell, Padget, Kelley-Baker, and Rider (2007) demonstrates that despite the inherent difficulties of surveying young children, these children can benefit from an alcohol-use prevention program that is carefully designed, implemented, and evaluated. The need for continued intervention and education for youth of all ages is crucial.

Research reviews (e.g., O'Conner, Dearing, & Collins, 2011; Johnston et al., 2010; Agnew, Mathews, Bucher, Welcher, & Keyes, 2008) suggest the following youth problem areas:

- Individual: other antisocial behaviors, low self-esteem, low social conformity, positive expectancies for drug effects
- Family: ineffective discipline, low warmth, high conflict, parental drug abuse, poor family management
- Peer: association with drug-using peers, low association with prosocial peers
- School: low intelligence, achievement and commitment to achievement
- Neighborhood: disorganized, high crime
- Socioeconomic status: financial difficulties, inability to purchase needs, delinquency

Troubled Teen 101 (2009), troubledteen101.com/, a website designed for parents in need of teen help describes the key components of effective treatment programs, which include the following:

Behavior Modification   Youth benefit from a program where appropriate behavior is reinforced and rewarded and in appropriate behavior is confronted and redirected, with consequences issued. Expectations should include holding youth to high standards and providing tight supervision, and opportunities for motivation and encouragement from an effective program.

Academics   Many youth are able to earn high school credit while they attend an accredited treatment program. Enrolling in a treatment program with an academic component provides educational advancement and encouragement.

Activities   Effective programs offer a balance of enriching activities. This may include: recreation, exercise, learning, personal development, and social opportunities.

Personal/Emotional Development   Youth should have opportunities to participate in introspective activities that help them make changes in their lives. An effective program will assist them in evaluating their lives and determining the need for change.

Family Involvement   Effective treatment programs provide opportunities for parental education as well as opportunities for family members to re-establish relationships. Some programs offer family workshops that allow parents and youth to participate together.

Partial Hospitalization

Partial hospitalization, occasionally referred to as *day treatment*, offers comprehensive substance-abuse treatment in a semirestrictive program where clients live at home and attend treatment during the day. Similar to other more restrictive treatment settings, partial hospital programs require completion of a detoxification program. Only clients *without* medical or psychiatric complications requiring inpatient care are admitted. These settings are for clients who need a level of restrictiveness between hospital inpatient/rehabilitation/residential and intensive outpatient. It is considered that the client should attend a daily, intensive, structured treatment program or otherwise be at high risk for relapse.

The SE Missouri Community Treatment Center (2008) provides partial hospitalization treatment and describes it as a more intense form of outpatient treatment. The treatment sessions in partial hospitals are usually longer than in outpatient treatment. Partial hospitalization patients go to sessions for 3–12 hours per day and 3–7 days per week. Most partial hospitalization programs are less than six weeks. After the partial hospital program is completed, most experts suggest continued support and counseling through weekly meetings. Weekly meetings could include the family and counseling might take place with the individual or in a group. This type of treatment is often very effective for many people because it combines the best parts of inpatient treatment (intensive care and strict goals), and outpatient treatment (the ability to continue working, being with family, a flexible schedule, and lower cost).

Partial hospitalization offers:

- a cost-effective level of care between full hospitalization/rehabilitation and intensive outpatient, and
- a professionally staffed structured environment providing treatment services.

Temporary Recovery or Halfway Homes

A recovery/halfway house is usually a community-based home or a building near a rehabilitation or residential facility. Resident clients rely on the safe and supportive group social structure of a transitional living arrangement with less monitoring than a more restrictive environment. Requirements for residence typically are abstinence, employment, attendance of 12-step recovery meetings, and possible urine testing to evaluate recovery progress and maintain a safe, sober house. Staff members are usually considered "paraprofessional," and most often are self-identified recovering alcoholics or addicts. Stays can vary ranging from several weeks to several months.

Recovery or halfway homes provide:

- a minimum structured transitional living in a recovering environment,
- an opportunity to save money to live independently, and
- help maintaining a connection with a recovering community while dealing with day-to-day trials.

Intensive Outpatient

Intensive outpatient treatment consists of substance-free treatment that can range from daily all-day activities to once-a-week meetings. In traditional comprehensive "intensive outpatient" programs, clients are initially enrolled to attend three evenings of 3-hour group therapy with 1 hour of family therapy per week. In addition, clients are expected to attend a certain number of AA/NA 12-step meetings established by treatment personnel.

Group therapy meetings can range in theme from managing stress to handling dysfunctional family patterns. Random urine testing is usually an integral part of these programs. Continued participation is based on abstinence as evidenced by self-report and/or urine testing. Completion is usually determined by documented behaviors such as length of abstinence, attendance in groups, and keeping scheduled individual and family counseling appointments. Intensive outpatient programs are typically 90- to 120-day commitments.

Weekly or biweekly outpatient settings are often for those clients who have successfully completed the intensive portion of treatment and demonstrated sustained abstinence, employment, and a sober/clean lifestyle (e.g., staying away from high-risk substance-using friends).

Intensive outpatient treatment provides:

- comprehensive treatment with off-site living arrangements while establishing or maintaining employment;
- graduated treatment services; and
- possibly longer-term, intensive treatment than hospitals and rehabilitation settings.

SAMPLE OF A THREE-PHASE INTENSIVE OUTPATIENT PROGRAM
Phase 1.

Schedule

Three to five evenings per week, 2 to 4 hours each night for an average of 6 weeks

Initial Tasks

Client completes medical evaluation

Assessment and diagnosis completed

Treatment plans developed and signed

Meetings with significant others of client

General Goals

Address denial

Share extent of substance abuse with treatment group

Demonstrate compliance with program

Outcomes

Completion of personal and family history

Assigned readings

Participation in self-help groups

Verification of abstinence (drug/alcohol screening)

Compliance with program expectations

Phase 2.

Schedule

Two nights per week, 1.5- to 3-hour group sessions for 6 weeks. Family/significant others attend "family group" and possibly individual family sessions.

General Goals

Uninterrupted abstinence

Replacement of substance abuse behaviors with recovery or routine activities and/or responsibilities

Outcomes

Sustained demonstrated willingness to change

Evidence of use of peer groups as support

Achievement and maintenance of treatment plans

Demonstration of nurturing self-care and respect of others

Assumption of consequences of own actions and ability to identify and engage in corrective actions

Phase 3.

Schedule

Introduction to weekly aftercare group sessions

One-and-a-half to 3 hours in length for 4 weeks

General Goals

Both an external and internal commitment to a substance-free lifestyle

Identification of ongoing recovery issues

Development of a posttreatment lifestyle plan that includes maintaining changes and expanding life changes in social, psychological, and spiritual realms

Outcomes

Active use of community-based self-help groups

Consistent demonstration of appropriate response to life stressors

Completion of a relapse prevention education series

Consistent ability to serve family, community, and self in a substance-free manner

Outpatient rehabilitation, a less restrictive environment, typically includes group therapy meetings three times per week. Homework is given to extend learning into home and work environments. Clients maintain their place of residence and employment while committing to a program of recovery that includes abstinence. If a client is unable to maintain sobriety and/or is not making sufficient progress, a more restrictive environment such as inpatient rehabilitation might be recommended.

OUTPATIENT DUI/DWAI/DUID PROGRAMS Driving under the influence (DUI), driving while ability impaired (DWAI), and driving under the influence of drugs (DUID) are some of the titles used by state legislatures to address the problem of driving intoxicated or drug impaired. Most states have well-defined penalties and treatments for the impaired drivers that vary from state to state.

Beginning in the mid-1970s, large institutions such as the National Institute on Alcohol Abuse and Alcoholism began funding pilot projects known as alcohol-driving countermeasures (ADC) programs. These were most often administratively placed under motor vehicle divisions or highway safety departments. In the late 1970s and early 1980s and with the onset of action groups such as Remove Intoxicated Drivers (RID), Mothers Against Drunk Driving (MADD) and Students Against Drunk Driving (SADD), treatment programs, and citizen advocacy groups collaborated to influence the development of more formal and strict mandated programs targeting impaired drivers. For the group Mothers Against Drunk Driving (MADD), the drinking age recently questioned by college presidents is not a topic for debate. MADD has long cast under-age drinking in black-and-white terms; many college officials see it as impossibly gray. In October, John M. McCardell Jr., a former president of Middlebury College, moved his fledgling nonprofit group, Choose Responsibility, from Vermont to Washington, D.C., with the hope that he too can start a movement that changes not only laws, but how Americans think about alcohol and young adults, just as MADD has done (Hoover, 2008).

Despite the involuntary nature of the clients attending DUI/DWAI/DUID programs (the majority are court ordered), they are considered the least restrictive treatment setting. Typical alcohol/drug education track programs are for 12 weeks with 90-minute group meetings, the basics of which are:

- describing the physiological effects of alcohol and drugs,
- describing the possible psychological consequences of use/abuse of drugs,
- defining the legal limits of blood alcohol levels,
- presenting current theories of alcohol and drug abuse and addiction, and
- developing alternatives to impaired driving.

The Importance of Matching Treatment to Client Needs

Thus far we have described a broad range of treatment settings available to the drug abuser. In practice, various treatment programs often provide similar services. The patient's diagnosis will play a part in selecting a treatment program. The descriptor categories, mild, moderate, and severe, will be significant factors influencing the treatment programs and settings selected for individuals classified with a Substance Use Disorder. Research provides little, if no, evidence of superior efficacy of one program or setting over another. Circumstances that affect treatment-setting choice include but are not limited to:

- ability to pay
- method of payment
- geographic availability of specific services
- current employment, housing, and family conditions
- previous treatment experiences

- reliability of assessment information
- availability of space in existing settings
- level of self-care
- current emotional and behavioral state

Overall, programs have only limited success in matching services to client needs, but when they do, receipt of substance abuse counseling and services predicts both remaining in treatment and reduced post-treatment substance use (Marsh, Cao, & Shin, 2009).

Helpful Hints for Clinicians: Know Your Facility Setting

- Know what organization accredits your facility (e.g., Joint Commission on Accreditation of Healthcare Organizations) and all its documentation requirements and procedures.
- Develop relationships with facility administrators.
- Study your orientation manual.
- Know your job description.
- Know how your facility gets reimbursed for services (e.g., insurance, private pays, state/national funds, HMOs).
- Know the expertise of the setting (e.g., detoxification, comprehensive treatment).
- Know the referral sources of the facility: how do clients enter your facility?
- Know how clients are assessed and diagnosed: who is responsible for such tasks?

This section provided an overview of the major treatment settings encountered in the field of substance abuse. (Table 6.1 summarizes the various treatment settings.) It was designed to prepare clinicians to make informed decisions about treatment options. The following section introduces the more specific clinical skill of treatment planning. Planning for treatment is an essential element of all treatment settings. It offers clear and concise expectations and guidelines for the client and clinician within their particular context or setting. Planning addresses the client's specific problems and answers the who, what, when, where, and how of treatment.

WHAT IS TREATMENT PLANNING?

Treatment plans are written documents that detail how problems are defined and treatments are formulated for the substance abuser. Each plan needs to be specific and individualized to meet the client's needs and goals and must be measurable in terms of setting targets that can be used to chart the client's progress.

Treatment planning, which began in the medical sector during the 1960s, was created to provide an analytical and critical way of thinking for counselors, clients, substance abuse treatment administrators, insurance companies, and government agencies. Treatment plans are for the benefit of all participants in treatment, including the substance-abusing client. It is very easy for the counselor and client to lose sight of the issues that initially brought the patient into treatment. The treatment plan

TABLE 6.1 Summary of treatment settings

Type of Setting	Characteristics
Medical detoxification and stabilization	Short-term, specialized medical care to screen for the presence of withdrawal symptoms and/or psychiatric conditions
	Promotion of safe withdrawal of substances and psychiatric stabilization
	Protection from self-harm and harm to others
	Referrals made for further substance abuse treatment
Dual-diagnosis hospital inpatient	On-site medical and psychiatric care
	24-hour nursing, milieu supervision, restricted environment
	Specialized assessment, evaluation, and treatment of dual-diagnosis disorders
	Individual and group counseling
Free-standing rehabilitation and residential programs	Short- and long-term on-site treatment stays
	Comprehensive, intensive, structured services
	Ancillary services
Partial hospitalization	Full-day treatment, 5 days per week
	Comprehensive, intensive, structured services
	Hospitalization and outpatient alternative
Temporary recovery or halfway homes	Transitional living supporting sober/clean lifestyle
	Recovering social environment
	Flexible stays
Intensive outpatient	Comprehensive, intensive structured services with off-site living arrangements
	Lower cost and less restrictive than inpatient treatment settings
Outpatient DUI/DWAI/DUID programs	Specific treatment protocols
	Court-referred clients
	Weekly 90-minute group meetings

serves to structure the focus of the therapeutic relationship and contract. However, treatment plans are designed to evolve and change and should be used as a dynamic document. They must be updated to reflect any changes occurring during substance abuse treatment such as:

- addressing problems present along with drug abuse
- exploring solutions for problems
- expanding the patients worldview
- projecting long-term goals
- using measurable objectives
- using a variety of resources and interventions

Treatment plans are also very helpful, particularly when many service providers (e.g., psychiatrist, social worker, individual counselor, family counselor, and nutritionist) are working with one substance-abusing client, encouraging effective and efficient information exchange. Treatment plans identify targets, identify interventions, suggest resources, clarify provider responsibilities, and provide indicators of progress.

How to Develop a Treatment Plan

The foundation of any treatment plan is the data or information gathered in a thorough assessment interview and testing. Assessment and diagnosis, usually conducted together in the beginning of treatment are often performed by the same clinician. Both activities are key parts of planning and the overall treatment plan.

This chapter describes a method initially developed and designed by Richard J. Laban in 1997 to address the needs of the substance-dependent client. Theoretically, Laban drew from medical, psychological, and social models of substance abuse treatment. He suggested that substance abuse/dependency treatment plans could be categorized into common problem domains that reflect the three major models of substance abuse.

Perkinson and Jongsma's (2009) recent publication, *The Addiction Treatment Planner*, is described as the established standard for writing effective and efficient treatment plans in the treatment of addictions. This planner offers new treatment planning and addresses many of the most common presenting problems, including ADHD, borderline traits, eating disorders, gambling, impulsivity, psychosis, social anxiety, and substance abuse. The book contains over one thousand pre-written treatment goals, objectives, and interventions and allows practitioners to track patient outcomes, measure patient satisfaction, as well as the convenience of choosing between newer evidence-based and traditional "best-practices" treatment approaches. A key resource of this text is a sample substance abuse/dependence treatment plan that conforms to the requirements of most third-party payers and accrediting agencies, including Commission on Accreditation of Rehabilitation Facilities (CARF), The Joint Commission (TJC), Council on Accreditation (COA), and the National Committee for Quality Assurance (NCQA).

Over the years the original Laban treatment plan has been modified. Modifications suggested by the authors are reflected below.

- Diagnosis and initial structured treatment plan
- Medical treatment (effects of drugs on the body and brain)
- Psychological considerations (mental health considerations)
- Relationship factors: family, peers, friends
- Readiness for change: denial and spirituality outlook
- Client cooperation and setbacks (relapse possibilities)
- Context of treatment (setting)
- Context of living conditions while in treatment
- Home environment after and during treatment

Problems frequently present themselves in one or more of the preceding areas. Since all plans are considered systemic, it is believed that problems presented in any one area will impact the plans' remaining components. The interrelationships of these areas, or domains, make it necessary for clinicians to be alert and to regularly communicate with each other. It is therefore important for clinicians to work from a systems perspective. They need to recognize the interdependence of services provided to clients.

Case Discussion (*Continued*)

Let us return to the case of our 17-year-old, polysubstance-abusing client Leigh. After her arrest and detoxification, she was admitted to a 30-day chemical dependency rehabilitation program. Her biopsychosocial assessment revealed a history of using alcohol and marijuana at parties and sometimes during school hours.

She has had some moderate school-related problems (e.g., lateness) and a shoplifting charge.

She described a new, well-defined group of peers who "I like to hang out with and party with." Some potential problem domains related to Leigh's situation might be as follows:

Relationship factors: gravitates toward unhealthy, drug-using peers

Home environment: disengaged relationship with father, financial stressors, and feelings of having to choose between parents

Medical treatment: potential dietary problems, disheveled appearance, and poor hygiene

It is important to have an accurate, reliable, and detailed assessment to identify problem areas and match them to the most fitting problem domain. Each problem domain, although often conducted separately, is considered part of the full treatment plan that is both time-consuming and inclusive.

The Elements of a Severe Substance Use Disorder Treatment Plan

Elements considered necessary for an effective severe substance use disorder treatment plan follow:

- Plan Identification (early treatment, comprehensive treatment, modified)
- Diagnosis of the problem
- Symptoms/Behavior
- Treatment/Individual goals
- Treatment Objectives
- Interventions/Action (kind and frequency)
- Contract (Signatures of participating parties, including the client)

Figures 6.2–6.4 provide examples of treatment plans.

Sample Substance Use Treatment Plan: Relationship Factors

Facility   Shady Pines Rehabilitation Center

Client name   Leigh

Diagnosis of the Problem   Client states that all friends drink and use drugs/she will find it difficult to change friends and remain sober/clean.

Symptoms/Behavior Patterns   Client cannot identify sober friends and is reluctant about giving up current group.

Treatment/Individual goals   Client will develop a healthy, sober/clean network of friends.

Client will identify peer changes necessary to avoid drugs and alcohol.

Intervention/Action (kind and frequency)   Client will devise a written plan addressing changes she needs to realize to remain sober/clean.

Initial: Master: Update:

Client Name:

Problem #:

You are at risk for having difficulties getting used to being in a drug-free and structured living situation here at [facility].

Indicators:

New patient in treatment here at [facility] and first time in treatment.

Long-Term Goal:

You will have a satisfactory and rewarding treatment experience at [facility].

Short-Term Goal:

You will understand the reason and importance for following all directions and treatment plan instructions.

Objective #:

You will display the ability to follow all directions and instructions to help you settle into treatment.

Due Date: _____   Date Completed: _____

Methods:

1. You will need to perform your daily assigned house chore posted in the _____ area on the bulletin board.
2. You will need to be at all scheduled group activities as indicated on your daily schedule 5 minutes before the group starts.
3. You will have an assigned buddy for your first week. After this, you will be assigned a new person to whom you will be a buddy. Learn all you can from your buddy this week.
4. You will report to the nurses' station for vital signs for first _____ days in treatment at 7:30 A.M., after lunch, and again at dinner time. The nurse will inform you of any changes in times.
5. You will need to review your Patient Handbook to familiarize yourself with the routine and expectations of _____. Bring any questions to your assigned counselor or any staff on duty.

Services and Frequency Provided:

Group therapy ___ x's weekly; individual therapy ___ x's weekly; activities group ___ x's weekly; therapeutic work assignment daily as assigned; daily attendance at AA and NA meetings; peer feedback group ___ x's weekly; family therapy ___ x's weekly; family program ___ x's weekly; medication lecture 1 x; ___ lecture series daily (indicate)

Client Signature: _____   *Date:* _____
Staff Signature: _____   *Date:* _____

FIGURE 6.2   Initial admission plan.

Source: Information from *Chemical dependency treatment planning handbook,* by R. J. Laban, 1997, Springfield, IL: Charles C. Thomas.

Initial: Master: Update:

Client Name:

Problem #:

You are preoccupied with legal matters and situations outside treatment that could interfere with your need to stay focused on recovery.

Indicators:

Self-disclosure during admission; repeated requests to call probation officer; comments to peers that your probation officer "pushed" you into treatment.

Long-Term Goal:

Stable and self-directed involvement in a recovery program.

Short-Term Goal:

You will understand the need to focus your full attention and energies on the treatment program in order for you to get well.

Objective #:

You will demonstrate an ability to maintain a 70% or greater focus in the treatment program over a 48- to 72-hour period.

Due Date: _____   Date Completed: _____

Methods:

1. You will write down, and prioritize, the five things in your life that continue to cause you the most pain. Discuss with your group these five situations and ask for feedback, specifically if they believe these issues are interfering with your ability to commit to a recovery program.
2. Write about your fears and preoccupations—that is, exactly what kinds of thoughts you have, how they affect your behavior (negatively), and how you have dealt with these in the past. Share with your group and ask them for feedback re positive alternatives.
3. Make a list of all those things you are focused on or worried about that are outside treatment. Next to each item, describe in detail the impact your addiction and behaviors have had on each area. Read this to your group and let them critique your level of honesty into the assignment. What does this tell you about your use and need for treatment?
4. You will be given [_____ days] to get settled into treatment, but will be expected to present a convincing appeal to your counselor and group at the end of this time telling them why you should be allowed to remain in treatment. This appeal needs to be convincing. When done, your group will respond as to how convincing you were, and the treatment team will make a decision.

Services and Frequency Provided:

Group therapy ___ x's weekly; individual therapy ___ x's weekly; activities group ___ x's weekly; therapeutic work assignment daily as assigned; daily attendance at AA and NA meetings; peer feedback group ___ x's weekly; family therapy ___ x's weekly; family program ___ x's weekly; medication lecture 1 x; ___ lecture series daily (indicate)

Client Signature: _____   *Date:* _____
Staff Signature: _____   *Date:* _____

FIGURE 6.3   Sample treatment plan 1.

Initial: Master: Update:

Client Name:

Problem #:

Your difficulty accepting the severity of your alcoholism and not engaging in a recovery program will put you at risk for future drinking.

Indicators:

[client] compares her drinking against others and states "I was never that bad."

Long-Term Goal:

[client] will acknowledge the truth of her chemical dependency as evidenced by active participation in a recovery program.

Short-Term Goal:

[client] will recognize that she needs treatment for herself and that she is chemically dependent.

Objective #:

[client] will verbalize her pledge to follow all treatment recommendations that will help her stay sober.

Due Date: _____   Date Completed: _____

Methods:

1. You will fill in answers for every question in the workbook on "Step 1," including 20 areas that ask for examples of powerlessness and unmanageability. You should answer all areas and share your results with your group. Read the explanation of these terms and ask any staff for assistance. You need to present 20 examples of powerlessness and unmanageability relating to your addiction. Share in therapy group and ask for honest and critical feedback.
2. You will review the progression chart for the Disease of Alcoholism and place a checkmark next to every item that you can identify with. Write down several personal examples for each as well on a separate sheet of paper. Identify the stage of your disease process (early, middle, and late). Explain in therapy group in what stage of addiction you see yourself and personal examples of items checked.
3. Give examples of how your denial system causes you to minimize what and how much you use and to blame external factors for your use. Discuss in the group and ask the group for examples of how they see you minimizing and blaming. When finished, talk about the feelings associated with this assignment.

Services and Frequency Provided:

Group therapy ___ x's weekly; individual therapy ___ x's weekly; activities group ___ x's weekly; therapeutic work assignment daily as assigned; daily attendance at AA and NA meetings; peer feedback group ___ x's weekly; family therapy ___ x's weekly; family program ___ x's weekly; medication lecture 1 x; ___ lecture series daily (indicate)

Client Signature: _____   *Date:* _____
Staff Signature: _____   *Date:* _____

FIGURE 6.4 Sample treatment plan 2.

1. Client will relate in therapy group 10 examples of high-risk situations and/or encounters. Client will describe how she will handle such situations. Role-play and group feedback will be elicited.
2. Client will write a plan stating how she plans to develop new sober friends. This plan will be developed with individual counselor and group feedback.
3. Client will meet with two outside AA members (selected by staff) and talk with them about their recovery and changes they made with friends who used drugs. Results will be presented in group.

Kind and Frequency   Group therapy five times weekly; individual therapy twice weekly; therapeutic work assignment daily as assigned; daily attendance of NA or AA meetings; family therapy once weekly; daily house meetings; daily lecture series

Client signature: _____   Date: _____

Staff signature: _____   Date: _____

External Reviewers of Treatment Planning: Health Care Accreditation Organizations and Managed Care

Clinics, hospitals, and free-standing treatment agencies seeking to qualify for third-party reimbursement must attain and maintain accreditation from entities such as the Joint Commission on Accreditation of Healthcare Organizations (JCAHO). The JCAHO's main purpose is to give its stamp of approval to substance abuse treatment programs (SATPs) and facilities that are providing respectful, ethical assessment, care, and education to clients and their families.

Acceptable care consists of a continuum of services that can provide a range of services extending from pretreatment to treatment to follow-up. To evaluate the adequacy of a program's continuum of care, Joint Commission surveyors (evaluators who site-visit settings to ensure compliance) expect evidence that the program affords access to an integrated system of treatment environments, interventions, and care levels.

When evaluating SATP functions, accreditation visitors/surveyors examine the structures and processes that are used in six areas of performance:

1. Do structures and processes improve the SATP system and care provision?
2. Are leaders providing the structure and program administrative activities that are critical to developing, delivering, and evaluating good health care?
3. Are there safe and supportive environments for clients and staff?
4. Is the atmosphere conducive to staff self-development for the purpose of improving care?
5. What is the quality of the processes by which health care providers communicate and document?
6. Are there appropriate and effective surveillance and infection prevention and control?

SATPs that are accredited and those considering accreditation consider accreditation visits very important. They are taken very seriously and can determine the viability of the organization and its ability to provide care to substance abusers. The JCAHO requires care standards that are divided into five major areas: treatment planning, medication use, nutrition care, rehabilitation care and services, and special treatment services.

JCAHO *requires* that SATP clinical staff write treatment plans. Its guidelines for treatment planning are the following:

- Use diagnostic tools such as the *DSM*5 to identify complex treatment needs of each client.
- Design a program intervention tailored to meet those needs.
- Develop treatment objectives that are reasonable, attainable, and written in measurable and objective terms.
- Determine patient goals for treatment and involve patients in developing their own treatment plans.

It is important to remember that JCAHO is only one of several accrediting bodies, and each has its own set of treatment planning standards. Clinicians should know the accrediting body that guides and monitors their facility and understand all aspects of this increasingly important element of delivering substance abuse treatment.

Insurance companies and managed care companies are insisting that counselors move quickly through assessing the problem, formulating treatment plans, and implementing interventions. Managed care companies function as health care "gatekeepers of services" for the people participating under their particular plans. The "gate" is the point at which insured individuals can begin to access their mental health and/or substance abuse treatment benefits. It is common today for counselors to interact with managed care professionals such as preauthorization specialists, care reviewers, primary care physicians, and employee assistance professionals.

A written treatment plan with complete progress notes can help when accountability of one's services is demanded. If a plan has uniformity, detail, and is written/signed it will gain credibility with lawyers, administrators, regulatory agency workers, and managed care case reviewers. These important nonclinical professionals are very much involved in the treatment of substance abuse/dependency. They often rely on the written word, whereas chemical dependency treatment counselors are trained to rely on the spoken word and nonverbal communication.

Helpful Hints for the Substance Abuse Counselor and Managed Care

- Know the various problem domains for substance abuse.
- Know the behavioral symptoms of addictive disorders.
- Know DSM diagnostic criteria and terminology. (*DSM*5 categories for a Substance Use Disorder)
- Know the limits and strengths of your treatment setting.
- Develop strong treatment planning skills.
- Know the language of managed care.
- Know the procedural requirements of each managed care company your facility interfaces with.
- Document, document, document.
- Use detailed standardized forms when possible.
- Communicate using behavioral language.

Case Discussions

Case 1 (Sandy and Pam).

The appropriate treatment setting for Sandy and Pam should be determined by evaluating the assessment and diagnosis information. Setting selection will depend on the answers to such questions as these: What is the severity of chemical dependency or phase of abuse for Sandy and Pam? What psychiatric symptoms or disorders might be present? Does Pam need detoxification? What *DSM*5 diagnosis might be appropriate? What descriptor category would be appropriate if diagnosed with a Substance Use Disorder? What previous substance abuse and/or psychiatric treatment have the mother and daughter had? If Pam's substance use is considered *severe,* would she be willing to attend treatment? If not, would involuntary procedures be necessary?

Both clients volunteered for family counseling and do not seem to be a danger to themselves or others. The extent of Pam's alcohol and drug use is uncertain, but if she attempts to stop using substances, she might be at risk medically and psychologically. A detoxification program might be necessary to ensure her safety. Pam's diagnosis and her willingness to attend treatment will help direct the setting. If psychiatric problems also exist for Pam, a dual-diagnosis program may be appropriate.

Treatment planning would identify several important problem areas for each family member such as substance abuse/dependency, enabling, and transgenerational patterns of coping. Modalities might include individual, family, and group counseling. Methods emphasizing solution-oriented approaches might incorporate "the miracle question," scaling questions, and discussions of previous attempts at abstinence. Pam and Sandy might also benefit from 12-step meetings and the development of a sober peer network.

Case 2 (Jose and Juanita).

Jose and Juanita reportedly have a long history of substance abuse (alcohol, cocaine, and marijuana). Such long-standing poly-substance abuse can be difficult to treat. Abstaining from all mind- and mood-altering substances might be overwhelming for such dependent individuals. Intensive, simultaneous inpatient or outpatient treatment would be recommended for both partners.

The logistics for arranging treatment for both partners could be complex. What if their diagnosis suggested that they *both* needed separate, free-standing rehabilitation programs? Would the spouses enter treatment voluntarily? What if one partner was willing and the other was not? Who would care for their daughters Sarita and Karen if both attended rehabilitation programs? Does the family have health insurance that would cover such extensive treatment?

Depending on their diagnoses, this couple may benefit from intensive outpatient programs that would enable them to live at home and attend treatment. Family therapy should be reconsidered in light of both parents possibly diagnosed with the severe category of a substance use disorder. Should family therapy continue while Jose and Juanita attend their treatment programs? What would be the benefits or concerns of continuing family therapy? Is it effective to continue family therapy while both parents may be abusing substances? How would the children be involved in their parents' substance abuse treatment?

Treatment planning would be very important for such a complex counseling scenario. Coordinating two separate treatments, while maintaining individual confidentiality, requires considerable planning and ongoing assessment and evaluation. The potential for confusion among treatment providers and

(Continued)

(Continued)

family members is high when many individual and family services are used at once. Providers would need to decide who gets what kind of information. Written documentation would be critical for providing clear, responsive, and effective substance abuse treatment. Getting everyone "on the same page" while respecting individual differences in treatment progression would be a focus for the treatment providers of this family.

CONCLUSION

The substance abuse/dependency treatment industry is a vastly diverse collection of team members who have organized themselves (e.g., research, clinical, administrative, and financial) to provide strategies for those who struggle with substance use disorders, substance abuse, or dependency. Treatment settings described in this chapter provide an overview of the diversity of how substance abuse treatment programs are delivered. New and innovative settings have emerged, as those in the military, to better meet the needs of individuals diagnosed with a substance use disorder. Treatment planning and its place with accreditation bodies and managed care companies continues to play an important role in the changing health care system—a system that has expanded in significance and sophistication.

This chapter presented guidelines to condense information and promote analytic/rational thinking and treatment planning. Study the sample treatment plans and comprehensive treatment settings with a critical eye as a springboard for ones' own professional creativity when working with clients. Substance abuse treatment, the level of drug use and abuse, and diagnostic classification systems such as *DSM*5 rapidly change, requiring constant vigilance in modifying and adapting treatment plans and treatment settings.

SAMPLE TREATMENT PLAN

CLIENT NAME: ROBERT LOPEZ

A. SUBSTANCE ABUSE HISTORY

Robert Lopez is a 38-year-old Hispanic male currently residing with his spouse and three children. He does not appear to be withholding information as he speaks openly and freely about his alcohol, drug, and life situations. He states that he is frustrated and exhausted with his chaotic lifestyle of drug use. Mr. Lopez appears to disclose sincerely, specifically regarding his abuse of substances.

Mr. Lopez states that his alcohol and drug experimentation began at the age of 10 when he experimented with the use of both alcohol and marijuana. He states that his use of both substances initially remained occasional with friends. He states his use of alcohol progressed to weekend use for approximately 8 years when he began consuming alcohol regularly. His use then progressed further from occasional to weekend use and further

still to 3 to 4 times per week, consuming 8 to 12 beers per sitting, while avoiding all types of liquor. He admits to drinking regularly but not abusively for the past 20 years. He does not perceive his consumption of alcohol as a severe problem as he does not feel that he is physically nor psychologically dependent on it. He denies any problems resulting from his consumption of alcohol. Mr. Lopez appears to minimize his problems with alcohol, as he perceives his use of marijuana as the most severe of his problems.

Mr. Lopez also discusses his experimentation with other substances. He admits to using cocaine two or three times in his life, but he did not enjoy its effects. He denies his use of cocaine ever becoming habitual. Mr. Lopez also admits to taking a "roche" pill once in his life but also did not like its effects. There is no progression of abuse of aforementioned drugs..

Mr. Lopez also speaks extensively about his history of marijuana use. He states that his use of marijuana began with friends at the age of 10. Soon he found himself seeking out fellow drug users and ultimately began smoking alone. He admits that his use of marijuana quickly became abusive. He states that he has been smoking marijuana regularly for the last 28 years, and that his use has been daily for the entire duration of its use. He continues by stating that it has been a significant part of his life. He specifies that he smokes on average 20 to 25 joints per day, before, during, and after work (when employed) as well as before bed. He acknowledges his cannabis addiction and admits to several unsuccessful attempts to discontinue his use. He becomes emotional when discussing his failed attempts at sobriety. He states that his use of marijuana has drastically impacted his life in its entirety. Mr. Lopez concludes by stating that he has been abstinent from the use of marijuana for the past month and has found it extremely difficult.

Mr. Lopez states he independently inquired about available resources to assist with his drug addiction. He is volunteering to submit to inpatient treatment and recognizes his needs. He is aware of the consequences of his continued use and fears those consequences but genuinely desires sobriety. Mr. Lopez admits to feeling frustrated and wanting to give up but has decided to give treatment a chance.

B. PSYCHOLOGICAL FUNCTIONING

Mr. Lopez appears for his appointment for assessment in a timely manner. He is casually yet appropriately dressed. He appears sober and lucid, but he displays a depressed mood and affect. He is oriented to time, place, identity, and situation. He speaks with a soft-spoken tone utilizing clear and organized speech. He remains cooperative throughout the duration of the interview and often expounds on questions posed. Mr. Lopez does not display defensiveness or attempts to conceal information. He admits experiencing feelings of depression, anxiety, and tension. He attributes his depression partly to the fact that he has not engaged in smoking and his being troubled by the consequences of his continued use. His facial expressions and posture contribute to his withdrawn appearance. He further displays his distress by breaking into tears while stating that he simply does not know what to do in order to discontinue his drug use and change his life. Mr. Lopez relays a sincere desire for treatment. He appears to have gained insight regarding his substance abuse problem throughout the years and currently displays no denial. Mr. Lopez denies current or previous suicidal or homicidal ideation. He also denies any problems understanding, concentrating, or remembering. There is some evidence of problems controlling violent behavior, which Mr. Lopez also attributes to being largely due to substance abuse. Intelligence and general functioning level appear within the average range. There is no evidence of thought disorders or psychosis currently or in his lifetime. Overall, Mr. Lopez displays a compliant demeanor and a hopeful outlook.

C. EDUCATIONAL/VOCATIONAL/FINANCIAL

Mr. Lopez states that he completed 11 years of formal education. He adds that he dropped out of school due to his negatively influencing peers and a great disinterest in obtaining an education. He admits to spending much of his time skipping classes to smoke with friends and consequently did not learn a great deal. He denies being involved in any scholastic activities. He states that he has not attempted to pursue either his GED or any other type of education. However, he feels that at this point in his life he would like to obtain his GED and recognizes that it would enhance his employment opportunities. Mr. Lopez states that painting is his profession; however, his employment history reveals primarily construction work and odd jobs. History of employment appears to be extremely unstable, which he states is largely due to his extensive use of drugs. He also acknowledges that his use of substance has impacted his desire and ability to expand his education and job skills. Furthermore, he attributes his inability to obtain or secure gainful employment due to his continued abuse of marijuana. He admits that his use of marijuana has prevented him from securing employment, as he cannot pass a drug screen, which is required by many employers prior to being hired. Mr. Lopez describes his employment as part-time employment, working irregular hours. He worked 15 of the past 30 days. As a result of his unstable employment history, Mr. Lopez and his family have experienced ongoing financial problems. Many of his financial problems are also due to the percentage of his finances that are consumed by the purchasing of drugs. He adds that this has caused him to rely heavily on his wife's income for support, as she has been the primary wage earner for their family. His wife is currently employed as a convenience store clerk and is working long hours to support the household. Mr. Lopez denies any need for employment counseling, as he believes that the root of his problem is his addiction to marijuana. He strongly believes if he obtains treatment for his substance abuse problem, the rest of his life will fall into place.

D. LEGAL HISTORY

Mr. Lopez is currently on community supervision for the offense of possession of marijuana. He has completed one year of his 5-year probation period. During his one year of supervision, he has committed several violations due to his submitting positive drug urine specimens. Criminal history revealed one other arrest for possessing a weapon (brass knuckles) six years ago, which was dismissed. He admits to being in possession of marijuana and assumes full responsibility for his actions. He admits to the use of marijuana, while denying any other sort of related activity, such as drug dealing. Mr. Lopez perceives his legal problems as extremely serious and feels that counseling or referral for these legal problems is of extreme importance. He continues to be at risk for further legal problems due to continued use of marijuana. He admits this risk and does not attempt to minimize it. He acknowledges that drugs have been a consistent part of his life despite the fact that this is his first documented drug charge.

E. SOCIAL HISTORY

Mr. Lopez states that he was raised in a traditional and humble Hispanic home in St. Paul, Minnesota. He resided with his maternal grandparents from the age of 6 until he was 19 years of age, while his six siblings resided with his parents. He states he has two brothers and four sisters, of which he is the eldest. Mr. Lopez described his childhood as lonely but happy. He states he did as he pleased, stayed out late and smoked pot, but always managed to keep to himself. He admits that he was given too much freedom, which contributed to his rebellion. Mr. Lopez states that he believes he had a close lifetime relationship with his mother, wife, siblings, children, and friends. He quickly added that his relationships were close, as he perceived them at the time, but realizes at this point that his drug addiction has negatively impacted each of his relationships. He states that his family—that is, his mother, wife, and children—recognize his drug addiction and have asked him on numerous occasions to discontinue his use. Mr. Lopez admits to disregarding their feelings for his addiction.

There is some evidence of substance abuse in Mr. Lopez's life. He admits to having one paternal and one maternal uncle whom he considers have a significant problem with alcohol. He states one of these uncles was an alcoholic and was murdered while he was drunk. He adds that of six siblings, only he and one brother have a drug problem. Mr. Lopez states that he has one brother who drinks 6–12 beers per day. He adds that all of his brothers and brothers-in-law smoke marijuana as well, which has often made it difficult for him to remain abstinent. He relayed his concern for the fact that his family engages in the use of substances as it drastically impacted his decisions. Mr. Lopez states that no one in his family has ever received counseling or treatment, nor does anyone see a need to do so.

Mr. Lopez is currently residing with his wife and three children and has been for the past 3 years. He states that only one of the three children is his biological child. Despite the fact that he resides with his family, he states that he spends most of his time alone and is satisfied doing so. He adds that he tries to spend this time alone because he knows he will be engaging in excessive smoking and would like to do so freely. Mr. Lopez admits that his drug use has negatively impacted his family of origin as well as his own family. He adds that he was in a previous 5-year relationship, which ended due to his drug use. He denies having any other children. Current relationships with mother, wife, and children appear extremely strained. Mr. Lopez admits to dissension between him and his wife because of his addiction as it has impacted all aspects of their relationship. Problems appear to have been persistent for years.

Mr. Lopez states he has only two close friends, both of whom engage in the use of marijuana. He states he spends leisure time fishing, playing basketball, or socializing with family members or friends, which often involve the use of alcohol, marijuana, or both. Mr. Lopez states that his religious preference is Pentecostal but is not active in church or related activities. He states that he attempted to attend church twice per week but only endured for 1 year and discontinued due to his use of marijuana. Mr. Lopez states his current church participation is occasional.

F. PHYSICAL HISTORY

Mr. Lopez denies having any medical problems in his life. There is no evidence of significant medical problems that would require intervention. Mr. Lopez appears to be in good physical condition.

G. TREATMENT HISTORY

Mr. Lopez denies ever having received any treatment or counseling for his substance abuse problem. He states he completed a drug education program before being referred to this short-term residential program. He states it was during this educational program that he learned of the different types of treatment programs and available resources. He states he independently inquired about local resources and treatment. Mr. Lopez volunteered for treatment and recognizes his need to obtain a substance-free lifestyle.

H. ASSESSMENT

Mr. Lopez was assessed as being in need of an intense short-term residential program. Criteria for admission was established by reviewing Mr. Lopez's history and current use of substances and the *DSM*5 criteria for substance use disorder (*severe*), were clearly met (criteria listed in Treatment Plan, Problem 1). Self-admission to 20 years of substance use warranted the need for treatment. SASSI-2 was also administered, which indicated a classification of severe substance use disorder. In addition, various life aspects have been negatively impacted by substance use, including employment, education, family, social, legal, and psychological. *DSM*5 criteria for Substance Use Disorder are met at the dependence level. It is recommended that Mr. Lopez participate in and successfully complete a 60-day inpatient treatment program where he can obtain education about the disease concept and recovery. In addition, he will have an opportunity to integrate family while establishing a support system that will be conducive to a healthy recovery.

Mr. Lopez's strengths include his personal motivation for treatment, personal insight, family support, and legal restrictions.

Mr. Lopez's inhibitors include substance-using associations, unstable employment history, and extensive substance abuse history.

I. TREATMENT PLAN

Diagnosis of the Problem 1: Substance Use Disorder; *severe* (based on *DSM*5).

Symptoms/Behavior: DSM criteria: tolerance as defined by a need for markedly increased amounts of the substance to achieve intoxication or desired effect; withdrawal symptoms are relieved by continued use of the substance; there is a persistent desire or unsuccessful efforts to cut down or control substance use; a great deal of time is spent in activities necessary to obtain the substance, and important social, occupational, or recreational activities are given up or reduced because of substance use. Additional indicators include: self-admission of substance dependence; extensive drug history; family/peer influence; related legal problems.

Treatment Goals/Individual Actions: Understand concept of addiction.

Alter life aspects that will lead to a drug-free lifestyle.

Objectives

- Attain an increased knowledge of addiction/disease concept.
- Gain and verbalize increased insight regarding the severity and negative impact of addiction on self, family, and society.
- Gain and implement knowledge obtained regarding relapse prevention process.
- Learn and verbalize plans to live a chemical-free lifestyle.

Due Date: _____   Date Completed: _____

Interventions/Actions

- You will participate in short-term residential program as directed.
- You will complete required assignments to increase substance use/abuse knowledge.
- You will identify and discuss the things that contributed to substance abuse.
- You will identify and list all those that have been harmed by your use/abuse of substances.
- You will identify high-risk behaviors and situations.
- Develop a plan to effectively cope with high-risk behaviors and situations.

Kind of Services and Frequency

- Daily 1.5-hour educational alcohol/drug lecture
- Daily Recovery Dynamics and 12-step work
- Daily 30-minute meditation
- Daily 30-minutes of relaxation
- Daily 30-minute physical education

- Weekly individual counseling sessions
- Weekly peer group counseling sessions
- Daily Alcoholics Anonymous (AA)/Narcotics Anonymous (NA) evening meetings
- Weekly Big Book study
- Life skills training
- Family focus lesson
- Relapse prevention lesson

Problem 2: Lack of insight regarding the impact of addiction on self and family/strained family relationships.

Symptoms/Behavior Patterns: Self-admission; family admission (wife, mother, children); lack of time spent with family; avoiding family responsibilities.

Goals: Gain insight regarding the impact of addiction on self and family/strained family relationships and begin the healing process.

Reestablish family relationships.

Objectives

- Make amends with family members.
- Improve communication with family.
- Prioritize family responsibilities.
- Spend leisure time in a productive manner and with family.

Due Date: _____   Date Completed: _____

Interventions/Actions

- You will work to understand the impact substance use/abuse has had on your family.
- You will write down how each of your family members has been hurt by your use/abuse of substances and related behavior such as now being home.
- You will learn how to communicate effectively and begin communicating effectively with family members.
- You will create a list of priorities and examine where family should be placed.
- You will work to amend family relationships as part of the 12-step program.

Kind of Services and Frequency

- Weekly individual counseling sessions
- Weekly peer group counseling sessions
- Daily Recovery Dynamics and 12-step work
- Weekly communication skills lesson
- Amend letters to family members
- Family therapy

- Health issues, HIV, STDs lesson
- Anger management lesson

Problem 3: Negatively influencing associations/lack of a support group

Symptoms/Behavior: Self-admission; family admission.

Goals: Avoid persons/places of disreputable or harmful character as required by conditions of probation.

Establish a positively influencing, sobriety-centered support system.

Objectives

- Associate with productive and sober persons.
- Develop substance-free lifestyle.
- Improve self-image.
- Reestablish family relationship.

Due Date: _____   Date Completed: _____

Interventions/Actions

- Recognize and verbalize the importance of maintaining a substance-free lifestyle.
- Establish/rekindle relationships with nonsubstance-using friends.
- Spend quality time with nonsubstance-using family members.
- Attend 12-step meetings, including AA/NA, during and after residential treatment.

Kinds of Services and Frequency

- Daily 30-minute meditation
- Daily personal spiritual inventory
- Weekly individual counseling sessions
- Weekly communication skills lessons
- Daily AA/NA attendance (obtain sponsor)
- Daily Recovery Dynamics
- Daily Big Book study
- Family integration
- Spirituality in Life lesson

Problem 4: Financial, predominantly due to unstable employment

Symptoms/Behavior: Self-admission; inability to obtain/secure stable employment; inability to pass preemployment drug screen; lack of motivation/desire to seek employment; smoking during work thus leading to feelings of lethargy; spending finances to support drug addiction.

Goals: Abstain from the use of substances and seek gainful employment.

Obtain gainful employment while maintaining a drug-free, productive lifestyle.

Objectives

- Abstain from the consumption of alcohol and/or illicit drugs.
- Pass drug screen.
- Keep interview appointments.
- Maintain a positive and motivated outlook.

Due Date: _____   Date Completed: _____

Interventions/Actions

- Participate in and complete residential treatment program.
- Improve communications and job skills to be utilized to secure gainful employment.
- Maintain sobriety to avoid employment threats such as positive drug screens and/or absence.
- Continue attendance at AA/NA support groups.

Kinds of Services and Frequency

- Weekly individual counseling sessions
- Weekly group counseling sessions
- Submit to weekly breath and urine tests
- Job skill program
- Daily personal inventory
- Report to community supervision officer on a weekly basis until employment is secured

Problem 5: Legal

Symptoms/Behavior: Documented drug-related crimes; submission of positive urine specimens.

Goals: Comply with conditions of probation and report to community supervision officer as required.

Abstain from criminal involvement and consequently successfully complete term of community supervision.

Objectives

- Cease criminal activity and involvement.
- Spend leisure time engaging in substance-free activities.

Due Date: _____   Date Completed: _____

Interventions/Actions

- Abstain from substance use and related activities.
- Maintain positively influencing relationships.
- Report to community supervision officer as required.
- Successfully complete community supervision.

Kinds of Services and Frequency

- Weekly individual counseling sessions
- Weekly group counseling sessions
- Weekly office visits with community supervision officer
- Weekly breath and urine tests
- Daily AA/NA attendance and provide verification to supervision officer
- Family integration

Treatment programming during the 60-day intensive treatment combines exercises and activities that include work on spirituality, physical fitness, meditation, 12-step programming, and education and process groups. In addition, cognitive therapy, psychodramas, art, family focused classes, life skills, individual and group counseling experiences are also utilized. Optional Bible study groups and religious services are also made available. A children's educational component is also provided for those who desire the services. The program utilizes an age-appropriate curriculum for those children affected by the family disease of chemical dependency.

Treatment modalities that are utilized in addressing the identified problems will include but not be limited to 12-step work, rational emotive therapy, reality therapy, relaxation, and stress reduction. In addition, the Jellinek model of the disease concept, work on communication skills, self-esteem, and relapse prevention are also emphasized.

J. DISCHARGE SUMMMARY

Mr. Lopez recognized the severity of his addiction upon admission; thus denial, in that respect, never inhibited his progress. He became more knowledgeable regarding the concept of addiction and the impact it has had on all life aspects. In addition, Mr. Lopez came to recognize the problems that have resulted from his drug use, including the negative impact it has had on his family, and he has verbalized his insight. He has formulated a well-organized relapse prevention plan that clearly outlines his relapse triggers, warning signs, high-risk situation, and coping strategies. In addition, Mr. Lopez has made amends with his wife, mother, and children, who were all an active part of his treatment experience and continue to serve as a significant part of his support system. He displayed great remorse while resolving his issues and has accepted responsibility for his actions while working vigorously to continue improving his relationships. Mr. Lopez has identified persons he will need to avoid to prevent being placed in high-risk situations. In addition, he has established a positively influencing support system. Mr. Lopez obtained a temporary NA sponsor and has initiated contact with church ministers and substance-free family members who will assist during his transition into society. Obtaining a sponsor and participating in AA/NA were not expected to be a problem to Mr. Lopez as he stated that there is a group that meets a mere three blocks from his home. In addition, Mr. Lopez has also arranged for employment with a previous employer who was willing to provide him with a secure position with an annual probationary period, during which time he will submit to regular drug screens and be required to attend weekly AA/NA meetings.

Mr. Lopez's community supervision officer and counselors were present at his graduation from the substance-abuse program to display their support, which greatly pleased him. He will be required to continue complying with all conditions of community supervision as well as participating in and satisfactorily completing departmental counseling as part of his aftercare plan. He will be referred to a weekly Relapse Prevention Program as well as three weekly AA/NA groups. He will be reassessed in 3-month intervals for 12 months. His prognosis at the time of discharge is good provided his relapse prevention plan is followed. He has maintained a positive attitude since his admission as well as throughout his treatment, and he has gained tremendous insight and genuinely desires sobriety.

Critical Thinking Questions

1. What would the treatment experience be like without a treatment plan?
2. If society changed in a manner that would allow only two treatment settings, which should they be?
3. In which treatment setting would you be most effective as a counselor and why? Describe personal characteristics, experiences, and skills that would make you effective in this setting.
4. You are an intake counselor and have mismatched a client and placed him in the wrong treatment setting 2 weeks ago. You placed him in an outpatient program instead of residential treatment. What would you do to correct this problem? Include a review of his progress thus far and implications for treatment planning.
5. Do you believe Robert Lopez will succeed during and after treatment? Review his treatment plan, and discuss both the contributors and threats to his success.

Case Study

Ana

Ana is a 37-year-old Hispanic female. She grew up in a traditional Hispanic home of a low socioeconomic status. Her mother was married five times, suffered from mental health issues, and abused alcohol until her untimely suicidal death at age 48. Her father was uninvolved in Ana's life, having little or no contact with her since the age of 5 when he and her mother divorced. She has a total of four siblings, all of whom have had extensive drug and legal histories. Ana is unemployed, but receives social security benefits due to her mental health disabilities. Due to her extensive drug addiction, she often uses her benefit money on drugs and finds herself homeless. She is currently addicted to crack cocaine, smoking being her preferred method of ingestion. In addition to her long-term cocaine addiction, Ana has been diagnosed with bipolar disorder and depression. Her addiction has led to legal problems including theft, assault, and prostitution, which have resulted in multiple incarcerations. She is unable to maintain healthy relationships as she tends to partner with other alcohol/drug addicts. Ana has undergone in- and out-patient treatment several times, usually court-ordered, each time returning to drug use.

Topics to be explored include the identification of a sound treatment plan that will increase the likelihood of long-term sobriety and constructive living; contributing factors to addiction and mental health problems; and medical stabilization. Ana's case reviews the treatment process in its entirety, with an emphasis on treatment planning. It will allow the reader to take an in-depth look at a common scenario of addiction complicated by mental health issues, and examine the contributors and inhibitors to relapse.

Critical Thinking Questions

1. What are some possible contributors and inhibitors to Ana's prior relapses?
2. What would the most appropriate treatment setting be for Ana?
3. What should Ana's current treatment plan address?

Case Study

Andrew

Andrew is a 23-year-old White male. He is a pilot with the Navy. He grew up in a middle-class household. His dad worked as a building contractor and his mother is a stay-at-home mom. He has two younger brothers, ages 17 and 14. Andrew is married to Elaine, who works as a hairdresser. Andrew was arrested for public intoxication on his 23rd birthday. His command was notified and immediately requested treatment for Andrew at the Navy base. Andrew was screened by the Substance Abuse Rehabilitation Program. He was diagnosed as substance abuse and required to complete a two-week treatment program, including substance abuse education, individual counseling, group counseling, and participation in AA meetings. Additional presenting issues include a history of alcoholism in

Andrew's family, and personal bouts of depression. Some of the topics to be explored include family history, peer influence, and career plans related to his stay in the military. These issues and others will be explored during treatment. Andrew's response to treatment will determine whether he is allowed to keep his rank or remain in the military.

Critical Thinking Questions

1. Considering the problems related to this case, what would be your first priority?
2. How does the fact that Andrew is in the military affect your treatment planning?
3. What are your markers of success considering the two week treatment for Andrew?

Treatment of Drug and Alcohol Problems in the Military

Personnel in the military use the same drugs as those individuals not in the armed services. These drugs include alcohol, marijuana, cocaine, heroin, and methamphetamine, among others. Due to the heightened stress issues of combat and repeated deployment, drug abuse during and after military service has come to the forefront. Subsequently, all branches of the military have substance abuse programs. These programs resemble civilian adult treatment for alcohol and drug abuse. Most include medicine, individual counseling, group therapy, education, and 12-step programs. They provide drug information, prevention activities, screening, testing, and full treatment (RTI International, 2006). Soldiers who fail to participate as directed by their commander, or do not succeed in rehabilitation, are subject to administrative separation.

Commanders must refer for evaluation all soldiers who they suspect as having a problem with drugs or alcohol, including knowledge of any convictions for Driving While Intoxicated (DWI) (About the Army Substance Abuse Program, 2005). Research studies concerning the success of programs in the military are scant, reflecting the general lack of comprehensive assessment of drug and alcohol programs outside of the military. A positive note is the involvement of the National Institute on Drug Abuse. NIDA research has recommended a set of principles to prevent and treat drug abuse. Research findings, as these are used by programs in the military in an attempt to reduce substance abuse and its consequences for service personnel (Volkow, 2009).

MyCounselingLab™

Go to Topic 5: *Treatment Setting and Treatment Planning*, on the MyCounselingLab™ site (www.MyCounselingLab.com) for *Substance Abuse Counseling*, Fifth Edition, where you can:

- Find learning outcomes for *Treatment Setting and Treatment Planning* along with the national standards that connect to these outcomes.
- Complete Assignments and Activities that can help you more deeply understand the chapter content.
- Apply and practice your understanding of the core skills identified in the chapter with the Building Counseling Skills unit.
- Prepare yourself for professional certification with a Practice for Certification quiz.
- Connect to videos through the Video and Resource Library.

APPENDIX: 12-STEP, 12-TRADITION GROUPS ADJUNCT SUPPORT FOR CLIENTS IN TREATMENT

Adult Children of Alcoholics (ACoA)
P.O. Box 3216, Torrance, CA 90510; (213) 534-1815
adultchildren.org/

Alcoholics Anonymous (AA)
Central office: Box 459, Grand Central Station, New York, NY 10163
Directories available for the United States, Canada, and international
aa.org/

Al-Anon and Alateen
Central office: Al-Anon Family Groups, P.O. Box 182, Madison Square Station, New York, NY 10010
Directories available for the United States, Canada, and international
al-anon.alateen.org/

Cocaine Anonymous (CA)
Central office: P.O. Box 1367, Culver City, CA 90239
Also listed: 6125 Washington Blvd, No. 202, Los Angeles, CA 90230; (213) 559-5833
ca.org/

Codependents Anonymous (CoDA)
P.O. Box 33577, Phoenix, AZ 85067-3577; (602) 277-7991
coda.org

Codependents of Sex Addicts (CoSA)
Central office: P.O. Box 14537, Minneapolis, MN 55414; (612) 537-6904
cosa-recovery.org/

Co-Dependents of Sex/Love Addicts Anonymous (Co-SLAA)
P.O. Box 614, Brookline, MA 02146-9998

Debtors Anonymous (DA)
P.O. Box 20322, New York, NY 10025-9992; (212) 642-8222
debtorsanonymous.org/

Emotions Anonymous
P.O. Box 4245, St. Paul, MN 55104; (612) 647-9712
emotionsanonymous.org/

Gamblers Anonymous (GA)
Central office: P.O. Box 17173, Los Angeles, CA 90017; (213) 386-8789
Directories available for the United States, Europe, and Australia
gamblersanonymous.org/

Gam-Anon Family Groups
P.O. Box 157, Whitestone, NY 11358
gam-anon.org/

Incest Survivors Anonymous (ISA)
P.O. Box 5613, Long Beach, CA 90805-0613; (213) 428-5599
National organization: (213) 422-1632
lafn.org/medical/isa/home.html

Narcotics Anonymous (NA)
P.O. Box 9999, Van Nuys, CA 91409; (818) 780-3951
na.org/

Nar-Anon Family Group
P.O. Box 2562, Palos Verdes, CA 90274-0119; (213) 547-5800
nar-anon.org/Nar-Anon/Nar-Anon_Home.html

Nicotine Anonymous (formerly Smokers Anonymous)
2118 Greenwich Street, San Francisco, CA 94123; (415) 922-8575
nicotine-anonymous.org/

Overeaters Anonymous (OA)
Central office: 2190 190th Street, Torrance, CA 90504
Also listed: P.O. Box 92870, Los Angeles, CA 90009; (800) 743-8703
oa.org/

Parents Anonymous (use volunteer professionals as resources)
6733 S. Sepulveda Blvd., No. 270, Los Angeles, CA 90045; (800) 421-0353
parentsanonymous.org/

Pill Addicts Anonymous
P.O. Box 278, Reading, PA 19603; (215) 372-1128
pillsanonymous.org/

S-Anon (patterned after Al-Anon)
P.O. Box 5117, Sherman Oaks, CA 91913; (818) 990-6910
sanon.org/

Sex Addicts Anonymous (SAA)
Central office: P.O. Box 3038, Minneapolis, MN 55403; (612) 339-0217
sexaa.org/

Sex and Love Addicts Anonymous (SLAA)
Central office: P.O. Box 529, Newton, MA 02258
Also listed: P.O. Box 119, New Town Branch, Boston, MA 02258; (617) 332-1845
slaafws.org/

SexAholics Anonymous (SAA)
Central office: P.O. Box 300, Simi Valley, CA 93062; (818) 704-9854
sa.org/

Sexual Compulsives Anonymous (SCA)
P.O. Box 1585, Old Chelsea Station, New York, NY 10011; (212) 439-1123
sca-recovery.org/

Survivors of Incest Anonymous (SIA)
World service: P.O. Box 21817, Baltimore, MD 21222
siawso.org/

Workaholics Anonymous
P.O. Box 661501, Los Angeles, CA 90066; (310) 859-5804
workaholics-anonymous.org/

7

Individual Treatment

DAVINA A. MOSS-KING, PH.D., C.R.C., C.A.S.A.C., N.C.C.

MyCounselingLab™

Visit the MyCounselingLab™ site for *Substance Abuse Counseling*, Fifth Edition to enhance your understanding of chapter concepts. You'll have the opportunity to practice your skills through video- and case-based Assignments and Activities as well as Building Counseling Skills units, and to prepare for your certification exam with Practice for Certification quizzes.

This chapter presents an overview of individual treatment and the current strategies that are being used in the field of chemical dependency. The individuals who are abusing or dependent on alcohol, tobacco, or other drugs (ATOD) attend individual treatment for various circumstances. Regardless of the reasons for individual treatment, clinicians are aware that the changes in health care and the approaches to treatment are different than in the past (Smith, Lee, & Davidson, 2010). In the past, insurance providers allowed an individual to receive inpatient treatment for 28 days and possibly an unlimited amount of time for outpatient treatment. Currently an individual obtains permission by the insurance provider for a specific amount of time for inpatient or outpatient treatment that might be significantly less time than in the past (Walker, 2009).

Because of the shortened treatment times, the counselor who assists the client to begin recovery will need to provide swift and efficient counseling techniques (Fields & Roman, 2010). As a counselor in training or as a seasoned counselor, new and more efficient techniques are imperative to accompany the changes in health care and to assist the client toward recovery. This chapter will provide information for the counselor to assist the client in the treatment and recovery process. Other chapters will explore group and family treatment strategies. It is important to note that individual treatment is most successful when group and family treatment are incorporated and when new and innovative counseling techniques discussed in this chapter are used. This chapter focuses on effective individual treatment approaches.

BEGINNING INDIVIDUAL TREATMENT

The first step for individual treatment is the individual's mental and emotional readiness for treatment (Ekendahl, 2007; Redko, Rapp, & Carlson, 2007). The person who abuses substances has an emotional attachment to his or her drug despite the duration of use. This attachment revolves around the individual using the drug of choice to cope with life's difficulties and missing the drug of choice when it is not available. Individual treatment addresses the issue of grief and loss in relation to the attachment from the beginning (Moss-King, 2009). The individual must cease the use of his or her substance and be willing to make a change in his or her lifestyle (Ekendahl, 2007; Lewis, Dana, & Blevins, 2010).

According to DiClemente (2006), an individual transitioning from addiction toward recovery encounters five stages of change: 1) precontemplation (not considering change); 2) contemplation (weighing all options for change and possibly ambivalent); 3) preparation (trying to change); 4) action (changing behaviors); and 5) maintenance (commitment and planning). To make changes and to be mentally prepared for treatment at any level, DiClemente says the individual must be at the stage of preparation, which is the stage at which the individual is attempting to change.

The preparation stage is also interrupting the drug usage as the individual begins counseling, whether in an inpatient or an outpatient treatment facility. The individual must be willing to separate from the drug itself along with any associations. These associations can include but are not limited to the emotional bond with using partners and the paraphernalia associated with the drug of choice (Moss-King, 2009).

The type of treatment the individual will receive depends in part on the resources available in the community and on the level of treatment that might be paid for by an individual's insurance. The American Society of Addiction Medicine (ASAM) identifies four levels of treatment: Level 1: Outpatient; Level 2: Intensive outpatient (IOP) and partial hospitalization program (PHP); Level 3: Medically monitored inpatient (residential) treatment; and Level 4: Medically managed inpatient treatment (Brooks & McHenry, 2009, p. 116). The level of treatment is normally chosen by the insurance carrier using the medical model to base their decision (Smith et al., 2010). Once the decision is made for the level of care, the counselor will need to counsel swiftly and cleverly, with particular regard for the participant's need within the constraints of the length and type of program chosen.

In some cases, individuals are coerced by the drug courts to attend treatment. These drug courts were developed to give individuals with substance abuse problems the opportunity to become clean and sober with the help of treatment facilities, and have proven to be successful (Patra et al., 2010). In other cases, people are forced to the preparation stage because of ultimatums given by family, friends, employers, or significant others. Sometimes the ultimatum is structured as a formal intervention, and other times the intervention is in the form of informal threats to job or family life.

Intervention

An intervention—an action or occurrence that causes an individual to try quitting the use of substances—can happen in many ways. For example, an individual stops smoking because of the educational materials he or she has read, or an individual's employment is in jeopardy because of continuous drug and alcohol use. Another example may be individuals who have been mandated into treatment by the court system and required to cease all forms of ATOD abuse. The process of an intervention can involve all significant people in the individual's life: the partner, children, siblings, parents, friends, supervisors and coworkers, minister, medical professionals, and any other support people in the person's world. It is in the individual's best interest to secure an agreement to seek immediate treatment (Doweiko, 2011). To be successful, interventions are structured to acknowledge the care and concern for the abuser but also to emphasize that continued abuse of ATOD substances has both limits and significant consequences.

Although it is possible to complete an intervention successfully without professional assistance, the level of emotional intensity usually requires that the planning and completion be performed under the supervision of a substance abuse counselor who is trained in the process of intervention. Significant others may need assistance of a professional in planning and completion of this intense situation to stay focused and to remember that there is "no malice" in this process even though a confrontation is occurring (Doweiko, 2011).

Individuals involved in the intervention decide to "break the silence" concerning the individual's behaviors and the effect of these behaviors on everyone involved. It is important to have as many significant people involved as possible in the intervention. Anyone who has ever tried to challenge a person addicted to ATOD substances one-on-one knows the frustration and power of the abuser's excuses, rationalizations, anger, projection, and denial. Therefore, the strength of the caring group becomes powerful. Each individual should bring specific situations or incidents involving the individual to the intervention, with a focus on facts or firsthand observation of behaviors. Owing to the emotions involved and the seriousness of the situation, participants may want to write down what they wish to express. With a large and well-prepared group of people present at the intervention, it becomes very difficult for the individual to manipulate the facts of any situation or to discount the seriousness of the situation.

ETHICAL AND LEGAL CONCERNS OF INTERVENTION: A WORD OF CAUTION   In today's litigious society, it behooves the substance abuse counselor to proceed with caution. As early as 1988, Rothenberg addressed the concern for a thorough diagnosis of an ATOD dependency before an intervention began. Should this be an independent diagnosis? Are there any legal sanctions for a substance abuse counselor who supervises an intervention without this diagnosis? It is possible that some families may use the intervention as a tool to control behavior (Doweiko, 2011). This alone raises some ethical issues, including the individual's right to leave at any time. What if the person being confronted decides to exercise this right? What are the ethical considerations if the individual is not fully informed of this right? It is imperative that all rules and actions should be stated at the outset. In addition, it is vital that all participants are fully aware of their rights and responsibilities before any intervention begins. Once the intervention has been completed the person most likely will begin individual therapy in a setting mentioned earlier.

In summary, no matter what path the individual takes to reach treatment, once the decision is made, effective treatment needs to take a holistic approach. All aspects of the individual's life—physical, emotional, behavioral, familial, and social—have been impacted by the ingestion of substances, and to be successful, treatment needs to address these areas. To facilitate this process, a variety of methods should be incorporated into the treatment planning. Effective treatment should include individual therapy, group therapy, family therapy, physical exercise, healthy nutritional plan, and a supportive environment. This chapter focuses on individual treatment approaches.

This next section will discuss the different individual therapies and the importance of a therapeutic alliance between the individual seeking substance abuse counseling and the therapist/counselor.

INDIVIDUAL THERAPY

An assortment of approaches are used in individual therapy with clients who abuse substances, including cognitive-behavioral therapy (Courbasson & Nishikaway, 2010), social skills training (Lewis et al., 2010), and behavior therapy (Carroll & Onken, 2007). Opinions differ among counselors as to which approach is the most effective. Research can be found in all of the cited literature to support each of the approaches. However, one concept is central to all therapeutic relations: counselor relationship. So before we examine some of these theoretical approaches in depth, it is important to discuss this central issue, also referred to as the therapeutic alliance.

Therapeutic Alliance

The therapeutic alliance, or the relationship between the client and counselor, is an essential component in therapy. The fundamental principle of the therapeutic alliance is listening to the ATOD individual without passing judgment verbally or nonverbally. The relationship is the variable for predicting client response and the counseling outcome. Duff and Bedi (2010) concluded that validation was an important part of the therapeutic alliance; that nonverbal communication and positive regard were both effective toward enhancing an individual's self-efficacy and bringing about a positive outcome. Another part of the therapeutic alliance is the language used by the counselor to create motivation toward behavioral changes in recovery. One therapy that illustrates this best is motivational interviewing, not only because of the type of counselor language employed, but also because of the emphasis on behavior, self-control, and mindfulness. These are examples of direct effect strategies, which are discussed in the following section.

DIRECT EFFECT STRATEGIES

Some strategies have a direct effect on the discontinuation of chemical use. Such therapies that have been effective in the past in individual therapy were aversion therapy, solution focus therapy, and reality therapy, which was later replaced by choice theory. Recent empirical evidence now favors motivational interviewing, cognitive-behavioral therapy, and mindfulness training, along with the use of pharmacotherapy.

Motivational Interviewing

Motivational interviewing (MI) was developed in the late 1980s by William Miller, Ph.D., and Stephen Rollnick, Ph.D. (2009). Motivational interviewing can be used during individual therapy because it is client-centered and directive. Two main goals for using MI are (1) to move the ATOD individual in the direction of making a positive change toward recovery, and (2) to resolve ambivalence by increasing internal motivation and increasing self-efficacy (Miller & Rollnick, 2009). The five principles of MI are (1) express empathy; (2) roll with resistance; (3) develop discrepancy; (4) support self-efficacy; (5) avoid argumentation (Moyers, Martin, Houck, Christopher, & Tonigan, 2009). According to Bandura (1994), the definition of self-efficacy is gaining confidence in one's self. Achieving self-efficacy is necessary for the individual to be successful with therapy and is emphasized at the beginning stage of recovery. As the ATOD individual gains confidence, he or she has hope to begin or continue recovery.

The success of MI in individual therapy relies heavily on the language of the therapist (Moyers et al., 2009). "Change talk" has been described as a technique in which the individual expresses the benefit for change and the hope that change will come in the future. The use of change talk is identified as the desire, ability, reasons, need, and commitment to a plan for change. Mostly, the individual begins to take note of his or her changing behavior in and out of the sessions, which are a microcosm of the continuous therapeutic work (Moyers et al., 2009). According to Vader, Walters, Houck, Prabhu, and Field (2010), therapists who used change talk showed better sobriety outcomes. The participants embraced change as well as sobriety.

The counselor will use certain techniques to elicit change talk and to improve client language to create a positive change as the individual works toward recovery. Those techniques include exploring the addiction; examining past experiences; looking forward to recovery and setting positive treatment goals; examining values along with behavior; identifying the positives and negatives of the current decision to change; and, finally, planning and committing to change (Moyers et al., 2009). Changes can include but are not limited to lifestyle changes and positive thoughts of self that are effective in maintaining abstinence.

Cognitive-Behavioral Therapy

Cognitive-behavioral therapy is "based on a theory of personality which maintains that people respond to life events through a combination of cognitive, affective, motivational, and behavioral responses" (Beck & Weishaar, 2005, p. 238). The goals of cognitive therapy are to "correct faulty information processing and to help patients to modify assumptions that maintain maladaptive behaviors and emotions" (Beck & Weishaar, 2005, p. 250). One of its primary techniques is self-control training. According to the National Institute on Drug Abuse (2009), an individual who abuses substances must change behavior by first altering his or her thinking or frame of reference. Individuals who abuse substances most likely began using alcohol and/or drugs as a means of coping with difficult or stressful situations, and cognitive-behavioral therapy can be used to teach new coping skills and strategies to prevent relapse.

The counseling session could involve the individual learning a relaxation technique, called mindfulness. This technique, which is discussed in the next section, can be used in conjunction with cognitive-behavioral therapy.

Mindfulness Technique

According to Brewer et al. (2009), the mindfulness technique is an avenue to effectively control stress and undesirable feelings that could result in a relapse. Individuals who are in early recovery have perennial impulsive thoughts that can lead to using the drug of choice if the individual gives in to these impulses. Kabat-Zinn (2005) defines mindfulness as "moment to moment non-judgmental awareness cultivated by paying attention in a specific way, that is, in the present moment, and as non-judgmentally and as openheartedly as possible" (p. 108). The individual who abuses substances is learning, through the language of the therapist, to "live in the moment" of the experience by using all senses, including the mind. O'Connell's (2009) study examined the use of mindfulness in an inpatient setting where the patients would "sit" with their emotions. This entailed focusing on a certain part of the body and meditating. The result of the study was that the participants were able to regulate their thoughts. Regulating their thoughts included, but was not limited to, the participant being aware of his or her addiction and the thought process of compulsivity. Although this study was completed in an inpatient residential facility, mindfulness can be an adjunct to treatment at all levels of care mentioned earlier in the chapter. Brewer et al. (2009) conducted a study comparing the effect that mindfulness and cognitive-behavioral therapy had on participants' responses to personalized stress. The results showed that mindfulness techniques were more effective than cognitive-behavioral therapy in reducing patients' response to psychological and physiological stressors.

Regardless of the therapeutic treatment used, some individuals who are involved in individual therapy will require an additive to maintain abstinence so they are able to focus on and commit to change. Certain medications can be prescribed or administered to prevent relapse and increase the quality of outpatient therapy. This next section will discuss medications during the detoxification as well as the recovery phase of treatment.

Pharmacotherapy

Medications can be used in conjunction with individual therapy in two ways. The first is to safely withdraw from a substance and the second is to prevent relapse.

DETOXIFICATION Medications may be prescribed to provide safe detoxification for an individual attempting to withdrawal from a substance. Individuals who are withdrawing from heroin are given methadone and sometimes also clonidine (trade name Catapres). A more recent form of detoxification being used in England for heroin addiction is the rapid opiate detoxification, for which the individual is given lofexidine. More research is needed in this area before it will be used in the United States.

Individuals who are detoxifying from alcohol are given benzodiazepine, or Phenobarbital, to ease the discomfort of the withdrawal symptoms and decrease the chances of seizures.

MEDICATION FOR RELAPSE PREVENTION After detoxification has been completed at a medically managed facility, an individual may continue taking medications to remain abstinent. These medications are measures for relapse prevention and maintenance while engaging in individual therapy.

Shearer (2007) argued that to effectively treat addiction, one must move beyond traditional psychosocial interventions. Along this vein, Mudunkotuwe, Arnone, and Abou-Saleh (2006) reviewed current literature and found that some medications are effective for alcoholics while in the acute withdrawal phase. Other drugs are proving to be effective for the prevention of relapse. Until recently, one of the most commonly used drugs in the treatment of alcoholism was disulfiram (trade name Antabuse). If this drug is taken regularly, the individual becomes violently ill when drinking alcohol. According to Krampe and Ehrenreich (2010), when participants received disulfiram in conjunction with therapy, they developed better coping skills along with a sober lifestyle. Disulfiram has been used for at least the past three decades, but emerging research on new medications has great promise for treating addiction. Gossop and Carroll (2006) report on the use of disulfiram to treat cocaine use. They found it to be an effective agent for reducing craving in cocaine addicts. Similar results were reported by Suh, Pettinati, Kampman, and O'Brien (2006) in their investigation of the use of disulfiram with alcohol dependence, cocaine dependence, and individuals who were addicted to both substances.

Mason, Goodman, Chabac, and Lehert (2006) reported on a study that examined acamprosate calcium (trade name Campral), which was approved in August of 2004 by the Food and Drug Administration. In a double-blind study, the authors observed that people who were addicted to alcohol and who took acamprosate calcium were more likely to remain abstinent than those who received a placebo. Morley et al. (2006) examined the use of acamprosate calcium and another drug, naltrexone, with alcohol-dependent patients. The authors found both drugs to be effective in maintaining sobriety.

Case Discussion

Case 2 (Jose and Juanita).

Since Jose and Juanita have not been able to stay sober past 14 days it is imperative to introduce them to the benefits of pharmacotherapy with regard to relapse prevention. The two admit that once they return to drinking, they continue until they are intoxicated. At this point, discussing disulfiram and educating them about the adverse effects if they decide to drink while taking the medication is appropriate. The discussion would continue with Juanita that disulfiram can be safely administered for individuals addicted to cocaine as well as alcohol.

For the opiate population, the use of suboxone, buprenorphine, and methadone are used as maintenance to sustain recovery (Finch, Kamien, & Amass, 2007). Individuals recovering from opiate addiction may choose to enroll in a methadone maintenance clinic, or they could receive suboxone or buprenorphine from a physician in an office-based setting. A combination of individual and group therapy and self-help groups is recommended as an adjunct to the medications.

Methadone maintenance is primarily administered in a clinic setting and has been in existence for many years as a treatment to cease opiate use. Research has proven that abstinence is associated with higher doses; as the doses decrease, there is a danger for depression and abusing other substances such as alcohol, cocaine, and benzodiaze-pine (Senbanjo, Wolff, Marshall, & Strang, 2009). Another alternative is that suboxone may be administered in an office setting prescribed by a physician. Suboxone is a pharmacotherapy treatment that is a combination of buprenorphine and naloxone. It can be used for detoxification but is intended for abstinence from the use of opi-ates, to mainly control cravings (Fareed, Vayalapalli, Casarella, Amar, & Drexler, 2010; Orman & Keating, 2009). Orman and Keating report that participants who received suboxone had negative urinalysis for opiates. Suboxone is usually recommended for recovering individuals who are fully committed to treatment and a lifestyle change as well. It can also be a physician's recommendation for pregnant women (Wesson & Smith, 2010).

Buprenorphine can also be administered as a pharmacological treatment option for opioid dependent individuals, and is administered in the office of a physician. According to Wesson and Smith (2010), participants who received buprenorphine had negative urine tests and were retained in 28 and 90 day treatment. Buprenorphine has been used success-fully on the opiate population. According to Ciccocioppo et al. (2007), the administration of the drug also reduces alcohol intake among a special breed of rats, so research has yet to determine whether it can be a successful type of pharmacotherapy for alcohol abuse.

In addition to direct effect strategies, broader strategies are required to help indi-viduals gain improved living skills at the same time as they reduce or eliminate their substance abuse.

BROAD SPECTRUM STRATEGIES

In this section we will examine harm reduction, coping skills training, life-skills train-ing, prevocational readiness training, and support groups. The purpose of these strat-egies is to incorporate them into individual treatment and to approach the client holistically while addressing concerns that could hinder individual treatment.

Harm Reduction

Harm reduction has been used in the substance abuse field since the 1920s. Its success has been mostly with the opiate intravenous user and the HIV population in association with the syringe exchange program in the United States, Canada, Great Britain, Australia, New Zealand, Switzerland, Spain, France, and Germany (Des Jarlais, McKnight, Goldblatt, & Purchase, 2009). Most recently, harm reduction has been associated with other substances such as marijuana and cocaine (Hathaway, Callaghan, Macdonald, & Erickson, 2009). Harm reduction includes education about the drug of choice along with therapy to encourage a decision in favor of abstaining or reducing harm. Some therapies that work well were mentioned earlier, such as motivational interviewing, solution focus counseling, and cognitive-behavioral therapy. Harm reduction does not limit itself only to substances; it also includes any activity that can cause harm to an individual. Harmful events can include but are not limited to safe sexual contact, HIV, and gambling, to name a few, and other behaviors that may result in public health risks (Marlatt, 1998). Harm reduction offers an alternative during individual therapy for the individual who abuses substances to reduce their risky behaviors in the event that he or she is not ready to separate from his or her drug of choice.

An organization that specializes in this approach is the Harm Reduction Coalition (HRC), a national advocacy and capacity-building organization that promotes the health and dignity of individuals and communities impacted by drug use. HRC advances policies and programs that help people address the adverse effects of drug use, including overdose, HIV, hepatitis C, addiction, and incarceration. The mission of the HRC states, "We recognize that the structures of social inequality impact the lives and options of affected communities differently, and work to uphold every individual's right to health and well-being, as well as in their competence to protect themselves, their loved ones, and their communities" (harmreduction.org/section.php?id=63). The HRC posts the Principles of Harm Reduction:

> Harm reduction is a set of practical strategies that reduce negative consequences of drug use, incorporating a spectrum of strategies from safer use, to managed use to abstinence. Harm reduction strategies meet drug users "where they're at," addressing conditions of use along with the use itself.

(harmreduction.php.?id=62, reprinted by permission)

The overall goal of harm reduction programs is to also assist the individual to identify coping strategies when faced with harmful events, and reduce risky behaviors. In order for these principles to be effective, the therapist must be a strong supporter of harm reduction and must develop a therapeutic alliance with the substance abuser that is non-judgmental. The next section discusses the therapeutic relationship and harm reduction.

Harm Reduction from the Therapist's Perspective

The harm reduction model is in favor of the individual making positive changes in his or her life. The individual who abuses substances can make positive changes with the assistance of the therapist and the possible therapeutic interventions chosen. Regardless of the therapy chosen, the therapeutic relationship is vital to move the client toward positive changes using the harm reduction model. According to Marlatt (1998) motivational interviewing, solution focus counseling, and cognitive-behavioral therapy are extremely compatible with the harm reduction model. Motivational interviewing has impact because its main goal is to motivate the person toward change. Cognitive behavioral therapy is congruous because it processes the individual's behavior in an attempt to change the thinking patterns that are harmful. Finally, solution focus counseling is congenial because its purpose is to focus on a problem and to create attainable solutions and goals. Solution focus counseling is also beneficial since some of the individuals involved with a harm reduction program may not be involved with individual therapy, but will seek recommendations from harm reduction staff while using their services.

Within the therapy session, goal setting is part of the relationship. One of the principles of harm reduction is to "meet the client where he or she is at." Therefore, setting long-range goals not only defeats the purpose of reducing harm, but it discourages the individual. A more effective procedure is setting proximal goals. Research conducted by Bandura and Schunk (1981) found that short-term goals were effective in self-motivating users toward long-term goals. Therefore, in a harm reduction model, proximal goals (short-term goals) may be developed with the individual during the therapy session or during a brief encounter based on the individual's stage of change or motivation.

Case Discussion

Case 3 (Leigh).

While working with Leigh in recovery planning, a harm reduction model would apply for her protection during multiple sexual encounters at various parties. Leigh does not recognize that being with multiple partners is inflicting self-harm as well as exposing her to venereal diseases and HIV, which constitute both a long-term and a short-term problem. Therefore, harm reduction education is salient to her safety and well-being. Leigh would be given the option of female and male protection as well as instructions on proper usage.

Despite the model that motivates individuals toward change, they will be challenged with handling life stressors without the use of their drug of choice and will need to continuously develop appropriate coping strategies. This next section will discuss the coping skills training as well as life skills training.

Coping Skills Training/Life Skills Training

Any individual who began to abuse substances early in life likely failed to learn social skills. Others may have lost these skills through long years of substance abuse or dependence. Substance abuse clients report that their abuse and/or dependence allow them to participate in situations that require or allow them to not adhere to social skills. As a result, one of the most important skills to be taught is social skills. These skills are needed for life's daily activities as well as work situations. Social skills can be taught through modeling, role play, and demonstration. Various forms of these techniques are available in treatment (Moos, 2008).

This next section will examine the importance of transitioning social skills training to prepare the substance-abusing individual for vocational readiness.

Vocational Readiness

Research has shown that recovery is successful if an individual is gainfully employed post-treatment (DeFulio, Donlin, Wong, & Silverman, 2009; West, 2008). An individual who is involved with competitive employment has an increased sense of self-worth, which assists him or her in obtaining clean and sober relationships. Counselors recognize that vocational issues are in the forefront of the substance-abusing individual's mind and if the vocational issues are not addressed, those individuals are more likely to discontinue treatment. Treatment agencies, however, address vocational issues on a limited basis, if any (West, 2008).

In West's (2008) study, mail surveys were collected throughout the United States. She concluded that 73% of the treatment agencies did not conduct vocational assessments for the individuals in treatment and did not provide vocational counseling as a standard practice. The success of maintaining recovery relies heavily on the substance abuser's ability to work and to fill the day with positive activities; therefore, working becomes a self-fulfilling activity.

In addition to filling his or her day with competitive employment, the person who abuses substances will also need to identify another means of developing a clean and sober social network. One excellent way to do this is to become involved in a social group for recovery. Such groups are Alcoholics Anonymous, Narcotics Anonymous, Cocaine Anonymous, and other self-help groups. This next section will discuss self-help groups and their positive effects incorporating spirituality and self-actualization.

Support Groups

Involvement in a 12-step self-help group is an excellent addition to individual treatment. The need for support is a central issue in recovery. The self-help groups are accessible and cost-effective. As a supplement to treatment these groups can motivate the individual to be clean and sober. It is important to note that success with these groups is excellent when included with individual treatment.

The 12-step self-help groups were established as a means of support for recovering substance abusers. Self-help groups provide peer support in which members understand the feelings and problems faced by a recovering person. Self-help groups provide not only support, but they also provide goal direction, social values that are positive, such as encouraging strong bonds with family, friends, work, and spirituality (Moos, 2008).

Self-help groups can be found on the Internet if a face-to-face group is not available or preferred. They provide on-line support for a variety of issues, including substance abuse.

The Alcoholics Anonymous 12-step model has included spirituality since its inception. The definition of spirituality is often related to a personal experience with a higher power (Mason, Deane, Kelly, & Crowe, 2009). Mason et al. (2009) state that as spirituality increases, craving to use the drug of choice decreases. In their study, spirituality was also positively correlated with self-efficacy. In this study, the definition of self-efficacy is the confidence to remain abstinent.

To take spirituality and self-efficacy one step further, they are both tied to self-actualization being the end result of both simultaneously. According to Maslow (1968), self-actualization is achieved when the lower needs are fulfilled. According to Rogers (1977), self-actualization is the process of moving forward in a constructive and self-enhancing manner when an individual receives positive regard from others and thinks positively of him- or herself. The utilization of self-help groups and spirituality with the development of self-efficacy can lead to self-actualization, which allows the individual to be self-aware of his or her ability as well as potential and take personal responsibility for recovery (Beaumont, 2009; Greene & Burke, 2007).

Now that we have the salient information related to individual therapy, imagine that you are a substance abuse counselor and you have Jodi for a client. This next section will discuss the case study using motivational interviewing, harm reduction, and suboxone treatment.

Case Study

Jodi

Jodi is a 22-year-old Hispanic female who has been addicted to heroin for five years. While on a binge three years ago, Jodi was raped and became pregnant. She gave birth to her daughter Natalie three months prematurely. Natalie is 2 and is currently involved in the foster care system because she was born addicted to heroin and there were no family members available to care for her. She lives with a foster family who has four other children. Jodi is able to visit her daughter weekly; however, for the past year she has visited only three times because she has been in active addiction.

Jodi uses heroin five to six times per day intravenously. She has attempted recovery twice. Jodi attempted an outpatient detoxification program but did not complete the treatment. Jodi then decided to attempt an inpatient detoxification program but she left treatment on the second day. She then began suboxone treatment but discontinued after one month. Jodi then returned to using heroin and has been actively using for the past nine months. She is currently using heroin daily and is prostituting to supply her habit, and is homeless. Jodi has not been honest with her counselors as to where she resides nightly.

Jodi has no contact with her parents. She states that her mother is currently in active addiction using crack cocaine and can't take care of Jodi's 15-year-old sister and 13-year-old brother. Jodi states that her father lives in another town but has had some problems with addiction in his past and is clean and sober now. She states that he went to a halfway house and has never returned to their home town and has not corresponded with her since she was 15. Jodi states that she became so saddened that her father would not contact her that she began smoking marijuana daily at the age of 15 and then began using alcohol

at age 17. She reports that she graduated to heroin at the age of 17 with a friend out of curiosity and became dependent very quickly.

Jodi received her GED at age 20 and had started a Certified Nursing Assistant Training Program at her local Educational Opportunity Center but did not complete because of addiction. She explained that she had time and attendance issues because of experiencing withdrawal.

Jodi has been arrested for prostitution in the past. She is not on parole or probation and has never been involved with drug court, but states that she fears the legal system.

Jodi expresses that she feels depressed all of the time because she misses her daughter and her siblings. When she is not using heroin, she misses the drug as well as her friends.

Jodi says that recently she attempted suicide by taking pills she purchased from a friend. Jodi states that her friends called the ambulance and she was taken to the hospital. She is very angry with her friends for saving her life. She does not foresee recovery in her future and feels that she cannot make changes fast enough to obtain custody of her daughter and assist her siblings.

Jodi had been diagnosed with post-traumatic stress disorder (PTSD) because of being raped three years ago. Jodi has never been officially treated for the PTSD in a group setting or individually.

Jodi has had past employment as a waitress and a telemarketer. She reports that she does not keep a job for a long period of time because of the addiction. Her long-term goal is to be employed as a certified nurse's assistant.

Jodi has not seen a physician for a physical since she was in an inpatient facility. At the time of her medical examination she was underweight, and had irregular menses.

(Continued)

(*Continued*)

Jodi has been treated in the past month at the emergency room for an abscess on her left forearm. The abscess was packed and an antibiotic was prescribed. Jodi stated that she did not take the full prescription and has noticed some redness and swelling.

Jodi's support system consists of her friends who are in active addiction. She has not attended a Narcotics Anonymous group since she was at the inpatient detoxification facility for two days.

Jodi has been referred to counseling from the Department of Family and Youth Services since her daughter is in foster care and she has agreed to attend counseling sessions biweekly.

Jodi states that she would like to begin a relationship with her daughter, and to develop better coping strategies when dealing with negative emotions. Jodi also states that she would like to live a clean and sober lifestyle.

Case Study (*Continued*)

APPLYING HARM REDUCTION

Since Jodi is attempting treatment, and as her counselor you are aware of her attachment issues to heroin and her inability to recover successfully in the past, it is important to provide her with the harm reduction model. She will also be given information regarding addiction issues in families and the long-term effects. This information will be directly related to her daughter, Natalie. Jodi will be given educational information regarding heroin and its long-term physical and psychological effect. Jodi will also be given information on syringe exchange programs in her area, to be provided with clean needles.

APPLY SUBOXONE TREATMENT/ SELF-HELP GROUP

Jodi had attempted suboxone treatment in the past; however, she was not successful. Since she has committed herself to obtaining custody of her daughter and will use individual counseling to reach her goal, suboxone treatment can be considered. As discussed earlier, an individual may be recommended for suboxone treatment when there is a

commitment to treatment and it is used to minimize the craving for using opiates. This form of treatment, because it reduces cravings, also helps the individual to concentrate on treatment goals during the individual sessions. Jodi states that she is motivated, and as a result she will be referred to a local physician who administers and monitors the medication in the office setting. As mentioned earlier in the chapter, the administration of medication and individual counseling is successful if a self-help model is available to support the substance abuser who is in recovery. As a result of this information, Jodi will be recommended to attend a Narcotics Anonymous meeting at least once a week to provide added support while she is making new lifestyle changes. The counseling technique that will be used to assist in these changes is motivational interviewing. This next section will illustrate how motivational interviewing can be used with this case.

APPLY MOTOVATIONAL INTERVIEWING

As mentioned in the beginning of the chapter, motivational interviewing is a counseling technique that can motivate an individual toward a positive lifestyle change. This is done by positive regard and language provided by the counselor toward the substance-abusing individual in session. The result of this positive regard is "change talk." After the initial assessment, you as Jodi's counselor are aware of her desire to be abstinent; however, you also acknowledge her resistance. As you counsel Jodi and give her the opportunity to discuss her substance problem, she reveals to you her fear of change and the uncertainty of the outcome as well as all the benefits of abstinence. As her counselor, you give positive regard by expressing the strides that Jodi is currently making by attending sessions and recognizing her current difficulties but encouraging her to continue with treatment and self-help groups. You and Jodi make a treatment plan to abstain from heroin that is visited each session. Imagine that you are on your fourth session with Jodi and she is still clean and sober. You acknowledge that this is a milestone and continue with encouragement and positive regard. Jodi is then beginning "change talk" because at this point she is recognizing her commitment and plan to a change by self-initiation and expressing optimism toward recovery. During the sessions, you and Jodi are both able to witness the "change talk" and the commitment to change. This commitment will allow Jodi to begin recovery and to maximize her sessions toward reaching her long-term goal of abstinence and obtaining custody of her daughter.

CONCLUSION

Individual therapy consists of creating an environment where lifestyle changes can begin. The beginning is the therapeutic relationship with the counselor and the individual who abuses substances. This therapeutic relationship is a partnership in which goals toward lifestyle changes can begin without the use of the individual's drug of choice. Treatment goals are created in session with collaboration of the individual and the counselor gradually moving toward change to effectively begin recovery. This gradual movement must begin with the substance-abusing individual making a commitment toward abstinence or reduction and discussing attachment as well as grief and loss issues with the counselor to eventually develop coping skills without the substance to provide security. Once the individual is ready to commit to change regardless of the counseling technique chosen by the counselor, the individual will gain self-efficacy toward maintaining abstinence. Along with the confidence gained during the individual sessions, the individual will acknowledge his or her self-worth and move toward self-actualization in recovery.

MyCounselingLab™

Go to Topic 6: *Individual Treatment,* on the **My**CounselingLab™ site (www.MyCoun-selingLab.com) for *Substance Abuse Counseling,* Fifth Edition, where you can:

- Find learning outcomes for *Individual Treatment* along with the national standards that connect to these outcomes.
- Complete Assignments and Activities that can help you more deeply understand the chapter content.
- Apply and practice your understanding of the core skills identified in the chapter with the Building Counseling Skills unit.
- Prepare yourself for professional certification with a Practice for Certification quiz.
- Connect to videos through the Video and Resource Library.

MyCounselingLab™ Exercises

Go to the Video and Resource Library on the **My**CounselingLab™ site for your text and search for the following clip:

Exploring Proximal Instead of Long-Term Goals

After you view the clip, consider your responses to the following questions:

1. Why are proximal goals easier for some clients to pursue?
2. Does the client seem open to proximal goals discussed in this clip?
3. How does Dr. Marlatt facilitate this discussion of proximal goals?
4. Is Dr. Marlatt effective in exploring the steps involved to accomplish goals and the potential roadblocks that might result?

8

Group Treatment in the Continuum of Care

STEPHEN SOUTHERN, ED.D., & BEVELYNNE THORNTON, B.S.

MyCounselingLab™

Visit the **My**CounselingLab™ site for *Substance Abuse Counseling*, Fifth Edition to enhance your understanding of chapter concepts. You'll have the opportunity to practice your skills through video- and case-based Assignments and Activities as well as Building Counseling Skills units, and to prepare for your certification exam with Practice for Certification quizzes.

Group treatment is the most common modality for the delivery of services to individuals and families recovering from substance use disorders. In many settings across the continuum of care, from hospitalization to outpatient counseling, the group format affords efficient use of treatment resources. Group treatment has been viewed traditionally as an essential tool in overcoming denial, minimization, and other thinking errors typically associated with substance abuse, chemical dependence, and other addictive disorders. Psychoeducational groups can provide the means for learning information about addiction, as well as social and coping skills needed to reduce risk of relapse. In the community, most follow-up treatment is conducted in the group format. Self-help groups such as Alcoholics Anonymous cultivate hope in order to assist persons throughout the treatment process with the desire to stop drinking. In the following sections, various group models and approaches will be described for treating substance use and related addictive disorders over the life span and across the continuum of care. We will explore case studies, treatment efficacy, pragmatics of group treatment, continuum of care, group dynamics, and origins of group work.

Examination of the potential benefits and risks of group treatment demands attention to characteristics of persons living with substance use and other addictive disorders. Models of group treatment have been associated historically with both philosophy and continuum of care. Psychoeducational approaches are associated with prevention efforts, especially in school settings. Self-help groups, especially those based on the 12 Steps and Traditions of Alcoholics Anonymous (Alcoholics Anonymous World Services, 2002; Weegman, 2004), are commonly offered in community settings including churches and club houses. Group psychotherapy may be conducted in inpatient, residential, and outpatient settings under the guidance and direction of a professionally trained leader. Although there have been equivocal results regarding the efficacy of matching client and intervention (Weiss, Jaffee, de Menil, & Cogley, 2004), efforts to construct groups according to client characteristics have been central to the development of group treatment.

The best outcomes in the treatment of substance use disorders and co-occurring disorders involve matching clients with stage of change, intervention, or counselor characteristics. Proponents of the therapeutic community and recovery models of treatment are especially committed to hiring counselors who share some of the characteristics and life experiences of the populations they serve (Ullmann & Townsend, 2007; Wormith et al., 2007). Other reviewers indicated that matching the type and intensity of the intervention with the stage of change of the client is essential in efficacy of group treatment modalities, especially among highly resistant offender populations (Gondolf, 2008; Levesque, Velicer, Castle, & Greene, 2008).

In addition, early identification and intervention with at-risk adolescents can disrupt the progression of problems with addictive disorders when the timing of intervention is matched with client needs (Magoon, Gupta, & Derevensky, 2005). Psychoeducational and preventive interventions work best in early stages of progression toward addiction while behavioral and cognitive-behavioral interventions fit highly resistant populations in which the addictive behaviors and corresponding cognitive distortions are deeply entrenched (Gondolf, 2008; Levesque et al., 2008; Magoon et al., 2005). Matching of client and counselor in terms of race, ethnicity, gender, age, life experience, previous involvement in the addiction, and participation in recovery may also facilitate the development of the therapeutic alliance and group cohesiveness (Gondolf, 2008; Kaduvettoor et al., 2009; Quintero, Lilliott, & Willging, 2007; Ullmann & Townsend, 2007). Nevertheless, multicultural sensitivity and competence can contribute to good treatment outcomes even when the life experiences of client and counselor differ substantially (Gondolf, 2008; Kaduvettoor et al., 2009). Inclusion of clients from similar backgrounds in group interventions enhances the vicarious learning and depth of sharing of participants (Gondolf, 2008; Kaduvettoor et al., 2009; Quintero et al., 2007). Therefore group interventions with addictive disorders have generally been based on the matching model of treatment, affording opportunities for clients and counselor to explore shared meanings associated with recovery from the disorder.

EVOLUTION OF GROUP TREATMENT

The earliest attempts to deal with the problems of substance use were fundamentally group approaches. The temperance movement, an international effort to reduce the alleged moral and social decline in society associated with drunkenness, emerged in the early 19th century from Europe and the United Kingdom to influence daily life in the United States (Siegal & Inciardi, 1995). By the mid-1800s, thousands of temperance groups and societies were dedicated to informing the community about the evils of drinking alcohol. The prevailing view shifted over the years from responsible choices in alcohol use to total abstinence and restriction of access to alcohol. The temperance movement crested with the passage in 1919 of the 18th Amendment to the U.S. Constitution, which prohibited the manufacture, transportation, and sale of intoxicating alcoholic beverages. The failure of government efforts to control alcohol consumption and reform social views about alcohol, as well as the rapid growth of organized crime involved in alcohol distribution, led to the 21st Amendment that repealed prohibition in 1933. The temperance movement evolved into other group-oriented attempts to reform society through women's suffrage, humane labor laws, environmental conservation, and civil rights.

The temperance movement introduced key concepts into the group treatment of alcoholism. Excessive and problematic use of alcohol was associated with lack of willpower, moral flaws within individuals, and threats to the fabric of society. The reform movement emphasized abstinence from alcohol intake, largely by controlling access to alcoholic beverages. Many of the Christian reformers who formed the temperance societies and organizations were women who had suffered hardships from drunken and abusive family members (Women's Christian Temperance Union, n.d.). Therefore, the moral outrage produced profound social and legal consequences for persons presenting substance use disorders. Significant stigma was associated with alcohol abuse and dependence. Problems with substance use were criminalized, resulting in incarceration and loss of societal privileges.

Temperance groups were effective in promulgating their views about alcohol abuse. Their well-intentioned efforts at reform applied principles of persuasion (e.g., Schein, 1961) in which group membership, propaganda, and indoctrination or reeducation battled the perceived evils of alcohol. Their efforts to control alcohol use by viewing some persons as weak or flawed and restricting access to substances continue to influence social views and legal policies in the United States. Although the "War on Drugs" failed to reduce or eliminate problems associated with substance use, actually increasing crime and incarceration (WGBH Educational Foundation, 2000), community views on substance use disorders tend to reflect the temperance philosophy in which problems are located within the individual. Abstinence and restriction of access to intoxicating substances remain central goals in most group treatment.

Alcoholics Anonymous (AA) emerged in 1935 from fellowship groups within a Christian education and spirituality movement (Alcoholics Anonymous World Services, 2002, 2007). Similar to temperance groups, AA fellowships emphasized spiritual and educational solutions to the problems of alcoholism. Injured by the prevailing moral model, members of AA groups rejected hierarchy and coercive influence, emphasizing instead group solidarity, collective governance, and self help. Self-help group treatment within AA and other 12-step groups (e.g., Narcotics Anonymous, Overeaters Anonymous, and Sex Addicts Anonymous) shifted attention from personal immorality to enlightened individual choices. Consumption of alcohol or drugs (or engaging in mood-altering addictive processes) in persons suffering from the disease of addiction produced insane thoughts and behaviors from which it was difficult or impossible to extricate oneself. Alcoholics Anonymous advocated turning over one's will and life to a Higher Power in order to escape from a life of despair and decline. Over the years, members of 12-step groups embraced the emerging disease model of addiction.

According to the disease model, initially articulated by Jellinek (1950) and adopted in 1956 by the American Medical Association, problems and consequences associated with alcohol use can be attributed to physiological dysfunction linked to difficulties with metabolism. The proliferation of the disease model contributed to the designation of signs and symptoms of the disease as it progressed. The progression of the disease demanded abstinence and defined several stages in the manifestation of substance use disorders. Today, genetic and biological theories (Goldman, Oroszi, O'Malley, & Anton, 2005; Martin & Bonner, 2005; Young, Rhee, Stallings, Corley, & Hewitt, 2006) explain the pathogenesis of substance use disorders from abuse to dependence in vulnerable individuals.

Self-help treatment groups are typically based on perceptions of shared concerns and characteristics associated with a common disease or diagnosis. Group leadership is shared among recovering individuals. New members are instilled with hope through the examples or models of persons who have maintained abstinence over long periods of time. Self-help group members move from sobriety toward states of serenity and well-being through spiritual disciplines and participation in meetings. However, members of AA and like-minded fellowships experience lifelong vulnerability to the underlying disease and could relapse with exposure to an intoxicating substance. Therefore, self-help groups contribute to rehabilitation through mutual support, structured spiritual disciplines and educational activities, and relapse prevention.

Recent social learning and cognitive-behavioral models of the etiologies of substance use disorders tend to redefine relapse prevention from abstinence to controlled use or harm reduction (Little, 2006; Little, Hodari, Lavender, & Berg, 2008; Marlatt & Donovan, 2005; Marlatt & Gordon, 1985; Marlatt & Witkiewitz, 2002; Witkiewitz & Marlatt, 2007). Social learning and cognitive-behavioral models of substance use disorders assert that abuse and dependence are learned behaviors under the functional control of contingent consequences. According to these models, alcoholism and other addictions emerge initially because intoxication produces euphoria and other powerful effects that are rewarding. In addition, substances may be used and abused to reduce anxiety, ward off depression, or bolster deficient social and coping skills. Over time, tolerance and withdrawal effects increase the likelihood that larger or more frequent doses of mood-altering substances may be required to produce the anticipated positive effects (i.e., positive reinforcement) or avoid aversive consequences (negative reinforcement). As chronic substance use produces increasing limitations for the dependent individual, resourceful family members may relieve the person of daily life responsibilities, contributing to "secondary gains" for sick role behavior (see Bowen, 1974).

Addictive roles and behaviors are maintained frequently by mistaken beliefs and irrational ideas that reflect the thinking patterns of individuals consumed by addictive lifestyles. In particular, persons living with substance use disorders tend to rely on denial and minimization, blunting or ignoring the emotional, behavioral, and interpersonal consequences of addictive behavior. Lacking nonaddictive coping and social skills, they come to rely increasingly on disturbed problem solving and decision making. The learning-based cognitive and behavioral approaches to group treatment involve close examination of expectancies and choices and development of alternative coping and social skills (Marlatt & Donovan, 2005).

The cognitive-behavioral model attempts to prevent relapse by reducing consequences associated with abuse and dependence, leading to harm reduction or controlled substance use in some cases. For example, initial efforts at group treatment for alcoholics focused on self-monitoring to reduce intoxication and training to acquire the skills needed to become a controlled social drinker (Sobell & Sobell, 1973). Harm reduction strategies have attempted to increase mitigating and incompatible behaviors and to revise policies concerning community services and legal consequences of various types of tobacco, alcohol, and drug use (e.g., deRuiter & Faulkner, 2006; Fry et al., 2006; Heather, 2006; Little, 2006; Little et al., 2008; McVinney, 2006; Sobell & Sobell, 2006).

Cognitive-behavioral and self-help approaches to group treatment offer opportunities for changing thoughts and behaviors through interpersonal exchanges. Various group principles and dynamics may be operating; however, these processes are not addressed intentionally. Rather, the group process is viewed as the means for delivering education, training, and support. Group psychotherapy, which tends to be based on psychodynamic, existential, and systems models (e.g., McCluskey, 2002; Yalom, 2005), focuses upon group dynamics, process, and structure as the treatment itself. Thus, group psychotherapy examines some of the complex interpersonal, even intergenerational, influences upon the addictive behaviors that are producing consequences in the present. All groups operate according to some social influence and interpersonal processes. Group psychotherapy (including experiential, analytic, and family systems approaches) views the group as the curative or healing force in recovery from substance use disorders and other addictions.

GROUP DYNAMICS, PROCESS, AND STRUCTURE

Any form of group treatment will involve some attention to basic characteristics of evolving interpersonal systems in which relationships produce meaning. Although information and services may be conveyed efficiently with little or no interaction among group members (e.g., a large lecture class), the presence of more than one person affects the dynamics. Group members can acquire new information and change thoughts and behaviors through observational and vicarious learning. Although they may appear to be passive or uninvolved, even silent members can influence group process. Before describing some of the particular types of group treatment, it will be beneficial to consider basic group dynamics, process, and structure, especially as these elements relate to the needs and characteristics of persons living with alcoholism and other addictive disorders.

Curative Factors in Group Treatment

Groups "supply a mixture of therapeutic factors not available in any other single modality of treatment" (Washton, 1992, p. 508). Yalom (2005) identified the curative factors in group psychotherapy by conducting research using a Q-sort technique with group members. The four highest-ranked factors in descending order were interpersonal input, catharsis, cohesiveness, and insight (or self-understanding). Other factors included interpersonal output, existential factors, universality, instillation of hope, altruism, family reenactment, guidance, and identification.

Interpersonal input refers to feedback shared among group members and between the counselor and client (Yalom, 2005). In this manner, each group member has the opportunity to gain information about one's personal style of interaction. Interpersonal input also confronts the addict's distorted worldview, providing corrective feedback and reinforcement of the new behaviors needed to overcome roadblocks to growth (Vannicelli, 1992).

Catharsis involves the release of genuine emotions, classically viewed as repressed from conscious awareness by ego defense mechanisms (Freud, 1966; Yalom, 2005). In psychoanalytic approaches, catharsis can be viewed as a "corrective emotional experience" in which habitual cognition and repetitive behavior patterns are disrupted, providing opportunities for acquisition of new thoughts and behaviors (Alexander & French, 1946). Releasing strong emotions or forbidden feelings can overcome injunctions learned in dysfunctional addictive families of origin (Hadley, Holloway, & Mallinckrodt, 1993; Sachs, 2003; Vannicelli, 1989). Catharsis permits the sharing of pain and shame of the past with nonjudgmental group members in the safe "holding environment" of group (see Winnicott, 1965).

Cohesiveness is a special quality of well-developed groups in which a member experiences being a part of a supportive system, larger than oneself. Cohesiveness develops over time as members take risks and share disclosures about themselves. The therapeutic factor of cohesiveness emerges in group psychotherapy following a transition stage associated with the expression of emotion, especially negative affects such as anger (Corey, 2004, pp. 97–105). However, cohesiveness or cohesion can refer to the integration of members into a whole in many types of groups, including workplace groups, community associations, and self-help groups.

Insight, or self-understanding, follows from participation in group as a contributing member. Having received feedback, released pent-up emotion (especially shame among addictive persons), and a shared cohesive sense of group identity, a client of group therapy gains sufficient insight to make meaningful changes in thoughts, feelings, and actions. Insight is more than superficial understanding or temporary change. Rather, insight represents a fundamental shift in perspective such that the alcoholic or addict is equipped to make meaning through life-changing choices.

The curative factors arise in groups emphasizing warmth, empathy, and support (Johnson, Burlingame, Olsen, Davies, & Gleave, 2005). The working alliance and self-esteem building possible in cohesive group process contributes to collective well-being and creates a climate for growth and change (Marmarosh, Holtz, & Schottenbauer, 2005). Some group treatments for alcoholism and addiction use excessive confrontation, especially in the absence of the aforementioned curative factors. A recent study (Karno & Longabaugh, 2005) demonstrated the benefits of less directiveness with reactant clients in alcoholism treatment. There must be a balance of warmth and support with strength-oriented direct feedback and occasionally confrontation. The curative factors individually and cumulatively foster the development of a group climate in which meaningful choices and changes arise.

The curative or therapeutic factors are cultivated intentionally in group psychotherapy, conducted by a professional leader in pursuit of individualized and shared goals for group members. However, the curative factors occur in self-help and spiritual groups, as well as psychoeducational and skills training groups. Similarly, there are group dynamics at the core of interpersonal systems. These dynamics may be anticipated and cultivated in therapies or identified in naturally occurring groups.

Group Dynamics

Group dynamics include an array of factors that facilitate or impede participation in a group as it develops from a collection of individuals toward a cohesive interpersonal system. Groups share characteristics with other systems such as families and organizations including boundaries, subsystems, hierarchy, roles, and rules (Agazarian, 1997; Connors & Caple, 2005; McCluskey, 2002; von Bertalanffy, 1968). Group treatment of persons living with substance use disorders is complicated by a core dynamic in which individual group members attempt to recreate their dysfunctional families of origin, typically affected by generations of alcoholism and other addictive disorders (Fox, 1962; Hadley et al., 1993; Kaufman, 1994; Yalom, 2005). According to object relations theory (e.g., Horner, 1991), group members project disowned or split-off parts of themselves based on relationships experienced in families of origin. These parts are projected onto other group members who may reenact conflictual roles. The structure, process, and evolution of the group are affected by the dynamic of "projective identification," resulting in attempts to resolve inner conflicts and concerns by engaging members in external struggles.

Boundaries determine the existence of the group as a system and the bonds or alignments among group members. Initially, the basic task of group treatment is forming the group. The boundaries of the group designate who will be considered members and what will be acceptable forms of interactions. A key characteristic associated with boundary setting is determining whether the group will be open or closed with respect to membership. A related consideration is whether the group will be time limited or ongoing based on planning for termination or setting the number of meetings or sessions.

Group treatment for alcoholism and other addictions ranges from recommendations for lifelong participation in 12-step, self-help groups to brief, specific involvement in psychoeducational groups. When the group itself is not the primary modality of treatment, then the boundaries will be rather permeable, permitting new members to come and go. For example, an inpatient psychoeducational group focused on understanding the disease of addiction may add new members on a daily basis and change membership entirely over a few weeks. On the other hand, group psychotherapy tends to be relatively closed in terms of membership. In group psychotherapy, the boundaries define clearly the patterns of interaction in order to facilitate the emergence of cohesiveness and productive work in the evolving group. Boundaries in group treatment ultimately shape the sense of "us-ness" or shared identity. When group members use "we" talk, there is evidence of the presence of boundaries.

Subsystems reflect specialized boundaries based on particular needs and functions of the group. While shared identity can be an asset to the developing group, senior members, based on longevity of sobriety or length of participation in treatment, address important needs for encouragement and installation of hope. In addition, stable, successful members constitute a resource for modeling and guidance through such vicarious learning processes as imitation (see Bandura, 1999; Kaduvettoor et al., 2009). In 12-step groups, some members represent a subsystem of potential "sponsors," who mentor newcomers to the fellowship. Subsystems occur in residential care when members participate in an overall therapeutic community, as well as specialized groups based on needs and available resources. The boundaries that determine subsystems afford structures, roles, and rules affecting development of formal and informal groups. Unplanned, informal groups such as cliques and collusions undermine the development of group cohesiveness and sense of community. One response to potential problems of group subsystems is the designation of hierarchy, which addresses the issue of decision making.

Hierarchy in group treatment is concerned primarily with leadership. Every system requires some means for organization. Complex systems require some leadership function to maintain order and regulate resources. Groups may have no formal or identified leader. Yet, one or more members can function as leaders depending upon the needs and circumstances of the group and personal characteristics of potential leaders (e.g., power, status, or influence). Other groups have clear leadership, such as therapy groups in which a professional leader organizes and guides the group process. Well-functioning groups maintain a minimum of hierarchal organization or leadership so that all members can contribute resources and receive rewards.

Leadership in group treatment of substance use disorders is an important consideration. Self-help groups, such as AA, eschew hierarchy in general and professional leadership in particular. The 12 Traditions of AA (Alcoholics Anonymous World Services, 2002) represented efforts to maintain anonymity, promote collective or mutual interests, reduce the impacts of individual personalities, and share lay leadership. Typically, the status of "chair" of an AA or 12-step meeting is periodically rotated. AA and similar fellowships rely on written guidelines, read by the chair at the start of each meeting, to maintain order and direction. Professional group leaders in alcohol and substance abuse treatment present a wide array of background characteristics and approaches.

Professional leaders typically have some training and supervised experience in selecting members, conducting groups, and evaluating progress. There are courses devoted to training for group counseling and therapy in most mental health professional degree programs. In addition, there exists some specialized training and credentialing in group counseling and psychotherapy (e.g., American Group Psychotherapy Association, n.d.; Bernard, 2000). Leaders of group treatment for substance use disorders should have knowledge and abilities needed to work with substance abusers, alcoholics, and addicts, as well (Cardoso, Pruett, Chan, & Tansey, 2006). Licenses and other credentials are available to demonstrate adequacy of preparation to offer services to this population. However, there is a criterion among providers of alcoholism and addiction treatment that may be more important than professional credential or training: whether the counselor or therapist is a recovering person.

There is a long-standing tradition in the treatment of substance use disorders that the professional should be involved in recovery from alcoholism or addiction. On one hand, having maintained sobriety or abstinence over a sufficiently long period of time represents a kind of experiential credential that is generally respected in treatment programs. On the other hand, professionals who have no life experience with addiction may be viewed as lacking understanding and received with some caution or skepticism. Conflict between the two approaches to professional preparation arises from the strength of the 12-step model in community, self-help settings, and within inpatient or residential treatment settings. In the recent past, medical and clinical directors of treatment programs were themselves strongly committed to the model and invested in their own recovery programs. Sponsors and peers in AA have been suspicious of some treatment approaches offered to recovering persons including pharmacotherapy and cognitive behavioral therapy. The controversy regarding the background needed to offer empathic services parallels concerns regarding the desirability of matching therapist and client according to cultural similarity. Generally, research has indicated that perceived similarity does facilitate empathic understanding of the counselor and disclosure of the client (Gondolf, 2008; Kaduvettoor et al., 2009; Quintero et al., 2007; Ullmann & Townsend, 2007; Zane et al., 2005). However, a professional leader need not be a recovering person to offer helpful and effective services through the group modality.

Effective group leaders tend to possess the following characteristics: presence in the "here and now," personal power or self-efficacy, courage, willingness to engage in reflection, capacity for self-disclosure, authenticity, stable sense of identity, creativity, enthusiasm, and belief in group process (Corey, 2004, pp. 26–28). There are basic leadership skills as well. Group leaders should be able to empathize, offer core dimensions of facilitative communication, confront discrepancies and incongruence, block harmful behavior, protect vulnerable members, set goals, provide guidance and direction, model effective problem solving and decision making, and give accurate feedback. Effective group leaders involve members in the group process, link individual efforts, identify themes and patterns of interaction, evaluate progress, and terminate the group effort (pp. 32–41). In addition, the nature of group treatment increases the importance of developing multicultural competence in order to respect diversity. Depending on the type and structure of the group, professionals should possess the willingness and skills to practice coleadership with another person. Recently, Weegman (2004) described the integration of 12-step and group analytic approaches to treatment through coleadership conducted by a psychoanalyst and a recovering person.

Leadership and hierarchy represent the core of group formation. In group treatment of substance use disorders leadership may be offered informally by peers and sponsors in the 12-step tradition. Professional leaders complete specialized training and supervision in group work with alcoholics and addicts in order to conduct therapeutic groups. Technicians can be trained to offer psychoeducational and some skills training groups. Group psychotherapy requires the most training and experience in order to construct the group as the treatment itself. Group leaders may be in recovery for addictive disorders or present relationship skills needed to be an effective helper. Recent research has indicated that the interpersonal skills and personal qualities of the therapist contribute more than particular techniques to effective treatment outcomes (Miller, Duncan, & Hubble, 1997). While the leadership role is central to the success of group treatment, there are other roles in the group process that should be examined.

Roles exist in complex social systems in order to respond to emerging needs and fulfill basic functions required to maintain the existence of the group. Roles would ideally be chosen rather than imposed or unconsciously adopted. Some treatment programs use the role of mentor (e.g., the "buddy system" in inpatient settings or the "sponsor" in AA) to orient the newcomer and involve the person in the treatment process. Some groups have specialized roles, such as the "secretary" in a democratic form of the therapeutic community, to perform ongoing duties. Powerful group dynamics can contribute to some members adopting dysfunctional roles. Group leaders must be careful to discourage the evolution of "scapegoat" or "rescuer" roles, which interfere with genuine self-expression and inhibit the development of the group.

Rules are created in social systems such as groups to reduce conflict, respond to recurring concerns, and establish norms for conduct. In leaderless and peer-led groups, rules and guidelines may take the form of written documents to which members may refer for guidance and direction. Professionally led groups augment the organization afforded by hierarchy by introducing basic rules for member interaction. For example, the success of group psychotherapy depends upon the maintenance of confidentiality. Without this rule, there would be little meaningful disclosure by members. Many groups develop a treatment contract in which expectations, rules, and guidelines are specified in order to ensure therapeutic process and promote group progress.

Specification of helpful rules and roles, hierarchy or leadership, subsystems, and boundaries contribute over time to the evolution of a well-functioning group. Although all modalities of group do not exhibit the same linear progression of dynamics and interactions, groups share some features of development.

Stages of Group Development

All groups develop over time from a loose collection of individuals to a social system with shared identity and mutual goals. Therefore, group treatment shares basic social–psychological characteristics with work groups, sports teams, gangs, neighborhood associations, and other systems or institutions. Group treatment is specialized to the extent the delivery of services emphasizes the group process, which changes predictably over time.

The stages of development in group treatment reflect what is known about the group therapy process in general (e.g., Corey, 2004; Yalom, 2005) and about the process of change among substance abusers and addicted people (e.g., Kaufman, 1994). Yalom (2005) described the formative development of the group in three stages. The initial stage consists of orientation, hesitant participation, search for meaning, and dependency. The following stage comprises conflict, dominance, and rebellion. The final stage that Yalom mentioned is characterized by the development of cohesiveness.

The initial task of a group, after group members define the process by which they plan to reach their goal, is to form some type of social connection. During this stage, the group members are basically trying to understand one another. They question how much of themselves they should actually reveal and what level of commitment they should make to the group. The counselor is often looked to as the authority figure in this initial stage, providing structure and direction for the group. Another characteristic of an evolving group is its members' desire for similarity. This is a demonstration of the therapeutic factor of universality. This is part of the preparatory work that will allow the group to delve deeper into the therapeutic process later. A group in the early stage of development is prone to giving advice (Yalom, 2005).

The second stage, which is characterized by conflict, dominance, and rebellion, can be defined as the storming stage. During this stage the group sets up guidelines of how the group should be structured, such as what behaviors are considered acceptable. As a result, a control hierarchy will emerge. Now, when members give advice, they are trying to move into a higher position. Group members often strive to be the counselor's favorite client in the group. This leads to resentment because the client will eventually realize that the counselor does not have a favorite. Anger and resentment that is felt toward the therapist must be addressed in order for the group to progress into the next stage (Yalom, 2005).

The third stage addressed by Yalom, is characterized by the development of cohesiveness. At this stage, the primary concern of the group is to create a sense of intimacy within the group. Where conflict was a negative hallmark of the previous stage, it is avoided in this stage of development. Group members are often so wrapped up in maintaining cohesion that they fail to express their criticism of others. In due course, members will be able to offer constructive criticism to each other. This is a hallmark of a mature group. Once the group matures past a certain point (i.e., a healthy amount of cohesion and criticism), its development can no longer be compartmentalized into stages. At this point, the formative group evolves into an advanced group, which is characterized by the members' "capacity for reflection, authenticity, self-disclosure, and feedback" (Yalom, 2005, p. 345).

Corey described six generic stages in the development of counseling groups. Corey (2004, pp. 79–105) defined three early stages of group development: (a) formation, (b) initial orientation and exploration, and (c) transition or dealing with resistance. There are three later stages in the development of a group: (d) working or cohesion and productivity, (e) consolidation and termination, and (f) evaluation and follow-up (pp. 106–128).

The formation stage in group treatment for substance use disorders is influenced by the type of group and the underlying philosophy of care. Self-help groups, such as AA, do not recruit members but rely instead on the principle of attraction. The only requirement for participation in AA is the desire to stop drinking. Psychoeducational groups, conducted in many treatment settings along the continuum of care (including prevention efforts in school and community), tend to base membership on attendance at scheduled sessions. Vulnerable or impaired persons (e.g., those completing detoxification in the hospital) may be held initially from psychoeducational groups. Disruptive and uncooperative clients or students may be asked to leave if their behaviors interfere with the learning process that characterizes this approach to group treatment. Cognitive and behavioral skills training groups may be somewhat open to changing membership of the group, but they may work best when there is closed or stable membership over the predetermined number of sessions (e.g., 8–14 meetings in many cases). Group psychotherapy, focusing on the evolution of the group as a system for change, requires careful member selection and screening, stability and consistency in terms of schedule and setting, and attention to informed consent or other aspects of voluntary treatment choice. Additional characteristics of group formation, according to type of group and setting along the continuum of care will be addressed in later sections.

Initial orientation and exploration depend upon the efforts of the group leader to supply necessary information and include members in the emerging group process. The group leader provides the initial structure for the group and helps members focus on goals. Rules and roles should be discussed. In self-help groups, structure and process can be facilitated by the reading of documents and reiterating of basic principles and traditions. In group counseling and therapy, self-disclosure and active participation of members, including the leader, will be helpful in establishing trust, the cornerstone of group treatment. Trust issues among substance abusers and addicts are significant because addiction is associated with shame and secrecy. There are major issues with self-disclosure and participation among clients who may be mandated to attend group treatment. Involuntary clients may require additional reassurance regarding rules and norms, especially the practice and limits of confidentiality. Ethical group leadership is essential to the ongoing development of the group.

The transitional stage of group development addresses resistance to change, expression of emotion, emergence of conflicts among members, and ambivalence or perceived lack of commitment. It is not necessary to vent feelings or expose underlying conflicts in all types of groups. For example, psychoeducational groups use lecture and structured discussion to manage conflict and limit extent of participation. Group psychotherapy can flourish with the successful transition through this stage of group development. There may be struggle for control of the group process, manifestation of character defects and distortions of group members, expression of strong emotion (especially defensive anger), and confrontation or challenge of group leadership. The group leader must be resilient, well prepared, and focused on group goals in order to navigate through this difficult stage.

The working stage emerges from the conflicts and difficulties to afford an enhanced sense of cohesiveness or cohesion. Group members fit together in mutually beneficial transactions. They share an identity and make comments indicating their investment in one another. A higher degree of cohesion prepares members for meaningful disclosure, existential relatedness, and emotional exploration (Yalom, 2005). Not all groups need closeness and intensity in order to accomplish its goals. Psychoeducational and skills training groups require sufficient bonding and commitment to ensure optimal attendance and participation. Yet, educational and skill-building groups can be productive. There are some characteristics of an effective working group regardless of type or purpose (Corey, 2004, p. 109).

Working groups tend to have a "here-and-now" focus. There is less storytelling and more direct communication if the working stage has been realized. Effective working involves regular attendance, completion of in-group and homework assignments, warmth and comfort, progress toward goal attainment, and expressed satisfaction with the process. During the working stage, the leader is much less active than in the initial development of the group. Overall, members are likely to exercise assertion and self-responsibility. If members are not involved actively in the process, group members, including the leader, make efforts to include them. The working stage will be time limited in some groups (e.g., a 10-week stress management group) and may continue over many sessions in open-ended group psychotherapy.

As the working stage closes, it is important to consolidate learning, transfer gains to natural settings outside the group experience, and prepare for termination. Since many substance abusers and addicts have experienced some profound losses by the time they enter group treatment, this could be a very difficult stage. In longer groups, the leader may encounter some reiteration of character defects or interpersonal conflicts in order to prolong the "unfinished business" of the group. Some members may have attempted in earlier sessions to wait until the end of meeting to share significant material. Therefore, the group leader must use structuring and other active approaches to bring the group to a good conclusion. In terminating the group, members will examine progress, share feedback, and offer near-future goals. In some forms of group treatment (e.g., therapeutic community or residential treatment), members will terminate by "graduating" from the ongoing group experience. The prospective graduate may apply for discharge, discuss progress and aftercare plans, and receive input from the group.

All group efforts should be evaluated and ideally there should be opportunities for follow-up. When members are discharged from treatment or terminate by some planned process, it is useful to evaluate the impact of the group on particular members and assess the process and outcomes of the group as a whole. This stage can be especially important for passive or minimally involved members, who may need referrals for follow-up care. When members drop out of treatment, especially when they stop attending without explanation, follow-up contacts should be made. Members who are dropping out should be encouraged to share their decisions with the group whenever safe and possible. There may be planned follow-up or booster sessions. Graduates of residential treatment may attend reunions or regularly occurring aftercare sessions. Some residential treatment centers for persons recovering from addiction maintain active alumni groups and follow-up programs (e.g., Betty Ford Center, n.d.). In self-help groups based on the AA model, participation is lifelong. Therefore, the member does not terminate the group experience. "Birthdays" or anniversary dates of sobriety are celebrated as milestones in recovery.

The generic group process moves through stages of development from formation to evaluation and follow-up. Some processes, such as setting ground rules and encouraging participation, are characteristic of any group. Other characteristics (e.g., lifelong AA meeting attendance) represent the special needs of persons living with substance use disorders. Risk of relapse is an ongoing concern in the progression of treatment. In addition to the basic stages of group development, there are several phases of group treatment for substance abuse and addiction.

Kaufman (1994, pp. 179–184) described three phases in group psychotherapy of addicted persons. The first phase involves engagement of individual members in the group process. This phase shifts from education and pretreatment experiences to interpersonal sharing. The second phase is concerned with developing the cognitive and behavioral skills needed to explore feelings, especially anxiety and depression. Cognitive distortions, such as absolutism (i.e., black-or-white thinking), blame, and perfectionism, emerge to block the demands of genuine intimacy and to defend against underlying shame. In the second phase of group treatment for addicts, members focus on building coping and social skills, as well as external resources for ongoing recovery efforts. The third phase of treatment emphasizes the interpersonal and system characteristics of an evolving group. Kaufman recommends *reconstructive group work* in order to deal with transference issues in the group and unfinished business from the past that can contribute to maladaptive behavior patterns or relapse. During this stage, conflicts and patterns of behavior are examined in depth. In some groups, catharsis, abreaction (the sudden expression of formerly repressed emotions or thoughts), or emergence of strong emotions will occur. Generally, the third phase of group treatment affords opportunities to examine character defects and make changes in personality. Successful group psychotherapy for addicts will result in increased ego strength, insight, resilience, and openness to new experiences.

Group development can be considered in terms of stages or phases. The stages and phases are not linear or invariant. There may be cycling through the various characteristics of the group process. From the systems perspective, the group can become more complex and resourceful over time with sufficient leadership and member investment. In well-functioning groups, a kind of synergy in which the whole is greater than the sum of the parts may be experienced. Group development takes into account structure and leadership: generally moving from higher to lower levels of structuring by the group leader. However, group development focuses on the process and content of group systems. There are some special structural considerations for group treatment of persons living with substance use disorders.

Structural Considerations

Process and structure work hand in hand in promoting the beneficial effects of group treatment and minimizing the potential costs and problems. Group treatment for substance use disorders must take into consideration important characteristics of the clients and treatment settings. Some basic structural considerations should be made in treatment planning for substance abusers, addicts, and their families.

A basic structural consideration is whether or not participation in group treatment is voluntary. Given the ongoing "criminalization" of persons presenting substance use disorders (see WGBH Educational Foundation, 2000), the justice system continues to produce a large number of mandated clients for whom involuntary treatment is a reality. For example, sex addicts who have legal consequences may be required to participate in specialized group treatment during incarceration or upon return to the community (Turner, Bingham, & Andrasik, 2000). Persons who receive consequences for driving under the influence of alcohol intoxication may be required to attend specialized DUI classes or AA meetings. Physicians and other professionals who have been deemed "impaired" by virtue of substance use or addictive behaviors may be compelled by physician health programs or their regulatory boards to participate in various forms of mandated treatment as a requirement for ongoing licensure (Fayne & Silvan, 1999). There are many involuntary clients in treatment for substance use and addictive disorders. Added to the basic issue of mandated treatment for involuntary clients are characteristic problems of substance abusers and addicts: minimization and denial of their problems.

Kaufman (1994), a skilled therapist of substance abusers (SAs), observed, "Rigidity and denial are greater in groups of SAs than in any other groups I have worked with except those of chronic schizophrenics" (p. 182). Obviously, clients who deny their problems and resist interventions are unlikely to receive full benefits from participation in group treatment. Because many substance abusers and addicts do not evidence much readiness for behavior change when entering treatment, it is helpful to examine the stages of change and means to enhance motivation.

Prochaska and colleagues (Prochaska, DiClemente, & Norcross, 1992; Prochaska & Norcross, 2001) described stages of change particularly relevant to recovery from substance use disorders: precontemplation, contemplation, preparation, action, maintenance, and termination. Miller and colleagues (Miller, 1995; Miller & Rollnick, 2002) developed some cognitive-behavioral strategies for enhancing motivation to change among alcoholics and addicts. Motivational interviewing (Burke, Arkowitz, & Menchola, 2003; Miller & Rollnick, 2002) has been effective in overcoming denial and resistance while preparing clients to participate in the treatment process. An example will help articulate the importance of motivation as a structural consideration for group treatment.

While juvenile delinquents with substance abuse problems are often treated in secure settings through mandatory participation in groups, treatment may produce iatrogenic effects such as increases in deviant and addictive behaviors, failure to engage in the recovery process, and escalation of anger and violence (Dishion, McCord, & Poulin, 1999; Stein et al., 2006). This group of clients faces many barriers to effective group treatment. Motivational interviewing has been used with adolescent clients in several treatment settings to decrease resistance and acting-out behavior, increase participation in the treatment process, and reduce substance use in general (Breslin, Li, Sdao-Jarvie, Tupker, & Ittig-Deland, 2002; Dunn, DeRoo, & Rivara, 2001; Stein et al., 2006; Tait & Hulse, 2003).

Motivational interviewing (see Amrhein, Miller, Yahne, Palmer, & Fulcher, 2003; Marlatt & Witkiewitz, 2002; Masterman & Kelly, 2003; Miller & Rollnick, 2002; O'Leary-Tevyaw & Monti, 2004) consisted of reflecting for adolescents in their own words reasons to change problem behaviors (Stein et al., 2006). The empathic counselor helps the client examine the decisional balance by providing feedback regarding benefits and consequences of ongoing use and countertherapeutic behavior. Individually tailored feedback heightens the discrepancy between the adolescent client's current behavior and future goals. Finally, motivational interviewing enhances the client's self-efficacy expectations for resisting inducement and provocation, as well as pursuing healthy and rewarding goals. The structural consideration to front-load Motivational Interviewing in group treatment enhances motivation to change, prepares clients for engagement in group process, and inoculates clients against negative and countertherapeutic behaviors (Stein et al., 2006).

Some other structural considerations are related to receptivity or amenability to treatment. Attrition is a fundamental concern in that members who terminate prematurely, similar to those who do not engage willingly in the treatment process, are unlikely to receive benefits or make meaningful changes. In general, women and older clients (36 years of age and older) tend to remain in treatment longer, with most dropouts occurring in the first 90 days (McKay & Weiss, 2001; Monras & Gual, 2000). A major contributing factor to attrition may be failure to attend to multicultural concerns. McNair (2005) offered recommendations for treating comorbid addictive behaviors (now labeled *co-occurring mental health and substance use disorders*) in African Americans, which may also apply for other cultural groups. McNair recommended that treatment professionals determine the cultural contexts and meanings associated with addictive behavior. In addition, it would be important to examine the contributions of racism and discrimination in the initiation of substance use and the pathogenesis of addictive disorders. Prejudice and discrimination can present barriers to accessing effective treatment as well as triggers for relapse. African Americans and members of other minority groups may have comorbid health concerns that demand concurrent attention. There are a variety of structural issues in group treatment for multicultural groups.

Structural considerations including motivation or readiness for treatment and attrition or premature termination affect the likelihood that there will be any benefits deriving from group treatment. Mandated treatment of offenders and involuntary clients raises special concerns regarding professional ethics and pragmatics of group work. The group treatment model offers a variety of treatment options along the continuum of care that can be matched with the needs of diverse clients.

GROUP TREATMENT IN THE CONTINUUM OF CARE

Group treatment can take many forms depending on the setting in which the service is offered and the placement in the continuum of care. The concept *continuum of care* represents a response of behavioral health care to demands for matching patient needs to effective modalities of treatment, frequently articulated by managed care or third party payers (Wong, Park, & Nemon, 2006). The continuum of care takes into account both the severity of the patient's presenting problem and the availability of cost-effective treatment resources. Clinical decision making regarding placement in the continuum of care reflects risk of harm or deterioration in functioning among clients and estimation of the sufficient intensity or *dose* of treatment to produce targeted outcomes (see Howard, Kopta, Krause, & Orlinsky, 1986).

In the acute phase of narcotic withdrawal for a chronic heroin addict, inpatient treatment for detoxification and stabilization may be indicated. However, inpatient care would not be recommended for an adolescent substance abuser, just beginning to suffer consequences of marijuana use. The adolescent patient could be referred to an outpatient counselor for help in clarifying problems and goals. The continuum of care ranges from a high degree of structure (monitoring, scheduling, and restricting average daily activities) to lower levels of professional guidance, planning, and control. Self-help groups have virtually no professional involvement. Therefore, they are lowest in behavioral health care structure and occupy a precontinuum level of care. Outpatient and community treatment programs represent the least restrictive level of professional intervention, whereas hospitalization is atop the continuum of care.

The continuum of care represents efforts to intervene in the course of addictive disease or to rehabilitate those persons adversely affected by abuse and dependence. However, some aspects of group treatment actually attempt to prevent the expression of substance abuse in vulnerable or at-risk populations. Prevention programs attempt to reduce risk factors for substance abuse or increase protective factors. Most prevention groups focus on improving parenting skills or assisting children and adolescents with developmental transitions (Dishion & Stormshak, 2007).

Prevention

A review of prevention groups for children and adolescents (Kulic, Horne, & Dagley, 2004) identified empirically-supported treatments to increase self-esteem, improve social and problem-solving skills, and avoid problem behaviors. Confirming the results of a meta-analysis of child and adolescent group treatment (Hoag & Burlingame, 1997), Kulic and colleagues found that groups provided a natural, developmentally appropriate modality for effective behavior change. The reviewers determined that 80% of prevention groups were offered in school settings. Typically, the groups used the guidance or psychoeducational format, although some counseling or interpersonal problem-solving groups were reported in the literature. Most of the group treatments included 8 to 12 sessions led by a professional over 1 to 3 months. A few studies reported good results by conducting prevention groups weekly over the school year. Only a third of the groups included in the analysis of Kulic and colleagues used a treatment manual. However, manualized treatment is becoming the norm for grant-funded, evidenced-based efforts.

Detoxification and Inpatient Treatment

Medical detoxification is the first stage of addiction treatment for persons requiring safe management of the acute physical symptoms of withdrawal associated with stopping drug use (National Institute on Drug Abuse [NIDA], 2000). It represents the beginning of treatment and should not be considered an end in itself. In the past, alcoholics and addicts completed detoxification under the surveillance and care of physicians, nurses, and the allied health team, typically in a 28-day inpatient treatment program. In recent times, inpatient stays as short as 5 to 10 days barely address the immediate physical needs of patients. Hospitalization represents a window of opportunity to provide treatment when the suffering addict has become aware of consequences. The basic treatment model has shifted from the 28-day hospitalization to residential treatment.

Residential Treatment

Residential care, offered in free-standing treatment centers or facilities operated by hospitals and behavioral health care institutions, has become the primary modality for treating alcoholism, drug addiction, and other addictive disorders. Many caregivers believe that it is beneficial to remove the alcoholic or addict from the demands and contingencies of daily life. Others perceive potential benefits from separating the newly recovering person from codependent family members who could contribute to relapse. The residential treatment center becomes the safe haven for intervening in an over-learned lifestyle or chronic course of deterioration.

The optimal length of residential treatment for alcoholism and other drugs is 3 months (NIDA, 2000); however, many residents will have resources for only 1 or 2 months. Whatever the length of stay, it is very important to address family issues during residential treatment. A convention of residential care involves conducting a "family week" program, every 4 to 6 weeks. Staff members conduct psychoeducational and support groups for spouses, parents, and other family members. The focus of family week may involve an intensive multifamily group in which residents and family members process feelings as they learn about addictive family functioning.

Partial Hospitalization and Day Treatment

Similar to residential treatment, partial hospitalization or day treatment uses predominantly groups for services delivery. As the name implies, the groups are conducted within the hospital setting. There is a high degree of structure with respect to scheduling and goal setting, but less monitoring than the surveillance associated with inpatient treatment. Groups are conducted during the work day, which typically overlaps the day shift of the hospital. Staff and resources may be shared with an inpatient unit or the day treatment program may be self-contained.

Day treatment represents a modality especially indicated for dual-diagnosis patients, possibly after being discharged from inpatient care. Dual-diagnosis patients benefit from the medication management afforded by partial hospitalization. Compliance with medication schedule and other aspects of the treatment regimen can be facilitated by participation in a medication management group, conducted by a doctor or nurse (Anton et al., 2006). Frequently, the mental status of a patient is impaired by withdrawal from one or more mood-altering drugs while attempting to treat an underlying mental disorder (e.g., depression or schizophrenia) with psychotropic medications. Therefore, dual-diagnosis patients need the highly structured schedule, examination by health care professionals, and gradual community reentry provided by partial hospitalization. As the patient stabilizes, aftercare can be tailored to individual needs and family resources.

Aftercare and Sober Living

After patients stabilize in day treatment or inpatient care, they are ready to pursue ongoing recovery. Similarly, graduates of residential treatment programs will require some aftercare to avoid relapse in minimally structured environments such as the home or workplace. Therefore, aftercare represents a plan to provide guidance and structure in the relative absence of physical monitoring.

Some hospitals and residential treatment centers provide aftercare via weekly or monthly sessions scheduled in the facilities. Having follow-up group sessions helps in transfer and generalization of gains realized during treatment. The most common modality for community aftercare is the self-help group, traditionally AA or a 12-step fellowship for another addictive disorder (e.g., Gamblers Anonymous for pathological gambling). However, other self-help groups are not based on the 12-step model, such as Rational Recovery and Moderation Management (Humphreys, 2003; Schmidt, 1996; Trimpey, 1996). Occasionally, churches and religious groups conduct their own treatment and recovery groups.

Some graduates of structured programs will benefit from referral to "halfway houses" or "sober living" environments. A halfway house or sober living arrangement represents an extension of the therapeutic community model of residential care. Recovering persons who reside in a halfway house or sober living apartment find support from peers. They maintain a healthy environment conducive to abstinence and personal growth. There are community meetings to discuss issues and concerns, study groups, and sharing of resources (e.g., transportation to 12-step meetings).

Outpatient Groups and Community Care

Inevitably, graduates of structured group treatment return to the community settings in which they practiced their addictive lifestyles. Relapse is frequently associated with stressors at home or work and through associations with persons who continue to abuse substances or engage in addictive behaviors (Gorski, 1993; Marlatt & Gordon, 1985). Most persons living with substance use disorders would benefit from some ongoing, community-based treatment in addition to regular participation in a self-help group.

Group treatment is ideally suited to meeting client needs along the continuum of care. Based on the severity of the presenting problem and the extent of available family and community resources, the client may require more or less structure in the treatment setting. Individuals who are at risk for severe withdrawal symptoms and other consequences need the structure of the hospital. Persons who are just beginning to suffer some consequences of substance abuse and have strong community and family supports would do best in outpatient programs. The level of group treatment can be adjusted along the continuum of care based on resistance, relapse, and other difficult behavior. Groups provide the means for treatment planning, effective participation, feedback and evaluation, and discharge or graduation. Completing structured group experiences typically prepare clients for optimal participation and targeted outcomes in the next (or less structured) level of care. While certain types of groups are associated with particular levels in the continuum of care, all of the groups have potential benefits in the comprehensive treatment of substance use disorders.

PRAGMATICS OF GROUP TREATMENT

Several types of groups may be conducted in various settings along the continuum of care. The groups share system properties and dynamics, although the process, structure, goals, and outcomes differ. The following sections provide an overview of types of groups, describing their organization and application.

Therapeutic Community

Therapeutic community is an approach to daily living based on specified principles and values. The therapeutic community movement developed in the United States, the United Kingdom, and Europe, evolving from hospital milieus and group homes into a myriad of contemporary forms (see Dodd, 1997; Pines, 1999; Soyez & Broekaert, 2005). In mental health settings, the therapeutic community afforded a model for patient participation in unit governance and decision making regarding member progress. The community also provided the means for instilling healthy values and recognizing contributions. In treatment for substance use and other addictive disorders, the therapeutic community developed to promote a sober lifestyle and spiritual development. Bloom (1997) described the development of a safe therapeutic community through creating sanctuary for addicted trauma survivors. The therapeutic community model has been used to provide group treatment of personality disorders and addictive behaviors in a population of impaired physicians.

The senior author was involved in the creation of a therapeutic community program to address the needs of disruptive physicians and other impaired professionals, who were referred from licensure boards, health advocacy groups, and employers. The participants were identified for referral based on problems with substance use, addictive behavior (e.g., sexual addiction), and unacceptable conduct in the professional workplace. Because physicians, attorneys, and other professionals tend to be intelligent and well educated and to enjoy privileges associated with high social status, they may present self-centered and abusive lifestyles that are difficult to change. The therapeutic community of this program is built upon core values intended to confront the entitlement and resistance of demanding professionals.

The core values of the Professional Enhancement Program included open, honest, and direct communication; inclusion of all members; accountability and personal responsibility; and empathy and support. Community meetings were convened by professional case managers although group members were encouraged to assume leadership roles. Members provided feedback to one another regarding perceived behavior and adherence to community values in the day treatment program, as well as life outside the hospital in the apartments where members live. Typical of therapeutic community, the medical and clinical directors, as well as other group leaders and staff members, were involved in community meetings. Program participants and staff members were held accountable to the value system that organizes treatment.

The group method of therapeutic community is based on shared governance, accountability to others, and expression of healthy values. The application of core values and principles also contribute to the organization and structure of nonprofessional self-help groups.

Self-Help Groups

In most areas of the United States, the major self-help groups are based on the 12 Steps and Traditions of Alcoholics Anonymous (Alcoholics Anonymous World Services, 2002). Alternative self-help groups, such as Rational Recovery (see Trimpey, 1996), developed in part due to the rejection of the spiritual orientation of AA. However, the grassroots movement of AA and similar groups has been phenomenal.

AA fellowships are offered daily in various community locations, especially churches and freestanding "club houses." Although the basic meeting format can take several variations (e.g., speaker meetings), the group process is organized around the reading of program literature by members, who rotate leadership or chairing of meetings. Typically, there are introductions ("My name is Bob, and I'm a recovering alcoholic") followed by a check-in when members offer personal contributions based on their desire to maintain abstinence. Meetings may have particular themes (e.g., gratitude) or focus on particular steps. A curative factor in AA seems to be the opportunity to tell one's story, overcoming years of secrecy and shame. AA members work with sponsors, who have realized long-term sobriety and serenity in the self-help program, to complete step work. As new members grow, they become sponsors of newcomers, sharing their spiritual awakening with others. Meetings, which last approximately 1 hour, close with rituals such as prayer or a group hug.

Self-help groups such as AA provide an opportunity to demonstrate commitment to recovery. Sponsors and other members who are able to maintain sobriety serve as models to newcomers, who are seeking hope and solutions. However, AA members do not give advice or engage in therapy-like "crosstalk" with one another. Rather, they share from their experience of what works. As one of the many slogans suggest, "Take what you like and leave the rest." Self-help groups provide vicarious learning opportunities, as well as ongoing spiritual encouragement.

Psychoeducational Groups

Psychoeducational groups apply principles of teaching to convey important information about addiction and recovery. Psychoeducational or didactic groups exist in most treatment programs for youth and adults. The group format is used due to its efficiency and cost-saving features. Typically, there are lectures with audiovisual aids, demonstration (e.g., a relaxation technique), and discussion. The lecture offers information needed by all clients or stimulates awareness and readiness to learn in newcomers. The Cannabis Youth Treatment (CYT) series of manualized interventions has been advocated as an evidenced-based approach for helping adolescent substance abusers.

CANNABIS YOUTH TREATMENT SERIES The Cannabis Youth Treatment (CYT) Series consists of two phases of manualized treatment, combining principles of motivational enhancement, cognitive-behavior modification, and relapse prevention (Sampl & Kadden, 2001; Webb, Scudder, Kaminer, & Kadden, 2002). The two volumes of information sheets, role play vignettes, diagrams, worksheets, and homework exercises are designed to be used with adolescent substance abusers, especially those for whom marijuana use is producing negative consequences. CYT has been used in community prevention programs, as well as agencies and institutions providing services to youths.

The first volume or treatment manual provides five sessions with all necessary resources to address motivation building, goal setting, marijuana refusal skills, enhancing social support and increasing pleasant activities, and planning for emergencies and coping with relapse (Sampl & Kadden, 2001). This manual presents some common treatment issues involved in conducting the psychoeducational group with recommendations for the counselor or facilitator. Advice is provided for dealing with monopolizers in group, members who present cognitive or perceptual impairment, and those who are inactive or withdrawn (Sampl & Kadden, 2001, pp. 83–92). The initial treatment manual can be accessed at no cost from kap.samhsa.gov/products/manuals/cyt/pdfs/cyt1.pdf.

The second treatment manual (Webb et al., 2002) used in group treatment is also available online at no cost from chestnut.org/li/cyt/products/CBT7_CYT_v2.pdf. This component in the CYT treatment series involves specific focus on cognitive-behavioral interventions. There are seven additional sessions, which build on the foundation of the initial five group sessions. The sessions include problem solving, anger awareness, anger management, effective communication, coping with cravings and urges to use marijuana, depression management, and managing thoughts about marijuana (and other drugs of abuse). This component of the treatment package is aimed toward dealing with real-life problems in the natural environment that may trigger relapse. In addition, there is a focus on dealing with crises and tolerating distress. Additional volumes in the CYT series address transitioning to the community from structured care settings, improving family communication and coping skills, and living drug free in the community.

The Cannabis Youth Treatment (CYT) Series uses an organized psychoeducational skill-building curriculum, even including motivational posters and worksheets. It begins with motivational enhancement, then moves increasingly from coping skills acquisition, to distress tolerance and relapse prevention. The entire program is evidence-based or supported by empirical studies of treatment efficacy. The second volume of resources can be used to incorporate the cognitive-behavioral interventions of relapse prevention.

Cognitive and Behavioral Interventions

Cognitive and behavioral interventions combine the didactic method of psychoeducational groups with systematic training in coping, social, and problem-solving skills. Virtually all cognitive-behavioral interventions can be translated to the group format. Typical cognitive-behavioral interventions in addiction treatment include stress management, assertiveness training, anger management, dispute resolution, problem solving and decision making, cognitive restructuring, and relapse prevention. Free (1999) compiled an array of cognitive therapy interventions for group therapy, including guidelines, resources, and homework materials.

Cognitive-behavioral interventions have focused specifically on cognitions, behaviors, and co-occurring conditions such as depression or other mental disorders that contribute to ongoing problems with substance use and addictive behavior such as eating disorders and pathological gambling (Kadden, 2001; Kotler, Boudreau, & Devlin, 2003; Toneatto, 2005; Toneatto & Ladoceur, 2003). *Co-occurring disorders* is the contemporary term for labels such as *comorbid disorders* or *dual diagnosis,* which could have negative connotations or impose a stigma on the client. In a Substance Abuse and Mental Health Services Administration Publication, *Tip 42: Substance Abuse Treatment for Persons with Co-Occurring Disorders* (Center for Substance Abuse Treatment, 2005, p. 6), *co-occurring disorders* refers to substance use disorders and mental disorders. The disorders may result in psychiatric diagnoses (e.g., Post Traumatic Stress Disorder) or refer to serious symptoms such as suicidal ideation. Treatment for co-occurring disorders frequently involves medication, intensive case management, and individual or group therapy. A goal of treatment is to ensure concurrent treatment of all substance use and mental symptoms or disorders such that the client can benefit from recovery from addictive disorders. Cognitive-behavioral interventions, most of which are evidence based, are used to treat co-occurring disorders. The treatment protocol may be retrieved at ncbi.nlm.nih.gov/books/NBK14528.

It is possible to integrate cognitive-behavioral interventions within a disease model or abstinence-oriented setting. Cognitive distortions, positive expectancies for substance use, and coping and social skills deficits can be addressed in any setting, whether or not there is a treatment goal of abstinence. Behavioral interventions have been combined with pharmacotherapies (e.g., administration of naltrexone for alcohol dependence), producing good outcomes (Anton et al., 2006). Cognitive-behavioral treatment can produce increases in coping skills and decreases in alcohol use; however, interactional treatment, focused on relationships, can produce similar gains (Litt, Kadden, Cooney, & Kabela, 2003). Cognitive and behavioral strategies can be combined to produce effective treatment packages for a variety of clients. The Seeking Safety model for treating PTSD and substance use disorders, especially in women and other vulnerable populations, is an excellent example of cognitive-behavioral intervention for co-occuring substance use and mental disorders.

SEEKING SAFETY   An evidenced-based, manualized cognitive-behavioral intervention for abused women presenting post-traumatic stress disorder and substance use disorder was constructed through federally funded research. The resulting program, Seeking Safety (Najavits, 2002, 2003), incorporates several cognitive-behavioral components into a treatment package. The evidence-based program builds safe coping skills to reduce risk of relapse and improve interpersonal functioning in dual diagnosis trauma survivors, especially women. The treatment program can be conducted in groups over 25 sessions including cognitive, behavioral, interpersonal, and case management objectives. The Seeking Safety program offers structure by means of explicit treatment guidelines, monitoring of client and therapist adherence, focus on skill building, and use of handouts and resources. The topics are relevant to trauma and addiction recovery. Some of the topics include Introduction to Treatment, Honesty, Community Resources, Setting Boundaries in Relationships, Taking Good Care of Yourself, Coping with Triggers, Recovery Thinking, and Creating.

Women recover from traumatic violence and addictive disorders in many different ways (Stenius & Veysey, 2005). Some potentially effective programs can be dehumanizing or retraumatizing. Vulnerable populations who present co-occurring disorders need safety and caring service providers who have experience dealing with the problems of trauma and addiction. Intensive monitoring and case management are needed to maintain treatment gains for complex co-occurring disorders (Rush, Dennis, Scott, Castel, & Funk, 2008). Interventions targeting specific psychiatric disorders and symptoms among chemically dependent persons can dramatically improve treatment outcomes and maintenance of gains at long-term follow-ups (Chi & Weisner, 2008; McCay & Weiss, 2001). Therefore, evidence-based cognitive-behavioral treatment can be individualized and followed up by case management monitoring generalization and maintenance of treatment benefits. Najavits (2009) reviewed the characteristics of psychotherapies for co-occurring trauma and substance use disorders.

Najavits's (2009) review of published models for concurrent treatment of co-occurring trauma and substance use disorders identified some general themes and program development implications. While many models have been developed only a few have been subjected to systematic empirical review and validation. Most treatments have demonstrated some positive impacts. Although it is unclear whether or not specialized treatment for women or type of underlying trauma is required, input from women and personal accounts emphasized tailoring of treatment for unique concerns. Najavits concluded that the culture of treatment should be gender sensitive, incorporating the lived experiences of women living with trauma and addiction. She also advocated increased access to treatment services for these vulnerable populations.

Seeking Safety and other cognitive-behavioral interventions emphasize the use of treatment manuals and skill-building exercises in order to demonstrate effectiveness. Blending psychoeducational materials and skills training, the interventions target particular behaviors and pursue measurable outcomes. Cognitive-behavioral approaches have been at the forefront of the movement for evidence-based practice (e.g., APA Presidential Task Force on Evidence-Based Practice, 2006). Another cognitive-behavioral approach, motivational interviewing (MI) has become a major model for treating resistant clients and others not ready for change in intensive, abstinence-based programs.

MOTIVATIONAL INTERVIEWING Traditionally, motivational interviewing has been used in individual therapy; however, recent research (Michael, Curtin, Kirkley, Jones, & Harris, 2006; Velasquez, Stephens, & Ingersoll, 2006) has examined the use of motivational interviewing in the group format. MI operates under the assumption that the client possesses the required element for change. The job of the therapist is to fashion an environment where the client's motivation and commitment to change can blossom and to help the client resolve the ambivalence toward change. The primary motivation interviewing principles can be summed up by the acronym FRAMES: feedback, responsibility, advice, menu of options, empathy, and self-efficacy (Little et al., 2008). Another principle of MI is the reduction of resistance so that the client will be able to convey his or her reasons for wanting to change. The attainment of this goal allows for the internal motivation of the client to become the primary precipitant of change. Other principles that the therapist strives for is to develop discrepancy, go along with resistance, convey empathy, and to support self-efficacy (Velasquez et al., 2006).

There are four primary clinical strategies used in MI: open questions, affirmations, reflections, and summaries (OARS). These strategies are used to encourage dialogue, communicate respect, convey empathy, and strengthen motivation. Another tactic used in MI is change talk. This can be accomplished by getting the client to examine the costs and benefits of changing their behavior and by exploring their inclination to change. There are four types of change talk: desire, ability, need, and reason. The desire to make a change is hallmarked by the words "I want." When clients realize that they have the ability to make a change, they tend to use words such as "I can." The recognition of a need to change is marked by "I have to" or "I need to" statements. Change talk about reasons for engaging in addictive behavior answers the question of "Why is change necessary?" The process of change talk can be illustrated by the following: Desire + Ability + Need + Reasons → Commitment to Change → Positive Change Outcome (Velasquez et al., 2006).

One of the primary goals of motivational interviewing is the reduction of ambivalence. One way to work toward this is to have the group discuss the inconsistencies between their present behavior and the behavior they desire. This aids in the development of change talk and serves as a stimulus for change process. The discussion of the clients' goals is a key to unlocking their internal motivation. Another activity that Michael et al. (2006) note is to get the group to discuss extensively the costs and benefits of their addiction. This form of self-evaluation aids the group members in determining if their current behavior is helping them to achieve their goals.

Before any type of treatment plan can be implemented, the client's enthusiasm toward change must be taken into consideration. The process for change can begin only if the person has a desire to change. The client may voluntarily seek out a change in their behavior, or may be coerced into treatment by an authoritative figure. Freyer et al. (2005) noted the difference between behavior change motivation and help-seeking motivation. A person's desire to seek out help for addiction is independent from the desire to actually change his or her behavior. For instance, it is likely that an individual, who is coerced into treatment by a court order or a family member, will have a high help-seeking motivation, but have a significantly lower motivation for behavior change (Freyer et al.). This is translated into low internal motivation, which is correlated to higher rates of recidivism (Brocato & Wagner, 2008). A negative correlation has been found between the severity of the addiction and the level of both types of motivation (Freyer et al.).

The transtheoretical model (TTM) of change is especially helpful with populations who are in the early stages of change, and have been characterized as having a lack of motivation, being noncompliant, and not accepting of help. Behavior change is a process that involves six stages: precontemplation, contemplation, preparation, action, maintenance, and termination (Prochaska, 2008; D'Sylva, Graffam, Hardcastle, & Shinkfield, 2010). An individual in the precontemplation stage has no intention of making a change anytime in the near future or by a person who has tried to change many times. Clients in this stage are usually noncompliant and resistant toward treatment. Self-monitoring of one's own behavior is the hallmark of the transition from this stage into contemplation (Brocato & Wagner, 2008), which is characterized by the intention to change one's behavior within the next six months. For people suffering from an addiction, the ambivalent relationship that they have with their substance of choice is evident in the contemplation stage. When action is to be taken within the next month, the individual is in the preparation stage of change. Persons in this stage typically have a plan of action ready for implementation. Once their plan is implemented and behavior modifications have been taking place for at least six months, the individual is recognized as being in the action stage. The maintenance stage is one of preventing relapse. It is in this stage that the temptation to delve back into the addiction becomes less intense (Prochaska) and internal motivation is higher. In both of these stages, self-reinforcement is an important factor in achieving their goal

(Brocato & Wagner). When the client reaches a place where temptation is no longer an issue, the new behavior has become second nature (Prochaska).

When entering into a group therapy setting, one of the first initiatives is to establish rapport with the clients (Michael et al., 2006). Yalom (2005) described movement toward cohesion as the key to a successful group. The cohesion of the group takes precedence over the individual needs of clients. In some cases, it may be necessary to remove members from the group if they pose a continued threat to the group's cohesion. It is important to note that if any type of change occurs, the clients will institute it. OPEN is an acronym that some counselors find helpful in starting a group. First, they *open* the group by stating the purpose, which is usually to gain knowledge about the members' thoughts, concerns, and choices. Next, it is essential to emphasize *personal choice*. The counselor provides an environment that is respectful and *encouraging* for all members. Finally, the fact that MI exemplifies a *non-confrontational approach* is stated. The collaborative nature of the group is another focal point (Michael et al.).

Once the groundwork for the group has been laid, it is important for the counselor to discuss using collaborative language so as to not appear as being superior to the group members. Along with this, counselors should practice reflective listening. Such reflections can be used to direct individual's comments to the whole group. The skill of reflective listening can also be used to combat resistance in the group by selectively highlighting the most positive parts. The pertinent comments of the client can be reinforced through the use of group summaries, which also reinforce change talk. More research is needed to determine the strengths and limitations of MI used in the group setting (Michael et al., 2006).

MI can be used to enhance other forms of treatment or as a stand-alone treatment for substance abuse. Some treatment programs may not complement MI. For instance, MI would not be suitable for use with a program that promotes abstinence as a principle component because MI employs successive approximations in order to build self-efficacy. Other aspects of MI are collaboration, evocation, and the conveyance of empathy and respect for autonomy. In the group format, learning opportunities occur when members disclose their views and experiences. To provide the most conducive environment for change, the counselor works to provide feedback in a positive way, promotes collaboration and respect, and redirects less helpful comments (Velasquez et al., 2006).

For individuals who have low behavior change motivation, a harm reduction therapy group may be helpful. It serves as a way to ease the client into treatment. Individual goals are set that support self-efficacy. This initiates the change process. Within the harm reduction group, the members support each other and are encouraged to talk about any concerns that they have. Such groups have a come as you are policy (Little, 2006; Little et al., 2008) and do not place the stipulation of change as a requirement for continued membership in the group. That being said, there are, however, four goals for members of the group: "(1) to learn more about their relationship with drugs; (2) to understand the interaction of drug use with other life issues of concern to them; (3) to make decisions about change; and (4) to use the group's help to make changes" (Little, p. 72).

By participating in group therapy, members are able to hear about the consequences of alcohol and drug use without actually having to experience them. Group members are able to appreciate the successful change efforts of their peers. Abstinence is viewed as only one form of success. In harm reduction, more emphasis is placed on the process and behavior than on the outcome or the drug use. The job of the therapist is to be a facilitator of self-exploration, decision making, and behavior change (Little, 2006). However, all conversation is to be member-driven. Little et al. (2008) adopted a drop-in format for their harm reduction group. This is more accommodating for clients with co-occurring disorders who are prone to not keeping appointments. It also lowers resistance to therapy because the client maintains authority.

Group Psychotherapy

Group psychotherapy was based historically on psychoanalytic and existential approaches to treatment (Yalom, 2005). Specialized group interventions tend to be time limited, eclectic, and focused on the "here-and-now" quality of member interactions (Kaufman, 1994). Group psychotherapy differs significantly from other forms of group treatment in that a highly skilled professional leader is required, and the group itself is viewed as the means for therapeutic change. Other modalities of group treatment tend to treat the group as a convenient or efficient vehicle for delivering services.

Group psychotherapy uses cohesiveness to create a safe, holding environment in which members may explore their feelings and their relationships with one another (see Winnicott, 1965). Members experience transference, projecting unfinished business from previous relationships, especially in one's family of origin, onto various group members and the group leader. Typically, attraction and repulsion contribute to conflict, overinvolvement, and withdrawal. Therefore, the psychotherapy group functions as a kind of laboratory in which one is able to examine, work through, and change relationships that express one's current capacity for intimacy. Members develop insight about their impacts on others, gaining empathy and hope in the process.

The senior author has conducted group psychotherapy for addicted trauma survivors in all levels of the continuum of care. The group addressed all addictive behaviors, including substance dependence, eating disorder, sexual addiction, pathological gambling, and self-injurious behavior. An explicit goal of the group was to gain sufficient internal and external resources to maintain abstinence in order to resolve underlying trauma issues. Most of the clients over the years had survived physical or sexual abuse, as well as shame issues from growing up in addictive or dysfunctional family systems. Most clients were voluntary, although a few members were court-ordered to attend some therapy as a condition of probation or parole. Many of the clients had completed inpatient or residential treatment for addictive behavior.

The Life Trauma Treatment Group, similar to Najavits's (2002, 2003) Seeking Safety, was conducted by means of a treatment manual, client worksheets, and home-work exercises. The group arose from consultation and administrative experiences within the Masters and Johnson Institute treatment programs (Southern, 2003). However, the emphasis was placed on the group process. In outpatient settings, the group met for two hours weekly and included 8 to 10 members. The author usually co-led the group with a woman in order to catalyze family and gender issues. Members maintained a personal journal, sharing entries as part of the group process, and completed experiential activities in and outside of group. Each member completed and presented a life history, First and Fourth Steps (sometimes organized around Carnes [1993] *Gentle Path* workbook), and relapse prevention plans. Progress was monitored by means of a checklist and members applied for graduation after completing designated tasks and demonstrating interpersonal competencies. While some version of the group existed for over 18 years, most members participated weekly for a period ranging from 6 to 24 months.

Ongoing group psychotherapy threatened recovery by uncovering trauma-related issues. Members were required to participate at least weekly in one or more 12-step fellowships (e.g., Alcoholics Anonymous, Overeaters Anonymous, Narcotics Anonymous, Sex Addicts Anonymous, and Co-Dependency Anonymous). Relapses were rare but did occur. Members who relapsed (or otherwise could not satisfy the terms of the group treatment contract) would discontinue group, receive additional treatment or care, complete assigned tasks, and apply to the group for reentry. Member selection and discharge were determined by consensus-seeking and democratic processes. Therefore, the ongoing program resembled in some ways a therapeutic community. The group did constitute an important resource and support with graduates returning after months or years to share their experiences and hope by telling their life stories.

Typical issues in the Life Trauma Treatment Group were similar to those identified by other authors (Cohen & Hien, 2006; Dayton, 2000; Evans & Sullivan, 1995; Najavits, 2002, 2003). Group members struggled with anxiety and depression, frequently associated with the grieving of losses. They explored past, present, and future relationships in order to discontinue patterns of dysfunctional behavior. Many of the members confused intensity with intimacy; therefore, they needed help with emotional regulation and stress management. The group was organized intentionally to include men and women (occasionally older adolescents), as well as victims and perpetrators of interpersonal violence. The composition of the group catalyzed feelings and emotions that could be experienced and expressed and conflicts that could be contained and worked through. Occasionally, leaders use Gestalt and psychodrama exercises to access material for group treatment (e.g., Dayton, 2000). Some professionals would not combine members of both genders, especially those presenting these relationship issues. According to the treatment model used for the group, addictive behaviors and relationships represented the best efforts of trauma survivors to ward off the pain and shame from the past by reenacting or repeating dysfunctional patterns (Southern, 2003). Therefore, this approach to group psychotherapy actually viewed addiction as an intimacy disorder requiring intensive relational treatment.

Relational Therapy and Family Groups

Relational therapy involves individuals and intimate others in a group process to examine bonding and boundaries. There are many anecdotes about persons in early recovery for addiction becoming involved in harmful codependent, romantic, and sexual relationships. Conventional wisdom in AA and other fellowships advise refraining from becoming involved in a new relationship during at least the first year of recovery. This creates opportunities to form relationships with oneself and a Higher Power, as well as bond with a sponsor. Yet, some self-help groups are notorious for "Thirteenth Stepping" in which members form intense, exploitative or sexual relationships with newcomers (Bogart & Pearce, 2003). Since most recovering alcoholics and addicts do not know how to maintain healthy boundaries in relationships, group treatment is indicated. Groups can help individuals, couples, and families avoid dynamics that contribute to replay of unfinished business and relapse.

The author has conducted many relational therapy, couple, and multifamily groups in residential treatment and intensive outpatient settings (e.g., workshops). One relational therapy group was formed in a residential treatment center following the discharge of five men and women who had become involved in an orgy in one of the resident's apartments. The treatment facility was co-ed, but had strict punitive rules prohibiting romantic and sexual relationships among members of the therapeutic community. The relational therapy group became a safe haven for discussing attractions, romantic feelings, and sexual urges. In addition, we examined issues related to current marriages and sexual experiences associated with alcohol and drug use. Occasionally, group members would confront and assist a pair who was in the process of establishing a secretive, shameful relationship, reversing the decompensation toward relapse. As many as 14 men and women participated weekly in the relationship therapy group. They gained information about healthy bonding and boundary setting, as well as insight about the repetition of harmful relationships early in the recovery process.

Another form of relational therapy offered by the author involved couples in recovery. Typically, alcoholics and addicts just entering treatment had to deal with relationship consequences. Spouses or partners may have ended their relationships or threatened termination due to the addict's abusive behavior and betrayal. Since addiction is a family disease, couples exhibited patterns of behavior, especially approach and avoidance conflicts, that contributed to relapse. Paradoxically, spouses and partners who attempted to control their loved ones' substance use by threatening to leave would end their relationships when the person attained sobriety or demand that the addict leave treatment. The addiction may have been the third element in a triangle that maintained a set level of conflict or dysfunction in the ongoing relationship (see Bowen, 1974). Therefore, partners of recovering addicts frequently need group treatment in order to improve their quality of life and spiritual development.

ALANON represents a corresponding 12-step group for partners and family members affected by alcoholism. In recent years, a fellowship for couples, Recovering Couples Anonymous, facilitated the exploration of dyadic issues associated with addiction and recovery. One program used a 12-week relational group therapy approach to reduce symptoms and enhance functioning in codependent partners by helping them to address family of origin and current relationship issues (Byrne, Edmundson, & Rankin, 2005).

Couples groups can be offered within the context of a larger family program (e.g., "family week" at a residential treatment center), a self-contained intervention (a "weekend couples retreat"), or an adjunct to ongoing treatment (e.g., an intensive outpatient codependency group). Whatever the schedule and setting, care should be taken to select couples who are ready for group and will likely benefit from the process. Each member of the couple should be adequately prepared, including individual consultation if needed, and free to provide informed consent. Because couples group work is demanding, the group therapist should be competent in group therapy, couples therapy, and addictions treatment. The group therapist should be skillful in pacing and structuring input so that shameful issues are not divulged prematurely and disclosures are not used to attack or injure the partner or another person. The best couples groups are built on an existential framework, dedicated to strengthening the pair bond, and include structured and unstructured exploration of intimacy issues (see Coche & Coche, 1990).

The senior author has conducted group therapy for recovering couples, based in part on Framo's (1992) family-of-origin therapy and a couples group psychotherapy model (Coche & Coche, 1990). The couples group therapy incorporated psychoeducational material (e.g., Fossum & Mason, 1986; Sternberg & Barnes, 1988), cognitive-behavioral interventions (e.g., Gottman, 1999), and sex therapy (Firestone, Firestone, & Catlett, 2006; Masters & Johnson, 1970; Schnarch, 1991). Because one of the predictable issues will be disclosing secrets, including infidelity, the group therapist must have an understanding of the dynamics of shame-bound systems and provide adequate structure and professional support (see Corley & Schneider, 2002).

Couples group therapy has been conducted as a component in a family therapy program, a workshop, and an ongoing psychotherapy group. The weekend workshop is an excellent modality involving intensive treatment (up to 20 hours), some opportunities for courtship and homework exercises outside of group, and a moderately high degree of structure for trust building. The author has conducted the workshop in several settings including a church fellowship hall, a residential treatment center, an outpatient clinic, a doctor's office, and a hotel. Each version of the workshop focused on a particular theme: communication, acceptance, conflict resolution, healing from betrayal, relationship contracting, and intimacy enhancement. The workshop addressing intimacy enhancement included a didactic component (e.g., an "Expressions of Intimacy" lecture), discussion group (gender differences in sexual preferences), communication skills training (practicing empathy), homework (sensate focus), process group (unstructured exploration), and wrap-up group (termination). Small groups were conducted according to gender and through random assignment although each couple was together for the majority of the workshop. The process groups were limited to five couples and remained together over the 3.5 days of the experience. Couples group therapy affords opportunities to learn more about one's style of intimacy, the partner's needs and preferences, and the promises and pitfalls of recovering couples.

The most common form of relational therapy in substance abuse treatment is multifamily groups. The multifamily group is a logical extension of the group therapy and couples group models. It involves combining family members of addicts into a recovery community where individuals and family members receive support. Multifamily groups help "families and patients to experience a sense of universality and cohesiveness as they realize they are not alone in their experience of the illness and recovery process" (Tantillo, 2006, p. 82).

Family programs in residential treatment centers, which are usually several days in duration, can be quite large. For example, if 20 residents are involved with family week with two to four family members, the community may be 60 to 100 persons. Such programs require careful planning and troubleshooting to maintain order and well-being. Lectures, groups, meals, and extracurricular activities must be planned. In addition, family members may need transportation from their accommodations and other forms of assistance. The scheduling of family week evokes considerable anxiety among clients and family members who may not have seen one another for weeks. High structure will be needed to contain anxiety, potential conflicts, and acting-out behavior.

During family week, a variety of multifamily groups are offered. Most programs include authoritative lectures from physicians and others regarding the disease concept, relapse prevention, and related topics. Psychoeducational programs can be conducted in lecture halls, auditoriums, or cafeterias. Therapy groups must be conducted in confidential and comfortable environments with as few interruptions as possible in order to foster cohesiveness and serenity. Specialized groups for couples, parents, and children (usually adolescent or adult children) may be offered to address their common concerns. One or more multifamily groups will likely involve each family system having the opportunity to reduce shame and embrace reality by addressing the extent or severity of the resident's addiction. Because secrecy, deception, denial, and minimization are associated with addictive family process (see Fossum & Mason, 1986), it is essential for family members to learn what the resident actually experienced in the addictive lifestyle and to understand the consequences.

In multifamily group, each family system is the center of attention as the addict reads or summarizes the history of drug use and family members are encouraged to share their thoughts and feelings. All family members in attendance benefit from the disclosure and processing of a single family unit. With each round of disclosure, family members deepen their understanding and insight while forming a cohesive recovery community. Following a day of multifamily group, members are exhausted but encouraged. They may attend ALANON meetings, family outings, and experiential activities as well.

The multifamily group and other family program treatment components attempt to prepare the family for the reentry of the resident or client and to support the involvement of all family members in treatment and recovery groups. Most couple and family groups are conducted through a large organization such as a hospital or residential treatment center. However, there are some community programs (e.g., the community mental health center) that are able to offer couple and family groups, psychoeducational groups, and workshops. Relational therapy may be a key ingredient in maintaining abstinence, especially during the critical first 90 days following release from structured or intensive treatment.

Several modalities of group treatment can be used to reduce risk of relapse, improve individual and family functioning, intervene in the pathogenesis of addictive disorders, resolve trauma and other underlying problems that fuel addiction, and facilitate ongoing growth and development. Some groups seem to fit a particular level in the continuum of care: psychoeducational groups in the school setting to prevent substance abuse. Other modalities, including cognitive-behavioral and psychotherapy groups can be found in any treatment settings. The group may be an efficient means for offering a given service or may represent the treatment itself. Group treatment is the most common and effective approach to recovery from addictive disorders. Groups offer therapeutic or curative factors, express known dynamics and processes, and produce some beneficial outcomes.

GROUP TREATMENT EFFICACY

Group treatment presents obvious benefits in terms of efficiency, relatively low cost in comparison to individual treatment, and compatibility with the needs and preferences of recovering people. Groups address the shared and unique concerns of children, adolescents, adults, couples, and families in various settings across the continuum of care. We have sufficient published data to determine the potential benefits and risks of group treatment for substance use disorders and other addictions.

Groups have produced gains in self-esteem and decision making, coping, and social skills in evidenced-based prevention programs for children and adolescents in school, hospital, and community settings (Hoag & Burlingame, 1997; Kulic et al., 2004; McKay & Weiss, 2001). Group treatment has been effective in preventing or delaying tobacco or alcohol use and reducing other risk factors for developing a substance use disorder (Center for Substance Abuse Prevention, 2005). Generally, adolescents benefit from group therapy (Hoag & Burlingame, 1997). However, treatment and prevention professionals should examine carefully member selection and group composition in order to avoid deviant socialization and antisocial peer influence (Dishion et al., 1999).

Groups have contributed to meaningful symptom reduction and behavior change in inpatient and outpatient settings for patients presenting schizophrenia, mood disorder, and other clinical syndromes (Dykeman & Appleton, 2002; Kosters, Burlingame, Nachtigall, & Strauss, 2006). Group treatment has been combined with pharmacotherapy with good results (Anton et al., 2006). A recent review of group therapy for substance use disorders (Weiss et al., 2004) established the potential efficacy of group treatment for substance abusers and addicts and highlighted some of the methodological problems in evaluating interventions for this population.

Weiss and colleagues examined the extant outcome studies comparing group with individual therapy modalities, treatment as usual, and no treatment. Some of the reviewed studies attempted to dismantle group treatment packages, examine duration and intensity of care, and compare types of group therapy. The reviewers found evidence in 24 sufficiently rigorous, prospective treatment outcome studies that group therapy was effective when compared to no treatment and "treatment as usual" conditions. There were no consistent differences between group therapy and individual therapy. No particular type of group therapy (e.g., skills training versus process-oriented groups) emerged as superior to others. Groups varying in duration and intensity (e.g., 6 hours per week in intensive outpatient vs. 12 hours per week in day hospital treatment) produced similar good results.

In spite of the widespread clinical application of group therapy, only 24 rigorous outcome studies evaluated impacts for substance use disorders. Although the findings were encouraging, the mixed results identified the need for ongoing research. It is difficult to study group treatment because of methodological issues: member recruitment and retention; group assignment (e.g., closed vs. open enrollment); interdependence of members; and lack of measures and data-analytic approaches (Morgan-Lopez & Fals-Stewart, 2006; Weiss et al., 2004). Nevertheless, group modalities offer efficient and effective treatment options for adults, couples, and families.

Groups with couples and multifamily group treatment experience many of the same curative factors afforded by group therapy for individuals. Couple and family groups share the challenges of implementation and evaluation that trouble any type of group treatment. In addition, couple and family groups introduce complexities of system dynamics as dyads, triads, and entire families become the units for analysis. In spite of difficulties in evaluating the outcomes of couple and family groups, there have been some promising results (see Chan, 2003; Tantillo, 2006; Thorngren, Christensen, & Kleist, 1998; Winters, Fals-Stewart, O'Farrell, Birchler, & Kelley, 2002). Similar to the findings of Weiss and colleagues, the reviewers found some benefits but no evidence of any one superior type of treatment modality. Group treatment involving partners, spouses, and family members fits the goals of recovery in the therapeutic community setting. Couple and family groups provide efficient means for psychoeducational and skills training efforts anywhere in the continuum of care. Multiple family group therapy presents many opportunities to implement family and systemic approaches. The presence of multiple family units could be a catalyst for sharing experiences, as well as a confounding factor in outcome research. Couple and family therapy groups extend recovery beyond the individual to family and community systems.

Community group treatment through participation in self-help groups such as Alcoholics Anonymous is a well-established modality. While there have been persuasive anecdotes and case studies for years, some treatment professionals have questioned the effectiveness of Alcoholics Anonymous. Recently, several studies established the efficacy of self-help recovery group involvement (Bogenschultz, Tonigan, & Miller, 2006; Galanter, 2006; Humphreys, 2006; Moos & Moos, 2006a, 2006b, 2006c; Suire & Bothwell, 2006; Timko, DeBenedetti, & Billow, 2006; Valliant, 2005). Collectively, these studies established that participation in Alcoholics Anonymous contributed to abstinence ranging from 6 months to 16 years. Supporting the promises of the fellowship, there were psychosocial benefits, increases in self-efficacy, less reliance on avoidance for coping, and spiritual growth.

The results of studies evaluating the effectiveness of group treatment were promising, but inconclusive. Given the relative paucity of rigorous studies, it appears that group modalities are more effective than no treatment or therapy as usual. There is no conclusive evidence that group therapy is more effective than individual therapy. However, the observed lack of differences argues for the efficiency and cost-saving features of group treatment. There is no clearly superior model or type of group approach. It is likely that psychoeducational, cognitive-behavioral skills training, and process-oriented groups contribute to meaningful behavior changes across the continuum of care. Couple and family groups have been underresearched, but they appear to offer special opportunities for partners, spouses, and family members to participate in recovery. Another approach to evaluating treatment involves estimation of relevancy and utility of groups for particular clients. Case studies provide rich sources of qualitative data.

Case Discussions

The case studies considered in other chapters, as well as the review of a unique Chapter Case Presentation (Robert), illustrate the relevancy and utility of group treatment. The case discussions explore application of several types of groups.

Case 1 (Sandy and Pam).

Sandy and Pam are repeating intergenerational problems with boundaries and relationships. Pam appears to be experiencing consequences of drinking, drug use, and participating in an abusive, addictive relationship. Pam, who is now 29 years old, recently moved back into her mother's home to get away from her boyfriend, although they maintain contact. Sandy only has 2 months of sobriety. Over the childhoods of Pam and her brother, Sandy had numerous sexual partners in the family home, a pattern repeated by the daughter. Sandy and Pam have been involved in some family counseling to "work on their relationship" and make amends.

Neither Sandy nor Pam have sufficient sobriety to benefit from therapy. The decision of Pam to return to her mother's home represents a fantasy solution to relationship problems and denial of her substance use problems. She will probably return to her boyfriend after a period of conflict with her mother, who will likely relapse in the process. The family therapist should encourage Sandy and Pam to attend independently 12-step groups for their substance use disorders. At some point in the future, either of them may benefit from self-help or therapy groups addressing adult child of alcoholic issues, as well as sex and love addiction. The therapist should consider referring Pam to an individual therapist who can offer Motivational Interviewing, possibly as preparation for her to enter residential treatment. It would be desirable for Pam to establish residence and identity separate from her mother and her boyfriend. Pam would be an excellent candidate for a relational therapy group within the safe boundaries of a residential treatment center.

Case 2 (Jose and Juanita).

This couple clearly shows signs and symptoms of polysubstance dependence. They are presently engaged in family therapy with the precipitating factor of escalating conflict between Sarita, a 15-year-old daughter, and Jose, her stepfather. Given Juanita's history of being sexually abused as a child and Jose's role as a parentified child in his family of origin, the family should be considered at risk for incest. Therefore, the therapist should explore carefully the family dynamics as well as the absence of Karen, the younger daughter, from the family session.

It will be difficult or impossible for the family to improve with both parents drinking and using drugs in the family home. The therapist should encourage each parent to become involved in treatment for substance use disorders. It is likely that Juanita will decompensate in any type of therapy given her childhood losses and abuse history. She would probably benefit from an inpatient stay followed by 60 to 90 days of residential treatment. Perhaps an extended family member

could offer assistance with childcare and monitoring of the family system if the mother leaves for treatment. Sarita may benefit from staying with her biological father. Ideally, Jose and the children would become involved in family week near the end of Juanita's stay at the residential center. Juanita could become involved in group therapy for sexual abuse concurrent with her addiction treatment.

Case 3 (Leigh).

Leigh is a 16-year-old referred to counseling for problems at school and a shoplifting charge. She moved to a new town and school, where she started the 11th grade, 8 months ago. During this period, she lost contact with her father and brother, as well as previous friends. She received excellent grades and participated in extracurricular activities at her previous school. She has a distant relationship with her mother, who works a lot and recently started dating Hank. Leigh has adopted a deviant, partying lifestyle in order to feel accepted by new peers. She abuses alcohol and drugs and engages in risky sexual behaviors. There is some indication that Leigh may have an emerging eating disorder. She has a co-occurring depression for which she receives an antidepressant.

Typically, someone like Leigh might be referred to an alternative high school or an intensive outpatient treatment program for substance abuse. Either of these referrals would be iatrogenic in that differential association with deviant peers would hasten the progression of her substance use and conduct problems. Leigh's constellation of symptoms represents a cry for help. She should be involved in family therapy with her mother and father to strengthen bonds and clarify boundaries. She may benefit from a referral to a specialist in eating disorders who can complete an in-depth assessment and make treatment recommendations if indicated. This is a case in which group treatment is probably contraindicated.

Case Study

Robert

Robert is a 45-year-old, White, married male. He is an affluent attorney and investment advisor who was negatively affected by the recent financial upheaval of the recession. He has been married for 10 years to a former model. The couple has twin 7-year-old sons who attend a prominent school near their estate. His lifestyle has been characterized by many markers of success. Recently, Robert's wife discovered he had a secret life involving affairs with prostitutes. He was forced to leave home and reside in a beachfront condominium he owned.

Robert continues to work 60 or more hours per week. He always excelled in undergraduate studies, law school, and his various professional endeavors. Now that he has lost significant funds in his real estate and market investments he is working feverishly to regain what he lost. Robert grew up in a privileged family, but his alcoholic father lost the family fortune in gambling and investments in unsuccessful businesses. He was notorious in their small community for a series of extramarital affairs that resulted in divorce. Robert always reported that he was deeply ashamed of his father with whom he had little contact when his father died two years ago concurrent with the onset of the recession and Robert's financial losses. Maladaptive coping with losses was an intergenerational theme in Robert's life.

During the early months of the recession, Robert consulted his family physician for weight loss, insomnia, and lack of energy. He was diagnosed with depression and received prescriptions for Celexa and Trazodone, which he used on an intermittent basis and occasionally when abusing alcohol. Robert drinks five or more cocktails each evening. He has begun to experience some blackouts associated with partying on the weekends. He has been frequently visiting clubs with escorts, bringing attention to his drinking and extramarital affairs. Now that he is separated and living in the beach condo, he has stopped conducting his business and spends much time in bars in the company of prostitutes he meets online.

Robert's wife secured a court order in which he had to complete a psychiatric evaluation in order to continue visitation with his sons. Robert explained his recent behavior by stating "I cannot stand to be alone." He minimized his alcohol use and attributed his problems to the financial collapse in his profession. The psychiatrist referred him to an intensive outpatient program for treatment of alcohol dependence and encouraged Robert to take his antidepressant medication as prescribed. His supervised visitation with his children was contingent upon his continuing participation in the treatment program.

Robert is considering dropping out of the group-oriented outpatient program. He is troubled by attending sessions three nights per week. In addition, he said that no one understands him in the group in group counseling sessions. Although there are employed men in the group, Robert said that none of them have ever dealt with the intensive demands of his profession. He presents himself as unique, entitled to special treatment, and mistreated by peers who have begun to confront his minimization of his problems. Robert has been asked to attend Alcoholics Anonymous group meetings although he has refused to attend. He is at risk for being discharged from the outpatient treatment program.

Robert presents alcohol dependence, co-occurring depression, history of compulsive work (workaholism), hypersexual behavior, and narcissistic personality traits. He has been resistant to an intensive outpatient program that emphasizes participation in confrontational groups. Robert, whose self-image of uniqueness and superiority makes it difficult to relate to other men resists group influence and genuine personality change. Although his depression is improving with medication compliance, he is unwilling to attend AA. He is at risk for dropping out or being discharged prematurely from treatment.

He would benefit from motivational interviewing (MI) in individual consultation in which he explores the costs and benefits of the decisions he makes. He would be better served in a group that emphasizes the four primary clinical strategies of MI: open questions, affirmations, reflections, and summaries (OARS). These strategies would encourage dialogue, communicate respect, convey empathy, and strengthen motivation to change. Then, Robert could move from the precontemplation stage of change toward preparation and action. While abstinence from alcohol use and hypersexual behavior would be goals of treatment, harm reduction strategies could be used to enhance exploration and reduce resistance. Robert would likely benefit from participation in a group in which there are attorneys, doctors, athletes, and other professionals who could "understand" his special qualities while providing vicarious models of successful change strategies. Although the aforementioned interventions may not fit with an older recovery model for abstinence through confrontation, it is unlikely the initial intensive outpatient program will be of assistance to Robert given his stage of change.

Critical Thinking Questions

The case of Robert introduced some complexities that are increasingly common in substance use disorder treatment. There are issues related to co-occurring disorders, intergenerational influences, relational dynamics, and child custody issues. His case emphasizes the importance of matching client needs and stage of change to type of intervention. In order to develop your case conceptualization of Robert, reflect on the following questions.

1. Should Robert be required to continue his participation in the intensive outpatient program and attend AA in order to continue visitation with his children? What is your rationale for this position?
2. What are his genuine barriers to full participation in the treatment process? What would be a reasonable treatment goal for Robert at this time?
3. How would Robert respond to admission to an inpatient treatment program for co-occurring disorders? Could this affect his long-term outcome in recovery?

MyCounselingLab™

Go to Topic 7: *Group Treatment* on the MyCounselingLab™ site (www.MyCounselingLab .com) for *Substance Abuse Counseling*, Fifth Edition where you can:

- Find learning outcomes for *Group Treatment* along with the national standards that connect to these outcomes.
- Complete Assignments and Activities that can help you more deeply understand the chapter content.
- Apply and practice your understanding of the core skills identified in the chapter with the Building Counseling Skills unit.
- Prepare yourself for professional certification with a Practice for Certification quiz.
- Connect to videos through the Video and Resource Library.

CONCLUSION

Discussions of the case studies and reviews of extant data confirmed that group treatment of substance use disorders can be effective. When the needs of particular clients are matched with the resources of groups, therapeutic gains are realized in an efficient manner. There are curative factors and dynamics that are shared by the various types of group treatment. However, processes and structures of group modalities across the continuum of care can be specialized according to population, problem, or setting. Group treatment is conducted in prevention, inpatient, residential, day treatment, aftercare, and outpatient settings. Curative and therapeutic factors are implemented in therapeutic community, self-help, psychoeducational, cognitive-behavioral, psychotherapy, and couple and family therapy groups. Increasingly, group treatment is evidence based, enlisting specific protocols, manuals and worksheets, and careful evaluation techniques. Qualities of the leader, opportunities for meaningful interaction, group climate, and ongoing group development contribute to the eventual outcomes of group treatment, regardless of the underlying philosophy, theory, or model. Nevertheless, the future of group treatment may depend upon innovation of measurement techniques that fit the complexities of group process and ongoing efforts to conduct rigorous trials of integrative treatment packages in specific settings.

The implications of the present review extend to clinical decision making and treatment planning. An important practice implication involves careful selection of group members to fit client needs for structure and intensity and to reduce iatrogenic effects, especially for adolescents. Each treatment setting would benefit from providing an array of groups that addresses client needs for motivation, information, skill building, corrective emotional experience, and relapse prevention. Although there have been some conflicts between abstinence-oriented and harm reduction approaches, cognitive-behavioral skill-building groups can be useful in recovery settings, while spiritually attuned 12-step groups can increase the benefit and meaning of manualized, evidence-based treatment packages.

In recent years, integrative treatment has included pharmacotherapy for co-occurring and addictive disorders. The transtheoretical model and motivational interviewing have helped professionals understand that treatment is not "one size fits all." Rather, interventions should be tailored to the stage of change and particular needs of clients. The psychotherapy integration movement has contributed innovative psychodynamic, ecological, and multicultural models for substance use disorder group treatment (Futterman, Lorente, & Silverman, 2005; Guajardo, Bagladi, & Kushner, 2004).

Based on what is known about the potential benefits of group treatment in the continuum of care, several recommendations are warranted:

- Most clients should receive pretreatment motivational interviewing and enhancement interventions to prepare them to become productive group members and to receive maximum benefits from the process. This may be an essential step for involuntary clients.
- When adolescents participate in prevention or treatment groups, the leader should be highly skilled and assure adequate structure to reduce risks for iatrogenic effects. Adolescents who are just beginning to experience consequences of substance use or addictive behaviors should not be referred to correctional groups or placed with delinquent peers.

- Group treatment should begin with careful clinical decision making and conclude with placement in the least restrictive level of care in the continuum. However, it is important to match intensity of treatment to genuine client needs in order to produce an adequate dose effect of group treatment.
- Given advances in understanding the genetic, biological, and neurological factors in the pathogenesis of addictive disorders, many treatment packages will include pharmacotherapy. However, psychotropic medications should not replace the essential human interactions afforded by group treatment.
- Group treatment should address spirituality and existential concerns. If possible, most clients will benefit from participation in Alcoholics Anonymous or another 12-step group concurrent with professional treatment.
- Optimal group treatment packages will apply principles of therapeutic community and build treatment packages from psychoeducational, cognitive-behavioral skill building, psychotherapy, and relational therapy interventions. There is no single form of treatment indicated for all persons. There is no particular group treatment technique that is clearly superior to other types of group.
- Optimal treatment for substance use disorders involves 90 days of treatment. This is a critical period for relapse prevention. Evidence suggests that ongoing involvement in self-help groups reduces relapse risk. Integrative treatment approaches should be considered. Harm reduction interventions and policies may be indicated. However, abstinence should remain a fundamental goal in most cases of substance use disorders. Substance use should be monitored during the course of group treatment.
- Special considerations are indicated for involuntary, correctional, multicultural, and co-occurring disorders clients. Also, women in recovery present special needs and require protections from exploitation in self-help groups.

9

Family Treatment

PATRICIA W. STEVENS, PH.D.

MyCounselingLab™

Visit the **MyCounselingLab**™ site for *Substance Abuse Counseling*, Fifth Edition to enhance your understanding of chapter concepts. You'll have the opportunity to practice your skills through video- and case-based Assignments and Activities as well as Building Counseling Skills units, and to prepare for your certification exam with Practice for Certification quizzes.

Through the years, systems theory and the addiction field have often been at odds with one another. Much of this disagreement has focused on whether addiction is an individual or a family problem—the old nature-versus-nurture argument. Is the addiction secondary to the dysfunction in the family (i.e., a result of it) or the primary cause of the dysfunction (i.e., the result of the individual's dysfunction)? Although how the clinician views the problem determines the primary focus of treatment, both conceptualizations are important factors in the success of treatment. The power of the family system to impact behavior of its members cannot be denied. On the cause/result debate, this author takes the position, like early family therapy theorists such as Bateson (1971) and others, that it is not an either/or proposition but a "both/and" problem. Basing this position on the already-stated philosophy that the etiology of abuse/dependency is "biopsychosociofamilial," it makes sense to incorporate all aspects of the client's life with special attention to the family into the treatment model. Furthermore, it may be less important for the counselor to determine the etiology of the problem than it is for the counselor to determine how the problem continues to maintain itself within the client's and family's life.

Over the years, research in the use of family therapy in the substance abuse field has been delineated into two separate tracks: working with the "alcoholic family" and working with the "substance abuse family." Research in the area of alcoholism has tended to focus on families of White middle-class males in their mid-40s. Research on families of substance abusers (individuals whose primary drug is not alcohol) has tended to focus on adolescents or young adults. Therefore, researchers may study the same family unknowingly but from two different perspectives: a parent with an alcohol problem and an adolescent who is using other substances that are currently in vogue (Zhou, King, & Chassin, 2009). As clinicians begin to assess individuals in treatment, we find that many young adults who are polydrug/designer users have alcoholic parents. This further substantiates the need to address multigenerational patterns that support chemical use along with individual issues as treatment plans are developed.

As the addictions field has expanded its research base, it has become increasingly apparent that family structure and dynamics play an important role in the continuation of substance use within a family (Doweiko, 2011; McCrady, 2006; McNeece & DiNitto,2005). Also, substance use increases other dysfunctional patterns of behavior in families such as domestic violence, child abuse, incest (Greenfield, 2007; Parrott & Giancola, 2006), increased criminal behavior, accidental injuries (Lapham, 2004/2005; Miller, Levy, & Cox, 2006). Further, many substance abusers and/or family members have dual-diagnosis issues (National Alliance on Mental Illness, 2011) which further compounds the treatment variables needed for success with the client and the family. Research supports that substance abuse in families impairs a child's physical, social, and psychological development in a way that may lead to an adult with mental illness or substance abuse issues (McCrady, Epstein, & Kahler, 2004).

While biological factors have been proven to be a factor in predisposition for use/abuse/addiction, new brain research called system biology further evidences the effect of the brain on drug use (Guo & Zakhari, 2008). However, even this brain model includes the impact of environment to the brain system. So we can safely assume that nurture (or lack thereof) explains a significant portion of these development and substance abuse issues (Collins, Maccoby, Steinberg, Hetherington, & Bornstein, 2000). Dramatic statistics have been gathered about substance-abusing families and the impact of childhood experiences on adult substance use (Anda et al., 2009; Doweiko, 2009; Felitti, 2004). Felitti's 2004 article, which is supported by the 2009 research, states that there is a significant correlation between adverse childhood experiences (ACE) and ATOD abuse (e.g., child abuse, alcoholic or drug-abusing parents). He states that a "male child with a score of 6 ACE as compared with a male child with an ACE of 0 has 46-fold (4600%) likelihood of becoming an injection drug user sometime later in life" and "a 500% increase in adult alcoholism is related in a strong, graded manner to adverse childhood experiences (in other words, the more ACEs the more likely the person is to be an alcoholic)" (pp. 6, 7). The U.S. Department of Health and Human Services (2006) study indicates that 50% of all addicted people had parents who were addicted, 50% of all adult children of alcoholics (ACOA) become alcoholics (as opposed to 10% of non-ACOAs), and about 50% marry a chemically dependent partner (vs. 13% of non-ACOAs). This study also concluded that a third of all American families have an immediate family member with an alcohol- and drug-related problem, that drugs are implicated in 50% to 90% of cases of domestic violence, and that drugs play a significant part in the violent or sexually inappropriate behavior between siblings. A Gallup Poll states that 1 in 12 Americans aged 12 and older admitted that they currently use illicit drugs and 42% of adults worry about drug use "a great deal" in the United States and 23% worry a "fair amount." The percentage who worry a great deal about drug use has consistently been among the top five concerns since Gallup began asking this question in March 2001 (Gallup Organization, 2005).

The cross-state analysis of the Center for Substance Abuse Treatment (CSAT) Outcomes and Performance Pilot Studies (TOPP-II) included primary data from 16 States and also found that 58.5% of persons admitted to treatment had a child younger than age 18 (Ahmed, 2006). Applying those prevalence data to the annual number of adults admitted to treatment results in the estimate that 1.09 million parents of minor children were admitted to substance abuse treatment in 2004. Further, it is estimated that 115,240 to 211,720 child victims in out-of-home care had parents with a substance use disorder (U.S. Department of Health and Human Services, 2006). This information clearly supports the need to work from a systems perspective, which declares that as the individual influences the family, so the family influences the individual in feedback loops that are always connected and never ending.

Family therapy with addicted families strives to stop the present, active abuse and to mitigate the multigenerational transmission process noted in these statistics. No matter what your belief about the etiology of addiction—biological, sociological, psychological—it clearly passes from generation to generation.

This chapter will discuss the general concepts underlying all systemic theories. It is beyond the scope of this chapter to detail the numerous and diverse theories available to the systems practitioner. Furthermore, the theory that one might choose to work with clients varies with the individual's beliefs, values, philosophy, and personality. To choose a particular systemic theory, the reader is referred to the vast literature available on these theories, which includes but is not limited to experiential/symbolic family therapy (Satir, 1967), structural family therapy (Minuchen, 1974), strategic family therapy (Jackson, 1960; Napier & Whitaker, 1988), Adlerian family therapy (Adler, 1927; Lowe, 1982), and transgenerational/Bowenian family therapy (Bowen, 1974). Goldenberg and Goldenberg (2008), Nichols (2009), and Gladding (2011) present excellent overviews of these systemic theories. The author hopes that the student will have access to classes whose primary focus is to detail these theories for use in general counseling as well as with substance abusers.

DEFINING FAMILY

Understanding the terminology utilized in the field of chemical dependency is difficult enough, but in today's society with so many different combinations of individuals, we must also define the word *family*. It is essential to understand and integrate that the definition of family varies from culture to culture but may also vary from individual to individual in the same culture. Much of the research in the family therapy field, as well as in the addiction field, has been focused on the White Anglo-Saxon Protestant definition of family as an intact nuclear family in which lineage (blood line) is important in tracing one's ancestry. However, because we know that ethnicity is no prerequisite for abuse or addiction, it behooves us to acknowledge the different cultural/personal definitions, expectations, and structures of families as we begin to work in this field (see Chapter 12).

One definition of family would be the traditional term *nuclear family*, which has been defined as the individuals with whom the person is currently living. Individuals in relationships come together from their respective "nuclear families" of origin (birth) to create this nuclear family. It is impossible to examine the roles, rules, rituals, boundaries, and subsystems in the current "nuclear family" without examining its interrelatedness with the family of origin. The present nuclear family becomes the family of origin for the next generation, shaping the multigenerational transmission process of behavioral patterns (Gladding, 2011).

The definition of family in our current society takes on many forms and structures. For the purpose of this chapter the definition of family will include "any combination of nuclear, extended, single-parent, reconstituted, gay and lesbian couples and/or any other form of family life. A family is composed of the people—regardless of their actual blood or legal relationship to the client—whom clients consider to be members of their family" (Johnson, 2004, p. 130). While this definition complicates the treatment plan that includes the family, it is truer to the client's view of the world, therefore more effective, than a family that is artificially defined by the treatment program or the social system values by which the provider lives.

GENERAL SYSTEMS CONCEPTS

A *system*, as defined by *Merriam-Webster's Collegiate Online Dictionary*, is "a regularly interacting or interdependent group of items forming a unified whole and/or a group of interacting bodies under the influence of related forces." To understand family functioning adequately, the individual behavior must be examined within the context of the family interactions. Virginia Satir (1967) first described this interaction using the example of a mobile or windchime. All pieces are connected yet independent to the extent that the mobile/windchime hangs in balance with pieces not touching. However, if moved, for example, by a breeze, the parts are shown to be interdependent because when one piece moves, it causes the other pieces to move as well. Each breeze may cause the pieces to move and "interact" in different ways. As the breeze diminishes and finally ceases, the pieces also stop moving and return to balance. This seminal example in the field still describes the interactiveness of family in a simple yet multifaceted manner.

The foundation of all family systems work comes from the literature by Bertalanffy (1968) on the functioning of all systems in the universe. Some of the original general systemic concepts of functioning need to be discussed to understand this idea of interdependence that Bertalanffy assigned to all systems—which, for our purposes, we will assign to families with whom we are counseling. The systems theory framework is based on several underlying concepts:

- All systems seek *homeostasis.*
- All systems incorporate *feedback loops* to function.
- *Hierarchy* is an integral part of systemic functioning, including all the *roles, rules,* and *subsystems* necessary. *Boundaries* are necessary to facilitate the existence of roles, rules, and subsystems.
- The system cannot be understood by reductionism but must be examined as an entity, synthesizing the component parts into a *whole.*
- *Change* in one part of the system creates change in all parts of the system.

And, when we define and conceptualize systems as families, mental health workers add a final concept that is specific to humankind:

- *Values* are passed down from one generation to another affecting the dynamics of the family system.

As the basis for all systems work, and concepts that still set the foundation for family work, a closer examination and understanding of these concepts in relationship to families is crucial. Understand that these systemic concepts are so interrelated that it is impossible to discuss one without examining all.

Homeostasis

The term *homeostasis* is used to define the natural tendency of families to behave in such a manner as to maintain a sense of balance, structure, and stability in the face of change (Gladding, 2011; Goldenberg & Goldenberg, 2010). Homeostasis is not equivalent to healthy functioning but represents a psychological and emotional comfortable/stable position for the family. Inherent in this definition is the assumption that change in one family member will create change in all other family members (Lewis, Dana, & Blevins, 2011).

There will be times when change requires the family to adjust. Systems, in this case families, have a natural resistance to change, which serves as a mechanism to avoid complete chaos during the change process. During these times families will need to renegotiate their roles, rules, and boundaries to fashion a new, more functionally balanced structure to manage these changes. If families are too resistant to change, they become rigid and decline into entropy. Conversely, too much flexibility produces chaos. Substance-abusing families demonstrate too much flexibility when the abuser is using. When the abuser stops, the roles, rules, and boundaries in the family must be renegotiated, and this scenario creates a crisis state for the family. Many times the family becomes very rigid. This cycle can continue ad infinitum in ATOD families.

Feedback Loops

The essence of systems is feedback loops. Feedback loops provide the communication that enables the system to continue functioning and to maintain homeostasis, to promote or resist change. They are the systems method of self-regulation and self-maintenance or, in simple terms, the communication between parts of the system or members of the family. Feedback serves two purposes: to move the system toward change and to bring the system back into balance.

Reinforcing feedback moves the system toward change. Sometimes called *positive feedback*, this interaction can be thought of as "heating up" the system. As feedback continues, it increases, sometimes exponentially, the system's move from the original balance. Just as a snowball gains size as it rolls downhill, so reinforcing feedback moves the system rapidly away from its first point of balance. Balancing feedback (sometimes called *negative feedback*), in contrast, brings the system back into balance. This represents the "cooling down" of the system. Balancing feedback brings the system back to its goal. How dissonant the system is from its goal determines how much feedback is necessary to regain homeostasis. A good example of balancing feedback is being thirsty. Your body begins in fluid balance but loses that balance as you exercise or sit in the hot sun. As a result, you experience the sensation of thirst, drink water, and your body then regains fluid balance. How thirsty (or out of balance) you are determines the amount of water you drink (balancing feedback) which in turn determines your return to fluid balance (Gladding, 2011; O'Connor & McDermott, 1997).

Hierarchy, Roles, Rules, Subsystems, and Boundaries

Hierarchy refers to the structure of the family, how the members are classified according to ability or rules and role definition within their cultural perspective. *Roles* may be determined by the individual's behaviors in performing rights and obligations associated with a certain position within the family and are usually related to complementary expected roles of others with whom the person is involved. It is through these roles, and their interaction, that families act out the covert and overt family rules.

Although roles vary, some generic rules appear to define the roles of being male, female, mother, father, husband, wife, and child within a familial structure. As children grow, they will experience childhood, adolescence, and young adulthood. Additionally, throughout the individual's life cycle, a person takes on a variety of roles: child, student, worker, spouse, partner, parent, retiree, grandparent, and so on. Marital and parental roles, in particular, are often derived from the family of origin. These old roles may or may not be suitable for the present family. This situation may create unbalance and conflict as the new family endeavors to shift and change roles. Therefore, as family members move in and out of these roles and as rules change, the family becomes unbalanced and attempts to reestablish homeostasis through feedback loops to create a new structure.

Rules are the mutual assumptions of the family as to how members should behave toward each other and the outside world. Rules within families may govern:

1) what, when, and how family members can communicate their experiences about what they see, hear, feel, and think, 2) who has permission to speak to whom about what, 3) the extent and manner in which a family member can be different, 4) the manner in which sexuality can be expressed, 5) what it means to be a male or female, and 6) how family members acquire self-worth and how much self-worth a member can experience.

Culture may not change how the family is governed but may well change the consequences of breaking the family rules. For example, a Euro-American family might punish (i.e., time-out) a child who "talks back," while an Asian family might use shame to correct the child who breaks the family rule.

Subsystems are the smaller systems within each system—systems within systems. Families are composed of multiple subsystems that assist the family in carrying out its day-to-day functions. Each subsystem contributes to the entire system's maintenance. Subsystems may be established by a variety of means: along generational lines (grandparents, parents, siblings), by mutual interest (who likes to read, play ball, shop), by sex (female-female or male-male), or by task (who cleans the house, who washes the car). Within each subsystem, a family member plays a particular role that has rules and expectations accompanying it. Family members, of course, can be in more than one subsystem, requiring the person to learn the appropriate role and rules for each subsystem (Gladding, 2011; Goldenberg & Goldenberg, 2010).

The clarity of the subsystem boundaries is more important than the constitution of the subsystem (Minuchen, 1974). For example, the marital (or partner) dyad is a primary subsystem. It is a closed system in the sense that there are certain duties and primary functions that are usually performed only by this marital subsystem (e.g., earning money, managing the home). With the birth of a child, this partnership changes and expands to become a parental subsystem with added duties and functions.

In effect, we now have two subsystems, the marital subsystem with responsibilities toward the relationship itself and the parental subsystem with parenting duties of care-taking, discipline, scheduling of activities, and so forth.

Boundaries, as already implied, define the subsystems. They are like fences: they keep things out and they keep things in. Boundaries exist between family members, between subsystems, and between the family and society. Boundaries can best be compared to a picket fence. It is strong enough to keep the dogs out of the garden but open enough to see the flowers across the street and to visit with friends who walk by your yard. In family systems, boundaries are on a continuum from clear and overly rigid to clear but flexible to unclear and diffuse. In families with overly rigid boundaries, communication is constricted and family members are disengaged or isolated. There is a lack of expressed love, a low sense of belonging, and a lack of family loyalty. In families with diffused boundaries, there is little if any recognition of autonomy. If one person feels, the whole family feels. There is an intense sense of family loyalty and belonging—to the exclusion of anyone outside the family.

Again, the clinician must be aware of cultural norms when evaluating families' boundaries. In Asian families, for example, the cultural expectation might be that the father is more disengaged (i.e., has more rigid boundaries). The opposite of disengagement, enmeshment, occurs when the boundaries are unclear and diffuse. Enmeshed families leave little room for difference; unity is stressed, and emotions are shared (if the mother cries, so does the child). In the Latino/Hispanic culture, what would be considered in the White culture as an "enmeshed" mother, is not only expected but highly valued (Minuchen, 1992). So, culture colors the perspective (and the pathology) of terms such as *disengagement* and *enmeshment*. It is also important to be aware of the messages about distance and closeness that are given in Western culture. For example, women are considered the nurturers of the family, but "too much" nurturing can create a "Mamma's boy," which is seen as dysfunctional in White society both for the mother (enmeshed) and the son. Fathers are not given this double message about closeness and distance with their children.

The families of substance abusers are often found disengaged, not rigidly enmeshed. Compared with normative data from nonclinical families, the families of substance abusers were significantly different on cohesion but not on adaptability. The paradox of this information is that to the outside world, these families may appear enmeshed, therefore tempting the therapist to ask the family to disengage. The result would be adolescents who feel even more disenfranchised from their family system.

Wholeness

Another systems concept is that of *wholeness.* Systems theorists believe that the system cannot be understood by dissecting it into its individual parts but only by observing the whole system. This concept of wholeness carries with it the idea of "emergent properties" (O'Connor & McDermott, 1997). These are the properties of the system that exist only when the system is whole and functioning; conversely, if you take the system apart, the emergent properties no longer exist. For example, H_2O is the chemical equation for water. When you dissect water into its component parts, you have hydrogen and oxygen, but when you combine these elements, you have water. Nothing in the individual elements or even in the idea of combining the elements prepares you for the wetness of water (the emergent property). Also, the picture on a television is the emergent property of that system. Take a TV apart, and you will not find the picture anywhere in the parts.

In families, emergent properties are the behaviors that, when operating as a system, each family member exhibits but, when separated into individuals, they may not exhibit. All of us have had the experience of talking with a friend about someone with whom the friend is involved. The dynamics of the relationship are explained through the eyes of the individual (or a "part" of the system). Then, when we see our friend and the other person together, the experience may be very different than what has been explained to us. This different experience of the functioning-couple system is the emergent property of that couple system.

Change

We have already discussed the concept of how *change* in one part of the system, or an individual, changes the other parts, or individuals, of the system. An important aside to this concept, especially for counseling, is always to expect side effects. Remember: with a family system, you can never change just one interaction or behavior because of this systemic effect. As stated earlier, when the abuser stops using (one behavior), it affects the behaviors of all the other members of the unit.

Values

One last concept that is important in working with family systems is that of values. V*alues* are the composite of the rules, roles, boundaries, and subsystems in both the nuclear family and the family of origin. Values may be shared or more strongly valued by one partner than by another. Examples of values are receiving an education, engaging in athletics, having musical ability, becoming wealthy, being a good wife and mother, and being the good male provider. Conflict occurs in families when mutually exclusive values are embraced—for example, a family that values male children has a female child. Cultural values are also superimposed on the family values, impacting the family values as well as individual members and their accomplishments and behaviors. More conflict occurs when these values are covert and not overt.

Not only is it important for therapists to understand the family value system, but it is imperative for them also to be aware of their own values, beliefs, and prejudices. Counselors do not leave their values at the door of the therapy room. These values are apparent in each intervention, question, or comment in therapy. The therapist's values can impact the client family system in both positive and negative ways. Therefore, it is necessary for the ethical therapist to recognize that there is no value-free therapy.

SYSTEMS AND ADDICTIVE FAMILIES

Now that we have described the major components of a system—and for our use— a family system, integrating these concepts into a description of an addictive family becomes much easier. Many addictive families share common characteristics. Secrecy (disengagement), for example, is extremely important. Denial of the problem is also paramount. Family members will go to extreme measures to keep the secret and to avoid dealing with the issue of alcohol/drug use. The family will readjust itself and redistribute responsibilities (change its rules and roles) to accommodate the user (new homeostasis). In fact, Ackerman (1983) states that the "key to surviving in an alcoholic home is adaptation" (p. 16).

We know that one of the developmental tasks of children is to learn to adapt to their surroundings. Therefore, the adaptation to a dysfunctional, chemically dependent system will create dysfunctional behaviors in children as they interact with outside systems and as they grow into adulthood. Taking into consideration this adaptation, one can easily understand the statistics given in the first part of this chapter in regard to ACEs and adult dysfunction.

Hypervigilance is also a characteristic of individuals in these families. Never knowing when or where the abuser will act out (no set role or rule) creates a constant state of fear for other family members. Lack of trust is a by-product of this unstable and uncertain atmosphere. Another feature of addictive families is the inability to express feelings. Because the user/abuser is the feeling carrier and the only one allowed to express feelings in the family, other family members lose the ability to identify and express appropriate feelings. This rule can especially create dysfunction in the child and in the child as an adult.

This may be an appropriate section in which to discuss *shame* as an integral part of a dysfunctional family. Alcoholic and substance abusing families are highly vulnerable to shame because these families construct elaborate mechanisms for denying the chemical use/abuse among themselves and with the outside world. Chemical use is also highly correlated with abuse, incest, and violence. These behaviors feed on secrecy, which in turn perpetuates the behaviors as well as the shame of the people involved in keeping the secret.

The Marital Dyad and Substance Abuse

Research into the dynamics of the marital dyad of substance-abusing couples provides interesting information. One study finds that marital adjustment in alcoholic couples may be driven more by the wives' abuse pattern than by the husbands' (Cranford, Floyd, Schulenberg, & Zucker, 2011).

One interesting study shows that marriage may be a protective factor for addiction but not for heavy drinking. Further, family history, antisocial behavioral tendencies and negative affect predicted the use of alcohol at the time of marriage, while changes after marriage were predicted by the drinking of one's partner (Leonard & Hornish, 2008). The marriage may provide the individual with a drinking partner and the two will adjust their drinking behavior until it matches. In the cases where this match does not happen, the alcohol will have a negative impact on the couple.

Issues of control are central to the alcohol-abusing marriage. Both partners are endeavoring to maintain control and to decrease the chaos in the relationship, but for their own purpose. The alcohol-abusing partner does not want the other person to leave, and the non-alcohol-abusing person is also often afraid of abandonment. Conditional love becomes a daily part of their lives. Behaviors are centered around "If you love me, you will [or will not]. . . ."

Communication in these marriages is often angry, hostile, and critical. They appear to have an extensive use of projection, display poor psychological boundaries, and use blame frequently. These marriages also have a "borderline personality" involving either intense love or hate, being totally in control or totally out of control, or being enmeshed or disengaged. These relationships tend to be highly symbiotic or, in the current jargon, codependent. These partners are so interrelated that they are inseparable emotionally, psychologically, and sometimes physically from each other and their drug(s) of choice (Capretto, 2007).

In the 1980s the term *codependency* became a household word. In the beginning it referred to anyone who had contact with the abuser. Then, it became the terminology used for "women who stayed in long term relationships with chemically dependent men and, somehow, were responsible for their partner's chemical dependency" (Johnson, 2004, p. 148). In systems terms, however, *codependency* simply refers to an adaptive function of a troubled family. The process explains how problems flow from one role to another as a family system tries to cope with an increasingly problematic person. The codependent(s) (nonusing) individual(s) are usually the people closest to the abuser and the first to react dysfunctionally. As the codependent becomes more vulnerable and reactive to the dependent (user), the user increases the drinking/drugging. Therefore, the codependent must become more reactive and protective, which does not allow the user to experience the consequences of the behavior. The user's rationalizations support the misunderstanding of the problem. However, this cycle engages both partners in self-deception, which allows the problem to remain hidden and progress (Craig, 2004).

An early definition by Gorski (1992) of *codependency* states that it is a "cluster of symptoms or maladaptive behavior changes associated with living in a committed relationship with either a chemically dependent person or a chronically dysfunctional person either as children or adults" (p. 15). Today we might say that these individuals overcompensate and try to manage the addiction. Common elements of this behavior include being overinvolved, obsessing over attempting to control the dependent person's behavior, gaining self-worth from the approval of others (many times primarily the chemically dependent person), and making great sacrifices for others. The multigenerational transmission pattern of this behavior is readily seen. No matter how abusive or unsatisfactory children saw their parents' relationship, they will likely repeat the pattern in their own relationships by seeking out abusers to marry or by becoming chemically dependent (Capretto, 2007).

Codependency continues to be a controversial topic in this field. Many believe that it does not exist, that the definition itself tends to blame the victim(s). Further, there is no clear clinical definition (Jaffe & Anthony, 2005). Doweiko (2011) views codependency as a continuum from totally dependent to totally disregarding the feedback of others. These individuals usually focus too much on the opinions of others, not knowing what they want or like, and are drawn into relationships with needy individuals.

As discussed earlier in the chapter, homeostasis is an important concept in a system. In order to maintain this balance, the non-abusing partner will shield the abusing partner as much as possible from any unpleasantness—making excuses to the boss for absenteeism, justifying lies to the children, and so forth. This pattern of preserving balance soon becomes a common coping mechanism within the marriage. This form of protection is sometimes called enabling. *Enabling* is anything done to protect the chemically dependent person from the consequences of his or her behavior (Capretto, 2007; Doweiko, 2011). It comes from attempts to adapt to the chemical use rather than confront it. Enabling can come not only from inside the marriage or family but it may come from sources outside the marriage, as it does not require a committed relationship. Codependence and enabling can be mutually exclusive. In other words, someone might enable the drinker and not be codependent—for example, a coworker or an employer.

These marriages also use alcohol and/or other drugs to triangulate their relationship. Bowen (1976) says that the smallest stable relationship is a triangle. In substance-abusing marriages, when the tension reaches an unbearable level, instead of bringing in a child or another family member as the third part of the triangle to defuse the tension, these couples include the drug of choice. For example, if a couple is arguing, they may decide to focus on the bad grade of their child instead of the underlying cause of their problem. For the addictive family, the drug becomes the third "person" in the relationship and one that is as loved (or more so) as the partner by the abuser.

Boundaries for these couples are not well defined, vacillating from overly rigid to overly diffuse. Communication is usually strained and incongruent with feelings. Subsystems may be cross-generational, with each partner seeking advice, consolation, or love from the mothers, fathers, sisters, brothers, or children.

Given these couple dynamics, it is not surprising that alcohol (or other drugs) is involved in many domestic violence incidents (Shipway, 2004). Some studies have shown a significant association between battering incidents and alcohol abuse (McCauley et al., 2004; O'Farrell, Fals-Stewart, Murphy, & Murphy, 2003). Men who drink alcohol and have a predisposition for physical violence toward their female partners are more likely to be violent on the days they drink alcohol. In fact, compared with days of no drinking, the odds of any male-to-female violence on days of heavy drinking by the male partners (drinking six or more drinks in 24 hours) are more than 18 times higher, and the odds of severe violence are more than 19 times higher (O'Farrell et al., 2003). The counselor who works with individuals who abuse alcohol and other drugs needs to understand how the dynamics of violence interacts with alcohol/drug abuse.

THE FAMILY AND SUBSTANCE ABUSE

From the overview of marital dynamics, it is apparent that such a marital partnership would impact children when they enter the system. Because family homeostasis and growth are organized around the chemically dependent person's behavior, children rarely have the opportunity for developmentally appropriate stages of life.

In his seminal work on alcohol family structure, Kaufman (1985) describes four different structures of alcoholic families: functional, neurotic enmeshed, disintegrated, and absent. The *functional* family is usually one in the early stages of abuse, and the abuse is connected to social or personal problems. Family members might talk about the chemical problem but are more concerned about other issues. The *neurotic enmeshed* family is the stereotypical alcoholic family. This family encompasses all the characteristics listed earlier for the alcoholic couple. Clues to the chemical use are apparent from the parental role reversal, the history of using in the family of origin, and the protection of the abusing parent by the child. The *disintegrated* family is the family in which temporary separation occurs between the abuser and other family members. This is usually the neurotic enmeshed family at a later stage. These families may present for therapy after the abuser has completed an inpatient or intensive outpatient program. Kaufman and Kaufman (1992) further separate the disintegrated family into two stages: the first stage involves the temporary separation, and the second stage is where chemicals are the focus of the family and conflict is open and apparent. The *absent* family is one with a permanent separation between the chemically dependent person and the other members. This situation is usually seen in chronic abusers or chemically dependent people.

Steinglass's seminal model (1980) of a family life history model evaluates the alcoholic family system using a developmental model. The author describes three developmental phases: early, middle, and late. This model echoes Jellinek's (1960) early model of the individual's development of alcoholism. In the *early phase*, the family is in the process of developing a solid family identity. They may over- or underreact to problems related to the alcoholism. In the *middle phase*, the family has already established identity. This family usually presents with a nonalcoholic problem and a vague history of abuse. They will develop short-term, rigid methods for maintaining homeostasis that incorporate the chemical use behavior in the system. *Late phase* families focus on the intergenerational issues regarding chemical use. The wife might ask the husband to resolve issues about his father's alcoholism before they have children, or the wife might need to "do something" about her alcoholic mother.

It is important to understand that the family with an alcoholic member "has alcoholism" in the same way that families with a mental or physical illness are impacted by those illnesses. Alcoholism regulates all behaviors in the family life. Therefore, if the primary regulatory relationship in the family is with alcohol or drugs, then other relationships in the family become secondary and do not prosper as well as in a family without ATOD. Because denial is an integral component of the ATOD family homeostasis mechanism, the family will blame factors outside of the family for their problems (e.g., loss of job, lack of money, problems at work/school, argument with friend). This externalization of blame reflects the powerlessness felt throughout the family system. The chemically dependent member functions to bring the family together as they bond against these outside issues through the crises that are caused by the abuse.

Families with ATOD problems utilize criticism, anger, blame, guilt, and judgment in the family communication process as is seen in the marital dyad. Parenting is inconsistent, and the boundaries are unclear and constantly changing. Rules and limits are also in flux depending on whether the ATOD family member is "wet" or "dry" (i.e., using or nonusing). Black (1981), whose work has never been empirically tested but is still utilized in the majority of treatment programs, self-help literature, and is anecdotally proven by most members of alcoholic families, states three rules that govern the alcoholic family: don't talk, don't trust, and don't feel. These three rules sum up the interactions seen within the alcoholic family. Family members develop survival roles to cope with the increasing dysfunction in the family. These roles build a wall of defenses around the individual members that allow each person to deny feelings and to fit into the family. The continuing action/reaction to the chemically dependent person is self-deluding. As the protective barriers increase, family members become more out of touch with themselves and with each other. These protective barriers serve the members of the ATOD family well, but they may become destructive behaviors as the person moves out of the family and into mainstream society and relationships without alcohol or drugs involved.

In most dysfunctional families, the identified patients or symptom bearers are the children. In alcoholic families, the parents are the symptom bearers. However, the adult chemically dependent person may have developed the problem in adolescence, thereby being the symptom bearer in his family of origin where parents were also using. Developmental neurologists have verified the brain growth that takes place in adolescence and continues into early adulthood, bringing to the forefront the question of how early use may alter normal brain growth and future behaviors (Ling, Rawson, & Shoptaw, 2006; Parekh, 2006).

It is important for the counselor working with these families to understand the process that the symptom (ATOD) serves in the family. It is also imperative to remember that no matter how sick it may appear to the outside observer, the established equilibrium represents that family's attempt to minimize the threats and disruption in the family system (family homeostasis). This comment is extremely important for clinicians as they endeavor to establish rapport and trust with these families. It is imperative *never* to discount the survival skills of the members of these families.

CHILDREN IN THE ADDICTED FAMILY

Long-term parental alcoholism appears to create the same type of dysfunction that exists in families with sexual, physical, or emotional abuse. This makes the children in these families at high risk for the development of a variety of stress-related disorders including conduct disorders, poor academic performance, and inattentiveness. Children in substance-abusing families are socially immature, lack self-esteem and self-efficacy, and have deficits in social skills. Furthermore, because these children live in chronic chaos and trauma, they might develop long-lasting emotional disturbances, antisocial personality disorders, or chemical dependence in later life. Children may become addicted to excitement or chaos and may develop inappropriate behaviors such as fire setting or, conversely, may become the "superresponsible" child in the family, taking on parental roles.

A number of factors affect the impact of the parental chemical dependence on children. One is the sex of the abusing parent: the impact of a chemically dependent mother is far different than that of an abusing father. Because mothers commonly have the primary care position in the family, this dynamic often creates a greater sense of loss and responsibility (parentified child) than does paternal chemical use. The second factor is the sex of the child. Again, males and females may respond differently. The sex of the parent in conjunction with the sex of the child is also a complicating factor, with mother–daughter, mother–son, father–daughter, and father–son pairings all having different dynamics. The third factor is the length of time the parent has been actively abusing. A fourth factor is the age of the child during the period of active abuse. Finally, the extent of the abuse/dependence on the chemical influences the effects on children.

Ackerman (1983), along with other, more recent researchers (Administration on Children, Youth, and Families, 2006; Kumper & Summerhays, 2006) in the field of resiliency believe that children can avoid the worst of the impact if they are able to find a parental surrogate. The impact that one stable, caring adult—whether a family member or not—can have in a child's life has since been researched and proven. The presence of such a person is one of the major factors in children who are resilient—who survive dysfunctional families and environments with healthy attitudes and behaviors. Factors that distinguish these children from less resilient children continue to be researched but may include the child's personal characteristics. Other factors that seem to impact a child's resilience are environmental factors and the support from the larger social system, such as religious influence, peer influences, and community or educational influences

"Children in families with alcohol and drug abuse may leave their families in many ways but they usually feel that although they never really belonged to the family they can never really leave" (Lawson & Lawson, 2004, p. 64). This comment best addresses the pseudomutuality that is a sustaining dynamic in the addictive family. It also expresses the problems experienced by these children as they move out into the world. This connectedness to the family of origin creates the highest probability for the child to re-create that family's dynamics in their present family. (For an in-depth understanding of this process, see David H. Olsen's work and the Circumplex Model of Marital and Family Systems.)

TREATMENT WITH ADDICTIVE FAMILIES

With compelling evidence of the family's impact in the etiology and maintenance of abuse and dependency, it seems appropriate to incorporate family systems therapy in the treatment process. However, many treatment programs do no more than pay lip service to family therapy. Partially, this may be due to the politics and available monies through managed care for substance abuse treatment today. Some treatment programs tend to compartmentalize individual and family therapy, offering a time-limited family component to augment ongoing individual treatment; some offer no family therapy. Artificial compartmentalization itself denies a holistic or systems approach to treatment.

Another issue is that many treatment facilities do not have clinicians trained in family systems theory. Therefore, counselors who are minimally trained in the theory and techniques of family theory are offering the "family therapy" component. In spite of these problems, family therapy can be a powerful adjunct in the treatment of substance abusers, from assessment, to detoxification, and through treatment and aftercare. One variation of family therapy that is often included in residential treatment is family week.

As already discussed, an underlying principle of systems theory, no matter which school of family theory that one adheres to, is that systems (in this case, families) are self-regulating and self-maintaining. This one sentence speaks volumes for the inclusion of family members in treatment. The identified patient (IP) or substance abuser would be unable to continue the behavior without a system (family or other significant support system) to maintain the behavior. This in no way implies that the system prefers the individual's continued use of drugs. Rather, it implies that the system accommodates and adjusts itself to the individual's use. The family may be traumatized by the consequences of the abuse but at the same time finds it essential that the individual continue using to maintain the system's homeostasis. Therefore, when the individual decides to stop abusing, the family balance is disrupted. Based on systems theory, without intervention the system will seek to return to its previous homeostasis or balance, which in this case includes a substance-abusing family member.

The value of including the family in assessment lies in the multiple perspectives that become available when family members are included. No longer does the clinician have to rely on the individual abuser's information about drug use; he or she now has access to a variety of information about the individual's patterns of behavior. Additionally, the clinician has information concerning the effects on the family's problem-solving skills, daily routines, and rituals or, more specifically, how the family maintains itself in the face of the dysfunctionality.

Although working with substance abuse families appears to be a long-term developmental treatment plan, many treatment programs (involving either inpatient or intensive outpatient care) are able to offer only one family week during the treatment period. Family week offers an excellent beginning for family change. The week is usually structured so that the morning meetings are with the dependent and the family and perhaps with a family group of three or so families. The afternoons are reserved for individual work with the dependent and the family, and also for leisure time.

Families must be prepared in many ways for the intensity of this week. First, they must be given the ground rules, which include the way in which the therapy will be structured (who will meet with whom and when), confidentiality limits, examples of healthy communication ("I" statements), and group norms and expectations. Furthermore, families need to understand that this is time to focus on immediate stressors and concerns. This week will be used to practice communicating honestly, expressing feelings, taking appropriate responsibility, and establishing appropriate boundaries. A relapse plan will be developed and discussed with the entire family.

Family week is usually a highly volatile and emotional week for all concerned, including the therapist. Families can observe how other families are handling their problems and learn from their strengths. They also learn from the therapists' role modeling as well as many of the interactive techniques that might be used, such as family sculpting, role playing, and reenactment. Family members are taught to interact more honestly and are allowed sufficient time to express their emotions.

Most families who have stayed together and get to family week usually survive family week together also. These families are then ready to continue therapy outside the treatment facility. This therapy will begin to explore the family-of-origin issues that assisted in the development of the chemical use.

It may also be important for the counselor to address the difference in the family's behavior patterns when an individual is using and when the individual is not using (wet and dry conditions). Developing a clear understanding of these behavior patterns can be essential in assisting the family in change.

The author shares with many other practitioners in the field the belief that meaningful psychotherapy can begin only after an individual stops using mind-altering drugs. Therefore, detoxification is a fundamental beginning for treatment. The family therapy approach to detoxification includes a contract with the entire family for detoxification that involves not only the abstinence of the individual but also a shift in the self-regulating patterns of behavior that have developed around the use of drugs in the family.

When an individual stops using alcohol or other drugs, the family is destabilized. Many times this new situation creates a crisis within the family. Sometimes other problems increase: an adolescent will begin to act out, a physical illness will become worse, or another family member's drug use will worsen. A systems approach recognizes the family's attempt at returning to balance and addresses these issues from that perspective. Just as the family learned to organize itself around the substance use, it must now reorganize itself when there is no substance use in the family. This reordering will require the restructuring of family rituals, roles, and rules. For many families, daily routines will be significantly altered without the presence of alcohol or other drug use. In the cases of long-term substance use, families may have no concept of ways of interacting in the world other than those that are centered around the abuser's behavioral shifts.

THE PROCESS OF TREATMENT

A few general considerations should be discussed before examining the process of working with chemically dependent families. Generally, systems theorists believe that a symptomology in the child or children helps stabilize or balance a dysfunctional marital partnership. Therefore, when the child's behavior becomes healthier (non-use) the marital distress level will rise greatly. Often, to maintain the homeostasis, the partners will manipulate the child's behavior back to chemical use.

A family member is always primarily loyal to the family, no matter how dysfunctional or "crazy" the family appears to outsiders. The counselor must be cautious of criticizing or demeaning the family in any way.

There is no ideal family structure. Each family has its own personality and structure. The level of chemical use may affect the system differently based on many factors, including the learned behaviors from the family of origin. High levels of abuse may not affect one family as profoundly as lower levels affect another. Remember: each family is a unique system. All of these families, to one degree or another, operate in a crisis mode. The family moves from one crisis to another as a normal part of daily functioning.

Families operate in an emotional field of past, present, and future. This three-tiered emotional field includes the family of origin, the present nuclear family, and the future generations of this family. Family therapy provides the unequaled opportunity to impact, or change, not only the present generation we have in treatment but, through changing the family patterns and structures, future generations as well.

To be effective when working with chemically dependent families, the counselor must first develop a framework or theoretical orientation within systems theories. This approach allows the counselor to organize the assessment, diagnosis, treatment planning, and goals of therapy. The basic goal of all systems theories is for the members of the family to achieve a higher level of functioning and to experience symptom relief.

PROGRAMS UTILIZING FAMILY THERAPY

While many treatment facilities are not utilizing family therapy to the maximum, there are multiple evidence-based programs available today. These programs are specifically designed to engage couples, families, and communities in treatment. SAMHSA's website (nrepp.samhsa.gov/ViewAll.aspx) provides a complete list of programs deemed to have high efficacy and low recidivism.

One such program is Multidimensional Family Therapy (MDFT), which focuses on adolescent substance abuse. MDFT utilizes treatment in four areas: the individual adolescent, the adolescent's family, members as individuals, the family unit, and how the unit interacts with the social environment. This particular program is solution-focused and strives to provide immediate practical outcomes that affect all aspects of the family's life.

As an evidence-based program, MDFT results indicate:

- 93% of youth receiving treatment reported no substance-related problem at one year post intake
- Reduction in negative attitudes/behaviors and improvement in school functioning
- Parents increased their involvement in teen's lives, improved their parenting skills, and decreased their stress (Liddle, 2002).

Another evidenced-based program is Alcohol Behavioral Couple Therapy (ABCT). ABCT is an outpatient treatment for individuals with alcohol use disorders and their intimate partners. It is based on two assumptions: Intimate partner behaviors and couple interactions can be triggers for drinking, and a positive intimate relationship is a key source of motivation to change drinking behavior. Using cognitive-behavioral therapy, ABCT aims to identify and decrease the partner's behaviors that cue or reinforce the client's drinking; strengthen the partner's support of the client's efforts to change; increase positive couple interactions by improving interpersonal communication and problem-solving skills as a couple; and improve the client's coping skills and relapse prevention techniques to achieve and maintain abstinence. This program is based on several research studies (McCrady et al., 2004; McCrady, Epstein, Cook, Jensen, & Hildebrandt, 2009; Powers, Vedel, & Emmelkamp, 2008).

The research indicated that in all groups over an 18-month period, there were significant increases in days of abstinence. Further, fewer days of heavy drinking were reported over a 12-month period.

How Successful Is Family Therapy?

Family therapy is successful if used in conjunction with individual and group therapy over the period of treatment and recovery. We all know that individuals get better in different ways and at different rates, so many variables play into the concept of success when working with the family system. For example, how long does the dependent person need to be clean, or clean and sober, to claim success? What is the difference? How many of the family members must be using new coping skills? For how long? By what means do we measure this: self-report or outsiders' observations? It would seem that at least three criteria must be met to approach success: the family has to value sobriety, the family has developed and implemented new problem solving skills, and the drug-using behavior has been accepted as the primary cause of the dysfunction.

Case Discussions

These case discussions incorporate the use of individual and group therapy (as discussed in Chapters 7 and 8) as well as systems theory to exemplify the integration of treatment modalities.

Case 1 (Sandy and Pam).

Neither Sandy nor Pam would be referred to residential treatment at this time. Although Pam may need detoxification, more information concerning her drug use pattern would be necessary to make this decision.

Sandy exemplifies an individual who has decided to stop drinking and now needs someone to facilitate structure and develop a plan of action to avoid a relapse. Using the biopsychosocial model of treatment, Sandy would be involved in individual therapy to address relationship issues and the possibility of posttraumatic stress disorder. Both Sandy and Pam would be invited to participate in group therapy as discussed in Chapter 8. Using a solution-focused model of therapy, the therapist would build on Sandy's strengths, emphasizing the fact that she has quit drinking on her own. The therapist would ask for other exceptions to times when Sandy was drinking and explore how she managed to stay sober during those times. A plan to continue these behaviors would be developed.

Because Pam and Sandy came in together to work on their relationship, the therapist would want to honor this request and continue to work with them from a systems perspective. Using the genogram previously developed, issues of transgenerational patterns of use would be explored. From a solution-focused model, the question would be how others in the family handled stress other than by drinking. Furthermore, communication and relational issues might be discussed both in group and in sessions including both Pam and Sandy.

Pam would be asked to contract to decrease her drinking and not to use cocaine over a negotiated period of time and also agree not to come to a session having had alcohol or cocaine. The goal would be complete abstinence as soon as possible. It would also be effective to ask Pam to contract not to see Sam for a given period of time. During this time frame, the therapist might work with Pam individually on relationship issues, transgenerational patterns of coping, and alternative behaviors to using alcohol and cocaine. It would also be appropriate to work with Pam on relaxation techniques for the anxiety attacks. Referral for medication is possible but not preferable since the goal of therapy is to learn to live productively without drugs.

The therapist would recommend that both Pam and Sandy attend AA/NA/Al-Anon meetings. The 90/90 schedule would be suggested (i.e., 90 meetings in 90 days). If an outpatient group were available, the therapist might suggest attendance for additional support and therapeutic involvement not available through a 12-step program.

Case 2 (Jose and Juanita).

As noted in Chapter 5, both Juanita and Jose meet the criteria for substance dependence. Their chronic use of drugs spans 23 years. If possible, the therapist might suggest short-term residential treatment for Juanita and Jose. This decision is based on the admitted inability to stop using, the environment in which Juanita works, and the admitted lack of desire to quit using completely. Placing this couple in a setting at least to detoxify might enable the therapist to begin to develop an abstinence plan. Additionally, it would allow breathing space to work with their daughters Sarita and Karen to explore what is actually happening with them.

Residential treatment may not be practical for both adults in the family; if so, intensive outpatient treatment would be recommended. A regimen of individual, family, and group sessions would be designed. Both adults need to address transgenerational substance abuse and child abuse issues as well as parenting issues in the present. A contract to remain clean and sober should be developed and a structure constructed with the family to implement the plan.

Sarita's acting-out behavior is an indication of the imbalance in the system. Also, Jose's inappropriate behavior with Sarita when drinking must be explored thoroughly. Although Karen is the quiet one, her "disappearance" from the family is also a concern for the therapist. Boundary issues and hierarchy should be discussed. Again, transgenerational patterns of abuse can be discussed and the implications for Karen and Sarita brought into the session.

The therapist must also be aware of the possibility that Sarita is already involved in drug use. Individual sessions with the girls would be an important asset in the treatment plan. The therapist would want to gather information about the day-to-day activities in the home, at school, and in other situations. Information about peers and activities would also be helpful. Referring Sarita to Alateen and Karen to a group for children would be beneficial if available.

Couples group therapy for Juanita and Jose would prove extremely beneficial. In this setting, couple and family issues as well as parenting can be discussed freely and with others in the same situation as well as benefiting from

(Continued)

(*Continued*)

the facilitation of a professional. Certainly a 12-step program would be an appropriate support for both Jose and Juanita.

Case 3 (Leigh).

In working with Leigh, several factors need to be considered. The first factor is Leigh's developmental stage. Normal adolescent growth includes rebellious and sometimes dangerous behavior. It most certainly includes behaviors that are unacceptable to the parents. Additionally, many changes have occurred in Leigh's life recently: Her brother left for college, and she has moved to a new area and a new school. Her mother's stress appears to have increased, creating increased conflict between Leigh and her mother.

The therapist might address Leigh's drug use and acting-out behavior as a symptom of her discontent with her present situation. An additional important concern, and also a symptom, would be the fact that Leigh is overly thin. The possibility of an eating disorder combined with the other issues must be carefully evaluated. If the therapist

determines that an eating disorder exists, a referral to an eating disorder specialist might be appropriate. Safety issues must be addressed in regard to all of Leigh's present behaviors.

Addressing Leigh's drug use as a symptom, rather than the problem, requires a different approach to treatment. Normalizing some of her behavior with Mom might take pressure off the situation. A "no drug" contract would be negotiated. Sessions with Mom would be scheduled to decrease the conflict and establish boundaries as well as connections. If possible, this therapist would also include the father. How to schedule these sessions would be determined after conversations with Leigh, Mom, and Dad. Mom and Dad appear to need some assistance with their relationship because Leigh feels in the middle of this situation, so parenting skills work would be one goal of therapy. Also, developing a plan in which Leigh spends quality time with her parents would be advantageous.

Leigh does not appear to need a 12-step program at this time. If a teen group were available, however, the support of other clean and sober teenagers might be beneficial.

Case Study

Amanda

Amanda is a 21-year-old single female who lives with her mother and her 17-year-old brother. Her dad is a truck driver who is on the road for weeks at a time. Amanda reports concern about her drug use but doesn't know what to do about it. She was recently arrested for her second DUI and is court mandated to residential therapy for two weeks. The residential facility has a family therapy weekend.

Amanda reports that when her dad is home, he drinks and watches the ball games on TV. When he gets drunk he yells at her, her

brother, and mom and throws things. Mom also drinks some when Dad is gone and a lot more when he is home. When they are both drunk, they fight both verbally and physically. Amanda says it is best just to get out of their way. The cops have been out to the house several times. Amanda usually leaves when they start fighting. Many times she goes to stay at her grandmother's house.

Amanda says she started drinking and smoking when she was 13, in the eighth grade. She and her friends would raid the liquor cabinet at home. At first it was every month or so, then more and more until they were drinking every day after school. She started smoking around that same time and spent her time trying to figure out where to get money for "smokes." Amanda says, "Other kids were talking about high school and the classes they were going to take, and I was just thinking about drinking and smoking and avoiding Mom and Dad."

Amanda now smokes about a pack a day, plus a couple of joints too. She has a cup of coffee in the morning before work and that's it. At night she drinks 3 or 4 beers plus a few shots of vodka. On the weekends is "when I really get down to partying. I've played around with lots of stuff. You know, trying to see what's out there. I've tried pot, coke, mescaline, XTC, mushrooms, meth. I've even shot up a few times. It's no big deal. When I'm partying, I like to mix things up a bit—alcohol and something else—maybe pot, maybe coke. Depends on what's going on and who's around. If I drink too much I black out. I've even OD'd a few times. I do like meth or speed though. If any drug is my favorite, aside from cigarettes and coffee, it'd be 'speed.'"

Amanda's parents took her to a doctor when she was 10. They told the doctor that she was out of control at home. Her teacher had complained of her lack of attention in school and outbursts of frustration both with the teacher and with the other children. The doctor diagnosed her with attention deficit disorder (see *DSM-4-TR* for criteria) and gave her Ritalin, which she took for 5 years and then quit. She is on no prescribed medication at this time.

Amanda describes her brother as a complete math "geek." He always got good grades, has never been in trouble; is responsible, dependable, healthy, and clean. Amanda states, "He's the prince charming and I'm the evil villain in the family."

Critical Thinking Questions

1. Based on the information Amanda gave you, what other information would you need to determine her level of drug use?
2. What dynamics in Amanda's family would you consider nature and/or nuture?
3. What would be your strategy for the family therapy weekend if all members attended? Who would you want to attend? What would you specifically want to know/observe?
4. Is there any information in Amanda's medical history that might lead you to suspect that some diagnosis other than substance abuse might be correct? How would you determine this? How would that affect your treatment?
5. What in Amanda's environment plays a role in her drug use?

MyCounselingLab™

Go to Topic 8: *Family Treatment,* on the MyCounselingLab™ site (www.MyCounseling Lab.com) for *Substance Abuse Counseling,* Fifth Edition where you can:

- Find learning outcomes for *Family Treatment* along with the national standards that connect to these outcomes.
- Complete Assignments and Activities that can help you more deeply understand the chapter content.
- Apply and practice your understanding of the core skills identified in the chapter with the Building Counseling Skills unit.
- Prepare yourself for professional certification with a Practice for Certification quiz.
- Connect to videos through the Video and Resource Library.

CONCLUSION

Family therapy addresses the systemic circumstances in which the individual exists. If we as clinicians believe that the etiology of substance abuse encompasses every aspect of the individual's life, then it is only reasonable that our treatment modalities mirror this belief. Family therapy not only can resolve issues in the family currently presenting for therapy but also, by addressing long-running patterns of behavior, can help prevent dysfunctionalities from arising in future generations. No one is suggesting that family/systems therapy alone be used in treatment but it is a *crucial part* of the collaborative framework for treating substance abuse.

10

Retaining Sobriety: Relapse Prevention Strategies

ROBERT A. DOBMEIER, PH.D.

PATRICIA STEVENS, PH.D.

MyCounselingLab™

Visit the **MyCounselingLab™** site for *Substance Abuse Counseling*, Fifth Edition to enhance your understanding of chapter concepts. You'll have the opportunity to practice your skills through video- and case-based Assignments and Activities as well as Building Counseling Skills units, and to prepare for your certification exam with Practice for Certification quizzes.

Individuals in recovery as well as the individuals involved in the treatment of recovering individuals recognize that sustaining a clean and sober life is significantly more difficult than eliminating the actual use of any alcohol, tobacco, or other drugs (ATOD). There is a high degree of consensus in the field that lapses usually are a common element in the recovery process. Many believe that "the rates of relapse vary between studies and across substances, but the tendency to experience a lapse is the modal treatment outcome" (Witkiewitz & Marlatt, 2007, p. 726). More research is beginning to emerge on substance abuse relapse and its prevention (Witkiewitz & Marlatt, 2004). The process of change in the modification of substance-abusing behavior includes influences related to the person, provider, intervention, and environment (DiClemente, 2007).

Recovery is defined not only as abstinence from mind-altering chemicals or nonproductive compulsive behaviors but also as changes in physical, psychological, social, familial, and spiritual areas of functioning. These changes are a process and not an event in the recovering individual's life. It is generally accepted that the dynamics that enable an individual to maintain sobriety are as different as the factors that initiate sobriety (Witkiewitz & Marlatt, 2004). Just as there are differences in individuals in the treatment process, there are differences in individuals in the recovery process. Unique individual differences as well as the stage of recovery affect the path that recovery takes.

Some important intrapersonal factors in the recovery process are self-efficacy, outcome expectancies, craving, and motivation toward positive behavior change and toward use of the substance. Coping behavior skills and intense negative and positive emotional states are intrapersonal forces that impact recovery. The availability of social support, particularly from significant others who do not abuse a substance, positively impacts the recovery outcome (Witkiewitz & Marlatt, 2004).

A recovery plan must take into account all of these factors. It would be fair to say that recovery, as with all changes in a person's life, is ultimately governed by the client's drives and motivation to change. Motivation is a key predictor of treatment success (Freyer-Adam et al., 2009). In substance abuse/dependency counseling, as in other areas of psychotherapy, the individual's motivation for change must be greater than that of the therapist's or significant others' for changes to take root (Wahab, 2010).

Many individuals are "dry" or "clean," referring to having completed withdrawal and being physically free of ATOD. However, this state should not be confused with recovery. Being physically without ATOD but making no other lifestyle changes most frequently leads to chronic lapses or relapse. And, even if individuals do not begin to use again, their behaviors mimic their active drug-using behaviors, particularly those observed in the precontemplation stage of active use. This is sometimes called "white-knuckle sobriety."

Relapse has many definitions. One early definition was a *breakdown or setback in a person's attempt to change or modify a target behavior* (Marlatt, 1985b). "[E]ssentially, when individuals attempt to change a problematic behavior, an initial setback (lapse) is highly probable. One possible outcome, following the initial setback, is a return to the previous problematic behavior pattern (relapse)" (Witkiewitz & Marlatt, 2004, p. 224). This definition provides insight into the changing view of relapse in research and treatment. *Merriam-Webster's Online Dictionary (2011)* defines relapse as "1. The act or an instance of backsliding, worsening, or subsiding; 2. A recurrence of symptoms of a disease after a period of improvement." A simple definition would be the continuous return to ATOD use or to the dysfunctional patterns of compulsive behavior.

Relapse can be seen from two dimensions. The first is the "event" of resumption of use; the second is the "process" whereby attitudes and/or behaviors are exhibited that indicate a likelihood of resumption of use. It is also true that these indicators vary widely from individual to individual and, therefore, may be difficult to recognize and identify. The decision to start use may also be influenced by the person's expectations for the initial effect of use (Hayaki, Anderson, & Stein, 2008).

Lapse is the initial return to use after a period of sobriety. This may be a single episode, or it may lead to relapse—as indicated in the word itself, to lapse and lapse again. A lapse is usually temporary, as opposed to a relapse, which is considered a return to uncontrolled use. Although AA defines a *lapse* as a failure in sobriety and indicates that the individual must begin their path to sobriety again, many mental health practitioners and other self-help groups believe that a lapse may be used to assist the client (and the therapist) in learning what factors motivate the client to return to substance use or relapse. This information can be used to develop a plan to prevent other lapses or a return to substance use. In truth, some clients gain valuable self-information from a lapse and are strengthened by this new knowledge.

As the concepts of both etiology and maintenance of dependency have changed, the view of relapse has changed. Most now view relapse as a normal part of the recovery process and as a learning experience for the recovering individual (Thakker & Ward, 2010). In fact, after treatment many individuals still use substances on an episodic basis and consider themselves successful in their struggle with ATOD. This model of recovery is based in the theory of harm reduction (Witkiewitz & Marlatt, 2006). We have progressed in our beliefs from the forced choice position of alcoholic/ nonalcoholic or clean/addict to understanding that use, misuse, abuse, and dependency is a continuum. Recovery is now considered a continuum, from total abstinence to drinking/using in moderation or socially.

Relapse is a part of treatment and recovery. Models that are discussed in this chapter could also be discussed in the chapters on individual and group treatment because the process of treatment is a continuum. The fact that we have chosen to discuss these models here indicates the importance that we place on relapse planning for all clients who abuse or are dependent on ATOD.

DETERMINANTS OF RELAPSE

The first 90 days after the individual stops using ATOD appear to be when clients are the most vulnerable to relapse. Clients have not developed strong coping skills this early in the process (some have been in controlled settings; others are in family systems that are dysfunctional and unable to appropriately support nonuse) and therefore tend to be unable to make healthy decisions in regard to their life choices (Doweiko, 2006; Marlatt & Witkiewitz, 2005; Thakker & Ward, 2010).

Although several models of relapse prevention will be discussed later in this chapter, it is interesting to note that all of these models incorporate, in some manner, common elements that are precursors of renewed substance use. The counselor should be aware that these different elements are overlapping and integrated. They represent every aspect of the client's life. No matter which model is chosen by the client or the counselor, recovery means a restructuring of the client's entire life system.

Environmental

When clients are in treatment, either residential or intensive outpatient, they usually believe strongly that they can abstain from use. This belief has its basis in the comfort of the protected and supportive atmosphere of treatment. When they return to their own environment, many times this protection and support are not as available as during treatment. Feelings of self-efficacy, an important aspect of recovery (Oei, Hasking, & Phillips, 2007; Senbanjo, Wolff, Marshall, & Strang, 2009), and control are replaced by anxiety, insecurity, and doubt.

High-risk situations—negative emotional states, interpersonal conflict, social pressure, environmental stimuli such as places and activities associated with former substance use lifestyles, and craving— threaten the client's control and increase the likelihood of a return to use (Fernández-Montalvo, López-Goñi, Illescas, Landa, & Lorea, 2007; Roffman & Stephens, 2005).

Fernández-Montalvo et al. (2007) reported that coping with negative emotional states accounted for 49.5% of relapses. Stressful conditions associated with substance-related environmental cues accompany increased craving, increased negative emotion, and decreased positive emotion, contributing to the risk of relapse (Fox, Bergquist,

Hong, & Sinha, 2007). Interpersonal factors such as conflict with others, which may be high during recovery as the client endeavors to decide which behaviors to engage in, accounted for 17.5% of relapses.

Interpersonal conflict refers to arguments or confrontation with family, friends, or other significant individuals in the client's life that lead to negative feelings. Negative emotions such as anger, anxiety, frustration, depression, and/or boredom may occur from these conflicts. Clients who have not developed new and more productive coping may resume substance use (An-Pyng, 2007). As you can see, environmental, intrapersonal, and interpersonal components interact to contribute to a high-risk situation for relapse.

Case Discussion

Case 2 (Jose and Juanita).

Working with Juanita and Jose in a recovery planning process would require specific attention to the environmental factors in their lives. Juanita is still working in a bar, and this situation will create social pressure and therefore will be a significant "trigger" for use. If Jose continues to associate with drug-using acquaintances, he may become vulnerable to cravings. They both admit that using is a mechanism for handling stressful events. Jose and Juanita will need to learn and practice new coping skills that will empower them to recognize environmental and related intrapersonal and interpersonal influences. It may be beneficial for a counselor to help Juanita and Jose to develop communication skills that allow them to talk with each other about the risks for relapse associated with Juanita's working at the bar and Jose's spending time with his drug-using associates. This could involve sharing with each other the dangers to their peace of mind, relationship with each other, family, and job stability that these environments represent.

Urges and craving for ATOD are also a part of the relapse process. *Craving* is a cognitive state where individuals relive the positive feelings of use through anticipation of use; *urges* are behavioral impulses to get and use ATOD (Marlatt & Witkiewitz, 2005). A craving, or jonesing, is the desire for a substance—drug wanting; an urge is being drawn to fulfill the desire—drug-seeking (Wanberg & Milkman, 2008). Urge surfing refers to going with the craving, without fighting it or giving in to it. It allows recognition of craving as a time-limited, normal experience that can be managed without relapsing (Ruiz, Strain, & Langrod, 2007). It is imperative that clients learn their cues or triggers and that they develop practical and effective methods for dealing with these situations. Doing so may well decrease the possibility of relapse (Baker, Piper, McCarthy, Majaskie, & Fiore, 2004).

Behavioral

Clients who have few or no coping skills to handle high-risk situations are more likely to return to substance use. Several studies emphasize the importance of teaching clients alternative coping skills to deal with these situations (Baker et al., 2004; Senbanjo et al., 2009). It is also important to teach the client new decision-making skills (An-Pyng, 2007; Litt, Kadden, Cooney, & Kabela, 2003). A sober lifestyle requires integration into a productive family life, work, recreation, diet and exercise, stress management, and handling the desire to use ATOD drugs again. Each of these represents stress in the client's life. Clients learn that abstinence does not mean an absence of problems in one's life; even if some of the problems were caused by use, others are a part of living. Learning to deal with stress in a healthy way is imperative to recovery.

Although many think that it is major life decisions or situations that cause one to return to use, the reason is usually much less dramatic. Dealing with daily life requires constant minidecisions that are impacted by a host of environmental, cognitive, affective, and interpersonal influences. It is the unforeseen minidecisions (taking a shortcut to work and driving by the dealer's house, not getting enough sleep, a conflict with the boss, etc.) that often lead the individual to relapse.

Case Discussion

Case 3 (Leigh).

Leigh is an excellent example of a client who needs to develop new coping skills. Leigh is responding to the stressful events in her life by using drugs and perhaps with the development of an eating disorder. Assisting her in learning how to make day-to-day decisions that decrease her anxiety would be essential to her sober lifestyle. The therapist might want to help her to increase her awareness of her life choices, assist her in developing new skills, and then facilitate the practice of these skills in individual, group, and family therapy. When Leigh becomes anxious about her belief that she is overweight, she can practice initiating a phone conversation with a friend or family member rather than exercising excessively. She might choose to listen to music, which she says has a calming effect on her.

Cognitive

Researchers have found a variety of cognitive variables that affect relapse. The person's attitude toward sobriety (motivation to quit or not) (Miller & Rollnick, 2009), perception of his or her coping self-efficacy (their belief that they have good coping skills) (Oei et al., 2007; Senbanjo et al., 2009), and expectation of relapse are important factors (Hayaki et al., 2008). AA and Narcotics Anonymous (NA) refer to "stinking thinking" or the faulty thinking of substance abusers that can contribute to relapse. Irrational beliefs both about self and the present circumstances create negative emotions for the client. Rational Recovery (RR) and Save Our Selves (SOS) utilize cognitive-behavioral terminology and interventions that support rational thinking. It may not be the actual thought or pattern of thinking, but more how the abuser interprets or manages situations that determines the outcome (Barry & Petry, 2009).

Affective

In their 2007 study, Fernández-Montalvo and colleagues identified negative affect as the major cause of relapse. Anxiety, depression, and other negative emotions have been shown to be major determinants of relapse. Fox et al. (2007) discovered that personal stress and alcohol cue imagery (mental representation of an alcohol-related stimulus), increased emotions of anxiety, anger, fear, and sadness, and decreased positive feelings of joy and relaxation, which in turn accompanied increase in stress and cue-induced alcohol craving in alcohol abusers. Much discussion continues about dual diagnosis of coexisting mood anxiety disorders with substance abuse in this field (see Chapter 5 for a full discussion on dual diagnosis).

The stress of everyday living can create negative emotions in the recovering person. Twelve-step programs use the acronym *HALT* (don't get too hungry, angry, lonely, or tired) to alert individuals to emotions that lead to reuse. AA tells members to "get off the pity pot" when they are overwhelmed by feelings of depression and hopelessness. For many clients, the purpose of using was to numb negative feelings. So, the first step in avoiding relapse is learning to recognize, label, and be able to communicate feelings in a productive way (Slaymaker & Sheehan, 2008). Relaxation techniques, meditation, assertiveness skills, and other emotion management skills will be important in reducing the risk of relapse.

Two very strong emotions that must be dealt with in recovery are shame and guilt. Guilt is "a feeling of culpability for offenses" (*Merriam-Webster*, 2011). It is a consequence of the dependency process both for the addict and for the significant others in the addict's life. When the guilt becomes tied to "who I am" and not "what I did," it is known as *shame*. Dealing with guilt and shame affects an individual's self-esteem through negative feedback. These emotions may become overwhelming in recovery and easily lead to relapse in an attempt to protect one's self from the feelings (Slaymaker & Sheehan, 2008).

Recognizing that positive emotional states also create stress is imperative when working with this population. Positive events such as a new job, a child's wedding, and a renewal of an intimate relationship may be seen as more stressful than negative events since the abuser may be familiar with negative emotions associated with negative events. In fact, success may be the most stressful event in recovery as it often heightens expectations that the individual be even more successful in the future. Recognition that one is feeling stressed, be it from positive or negative emotions, and learning behaviors that help to calm one such as taking a walk are important skills to learn.

Interpersonal Determinants

The lack of a supportive family or social network has been highly correlated with a return to substance use (An-Pyng, 2007; Fernández-Montalvo et al., 2007). The support of a partner to accomplish abstinence goals is particularly relevant to success (Marlatt & Witkiewitz, 2005). Many times the primary significant other is also an active substance abuser, and, as noted earlier in this book, many of these individuals come from families with substance abuse problems that span generations.

The family is usually the primary relationship and, therefore, the relationship that is most harmed in the process of abuse and dependency. Broken promises, hurts, isolation, and in many cases verbal, physical, and/or sexual abuse have been present. Taking responsibility for the behaviors and mending the relationships are a large part of recovery. Research indicates that family involvement in treatment is critical; families who are involved support rather than sabotage the process (Slesnick & Prestopnik, 2009). If the family is not engaged in the recovery process along with the recovering individual, the results can be devastating (Kinney, 2009). If they fail to support the recovering individual's efforts to make changes in lifestyle, family members risk contributing to a relapse (see Chapter 9 on codependency and enabling behaviors). There has been a remarkable increase in the use of nonmedical prescription drugs among adolescents. Among illicit drugs, only marijuana is used more regularly by this age group. In a study of a nationally representative sample Ford (2009) discovered that teens with strong bonds to family are not as likely to continue or to start abusing prescription drugs.

Work and leisure time are two other components that may create a problem in recovery. Many times the individual has lost a job or been demoted due to the substance abuse problem. Finding satisfying work is an important component of avoiding relapse. Leisure time for substance abusers has previously meant looking for their drug of choice, using the drug, or hiding the fact that they were using. Without these activities, recovering individuals find themselves with lots of time on their hands. Boredom, because of a lack of social support or activities, is a significant factor in relapse. Work and leisure-time activities have been shown to be resources for preventing relapse (Ruiz et al., 2007).

Summary

It is easy to see that recovery, like abuse, addiction, and treatment, is a complex system. Every aspect of the individual's life has been affected by substance use. Every aspect must now be examined and redefined. Change, positive or negative, creates stress. Stress, without appropriate coping skills, may lead to relapse. So, again, we see the convolution of so many elements of the client's life that are involved in relapse and relapse planning and management.

MODELS OF RELAPSE PLANNING AND MANAGEMENT

Several models of relapse prevention have developed through the years. The first model was Alcoholics Anonymous. This model has become the framework for a multitude of self-help/support groups including Narcotics Anonymous (NA), Cocaine Anonymous (CA), Sex Addicts Anonymous (SAA), Gamblers Anonymous (GA), and Overeaters Anonymous (OA), to name a few. Through the years, other researchers and recovering people have developed different models of relapse prevention (e.g., Rational Recovery, Women for Sobriety, Moderation Management, and Secular Organizations for Sobriety/ Save Our Selves). We will first discuss the overarching models of recovery that are shown to be of value in the literature: the disease model, a developmental model, and a cognitive-behavioral/social learning model for maintaining sobriety. These models are used in treatment and in aftercare programs as well as being components of some of the self-help groups that have been established throughout the world. After this discussion, examples of the current available self-help organizations will be presented.

The Disease Model

Addictionology, the study of the addiction process, began with one of the earliest models to explain alcoholism—the disease model. It was developed by Jellinek in the 1940s and his seminal work, *The Disease Concept of Alcoholism*, was published in 1960. Jellinek concluded that individuals suffering from alcoholism had a physiological problem with alcohol. He believed that the physical, emotional, and cognitive problems were a result of this physiological disease, not because of a lack of moral fortitude (the previous belief being that one who was alcoholic lacked morals). In the 1940s, this was cutting-edge research that shifted the focus from the individual's willpower to abstain from the drug (alcohol) to the drug's effect on the body. The disease model, adopted by some as a way to understand attachment to alcohol, other substances, or activities (e.g., gambling, sexual risky behaviors), conveys that the behavior is a sickness or illness that the individual cannot control without intervention (Shaffer & LaPlante, 2005). The acceptance of alcoholism and, by association, other drug addiction, as a disease by the American Medical Association in the 1950s put treatment centers on the same level as medical and psychiatric care facilities.

The public and treatment personnel have widely and enthusiastically accepted the concept of the disease model through the years. The concept has been utilized to explain all addictions. Alcoholism and addiction are seen as a disease that is progressive and irreversible (see Chapter 4 for a view of Jellinek's chart of the disease process). Under this premise, the only "cure" for the disease is total abstinence. In this model of addiction and recovery all "slips" or "lapses" are viewed as a setback. Relapses constitute a return to the disease and negate all progress that the person has made in recovery before the relapse. Recovery must start again at the beginning as one has "become ill" again and the disease process has restarted. Therefore, abstinence equals a healthy lifestyle and relapse equals sickness. Alcoholics Anonymous adopted the disease model of addiction and recovery.

Developmental Models

The developmental theorists integrate concepts of the disease model with a developmental model of recovery. Gorski and Miller (1986) developed a six-stage/nine-step model of recovery. Known as the CENAPS (Center for Applied Sciences) Model of Relapse Prevention (Gorski, 1990, 2007), it is based on the belief that substance abuse creates dysfunction at every level in an individual's life. It is, therefore, imperative in relapse prevention to focus on treatment at each of these levels. This model has been used extensively in private treatment facilities. The model addresses the need for client responsibility of behavior including triggers for relapse and coping behaviors other than ATOD use. It is based on the 12-step model of AA and used by Minnesota Model treatment facilities. (For more information regarding the Minnesota Model, see the National Institute of Drug Abuse website at nida.nih.gov/ADAC/ADAC11.html.)

THE GORSKI MODEL This model takes into consideration that relapse is a progression of behaviors that allows the substance use to be reactivated if intervention does not take place. Gorski (2007) views addiction as a chronic and progressive disease and advocates for change in all aspects of an individual's life for recovery to happen. Another aspect of this developmental model, which borrows from the AA model, is the belief that individuals must admit they have a problem and then abstain from substance use. Gorski and Miller (1986) believe that this model works best for patients who have been in treatment and relapsed.

The six stages of the developmental model are as follows:

1. *Transition* The individual begins to experience more severe symptoms and dependency and recognizes the need for treatment and seeks it.

2. *Stabilization* This is the beginning stage of treatment and may include detoxification. The individual is stabilized, and immediate problems are solved to facilitate the termination of substance use.
3. *Early recovery* The client is becoming aware of how the use of substances affected thinking and begins to manage feelings without use.
4. *Middle recovery* A balanced lifestyle change begins.
5. *Late recovery* The client has used the counseling process to understand core psychological issues that might create relapse potential.
6. *Maintenance* Maintenance is a lifelong process of sharpening coping skills to deal with life problems (Gorski, 2007).

Gorski and Miller (1986) and later Gorski (1990, 2007) developed nine steps or principles to facilitate relapse prevention. Skills are needed at each stage of recovery, and the role of the counselor is to assist the client with each of these steps or principles:

1. The first step is to stabilize the client or assist the client to develop a daily structure. This is a mechanism to solve immediate problems and to assist the client to begin to live without substance use.
2. The second principle is teaching the client continual self-assessment. This provides a means to understand the previous relapse pattern and to intervene in that pattern.
3. Educational information is given concerning the disease and the biopsychosocial models of dependency.
4. The counselor helps the client identify the warning signs of an impending relapse.
5. After identification of warning signs, the counselor facilitates the client's ability to manage his or her own warning signs.
6. The client creates a set of activities to use when these warning signs appear to avoid relapse.
7. The relapse dynamic is interrupted. Problems that are associated with the warning signs are discussed and solved.
8. The counselor may well have been working throughout this process with family and friends. At this point, significant others become involved in the relapse planning program.
9. The final step is a consistent follow-up over a minimum of 2 years and reinforcement by the counselor of the client's progress during this time.

Similar to the AA model, the developmental model is structured with the assumption that relapse problems and warning signs will change as the individual progresses through the stages of recovery. These changes will necessitate the reworking of these steps or principles with each developmental stage of recovery.

THE STAGE MODEL Prochaska, DiClemente, and Norcross (1992) also suggested a developmental stage model of recovery. This model incorporates five definite stages of recovery. The model assumes that change is intentional on the part of the individual. Ten change processes were identified as operational across many psychotherapy theories. These include consciousness raising, self-reevaluation, self-liberation, stimulus control, and helping relationships (Prochaska et al.). The stages of change are precontemplation, contemplation, preparation, action, and maintenance.

Precontemplation is the stage in which the individual has no intention to change behavior. One is unaware or underaware of problems related to use or addiction. Others close to the person usually recognize that a problem exists. *Contemplation* represents the stage of awareness that a problem exists and one is thinking seriously about addressing it but has not yet committed to taking action. People can remain stuck in this stage for a long time. *Preparation* is the stage of intention along with behavioral criteria (e.g., intending to take action in the next month and beginning to try out cutting down on smoking). One is still uncertain about a criterion for effective action, e.g., total abstinence from alcohol. *Action* is the stage in which one modifies behavior, experiences, and the environment to allow recovery from the addiction. It requires much commitment of time and energy. Typically, one is in the action stage of change up to six months. *Maintenance* is the stage in which one strives to prevent relapse and consolidates the gains made in the action stage. Maintenance is a continuation and development of the change initiated in the action stage. Remaining free of the addictive behavior and ongoing engagement in alternative constructive behaviors for more than six months are the criteria for entry to the maintenance stage (Prochaska et al., 1992).

This transtheoretical model assumes that change is cyclical and dynamic. The individual typically has to cycle through stages multiple times to achieve abstinence (see Figure 10.1). According to Doweiko (2006) approximately 40% of the substance-abusing population falls into the precontemplative stage and another 40% in the contemplative stage. Only 20% of the substance-abusing population falls within the last three stages of this model.

Prochaska and his colleagues have applied their stages of change model to a number of addictions including nicotine, heroin, alcohol, eating, and bullying (e.g., DiClemente, 2007; Prochaska, Evers, Prochaska, Van Marter, & Johnson, 2007). Given its intuitive accuracy and a growing body of empirical evidence of its effectiveness, numerous researchers (e.g., Ferrer et al., 2009; Meyer et al., 2008) and practitioners have applied the stages of change model to a host of addictions, compulsive habits, and behavior problems.

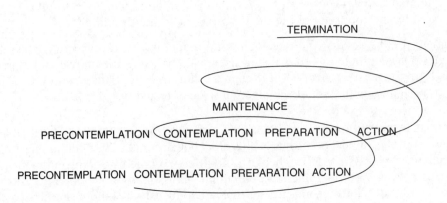

FIGURE 10.1   A spiral model of the stages of change.

Case Discussion

Case 3 (Leigh).

Leigh does not recognize the harmful effects of her using alcohol, pot, and other drugs. She is not interested in looking at her substance use and its impact on her life. As for the counseling, she simply wants to "get this done." This lack of recognition and interest would best be described as Prochaska et al.'s precontemplative stage. A counselor working with Leigh might use psychoeducational methods to help her to realize the association of family losses with her substance abuse and subsequent falling grades, deteriorating hygiene, and emotional turmoil. The counselor could also work with Leigh's mother to strengthen parenting skills and ways to engage Leigh in discussion about constructive ways to meet her needs other than substance use.

A Cognitive-Behavioral/Social Learning Model

The cognitive-behavioral model (Marlatt, 1985a; Witkiewitz & Marlatt, 2004) is based on social learning theory (Bandura, 1969, 1977). Social learning theory holds that substance use and abuse are learned behaviors in which use has been increased in frequency, duration, and intensity for psychological benefit (Barry & Petry, 2009). In other words, use is associated with reinforcement, either immediate or delayed.

SOCIAL LEARNING THEORIES The primary learning principle in social behavior is operant conditioning, in which behavior is shaped by the stimuli that follow. Social behavior is taken on through direct conditioning and through modeling of the behavior of others. Behavior is strengthened through reward (positive reinforcement) and avoidance of punishment (negative reinforcement). Influences on one's substance-using behavior come from interaction with those groups that control reinforcement and punishment, such as substance-using acquaintances, family, and work companions. Individuals learn from these significant groups' definitions (norms and attitudes) of a behavior as good or bad, for example, getting high. Substance-using behavior results when greater reinforcement of social acceptance and the other benefits of use are greater than any punishing contingencies (Akins, Smith, & Mosher, 2010).

Another social learning theory perspective examines the effect of psychological stress on substance use. This theory asserts that substance use is a mechanism, learned through reinforcement and modeling, to reduce stress. As substance use continues, the individual may use more frequently and at higher dosages to avoid withdrawal (Preston, 2006).

The importance of self-efficacy must not be overlooked in any discussion of social learning theory (Bandura, 1969, 1977). Self-efficacy reflects the individual's belief that it is within one's capacity to not use the substance that has created dependency. Research substantiates the interactive effect of self-efficacy with other treatment variables on alcohol treatment outcome—abstinence confidence, self-consciousness, and coping with stress (Krampe et al., 2008). A meta-analysis assessed interventions that enhanced self-efficacy and subsequent reduction of substance abusing behavior (Hyde, Hankins, Deale, & Marteau, 2008). Significant outcomes were found in favor of self-efficacy targeted advocacy interventions for addictions to smoking, heroin and methamphetamine, steroids and accompanying prevention behaviors. Mixed outcomes on interventions that strengthen self-efficacy were discovered in studies that looked at the following areas: cognitive-behavioral relapse prevention with a focus on alcoholism as a disease of the spirit, mind, and body; computer-generated smoking cessation self-help materials for a group of primarily female smokers; and social cognitive theory training focused on substance abuse and strategies to create change in schools and communities that yielded a greater increase in self-efficacy for girls, but not for boys (Hyde et al.).

Therefore, if high self-efficacy is positively correlated with abstinence, then a crucial element in relapse prevention would be the development of a strong sense of capacity to handle situations. Self-efficacy theory provides that "hands-on" practice handling situations of ever-increasing difficulty creates a sense of ability to manage risks of using.

COGNITIVE-BEHAVIORAL MODEL   Marlatt and his colleagues have developed the most widely used cognitive-behavioral model of relapse prevention based on social learning theory. The premise of the relapse prevention (RP) model is that individuals attempting to stop or reduce substance use will face risks of relapse (Marlatt & Gordon, 1985; Witkiewitz, Marlatt, & Walker, 2005). Although this model was initially developed to identify the challenges of maintaining abstinence for substance abusers, it has been used with other compulsive or addictive behavior patterns, including gambling, sexual addiction, and eating disorders. When individuals attempt to change a problematic behavior, an initial return to the behavior, lapse, is common. A return to the addictive behavior pattern is relapse. An alternative outcome to the lapse, prolapse, is getting back on track with the positive change.

In this model, relapse may be viewed as an opportunity for transition to a new level. In contrast to the AA model, relapse is not seen as a failure but as a learning tool for the individual. The lapse is used as a means to assess the antecedents to the lapse and to formulate a more successful coping strategy for the future. One of the most important factors in determining whether the individual will return to substance use is the individual's perception of the lapse. The client may see this as a failure or as a way to learn and develop stronger skills (Witkiewitz et al., 2005).

The RP model is useful with any behaviors that are part of a compulsive habit pattern and makes the following assumptions about attempts to change the problem behavior:

1. The individual's addictive behavior emerges from one's thought processes.
2. There are multiple cognitive, affective, social, environmental, spiritual, and neurological influences that bear on the outcome of attempts at abstinence.
3. There is often ambivalence about giving up the substance or habit.
4. Multiple treatment episodes are usually required before one is able to discontinue or control the addictive behavior.
5. Successful attempts at abstinence and other kinds of behavioral change need to be generalizable to multiple settings.
6. Individuals who have been addicted need to discover positive experiences in their lives without use (Thakker & Ward, 2010).

Thakker and Ward (2010) recommend that in addition to abstinence or moderation of use or habit, individuals in recovery have a need to experience good things in themselves and in the world. Lack of hope, inspiration, and joy can contribute to negative emotions that increase the risk of returning to old behaviors. Ward and Stewart (2003) in their Good Lives Model (GLM) recognize 10 primary goods that every individual needs to pursue: healthy living, knowledge, excellence in play and work (mastery experiences), excellence in agency (autonomy and self-directedness), inner peace (freedom from emotional turmoil and stress), friendship (intimate, romantic, and family relationships), community, spirituality (meaning and purpose in life), happiness, and creativity. Relapse prevention underscores the need for lifestyle or systemic change for the client. Exercise, biofeedback, meditation, stress management techniques, assertiveness training, and relaxation skills are a few examples of participatory changes. Cognitive restructuring, imagery, and self-talk might also be implemented. A balanced lifestyle is emphasized throughout this model.

Abstinence violation effect (AVE) is an important cognitive concept in cognitive behavioral/social learning theory of relapse (Barry & Petry, 2009; Curry, Marlatt, & Gordon, 1987). AVE occurs when an individual, having made a personal commitment to abstain from using a substance or to cease engaging in some other unwanted behavior, has an initial lapse whereby the substance or behavior is engaged in at least once. Some individuals may then proceed to uncontrolled use. The AVE occurs when the person attributes the cause of the initial lapse (the first violation of abstinence/lapse) to internal, stable, and global factors within (e.g., lack of willpower or the underlying addiction or disease).

AVE creates cognitive dissonance (the contrast between what people believe about themselves and how they behave). AVE also involves self-attribution effect. In other words, how does the person explain the lapse? Is it a personal weakness, a unique response, a lack of discipline, or a mistake that can be corrected? The explanation of the event may either create more or less guilt, conflict, or a sense of personal failure. The higher the AVE, the more likely the person is to continue the relapse. Conversely, a weaker AVE creates a situation where the client may be able to choose an explanation for the behavior that will result in more sense of control with regard to changing the behavior. For example, if the explanation of the lapse is "I drank because of an unusually high level of stress about my marriage and my legal status that does not happen often in my life," the individual may well be able to utilize learned coping mechanisms to avoid a lapse when future high stress appears.

The aim of relapse prevention is to teach people how to minimize the size of the relapse (i.e., to weaken the AVE) by directing attention to the more controllable external or situational factors that triggered the lapse (e.g., high-risk situations, coping skills, and outcome expectancies), so that the person can quickly return to the goal of abstinence and not "lose control" of the behavior.

While all the aforementioned concepts and steps are part of the Marlatt model, his most recent reconceptualization of the model is multidimensional and complex, recognizing the systemic nature of treatment and recovery (see Figure 10.2). The model is dynamic in nature rather than the linear model proposed in the 1980s. It recognizes the integration of a variety of factors as well as timeliness in these factors. Tonic, or ongoing processes (Marlatt et al., 2005), frequently accumulate over time, thereby increasing the risk for relapse. They might include distal risks such as family

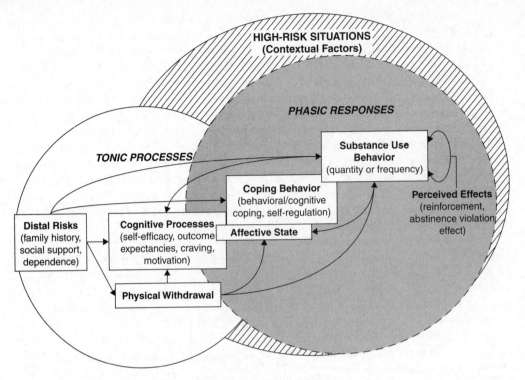

FIGURE 10.2   Dynamic model of relapse. (This is currently on p. 289 of Stevens & Smith, 4th edition):

Source: Witkiewitz, K., & Marlatt, G. A. (2004). That was Zen, this is Tao. *American Psychologist, V* 59(4), 224–235.

history and social support, cognitive processes such as self-efficacy, and physical withdrawal. Phasic response (Marlatt et al.) comprises immediate, situational behavioral/cognitive coping, affective states, and perceived effects of substance use. It is the core of the system where behavioral responding will result in a sudden change in substance use behavior. Witkiewitz and Marlatt (2004) state that the "clinical utility of the proposed model depends on clinicians' ability to gather detailed information about an individual's background, substance use history, personality, coping skills, self-efficacy, and affective state" (p. 231).

How the individual and one's supports understand the causes and implications of relapse as represented by these three models, will heavily influence their response to relapse and how they go about attempting to manage it.

SELF-HELP RECOVERY ORGANIZATIONS: ADJUNCTS TO PROFESSIONAL INTERVENTION

This text focuses on the use, abuse, and dependence of ATOD. Many self-help groups exist that focus on other addictions (gambling, eating, sex, etc.), but this chapter will review only those that specifically focus on substance abuse. Although we may mention the other groups as examples of 12-step programs available, the focus here remains on ATOD.

Alcoholics Anonymous Model

Alcoholics Anonymous (AA), as mentioned earlier, was the first self-help organization founded to assist alcoholics in recovery. It continues to be the model of recovery most widely used in treatment facilities and for individuals who may choose to start recovery on their own. Even if individuals are in long-term outpatient care, it is unusual not to include AA as an adjunct to the therapeutic process. AA's concepts are also the basis for many other self-help programs.

AA was officially founded on June 10, 1935. The groundwork for the organization was laid earlier, however, when Carl Jung, the famous psychologist, sent Ronald H. to the Oxford Group, a popular nondenominational religious group of the time, to find a spiritual awakening that therapy could not provide. Ronald H. was able to maintain his sobriety and to assist his friend, Edwin T., to do the same. Edwin T. was a friend of Bill W. At this time, Bill W. was still drinking but later was hospitalized for detoxification. After his release, he read *The Varieties of Religious Experiences* by William James, which became the foundation for the Twelve Steps of AA. During a business trip at a later date, Bill W. was fighting to keep his sobriety and, being in Akron, Ohio, was referred to Dr. Robert H. Smith (Dr. Bob). Reluctantly, Dr. Bob agreed to see him. Dr. Bob was still drinking at this time, but Bill W. found himself reaching out to him with the message of his own sobriety. Through their subsequent conversations and friendship, both remained sober and founded what we know today as Alcoholics Anonymous (White & Kurtz, 2008). Although Jellinek's model of the disease concept was not well known until the 1950s, most of the concepts of AA are based in this belief.

In 1937 the fellowship had 40 members and by 1941 membership had grown to 8,000 (White & Kurtz, 2008). The early members wrote about their struggle to maintain sobriety, publishing the first edition of the book *Alcoholics Anonymous* in 1939. Included in this first edition of the "Big Book" were the Twelve Steps and Twelve Traditions of the organization. AA has developed into a fellowship of over 2.1 million individuals all over the globe (Alcoholics Anonymous, 2010). AA members often say "wherever you can find a liquor store, you can find an AA group."

The cornerstone of the AA model is the paradoxical belief that to gain control of one's life, one must give up control to a Higher Power. Although God is mentioned in AA, members believe that one's Higher Power can be many things or beings. Distinguishing between spirituality and religion, AA believes that addiction is a spiritual disease as well as a physical one. By embracing spirituality, not a specific religious dogma, AA allows all individuals to embrace a Higher Power of their own choosing. AA is a spiritual program of living.

Fundamental in the 12-step philosophy is the belief that abstinence from substance use is not enough. Individuals must be willing to make attitudinal and behavioral changes in their lifestyle. The AA model is designed to enable individuals to address every aspect of their lives—physical, emotional, social, and spiritual—and to make positive changes in each of these areas. The twelve steps of recovery are the foundation for these changes (see Table 10.1). Having made these changes, the individual will then reach out to others in an effort to offer assistance in recovering from a substance-using lifestyle. The Twelve Traditions are also an important component of AA. These traditions govern the operation of AA.

TABLE 10.1 The twelve steps of alcoholics anonymous

1. We admitted we were powerless over alcohol—that our lives had become unmanageable.
2. Came to believe that a Power greater than ourselves could restore us to sanity.
3. Made a decision to turn our will and our lives over to the care of *God as we understood Him*.
4. Made a searching and fearless moral inventory of ourselves.
5. Admitted to God, to ourselves, and to another human being the exact nature of our wrongs.
6. Were entirely ready to have God remove all these defects of character.
7. Humbly ask Him to remove our shortcomings.
8. Made a list of all persons we had harmed, and became willing to make amends to them all.
9. Made direct amends to such people wherever possible, except when to do so would injure them or others.
10. Continued to take personal inventory and when we were wrong promptly admitted it.
11. Sought through prayer and meditation to improve our conscious contact with God as we understood Him, praying only for knowledge of His will for us and the power to carry that out.
12. Having had a spiritual awakening as the result of these steps, we tried to carry this message to alcoholics, and to practice these principles in all our affairs.

Source: The Twelve Steps are reprinted with permission of Alcoholics Anonymous World Services, Inc. (A.A.W.S.). Permission to reprint the Twelve Steps does not mean that A.A.W.S. has reviewed or approved the contents of this publication, or that A.A.W.S. necessarily agrees with the views expressed herein. A.A. is a program of recovery from alcoholism *only*—use of the Twelve Steps in connection with programs and activities which are patterned after A.A., but which address other problems, or in any other non-A.A. context, does not imply otherwise.

AA OUTCOME STUDIES   Many recovering individuals and professionals in the field view AA as the single most important component of recovery. A number of longitudinal and well-designed studies conducted between 1989 and 2001 with focused measures of AA exposure, drinking behavior, and secondary outcomes concluded that the AA experience is multidimensional and that the latent construct representing AA participation was a strong predictor of positive outcome (Tonigan, 2008). In a meta-analysis (Forcehimes & Tonigan, 2008) of 11 studies that looked at the degree of change in self-efficacy in predicting drinking reductions among attendees, changes in self-efficacy were not uniform across AA settings and the magnitude of benefit associated with self-efficacy was heterogeneous across studies. Additional research is needed to determine the nature of the mediating effects. A study by Gossop, Stewart, and Marsden (2008) involved follow-up interviews at 1 year, 2 years, and 4 to 5 years with 142 alcohol- and drug-dependent clients following residential treatment. Those who attended NA or AA more frequently were more likely to be abstinent from opiates and alcohol when compared both to those who did not attend and those who attended infrequently (less than weekly).

Women's groups and minority groups who feel disenfranchised have leveled criticism about the AA program. Many women believe AA perpetuates the powerlessness of women in steps 1 through 3. Minority groups believe that AA serves the White middle class and does not address ethnic issues in their philosophy. It would appear that some research supports this theory—that AA is most effective with socially stable White males over 40 years of age, who are physically dependent on alcohol and prone to guilt, and who are the first born or only child (Doweiko, 2006). However, most research does not support this view, and most believe that this conclusion is not reliable in predicting successful membership in AA. In a study conducted by Moos, Moos, and Timko (2006) of 461 individuals with alcohol use disorders (50% women), women were more likely than men to participate in treatment and in AA, and to achieve better alcohol-related and lifestyle outcomes. Women benefited more than men from extended participation in AA. Women and men who participated in treatment and/or AA for a longer period were more likely to have a successful recovery. Kelly, Kahler, and Humphreys (2010) conducted a study of why male veterans who are substance abuse disorder patients drop out of or never attend 12-step mutual-help groups such as AA. Comorbid psychiatric problems and, to a lesser extent, spiritual concerns, were found to be obstacles. The needs of individuals striving to recover from an addiction are complex and the varied contextual influences that play a role in abstinence and relapse make it impossible to arrive at overly simple prescriptions for referral to self-help and treatment sources. Some clients may be better served through different approaches, but it behooves the mental health practitioner to be aware that many individuals are served well by AA.

Spirituality as a Resource

Many authors, leaders, and individuals associated with recovery from addictions advocate the valuable contribution of spirituality in one's striving to maintain abstinence or moderation in use. Many others have reacted to the spiritual emphasis in AA and have sought alternative self-help groups in an effort to approach sobriety outside of a context of spirituality. This suggests the importance of raising the question of the nature of spirituality. Galanter (2006) referred to the unique role of spirituality in its "promotion of meaningfulness in recovery from addiction" (p. 286). Spirituality is the search for meaning; those undergoing recovery usually are faced with essential questions about purpose, identity, and responsibility. Spirituality can be a helpful resource for understanding a past lifestyle of substance abuse or dependence and for making decisions about a future free from addiction. Galanter, seeking to clarify the nature of spirituality and religion, offers that religion has a creed that its members are expected to follow and spirituality is a way of living sought by the individual through one's own experience. A spiritual view often understands God as loving and a religious view understands God as judgmental. The Association for Spiritual, Ethical, and Religious Values in Counseling (ASERVIC, n.d.) states in a white paper that "spirituality is innate and unique to all persons . . . moving the individual toward knowledge, love, meaning, peace, hope . . . " (p. 1). Religion is the "organization of belief which is common to a culture or subculture," which includes lifestyle, ritual activities, and institutions (p. 1). While spirituality is usually expressed through culture, it both precedes and transcends culture. A person can be spiritual, religious, or both.

Hagedorn and Moorhead (2010) offer that addictions frequently develop as a result of emotional pain from one's past, e.g., abuse or demeaning criticism, which may result in perfectionism. Spirituality can be a resource to fill the hole created by the hurt. Mindfulness, paying close attention to the present, can help the individual seeking to recover and avoid relapse. Getting in touch with one's feelings, recognizing cravings and urgings, and seeking positive thoughts can empower the individual in one's goal of abstinence. Horton-Parker and Fawcett (2010) recommend the following mindfulness exercises that facilitate control and balance through spirituality: Focus on breathing, body scan, observing thoughts and feelings, and walking meditation. Women for Sobriety emphasize spiritual growth through meditation, discovery of self, caring and love toward self and each other, establishing life priorities, and treasuring each moment.

AA-Associated 12-Step Programs

Using the AA model of recovery as a basis, several 12-step programs have been developed, such as Narcotics Anonymous (NA), Cocaine Anonymous (CA), Gamblers Anonymous (GA), Sex Addicts Anonymous (SAA), and Overeaters Anonymous (OA). All are based on the AA philosophy and use a variation of the Twelve Steps of AA. The difference in these groups is their scope. NA, for example, is all-inclusive with its definition of addiction. It includes any mood-changing, mind-altering substance. CA limits its membership to individuals who identify cocaine as their primary drug or drug of choice, GA focuses on gambling as an addiction, and SAA focuses on sexual addictions. OA is directed toward individuals who have compulsive eating habits. Al-Anon, Alateen, and Nar-Anon are examples of support groups for partners and families of substance users. Al-Anon was founded by Lois W. (Bill W.'s wife) in 1954. While the substance abuser is in AA or NA, families meet to share experiences and discuss problems. These groups use the same 12 steps as they work toward their own recovery process. Alateen, which began in 1957, is for teenagers who live in alcoholic or drug-abusing families and for substance-using teenagers. It also uses the 12-step model and has its own Big Book. It was started to create an opportunity for youth to come together for support, share experiences, learn about dependency, and develop problem-solving skills. The model has been used to develop 12 steps for even very young children.

Moderation Management (MM)

Moderation Management (MM) groups were started in 1994. As you read further about MM, you will discover that it is clearly based in the cognitive behavioral theory. Furthermore, unlike AA, this group does not rely on abstinence for success but sees moderate use as success. They are clear, however, that MM is not for individuals who are chemically dependent (see Chapter X for the *DSM* definition of dependence). Rather, these groups function well for problem users (misuse, abuse). The National Institute on Alcohol Abuse and Alcoholism (2004) reported that among problem drinkers there are more who meet the criteria for alcohol abuse (4.65%) than alcohol dependence (3.81%) in the United States. The former are included among the population that MM serves. MM acknowledges that 30% of its members go on to become members of an abstinence-based group (Kinney, 2009). For women and minorities who may feel like victims already, MM may be a beneficial alternative to traditional approaches that are based on the disease model and its reliance on the concept of powerlessness.

MM has specific guidelines for participation in the program (see Table 10.2). Counselors need to work closely with clients who are involved in MM and be aware of possible limitations to the program. Contracting with the client about consequences of not following the MM guidelines, what will be considered evidence that they are in compliance, and how much failure will be tolerated are important pieces of working with clients in MM.

TABLE 10.2 MM suggested guidelines for moderate drinking. (Moderation Management, 2011)

A moderate drinker

- considers an occasional drink to be a small, though enjoyable, part of life.
- has hobbies, interests, and other ways to relax and enjoy life that do not involve alcohol.
- usually has friends who are moderate drinkers or nondrinkers.
- generally has something to eat before, during, or soon after drinking.
- usually does not drink for longer than an hour or two on any particular occasion.
- usually does not drink faster than one drink per half-hour.
- usually does not exceed the 0.055% BAC moderate drinking limit (see Note 1 below).
- feels comfortable with his or her use of alcohol (never drinks secretly and does not spend a lot of time thinking about drinking or planning to drink).

MM recommends that if one makes a healthy decision to drink less and to stay within moderate limits, one should not experience any health, personal, family, social, job-related, financial, or legal problems due to alcohol. The suggested guidelines allow for a degree of individual interpretation, because moderation is a flexible principle and is not the same for everyone. The suggested limits below, however, are more definite (Moderation Management, 2011).

Suggested Limits (Moderation Management, 2011)

- Strictly obey local laws regarding drinking and driving.
- Do not drink in situations that would endanger yourself or others.
- Do not drink every day. MM suggests that you abstain from drinking alcohol at least 3 or 4 days per week.
- Women who drink more than 3 drinks on any day, and more than 9 drinks per week, may be drinking at harmful levels. (See Note 2 below for definition of a "standard" drink.)
- Men who drink more than 4 drinks on any day, and more than 14 drinks per week, may be drinking at harmful levels.

Notes

1. Blood Alcohol Concentration (BAC) charts are available at MM meetings.
2. Standard drink: one 12 oz-beer (5% alcohol), one 5-oz glass of wine (12% alcohol), or 1 1/2 oz of 80-proof liquor (40% alcohol).

These "number of drinks" limits are LIMITS and not TARGETS. Blood Alcohol Concentration (BAC) charts are more accurate than number of drink limits because they take into account weight, sex, and rate of drinking. If you are very light in weight use the BAC upper limit of .055%. Some researchers advise a limit of one drink per day for older adults (55+).

These limits offered on the MM website are based on research published in 1995 in the *American Journal of Public Health,* by Dr. Martha Sanchez-Craig, Addiction Research Foundation, Toronto, Canada and other published limits.

Nine Steps Toward Moderation and Positive Lifestyle Changes (Moderation Management, 2011)

1. Attend meetings or on-line groups and learn about the program of Moderation Management.
2. Abstain from alcoholic beverages for 30 days and complete steps three through six during this time.
3. Examine how drinking has affected your life.
4. Write down your life priorities.
5. Take a look at how much, how often, and under what circumstances you had been drinking.
6. Learn the MM guidelines and limits for moderate drinking.
7. Set moderate drinking limits and start weekly "small steps" toward balance and moderation in other areas of your life.
8. Review your progress and update your goals.
9. Continue to make positive lifestyle changes and attend meetings whenever you need ongoing support or would like to help newcomers.

Source: Moderation Management [Online]. Available: http://www.moderation.org/readings.shtml. Used by permission.

This harm reduction model has received much interest in the treatment and recovery field. In their extensive review of the literature, Witkiewitz and Marlatt (2006) conclude that "empirical data and qualitative reports support the effectiveness and efficacy of harm reduction approaches to alcohol treatment" (p. 291). Other researchers have come to the same conclusion.

Case Discussion

Case 1 (Sandy and Pam).

In their desire to manage their alcohol and drug use, Sandy and Pam have considered limiting their use of substances. Sandy is disposed to using in moderation rather than seeking total abstinence. She will have to be realistic about her capacity to use in a way that keeps her from falling into old habits of drinking and abusing pills when she is experiencing stress. Sandy may want to consider participating in Moderation Management. A counselor working closely with Sandy might assist her to develop alternative coping skills such as hobbies, interests, and other ways to relax. Given her prior association with AA and her desire to be abstinent from alcohol and other substances, Pam may want to pursue her association with AA. Given Sandy's and Pam's desire to build their relationship, to learn to relate with men in less destructive ways, and to learn to deal with stress without turning to substances, they will need to be honest with each other about their differing values of abstinence versus use in moderation.

Rational Recovery

Rational Recovery (RR) developed as an alternative for individuals who had difficulty with the spiritual aspect of AA. Also based in cognitive-behavioral theory, it is a secular program that deemphasizes the need for any higher power in the recovery process. This program was developed beginning in 1988 by Jack Trimpey (1996) and is based on the work of Albert Ellis. RR uses the framework of rational emotive therapy to combat the irrational thoughts and beliefs of recovering individuals. Trimpey takes the irrational beliefs about alcoholism and drug use and reframes them into rational beliefs and ideas. These irrational thoughts are labeled as "the Beast," and individuals use a "Sobriety Spreadsheet" to combat the Beast. RR has a "Little Book" that emphasizes the individual's ability to make good life choices. In 1994, RR changed its name to Self-Management and Recovery Training (SMART).

Research on the effectiveness of RR indicates a high (73%) abstinence rate for 3 months following attendance. One limitation of this study is that the population was largely well educated and employed, creating concern about the generalizability of the results to other populations (Gallant, Egelko, & Edwards, 1993). Schmidt, Carns, and Chandler (2001) discovered that a group of 10 subjects who participated in RR showed significant diminishing of symptoms associated with alcohol/drug dependency, including enhancing their openness and decreasing denial. Additional research on the effectiveness of SMART/RR is needed to assess its role among current treatment and self-help strategies.

Secular Organizations for Sobriety/Save Our Selves (SOS)

SOS was founded in 1985 by James Christopher, the sober son of an alcoholic. Christopher wrote an article entitled "Sobriety Without Superstition" in *Free Inquiry* (The SOS Story, 2011). He received an overwhelming amount of response from the article and decided to found SOS. The response has continued to be great from the public, and SOS has also received recognition in the treatment field. In November 1987, the California courts recognized SOS as an alternative to AA in sentencing offenders to mandatory participation in a rehabilitation program. SOS now has chapters in 21 foreign countries and in all states in the United States (SOS Meetings, 2011).

SOS claims to be a self-empowerment approach that is based on the belief that sobriety is an issue apart from any other issues in the person's life. Sobriety is "Priority One, no matter what." Anyone who is interested in sobriety is welcome at a meeting. All meetings are self-supporting and separate from other meetings. SOS avoids outside involvement. The organization also provides online real-time chats to assist individuals in their time of need.

The suggested guidelines for sobriety from SOS are as follows:

1. To break the cycle of denial and achieve sobriety, we first acknowledge that we are alcoholics and addicts.
2. We reaffirm this truth daily and accept without reservation the fact that, as clean and sober individuals, we cannot and do not drink, or use, no matter what.
3. Since drinking and using is not an option for us, we take whatever steps are necessary to continue our Sobriety Priority lifelong.
4. A quality of life—"the good life"—can be achieved. However, life is also filled with uncertainties. Therefore, we do not drink or use regardless of feelings, circumstances, or conflicts.
5. We share in confidence with each other our thoughts and feelings as sober, clean individuals.
6. Sobriety is our Priority, and we are each responsible for our lives and our sobriety (cfiwest.org/sos/brochures/overview.htm).

The website further states that the organization is not a spin-off of any religious group, has no hidden agenda, and is only concerned with sobriety and not religiosity. In a national survey of self-help participation Atkins and Hawdon (2007) ascertained that involvement in all support groups significantly strengthened the likelihood of remaining sober. Complementarity of the subject's beliefs with those of the group they attended was associated with more frequent participation, contributing to greater number of days clean. Whereas, religious respondents participated more in 12-step groups and Women for Sobriety, nonreligious respondents were significantly more likely to participate in secular groups. Religiosity had little influence on SMART Recovery participation, but did decrease participation in SOS.

As a young organization, SOS has not been empirically studied to ascertain effectiveness of the methodology. However, it holds appeal to those who fault AA for its religious (not spiritual) leanings. It also would be considered a cognitive-behavioral type of self-help group with a good dose of willpower added to the mix.

Women for Sobriety (WFS)

WFS was founded in July 1976 by Jean Kirkpatrick, one woman on her journey toward sobriety. It is a group founded by women for women. WFS recognizes the unique issues related to women striving to reach sobriety and uses behavioral methodology to assist with those issues. WFS promotes behavioral changes through positive reinforcement, cognitive strategies, and use of the body's healing powers through meditation, diet, and relations techniques.

WFS Statement of Purpose

1. Women for Sobriety is an organization whose purpose is to help all women recover from problem drinking through the discovery of self, gained by sharing experiences, hopes and encouragement with other women in similar circumstances.
2. Women for Sobriety is unique in that it is an organization of women for women. It recognizes woman's emerging role and her necessity for self-esteem and self-discovery to meet today's conflicts.
3. Women for Sobriety is not affiliated with Alcoholics Anonymous. Members of Women for Sobriety sometimes belong to AA. However, each organization has its individual purpose and should be kept separated.
4. Women for Sobriety believes that drinking began to overcome stress, loneliness, frustration, emotional deprivation, or any number of other kinds of harassment. Dependence and addiction resulted. This physiological addiction can only be overcome by abstinence. Mental and emotional addiction are overcome with the knowledge of self gained through Women for Sobriety.
5. Women for Sobriety members live by the Women for Sobriety philosophy: Forget the past, plan for tomorrow and live for today.
6. Membership in Women for Sobriety requires a desire to stop drinking and a sincere desire for a new life.

It is interesting to note the positive reframe of the traditional 12 steps of AA in WFS's 13 statements:

"New Life" Acceptance Program

1. I have a life-threatening problem that once had me.
   I now take charge of my life and my disease. I accept the responsibility.
2. Negative thoughts destroy only myself.
   My first conscious sober act must be to remove negativity from my life.
3. Happiness is a habit I will develop.
   Happiness is created, not waited for.
4. Problems bother me only to the degree I permit them to.
   I now better understand my problems and do not permit problems to overwhelm me.
5. I am what I think.
   I am a capable, competent, caring, compassionate woman.
6. Life can be ordinary or it can be great.
   Greatness is mine by a conscious effort.
7. Love can change the course of my world.
   Caring becomes all important.
8. The fundamental object of life is emotional and spiritual growth.
   Daily I put my life into a proper order, knowing which are the priorities.
9. The past is gone forever.
   No longer will I be victimized by the past, I am a new person.
10. All love given returns.
    I will learn to know that others love me.
11. Enthusiasm is my daily exercise.
    I treasure all moments of my new life.

12. I am a competent woman and have much to give life.
    This is what I am and I shall know it always.
13. I am responsible for myself and for my actions.
    I am in charge of my mind, my thoughts, and my life.

(Reprinted with permission from Women for Sobriety, Inc. P.O. Box 618. Quakertown, PA 18951. Womenforsobriety.org. 215-536-8026 (c) WFS, Inc.)

WFS's philosophy rests in the empowerment of women to seek their own wellness and prosperity. This women's group grew out of the belief that the traditional AA 12-step program was disempowering to a group that was already disempowered in many ways by societal norms. Therefore, empowerment and self-reliance are cornerstones of this movement.

Self-Help for Dually Diagnosed Persons

Over 5 million adults in the United States have co-occurring substance abuse and mental health disorders (Magura, 2008). Nearly 50% of persons diagnosed with a serious mental illness have a co-existing substance abuse or dependence disorder (Horsfall, Cleary, Hunt, & Walter, 2009). Self-help groups for individuals with a substance abuse problem have often not been accepting of those who have a co-existing mental disorder due to perceived transference of addiction from alcohol or another substance of choice to psychotropic medication. Double Trouble in Recovery, Dual Recovery Anonymous, special AA meetings for alcohol-dependent individuals with a mental disorder, and Self-Management and Recovery Training (SMART) are self-help groups that have been started to help dually diagnosed individuals. Double Trouble in Recovery was started in New York State in 1989 and has over 200 group meetings in 14 U.S. states, including Georgia, Colorado, New Mexico, and New Jersey (Laudet, 2008). Davidson et al. (2008) proposed a dual recovery focus that emphasized initiating recovery from addiction, establishing mutual relationships, and renewing hope, confidence, and commitment; understanding, accepting, and redefining self; and managing symptoms and triggers, overcoming stigma, community involvement, and becoming an empowered citizen. As stated earlier in this chapter, while there are a multitude of other self-help groups in the world, we have endeavored to provide an overview of the most well known in the field of substance abuse. As the reader can readily recognize, the majority of these groups recognize that abstinence is an essential component of a clean and sober lifestyle.

I would be remiss if I did not close this chapter with a concept that is so often ignored in both treatment and recovery—yet it may well be the basis for long-term sobriety and contentment in each of our lives.

A Well-Rounded Life with Joy

A generation ago Zackon (1988) proposed the question, "What is the relationship between joylessness and relapse?" (p. 69). In our diligent and caring quest to teach the individual all the cognitive and behavioral skills necessary to stay clean and sober, we may be overlooking an intrinsically important aspect of recovery. Becoming clean and sober requires the substance abuser to give up a lifestyle that is "psychologically comfortable" and to enter unfamiliar territory. Abusers must leave friends who shared a value system and created a sense of community for them. The recovering individual many times does not know how to experience joy or enjoyment with everyday living. Many common social situations are uncomfortable. Friends are few, if they exist at all. Typically, addicts must learn to manage their "pleasure threshold"—in other words, learn to enjoy more moderate stimulation than that commonly accompanying substance abusing lifestyles.

Also, early recovery means detoxification and withdrawal symptoms that may linger. It also entails facing the pain of one's life before, during, and now after the drug use. Destroyed relationships, financial and legal problems, expectations from everyone, physical pain, and the consistent—and sometimes strong—drug cravings create a heavy burden of unhappiness that drains energy and prolongs the lack of joyfulness in the individual's life. So it becomes incumbent on the counselor not to overlook the relearning of pleasure in the recovery process. Relearning takes time, and counselors need to remember that this relearning can be blocked by guilt and shame or simply by lack of money to participate in activities. Ward and Stewart (2003) in their "good lives model" recognize the need for the recovering individual to balance efforts to manage the risk of relapse with positive and joyful aspects of human life such as excellence in play and work, physical activity, rewarding intimate, romantic, and family relationships, spirituality, and creativity. In relapse prevention models and programs, counselors should emphasize and systematically support their clients' "good lives." This may mean that counselors take the nontherapeutic role of "coach" in social and leisure activities. Aftercare groups, AA, NA, and other social support groups can provide much-needed participation for recovering individuals.

Case Study

Robert

Robert is a 34-year-old African American male who identifies himself as gay. He has been in a number of gay relationships since his early 20s, none of them lasting longer than six months. He currently lives with Larry, a 41-year-old man, whom he has known for four months. Robert is the father of two children, a son born to his girlfriend whom he hung around with in high school and a daughter conceived during a brief affair when Robert was 20 years old. Robert reports that he can remember being attracted to and associating with men during his teen years, when he was also dating women. Robert is the third son and fifth of eight children born to his mother. Robert had occasional contact with his father as a child, but has not seen him in more than 10 years. Robert's father had a drinking problem and was diagnosed with cirrhosis of the liver the last time Robert heard about him. Robert has not seen his children in many years and has had no contact with his mother or siblings for over two years.

Robert reports that he started smoking reefer when he was around 11 years old. During his teens he would drink wine and liquor with friends and often by himself. Robert also used heroin and cocaine. He has undergone detox for alcohol, heroin, and cocaine "enough" times since his early 20s. Robert participated in chemical dependency rehabilitation for almost two months in 2004. A history of unemployment has been interrupted occasionally with short-term employment as a cook and as a maintenance worker. Robert has had bouts of depression on and off. He was hospitalized for suicidal behavior when he was 27 years old following his being diagnosed with HIV. Subsequent testing has failed to detect a presence of the virus.

The longest period of abstinence from substances that Robert has achieved is one year. He had been attending AA meetings and was feeling supported by his sponsor to whom he was introduced during one of his detox treatments. Robert relapsed on alcohol when his sponsor moved to another city and Robert did not feel that he could connect with his new sponsor. Robert states that he believes in a higher power, but has mixed feelings about God and religion. He was raised in the Baptist Church and accepted their teachings about God and Jesus Christ. However, the alienation that he experienced in two churches when the congregations learned that he was gay created doubt about God's love for him. The teaching that homosexuality is a sin has made Robert feel that he is not wanted by God or by Christian churches. Robert was recently referred to a drug court following his arrest for possession of barbiturates. He was mandated by the judge to attend intensive outpatient treatment and to participate in a self-help group, or be sentenced to jail. In assessing Robert, a substance abuse counselor viewed Robert as being somewhere in between a precontemplative and contemplative stage of recovery. Robert states that he recognizes that he has a number of relationship, career, and health problems that are related to his use of substances. He is losing hope that he will be able to change his life. He wonders if going to jail would be any worse than what he is currently facing. When he told the drug court coordinator about his ambivalence toward AA, he was informed about Double Trouble in Recovery, a self-help group for individuals facing substance dependence and mental illness. Robert wonders how he would be accepted in the Double Trouble group. He feels that he has failed each time that he has attempted to achieve sobriety. He would like to find a self-help group where he does not have to hide his being gay.

Critical Thinking Questions

1. Robert is facing a number of difficulties—addiction, depression, hopelessness, and alienation from the church, a previous diagnosis of HIV, unemployment, and estrangement from his family. What problem does he need to address first? Provide a rationale for your choice.
2. What model/s of relapse planning and management is most relevant to Robert's situation? What, if any, self-help recovery program/s would you recommend?
3. In your view, what role, if any, should spirituality have in recovery from an addiction?
4. What should Robert do about his alienation from the church? He states that faith in God is important to him, but he has been told that homosexuality is an abomination.
5. How could a well-rounded life with joy become part of Robert's recovery from addiction? What could a counselor do to assist Robert to discover joy in recovery?

MyCounselingLab™

Go to Topic 9: *Retaining Sobriety: Relapse Prevention Strategies*, on the MyCounselingLab™ site (www.MyCounselingLab.com) for *Substance Abuse Counseling*, Fifth Edition where you can:

- Find learning outcomes for *Retaining Sobriety: Relapse Prevention Strategies*, along with the national standards that connect to these outcomes.
- Complete Assignments and Activities that can help you more deeply understand the chapter content.
- Apply and practice your understanding of the core skills identified in the chapter with the Building Counseling Skills unit.
- Prepare yourself for professional certification with a Practice for Certification quiz.
- Connect to videos through the Video and Resource Library.

MyCounselingLab™ Exercises

Go to the Video and Resource Library on the MyCounselingLab™ site for your text and search for the following clip:

Finding Healthy Alternatives to Substance Use

After you view the clip, consider your responses to the following questions:

1. How does the client respond to Dr. Marlatt's question of what would be more important than using heroin?
2. What characteristics do positive alternatives to substance abuse have to have in order to be effective?
3. How would you use those things that are important to the client to help him in the recovery process?

CONCLUSION

The determinants of substance abuse relapse and prevention models share commonalities. Relapse prevention skills, cognitive and behavioral, are important in creating a clean and sober lifestyle. However, simply put, the intentionality and joy with which the individual is living life may be the necessary component that creates hope, inspiration, and motivation needed to stay focused and flexible in one's recovery goals.

11

Working with Selected Populations: Treatment Issues and Characteristics

CONNIE TAIT, PH.D.

MyCounselingLab™

Visit the **MyCounselingLab™** site for *Substance Abuse Counseling*, Fifth Edition to enhance your understanding of chapter concepts. You'll have the opportunity to practice your skills through video- and case-based Assignments and Activities as well as Building Counseling Skills units, and to prepare for your certification exam with Practice for Certification quizzes.

This chapter will address treatment issues and characteristics of six groups of individuals. The underlying criteria for selecting the groups was the power differential among these groups and the influence of societal perceptions and actions that have limited their full participation in mainstream society. Obviously, other groups could be included, but because of space constraints, the discussion will concern women, gay/lesbian/bisexual/transgender individuals, people with disabilities, children and adolescents, older adults, and the homeless.

CHILDREN AND ADOLESCENTS

Research from the National Institute on Drug Abuse (NIDA, 2007a) has shown that for most children, the key risk periods for drug abuse occur during major transitions in children's lives. Such transitions could include such vulnerable life periods as moving from one developmental stage to another, moving, or parents divorcing. Another major transition for children is when they leave the security of the family and enter school. Exposure to risks can start before a child is born if the mother is using drugs during pregnancy. As children advance from elementary school to middle school or junior high, they often face social challenges, such as learning to get along with a wider group of peers. It is at this stage, early adolescence, that children are likely to encounter drug use for the first time. When they enter high school, adolescents again face social, emotional, and educational challenges. Because of a greater exposure to available drugs, drug users, and social activities involving drugs, adolescents face an increased risk to become involved with illegal substances.

Substance use during childhood is rarely studied because of perceived infrequent use at these ages (Dunn & Mezzich, 2007). NIDA, through its Monitoring the Future Study, estimates drug use among 12- to 17-year-olds but not among younger children. However, the younger people start using alcohol and drugs, the more likely they will develop problems with such use (NIDA, 2007a). The National Survey on Drug Use and Health (Substance Abuse and Mental Health Service Administration [SAMHSA], 2006b) reported that children are already abusing drugs by age 12 or 13, which likely means that some may have begun even earlier. Early abuse includes such drugs as tobacco, alcohol, inhalants, marijuana, and prescribed medications.

Research conducted by the Partnership/MetLife Foundation Attitude Tracking Study (Partnership for a Drug-Free America, 2009) tracked drug use and drug-related attitudes among seventh- through 12th-grade students. The study showed a reversal of the decline in teen abuse of drugs and alcohol that had been seen since 1998. The Partnership study points to marked upswing in the use of drugs that teens encounter at parties and in other social environments. An increase was found in the use of alcohol, ecstasy, and marijuana. The resurgence in teen drug and alcohol use comes at a time when prodrug use is seen in films, television, and online and when funding for federal prevention programs has been declining.

Research from the National Institute on Drug Abuse (2007a) indicates that signs of risk can be seen as early as infancy or early childhood, including aggressive behavior, lack of self-control, or a difficult temperament. Negative behaviors have led to more risks, academic failure, and social difficulties, putting children at greater risk for drug abuse. Family situations also increase a child's risk for later drug abuse, when there is

A lack of attachment and nurturing by parents and caregivers

Ineffective parenting

A caregiver who abuses drugs

These problem behaviors tend to cluster in children raised in dysfunctional families by parents who were also raised in dysfunctional or overstressed families. In addition, studies have shown that children with poor academic performance and inappropriate social behaviors at ages 7 to 9 are more likely to be involved with substance abuse by the age 14 or 15 (NIDA, 2007a).

Even though there appears to be a trend toward younger children abusing substances, Dunn and Mezzich (2007) stress that early adolescence is a period of greatest vulnerability because of the youth's increasing desire for autonomy leading to increased conflicts within the family. This may also lead to negative peer influences and the potential for increased risk of substance abuse.

Adolescence is a developmental period that is characterized by psychological, social, and biological change. The transition period between childhood and adulthood is characterized by internal and external changes that are often manifested by a barrage of emotions. Shillington et al. (2005) noted that adolescence is a time when many youth experiment with risk practices. These practices, such as substance abuse, sexual risk-taking, and violence carry potential risks for adverse health outcomes. The consequences of adolescents' risk-taking behaviors include drug addiction, pregnancy, legal problems, school attrition, and sometimes death.

Although most adolescents experience transitory problems they can resolve, others with poor coping skills are vulnerable to intense emotional pain, with drug use becoming a way to cope with both internal problems (stress, depression, low self-esteem) and external problems (school, family, workplace) (McWhirter, McWhirter, McWhirter, & McWhirter, 2007).

Youth involved with alcohol and drugs pose a major problem not only to themselves but also to the community as a whole. Since 1975, the Monitoring the Future (MFT) survey has measured drug, alcohol, and cigarette use and related attitudes among adolescents. Initially, the survey included 12th graders only, but in 1991 that was expanded to include eighth and 10th graders. The 2009 MFT (NIDA, 2010) survey encompassed about 46,000 eighth-, 10th-, and 12th-grade students in more than 389 public and private schools nationwide. Table 11.1 provides data from the Monitoring the Future survey. Clearly, the problems of substance abuse are widespread among American youth. The positive findings show that cigarette smoking is at its lowest point in the history of the survey. Methamphetamine, amphetamines, cocaine, and alcohol also showed declines over the past year use. Areas of concern are marijuana use as prevalence rates remain consistently high. Smokeless tobacco increased significantly among 10th graders. Past-year nonmedical use of Vicodin and OxyContin increased during the last five years among 10th graders and remained unchanged among eighth and 12th graders. In 2008, 9.3% of youths aged 12 to 17 were current illicit drug users (SAMHSA, 2009).

The 2009 MFT also found that by eighth grade, approximately 41% of children had used alcohol, 26% had used tobacco, and 16.5% had used marijuana. Furthermore,

TABLE 11.1 Monitoring the future: Overview of key findings. "Trends in Lifetime Prevalence of Use of Various Drugs for Grades 8, 10, and 12 Combined."

Any illicit drug	33.2%
Any illicit drug other than marijuana	16.5%
Any illicit drug including inhalants	37.9%
Hallucinogens	5.3%
Alcohol	54.6%
Been drunk	35.9%
Cigarettes	31.2%
Smokeless tobacco	13.5%
Marijuana	29%

Source: *Monitoring the Future National Results on Adolescent Drug Use: Overview of Key Findings, 2009,* by L. D. Johnston, P. M. O'Malley, J. G. Bachman, & J. E. Schulenberg. Bethesda, MD: National Institute on Drug Abuse.

about 25% of all school-age youth are children of alcoholics. These percentages are down slightly from the 2002 MFT.

The Partnership for a Drug-Free America (2009) reported alarming levels of abuse of prescription and over-the-counter drugs among young people. The report stated that many teens think these drugs are safe because they have legitimate uses, but taking them without a prescription to get "high" or "self-medicate" can be as dangerous and addictive as using street narcotics and other illicit drugs. The Partnership's research showed that most youth know these drugs are easy to get, whether taken from home, a friend's medicine cabinet, or purchased via the Internet.

Some youth may be experimenting with drugs, others attempting to ease the stress of adolescence, and others modeling the behavior of family members and peers. Regardless of the reasons, the consequences of substance abuse are serious. McWhirter et al. (2007) have stated that early and risky sexual involvement, school dropout, unemployment, and underemployment are associated with high levels of drug use. These adolescents enter into adult roles before they are ready and continue without critical life skills.

Risk Factors

No single profile identifies who will or will not use alcohol and drugs. Adolescent substance abusers have different personality types, family histories, socioeconomic levels, and life experiences. According to research conducted by NIDA (2007a), risk factors can increase a youth's chances for drug abuse, while protective factors can reduce the risk. A risk factor for one person may not be a risk factor for another person. Studies have indicated that although most youth do not progress beyond initial use, a small percentage rapidly escalate their substance abuse. In general, risk factors can be seen as operating in five domains or settings: (a) individual; (b) family; (c) peer; (d) school; and (e) community. Conclusions from the research indicate that the more risks a child is exposed to, the more likely the child will abuse drugs.

Dunn and Mezzich (2007), McWhirter et al. (2007), and Putnam (2007) identified risk factors from the following domains:

- Early and persistent behavior problems
- Low commitment to school/lack of school bonding
- School failure
- Deficits in behavioral–affective regulation
- Lack of social competence
- Negative peer influence
- Low parental involvement
- Sensation seeking
- Family history of alcohol or drug use
- Low self-esteem
- Poverty
- Community and interpersonal violence

NIDA (2007a) noted that an important goal of prevention is to change the balance between risk and protective factors so that protective factors outweigh risk factors. Having protective factors in the multiple domains is particularly important in buffering adolescents from the effects of earlier circumstances that place them at risk.

Family members are a significant factor in adolescent development as they are role models and major sources of support. Among the most frequently identified protective processes against child and adolescent substance use and abuse are (a) parent–child attachment, (b) parental supervision, and (c) communication of family values (Kumpfer, Alvarado, Tait, & Whiteside, 2007). Family interventions that decrease family conflict and improve involvement and parental monitoring should reduce later youth problem behaviors.

The second-most-important socializing agent for children, after the family, is the school. What is happening or not happening in schools has an impact with youth using illicit drugs. Dunn and Mezzich (2007) identified school bonding and achievement as critical protective factors. The major factor that contributes to school bonding (which entails commitment, attachment, and belief) is involvement. The degree of involvement is determined by opportunities for reinforcement of involvement in a rewarding social environment. The researchers found that students bond more readily in a positive social environment that discourages the use of drugs. Decrease in drug use is found in schools where a positive school climate exists in which students feel rewarded for achievement, perceive opportunities for involvement, feel respected and heard, and feel capable of influencing school policy and in which clear policy exists (Sankar-Gomes & Malley, 2006).

In addition to protective influences, factors related to resiliency also need to be explored. Reivich (2010) defined resilience as the ability to persist in the face of challenges and bounce back from adversity. The following factors were found to increase resiliency:

- Optimism and hope
- Self-efficacy
- Strong self-regulation skills
- Problem-solving skills
- Adaptability
- Self-regulation
- Sense of humor
- Easy temperament
- Close relationships among family members
- Low discord between parents
- Warm and structured parenting style

The research on resilience shows that youth with strong resilience skills do better in a variety of domains compared to those with less resilience. A number of programs are attempting to incorporate resiliency training into adolescent substance abuse prevention programs.

Prevention and Intervention

Effective identification and assessment of substance abuse is a crucial early step in both treatment and prevention programs. According to Califano (2007):

> Over the past decade, extensive research has demonstrated that the route to a drug-free America is through our children. We know that the earlier a child starts to smoke, drink, or use drugs, the greater the chances that child will get hooked. However, a child who gets through age 21 without smoking, using illegal drugs, or abusing alcohol is virtually certain never to do so. And, for better or worse, the greatest influences on children appear to be their parents and their schools.

TABLE 11.2 Research-based drug abuse prevention programs		
Type	**Approach**	**Effective Program**
School + family based	Sense of Community	Caring School Community Program (Schaps, E.)
Elementary School	Improve performance	Classroom-Centered & Family-School Partnership Intervention (Ialongo, N.)
Parenting	Parent Education	Guiding Good Choices (Hawkins, J. D.)
Middle School	Social Skills	Life Skills Training (Botvin, G.)
Elementary School	Enhancing protective factors	Skills, Opportunities, and Recognition (Hawkins, J. D.)
Youth 10–14 years	Family strengthening	The Strengthening Families Program (Molgaard, V.)
Youth 6–11 years	Family strengthening	The Strengthening Families Program (Kumpfer, K.)
High School	Dropout prevention	Reconnecting Youth Program (Herting, J. R.)
Community-based	Legal	Community Trials Project (Holder, H. D.)
Community-based	Coalitions	Communities That Care (Hawkins, J. D.)

Source: Information from *Preventing Drug Use among Children and Adolescents. A Research Based Guide for Parents, Educators, and Community Leaders,* Second Edition, NIDA, 2007.

Prevention efforts should be interrelated activities that include the home, school, and community. Szapocznik, Tolan, Sambrano, and Schwartz (2007) noted that evidence-based prevention programs have been designed to focus on four important domains: parental investment in the child/adolescent, child/adolescent social competence, child/adolescent self-regulation and control, and child/adolescent school bonding and academic achievement.

Table 11.2 lists types of prevention programs with examples of each. These efforts need to extend beyond providing information and specifically address the individual and environmental risk factors.

Family support programs that encourage involvement of the parents in their children's lives are a major key to making adolescents less vulnerable to alcohol and drugs. Regardless of the parents' relationship to their child, they need to be involved in the solution. NIDA (2007a) stated that family-based prevention programs should enhance family bonding and relationships and include parenting skills; practice in developing, discussing, and enforcing family policies on substance abuse; and training in drug education and information.

Prevention programs designed to increase positive peer relationships focus on an individual's relationship to peers by developing social competency skills. These skills include peer-relationships, self-efficacy and assertiveness, strengthening personal commitments against drug abuse, communication, and drug resistance skills (NIDA, 2007a).

Schools are a crucial element in the prevention of substance use by youth. McWhirter et al. (2007) indicated that prevention programs in schools focus on improving academic and social-emotional learning to address risk factors for drug abuse, such as early aggression, academic failure, study habits and academic support, and school dropout. School-based prevention programs should be integrated within the school's own goal of increasing academic performance. Most curricula include the support for positive peer relationships and an education component designed to correct the misperception that most students are using drugs. The research found that when youth understand the negative effects of drugs (physical, psychological, and social) and when they perceive their friends' and families' social disapproval of drug use, they tend to avoid initiating drug use. A comprehensive drug prevention curriculum for kindergarten through grade 12 is essential to teach students that drug use is wrong and harmful and to support and strengthen resistance to drugs.

In combination with prevention efforts, effective treatment approaches should be designed to meet adolescents' specific needs. Gans, Falco, Schackman, and Winters (2010) noted that teenagers have different patterns of substance use, unique developmental and social issues, and a higher prevalence of co-occurring disorders. Adolescent treatment programs need to address the various factors that affect the adolescent's life, including education, family, recreation, peers, juvenile court, probation, and mental and physical health. It is recommended that the first step in finding the appropriate help is an initial screening followed by an in-depth assessment of the presenting symptoms and needs. Assessments should cover psychological and medical problems, learning disabilities, family functioning, and other aspects of youths' lives.

It has been suggested that treatment programs contain the following elements (U.S. Department of Health and Human Services [DHHS], 2005):

- Services should address all aspects of youths' lives: school, home, public activities.
- Parents should be involved in the youths' drug use treatment.
- Programming should reflect developmental differences between adolescents and adults.
- Treatment programs should build a climate of trust.
- Staff should be well trained in adolescent development, comorbidity issues, and substance use.
- Programs should address the distinct needs of youths based on gender and ethnicity.
- Information should be provided on continuing care (relapse prevention, aftercare plans, and follow-up).
- Rigorous evaluations to measure success and improve treatment services should be included.

Sussman, Skara, and Ames (2008) note that the research literature on adolescent substance abuse indicates that there is more work needed to advance knowledge in this area. It seems that no single treatment approach is likely to be appropriate and effective for all adolescents. However, it is suggested that all treatment programs include some type of continuing care or self-care component. It is also recommended that programs encourage adolescents to form attachments with non-drug users in their communities who will assist them in finding leadership or service opportunities that enable them to contribute to their communities.

WOMEN

The use of ATOD and the misuse of prescription medications are taking a serious toll on the health and well-being of women and their families. Stevens, Andrade, and Ruiz (2009) noted that historically data has shown a smaller percentage of women use alcohol and illicit substances than men. However, the research indicates that substance use among women has been a hidden issue and not realistically acknowledged by society prior to the mid-1960s. The proportion of women among substance abuse treatment clients has increased over the past decade, and female clients currently constitute about one-third of the treatment population. As was the case from 2002 through 2009, the rate of substance dependence or abuse for males aged 12 or older in 2010 was about twice as high as the rate for females. For males in 2010, the rate was 11.6%, which was similar to the 11.9% in 2009, while for females, it was 5.9% in 2010, which did not differ significantly from the 6.1% in 2009. Among youths aged 12 to 17, the rate of substance dependence or abuse among males was similar to the rate among females in 2010 (6.9 vs. 7.7%) (Substance Abuse and Mental Health Services Administration, 2011).

The history of substance abuse among women suggests that addiction among women is closely connected to negative and sanctioned socialization and with experiences of disempowerment (White & Kilbourne, 2006). Throughout history, women have experienced varied forms of oppression, from economic to personal, which injure women in unique ways (Lanzetta, 2005). Oppression invades women in such a way that it is difficult to identify the source of their pain. Women may react in unhealthy ways by numbing the feelings through the use of prescribed, legal, or illicit substances (Stevens, 2006).

Women frequently initiate substance use as a result of traumatic life events such as physical or sexual violence, sudden physical illness, an accident, or disruption in family life (Stevens et al., 2009). Those women reported that the traumatic experiences occurred before substance use. In one study (Stevens et al.), of the 80 women enrolled in a treatment program, 74% reported having been raped and 80% reported having been physically assaulted.

Lanzetta (2005) and White and Kilbourne (2006) stated that social stigma and shame continue to be associated with women's substance use. Society's expectation for women is to provide the moral foundation for the family, be the caretakers and nurturers. These expectations discourage women from admitting their drug problems and seeking professional help.

Risk Factors

Agrawal (2005) reports that women (18–49 years of age) who are married have a lower rate of alcohol or illicit drug abuse or dependence than unmarried women. History of divorce is positively associated with illicit drug use, not dependence. In addition, to some degree, partners influence each other's drinking and drug use. Women dependent on illicit drugs are more likely to have partners who use illicit drugs. Some women use alcohol and drugs to have an activity in common with their partners or to maintain the relationship.

Data from the Gender Research (2011) suggests differences in the mental health of adult substance abusers, indicating that women are more likely than men to have co-occuring mental and substance use disorders. For women, anxiety disorders and major depression continues to be positively associated with substance use, abuse, and dependence and are the most common co-occuring diagnoses. Other common mental disorders are eating disorders and post-traumatic stress disorder (PTSD), a common result of violence and trauma (Gender Research, 2011).

The use of alcohol, tobacco, and drugs can affect a pregnant woman in a variety of ways, from obstetric complications, miscarriage, or significant problems for the fetus. Above all other drugs, alcohol is the most common cause of malformation to the embryo or fetus in pregnancy. Maternal alcohol use contributes to a range of effects such as fetal alcohol spectrum disorders (FASDs) and fetal alcohol syndrome (FAS).

According to the Center for Substance Abuse Treatment (CSAT) (2009), women are more sensitive to the consumption and long-term effects of alcohol and drugs than men. From absorption to metabolic processes, women display more difficulty in physically managing the consequences of use. With higher levels of alcohol and drugs in the system for longer periods of time, women are more susceptible to alcohol and drug-related diseases and organ damage. CSAT (2005) research indicates that there are different vulnerabilities at different ages for women. Adolescent women are more likely than adolescent males to experience cognitive impairment despite less alcohol consumption. Women of child bearing age are more likely to experience infertility with heavier drinking. Postmenopausal women are more likely to exhibit significant hormonal changes with heavy consumption of alcohol, leading to higher risks for breast cancer, osteoporosis, and coronary heart disease. Older women are more sensitive to alcohol and tend to display a decrease in tolerance and alcohol metabolism.

Women have a greater reluctance than men to admit they have a problem with alcohol and/or drugs. They often confront barriers to finding, entering, and completing treatment programs. Society imposes some of the barriers, while others are internal within the woman herself. Many drug-using women do not seek treatment because they fear not being able to take care of or keep their children, they fear reprisal from their spouses or partners, and they fear punishment from authorities (Brady & Ashley, 2005). Those who have been most successful have had the help and support of significant others, family members, friends, treatment providers, and the community.

Prevention and Intervention

Reports concerning treatment of women have shown the following: (1) women experience a number of barriers to receiving treatment, (2) women are more vulnerable than men to some of the physiological effects of substance abuse, and (3) substance abuse among women is more often rooted in psychosocial problems and traumatic life events (Gender Research, 2011).

CSAT (2009) studies suggest that treatment programs for women include diverse services that aim to reduce the barriers women face entering and staying in treatment and to address the specific substance abuse-related problems of women. Barriers can include child care, stigmatization, and inability to pay for treatment. Retention in treatment is influenced by many factors. For women these include support from a partner, age (under 21 not as likely to complete treatment), education (high school education more likely to stay in treatment), and being of color (show lower retention rates).

Gender sensitive treatment (CSAT, 2005; Stevens et al., 2009) include the following:

- Ancillary services, such as child care or transportation services
- Prenatal care and well-baby care
- Admission for women only to be more focused on women's issues
- Mental health services
- Trauma
- Grief and loss
- Family issues
- Oppression
- Economic constraints
- Life skills training
- Medical treatment

Some studies (CSAT, 2005; Gender Research, 2011) have shown that women who abuse substances benefit more from supportive therapy with a collaborative approach. Positive treatment outcomes have been associated with the therapist characteristics of warmth, empathy, staying connected during treatment crisis, and the ability to manage countertransference during therapy. Women need a treatment environment that is supportive, safe, and nurturing. The therapeutic relationship should be one of mutual respect and compassion with an atmosphere of hope, optimism, and support.

Stevens et al. (2009) encourage a focus on empowerment with service providers thinking in terms of wellness versus illness, competence instead of deficits, and strengths versus weaknesses. Programs should provide opportunities for women to establish a sense of self-empowerment, self-efficacy, and self-control to assist them in gaining the skills and resources that they need to take control of their lives.

During the recovery process, women need the support of the community and encouragement of those closest to them to assist with possible relapses. After completing treatment, women also need the services to assist them in sustaining their recovery and in rejoining the community.

In addition to entering a treatment program, a number of protective factors have been identified that are associated with a reduced risk for substance abuse (Agrawal, 2005). Protective factors that may prevent initial and continued use of substances include the following:

- Parental Warmth: The likelihood of a woman to seek out the use of substances may be lessened if her family of origin is characterized by warmth and caring.
- Spousal or Partner Support: Spousal support or partner support can help mitigate the initial use or abuse of alcohol for women.
- Spiritual Presence: Women with a spiritual presence in their lives are possibly at a lower risk of substance abuse or dependence.
- Coping Skills: Coping skills and resiliency, including seeking support from others, are protective factors that may mitigate the use or abuse of substances.

The National Institute on Drug Abuse (2007b) states that the best substance abuse and treatment message is that "one-size fits-all" approaches do not always work. Treatment approaches for women need to be more tailored and effective in recognizing gender implications.

THE GAY/LESBIAN/BISEXUAL/TRANSGENDER COMMUNITY

The psychosocial stress of being a homosexual man or woman (hereafter also referred to as gay/lesbian/bisexual/transgender, GLBT) in a society dominated by a heterosexual orientation places GLBT individuals at high risk for alcohol and drug abuse. According to McCabe, Bostwick, Hughes, West, and Boyd (2010), a minority stress model indicates that discrimination, internalized homophobia, and social stigma can create a hostile and stressful social environment for GLBT individuals, which contributes to mental health problems, including substance abuse disorders. There is a lack of reliable data on how many GLBT are in the population for several reasons: (1) because population surveys on health issues do not routinely ask sexual orientation or gender identity questions, (2) there is a reluctance to disclose sexual orientation and substance use, and (3) using convenience samples, which may bias results because the data are collected in gay bars, from GLBT events, and at HIV service organizations.

Healthy People 2010 stated there is evidence to suggest that GLBT individuals perceive themselves to be at increased risk for alcoholism and substance abuse. Some studies have indicated that when compared to the heterosexual population, GLBT are more likely to use drugs, have higher rates of substance abuse, and are more likely to continue drug abuse into later life (Cabaj & Smith, 2009; CSAT, 2009). Although GLBT have been shown to use all types of drugs, certain drugs appear to be more popular in the GLBT community. For example, gay men are significantly more likely to have used marijuana, stimulants, sedatives, cocaine, and party drugs than men in the general population. What little information is available concerning lesbian substance use, however, suggests that substance abuse in lesbians occurs at a higher rate than in heterosexual women and could equal the rates of occurrence in gay men (Center for Substance Abuse Treatment, 2009).

Like the general population in the United States, substance abuse in the GLBT community is associated with a myriad of public health challenges, including human immunodeficiency virus (HIV) and acquired immunodeficiency syndrome (AIDS), sexually transmitted infections (STIs), violence, and chronic disease conditions such as cirrhosis of the liver (Gay and Lesbian Medical Association [GLMA], 2010).

CSAT (2009) states that having a general understanding of heterosexism and homophobia is important for health care providers in working with the GLBT population. Heterosexism and homophobia are forms of bigotry against GLBT people. Heterosexism resembles racism or sexism and denies, ignores, denigrates, or stigmatizes nonheterosexual forms of emotional and affectional expression, sexual behavior, or community. Homophobia is defined as the irrational fear of, aversion to, or discrimination against GLBT behavior or persons. Internalized homophobia describes the self-loathing or resistance to accepting a GLBT sexual orientation and is an important concept in understanding GLBT clients. The negative effects of these attitudes include the following: self-blame, negative thoughts about oneself, internal anger, self-deprecation, hopelessness, despair, and self-victimization.

Gay/Lesbian/Bisexual/Transgender Identity Development

McNally (2009) states that "coming out" refers to the experience of some but not all gay men and lesbians as they work through and begin to accept a stigmatized identity. Coming out is a way of transforming a negative self-identity into a positive identity. This process can be very important to people recovering from substance abuse. Feeling positive about oneself is at the heart of recovering from addiction.

The coming-out journey begins with an early awareness of feelings of difference to the development of an integrated identity, which takes many years. The reasons that people move from stage to stage, or fail to move, are very complex. Stage models can provide a useful description of the process and suggest a way of looking at how substance use and recovery interact with being gay or lesbian (McNally, 2009).

Cass's (1979, 1984) seminal theoretical model of homosexual identity formation has become the foundation for other GLBT models. It provides an understanding of the six stages of development an individual moves through to develop integrated GLBT identity. The model is based on two broad assumptions: (a) identity is acquired through a developmental process, and (b) change in behavior stems from the interaction between individuals and their environment.

The first stage of identity confusion is characterized by confusion, turmoil, and doubt as individuals begin to question their sexual orientation. Identity comparison, the second stage, occurs when they have accepted the possibility of being homosexual. In the third stage of identity tolerance, individuals increase their commitment to a homosexual identity but keep public and private identities separate. The fourth stage of identity acceptance is characterized by acceptance of a homosexual identity rather than a tolerance for this identity. Disclosure of homosexual identity remains selective. Identity pride is the fifth stage, characterized by anger, pride, and activism, which leads to immersion in the homosexual culture and rejection of the values of the heterosexual community. Finally, identity synthesis occurs with a fusion of the homosexual identity with all other aspects of self, as individuals no longer dichotomize the heterosexual and homosexual world.

This model can assist both clients and professionals in having a better understanding of the challenges of each developmental stage and the particular supports that might be necessary to reach an integrated identity. McNally (2009) cautions that stage models are general guides to help counselors understand the coming-out process. The models are not linear, and people do not necessarily move through them in order. One stage is not better than another, and people should not be seen as more advanced and mature if they are in a later stage. In fact, Cass (1984) has even made revisions to the model based on a lack of empirical evidence for some of the stages. However, the model is useful in approaching the complexity of sexual orientation and identity formation.

Risk Factors

CSAT (2009) discusses the following factors that may explain the etiology of problem substance use in GLBTs:

- Prejudice and discrimination: The effects can result in feeling isolated, fearful, depressed, anxious, and angry. GLBT people may be victims of antigay violence and hate crimes such as verbal and physical attacks

- Cultural issues: The GLBT person from an ethnic or racial minority makes coping with one's sexual orientation even more complex and difficult due to cultural traditions, values, and norms
- Legal issues: Disclosure of one's sexual orientation can lead to employment problems, denial of housing, and loss of custody of children
- Accessibility: Due to homophobia and discrimination, some GLBT persons may find it difficult or uncomfortable to access treatment services
- Families of origin: There may be unresolved issues with a family resulting from the family's reaction to disclosure of one's sexual orientation, which may have a devastating effect on the GLBT individual
- Health issues: GLBT individuals may face a variety of additional health problems such as co-occurring mental health disorders, PTSD, HIV/AIDS, sexually transmitted infections, hepatitis, and injuries
- Gay bars: Discrimination has often limited GLBT people's social outlets to bars, private homes, or clubs where alcohol and drugs often play a prominent role.

Health care providers need to be aware of the myriad of issues specific to the GLBT population. Providers can enhance treatment and recovery by being knowledgeable about their client's unique needs and being sensitive to issues surrounding identity, homophobia, and heterosexism (McCabe, 2009).

Prevention and Intervention

According to Cabaj and Smith (2009), substance abuse treatment for a GLBT client is the same as that for other individuals and primarily focuses on stopping the substance abuse that interferes with the well-being of the client. However, some GLBT clients will need to address their feelings about their sexual orientation as a part of their recovery. They may be dealing with coming out, societal stigmas, death and dying, relationships, and homophobic families, employers, and work colleagues. It is important that treatment providers understand that the recovery process for some GLBT persons is accepting themselves as gay, lesbian, bisexual, or transgender and feeling comfortable in society.

Substance abuse treatment programs are often not equipped to meet the needs of this population. Heterosexual treatment staff may be uninformed about GLBT issues, may be insensitive to or antagonistic toward GLBT clients, or may falsely believe that sexual identity causes substance abuse or can be changed by therapy. These beliefs by treatment staff become barriers to treating the GLBT client.

Brooks (2009) and Cabaj and Smith (2009) discuss aspects of substance abuse treatment that are sensitive to the needs of GLBT population. They suggest that programs incorporate the following strategies and considerations:

- Screen staff to ensure they are willing to work with GLBT individuals
- Education and training of treatment program staff on issues, appropriate services, and about state and local laws and regulations regarding GLBT persons
- Referral to "gay friendly" self-help groups such as Alcoholics Anonymous for GLBT persons
- Establish written policies that ensure that information about sexual orientation is confidential

- Encourage GLBT clients to carefully consider disclosing their sexual orientation and substance abuse histories to others unless they are fairly sure how the information will be received
- Treat the partners of GLBT clients as they do members of traditional families
- Consider the impact of anti-GLBT bias and internalized homophobia on the client when developing treatment plans
- Promote self-respect and personal dignity by ensuring that the service delivery program does not stigmatize the clients further
- Promote healthier behaviors of safer sexual behaviors, strengthen supportive relationships, and comply with medication regimes

McCabe (2009) stresses providing support for GLBT clients and their families as a significant element of treatment. However, a GLBT client may have unresolved issues with his or her family of origin stemming from the family's reaction to the disclosure of his or her sexual identity. Responses can range from abusive, rejecting, or avoiding, to tolerant, supportive, or inclusive. As with all clients, counselors need to review the client's role in his or her family of origin, because unresolved issues can act as emotional triggers to a relapse. Questions regarding families should be asked with sensitivity. A support group that works with GLBT families known as PFLAG (Parents, Families, and Friends of Lesbians and Gays) may be helpful and may provide a supportive environment to explore family issues.

Alcoholics Anonymous reports over 500 GLBT groups throughout the United States. Most major metropolitan communities have outpatient centers that provide chemical dependency services for GLBT. The National Association of Lesbian and Gay Addictions Professionals (NALGAP) operates to create a network for support and communications among addiction professionals to educate agencies and organizations about GLBT and addictions, act as a clearinghouse for resources, raise the GLBT community's consciousness and combat its denial of the problem of addictions, and strive to improve substance abuse treatment for GLBT (CSAT, 2009). Counselors can encourage clients to establish a GLBT support system, be familiar with community resources, and make the information available.

Substance abuse treatment providers, counselors, and administrators need to become aware of the issues facing GLBT clients. With this knowledge, they can design quality treatment programs that provide effective, ethical, and informed care for GLBT clients. Outcomes will improve and providers will reach a previously underserved population (CSAT, 2009).

PEOPLE WITH DISABILITIES

Estimates of people with disabilities vary, depending on how *disability* is operationally defined. The general definition for people with disabilities, supported by the Americans with Disabilities Acts of 1990 and 1991, include individuals with physical or mental impairment that substantially limits one or more major life activities. Utilizing the statutory definition (Americans with Disabilities Act of 1990, 1991) it has been estimated that at least 54 million people in the United States have one or more physical or mental disabilities and this number is increasing as the population grows older. Five percent of children age 5 to 17 have disabilities; 10% of people age 18 to

64 have disabilities; and 38% of adults age 65 and older have disabilities (U.S. Bureau of the Census, 2008). In 1990 the Americans with Disabilities Act (ADA) (1991) was enacted, which guaranteed equal opportunity for people with disabilities in public accommodations, commercial facilities, employment, transportation, state and local government services, and telecommunications.

Smart (2009) describes four broad categories of disability:

Physical

- Visual impairments
- Hearing impairments
- Dual sensory loss, such as deaf/blindness
- Mobility impairments
- Health disorders

Intellectual

- Mild mental retardation
- Moderate mental retardation
- Severe mental retardation
- Profound mental retardation

Cognitive

- Traumatic brain injury
- Learning disabilities

Psychiatric

- Mental illness
- Autism
- Substance abuse

West, Graham, and Cifu (2009) note that substance abuse by persons with disabilities has been a largely overlooked issue. This is particularly troublesome given the high rate of use and abuse by this population. The rates of alcohol and other drug abuse have consistently been greater than those of the general population. Among persons with developmental disabilities such as mental retardation and autism, rates of abuse have been estimated to be as high as 14% (Winkel, 2011). Individuals with visual impairments and those with auditory impairments both have rates of abuse that are at least 50% or more. Particularly high rates of substance abuse are also found among persons with traumatically acquired disabilities. In many cases, substance abuse predates the disabling condition, and 60% of traumatic brain injuries and spinal cord injuries are acquired while being intoxicated.

While prevalence indicators note the rates of substance abuse and addiction in this group to be greater than nondisabled, the participation of people with disabilities in treatment is thought to be minimal. There is a continual concern about the ability of people with disabilities to access substance abuse treatment services (West, Luck, & Capps, 2007).

Risk Factors

Capuzzi and Gross (2005) stated that people with disabilities face numerous problems that can be seen to arise as a result of (a) the disability itself, (b) the environment in which the disability is experienced, (c) the individual's response to the disability, or (d) the response of family members and others in the social environment. Substance abuse behaviors need to be identified as to whether they are a consequence of, or a response to, the disabling event or whether individuals participated in the same behaviors prior to the disability. Other contributing factors appear to be frustration, oppression, or social isolation that some individuals with disabilities experience and seek to escape through substance abuse.

Livneh and Antonak (2007) examined the psychological adaptation to having a disability. Many disability- and nondisability-related factors interact to create a profound effect on the lives of those with disabilities, which may lead to substance abuse:

Stress   Persons with disabilities normally face an increase in both the frequency and severity of stressful situations. Stress may increase due to the need to cope with daily threats such as independence, fulfillment of life roles, and economic stability.

Crisis   The sudden onset of many disabilities, loss of valued functions, or a life-threatening diagnosis is highly traumatic. The psychological consequences of crisis may be long lasting and evolve into pathological conditions.

Loss and Grief   The crisis experienced following the onset of a traumatic or progressive disability triggers mourning for the loss of function. The individual expresses feelings of grief and despair.

Body Image   The onset of a disability may alter or distort one's body image, self-perception, and self-concept, leading to feelings of anxiety, depression, and cognitive distortions.

Stigma   Stereotypes and prejudice can increase the stigma associated with having a disability. *Handicapism* is defined as a set of assumptions and practices that promote the differential and unequal treatment of people because of apparent or assumed physical, mental, or behavioral differences (Smart, 2009).

Livneh and Antonak (2007) identified the following most frequently experienced psychosocial reactions to a disability that affect one's ability to cope:

- Shock
- Anxiety
- Denial
- Depression
- Anger/Hostility

Understanding how people navigate the process of adapting to an acquired disability and applying this understanding in the form of effective clinical interventions is critical to successful treatment outcomes (Bishop, 2007).

Prevention and Intervention

The Office on Disability (2010) stated that existing substance abuse prevention, intervention, and treatment services are not sufficiently responsive to the needs of people with disabilities. As a result, access to education, prevention, and treatment services for substance use and abuse can be limited, incomplete, or misdirected. It was also noted that treatment centers are often inaccessible in the following ways to those with physical disabilities:

- Transportation and sheer distance can complicate access to specialized treatment centers.
- Cultural insensitivity by health care providers may prevent persons with disabilities from seeking education, risk management, and treatment for substance abuse.
- Effective communication may be frustrated due to limited availability of assistive supports, such as interpreter for persons who are deaf or hard of hearing.
- Often health care providers focus solely on a person's disability and may fail to discuss substance abuse prevention/intervention.

Interventions need to be designed that are sensitive to the particular disability and life circumstance of the individual. Substance Abuse for Disabled Persons (2006) stressed the need for counselors who have specific training for working with people who are mentally or physically disabled with some cross-training in substance abuse services to satisfy the demand for more specialized programs. It is recommended that substance abuse treatment for people with disabilities include the following:

- Family psychoeducation
- Disability and medication management and education
- Independent living skills education
- Anger and stress management
- HIV risk reduction, counseling, and testing
- STD and infectious disease education
- Interpreted self-help meetings for the deaf and hard of hearing
- Health and wellness education
- Case management and crisis intervention
- Educational, vocational, and residential referrals
- Medical and psychiatric services
- Domestic violence and victim assistance counseling
- Development of social support networks
- Self-esteem and body image

There are few substance abuse treatment options for people with disabilities and a lack of cross-training and guides to best practices for staff who serve this population. Changes in policy, advocacy, and attitudes are necessary for specialized programs to catch up with traditional treatment programs. Treatment for special populations is more expensive because of the need for smaller group sizes, modified materials, and additional staff. If more programming options were available, treatment services could be better customized. As people with disabilities leave treatment programs, they face the same challenges that many people with substance abuse issues face, except to a greater degree. They face a shortage of sober living arrangements, employment opportunities, leisure activities, and support systems. All programs should be fully accessible; physically, attitudinally, and programmatically (*Substance Abuse Treatment for Disabled Persons*, 2006).

OLDER ADULTS

By 2050 it it estimated that people 65 and over will comprise 21% of the U.S. population (Kinney, 2009). Older adults are the fastest growing section of the population. The baby boomer cohort, people born from 1946 to 1964, is the first in U.S. history with a majority of individuals who have used illicit drugs some time in their lives. As a result, an increase in substance abuse among older adults could be expected. Therefore, it is estimated that older adults in need of substance abuse treatment will more than double from 1.7 million in 2000–2001 to 4.4 million in 2020 (Blank, 2009; Kinney, 2009).

Older adults use a high number of prescription and over-the-counter (OTC) medications, which increases their risk for inappropriate use. Overuse, underuse, or irregular uses of prescription or OTC drugs are all forms of drug misuse. Factors such as coexisting drug, alcohol, or mental health problems, old age, and being female can increase vulnerability for misusing prescribed medications (Bartels, Blow, Brockmann, & Van Citters, 2005).

Although the use/abuse of alcohol generally declines in old age, it still remains a major problem for some older adults and is often an underreported and/or a hidden problem. The misuse of alcohol among older adults, including drinking above age-recommended limits, binge drinking, or combining alcohol with other medications is a growing concern. Rates of heavy alcohol use have been shown to be higher among baby boomers than in earlier cohorts (Gfroerer, Penne, Pemberton, & Folsom, 2003). It is estimated that 1 in 5 older Americans (19%) may be affected by combined difficulties with alcohol and medication misuse. Accurate identification of alcohol misuse and risky drinking behaviors is important in the prevention and early intervention of alcohol misuse by older adults (SAMHSA, 2006a).

Nicotine addiction often co-occurs with other substance use and can be an indicator of other substance use. Smoking in older adult problem drinkers is more prevalent than in the general older adult population. Some studies indicate the smoking among alcohol-dependent older individuals generally is above 80% (SAMHSA, 2006a). It is estimated that 60% to 70% of older male alcohol users smoke a pack or more a day of cigarettes (SAMHSA, 2006a).

Risk Factors

Various biological, psychological, and social changes that accompany aging make older adults uniquely vulnerable to problems associated with substance abuse. Some of these include loneliness, diminished mobility, impaired sensory abilities, chronic pain, poor physical health, and poor economic and social supports (Bartels et al., 2005). Additionally, the societal stigma about growing old can foster low self-esteem and self-doubt. There is a notion that for older adults there is no play or fun, no money, no usefulness, and no attractiveness (Kinney, 2009).

Physical changes take place in the body as it ages. Some of these changes directly relate to the body's ability to metabolize drugs. Kinney (2009) states that with normal aging, total body water content decreases and the proportion of body fat increases. Alcohol is rapidly distributed in body water after ingestion. With the decrease in body water as we age, the volume for distribution decreases, and therefore the amount of alcohol that reaches the central nervous system increases.

In addition to the increased acute effects of alcohol, a variety of other physical changes make older adults more vulnerable to the medical consequences of use. By age 75, there is a 50% reduction in lung capacity, the kidneys work at only 45% of their previous capacity, and heart function is reduced by 35% (Kinney, 2009).

Another major risk factor is the change in social support and work-related activities for older adults. They have fewer family responsibilities and work-related duties. Many families live far apart, and when older friends begin to die, the person is left with a small or no social support network. Also, many older adults are retired, leaving the days empty of structured activity and creating the need for a substitute activity. Sometimes the activity is alcohol or other drug consumption.

Kinney (2009) states that one of the greatest psychological stressors older adults face is loss. There is loss that comes from the illnesses and deaths of family and friends, loss of money through earned income, loss of status due to retirement, and loss of body functions and skills. The result of these losses is that self-respect, dignity, and self-esteem are threatened.

Bartels et al. (2005) note that one in four older adults has a significant mental disorder. The most common mental health problems are depression, anxiety disorders, and dementia. Older adults also have the highest suicide rate of any age group, with the greatest risk among men, often with the presence of alcohol use and depressive symptoms. Health care providers tend to overlook substance abuse and misuse among older patients while older adults and their families tend to hide their substance abuse and are less likely to seek help (Bartels et al., 2005).

Prevention and Intervention

Many older people are unaware of the effects of aging in combination with the use of alcohol and other drugs. Therefore, beginning with an educational discussion may be extremely helpful. Counselors should ask specifically about the frequency and quantity of use, as well as OTC medications, prescriptions, and alcohol use. Possible symptoms of use should not be ignored. Hesitancy to confront an older adult and not wanting to take away "their last pleasure" sets the stage for denial and enabling behavior on the part of the clinician or family member.

Older adults need the same type of rehabilitation services as younger persons: education, counseling, and involvement in self-help groups (Kinney, 2009). Some recent studies have shown that programs designed for older adults enhance outcomes by reducing treatment dropout, increasing rates of aftercare, and by dealing with relapses if they occur.

Korper and Raskin (2008) indicate that evidence supports a variety of pharmacological and psychotherapeutic interventions for substance abuse problems and psychiatric disorders in older persons. Promising treatment practices include brief alcohol interventions, home- and community-based mental health outreach, integration of substance abuse, mental health, and primary care services, geriatric mental health consultation and treatment teams in nursing homes, support interventions for family and caregivers, and a variety of pharmacological interventions (Korper & Raskin, 2008).

Recommendations (Korper & Raskin, 2008) support including the following into substance abuse treatment for older adults:

- Age-specific group treatment that is supportive and nonconfrontational with focus on self-esteem building
- Coping with depression, loneliness, and loss

- Rebuilding the client's social support network
- Pace and content of treatment appropriate for the older person
- Staff members who are interested and experienced in working with older adults
- Linkages with medical services, services for the aging, institutions for treatment, and case management

Other recommendations included providing an environment of respect for older clients, taking a broad and holistic approach to treatment, keeping the treatment program flexible, and adapting treatment in response to gender and ethnicity.

Kinney (2009) stresses the importance of groups in substance abuse treatment for older adults. Groups can reduce the sense of isolation, enhance communication skills, provide a setting for problem solving, and address issues of denial. Small-group sessions or individual therapy within a treatment program can help develop skills for coping with loss, enjoying leisure time, and developing new relationships.

SAMHSA (2006a) recognizes that substance abuse problems among older adults are associated with increased health care usage and expenditures. Prevention and early intervention programs, including those focused on risk and protective factors, are promising approaches to maximize health outcomes and minimize health care costs of older adults. A range of prevention/intervention strategies for older adults include prevention education for those at risk, accurate identification and screening tools, brief advice during medical visits by primary care providers, and structured brief intervention protocols.

The growth in the aging population will have a significant impact on health services for treatment of substance abuse and mental health. It is essential that improved tools and programs specific to the needs of older adults be developed and implemented.

HOMELESSNESS

Homelessness is one of our most pressing and complex social problems. It is estimated that 842,000 people are homeless on a given night and 2.3 to 3.5 million are homeless over the course of a year (National Law Center, 2010). The recession will force 1.5 million more people into homelessness over the next few years (National Law Center, 2010). An estimated 20% to 25% of these people have a serious mental illness, and one-half of this subgroup also has an alcohol and/or drug problem. Minorities, especially African Americans, are overrepresented among homeless persons with mental illness (National Coalition for the Homeless, 2009).

The definition of *homeless* is provided by the Stewart B. McKinney Homeless Assistance Act (PL 106-400). A homeless person is one whose nighttime residence is

- A supervised publicly or privately operated shelter designed to provide temporary living accommodations (including welfare hotels, congregate shelters, and transitional housing for the mentally ill)
- A public or private place not designed for, or ordinarily used as, a regular sleeping accommodation for human beings (for example, cars, campgrounds, motels, and other temporary places)
- A doubled-up accommodation (i.e., sharing housing with other families or individuals due to loss of housing or other similar situations)

The stereotype of homelessness is often the "bag lady" or single man living on the street. However, since the early 1980s, there has been an alarming rise in family homelessness with approximately one out of 50 children, or about 1.5 million, being homeless each year (National Center on Family Homelessness, 2009). Being homeless can range from acute/short-lived through chronic homelessness with extreme poverty.

Johnson and Chamberlin (2008) noted that some studies indicate that substance abuse is a risk factor for homelessness, whereas others suggest that homelessness leads to drug use. This is the debate about substance abuse as either a cause or consequence of homelessness. Newly homeless people encounter an environment where substance use is accepted as the norm. For some individuals, involvement with drugs stems from their socialization into the homeless culture. Some become homeless with a substance abuse problem. For others, substance use emerges as a means of coping with the uncertainty, instability, and chaotic conditions of their daily lives. Substance abuse and homelessness is a complex issue because there is considerable variation between individual cases, and homelessness is caused by more than one factor.

It has been estimated that 38% of homeless people were dependent on alcohol and 26% abused other drugs. Alcohol abuse is more common in older generations, while drug abuse is more common in homeless youth and young adults (National Coalition for the Homeless, 2009). A survey conducted by the United States Conference of Mayors (2008) asked cities for their top three causes of homelessness. For singles, the causes were 1) substance abuse, 2) lack of affordable housing, and 3) mental illness. For families, the three most commonly cited causes were 1) lack of affordable housing, 2) poverty, and 3) unemployment.

The National Coalition for the Homeless (2009) state that 20% to 25% of the homeless population in the United States suffers from some form of severe mental illness. In comparison, only 6% of the American general population is severely mentally ill. In addition, half of the mentally ill homeless population also suffers from substance abuse and dependence. Some mentally ill people self-medicate using street drugs, which can lead to addiction and disease from injection drug use. Poor mental health can also affect physical health, especially for the homeless. The combination of mental illness, substance abuse, and poor physical health make it difficult for people to obtain employment and residential stability.

Risk Factors

The National Alliance to End Homelessness (2011) points out that while circumstances vary, homelessness occurs when people or households are unable to acquire or maintain housing they can afford. The alliance has focused on four main groups that often suffer from homelessness and its effects:

- *Families* Homeless families are similar to other poor families. Often, families become homeless due to some unforeseen financial crisis—medical emergency, car accident, or death in the family—that prevents them from being able to keep their housing. Most homeless families are able to bounce back fairly quickly with community assistance.
- *Youth* Young people often become homeless due to some familial disruption, including divorce, neglect, or abuse. A large majority experience short-term homelessness and return back home or to family/friends. Homeless youth are

particularly at risk due to their exposure to crime, violence, sexual victimization, and criminal involvement while on the streets.

- *Veterans*   20% of the homeless population is made up of veterans. On any given night, 200,000 veterans are homeless. Veterans often become homeless due to war-related disability. For various reasons (physical disability, mental anguish, post-traumatic stress disorder, stress, substance abuse) many veterans find it difficult to readjust to civilian life. Any and/or all of these difficulties may lead to homelessness.
- *Chronic Homelessness*   Chronic homelessness involves either long-term and/or repeated periods of homelessness coupled with some sort of physical or mental disability. These individuals often end up living in shelters. It is a common misconception that this group represents the majority of homeless; rather they account for about 20% of the entire homeless population.

These four groups do not represent the entire homeless population. Other groups experiencing homelessness are nonchronic single adults, survivors of domestic violence, and former prisoners reentering society.

The National Coalition for the Homeless (2009) noted that homeless persons with substance abuse problems are at a higher risk for HIV infection and are more likely to have serious health problems and severe mental illness, to be arrested, to be victimized on the streets, and to suffer an early death. Alcohol and drug abuse are frequently cited as a major obstacle to ending an individual's homelessness. Many homeless people have become estranged from their families and friends. Without a support network, recovering from substance abuse is very difficult.

In the past 11 years, the National Coalition for the Homeless (2010) has documented over a thousand acts of violence against homeless individuals with 43 known deaths. These crimes are believed to be hate crimes against homeless individuals. The Coalition noted that since the homeless community is treated so poorly in our society, many more attacks go unreported.

The National Coalition for the Homeless (2006) indicated that there are numerous barriers to treatment and recovery opportunities. Homeless people typically do not have health insurance, including Medicaid. This means that few homeless people with addictive disorders are able to find the resources necessary to pay for their own treatment or health care. In addition, there are extensive waiting lists for publicly funded addiction treatment in most states.

The Coalition also noted that other barriers to treatment include lack of transportation, lack of documentation, lack of supportive services, and abstinence-only programs. Absolute lifetime abstinence is not a reality for the majority of people with addictive disorders, so a single focus on it has served as a barrier to the course of treatment.

Treatment

According to the United States Conference of Mayors (2008), additional substance abuse services were reported as one of the top three items needed to combat homelessness. Substance abusers who are homeless have different needs than those who are housed, and programs need to be created that address these needs. Few federal substance abuse treatment and prevention programs target funds specifically to the homeless population. Much of public policy has favored a punitive approach to substance abuse, even though health experts agree that treatment and prevention are effective (Rawson & McCann, n.d.).

Lee and Petersen (2009) noted that homeless substance abusers often report feeling dehumanized, disrespected, and treated as a second-class citizen. Added to their sense of isolation and disadvantage, the replication of these attitudes in social service agencies can further alienate individuals who may need the services the most. When homeless individuals feel humanized and treated with respect, they are more receptive to treatment services.

Another important factor in successful substance abuse treatment is housing. According to Didenko and Pankratz (2007), stable housing during and after treatment decreases the risk of relapse. Substance abuse treatment on its own is inadequate and needs to be combined with supported housing opportunities. Supportive housing programs offer services such as mental health treatment, physical health care, education and employment opportunities, peer support, and daily living and money management skills. In addition, supportive housing programs include outreach and engagement workers, a variety of flexible treatment options, and service to help people reintegrate into their communities.

Case Study
James

Background:
James is a White middle-class male in his mid-60s who was forced to retire early. His wife passed away five years ago and he currently lives with his son and daughter-in-law. During this time he has spent some time in a psychiatric facility due to depression, disorientation, suicidal ideation, and overuse of prescription drugs. As part of his recovery, James participates in a day-treatment program. As an outpatient he is involved in individual therapy a couple of times each week and his therapy has continued for several months.

Presenting Problem:
James has discussed a number of current life issues, including the following:

- James feels depressed most of the time and often wishes he could die so that he will not have to feel the loneliness, emptiness, and the general feeling of being down and hopeless. He says that

he does not have much to look forward to in his life; there is only a past that is filled with mistakes and regrets.

- James was very dependent emotionally on his wife and when she died of cancer a big part of him died. He continues to feel lost and like a child in so many ways. He does not feel close to anyone, and he is convinced that his presence in his son's home is a burden.

- Before he was forced to retire, James taught high school English. When he was involved in this work he felt good because he had some measure of worth. He enjoyed working with young people, especially teaching them literature and encouraging them to think about the direction of their life. He was rated a fantastic teacher, well liked by his students. After his wife died, James went into a long and deep depression; coupled with

(Continued)

(*Continued*)

his age, this resulted in his dismissal and the beginning of his retirement years.

- For James, retirement is next to death. He feels "put out to pasture," simply passing time without getting in people's way. His major problem is the emptiness and lack of purpose for living. He is searching for something to take the place of his wife and his job, yet he sees little chance that he will find a substitute that will bring any meaning to his life.
- James has abused alcohol and prescription drugs off and on during the past five

years. He finds that using substances is a "good" way to ease his pain, loneliness, emptiness.

Critical Thinking Questions

1. What are the primary and secondary issues and why is James experiencing difficulties?
2. What would be your action plans and goals for James?
3. Describe your theoretical orientation, interventions, and anticipated outcomes.

MyCounselingLab™

Go to Topic 10: *Working with Selected Populations*, on the **MyCounselingLab**™ site (www.MyCounselingLab.com) for *Substance Abuse Counseling*, Fifth Edition, where you can:

- Find learning outcomes *Working with Selected Populations*, along with the national standards that connect to these outcomes.
- Complete Assignments and Activities that can help you more deeply understand the chapter content.
- Apply and practice your understanding of the core skills identified in the chapter with the Building Counseling Skills unit.
- Prepare yourself for professional certification with a Practice for Certification quiz.
- Connect to videos through the Video and Resource Library.

CONCLUSION

A growth in alcohol and drug use behaviors has been witnessed in women, people with disabilities, GLBT, children and adolescents, the homeless and the aged. A common theme for treatment among these groups is identification and early intervention. All these groups share the experience of being marginalized within our society, which in turn influences self-esteem as well as self-efficacy skills. These issues, then, are not only individual issues but issues of social importance. Interventions need to be designed to meet individual and group needs, and professionals must act as change agents within their communities and society. As change agents, helping professionals can assist in challenging myths and educating the community of particular individual and group needs revolving around ATOD behaviors and risk factors for the groups presented in this chapter.

12

Working with Diverse Cultures: Exploring Sociocultural Influences and Realities in ATOD Treatment and Prevention

JOHN JOSEPH PEREGOY, PH.D.

MyCounselingLab™

Visit the **My**CounselingLab™ site for *Substance Abuse Counseling,* Fifth Edition to enhance your understanding of chapter concepts. You'll have the opportunity to practice your skills through video- and case-based Assignments and Activities as well as Building Counseling Skills units, and to prepare for your certification exam with Practice for Certification quizzes.

This chapter presents a background for viewing factors that affect diverse cultural groups related to substance use and abuse, prevalence, and effective prevention and intervention strategies. The groups discussed in this chapter are limited to minority/ethnic cultures that have historical roots and are prevalent in the United States, and that share a history of oppression.

The assumption at the foundation of this chapter is simple yet often overlooked in the implementation of individual and community alcohol, tobacco, and other drug (ATOD) interventions: Programs designed for particular groups *need* to be developed within the sociocultural worldview in which they are applied. Substance abuse cannot be addressed without examining the dynamics that influence the context and systems in ethnic communities, which include issues of poverty, the lack of health and child care, education, unemployment, covert and overt racism, within-group diversity, and the role and level of acculturation. The individual (level of acculturation, knowledge, identity and commitment to culture), group (minority group membership and subgroup membership), and community and environmental factors (the social system at large, economics in the community, etc.) influence how the individual creates and makes sense of his or her world, and the role ATOD plays in one's life. The Substance Abuse and Mental Health Services Administration (SAMHSA), a federal program, and other funding and research organizations have adopted similar assumptions regarding treatment and research (SAMHSA, 2010; Trimble, 2010a).

The vast majority of treatment facilities are not linguistically or culturally skilled, and practitioners with multicultural skills are limited. Efforts to train practitioners are ongoing. For example, the National Institute on Drug Abuse (NIDA) (2011) and others offer culturally appropriate fellowships and research opportunities, yet this is not enough. Training programs need to go beyond what is currently provided and recognize the necessity to expand multicultural competence in their programs.

Cultural/ethnic group divides the chapter into sections. Each section has subsections that provide a demographic overview, which may include cultural values and sociocultural perspectives, risk factors affecting each group, barriers to treatment, and considerations in prevention and intervention with each group.

AMERICAN INDIANS AND ALASKAN NATIVES

American Indians and Alaskan Natives are a heterogeneous group made up of 569 federally recognized tribes and a number of tribes that are not federally recognized (Pereguy & Gloria, 2007). The most recent census data indicate that there are 4.9 million (1.6% of the U.S. population) American Indians and Alaskan Natives (U.S. Census Bureau, 2010). About 41% of American Indians and Alaskan Natives were younger than 29 years of age compared with 29% of the total U.S. population. Of this population, 57% of the population can be considered in the childbearing years (ages 10 to 44). This group is growing and exceeding demographic projections. If the current rate of population growth continues, it is projected that by 2050, the Indian/Native population will reach 8.6 million, doubling today's number (U.S. Census Bureau, 2010). High school graduation rates are low, about 50% versus nearly 70% for the general U.S. population (Pamber, 2010). In addition, income for Indians/Natives is about 62% of the national average, with their poverty rate being about three times the national average (U.S. Census Bureau, 2010).

Each tribe has unique customs, values, and religious/spiritual practices; these vary between each tribe. A tribe's commitment to traditionalism ranges from very traditional, in which members speak their tribal language at home, to tribes that use English as their first language. Some historians have said that the intent of Indian education in the 1800s and early 1900s was to kill the Indian and save the child (Morning Edition, 2008). This has resulted in varying degrees of loss of custom and language amongst tribal peoples. About 67% of all American Indians and Alaskan Natives live outside a reservation. With this shift to the cities, an increase in interethnic and intertribal marriages has occurred. This diversity is also compounded by the fact that more than 60% of all Indians are of mixed background, the result of intermarriages among African American, White, Hispanic/Latino, and Asian and Native Hawaiian and Pacific Islander populations (Kochanek, Xu, Murphy, Miniño, & Kung, 2011).

Since the late 1950s more Indians/Natives have been moving to urban settings. A person who meets tribal enrollment criteria and is registered on the rolls of the tribe is entitled to services from the tribe, has voting rights within tribal elections, and has eligibility for government services provided by treaty agreements. Enrolled tribal members who have moved to the city are subject to many of the same social pressures and urban survival.

Alcohol use is a relatively new phenomenon in Indian/Native life. With the arrival of Columbus and the principle of Manifest Destiny, alcohol has eroded the bedrock of individuals, families, communities, and tribes, yesterday and today. Reliable data on the extent and pattern of drug use (including alcohol) among American Indians have been scarce and compounded by questions about the generalizability of findings (Witko, 2006). The greatest proportion of adults who drink are between the ages of 15 and 29, and drinking behaviors appear to decline after age 40. Falk and Hiller-Sturmhöfel (2006) reported that Indian/Natives' incidence of drinking is not greater than their White counterparts', but binge drinking among Indian/Natives is high. Substance abuse behaviors may taper off with age, and the data indicate that there is a slight decrease in lifetime prevalence. Yet, for those who drink heavily, the behavior is killing.

Alcohol and other drug use in the Indian/Native communities takes a drastic toll. Many Indian/Native deaths—including accidental deaths, homicides, suicides, and terminal health status, such as cirrhosis and other liver diseases—can be attributed to alcohol and substance abuse. Alcoholism death rates for Indians/Natives range to about six times that of the national average (Indian Health Service [IHS], 2006). In reviewing the 10 leading causes of death in the Indian/Native communities, researchers found that alcohol use was directly implicated in four: accidents, cirrhosis of the liver, homicides, and suicides. Nearly one-third of all outpatient visits to Indian Public Health Services were related to substance abuse or dependence (IHS). For those over 18 years of age, this population experiences nearly three times more average distress than Whites in their everyday life (Centers for Disease Control and Prevention [CDC], 2009).

Infant mortality rates have dropped in Indian country from 27.7% per 100,000 births to 6.7% during this decade (IHS, 2006). Indian Health Service has identified that age-adjusted mortality rates were considerably higher for Indians/Natives than for all other races. For example, the following rates were identified but are by no means exhaustive: alcoholism was nearly 600 times greater, accidents over 200% greater, suicide within specific age groups is up to 10 times greater (U.S. Department of Health and Human Services, 2007), and homicide was 41% greater than the national average (U.S. Department of Justice, 2011).

Nationally, across all crime categories, victims report that perpetrators were perceived to have been under the influence of alcohol or drugs, regardless of the race of the perpetrator. The average annual number of victimizations for Indians/Natives aged 12 and older are nearly 2.5 times higher than the rest of the nation. A report by the Bureau of Justice Statistics (U.S. Department of Justice, 2011) observed that intimate and family violence involves a comparatively high level of alcohol and drug abuse by offenders as perceived by the victims. Indian/Native victims of intimate and family violence, however, are more likely than others to be injured and need hospital care.

The rate of victimization among Indian/Native women was more than double all women. This group was more likely to be victims of assault, including rape/sexual assault committed by a stranger, not a family member or person known to the victim. Sixty percent of the time the perpetrator was reported to be White. Acts of violence toward Indian/Native people, regardless of assailant, were implicated with alcohol (U.S. Department of Justice, 2011).

Another issue related to substance abuse concerns the affect on maternal and infant health. Fetal alcohol syndrome (FAS) and fetal alcohol effects (FAEs) are consequences of women consuming alcohol during pregnancy. The child can then suffer from neurosensory and developmental disabilities. Although FAS and FAE occur in every cultural community and socioeconomic group, the occurrences vary by subpopulation. FAS is estimated to occur in the general population at about 1 in 750 live births. FAS and FAE effects vary by tribe, yet American Indians/Alaskan Natives are hardest hit. Studies from the Centers for Disease Control show that the fetal alcohol rate among Indians is 30 times greater than Whites (Robertson, 2007). It appears that the impacts vary. Speculation regarding the influence of the male donors' influence on the constellation of FAE effects during conception has not found strong support in the research.

Cultural Values

Keeping in mind the heterogeneity that exists in Indian country, values shared across different tribes will be presented. This information is presented here not to perpetuate stereotypes but rather to explore your clients' worldview and sociocultural orientation. As discussed elsewhere, Indians/Natives differ in their level of acculturation and Indian/Native identity.

Hall, in his seminal work (1984) identified Indians/Natives as living in high-context cultures. For the traditional Native, this means that they implicitly embed meanings at different levels of the sociocultural context, value a group sense, tend to take time to cultivate and establish a permanent personal relationship, emphasize spiral logic, value indirect verbal interaction, and are more able to read nonverbal expressions.

Values most cited in the literature for American Indians and Alaskan Natives include sharing and generosity, cooperation, noninterference, time orientation, spirituality, humor, and humility (Peregoy, 2009; Sue & Sue, 2007).

Sharing is a mechanism to gain both honor and respect. It is a value embedded across tribes. Generosity is tightly intertwined with sharing. Accumulation of wealth is a hollow activity if it cannot be shared with others. At the same time, sharing and generosity play a role in substance abuse and use. Strategies to deal with ATOD use need to consider this value in using behaviors and group interaction (Sue & Sue, 2007).

Cooperation is grounded in the value of group and others. Group includes the tribe, clan and family system, the extended family, and tribal group takes precedence over outside influences. The tribe is not perceived as made up of separate individuals, but rather as a whole entity in and of itself. As such, actions reflect upon the tribe and family. One considers one's self in relation to the tribe and family. Accusing someone as acting as if he or she has no family is an insult in the Indian community. This insult highlights the importance of cooperation and the value of family and infers the extended family, clan, and tribe.

Noninterference is a value based in a sociospiritual orientation. It is grounded in the belief that as human beings we intrinsically know the right way to act or are at least capable of learning to act in a good way on our own. This value highlights the importance of learning by observation, and observing rather than acting impulsively. As a result, rights of others are respected, which then influences parenting style. This parenting style values children making their own decisions, to the extent that our social services systems (based on Euro-American values) sometimes view this behavior as child neglect or, at the very least, as "permissive." In part, the Indian Child Welfare Act was passed in 1974 to support Indian/Native parenting practices and protect families from being separated due to cultural misinterpretation by social service agencies.

Time orientation is an often misunderstood construct. The myth surrounding the concept of time in Indian country is that Indians/Natives do not care about time or, in the therapeutic relationship, are resistant to therapy. This is due to the imposition of a linear concept of time, which is largely Euro-American (i.e., If I miss an appointment, that moment will never be available in the same way or have the same meaning as if I had been "on time"). To begin to understand the concept of Indian time, one needs to understand the Indian/Native as being and becoming, a construct borrowed from the social work literature. The individual operates actively on two levels: one is the here and now, the other is a spiritual plane, both active simultaneously, with the spiritual world consciously or unconsciously. Time is seen as a spiral, with no value on up or down or sideways. The spiral overlaps, so if an appointment is missed "in the here and now," the opportunity for the same life experience will return. This concept makes sense within the concept of being and becoming.

Spirituality in Indian country is a belief that spirit, mind, and body are all interconnected. The belief is that there is a Higher Being, or Creator, and that all things have spirit.

Humor is seen as a value. Humor serves many purposes in the Indian/Native world. It can be used as a form of social control through storytelling, a path to relieve stress, and to create an atmosphere of sharing and connectedness.

Humility, the last value to be mentioned, is central to recognizing one's place in the circle of life. Modesty and humility are essential to a harmonious way of life, reflecting a balanced perspective of oneself in relation to others and the spirit world.

Risk Factors

The elements underlying Indian/Native substance abuse are complex and fall into three primary categories: biological, psychological, and sociocultural. Biological factors include physiology, or the body's response to substances that influence substance dependence. Psychological factors include an individual and community's response to the stresses of oppression and other stressors that affect sobriety or abuse. Sociocultural factors include a community's values surrounding ATOD use, and the acceptance or sanctions used in the cultural milieu to manage use and/or abuse.

Sociocultural factors encompass culturally influenced perceptions in response to larger social pressures as they relate to substance use. Education levels are low—the average education is completion of the ninth grade, while only 50% obtain a high school diploma, unemployment rates exceed 90% on some reservations, and family income is about one-third of the national average. The comparison of family income is faulty in that it does not take into consideration cultural obligations to extended family members and is therefore an overestimate of available resources in many instances (Peregoy, 2009).

The literature on Indian/Native substance use often cites stress as a precipitating or causal factor in alcohol and drug abuse (Hawkins & Walker, 2005). This stress has been referred to as *acculturative stress*, defined as the demands to integrate into and identify with a more dominant culture. Simultaneously, *deculturative stress* also takes place, defined as stress resulting from the loss or devaluation of historical tradition (Peregoy, 2009). Suicide, where rates in the Indian/Native community can be five to 10 times higher than the national average, is thought to be partly due to acculturative and deculturative stress. This phenomenon can be seen in two disparate examples; the first at the Standing Rock Sioux Reservation and the second on the Red Lakes Reservation. Between January and July of 2010 there were ten recorded suicides, primarily among young people on the Standing Rock Sioux Reservation (Health and Human Services [HHS], 2011). An earlier incident occurred on March 21, 2005 at Red Lakes; this was the homicide of eight youth and the suicide of the young gunman. Acculturation and deculturative stress contributed to these horrific events making suicide and cluster suicide daily concerns for many tribes and their people.

Acculturation can be viewed as the outcome of processes that occur at multiple levels in a society, starting with the acquisition of foreign (mainstream) beliefs and values, producing stress that may be alleviated by substance use and abuse. High rates of substance abuse, family disruption, criminal behavior, and mental illness can be attributed to deculturative stress.

Several researchers have proposed using a social integration model for understanding how communities influence substance use (Cleveland, Feinberg, & Greenberg, 2010). The assumption underlying this approach is the belief that cohesive, well-integrated communities provide mitigating influences on stress, whereas poorly integrated communities tend to demonstrate high levels of stress and concomitant substance abuse. Alcohol may become a primary coping response for some individuals and communities, and peer groups may be as powerful an influence as any other factor.

The costs of substance abuse go beyond the emotional and physical dangers and include the use of scarce economic resources. Money that is spent on drugs and alcohol becomes unavailable for individual or family purchases. Also, reservation economies are affected by economic leakage, the drain of reservation resources being spent outside the reservation economy.

Barriers to Treatment

Barriers exist in the provision of services offered in the non-Indian community, including historical distrust; difficulties in cross-cultural communication stemming from a lack of shared meaning; the use of extended family systems, which can be misunderstood as child neglect or social instability within the family unit; and unfamiliarity of non-Indian counselors with Indian/Native conversational styles among traditional and transitional family groups (Peregoy & Gloria, 2007; Sue & Sue, 2007). These groups do not emphasize personal issues and may refer only peripherally to matters of great importance to the family.

Non-Indian agencies have not demonstrated the ability to cross-culturalize their services to benefit Indian/Native families (Trimble, 2010b; Hawkins & Walker, 2005).

There is some resistance to providing home-based services, which is interpreted by the Indian community as a fear of cultural differences on the part of non-Indian providers. This matter speaks to the need for cultural sensitivity on the part of the non-Indian service provider.

Prevention and Intervention

In order for programming to be effective, from prevention to rehabilitation, it needs to be developed within the context of the community and the individual. Traditional healing practices, such as the sweat lodge, the talking circle, and other traditional ceremonial or religious activities, have been found to aid American Indian clients (Blume & Escobedo, 2005). These programs appear to be successful for clients who have a strong attachment to traditional Indian/Native cultures. These approaches would not be applicable to clients who do not have a strong attachment to Indian/Native culture and religion. Before implementing services for any client, it is important to understand his or her level of acculturation and commitment to traditional Indian/Native religions.

Prevention programming could take several other paths to be effective, including offering alternatives to substance use by strengthening community projects such as recreational opportunities, cultural heritage programs, and employment opportunities and training (Cleveland et al., 2010) and incorporating tribal centric treatment programs (Blume & Escobedo, 2005).

Elements that run consistently through the literature for prevention and intervention programs divide programming into two areas: on-reservation and off-reservation programming. Intervention specialists and providers need to have:

- knowledge of Indian/Native characteristics, such as tribalism (an attitude toward other tribes), identity issues, level of acculturation of the client and the community they come from, and issues surrounding biculturalism, which is essential for integrating mainstream and traditional healing techniques;
- an understanding that there is no single explanation for Indian/Native substance abuse; and
- that a treatment orientation based on the notion that alcoholism is a disease excludes the social and cultural aspects of drinking (Thomas, 2005).

Counselors also have a better chance of reducing the frequency of ATOD abuse if they acknowledge that substance abuse is learned in a cultural context (Spillane & Smith, 2010).

Communities need to respond to ATOD issues in a comprehensive fashion. Communities, both urban and rural/reservation, can begin to develop a comprehensive ATOD plan by (a) forming a consensus of the problem, (b) defining safe drinking practices, (c) determining and promoting specific safety provisions, and (d) building support for a comprehensive prevention plan.

Many people who have a thorough understanding of these issues argue that strong community policies need to be developed that are comprehensive, consistent, and clearly defined in relationship to alcohol. This argument describes the necessity to use a public health approach integrating all major institutions, such as the family, school, religion, law enforcement, courts, health services, and the media. The communities, through culturally appropriate facilitation, need to incorporate activities to identify both protective and risk factors in the community (Cleveland et al., 2010; Spillane & Smith, 2010).

ASIAN AMERICANS

The Asian, Native Hawaiians, and Pacific Islanders (ANHAPI) population is growing rapidly in the United States and was projected to be 16 million in 2009 (these population figures represent both individuals who identified as Asian or in combination with one or more races). The ANHAPI population increase is due to changes in immigration laws that occurred in 1965 and the entry of Southeast Asian refugees since 1975. The ANHAPI population grew at about 72% compared with the growth of the general population of about 13% during the period between 1990 and 2005 (U.S. Census Bureau, 2010).

This is a diverse population, consisting of at least 40 distinct subgroups that differ in language, religion, and values (Sue & Sue, 2007). The larger ANHAPI groups, in numbers, in the United States are Chinese, Filipinos, Koreans, Asian Indians, and Japanese, refugees and immigrants from Southeast Asia including Vietnamese, Laotians, Cambodians, and Hmongs, and Pacific Islanders include Native Hawaiians, Guamanians, and Samoans. Between-group differences within the ANHAPI populations may be great, but within-group differences also compound the difficulty of making any generalizations about this population. Individuals differ on variables such as migration or relocation experiences, degree of assimilation or acculturation, identification with the home country, use of their native language and English, composition and intactness of the family system, amount of education, and adherence to religious beliefs (Sue & Sue, 2007). This diversity has made the challenge of culturally competent substance abuse treatment services a complex one for providers.

Educational attainment for the percentage of single race Asians 25 years of age or older who hold a bachelor's degree or higher is 50%. At least 85% of single race ANHAPI 25 years of age or older hold at least a high school diploma. Twenty percent of ANHAPI 25 years of age or older hold a graduate or professional degree (Le, 2011). These percentages attest to the value ANHAPI cultures place on education in the United States. This educational status has fueled the "model minority" myth promulgated during the 1980s (Chou & Feagin, 2008), suggesting that the model minority myth has infiltrated the arena of research as a bias (Guofang & Wang, 2008).

The health statistics across cultures for Asian, Native Hawaiians, and Pacific Islanders reveals coronary heart disease at 2.9%, diabetes at 8%, and hypertension at 21% of the population. Research and information on alcohol and other drug use among ANHAPI is relatively small but suggests that these populations use and abuse substances less frequently than do members of other racial/ethnic groups (Chen, 2006). This observation can be partially attributed to the "model minority" stereotype held by drug researchers and mental health professionals that Asians do not have drug problems and therefore are in little need of study (Chang & Subramaniam, 2008). Chen suggested that the "model minority" belief only adds pressure on Asian Americans. Some ANHAPI immigrants have found success in society, while 12.5% live at or below the poverty level, struggling to survive. Households are not necessarily the average U.S. nuclear family size of 3.2 (U.S. Census Bureau, 2011); many more persons can live under one roof contributing to the total income for the household. This fact confounds income levels, as a household reporting $85,000 per year may represent four or five fully employed persons under one roof. The model minority concept can create pressure, as we find many persons of ANHAPI origin feeling nervous, tense, and depressed as they compete with everyone around them. Help-seeking is not culturally central to many of the ANHAPI cultures (Trinh, Rho, Lu, & Sanders, 2009; Chen, 2006; Sue & Sue, 2007).

Suicide can be a response to the constellation of stressors experienced by any acculturating group. Suicide ranked as the eighth cause of death for ANHAPI groups, compared to the overall population as the 11th-greatest cause of death. The highest rate of suicide is found among men 85 years of age and older, followed by women 75 years of age and older (Suicide Prevention Action Network USA, 2011). One question that emerges is about the cause of elder suicide within these populations. Culture of origin stressors competing with the stressors of acculturation can certainly be a factor.

The report *Prevalence of Substance Use among Racial and Ethnic Subgroups in the United States* was released by the Substance Abuse and Mental Health Services Administration (SAMHSA) providing national estimates of ATOD use (2008). The overall rate of past-year illicit drug use for the total U.S. population (age 12 and older) was 11.9%. Relative to the total U.S. population, Asian, Native Hawaiians, and Pacific Islanders reported use at 6.5%. Prevalence of dependence on alcohol for those 12 and older, among ANHAPI, was 1.8%, and prevalence of cigarette use was 21.7%. This report analyzes racial/ethnic patterns of substance use in the United States using a more detailed classification of race/ethnicity than has been possible in previous reports that used the National Household Survey on Drug Abuse (NHSDA). Asian, Native Hawaiians, and Pacific Islanders (ANHAPI) are consistently relatively low in need for illicit drug use treatment (SAMHSA, 2010). This statement by no means infers that there is not a need for culturally appropriate mental health services for those members of the ANHAPI populations that suffer ATOD abuse.

A report by SAMHSA (2010) using the National Household Survey on Drug Abuse (NHSDA) supports previous research in showing that Asian, Native Hawaiians, and Pacific Islanders' prevalence of substance use, alcohol dependence, and need for illicit substance abuse treatment, while clearly high enough to warrant attention, are low relative to those of the total U.S. population. For example, the percentages of ANHAPI aged 12 and older who used cigarettes, alcohol, and any illicit drug in the past year equaled about 22%, 53%, and 6.5%, respectively, as compared with about 31%, 66%, and 12% in the total U.S. population aged 12 and older. As in the total U.S. population, males have a higher prevalence than females for every substance, but the gender gap is larger among ANHAPI than in the total U.S. population. For example, the percentages of ANHAPI males and females using cigarettes in the past year equal about 30% and 14%, respectively, as compared with 34% and 28% among males and females in the total U.S. population. Given the extensive ethnic diversity of the category used here, these data should be interpreted with caution; averages for the overall group may mask significant variations in the prevalence of substance use among subgroups (SAMHSA, 2010).

Cultural backgrounds and norms governing ATOD-using styles in various cultures differ. Mosher and Akins (2007) noted that Asian drinking is thought to be more social than solitary, occurring in prescribed settings (usually with food) to enhance social interaction rather than as a method of escapism and within the context of moderate drinking norms. Asian women are expected to drink little or no alcohol. It is true that drinking attitudes and customs of the various Asian American cultures are similar in their encouragement of moderation and that no Asian American culture advocates or encourages excessive alcohol use. These views may account for a significantly lower prevalence rate of alcohol use among Asian American groups than that of Whites. When disaggregating data, we see differences in Native Hawaiian and Pacific Islander (NHPI) patterns of ATOD use.

Native Hawaiian and Pacific Islander (NHPI) use of alcohol, tobacco, and other drugs appears to parallel that of American Indians and Alaskan Natives (AI/AN). When looking at binge drinking and alcohol consumption, NHPI is very similar to that of AI/ANs (Mosher & Akins, 2007). "This is interesting because of some of the shared elements between the two groups, i.e., colonialism, cultural conflict and cultural displacement" (Mosher & Akins, 2007, p. 192).

Cultural Values

To fully understand the Asian, Native Hawaiian, and Pacific Islander (ANHAPI) client, a mental health professional absolutely must consider culture in the counseling process (Mosher & Akins, 2007). Although ANHAPI immigrants and refugees form diverse groups, certain commonalities can be generalized to the Asian, Native Hawaiian, and Pacific Islander populations. Sue and Sue (2007) and Chang and Subramaniam (2008) have discussed the following salient cultural values operating among these groups:

- *Filial piety*   Filial piety is the respectful love, obligation, and duty to one's parents. Asian children are expected to comply with familial and social authority even if they must sacrifice their personal desires and ambitions. As children become acculturated into the dominant U.S. culture, pressure to meet parental obligations and expectations can lead to stress and conflict.
- *Shame as a behavioral control*   Traditionally, shaming is used to help reinforce familial expectations and proper behavior within and outside the family. Individuals who behave inappropriately will "lose face" and may cause the family to withdraw support. With the importance of interdependence, the withdrawal of support can cause considerable anxiety in having to face life alone.
- *Self-control*   The Confucian and Taoist philosophies emphasize the need for moderation—to maintain modesty in behavior, be humble in expectations, and restrain emotional expression. Love, respect, and affection are shown through behaviors that benefit the family and its members. Hence, the ANHAPI client may lack experience in identifying and communicating emotional states.
- *Awareness of social milieu*   Individuals tend to be very sensitive to the opinions of peers, allowing the social norms to define their thoughts, feelings, and actions. One subordinates to the group to maintain solidarity. Social esteem and self-respect are maintained by complying with social norms.
- *Fatalism*   Asians, Native Hawaiians, and Pacific Islanders may accept their fate and maintain a philosophical detachment. This silent acceptance contributes to their unwillingness to seek professional help. Mental health professionals often misconstrue a fatalist view of life, "what will happen, will happen," as resistance to treatment.

- *Role and status* The hierarchy of the Asian, Native Hawaiian, and Pacific Islander family and community is based on a cultural tradition of male dominance. Men and elders are afforded greater importance than women and youths. The father makes the major decisions, and the mother is responsible for the children. The greatest responsibility is placed on the eldest son, who is expected to be a role model for younger siblings and help raise them. Upon the death of the father, the eldest son takes on the family leadership. Fewer demands are placed on daughters, because they leave their family of origin upon marriage. Therapy with Asian Americans must take into account family hierarchy and the demands placed on each member.
- *Somatization* Asians, Native Hawaiians, and Pacific Islanders perceive problems as difficulties with physical health. Physical illness is believed to cause psychological problems. Complaints such as headaches, stomachaches, and muscle aches are often expressed in response to stressors. Mental health professionals must take into account physical complaints as real problems to improve other aspects of the client's life.
- *Interdependence* The culture has a relational orientation and a cultural frame in which one is defined with his or her continued interdependence with the group and where the group needs are held above those of the individual.

Risk Factors

ATOD-using behavior is influenced by many cultural and situational variables pertinent to ANHAPI groups. Such variables identified in the literature include cultural values, traditions, attitudes, and beliefs (Costello, Swendsen, Rose, & Dierker, 2008); the degree to which one is socialized to the native culture and the degree of acculturation to the dominant values of the host culture (acculturation can lead to conflicts, including conflict across a generations) (Rosario-Sim & O'Connell, 2009; Le, 2009); family conflicts; role conflicts; alienation and identity conflict; racism (Alvarez, Juang, & Liang, 2006); and other factors related to immigration and refugee status combined with economic stressors. In addition to these risk factors, Asians', Native Hawaiians', and Pacific Islanders' personal and social problems may be caused by their immigration/refugee status (Abe-Kim et al., 2007):

- *Feelings of personal failure* For many immigrants there is great stress placed on basic survival needs and adjustment. This detracts from individual and family life just when the family member is needed most. Often immigrants are underemployed, reducing the social status that they held in the home country.
- *Family role reversals* In families in which the parents do not speak English, children may be forced to accept adult responsibilities, such as being the spokesperson for the family. This is a role reversal for the father, who is traditionally the family authority. Youth may lose respect for their elders because they are unable to assume the traditional roles or provide financial support. The impact on the family can be depression, alienation, family conflicts, and ATOD abuse.
- *Economic stress* Many immigrant Asian families are unable to support themselves financially owing to a lack of job skills, low English proficiency, and large family sizes. Several of these families are also supporting their extended family in their native countries, contributing to additional economic pressures and subsequently the risk of ATOD abuse.

Asian American mental health experts generally agree that Southeast Asian refugees are at the highest risk of these and other even more severe stressors (Abe-Kim et al., 2007). These authors and others have discussed the impact of refugees who experienced traumatization from political violence: witnessing family members or friends tortured and/or murdered; and uprooting. They have encountered repression, torture, violence, separation and loss, hardships, and exile. These experiences are so painful that the refugee is likely to suffer psychological dysfunction in both the short and long term. Symptoms of mental and emotional distress common among refugees include insomnia, eating disorders, moderate to severe depression, culture shock, and homesickness. These symptoms are characteristic of post-traumatic stress disorder (PTSD). Upon arrival in the United States, refugees experience what can be a new constellation of stressors. The sources of stress that emerge can include unemployment, underemployment, poverty, shifting family roles related to employment, loss of status from their community of origin, and a host of other issues common to refugees (Le, 2009; Rosario-Sim & O'Connell, 2009). The use of alcohol and drugs can be seen as helpful for dealing with sadness and forgetting painful memories (Juthani & Mishra, 2009).

Sue and Sue (2007) proposed three categorizations of Asian Americans, with distinct approaches in adjusting to the conflicts of acculturation. *Traditionalists* maintain loyalty to their ethnic group by retaining traditional values and living up to the expectations of the family. *Marginal persons* view their ethnicity as a handicap and attempt to become over-Westernized by rejecting traditional Asian values. This type of adjustment often leads to an identity crisis and a marginal existence, because these individuals cannot completely shed certain traditional ways. The third group, individuals attempting to develop a *new identity*, incorporate positive aspects of the Asian culture with the current situation. They have a need to attain self-pride by reversing the negatives of racism and discrimination in the United States. They may become politically or militantly involved to expose and change cultural racism in the United States.

Accurate assessment of an individual's acculturation level assists the therapist in data collection, analysis, interpretation, and determination of whether the client will return for future therapy (Sue & Sue, 2007). Awareness of the influence of generational status in the United States will aid the therapist in understanding individual struggles and perhaps family issues as well. Understanding the culture of Asian Americans and potential adjustment problems is a necessary first step in providing sensitive interventions to facilitate a positive therapeutic experience (Juthani & Mishra, 2009).

Prevention and Intervention

The use of mental health services by Asian Americans remains quite low because of the stigma and shame of talking about one's problems (Chen & Mak, 2008; Peregoy, 2009). Prevention and treatment programs for this population will be most effective if they reflect the values and norms of the population being served. To be successful, recovery programs for Asians, Native Hawaiians, and Pacific Islanders should address a variety of important issues: language, socioeconomic, cultural, and geographic barriers to treatment; status and length of time in the United States; refugee or immigrant status and history, and level of acculturation or assimilation into mainstream American culture. Addressing the following areas would lead to an increased possibility of successful treatment:

- Acknowledge the diversity, including the conflicts, shared values, and attitudes, of the many cultures within the Asian, Native Hawaiians, and Pacific Islander populations.
- Involve community members in treatment efforts whose voices command the respect of both parents and youth, such as elders, teachers, doctors, business leaders, community leaders, and youth role models.
- Help recent immigrants adapt to the English language and American culture.
- Acknowledge and respect prevention/healing practices of traditional cultures. Treatment should incorporate culturally-based support systems in families and communities, as well as Eastern and Western wellness models.
- Conduct outreach about important substance abuse treatment issues in newspapers, magazines, and media that provide information in Asian/Pacific Islander languages.
- Provide education to young people on ethnic heritage and customs to promote positive cultural identity, self-esteem, and family communications. Education for parents on U.S. life and substance abuse issues will help them understand their children's acculturation and the stressors related to that process.

Sue and Sue (2007) recommended giving Asian/Pacific Islander clients an overview of the counseling process to familiarize them with roles and expectations. The following guidelines, drawn from the literature, suggest how mental health professionals could proceed with clients:

- Use restraint when gathering information. Because of the stigma against mental illness, the therapist should refrain from asking too many personal questions during the initial session.
- Do a thorough analysis of current environmental concerns, such as the need for food and shelter. Clients may need information on services that are available to them. Assess financial and social needs.
- Assess clients' worldviews, the way they view the problem, and determine appropriate solutions.
- Focus on the specific problem brought in by clients, and help them develop goals for treatment.
- Take an active and directive role. Because of cultural expectations, clients will rely on the therapist to furnish direction.
- In working with families, consider the intergenerational conflicts. Be willing to accept the hierarchical structure of the family.
- Focus on concrete resolution of problems, and deal with the present or immediate future.
- In the case of refugees, do a careful history and gather information on their family life in their home country, their escape, and how this was experienced. Also important to refugees are the adjustment to the new culture, their methods of coping, and any marital or family problems that have developed.

Undoubtedly, more research is needed to increase our understanding of the causes of ATOD use among various Asian, Native Hawaiian, and Pacific Islander groups and effective prevention and treatment approaches. Mental health professionals must educate themselves about cultural differences if they are to provide services to address the unique needs of this population. The Substance Abuse and Mental Health Services Administration has recognized the need for developing culturally appropriate services to ANHAPI populations and has funded community developed programs for developing resiliency in youth and families. This is a beginning; it will take time to develop programming and services to effectively meet the needs of both immigrants and refugees.

AFRICAN AMERICANS

African Americans constitute about 14% of the total U.S. population. This percentage translates into approximately 41.8 million people of African descent and identity in the United States today (U.S. Census Bureau, 2011). Wide gaps exist between African Americans and the general population in the arenas of education, employment, and income.

In 2011, about 84% of Blacks 25 years of age or older held at least a high school diploma. Of all individuals identifying as Black and identifying with more than one other racial identifier, 19% held bachelor's degrees in 2009, and 1.5 million had advanced degrees. Ten years earlier only about 900,000 Blacks held advanced degrees. In 2008, 2.5 million Black students attended college. This is roughly twice as many as the number that attended college 25 years earlier (U.S. Census Bureau, 2011).

Among Black households (a household can include both related and unrelated persons including children) 64% contained families. There were 86 million Black family households. Of these, 44% were married couples. This does not include households of unmarried parents. This statistic challenges one of the mainstream misconceptions of the Black family: that the Black family is made up of a single-parent household. About 1.3 million single-race Black grandparents lived with their own grandchildren who were 18 years of age or younger. Of this number, 50% were also responsible for their grandchildren's care (U.S. Census Bureau, 2011). With an annual median income for Black households of $32,548 for the year 2009, we saw a drop of income for the same households of about $1,500 from the previous year. This is compared to an annual median income for Whites for the year 2009 of $51,861 (U.S. Census Bureau, 2010).

As a minority group, African Americans' disadvantaged status, racism, and poverty contribute to the following statistics. Incarceration for young African American men in their 20s who were high school drop-outs is about 37%. A full 33% of all Black men will spend time in jail or prison in their lifetime, compared with 1 in 87 of all White males. African American women represent 12% of the general female population but represent 50% of females in prison. This is due in part to the "war on drugs" (Williams, 2011). The life span of African Americans is on average 5.6 years shorter than the average White person (combined male and female average is 77.8 years of age) (Edlin & Golanty, 2010).

Educationally, the opportunities for African American youths have yet to improve significantly, especially in urban areas (Banks & McGee Banks, 2010). Only about 50% of Black children graduate high school, compared to 73% for White children. A variety of theories exist for this education/learning gap: that teachers are not sensitive to cultural differences; the curriculum may also not be meaningful to the experiences of minority group children; teaching/working conditions in lower income schools is not conducive to learning; lack of appropriate supplies; etc. (Banks & McGee Banks, 2010).

Drug abuse may also contribute to the lack of achievement for some African American children.

For many urban African American adolescents, life is complicated by problems of poverty, illiteracy, and racism (Palmer, Davis, Moore, & Hilton, 2010). For Black youth, unemployment is three times as likely than for White youth, and for Black men it is twice as likely as for White men (Pollard, 2011). Among African American males aged 15 to 34, homicide was the leading cause of death. Homicide is the second leading cause of death for Black males aged 10 to 14 years of age (Karch, Dahlberg, & Patel, 2007).

Although many of these statistics are bleak, it appears that much of our literature is based on individuals of the lower class, welfare recipients, or unemployed, while failing to examine other segments of the African American population. More than a third of all Blacks are now middle-class or higher. They tend to be well educated, professionals, homeowners, and married (Hardaway & McLoyd, 2009). The success of this portion of the population is not without frustrations, many may feel bicultural stress. Middle-class African Americans can experience feelings of guilt for having made it, frustrations from surpassing the present effects of past discrimination accompanied by feelings of isolation.

Risk Factors

African Americans have been particularly vulnerable to the negative social and health consequences of substance abuse. Research suggests that Black youth experience an earlier onset of alcohol use and other drug problems, a greater likelihood of being routed to the criminal justice system than to treatment for problems caused by substance abuse, and higher rates of illnesses, such as liver cirrhosis and esophageal cancer. Crack cocaine has compounded the problems associated with substance abuse.

There is increasing concern that African Americans who are concentrated in urban environments may be at greater risk for the transmission of HIV due in part to the high level of intravenous heroin and cocaine use and the exchange of sexual favors for crack cocaine. Kyomugisha (2006) pointed out that the number of crack cocaine users among Blacks has risen in the past decade. Blacks represent the majority of users. Black women are 15 times more likely to test positive for HIV than White women (Kyomugisha, 2006).

African Americans have historically been underserved by traditional counseling services (Constantine & Sue, 2007). The reasons suggested for this gap in service are poverty, lack of accessible facilities, lack of awareness of service facilities or their purpose, and the absence of culturally acceptable treatment models.

Other problems that African Americans face that can lead to depression, substance use, and other mental health problems include the following:

- Adverse effects of myths and stereotypes regarding the African American culture
- Historical and contemporary racism and discrimination
- Low self-esteem, confusion about cultural identity, and feelings of rejection from years of discrimination
- Lack of education
- Communication problems
- Differing cultural characteristics and customs
- Unequal employment and housing opportunities

- Underemployment, unemployment, and low socioeconomic status
- Increasing number of one-parent or female-headed households
- Living in high-stress environments, such as those with low income, high rates of crime, and high unemployment

Cultural Values

The African American family has been identified as having strengths that help overcome oppressive societal conditions and contribute to both family/community cohesiveness and resilience. These seminal findings were identified as strengths in the early 1970s and they have been supported by other investigators (Constantine & Sue, 2007). These strengths include (a) collectivism that can be seen as strong kinship bonds across a variety of households; (b) strong work, education, and achievement orientation; (c) a high level of flexibility in family roles, and developing familylike relationships with people outside of the biological family; (d) a commitment to spiritualism reflected through a strong commitment to religious values and church participation; and (e) "diunital" views of the world, where it is important to integrate all elements in life, striving for balance.

As a group, African Americans tend to be more group centered and sensitive to interpersonal matters and to emphasize community, cooperation, interdependence, and being one with nature. In contrast, White middle-class values stress individuality, uniqueness, competition, and control over nature (Sue & Sue, 2007).

Many African Americans have an extended family network that provides emotional and economic support. Among families headed by females, the care of children is often undertaken by a large number of relatives, older children, and close friends (Raphel, 2008; U.S. Census Bureau, 2011). African American men and women value behaviors such as assertiveness, and within the family, men are more accepting of women's work and willing to share in the responsibilities traditionally assigned to women. Many African American families have instilled positive self-esteem in their children despite the problems with racism and prejudice (Hardaway & McLoyd, 2009; McLoyd, Hill, & Dodge, 2005).

As in many ethnic minority cultures, older adults in the Black culture in America play vital roles in the family beyond caregiving, community leadership, and are respected for their knowledge and experience. Younger family members experiencing difficulties are often referred to their grandparents for counsel. Many grandparents accept the responsibility for rearing their grandchildren while the parents work or acquire education. In addition, older African American family members play a significant role in passing on cultural values, customs, and traditions to their children (Hardaway & McLoyd, 2009; McLoyd et al., 2005).

Spirituality and religion are essential elements of the African American way of life. African American churches have always been more than houses of worship, and the African American minister has been more than a preacher. The church has historically served as a spiritual, intellectual, and political arena for the African American community, and the ministers have traditionally served as teachers, counselors, and political activists. The churches are agents for transmitting traditional values, strengthening family ties, and providing opportunities to learn about their ancestry. Spirituality differs from religion and is a personal commitment to a higher being. This, too, is a strong value among African Americans (McLoyd et al., 2005; Bell-Tolliver, Burgess, & Brock, 2009).

Barriers to Treatment

African Americans who seek treatment are often thought to have a negative view of mental health services. Some potential Black clients may have distrust for the therapeutic relationship and service delivery organizations due to a prolonged history of systematic mistreatment and racial oppression that has treated the Black American as a marginal person. African Americans underuse counseling services because they perceive counselors as insensitive to their needs, believe that counselors fail to provide equal energy and time working with underrepresented groups, and feel that counselors do not accept, understand, or respect cultural differences (Constantine & Sue, 2007; Ponterato, Casas, Suzuki, & Alexander, 2009).

Counselors also need to understand that African Americans often rely heavily on their church for help. Mental health professionals are becoming increasingly open to the advantages of religious involvement and how a strong spiritual base can support resilience to life's problems (McLoyd et al., 2005).

Other barriers that contribute to underusing mental health services for the African American community include (a) the lack of a historical perspective on the development of the family and support systems within the African American community, (b) a lack of awareness and understanding of the unique characteristics of the value systems of African American families, and (c) communication barriers that hinder the development of trust between the African American client and the non-African American therapist (Bell-Tolliver et al., 2009).

Prevention and Intervention

Prevention and intervention strategies for Black Americans that meet the needs of the individual, family and community will prove successful over those strategies that focus on the individual alone. Mental health professionals must be capable of analyzing adaptive behavior patterns, the cultural rituals of alcohol and drug use, and the specific sociopolitical influences of substance abuse with African Americans. The counselor's process, goals, and expectations need to fit the worldview of the African American client.

Because of past experiences with racism and prejudice, African American clients are often distrustful of White counselors. Richardson, Bethea, Hayling, and Williamson-Taylor (2009) noted that to make headway, the therapist must establish a trusting relationship. African American clients are especially sensitive to interpersonal processes and will test the relationship. They may directly challenge the therapist's values and qualifications or act in a very guarded and aloof manner. These behaviors are part of a protective mechanism. A relationship may develop if the counselor can respond in a straightforward manner. Self-disclosure is very difficult for many African American clients since it leaves them vulnerable to racism (Constantine & Sue, 2007; Bell-Tolliver et al., 2009).

African Americans have traditionally relied on the support of the family, church, and the community (SAMHSA, 2010). Culturally sensitive and relevant treatment programs and materials specifically targeting African Americans are essential to successful programs. Inclusion of the family system in the treatment process to explore sources of strength is an important first step. Spirituality is also recognized as a tool in the treatment of African Americans. A strong spiritual leader may be included as reflective of the community culture and as an extended family member.

In working with African American youth and adults, McLoyd et al. (2005) suggested the following:

- It is often beneficial to bring up the client's reaction to a counselor of a different ethnic background.
- If the client was referred, determine the feelings about counseling and how it can be made useful.
- Identify the expectations and worldview of the African American client. Determine how the individual views the problem and the possible solutions.
- Establish an egalitarian relationship. Most African Americans tend to establish a personal commonality with the counselor.
- Determine how the client has responded to discrimination and racism in both unhealthy and healthy ways. Also examine issues around racial identity.
- Assess the positive assets of the client, such as family, community resources, and church.
- Determine the external factors that might be related to the presenting problem. This may involve contact with outside agencies for assistance.
- Help the client define goals and appropriate means of attaining them. Assess ways in which the client, family members, and friends handled their problems successfully.

HISPANICS

The term *Hispanic* was generated as a U.S. government catch phrase to conveniently classify different subgroups and subcultures of people who are of Cuban, Mexican, Puerto Rican, and South or Central American descent. Although Hispanics do have much in common (language; religion; customs; and attitudes toward self, family, and community), the subgroups have considerable variation in ethnic origins, socio-economic groups, dialects, immigration status, and histories (Peregoy, 2009). Hispanics accounted for one-half of the nation's growth. The Hispanic growth rate (24.3%) was nearly three times that of all races (6.1%) in the United States (U.S. Census Bureau, 2011).

The Pew Hispanic Center reported 50.5 million Hispanics in the United States (2011). Nearly two-thirds of the population (64%) are of Mexican descent, 9% from Puerto Rico, 3.4% Cuban, and about 7.6% from Central American countries (U.S. Census Bureau, 2011). These numbers reflect a population increase of 46.3% since the 2000 census (Pew Hispanic Center, 2011). This increase has been attributed to both immigration and high fertility rates. The census data do not reflect undocumented Hispanics who choose to "pass" because of fear of deportation or for economic, political, or personal reasons (Goffman, 1963); they represent an estimated 11.2 million undocumented immigrants (Pew Hispanic Center, 2011).

The average age for Hispanic males is 27 and the average age for females is 27.6 years of age. Sixty percent of all Latinos were native born, a full 40% were foreign born. There is little age difference at age of first marriage from the U.S. population in general. Seventeen million Latinos were under the age of 17, representing 23% of this age group (Pew Hispanic Center, 2011).

About 25% of the population 25 years of age or older, do not have a high school diploma or GED. The median earnings for males is $27,490 and for females it is $24,738 (U.S. Census Bureau, 2011). Health status and disparities are large among this population. Hispanic and Black youth under 18 experience poverty at a greater rate than their peers (CDC, 2011).

The eight top leading causes of death for Hispanics are heart disease, cancer, unintentional accidents and injuries, stroke, diabetes, chronic liver disease, and homicide (CDC, 2011). Mexican Americans suffer more from diabetes than do those with origins in Puerto Rico. Puerto Ricans suffer disproportionately from others, suffering from a greater incidence of asthma, HIV/AIDS, and infant mortality (CDC, 2009).

Hispanic drug use increased from 6.2% in 2008 to 7.9% in 2009 (SAMHSA, 2010). Early research failed to delineate between Hispanic subgroups. Current research overcomes some of the methodological weakness that prior research included across subgroups. Earlier, generalizations emerged that Hispanics were more likely to use drugs than other groups. The most recent information, however, indicates that although portions of the Hispanic community have been affected by serious drug problems, the Hispanic population as a whole (use rate of 7.9%) is not more likely to use drugs than other groups (White use rate is 8.8%) (SAMHSA, 2010). Variability among the seven Hispanic American subgroups was significant for substance use, alcohol dependence, and the need for illicit drug abuse treatment. Mexican Americans and Puerto Ricans exhibited higher prevalence of illicit drug use (including marijuana and cocaine), heavy alcohol use/dependence, and the need for illicit drug use treatment. Caribbean Americans, Central Americans, and Cuban Americans, however, showed lower prevalence. South Americans and other Hispanics reported prevalence close to the total population (SAMHSA, 2010). Many of the factors associated with substance abuse among other oppressed minority groups in the United States appear to operate for Hispanics as well.

Research has shown that Hispanics suffer the full impact of the "culture of poverty," which has been described as living under the impact of multiple oppressions. These factors include low income, unemployment, underemployment, undereducation, poor housing, prejudice, discrimination, and cultural/linguistic barriers. In addition to the stress of the culture of poverty, many Hispanics also experience acculturation stress. The intergenerational transition from one's culture of origin to the development of bicultural abilities places stress and strain on the individual and the family system (Martinez, 2006).

One pattern of acculturation is known as *cultural shift,* whereby an individual substitutes one set of practices with alternative cultural characteristics. Generally, this shift occurs out of the necessity to acculturate to the dominant society and is an act of survival rather than choice. A dramatic point of stress in the acculturational process is a shift from a culture that values family unity and subordination of the individual to the welfare of the group, to the highly individualistic culture predominant in U.S. society. If ATOD abuse is used to cope with stress, then levels of drug use will vary depending on the level of acculturation (Saint-Jean, Martinez, & Crandall, 2008).

Cultural Values

Discord and family disruption have been identified as an antecedent of substance use and abuse among Hispanic adolescents and young adults (Peregoy, 2009). To gain insight into the Hispanic individual, investigation of *la familia* is paramount, because the family is the basis of Hispanic cultures. Often divided by generation, the immigrant's status tends to guide the adherence to the values and mores of one's culture of origin. The difference between the cultural orientation of the family and the cultural identity of the child may cause intergenerational conflicts. For example, immigrant families tend to develop a family struggle in which younger members struggle for autonomy (i.e., an American value) and the older family members struggle for connectedness (i.e., a Hispanic value) (de Arellano & Danielson, 2005).

The acculturation process can produce tremendous amounts of stress for the individual and place dramatic strains on the family system. Those who have immigrated alone, leaving behind their extended family support system, face the potential of adjustment problems (Peregoy, 2009).

Hispanics underuse mental health services and tend to terminate therapy after one contact at a rate of more than 50% (Smith-Adock, Daniels, Lee, Villaba, & Arce, 2006). Sue and Sue (2007) suggest that ineffective and inappropriate counseling approaches to the values held by this group are often reasons for early termination. Certain unifying cultural values distinguish Hispanics from the dominant culture. An increased awareness of the cultural concepts can foster a positive therapeutic experience for the Hispanic client.

The Hispanic family provides support, identity, and security for its members. The strong sense of obligation ensures that the family's needs as a unit supersede individual needs. Garza and Watts (2010) note that children are expected to be obedient and are not generally consulted on family decisions, and adolescents are expected to take responsibility for younger siblings at an early age.

The Hispanic nuclear family is embedded in the extended family consisting of aunts, uncles, grandparents, cousins, godparents, and lifelong friends. During times of crisis, the family is the first resource for advice before help is sought from others. The downside, however, is that the extended family system can serve as a stressor due to the emotional involvement and obligations with a large number of family and friends. Nonetheless, this strong tie highlights the importance of enlisting the family in therapy.

The cultural value of personalism defines an individual's self-worth and dignity from inner qualities that give self-respect. The Hispanic culture values the uniqueness of inner qualities that constitute personal dignity. This sense of self-respect, self-worth, and dignity in oneself and others demands showing and receiving proper respect. A therapist who conveys personalism develops trust and obligation with the Hispanic client (Garza & Watts, 2010; de Arellano & Danielson, 2005).

Sex-role norms and hierarchy within the family unit continue to influence both Hispanic men and women; however, acculturation and urbanization appear to be affecting both of these standards. Traditionally, males are expected to be strong and dominant providers, whereas females are more nurturant, self-sacrificing, and submissive to males. Some Hispanic women are more modern in their views of education and work but remain traditional in their personal relationships (Garza & Watts, 2010; Sue & Sue, 2007).

In addition to sex roles, a hierarchy of leadership and authority is related to gender and generation. The father's role is one of superior authority, and the mother's role can be viewed as the center of the family and purveyor of culture. Roles appear to include egalitarian decision making and indirect assertion by women, which may serve to preserve the appearance of male control. Children are expected to obey their parents, and younger children are expected to obey older siblings who are role models. Understanding the roles and hierarchy of each Hispanic family is vital in assisting with problem solving, renegotiation, and redefinition of power relationships (Garza & Watts, 2010).

Spiritual values and the importance of religion can be a strong influence on the behavior of Hispanics. Spiritualism assumes an invisible world of good and evil spirits who influence behavior. The spirits can protect or cause illness, so an individual is expected to do charitable deeds to be protected by the good spirits (Furman et al., 2009; Peregoy, 2009).

Catholicism is the primary religion for Hispanics. Traditional adherence to the religious values of enduring suffering and self-denial may prevent some Hispanics from seeking mental health treatment. Catholicism, like many other religions, has powerful moral and social influences on day-to-day living. Religion and shared spiritual beliefs and practices are built on the idea of natural and supernatural forces that link an individual to a greater power. The three main healing/spiritual systems among Hispanics in the United States include *curanderismo* (Mexican American indigenous healers), *espiritismo* (Puerto Rican), and *santeria* (Cuban). Under each of these systems, life is governed by thoughts, intentions, and behaviors. Harmony is a unifying balance; failure to follow prescribed rules of belief can lead to imbalance and stress, including suffering, sickness, and bad fortune. Therapy can be augmented by enlisting other support systems, such as the church or folk healers (*curanderos/-as*). The reader is cautioned that when working with indigenous healers, traditional healing practices need to be understood. For example, *curanderas* on the California–Mexico border were prescribing dried rattlesnake meat for HIV-positive clients. Many of these clients contracted salmonella poisoning as a result (Alarcon & Ruiz, 2010).

Barriers to Treatment

Barriers to treatment for Hispanic groups include the disproportionate number of Hispanics enrolled in programs that emphasize pharmacological treatment rather than psychological treatment (Alarcon & Ruiz, 2010). This barrier may be due to the economics of treatment costs or the failure of treatment programs to operate effectively across cultural milieus. Several factors influence the inability of service agencies to respond to the needs of Hispanics.

First, cross-cultural counseling has been recognized as a viable force in the mental health field. The responsibility of this approach requires that mental health professionals be familiar with standard models of treatment in the field and that these models be analyzed as to how they may complement or belittle cultural beliefs and perspectives. These perspectives would include, for example, the view of alcoholism as a disease as well as the belief that an individual who abuses it is morally weak. The latter view is not consistent with the disease model of alcoholism but is a common perspective among Hispanics. Moreover, cultural perspectives, across and within groups, and gender-role expectations need to be understood. The perspective in some Hispanic cultures that alcohol use/abuse for men maintains a romantic element puts abuse in a different light within a cultural lens (Alarcon & Ruiz, 2010; Furman et al., 2009).

Cultural perspectives such as this one have implications for service delivery at all levels. As an example, working with a self-referred Hispanic male who believes these cultural values, the mental health worker may need to help him work through the shame of being morally weak within a traditional concept of machismo. In addition, an understanding of the meaning of substance abuse behaviors and their social contexts may produce an awareness of how competing values cause stress and influence substance abuse coping responses. Bilingual language ability and bicultural skills have been identified as essential elements in the provision of services to Hispanic groups, which, until the early 1980s, were vastly underrepresented in service delivery (Furman et al., 2009; Sue & Sue, 2007). This problem speaks to the need for training programs to actively recruit and train Hispanics into the human services professions.

Immigrant legal status can also be a barrier if individuals have entered the country illegally. These individuals may not seek assistance owing to fear of deportation. This group may be at particular risk for substance abuse, especially if they do not have well-developed support systems in place (Sue & Sue, 2007).

When considering Hispanic substance abuse behaviors together with the effect of ethnic minority status and stresses of recent immigration or refugee status to the United States, earlier models of ATOD use are not sufficient to explain substance abuse behaviors of Hispanics. Acculturational stress, socioeconomic status (SES) and poverty, role strain and conflict, unemployment, and discrimination are all factors that play into drug use and abuse (Furman et al., 2009).

Current research findings provide a better perspective on substance use patterns based on gender and age among Hispanic populations. Hispanic men are more likely to use the drugs previously mentioned than Hispanic women. Data also reveal sex differences in use and experimentation up to age 35 with substance use among Hispanic populations, with males more likely to use and experiment with substances than females. One hypothesis that may contribute to this difference of use in age and sex is that older cohorts were probably raised with stronger traditional norms discouraging drug use among women, whereas those in younger cohorts appear to be experimenting and using at higher rates (SAMHSA, 2010). Other possible explanations may be the level of acculturation or the belief in machismo and risk taking, and for younger Hispanics, the influence of peer pressure combined with stages of development.

Contrary to popular myth, data on national drug use patterns indicate that Whites have the highest lifetime use of cigarettes, alcohol, hallucinogens, and stimulants, regardless of age (SAMHSA, 2010). Another study also revealed differences among subgroups of Hispanics. For example, Puerto Ricans between the ages of 18 and 34 had the highest rates of lifetime drug use (SAMHSA, 2010). Puerto Ricans reported greater use of cocaine than Whites, African Americans, or any other Hispanic subgroup. It has been documented that inhalant use is much lower among Hispanic populations than current stereotypes would suggest (SAMHSA, 2010). From these differences it is hypothesized that subcultural experiences may be critical to substance use and that socioeconomic status and level of urbanization may be causal factors related to abuse and lifetime prevalence. Acculturation, too, is important in assessing abuse patterns. Acculturation levels have been associated with greater lifetime rates of substance use.

Prevention and Intervention

Although research on treatment for Hispanics in general and respective subgroups has increased over the past 20 years, less is known about long-term effects of intervention; the following recommendations are drawn from the literature and presented as a guide. Prevention and intervention with Hispanic groups need to be culturally sensitive to the individual client's life circumstances, including the level of acculturation, availability of natural support systems, and environmental conditions. In addition, mental health professionals working with Hispanic populations need to incorporate into the counseling process such cultural concepts as *confianza* (trust), *dignidad* (dignity), and *respeto* (respect); current time orientation; preference for action-oriented advice; and the belief that human beings are at the mercy of supernatural forces (Furman et al., 2009).

Primary prevention programming can use characteristics of Hispanic communities such as strong family units and extended family ties to support efforts aimed at adolescents and adults. Programming that addresses anticipated stressors or themes of conflict and that focus on strengths and skills for optimum functioning will enable individuals to combat potential negative effects of acculturational stressors. Peer pressure has been cited as a strong factor in substance abuse (Lewis-Fernandez, Das, Alfonso, Weisman, & Olfson, 2005). Community and school programming that focuses on leadership skills and problem solving can be helpful if they are continuous and provide consistent opportunities for youth to explore their own creativity. In rural areas it has been suggested that community-based approaches should focus on educational systems (SAMHSA, 2010).

Case Study

Marian White Horse

Marian is a professional with a master's degree in health sciences. She works for the local Indian Center providing wellness programs in the Native community. Marian describes herself as bicultural, being active not only within the urban Indian community but also visiting her home reservation for ceremonies.

Marian is 37 years old. She is a single mother with no support and little contact with her ex-husband. They have been divorced for 12 years. Marian is raising Jessie, their daughter, alone. Jessie spends summers with her grandparents who still live on their home reservation. She spends the school year living with her mother. Marian's parents are respected elders in the community, sought after by members for spiritual guidance, they also lead several ceremonies for the community members.

Marian attended a tribally controlled college and completed her bachelor's degree there. She then attended a graduate school with a strong Native American support program, completing her master's degree within

(Continued)

(Continued)

two years. She attributes her success to the academic, social, and spiritual support she received throughout her program of study.

Marian reports sleepless nights with bad dreams related to her family and daughter. She has difficulty concentrating at work and describes a consistent state of anxiety with a generalized sense of doom. She reported that these feelings started about 3 months ago. Coincidently, she heard through the community grapevine that her ex-husband was in town and carried ill will toward her and her family. It has been rumored that her ex-husband has become a shaman's apprentice and has studied the dark arts contrary to the community's wishes.

Critical Thinking Questions

1. Given your reading, identify four assumptions you would make about this

case and support your assumptions through the literature.
2. Identify all of the possible people who are directly and indirectly involved in this case. Briefly describe how they are—or should be—involved, and why.
3. What are the cosmologies at play in this case and how can they be integrated given the basic foundation of confidentiality?
4. Using a systems perspective, what are the complementary systems and competing systems at play in this case?
5. What are the physical, mental, and spiritual issues associated with working with diverse cultures? Given the issues you have identified, what health workers (including indigenous healers) should be involved in this case? How are you going to identify these players and integrate them into your treatment plan?

MyCounselingLab™

Go to Topic 11: *Working with Diverse Cultures,* on the **MyCounselingLab™** site (www .MyCounselingLab.com) for *Substance Abuse Counseling,* Fifth Edition, where you can:

- Find learning outcomes for *Working with Diverse Cultures,* along with the national standards that connect to these outcomes.
- Complete Assignments and Activities that can help you more deeply understand the chapter content.
- Apply and practice your understanding of the core skills identified in the chapter with the Building Counseling Skills unit.
- Prepare yourself for professional certification with a Practice for Certification quiz.
- Connect to videos through the Video and Resource Library.

CONCLUSION

Four themes emerge from the selected groups presented in this chapter. The first is the broad effect of stressors—environmental, social, and cultural—on, among, and within group interactions. This theme challenges us as mental health workers to expand our understanding of the interplay of populations outside the mainstream with those who have full participation within the mainstream.

The second theme can be summed up as perception, which is influenced by culture. This theme requires investigation into cultural and environmental conditions as they relate to community perceptions of alcohol and other drug behaviors. The question that arises from this theme is how to mobilize a community against the detrimental effects of substance abuse behaviors within a culturally relevant and meaningful approach.

The third theme speaks to acculturation and identity development. All the groups presented in this chapter, at some level, need to learn to cope with the development of bicultural skills. I believe that the learning of bicultural skills and the appreciation of diversity are not only the responsibility of selected populations but also the necessary responsibility of us all.

Finally, the fourth theme to emerge is the multiplicity in ways of knowing, which are influenced by society, culture, socioeconomic status, age, and cultural, social, religion/ spirituality and gender identity development.

All these themes speak to the need of mental health workers to challenge their perspective of the world and develop an awareness of how one perceives culturally different clients. In developing this awareness, counselors need to gain an understanding of the history and background of their clients to address their issues within the context in which they are presented. By doing so, they will not only serve their clients' needs more fully but also empower them within the process.

13

Prevention

ROBERT L. SMITH, PH.D., FPPR, NCC, CFT

MARGARET SHERRILL LUTHER, PH.D., LPC, LMFT, NCC, CCDS

MyCounselingLab™

Visit the MyCounselingLab™ site for *Substance Abuse Counseling*, Fifth Edition to enhance your understanding of chapter concepts. You'll have the opportunity to practice your skills through video- and case-based Assignments and Activities as well as Building Counseling Skills units, and to prepare for your certification exam with Practice for Certification quizzes.

In recognizing that substance use and abuse embraces a range of needs, different populations are associated with particular levels and classifications of interventions. A general history of the public health perspective of substance abuse prevention is offered, and an outline of past models clarifies the development of components of current efforts such as recognizing the importance of environmental and cultural variables as well as discerning risk and protective factors. Comprehensive prevention programs are analyzed and how these can be more effectively promoted through community collaboration is explored.

Alcohol, tobacco, and other drug (ATOD) abuse touches every level of our culture and national experience: individual, family, school, and community. Early prevention is necessary as children often use and abuse legal drugs such as caffeine, alcohol, tobacco, and illegal drugs like prescribed medications despite evidence of adverse health outcomes. Illegal drugs, such as marijuana, cocaine, and heroin, as well as over-the-counter and prescription drugs are used for purposes of recreation or self-medication despite their addictive potential, known health risks, and potential legal and financial penalties. Therefore, every age and ethnic group is affected as well as both sexes; no one—neither children, teens, adults, nor older adults—seems immune.

Previous chapters of this text have presented some of the costs of ATOD abuse. Other information regarding drug use and its negative consequences is clear and compelling.[1] For example, the Youth Risk Behavior Surveillance System (YRBSS), an arm of the Centers for Disease Control (CDC), published the following data from its 2009 survey of students in grades 9–12 (U.S. Department of Health and Human Services, 2009).[2]

- Across the nation, for current alcohol use, 41.8% of students had at least one drink of alcohol in the 30 days preceding the survey. Of this group, 42.2% obtained the alcohol by someone giving it to them. Nationally, 72.5% of students had tried at least one drink of alcohol during their life. The prevalence of females trying alcohol (74.2%) was higher than for male students (70.8%). The national rate for students having tried alcohol (other than a few sips) before age 13 was reported to be 21.1%.
- And, 24.2% of high school students had engaged in binge-type drinking, specifically five or more drinks in a row, within a couple of hours, on at least one occasion in the 30 days prior to the survey. White (27.8%) and Hispanic (24.1%) students were significantly more likely than African American (13.7%) students to report this kind of drinking.
- Over one-third of students (36.8%) had tried marijuana at some point in their lifetime, nationwide, and 20.8% were considered "current users" or had used marijuana on one or more days in the month preceding the survey.
- Nationally, 6.4% of students had used some form of cocaine during their lifetime (powder, crack, or freebase), and 11.7% acknowledged some inhalant use (sniffing glue, breathing contents from aerosol sprays, inhaling paint fumes). In addition, 6.7% of students reported having tried ecstasy (or MDMA) at least once, 4.1% reported using methamphetamines (called speed, crystal, crank, or ice) during their lifetime, while 8.0% had used hallucinogenic drugs (LSD, angel dust, PCP, mescaline, or mushrooms) at some point in their lifetime.
- Nationwide, 46.3% of students had tried smoking a cigarette, and 19.5% had smoked a cigarette at least once during the month preceding the survey. As for frequent current cigarette use, 7.3% of students smoked during at least 20 days during the month before the survey. In general, current cigarette use prevalence was highest among White students at 22.5%, followed by Hispanic (18.0%) and Black (9.5%) students. Initial use before 13 years old, of having smoked a whole cigarette, was reported at 10.7%. During the month prior to the survey, 8.9% of students had used forms of smokeless tobacco (such as chewing tobacco, snuff, or dip.)

---

[1] The latest information on U.S. drug use and its consequences is available from many sources, both governmental and private, some of which are listed at the end of this chapter. Several sources are available online, such as data from (a) the *Monitoring the Future* surveys sponsored by the National Institute on Drug Abuse, (b) the *National Household Survey* and the *Drug Abuse Warning Network*, sponsored by the Substance Abuse and Mental Health Services Administration, and (c) *Pulse Check*, sponsored by the Office of National Drug Control Policy (ONDCP). See the listing of data sources compiled by ONDCP at www.whitehousedrugpolicy.gov/drugfact/sources.html.

[2] The Youth Risk Behavior Survey (YRBS) data and research procedures may be obtained by contacting the CDC website at www.cdc.gov/HealthyYouth/yrbs/index.htm. Health, education, and prevention officials use YRBS data to (a) assess trends in health risk behaviors among youth, (b) monitor progress toward the 15 national objectives of *Healthy People 2010*, and (c) assess and revise prevention policies and programs in schools and communities. Research data regarding other populations are also available at the main CDC site.

Case Discussion

Case 3 (Leigh).

Imagine that you are Leigh's counselor at the new school she is attending. You are called to a "special" evening meeting at the invitation of the principal; a number of concerned parents and community representatives are also attending. The topic is a perceived rise in drug use among students at the school. The goal is to formulate some way to address the problem.

You have gotten to know Leigh only recently. Her acknowledgment of "smoking some dope" every so often and drinking with friends rings true to you; you know that she is "hanging out" with other students about whom you are increasingly concerned. You are also aware of too many students in the school who live with ongoing parental conflict or are struggling with marital separation or divorce. You know other students who seem withdrawn and isolated or who are experiencing academic difficulty for no apparent reason. You have come to think of Leigh, her new friends, and these other students as at risk for a whole variety of problems. Your hope is that the meeting will shed some light on these concerns.

The meeting begins with the principal and several community leaders presenting anecdotal evidence of drug use among students at several other schools in the region. The local police chief and a juvenile officer speak about increased incidences of drug sales and arrests within the community. Several teachers address their concerns about students in academic difficulty and a growing sense that some of the students are distracted and uninvolved in the classroom. Several parents speak to their worries about peer pressure and their children's "friends." They demand that something be done.

As the meeting progresses, there are calls for more drug information for students, for student assemblies at which the police warn of impending trouble for students caught using or selling drugs, and for classroom presentations by recovering addicts who can portray the perils of drug addiction. There are calls for action by law enforcement against street dealers and even against bar owners and alcohol distributors who are suspected of providing alcohol to underage persons. Although many of the parents seem unwilling to acknowledge a potential problem with their own daughters or sons, they do insist that the school and community agencies do "something" about the problem.

The principal turns to you as the school counselor to help provide a "way forward." He asks you to chair a working group of teachers and parents, charged with constructing a prevention program to be implemented in the fall. What resources are available to you and the working group? What approaches make the most sense? What students would you target for intervention? How can you find out what is most likely to work? What would be the first step to take in this process?

- Nationally, 34.2% of students reported they were currently sexually active, and among these, 21.6% had drunk alcohol or used drugs before the last intercourse. Males (25.9%) were significantly more likely to report this than female students (17.1%).

As families, schools, and communities focus on the consequences of ATOD abuse and addiction, counselors will increasingly be called on to help in addressing these difficult problems. Not only will counselors be asked to help in assessing and treating affected individuals and their families, they will also become involved in efforts to *prevent* abuse and the consequences that inevitably result.

This chapter is intended to help those who are concerned with this problem and are ready to work in the area of prevention/education. It is designed to provide a broad introduction to foundational terms, concepts, and currently accepted approaches in the ATOD prevention field. Resources and a basic way to proceed with effective, state-of-the-art prevention is presented. Guidelines are offered for those counselors who may wish to establish or collaborate in effective prevention programming in their schools or communities.

Programs of prevention can be targeted to many different problems, age groups, and populations. Drunk driving programs, HIV/AIDS prevention programs, antismoking programs in the early school years, cancer awareness programs of various kinds—all indicate the range of possible prevention efforts. This chapter, however, focuses mainly on prevention of ATOD abuse among children, teens, and young adults. Nevertheless, the basic principles are applicable across the range of prevention initiatives. The basic perspective of the chapter is the *public health model* of prevention.

TYPES OF PREVENTION

ATOD use, and the problems that result from it, are best viewed on a *continuum* that ranges from incidents of misuse, through a pattern of increasing or chronic abuse, moving toward ATOD dependence. Each individual has a different history of involvement with and use of drugs. For example, some use can remain chronic at a point along the continuum, while other use seems to progress. Each person's history and pattern of use present an individualized picture of interacting factors, including environmental and social along with genetic and biological characteristics.

Once a need for prevention is perceived, initial questions involve *who* should be the targeted audience and *what goals* should be set. Understanding some basic classifications can help in formulating a response to those questions. That is, these classifications, as they relate to ATOD abuse, can help in clarifying the goals and objectives of prevention efforts.

The traditional and widely accepted public health model of prevention speaks of three important classifications: primary, secondary, and tertiary prevention (Botvin & Griffin, 2007). *Primary* prevention is targeted at those with little or no experience with alcohol, tobacco, or other drugs. The goal of primary prevention is to prevent or delay the beginning of use by this population. Persuading young school-age children not to smoke is one example. Identifying those who may be at risk for ATOD use and helping mitigate the elements of risk in their lives is another goal. *Secondary* prevention is for novice or experienced users and those who may already be showing signs of difficulty. Identifying those who are experimenting with ATOD and helping them to discontinue or limit their use is one form of secondary prevention; "harm reduction" strategies that diminish the type or frequency of negative consequences from ATOD use is another. Alcohol abuse prevention programs in college settings are an example of secondary prevention. *Tertiary* prevention addresses persons at the more advanced stages of ATOD abuse and/or addiction. It encompasses the same goals as treatment and relapse prevention.

The Institute of Medicine (IOM) developed a slightly different classification scheme that is also helpful in prevention planning (Botvin & Griffin, 2007). At the *universal* level, ATOD education and prevention efforts are targeted to the general population, whereas specifically defined at-risk populations are addressed at the *selective* level of prevention. Persons or groups who already show problems as a result of ATOD use and who require intervention to halt or ameliorate these difficulties are targeted at the *indicated* level. Today, the accepted prevention paradigm is a *comprehensive* delivery of programs and services.

PREVENTION: A BRIEF HISTORY

Early prevention efforts in the 1960s and 1970s focused on classroom education, dissemination of information to potential users, and scare tactics. The rationale for these efforts was a basic belief: If potential or experimenting users received accurate information about the perils and consequences of drug use, their attitudes toward use and abuse would change and they would modify their behavior. Information has taken place in several forms including lectures by physicians, law enforcement officers, pharmacists, and recovering persons, often including displays of various drugs and drug paraphernalia. Presentations were sometimes supplemented by an array of scary anti-drug films, descendants of the famous *Reefer Madness* of the 1930s. Often these lectures were accompanied by dire warnings of possible consequences, stereotyping of users, overstatements about the "likely" addiction that would follow from experimentation, and moralizing about the destructive lifestyle that would affect those who used. It is not uncommon even today to hear parents or school personnel recommend variations of this same approach as they become aware of abuse in their community.

Although well intentioned, these early efforts were based more on fear, zeal, and moralistic attitudes than on scientific knowledge. For the most part this early approach is currently viewed as unproductive. Nevertheless, providing accurate information to potential drug users continues to be one element of ATOD prevention. As part of a more comprehensive prevention effort, providing information may be important depending on the kinds of information presented, the characteristics and needs of those targeted for information, as well as the context within which this information is given. A consistent problem with school-based programs in providing appropriate information is the ability to administer a curriculum with fidelity to the guidelines as prescribed by the authors (Payne, Gottfredson, & Gottfredson, 2006). Because of the wide variety in the quality of implementation, this is an area that needs future study when applied to programs of proven usefulness (Dusenbury, Brannigan, Hansen, Walsh, & Falco, 2005).

The 1980s saw the development of a variety of newer approaches to drug prevention and education. Moving beyond the traditional information-based approaches, these newer methods included *affective education* (helping students identify and express their feelings; helping them feel valued and accepted; building self-esteem), *values clarification* (assisting students in decision-making skills), teaching *alternatives* to drug use (e.g., relaxation, meditation, exercise, involvement with the arts), and development of personal and social *skills* (e.g., problem solving, self-management, and leadership skills; recognition of peer pressure and methods of resistance). The basic belief undergirding these programs was that adolescents and others would be deterred from using drugs if their self-esteem, social and communication skills, and decision-making, problem-solving, and resistance tools were improved.

Many of these approaches showed some initial promise, but rigorous evaluation was still spotty or gave ambiguous results. As early as 1984, a review of prevention programs suggested the need for more adequate evaluation, again debunked the supposed benefits of solely educational-based models, and criticized existing approaches for lack of success in actually preventing substance abuse (National Institute on Drug Abuse [NIDA], 1984). Both program content and delivery were investigated, with participatory and interactive learning needed. In our review of the Life Skills Training (LST) prevention program, these approaches continue to be important today but implementation fidelity is an important component to success (Botvin & Griffin, 2007).

A vigorous debate arose about the effectiveness of primarily didactic approaches, as can be seen in the case study of Project D.A.R.E. (Drug Abuse Resistance Education). Begun in 1983 as a joint project of the Los Angeles Police Department and local school districts, D.A.R.E. featured uniformed police officers presenting a multisession program of information and affective prevention with the delivery focused on fifth and sixth graders (Rosenbaum, 2007). The program spread rapidly across the country during the 1980s and 1990s, and according to the D.A.R.E. website, it still has consistently widespread use in schools across the country.[3] Multiple theoretically important prevention components are incorporated: building self-esteem, helping students to recognize and resist peer pressure, practicing specific strategies for resistance, utilizing alternative ways of coping, emphasizing information about the consequences of ATOD use. Nevertheless, increasing pressure was brought to bear on the program as studies showed a lack of effectiveness (Rosenbaum, 2007); even the U.S. surgeon general and the National Academy of Sciences offered criticism. Pan and Bai (2009) underscored previous research findings, with a meta-analysis of studies on D.A.R.E. from 1983 to 2005. The ineffectiveness of the DARE program on drug use as well as psychosocial behavior was confirmed and findings were consistent with earlier investigations.

In 2001, the D.A.R.E. model was revamped and financed by a $13.6 million grant from the Robert Wood Johnson Foundation, launching "new D.A.R.E." Officials unveiled a new curriculum, D.A.R.E.-Plus, aimed at extending its presentation to include older students and its impact into the college years and beyond. According to information from D.A.R.E. (2006), an evaluation by the University of Akron of 83 high schools and 122 middle schools in six cities, showed the new D.A.R.E. curriculum ". . . may be effective in reaching those adolescents who are at elevated risk for substance abuse" (p. 4). Little information regarding methodology was available from D.A.R.E. sources.

Later, prevention efforts began to shift toward intervention into the *environment* of (potential) users, focusing on the social environment in which students and potential users live and the temptations that they face (Van Wormer & Davis, 2008). Programs that were undertaken using this view included sensitivity to the social and interpersonal environment of students (e.g., family, school, neighborhood, peers), exploration of risk and protective factors that are important in these environments and are related to individual development and life transitions, training in "refusal" skills, and "normative education" (or social marketing) that was intended to correct misperceptions about the social norms governing use within peer and social groups.

---

[3] D.A.R.E.'s 2009 Annual Report states that the program is used in over 72% of school districts around the country, and 44 other nations.

A variety of social influences affect drug use. All communities or groupings of people have social norms about a variety of things from acceptable language and dress, to rules of proper conduct, values, and beliefs about ATOD use. *Norms* are perceived rules of behavior or values that influence a person's attitudes and actions. In prevention terms, norms set limits or establish guidelines that are the background or framework for ATOD use/abuse. Another aspect of the environmental or ecological perspective of prevention work is embedded systems offering reciprocal causality. Individuals are influenced by families, which in turn, are influenced by social networks, and vice versa. An environmental intervention at one level may also produce bidirectional change at another level. Accordingly, social norms are properties of large communities as well as of small subgroups, and the norms may conflict between groups. Although norms can influence a person's behavior and attitudes directly, they can also be *misperceived* and still exert influence. For example, teens may overestimate the number of their peers who smoke, drink, use drugs, or engage in sex and this can powerfully influence an individual's attitudes toward ATOD use. Normative education attempted to present factual information about students' social environments, creating a more realistic picture of social norms as they actually exist and reducing the "everybody does it" belief and prodrug attitude.

The development of a broad-based and proactive prevention perspective on college campuses underscored the importance of normative education within the context of comprehensive approaches (Van Wormer & Davis, 2008). The prevention model incorporated strategies of earlier models of ATOD prevention, providing services to prevent abuse among nonusers (primary prevention), reducing the likelihood that at-risk individuals will develop problems (secondary prevention), and helping abusers into recovery (tertiary prevention). Thus, the proactive prevention model utilized many strategies and approaches associated with other models, but it incorporated these activities into a more comprehensive, campuswide program that emphasizes the strengthening of already-existent healthy behaviors and a harm-reduction view of environmental factors. The proactive prevention model is distinguished from previous approaches by its two main components: emphasizing the importance of providing accurate information about communities and normative environments, and focusing on healthy, positive attitudes and behaviors of community members.

An example of an environmental approach carried to an extreme, however, was the "Just Say No" campaign of the Reagan administration (precursor of the original D.A.R.E. curriculum), coupled with the strategy laid out in the 1987 publication of *What Works: Schools without Drugs* by the U.S. Department of Education. This approach was typical of the more hard-line approaches encouraged by the "war on drugs" in the late 1980s and early 1990s, which emphasized the role of law enforcement and supply reduction tactics (e.g., increasingly harsh legal penalties for drug-related offenses, forfeiture laws, interdiction of drugs at the nation's borders) over the use of more long-term demand reduction strategies such as prevention, education, and treatment (Van Wormer & Davis, 2008).

Of course, throughout this brief history of efforts at ATOD education and prevention, a focus on drug *availability*—another form of the environmental approach—has been woven into the mix, having its roots as far back as the early temperance efforts of the mid- to late 1800s. This group of prevention efforts has involved legal, law enforcement, and policy initiatives intended to limit the access of youthful and other users to a variety of substances. These efforts involve such initiatives as the pricing of some substances (e.g., taxation of cigarettes and alcohol), regulation of distribution outlets (e.g., state stores and licensing systems for wholesale and retail purchase of alcohol), minimum drinking age laws, warnings in advertisements and labeling on alcohol and cigarettes, and "dram shop" or "social host" liability (i.e., the legal and financial liability of alcohol servers for the damage that intoxicated or underage patrons may inflict on themselves or others). These efforts at limiting availability and access have questionable results when utilized as stand-alone prevention efforts (Van Wormer & Davis, 2008).

Although many of these basic approaches—information-based, affective, social influence, environmental—may have limited effectiveness when used in isolation, nevertheless they show promise as part of an overall comprehensive strategy. Integration of these approaches into a coherent prevention strategy, directed toward clearly defined populations, having appropriate goals, and rigorously evaluated for effectiveness, is viewed as the more accepted way of proceeding today.

In 1986, with the assistance of the federal government in its new "drug-free schools and communities" initiative, many school districts and local communities received financial assistance to enhance prevention efforts, and a number of research efforts were undertaken. However, long-term impact of these programs is still not in evidence. There is a need for more comprehensive, multimodal programs with a broad perspective (Capuzzi & Stauffer, 2012).

COMPREHENSIVE PREVENTION

We recommend a comprehensive approach to ATOD prevention. Most comprehensive approaches to prevention incorporate a number of germane characteristics.

Comprehensive prevention strategies attempt to address *multiple levels of intervention* and *multiple populations*. Depending on the context and the ATOD issues at hand, all levels of prevention—primary, secondary, and tertiary; universal, selected, and indicated—are considered, and a variety of affected populations are addressed. All possible constituencies who are involved, for example, at-risk populations, secondary-effects sufferers, and "special" populations (e.g., minorities, people with disabilities, women) are targeted for prevention efforts. A comprehensive strategy takes into account a variety of factors that may be involved in the problem and the available theories for addressing these factors, integrating *multiple strategies* considered helpful in meeting current needs (e.g., information dissemination, affective programming, self-esteem building, skill development, normative education, etc.). With this effort the strategy envisions utilizing a number of different resources and personnel in a *collaborative* effort.

Comprehensive prevention strategies incorporate a view of the broader *environment* and ecology within which the problem resides. It is essential to consider issues of *diversity* in the planning and implementation of programs. Prevention efforts need to be *developmentally appropriate* as well as attending to the *effects and consequences* of ATOD abuse on other areas of living, including on the community's values and resources. The impact of abuse is multiple, and consequently so are the needs. The resources and interventions to address multifaceted problems should come from multiple perspectives. For example, VanderWaal, Powell, Terry-McElrath, Bao, and Flay (2005), using key informant interviews and student surveys from 508 communities, found that adult-supervised after-school activities, regular use of recreational facilities after school, along with community activities to reduce substance abuse, including work by student-led organizations to prevent alcohol abuse, showed a reduction in use of alcohol, tobacco, and marijuana over the preceding 30 days.

Finally, comprehensiveness presumes that prevention is a *long-term effort* and requires exposure to health-based messages over time. There is no such thing as a "quick fix" or magic solution. Rather, a long-term commitment is required along with flexibility and the ability to adapt to change, build on success, and respond to failure. This requires particular attention to initial goal setting and objectives that are measurable and outcome-based, including ongoing evaluation systems that are tied to program revisions.

COMMUNITY PREVENTION

Comprehensive, coordinated prevention programs possess a complementary set of strategies to prevent ATOD abuse. An example of such a program is the CASASTART, formerly Children at Risk, from the National Center on Addiction and Substance Abuse at Columbia University (CASA) (2006), which derived the program's acronym from the program title Striving Together to Achieve Rewarding Tomorrows. This program is considered to provide a successful comprehensive model to substance abuse prevention, and is a useful comparison to primarily school-based approaches (Roe & Becker, 2005). Developed by Lawrence F. Murray, CASASTART fits the profile in "Steps to an Effective Program." At present, CASASTART has been used in 25 cities across the nation and on a Native American reservation. The program has a history of high rankings from governmental departments such as the U.S. Department of Education Expert Panel on Safe Disciplined and Drug-Free Schools earning Exemplary Program status, the U.S. Department of Health and Human Services Center for Substance Abuse Prevention and U.S. Department of Justice Office of Juvenile Justice and Delinquency Prevention as a Model Program (National Center on Addiction and Substance Abuse at Columbia University [CASA], 2010). A 2005 British review of prevention programs located 759 studies via electronic database and narrowed their parameters to include 16 investigations that focused on drug-use behavior along with offering long-term follow up (Roe & Becker, 2005). Of these, Children at Risk was found to be the most effective, underscoring the efficacy of multiple-component programs in meeting multifaceted problems of substance abuse.

Program structure includes (CASA, 2007):

- CASASTART works to enhance protective factors through intensive case management of a wide range of services used to mitigate risk and deter 8- to 13-year-old youth from substance abuse and criminal involvement. After a thorough assessment to ascertain the unique needs of a particular neighborhood, the program offers help from different sectors creating a strong web of social support to both the child and family to address risk factors and promote resilience (CASA, 2006, 2007).
- *Case management* Case managers carry a small load of 15 families and are seen as the fulcrum of the program. The case managers provide counseling, case plans, service referrals, and coordination. More specifically, case managers teach and advocate with parents in social, educational, and legal systems; implement

recreational and after-school programs; arranging transportation; and helping with life skills training/advocacy such as intervention to prevent a loss of utility service.

- *Family services*   Families articulate their own needs and array of services that are needed under the direction of the case manager who can provide parenting training, stress/coping skills management, substance abuse and mental health treatment referrals, as well as support in finding job training, employment services, social support resources, and educational programs to meet their specialized goals.
- *Educational services*   Case managers work with families to establish educational goals for the children. Students consistently attend tutoring and homework assistance to improve functioning in school and academic pursuits.
- *After-school and summer activities*   CASA offers recreational programs, field trips, and special events on weekends or during the summer to enhance cultural identity, and life skills/youth development programs, plus other applicable training/education opportunities.
- *Mentoring*   Collaboration with local agencies allows children to establish relationships with a supportive adult outside of the family.
- *Incentives*   Awards celebrating accomplishments such as celebrations, or even small stipends, contribute to continued motivation and excitement about accomplished goals such as attendance at school or mentoring.
- *Community policing and enhanced enforcement*   Law enforcement personnel expand their efforts within the target community to build positive relationships such as creating safe corridors for school access, mentoring, and making educational presentations.
- *Juvenile justice intervention* (only for youth involved with this)   Relationships are established with justice staff to coordinate services for children who have experienced more serious difficulties and became involved with the justice system.

As described above, CASASTART involves multiple community resources that are accessed according to community and family needs. The primary partners are a "lead" social service agency, a school, and local law enforcement staff. The first step in this process is to assess community need in the area of interest. This is followed by the lead agency working collaboratively with other social, educational, and governmental agencies to use the structure of program components to weave productive interventions for their specific families using services (CASA, 2007). Through an intensive yet flexible format, CASASTART offers a *universal* approach to children and family members in a general area, with those who are at risk needing more *selective* interventions. In the family treatment plan, the case manager is able to incorporate goals specific to those at the *indicated* level of need such as parents with chemical dependency problems or youth involved in juvenile justice for substance abuse. Likewise, children and family members involved in CASASTART would most likely fit with *primary* or *secondary* prevention approaches for education and services, but through the flexibility of case management and individualized treatment plans, the case manager would be able to incorporate *tertiary* interventions for those with more intensive and long-standing problems.

The initial planning and assessment phase is a challenging undertaking on its own merit. Establishing productive working relationships with a loose confederacy of agencies takes skill and commitment. Overcoming obstacles such as these requires close communication and supervision from CASA staff, which maintains a consistent presence through the establishment and implementation of the program (CASA, 2007). CASASTART incorporates existing resources into a new framework that serves as a vehicle for clarification of need and offers a flexible implementation of tailored services.

RISK AND PROTECTIVE FACTORS

Multiple and individually expressed factors that interact in the etiology and maintenance of ATOD use and abuse suggests the need for multiple, integrated strategies. This point argues for the need for comprehensive prevention. One approach receiving attention that includes multiple factors in prevention is the emphasis on *risk and protective factors* as they relate to ATOD use and abuse (Burrow-Sanchez, 2006). This approach, as related to culturally diverse groups, is supported by Okamoto et al. (2006) and Wang, Matthew, Bellamy, and James (2005).

In constructing or evaluating ATOD prevention programs, particularly those aimed at youth and young adults, it is important to consider *risk* factors that may predispose vulnerable individuals or groups to use/abuse, and *protective* factors that may inoculate individuals or groups from use or problems of abuse (Burrow-Sanchez, 2006). A brief summary of such factors is provided in Table 13.1. A classical example of

TABLE 13.1 Risk and protective factors: ATOD abuse*

Levels	Risk Factors	Protective Factors
I. Agent	Early onset of use Choice of drug Experimentation "Gateway" effect	Delayed onset of use
II. Host		
1. Biomedical	Genetic vulnerability Physiological vulnerability Age Sex Race/ethnicity	
2. Personality/ character	Novelty and thrill seeking/risk taking Alienation and rebelliousness Poor impulse control Poor coping skills Co-occurrence of psychiatric disorders High stress (inter- or intrapersonal, life transitions) Misperceptions of peer use Particular life challenges (e.g., homosexuality, disability, oppression)	Self-esteem and internal locus of control Self-discipline Problem-solving and critical thinking skills Sense of humor

Levels	Risk Factors	Protective Factors
3. Behavioral/ attitudinal	Social marginalization ("failure to fit in")	Positive peer influence
	Early antisocial behavior	Effectiveness in work, play, and relationships
	Perceived "invulnerability"	Perceived dangers of ATOD use and consequences
	Favorable attitudes toward ATOD use	Healthy expectations and positive assessment of future
	Susceptibility to peer influence	
	Friends who use ATOD	Relationship with caring adult
	Perceived benefits (e.g., social acceptance, anxiety reduction, performance enhancement)	Positive moral values
		Opportunities to contribute positively
	Other risky behaviors (e.g., risky driving, violence)	Religious involvement
III. Environment		
1. Family	Family dysfunction/trauma/major loss	Family bonding ("nurturing attachments")
	Lack of caring	Clear and high expectations
	Lack of clear behavioral expectations	Parent communication and involvement
	Poor supervision	Consistent praise/low criticism
	Inconsistent or excessive discipline	"Quality" time
	Low expectations for individual success	"Responsible decisions" message
	Permissive parental attitudes re ATOD use	Influence of older siblings
	Influence of older siblings	Healthy stress management
	History of ATOD use	Sharing responsibilities
2. School	Alienation	Involvement (e.g., athletics, extracurricular activities)
	Poor performance	School performance
	Learning problems (e.g., ADHD)	Positive school climate
	School dropout	
3. Community	Availability	Access barriers (e.g., pricing, age restrictions)
	Unhealthy/ambivalent social norms	Clear messages re use
		Drug-free alternatives
		Opportunities for prosocial action (e.g., mentoring, peer support, community service)
4. Other	Media/advertising portrayals of ATOD	Healthy norms in larger community (e.g., media)
	Societal institutions disintegrating, ignoring youth needs, or having lack of appeal	Cultural focus on healthy decisions
		Honest and comprehensive ATOD education
		Religious involvement

*No single risk factor is determinative; multiple factors interact in an additive manner.

Case Discussion

Case 3 (Leigh).

Leigh is already "experimenting" with pot and alcohol (*agent*), and alludes to using other drugs. While she may or may not have a bio-medical "vulnerability" to ATOD use, she may well be experiencing high levels of "stress" owing to her family situation and move to a new school; she has found new "friends who use" and is likely to have "favorable attitudes" toward ATOD use as well as a sense of "perceived benefits" that result from use (*host*). Her difficulties with several important social systems such as family and school, as well as the potential "availability" of ATOD in her environment, are also some of the risk factors (*environment*) in her at-risk picture.

Although no one risk factor can predict a person's ATOD use or abuse, the cumulative effect of a number of risk factors—and the timing of their occurrence in individual and family development across the lifespan—may help counselors and others identify those who are vulnerable and may help in beginning to think through how to help.

The risk-based approach suggests that there will be some benefit to addressing certain risk "targets" for prevention intervention, such as family relationships, school environment, peer relationships, and the wider community. Individual "risk characteristics" may also be addressed, such as social marginalization, misperceptions of peer use, and individual coping skills. Prevention planners must be prepared to address these targets through a variety of interventions. Sharing accurate information, developing self-esteem and resistance skills, using normative education, building effective parent networks, working with community leaders to change the availability and access to alcohol and other drugs—any one of these strategies may be appropriate in meeting the needs of those involved.

A comprehensive approach to ATOD prevention suggests that reducing risks can be complemented by a strategy of enhancing resiliency. Here the value of "protective" factors comes to the forefront. These factors tend to inoculate potential users against the need, desire, or social influence that lead to use/abuse; they are associated with reduced potential for use. A review of the column labeled "Protective Factors" in Table 13.1 suggests a number of potential strategies for enhancing personal and social resiliency. Each of the strategies utilized in the Youth, Parent, and School components was intended to achieve this dual purpose.

a protective factor is the influence of family on attitudes about substance use (Burrow-Sanchez, 2006). Parents who monitor their children's activities, have strong bonds, and consistently enforce rules of behavior lower the risk that their children will use drugs (Burrow-Sanchez, 2006; Wang et al., 2005).

An ATOD prevention model utilizing risk and protective factors ought to encompass the *agent* (e.g., alcohol or marijuana) involved, the *individual* (host) who uses, and the *environment* (social context, immediate surroundings, local community, society) in which an individual obtains or uses psychoactive substances. The model emphasizes the interactive nature of these elements and suggests interventions at any level that may address or reduce risk.

Risk factors are considered to be characteristics that occur statistically more often for individuals who develop ATOD problems, either as adolescents or as adults. They are indicators of potential problems and may be helpful in identifying those who are vulnerable to developing ATOD difficulties. One way to utilize Table 13.1 is to review the column "Risk Factors," organized according to agent, host, and environment.

LIFE SKILLS TRAINING (LST): EFFECTIVENESS OF A COMPREHENSIVE PREVENTION APPROACH

Created by Gilbert Botvin of Cornell University Medical College and his colleagues over 30 years ago, and further described in the Life Skills Training (n.d.) website, LST is seen as a widely researched and evaluated, evidence-based, prevention program available for use with children and youth. It has been recognized as a Model/Exemplary program by agencies including the U.S. Department of Education and Center for Substance Abuse Prevention (National Health Promotion Associates, 2010). It is a *primary* prevention, school-based, *universal* classroom program that addresses a number of critical prevention components (e.g., risk and protective factors, general and social skills, drug resistance information and skills, and normative education) in an integrated manner (Redmond et al., 2009; Spoth, Randall, Trudeau, Shin, & Redmond, 2008).

The program was initially developed as a cigarette smoking prevention intervention, involving prevention professionals in an initial set of 10 class sessions. Over time, through the use of multiple studies in a step-by-step progression, the program broadened its base—and its effectiveness—to include (a) *program adaptation,* expanding the number of initial sessions and adding "boosters" in subsequent years; (b) *expanded coverage* of drugs used and abused (beyond tobacco and including alcohol, marijuana, and other illicit drugs) and addressing prevention of aggressive and violent behaviors; (c) *diversity of program providers,* utilizing prevention professionals, trained teachers, and/or peer leaders; (d) *expanded outreach to minority and inner-city populations* from initial testing with primarily White and suburban populations; and (e) *focused attention both on actual drug use behavior,* as well as supposed mediating variables (such as advertising knowledge and critical thinking), *and on durability* or the potential long-term effectiveness beyond the years immediately following the program. Primary focus is given to fostering a knowledge base, promoting avoidance of substance use, and skills development including social skills, self-management, and social resistance strategies (National Health Promotion Associates, 2010; Redmond et al., 2009; Spoth et al., 2008).

Early large-scale trials indicated that the LST approach produced significant prevention effects on cigarette smoking, heavy drinking, and marijuana use as well as on variables that are believed to influence drug abuse risk. Indicators pointed to the program's impact being heightened if skills training and drug resistance strategies were tailored and culturally focused on the needs of specified populations. Longitudinal research on the success of LST with adolescent methamphetamine use, measured at 4.5, 5.5, and 6.5 years past baseline, were seen in 597 public school students from the Midwest (Spoth, Clair, Shin, & Redmond, 2006). Further long-term research over 5½ years exploring the efficacy of LST combined with family-based programming with 1,677 seventh-grade students showed positive outcomes for one or both intervention groups regarding initiation of use of ATOD (Spoth et al., 2008). Similarly, long-term follow-up research on the use of LST applied toward drug use and high-risk sexual practices found a direct effect on high-risk sexual practices and significantly reduced levels of alcohol and marijuana intoxication, which was in turn associated with reduction in later high-risk sexual behavior (Griffin, Botvin, & Nichols, 2006).

The basic structure of the program is geared toward middle or junior high school students and consists of 15 to 17 class periods (approximately 45 minutes each) in the first year. "Booster sessions," 10 in the following year and 5 in the next, are utilized. The program has three major components: general self-management skills (e.g., problem solving, decision making, critical thinking, coping strategies), general social skills (e.g., effective communication, developing healthy friendships), and information/skills that specifically address drugs and their use (e.g., awareness of social influences to use, normative education tactics). These are presented to students, using methods such as skills training, instruction, group discussion, and behavioral rehearsal. All three components are intended to promote drug resistance as well as antidrug attitudes and norms (National Health Promotion Associates, 2010; Redmond et al., 2009; Spoth et al., 2008). Curricular materials, such as a teacher's manual and student guides, are available along with training workshops for prevention providers. Both adult providers training and training for peer leaders are available (see the LST website at lifeskillstraining.com).

The components combine the best of a number of approaches such as the development of personal and social skills, affective education, resistance training, and normative education into a coordinated curriculum. The program is developmentally appropriate, utilizing multiple levels of interventions and multiple strategies while addressing the effects and consequences of ATOD use and abuse. The commitment to long-term utilization of this approach is strong, with a solid history of proven effectiveness.

Yet, one of the discouraging elements of contemporary prevention work is that a number of proven programs like LST are not widely used in "real-world" prevention. Programs without clearly proven effectiveness (e.g., D.A.R.E. or Here's Looking at You 2000) are used more often (Saxe et al., 2006). Although there may be a number of reasons for this, the wider dissemination of proven and effective prevention programs remains a high priority for the future of prevention efforts. And, the availability of information on evidenced-based programming is expanding. With research-based models becoming the accepted standard for programs, there are a number of "clearinghouse" websites from governmental, educational, and private entities that offer information on evidence-based programs with many providing useful rating scales. Examples of these resources for mental health and social service practitioners, educators, and policymakers are RAND Corporation's (2005) Promising Practices Network at promisingpractices.net/about_ppn.asp; Office of Juvenile Justiceand Delinquency's Prevention's Program Guide at ojjdp.gov/mpg/mpgProgramDetails.aspx?ID=615; National Institute on Drug Abuse (NIDA) at nida.nih.gov/. U.S. Department of Education (2007) Office of Safe and Drug-Free Schools programs at 2.ed.gov/osdfs; and Substance Abuse and Mental Health Services Administration, (SAMHSA) (2010) National Registry of Evidence-Based Programs and Practices (NREPP) at nrepp.samhsa.gov.

STEPS TO AN EFFECTIVE PREVENTION PROGRAM

At a practical level, it is important to understand that prevention strategies must be built on a sound planning process. For a comprehensive strategy to succeed, it is essential that planning be conducted and/or affirmed by a representative group of stakeholders, members of the community who represent various important constituencies—for

Case Discussion

Case 3 (Leigh).

A comprehensive prevention program in Leigh's school may begin to take shape as the counselor's "working group" considers a set of complementary and integrated strategies. Informed by the risk and protective factors approach, these strategies might include the following:

- Identification of those already using and assessment of the risk factors that may be most powerfully operative. Establishment of peer intervention and peer support programs (e.g., student assistance programs [SAP], children-of-divorce support groups) to address risks and to establish positive connections among youth and between students and school (*secondary prevention; selected level*) may be needed.
- Assessment of the needs of the general student population and providing accurate information about the risks and consequences of ATOD use/abuse. Utilization of a proven prevention approach that addresses multiple populations and integrates accurate information with affective, social influence, and normative education strategies (*primary prevention; universal level*).
- Parent programs that share accurate ATOD information, address parent concerns about how to discuss drug use with their children, and connect parents with one another in a caring network of mutual support (*primary and secondary prevention; universal level*).
- Identification of students and families experiencing dysfunction, demonstrating high levels of stress or conflict, and/ or having histories of ATOD abuse; provision of services for counseling or intervention (*tertiary prevention; indicated level*).
- Creating school policies and teacher in-service programming to help in identifying at-risk students and creating involvement of school personnel in "student success- and support-oriented" initiatives, such as providing peer education, forming personal relationships with caring adults, and establishing student service organizations with opportunities to make positive contributions to the community (*primary prevention; universal level*).

These strategies and more may become part of an overall comprehensive prevention plan in Leigh's school that is sensitive to risk and protective factors in the lives of youth. Additional questions that need to be addressed include, What specific program components would most effectively address a list of Leigh's risk factors? How would these various components be put into the structure of a comprehensive program? How would program staff facilitate family participation? How would overall effectiveness be gauged?

example, schools, law enforcement, media, health service organizations, families, churches, and so forth. The use of community collaborations is recommended. From experience in various community collaborations focusing on effectively harnessing resources for substance abuse prevention, the authors recommend the questions shown in Table 13.2 as a springboard for discussion.

TABLE 13.2 Considerations in comprehensive prevention planning	
Procedures	**Questions for the Planning Process**
Needs clarification	What salient patterns of ATOD problems and co-occurring disorders appear in our community? What specific factors (e.g., socioeconomic and multicultural influence) affect these patterns?
Assessment	Are recent statistics and other sources of reliable information available, or is funding/planning needed for additional investigation (e.g., surveys)?
Goals	In concrete terms, what needs to be accomplished? What can realistically be achieved in the short term, and what is designated as long term?
Objectives	With further clarification and evaluation of desired results, what is specifically measureable and in what workable timeframe?
Resources	Stakeholders investigate which resources are attainable from which parties (e.g., facilities, finances, staff). What additional resources are needed to meet stated objectives?
Funding sources	Stakeholders analyze financial existing resources and consider options for expanding funding as needed.
Leadership and organization	Which stakeholder offers the most productive resources for each task? Is there an equitable distribution of responsibilities among participants?
Action	Are program components evidence-based? How to maintain consistent forward movement in program implementation? Is the timetable being followed?
Monitoring and evaluation	Are the prevention strategies adhering to stated goals? Are objectives being met? How is progress being measured? Are stakeholders able to evaluate progress, or will additional parties be needed?
Modification	Are goals/objectives being met? (Is it working?) What changes are needed, and how/by whom will they be implemented?

Notice that effective prevention planning begins with needs clarification, assessment, and development of goals and "measurable" objectives buttressed by consistent evaluation procedures. These early steps are essential, and prevention planners must be willing to expend the time and effort to pursue them thoroughly (Botvin & Griffin, 2007). Affirmation and acceptance by community leaders ("gatekeepers," such as school administrators and parents) of the needs, goals, and objectives that are developed in these steps are essential for program success. Notice, too, that these steps are tied to ongoing evaluation and program modification. Without clear and measurable objectives, effective evaluation will falter.

Prevention planners should have no illusions, however, about the ease or time frame required to achieve these first three steps. School personnel, and even parents, can be hesitant about conducting a thorough needs assessment. Although it may seem obvious that prevention initiatives require a sound understanding of the extent and scope of the problem in a particular setting, this information can also be disquieting and may be perceived as damaging in the short term from a public relations point of view. In addition, gatekeepers themselves may need to be educated about the approaches and underlying assumptions that guide selection of specific goals and objectives. Here, prevention planners may have to confront misperceptions about the effectiveness of some "commonsense" strategies on a long-standing structure (e.g., information dissemination and scare tactics) and will have to address potential strongly held value positions among gatekeepers to win their assent and support (Rosenbaum, 2007). Discussions of issues such as the (potential) objective of "zero tolerance" versus "responsible decisions," or "abstinence" versus "harm reduction," will inevitably have to occur. Winning the support of gatekeepers will take time in such cases but is critical for long-term program support, resource collection, implementation, and effectiveness.

In addition, having clearly held and affirmed goals and objectives will be necessary for evaluation of program effectiveness. A well-thought-out plan of evaluation can help in assessing program successes, in addressing program failures, and in revising program delivery to increase positive outcomes. This, too, will take time and energy but is essential in achieving prevention goals.

A sound planning process is only the first step, however, in constructing an effective and comprehensive prevention program. Planning, implementation, evaluation, and ongoing program revision are the hallmarks of the best programs. Prevention providers will benefit from a careful review of these important attributes.

The evaluation of the productivity of community collaborations has produced mixed results, with the addition of observations about methodological problems with adequate analysis of these partnerships (Saxe et al., 2006). Various problems arise when a group is formed of representatives from different constituencies in the community, each with motivations that are both individual-organization driven as well as joining the cooperative desire for the success of the coalition as a united entity (Saxe et al., 2006). An example of a program that had the commonsense appearance of a successful strategy was the Robert Wood Johnson Foundation development of Fighting Back, a national effort intended to reduce the demand for alcohol and drugs through the vehicle of community collaborations, to be implemented in 14 sites, but was not shown to reduce rates of substance use and associated problems (Saxe et al., 2006). Though the use of community partnerships is intuitively appealing, and such grassroots campaigns are seen as an effective and efficient means to clarify needs, avoid duplication of services, enhance communication and cooperation between entities, and promote research, the effectiveness of this approach remains in question.

IMPLICATIONS FOR COUNSELING

Counselors are increasingly called upon to be advocates of change in today's world, and this mandate includes involvement in collaborating with different stakeholders in devising and promoting prevention strategies. Working with high-risk youth and highlighting ATOD abuse in the community and schools are important ways in which counselors can help.

It is critical that counselors have the knowledge base and skills necessary for prevention work. As such, the task of training tomorrow's professional counselors, particularly in the areas of social change, advocacy, and prevention, is the responsibility of today's counselor educators. Training standards for the best counselor education programs (e.g., those approved by the Council for the Accreditation of Counseling and Related Educational Programs [CACREP]) recognize the need for specialization and include provisions for overall health promotion and prevention. The 2009 CACREP standards included a recognized specialization area in addictions counseling. Nevertheless, we maintain that there is still a gap in the preparation of counselors in the area of ATOD abuse, addiction, intervention, and prevention and the need for a move toward more uniformity of standards and credentialing (Miller, 2010).

> Currently, the United States credentialing process is a checkered, chaotic system because of the variation of standards . . . [I]n order to navigate the complexities of addiction treatment, a counselor must have a certain level of professionalism. Increasingly, a simple, grassroots fashion of counseling is becoming less acceptable. In addition, an addictions counselor must be able to work with organizations outside of the field . . . Finally, the process of credentialing forces the professional to expand, organize, and clarify his or her knowledge about the addiction counseling field, and employers are increasingly requiring it of their practitioners. (Miller, 2010, pp. 393, 395)

Regarding ATOD use and abuse, it is clear that counselor training and education for prevention ought to emphasize knowledge about, and advocacy for, prevention programs and approaches that actually work to prevent use and abuse. It is difficult to understand why many schools continue to use drug prevention programs that have proven to be ineffective, as well as showing a wide range in the quality of implementation in properly facilitating proven curricula with fidelity (Dusenbury et al., 2005; Payne et al., 2006; Rosenbaum, 2007). Acquainting counselors in training with those prevention programs that have demonstrated efficacy, as well as underscoring the importance of quality implementation for both client progress and program evaluation, would go a long way to enhance the effectiveness of substance abuse prevention efforts (Botvifn & Griffin, 2007; Spoth et al., 2008).

Case Study

Marci and Joey

Marciela, 19-year-old female, of bicultural background (Latina and Anglo), is struggling socially and academically during her senior year of high school, and lives with her siblings in her parents' suburban home in a small southern city. Mr. and Mrs. Soliz are small-business owners, operating a retail store featuring the sale and installation of home water and air filtering systems. Mrs. Soliz works part-time as an administrator and bookkeeper for the business, and considers her "main job" to be caring for their four children, which includes Marci's siblings, 16-year-old Joey and "the twins," Suzi and Marcos at 12 years of age. With the faltering economy, Mr. and Mrs. Soliz have been logging long hours at the store, and rely on Marci and Joey to help with the store on a part-time basis as well as supervising the twins while their parents are at work. Typically, the parents are known to drink alcohol minimally, only a few times each year, usually on holidays or during celebrations with extended family.

Marci failed the 10th grade because of absences and poor grades that coincided with the start of using alcohol and marijuana. She explained to her counselor that it was "boring at home" because of the Soliz's extended hours at the store. Marci expanded that she and her friends were able to effectively ". . . watch the younger kids okay and still smoke a little [marijuana]." Marci has gone through periods of sobriety during the last three years, sometimes lasting as long as six months. She vacillates between recognizing the detrimental effects of alcohol and marijuana on her academic and social life, and minimizing her misuse as "no big deal." Marci reported that she feels "invisible" at school except to her small circle of close friends.

Joey, known for his outgoing personality, has been a class leader in student government and athletics; he is part of the "popular crowd" at the high school. Joey received scholastic and athletic notice at the yearly awards banquets. However, during the recent semester, Joey's grades in some of his classes have begun to fluctuate. Mr. and Mrs. Soliz have talked to their son about "partying" with his friends repeatedly. Additionally, Mrs. Soliz is often frustrated by her inability to personally supervise her children at home because she is needed at the family business. When she is on "home duty" Mrs. Soliz is frequently out of the house, driving the twins to their extracurricular activities of soccer and piano lessons.

Marci has been feeling much self-recrimination, blaming herself for the negative consequences of her brother's experimentation with alcohol and tobacco. Joey recently got a warning ticket from a police officer for approaching a man at a convenience store, asking that beer and cigarettes be purchased for his friends. Mr. and Mrs. Soliz grounded Joey for six weeks, not allowing him to drive anywhere except to school and work. At this point, they noticed that Marci seemed more reticent and withdrawn lately. Mr. and Mrs. Soliz have discussed starting family counseling in addition to Marci's individual therapy.

Mr. and Mrs. Soliz talked to the parents of Joey's friends who were involved in the incident, alerting them to their children's use of alcohol. Though hesitant at first, they further expressed concerns about the effects of ATOD on Marci and their desire to avoid a similar outcome with her siblings. Several adults agreed that a more formal prevention effort would be helpful to support whatever response was chosen by each family. An informal meeting at the high school was scheduled with concerned parents, teachers, and administrators to outline a program strategy. Questions arose about which outside agencies should be approached as additional resources for services. If a community agency became involved, would that help defray costs for the high school and provide additional resources such as staff and materials? Regarding levels of intervention, would the same program components be appropriate for Marci and Joey, or would different approaches be needed?

Critical Thinking Questions

1. If you were a parent or administrator on the committee, which level of intervention would you consider important? In addition to *primary* services, would *secondary* prevention be appropriate for Joey and his friends? Are Marci's needs considered *tertiary* yet? Should the committee take a more *universal* tactic in educating children of different ages as well as other family members, or would it be more effective to take a *selective* approach by pinpointing high-school-aged adolescents, particularly those who have been experimenting with alcohol and marijuana? What resources are needed, and what would be the availability of personnel and funding for implementation?

2. As a participant at the strategy meeting, how would you suggest that the group coordinate the program and maintain accountability when there are multiple organizations involved such as a school and community agencies? What would be workable funding sources, and how should this be managed? In planning a prevention program, how would you

(Continued)

(Continued)

ascertain whether someone's interests were more self-involved or directed toward the benefit of the group? In recognizing the benefits and challenges of community collaborations, how many partnering entities should be included? Who should be approached?

3. In choosing components for the program, which risk and protective factors come forward in the discussion? Should the prevention program encompass a larger area of the city such as multiple schools, or the smaller community of one campus? Once they clarify the prevalence of ATOD use at their school and community, should the program promote normative education or embrace a position of abstinence? What about additional training such as life skills or communication education? How specific should the goals be, and how would you measure effectiveness? Should parents or school staff be trained to run the prevention program, or should counselors from community agencies facilitate various services? How would you design and implement a program to offer the most efficient use of funds?

CONCLUSION

This chapter was designed to provide the foundational concepts, trends, and knowledge that will enable mental health providers to participate in ATOD prevention and education programming. This work is both exciting and challenging. It is an essential element of the role as an advocate of change.

Building on lessons learned from the past, today's prevention efforts need to be comprehensive and collaborative that are based upon current knowledge of evidenced-based practices. The most effective prevention programs are integrated and include a coordinated set of strategies that enhance the health and total well-being of persons to reduce the risk of destructive behavior and its consequences.

MyCounselingLab™

Go to Topic 12: *Prevention*, on the MyCounselingLab™ site (www.MyCounselingLab .com) for *Substance Abuse Counseling*, Fifth Edition where you can:

- Find learning outcomes for *Prevention* along with the national standards that connect to these outcomes.
- Complete Assignments and Activities that can help you more deeply understand the chapter content.
- Apply and practice your understanding of the core skills identified in the chapter with the Building Counseling Skills unit.
- Prepare yourself for professional certification with a Practice for Certification quiz.
- Connect to videos through the Video and Resource Library.

MyCounselingLab™ Exercises

Go to the Video and Resource Library on the MyCounselingLab™ site for your text and search for the following clip:

Addressing and Acknowledging Motivation

After you view the clip, consider your responses to the following questions:

1. What activities would you suggest that might help this client avoid the use of drugs?
2. What kind of structured program would you design for this client, including assessing risk and identifying protective factors?
3. How would you assess the success of your prescribed prevention program?

Select Websites on ATOD Prevention and Education

For the student or experienced professional who wants to learn more, a number of prevention-related websites are provided here. These are only a small sampling of the information and resources that are available, yet they will help concerned counselors to continue their own development in this important area of professional work.

Government Sites:

Centers for Disease Control and Prevention (CDC): cdc.gov/

National Education Association Health Information Network: neahin.org/programs/substance/index.htm

National Institute on Alcohol Abuse and Alcoholism (NIAAA): niaaa.nih.gov/

National Institute on Drug Abuse (NIDA): nida.nih.gov/

National Institutes of Health (NIH): nih.gov/

Substance Abuse and Mental Health Services Administration (SAMSHA), Department of Health and Human Services: samhsa.gov/

U.S. Department of Health and Human Services (HHS): hhs.gov/

University-Based Sites:

Higher Education Center for Alcohol and Other Drug Prevention: higheredcenter.org/

National Center on Addiction and Substance Abuse [CASA] at Columbia University: casacolumbia.org/templates/Home.aspx

School of Public Health, Harvard University/College Alcohol Study: hsph.harvard.edu/cas/

Miscellaneous:

American Council for Drug Education (ACDE): acde.org/

American Society of Addiction Medicine (ASAM): asam.org/

Drug Policy Alliance: drugpolicy.org/about/

Partnership for a Drug-Free America (PDFA): drugfree.org/

Partnership for Responsible Drug Information: prdi.org/

REFERENCES

Chapter 1

American Psychiatric Association. (2001). *Diagnostic and statistical manual* (5th ed.). Washington, DC: Author.

Booth, M. (2005). *Cannibis: A history*. New York: Picador.

Centers for Disease Control and Prevention. (2006). *Hepatitis C: Treatment guides 2006*. Retrieved from http://www.cdc.gov/std/treatment/2006/hepatitis-c.htm

Centers for Disease Control and Prevention. (2007). *HIV/AIDS surveillance report* (Vol. 17). Atlanta: Author.

Centers for Disease Control and Prevention. (July, 2010). *'HIV in the United States'*. Atlanta: Author.

Chafetz, M. E. (1965). *Liquor: The servant of man*. Boston: Little, Brown.

Chouvy, P. A. (2010). *Opium: Uncovering the politics of the poppy*. Cambridge: Harvard University Press.

Doweiko, H. (2011). *Concepts of chemical dependency* (7th ed.). Pacific Grove, CA: Brooks/Cole.

Drug Abuse Warning Network. (2009). Drug Abuse and Emergency Room Visits. Retrieved from http://www.suite101.com/content/drug-abuse-and-emergency-room-visits-2008-update-a90546

Eliason, M. J. (2007). *Improving substance treatment: An introduction to the evidence based practice movement*. Thousand Oaks, CA: Sage.

Fernandez, H. (2011). *Heroin: Its history, pharmacology, and treatment*. Center City, MN: Hazeldon.

Goode, E. (2007). *Drugs in American society*. Columbus, OH: McGraw-Hill.

Harris, N. (2004). *Amphetamines (History of drugs)*. Farmington Hills, MI: Greenhaven.

Hettema, J., Steele, J., & Miller, W. R. (2005, April). Motivational interviewing. *Annual Review of Clinical Psychology, I*, 91–111.

Kane, H. H. (1883). A hashish-house in New York, *Harper's Monthly, 67*, 944–949.

Karch, S. B. (2005). *A brief history of cocaine* (2nd ed.). Boca Raton, FL: CRC Press.

Lewis, J. A., Dana, R. Q., & Blevins, G. A. (2011). *Substance abuse counseling* (4th ed.). Pacific Grove, CA: Brooks/Cole.

Merriam-Webster. (2011). *Merriam-Webster collegiate edition dictionary* (11th ed.). Springfield, MA: Author.

Miller, W. R., & Carroll, K. M. (2006). Drawing the scene together: Ten principles, ten recommendations. In W. R. Miller & K. M. Carroll (Eds.), *Rethinking substance abuse: What the science shows, and what we should know about it* (pp. 293–311). New York: Guilford Press.

National Insitute of Drug Abuse. (2000). *NIDA Notes, 15*(1).

Norton, M. (2010). *Sacred gifts, profane pleasures: A history of tobacco and chocolate in the Atlantic world*. Ithaca, NY: Cornell University Press.

Scaros, L. P., Westra, S., & Barone, J. A. (1990). Illegal use of drugs: A current review. *U.S. Pharmacist, 15*(5), 17–39.

Substance Abuse and Mental Health Services Administration. (2010a). *The DAWN report*. Retrieved from http://dawninfo.samhsa.gov/pubs_94_02/short-reports/files/TDR_EDvisits_glance_1994_2001.pdf

Substance Abuse and Mental Health Services Administration. (2010b). National survey on drug use and habits. *Illicit Drug Use among Persons Arrested for Serious Crime*, December 16, 2005. Retrieved from http://www.oas.samhsa.gov/2k5/arrests/arrests.htm

Substance Abuse and Mental Health Services Administration. (2010c). *National Youth Risk Survey, 1991–2009*. Retrieved from http://www.cdc.gov/HealthyYouth/yrbs/

Substance Abuse and Mental Health Services Administration. (2010d). *Results from the 2009 National Survey on Drug Use and Health: Volume I. Summary of National Findings* (Office of Applied Studies, NSDUH Series H-38A, HHS Publication No. SMA 10-4856 Findings). Rockville, MD: Author.

U.S. Department of Health and Human Services. National Institute of Allergies and Infectious Diseases. (2006). *HIV infection in women, May, 2006*. Retrieved from http://www.niaid.nih.gov/factsheets/womenhiv.htm

U.S. Department of Transportation. (2009). Traffic Safety Facts. National Highway Traffic Safety Administration.

Weinberg, B. A., & Beale, B. K. (2002). *The world of caffeine: The science and culture of the world's most popular drug*. New York: Routledge.

Weisheit, R., & White, W. (2010). *Methamphetamine: Its history, pharmacology, and treatment*. Center City, MN: Hazeldon.

Williams, M. E. (2004). *Hallucinogens (The history of drugs)*. Farmington Hills, MI: Greenhaven.

World Health Organization. (2005). *Epidemiological fact sheets by country*. Retrieved from http://www.who.int/hiv/pub/epidemiology/pubfacts/en/

Yacoubian, G. S. (2003). Correlates of benzodiazepine use among a sample of arrestees surveyed through the Arrestee Drug Abuse Monitoring (ADAM) Program. *Substance Use & Misuse, 38*(1), 127–139. doi:10.1081/JA-120016569

Chapter 2

American Counseling Association. (2005). *Code of ethics*. Alexandria, VA: Author.

American Counseling Association. (2010). *Licensure requirements for professional counselors*. Alexandria, VA: Author.

American Mental Health Counseling Association. (2010). *Code of ethics*. Alexandria, VA: Author.

American School Counselor Association. (2002). *Confidentiality position statement*. Retrieved from http://www.mtschoolcounselor.org/MT_School_Counseling_Program_Model/files/ASCA_Position_Statements.doc

American School Counselor Association. (2010). *Ethical standards for school counselors*. Alexandria, VA: Author.

Arredondo, P., Toporek, M. S., Brown, S., Jones, J., Locke, D. C., Sanchez, J. and Stadler, H. (1996). Operationalization of the Multicultural Counseling Competencies. AMCD: Alexandria, VA.

Broderick, E. B. (2007). *Report to Congress: Addictions treatment workforce development*. Retrieved from www.pfr.samhsa.gov/docs/Report_to_Congress.pdf

Burrow-Sanchez, J. J., Jenson, W. R., & Clark, E. (2009). School-based interventions for students with substance abuse. *Psychology in the Schools, 46*(3), 238–245.

Chamberlain, L. L., & Jew, C. L. (2005). Assessment and diagnosis. In P. Stevens & R. L. Smith (Eds.), *Substance abuse counseling: Theory and practice* (3rd ed., pp. 123–152). Upper Saddle River, NJ: Pearson/Prentice Hall.

Code of Federal Regulations, 42, 6-25. (1994). Washington, DC: U.S. Government Printing Office. (2010). E-code available at http://ecfr.gpoaccess.gov/cgi/t/text/text-idx?c=ecfr&sid=02b3d31742318b503b8d4ba0111d0e35&tpl=/ecfrbrowse/Title42/42cfr2_main_02.tpl

Coleman, P. (2005). Privilege and confidentiality in 12-step self-help programs: Believing the promises could be hazardous to an addict's freedom. *Journal of Legal Medicine, 26*, 435–474. doi: 10.1080/01947640500364713

Cox v. Miller, 537 U.S. 1192 (2003).

Family Educational Rights and Privacy Act. (1974). 20 U.S.C.A. Section 1232g. [Buckley Amendment.] (1991). Implementing regulations 34 *CFR* 99.3. Fed. Reg. 56, Section 117, 28012.

Forester-Miller, H., & Davis, T. (1996). *A practioner's guide to ethical decision making*. Alexandria, VA: American Counseling Association. Retrieved from http://www.counseling.org/Resources/CodeOfEthics/TP/Home/CT2.aspx

Glosoff, H. L., & Kocet, M. M. (2006). Highlights of the 2005 ACA *Code of Ethics*. In *VISTAS: Compelling Perspectives on Counseling 2006* (pp. 5–12). Alexandria, VA: ACA Press.

Glosoff, H., & Pate, Jr., R. H. (2002). Privacy and confidentiality in school counseling. Special issue: Legal and ethical issues in school counseling. *Professional School Counseling, 6*, 20–27.

Health Insurance Portability and Accountability Act of 1996 (HIPAA), Pub. L. 104-191, Sec. 261–264.

Henricksen, Jr., R. C., & Trusty, J. (2005). Ethics and values as major factors related to multicultural aspects of counselor preparation. *Counseling and Values, 49*, 180–192.

Herbert, P. B., & Young, K. A. (2002). *Tarasoff* at twenty-five. *Journal of the American Academy of Psychiatry and the Law, 30*, 275–281. Retrieved from www.jaapl.org/cgi/reprint/30/2/275.pdf

Illinois State Board of Education. (n.d.). *No Child Left Behind*. Retrieved from http://www.isbe.state.il.us/nclb/htmls/ppra_ferpa.htm

Individuals with Disabilities Education Act of 1997. (1997). Pub. L. No. 105-17, 34 *CFR* 300–574.

International Association of Marriage and Family Counselors. (2005). *Ethical Code of the International Association of Marriage and Family Counselors*. Retrieved from http://www.iamfconline.com/PDFs/Ethical%20Codes.pdf

Kaplan, L. E. (2005). Dual relationships: The challenges for social workers in recovery. *Journal of Social Work Practice in the Addictions, 5*(3), 73–90. doi: 10.1300/J160v05n0306

Kenney Hollander, J., Bauer, S., Herlihy, B., & McCollum, V. (2006). Beliefs of board certified substance abuse counselors regarding multiple relationships. *Journal of Mental Health Counseling, 28*(1), 84–94.

Kerwin, M. E., Walker-Smith, K., & Kirby, K. C. (2006). Comparative analysis of state requirements for the training of substance abuse and mental health counselors. *Journal of Substance Abuse Treatment, 30,* 173–181. doi: 10.1016/j.jsat.2005.11.004

Lawrence, G., & Robinson Kurpius, S. E. (2000). Legal and ethical issues involved when counseling minors in nonschool settings. *Journal of Counseling & Development, 78,* 130–136.

Lipari v. Sears, Roebuck & Co., 836F.2d 209 (1987).

National Addiction Technology Transfer Center. (2010). Licensing and certification requirements. Retrieved from http://www.nattc.org/getCertified.asp

National Association of Alcoholism and Drug Abuse Counselors. (2008). *Code of ethics.* Arlington, VA: Author.

National Board for Certified Counselors. (2005). *Code of ethics.* Retrieved from http://www.nbcc.org/Assets/Ethics/nbcc-codeofethics.pdf

National Board for Certified Counselors. (2011). *Exam for master of addictions counselor application.* Retrieved from http://www.nbcc.org/extras/pdfs/apps/macapp.pdf

Office for Civil Rights. (2003). *Summary of the HIPAA privacy rule.* Retrieved from http://www.hhs.gov/ocr/privacy/hipaa/understanding/summary/

Protection of Pupil Rights Amendment. (1994). Goals 2000: Educate America Act. 20 USC, Section 1232h.

Remley, T., & Herlihy, B. (2010). *Ethical, legal, and professional issues in counseling* (3rd ed.). Upper Saddle River, NJ: Pearson Education.

Rubin, S. E., Wilson, C. A., Fischer, J., & Vaughn, B. (1992). *Ethical practices in rehabilitation: A series of instructional modules for rehabilitation education programs.* Carbondale, IL: Southern Illinois University.

Schank, J. A., Helbok, C. M., Haldeman, D. C., & Gallardo, M. E. (2010). Challenges and benefits of ethical small-community practice. *Professional Psychology, Research & Practice, 41*(6), 502–510. doi: 10.1037/a0021689

Schwartz, R. C., & Smith, S. D. (2003). Screening and assessing adolescent substance abuse: A primer for counselors. *Journal of Addictions & Offender Counseling, 24,* 23–34.

Smith, R. L., & Capps, F. (2005). Research and contemporary issues. In P. Stevens & R. L. Smith (Eds.), *Substance abuse counseling: Theory and practice* (3rd ed., pp. 339–372). Upper Saddle River, NJ: Pearson/Prentice Hall.

Stevens, P. (2005). Family therapy in substance abuse treatment. In P. Stevens & R. L. Smith (Eds.), *Substance abuse counseling: Theory and practice* (3rd ed., pp. 213–238). Upper Saddle River, NJ: Pearson/Prentice Hall.

Stone, C. (2001). *Ethics and law for school counselors.* ASCA: Alexandria, VA.

Substance Abuse and Mental Health Services Administration. (2005). *A national review of state alcohol and drug treatment programs and certification standards for counselors and prevention professionals.* Rockville, MD: U.S. Department of Health and Human Services.

Sue, D., Arredondo, P., & McDavis, R. (1992, March). Multicultural counseling competencies and standards: A call to the profession. *Journal of Counseling & Development, 70*(4), 477–486. Retrieved from Academic Search Premier database.

Sue, D. W. & Sue, D. (1990). *Counseling the culturally different.* New York: John Wiley and Sons.

Tarasoff v. Regents of the University of California. 17 Cal. 3d 425, 131 Cal. Rep. 14, 551 P. 2d 334. (1976).

Toriello, P. J., & Benshoff, J. J. (2003). Substance abuse counselors and ethical dilemmas: The influence of recovery and education level. *Journal of Addictions & Offender Counseling, 23,* 83–98.

U.S. Department of Education. (2009). Federal regulations. Retrieved from http://www.ed.gov/policy/gen/guid/fpco/pdf/ferparegs.pdf

White, W. L. (2008). Alcohol, tobacco and other drug use by addictions professionals: Historical reflections and suggested guidelines. *Alcoholism Treatment Quarterly, 26*(4), 500–535. doi: 10.1080/07347320802347228

Chapter 3

Adinoff, B., Devous, Sr. M. D., Williams, M. J., Best, S. E., Harris, T. S., Minhajuddin, A., Zielinski, T., & Cullum, M. (2010). Altered neural cholinergic receptor systems in cocaine-addicted subjects. *Neuropsychopharmocology,* 35, 1485–1499. doi:10.1038/npp.2010.18

American Cancer Society. (2010). Alcohol and Cancer. Retrieved from www.cancer.org

Amphetamine Epidemics. (2011). Retrieved from eNotes.com. http://www.enotes.com/amphetamine-epidemics-reference

Bartholomew, J., Holroyd, S., & Heffernan, T. M. (2010). Does cannabis use affect prospective memory in adults? *Sage Journals Online.* Retrieved from http://jop.sagepub.com/content/24/2/241.abstract

Bhattacharyya, S., Fusar-Poli, P., Borgwardt, S., Martin-Santos, R., Nosarti, C., O'Carroll, C., & McGuire, P. (2009). Modulation of mediotemporal and ventrostraital function in humans by Δ9-tetrahydrocannabinol. *Archives of General Psychiatry*, 66, 442–451. Retrieved from http://archpsyc.ama-assn.org/cgi/content/abstract/66/4/442

Buckholtz, J. W., Treadway, M. T., Cowan, R. L., Woodward, N. D., Benning, S. D., Li, R., Ansari, M. S., . . . Zald, D. H. (2010). Mesolimbic dopamine reward system hypersensitivity in individuals with psychopathic traits. *Nature Neuroscience*, 13, 419–421. doi:10.1038/nn.2510

Bullmore, E., & Sporns, O. (2009). Complex brain networks: Graph theoretical analysis of structural and functional systems. *Nature Reviews. Neuroscience,*10, 186–198. doi: 10.1038/nrn2575

Buttigieg, J., Brown, S., Zhang, M., Lowe, M., Holloway, A. C., & Nurse, C. A. (2008). Chronic nicotine in utero selectively suppresses hypoxic sensitivity in neonatal. *The Journal of the Federation of American Societies for Experimental Biology*, 22, 1317–1326.

Campbell, N. D. (2010). Toward a critical neuroscience of 'addiction.' *BioSocieties*. 5, 89–104. doi: 10.1057/biosoc.2009.2

Centers for Disease Control and Prevention (CDC). (2005). General Alcohol Information. Fact Sheet. Atlanta, GA: CDC. Retrieved from www.cdc.gov/alcohol/factsheets/general_information.htm

Choy. Y. (2007). Managing side effects of anxiolytics. *Primary Psychiatry*, 14(7), 68–76.

Cosgrove, K. P., Batis, J., Bois, F., Maciejewski, P. K., Esterlis, I., & Staley, J. K. (2009). Beta2-Nicotinic acetylcholine receptor availability during acute and prolonged abstinence from tobacco smoking. *Archive of General Psychiatry*, 66(6), 666–676. doi: 10.1001/archgenpsychiatry.2009.41

Cowan, R. L., Haga, E., Deb Frederick, B., Dietrich, M. S., Vimal, R. L. P., Lukas, S. E., and Renshaw, P. F. (2006). MDMA use is associated with increased spatial **fMRI visual cortex activation in human MDMA users.** *Pharmacology Biochemistry and Behavior.* 84: 2, 219–228.

DEA/OD/ODE, U.S. Department of Justice, Drug Enforcement Administration, Office of Diversion Control. (2010). *Benzodiazepines.* Retrieved from http://www.deadiversion.usdoj.gov/drugs_concern/benzo_1.html

Doidge, N. (2007). *The brain that changes itself.* New York: Viking.

Drake, J. (2009). Fetal alcohol syndrome testing expands. *e! Science News.* Retrieved from http://esciencenews.com/articles/2009/03/19/fetal.alcohol.syndrome.testing

FDA Commissioner Testified: Tobacco companies spiking cigarettes to addict smokers. (2009). *eSmoke.* Retrieved from www.esmoke.net/news

Geibprasert, S., Gallucci, M., & Krings, T. (2009). Addictive illegal drugs: Structural neuroimaging. *American Journal of Neuroradiology*, 31, 803–808. doi:10.3174/anjnr.A1811

Hanlon, C. A., Wesley, M. J., & Porrino, L. J. (2009). Loss of functional specificity in the dorsal stratum of chronic cocaine users. *Drug Alcohol Dependence*, 102(1–3), 88–94. doi:10.1016/j.drugalcdep.2009.01.005

Hanlon, C. A., Wesley, M. J., Roth, A. J., Miller, M. D., & Porrino, L. J. (2010). Loss of laterality in chronic cocaine users: Am fMRI investigation of sensorimotor control. *Psychiatry Research: Neuroimaging*, 181(1), 15–23. doi:10.1016/j.pscychresns.2009.07.009

Hassan, H.E., Meyers, A.L., Lee, I.J., Chen, H., Coop, A., & Eddington, N. D. (2010). Regulation of gene expression in brain tissues of rats repeatedly treated by the highly abused opioid agonist, oxycodone: microarray profiling and gene mapping analysis. *U.S. National Library of Medicine National Institutes of Health*, 38(1):157–167.

Hester, R., Nestor, L., & Garavan, H. (2009). Impaired error awareness and anterior cingulated cortex hypoactivity in chronic cannabis users. *Neuropsychopharmacology*, 11, 2450–2458. doi: 10.1038/npp.2009.67

Hsu, C. W., Chen, C. Y., Wang, C., & Chiu, T. H. (2009). Caffeine and a selective adenosine A2A receptor antagonist induce reward and sensitization behavior associated with increased phosphor-Thr75-DARPP-32 in mice. *Psychopharmacology*, 204. 313–325. doi: 10.1007/s00213-009-1461-3

Johnson, P. M., & Kenny, P. J. (2010). *Addiction-like reward dysfunction and compulsive eating in obese rats: Roles for dopamine D2 receptors.* Nature Neuroscience. Retrieved from http://www.nature.com/neuro/journal/vaop/ncurrent/index.html

Johnston, L. D., O'Malley, P. M., Bachman, J. G., & Schulenberg, J. E. (2011). Monitoring the future national results on adolescent drug use: Overview of key findings in 2010. Ann Arbor, MI: Institute for Social Research, University of Michigan.

Lau, B. W-M., Yau, S-Y., & So, K-F. (2011). Reproduction: A new venue for studying function of adult neurogenesis?. *Cell Transplantation*, 20(1), 21–35.

Licata, S. C., & Renshaw, P. F. (2010). Neurochemistry of drug action: Insights from proton magnetic resonance spectroscopic imaging and their relevance to addiction. *Academic Science*, 1187, 148–171. doi: 10.1111/j.1749-6632.2009.05143.x

Mehra, R., Moore, B., Crothers, K., Tetrault, J., & Fiellin, D. (2006). The association between marijuana smoking and lung cancer. *Archives of Internal Medicine*, 166, 1359–1367.

Meyer, K. D., & Zhang, L. (2009). Short and long-term adverse effects of cocaine abuse during pregnancy on the heart development. *Therapeutic Advances in Cardiovascular Disease*, 3(1), 7–16.

Naloxone 'Reboots' Opioid Pain-Relief System. (2010). Pain Treatment Topics. Retrieved from http://updates.pain-topics.org/2010/11/naloxone-reboots-opioid-pain-relief.html

National Institute on Drug Abuse. (2009a). *Neuroscience Consortium.* Retrieved from http://www.drugabuse.gov/about/organization/nswg/NSWG.html

National Institute on Drug Abuse. (2009b). *Neuroscience Consortium – Scientific Goals.* Retrieved from http://www.drugabuse.gov/about/organization/nswg/goals.html

National Institute on Drug Abuse. (2009c). *NIDA Info Facts: Hallucinogens – LSD, peyote, psilocybin, and PCP.* Retrieved from http://drugabuse.gov/infofacts/hallucinogens.html

National Institute on Drug Abuse. (2009d). *NIDA InfoFacts: MDMA (ecstasy).* Retrieved from http://drugabuse.gov/infofacts/ectasy.html

National Institute on Drug Abuse. (2009e). *NIDA InfoFacts: Prescription and over-the-counter medications.* Retrieved from http://teens.drugabuse.gov/facts/facts_rx2.php

National Institute on Drug Abuse. (2009f). *NIDA Info-Facts: Steroids (anabolic-androgenic).* Retrieved from http://drugabuse.gov/infofacts/steroids.html

National Institute on Drug Abuse. (2009g). *NIDA Info-Facts: Stimulant ADHD medications – Methylphenidate and amphetamines.* Available at http://www.drugabuse.gov/infofacts/ADHD.html

National Institute on Drug Abuse. (2009h). *PCP/ Phencyclidine.* Retrieved from http://www.nida.nih.gov/drugpages/pcp.html

National Institute on Drug Abuse. (2010a). *Drugs, brains, and behavior – The science of addiction.* Retrieved from http://www.drugabuse.gov/science of addiction

National Institute on Drug Abuse. (2010b). *CNS depressants.* Retrieved from http://www.drugabuse.gov/researchreports/perscription/prescription3.html

National Institute on Drug Abuse. (2010c). *NIDA InfoFacts: Cigarettes and other tobacco products.* Retrieved from http://www.drugabuse.gov/infofacts/tobacco.html

National Institute on Drug Abuse. (2010d). *NIDA InfoFacts: Club drugs (GHB, ketamine, and rohypnol).* Retrieved from http://www.drugabuse.gov/infofacts/clubdrugs.html

National Institute on Drug Abuse. (2010e). *NIDA InfoFacts: Cocaine.* Retrieved from http://www.drugabuse.gov/infofacts/cocaine.html

National Institute on Drug Abuse. (2010f). *NIDA InfoFacts: Heroin.* Retrieved from http://www.drugabuse.gov/infofacts/heroine.html

National Institute on Drug Abuse. (2010g). *NIDA InfoFacts: Methamphetamine.* Retrieved from http://www.drugabuse.gov/infofacts/methamphetamine.html

National Institute on Drug Abuse. (2010h). *Methamphetamine.* Retrieved from http://www.nida.nih.gov/drugpages/methamphetamine.html

National Institute on Drug Abuse. (2010i). *Research Report Series Cocaine: Abuse and addiction - Letter from the director.* Retrieved from http://www.nida.nih.gov/ResearchReports/Cocaine/cocaine.html

National Institute on Drug Abuse. (2010j). *Research Report Series: Inhalant abuse.* Retrieved from http://www.drugabuse.gov/PDF/RRinhalants.pdf

National Institute on Drug Abuse. (2011). Epidemiological Trends in Drug Abuse: Proceedings of the Community Epidemiology Work Group. Highlights and Executive Summary. Retrieved from http://www.nida.nih.gov/pdf/cewg/CEWGJan2011_508.pdf

Ormrod, J. E. (2008). *Human learning.* Upper Saddle River, NJ: Pearson Education.

Paulozzi, L. J. (2006). Opioid analgesic involvement in drug abuse deaths in American metropolitan areas. *American Journal of Public Health*, 96(10), 1755–1757.

Quickfall, J., & Crockford, D. (2006). Brain neuroimaging in cannabis use: A review. *Journal of Neuropsychology & Clinical Neurosciences*, 18, 318–332. doi: 10.1176/appi.neuropsych.18.3.318

Rais, M., Wiepke, C., Van Haren, N., Schnack, H., Caspers, E., Hulshoff, H., & Kahn, R. (2008). Excessive brain volume loss over time in cannabis-using first-episode schizophrenia patients. *The American Journal of Psychiatry*, 165, 490–496. doi: 10.1176/appi.ajp2007.07071110

Raj, V., Liang, H., Woodward, N., Bauernfeind, A., Lee, J., Dietrich, M., Parks, S., & Cowan, R. (2009). MDMA (ecstasy) use is associated with reduced BOLD signal change during semantic recognition in abstinent human polydrug users: A preliminary fMRI study. *Journal of Psychopharmacology, 24*(2), 187–201. doi: 10.1177/0269881109103203

Rio, K. (2011). MDMA—The ecstasy. *The Journal of Young Investigators: An Undergraduate, Peer-Reviewed Science Journal, 21*(5).

Rogers, P. J., Hohoff, C., Heatherly, S. V., Mullings, E. L., Maxfield, P. J., Evershed, R. P., Deckert, J., & Nutt, D. J. (2010). Association of the Anxiogenic and Alerting Effects of Caffeine with ADORA2A and ADORA1 Polymorphisms and Habitual Level of Caffeine Consumption. *Neuropsychopharmacology, 35,*1973–1983. doi: 10.1038/npp.2010.7

Scholz, B., Kultima, K., Mattsson, A., Axelson, J., Brunström, B., Halldin, K., Stigson, M., and Dencker, L. (2006). Sex-dependent gene expression in early brain development of chicken embryos. *BMC Neuroscience, 7*(12).

Sherman, C. (2006). Drugs affect men's and women's brains differently. *National Institute on Drug Abuse, 20*(6).

Sigmon, S. C., Herning, R. I., Better, W., Cadet, J. L., & Griffiths, R. R. (2009). Caffeine withdrawals, acute effects, tolerance, and absence of net beneficial effects of chronic administration: cerebral blood flow velocity, quantitative EEG, and subjective effects. *Psychopharmacology, 204*, 573–585. doi: 10.1007/s00213-009-1489-4

Sproule, B. (2009). Changing patterns in opioid addiction. *Canadian Family Physician*, 55.

Staff. (2009). *Migraine attacks may become more frequent due to certain medications.* Daily RX Relevant Health News. Retrieved from http://dailyrx.com/news-article/migraine-attacks

Substance Abuse and Mental Health Services Administration. (2010). *Results from the 2009 National Survey on Drug Use and Health: Volume 1. Summary of National Findings (Office of Applied Studies), NSDUH Series H-38A, HHS Publication No. SMA 10-4856 Findings. Rockville, MD.*

Tobias, M. C., O'Neill, J., Hudkins, M., Bartzokis, G., Dean, A. C., & London, E. D. (2010). White-matter abnormalities in brain during early abstinence from methamphetamine abuse. *Psychopharmacology, 209*(1), 13–24. doi: 10.1007/s00213-009-1761-7

Veterinary Practice News. (2010). Generic ketamine approved by FDA. Retrieved from www.veterinarypracticenews.com/vet-breaking-news/

Volkow, N. (2005). Inhalant abuse: Danger under the kitchen sink. *National Institute on Drug Abuse, 20*(3).

Volkow, N. (2006). Steroid abuse is a high-risk route to the finish line. *National Institute on Drug Abuse, 21*(1).

Welch, K. A., Mcintosh, A. M., Job, D. E., Whalley, H. C., Moorhead, T. W., Hall, J., . . . Johnstone, E. C. (2010). The impact of substance use on brain structure in people at high risk of developing schizophrenia. *Oxford Journals.* doi: 10.1093/schbul/sbq013

Xue, G., Lu, Z., Levin, I., Weller, J., Li, X., & Bechara, A. (2009). Functional dissociations of risk and reward processing in the medial prefrontal cortex. *Cerebral Cortex, 19*(5), 1019–1027. doi: 10.1093/cercor/bhn147

Yucel, M., Solowij, N., Respondek, C., Whittle, S., Fornito, A., Pantelis, C., & Lubman, Dan. (2008). Regional brain abnormalities associated with long-term heavy cannabis use. *Archives of General Psychiatry*, 65, 694–701. Retrieved from http://archpsyc.ama.assn.org/cgi.content/abstract/65/6/694

Zacny, J. P., & Gutierrez, S. (2003). Characterizing the subjective, psychomotor, and physiological effects of oral oxycodone in non-drug-abusing volunteers. *Psychopharmacology, 170*(3), 242–254.

Chapter 4

Addolorato, G., Leggio, L., Abenavoli, L., & Gasbarrini, G. (2005). Neurobiochemical and clinical aspects of craving in alcohol addiction: A review. *Addictive Behaviors.* 30, 126–130. doi: 10.1016/j.addbeh.2004.12.011

Agrawal, A., Edenberg, H. J., Foroud, T., Bierut, L. J., Dunne, G., Hinrichs, A. L., . . . Dick, D. M. (2006). Association of GABRA2 with drug dependence in the collaborative study of the genetics of alcoholism sample. *Behavior Genetics 36*(5), 640–650. doi: 10.1007/s10519-006-9069-4

Agrawal, A., Hinrichs, A. L., Dunn, G., Bertelsen, S., Dick, D. M., Saccone, S. F., . . . Bierut, L. J. (2008). Linkage scan for quantitative traits identifies new regions of interest for substance dependence in the collaborative study of the genetics of alcoholism (COGA) sample. *Drug and Alcohol Dependence, 93*, 12–20. doi:10.1016/j.drugalcdep.2007.08.015

Agrawal, A., & Lynskey, M. T. (2006). The genetic epidemiology of cannabis use, abuse and dependence. *Addiction, 101*(6), 801–812. doi: 10.1111/j.1360-0443.2006.01399.x

Agrawal, A., & Lynsky, M. T. (2008). Are there genetic influences on addiction: Evidence from family, adoption, and twin studies. *Addiction, 103*(7), 1069–1081. doi: 10.1111/j.1360-0443.2008.02213.x

Alcoholics Anonymous. (1976). *Is there an alcoholic in your life?* Retrieved from www.aa.org/pdf/products/p-30_isthereanalcoinyourlife1.pdf

Akins, S., Smith, C. L., & Mosher, C. (2010). Pathways to adult alcohol abuse across racial/ethnic groups: An application of general strain and social learning theories. *Journal of Drug Issues 40*, 321–351.Retrieved from http://www2.criminology.fsu.edu/~jdi/

Alcoholics Anonymous. (2002). *The 12 steps of alcoholics anonymous.* Retrieved from aa.org/en_pdfs/smf-121_en.pdf

Ameisen, O. (2008). *The end of my addiction.* New York: Farrar, Strauss and Giroux. http://us.macmillan.com/FSG.aspx

American Medical Association. (1966). Drug dependencies as diseases. *Policy Finder. H-95.983. Chicago: American Medical Association, (2011).* Retrieved from www.ama-assn.org

American Psychiatric Association. (2010). *DSM-V development: Substance-related disorders.* Retrieved from http://www.dsm5.org/ProposedRevisions/Pages/Substance-RelatedDisorders.aspx

Babor, T. F., & Caetano, R. (2006). Subtypes of substance dependence and abuse: Implications for diagnostic classification and empirical research. *Addiction, 101* (Suppl. 1), 104–110. doi: 10.1111/j.1360-0443.2006.01595.x

Babor, T.F., Hofmann, M., Del Boca, F., Hesselbrock, V., Meyer, R., Dolinsky, Z., & Rounsaville, B. (1992). Types of alcoholics, I. Evidence for an empirically-derived typology based on indicators of vulnerability and severity. *Archives of General Psychiatry, 49*(8), 599–608.

Bandura, A. (1977). *Social learning theory.* Englewood Cliffs, NJ: Prentice-Hall.

Beauvais, F., Jumper-Thurman, P., & Burnside, M., (2008). The changing patterns of drug use among American Indian students over the past 30 years. *American Indian and Alaska Native Mental Health Research, 15*(2), 15–24. Retrieved from http://www.ncbi.nlm.nih.gov/pubmed/19085827

Becker, H. C. (2008). Alcohol dependence, withdrawal, and relapse. *Alcohol Research & Health, 31*(4), 348–361. Retrieved from http://www.niaaa.nih.gov

Bryson, E., & Silverstein, J. (2008). Addiction and substance abuse in anesthesiology. *Anesthesiology, 109*(5), 905–917. doi:10.1097/ALN.0b013e3181895bc1

Burrow-Sanchez, J. J. (2006). Understanding adolescent substance abuse: Prevalence, risk factors, and clinical implications. *Journal of Counseling Development, 84*, 283–290. Retrieved from http://goliath.ecnext.com/coms2/gi_0199-5645510/Understanding-adolescent-substance-abuse-prevalence.html

Calabrese, E. J. (2008). Addiction and dose response: The psychomotor stimulant theory of addiction reveals that hermetic dose responses are dominant. *Critical Reviews in Toxicology, 38*, 599–617. doi:101080/104084402026315

Carbaugh, R. J., & Sias, S. M. (2010). Comorbidity of bulimia nervosa and substance abuse: Etiologies, treatment issues, and treatment approaches. *Journal of Mental Health Counseling, 32*(2), 125–138. Retrieved from http://findarticles.com/p/articles/mi_hb1416/is_2_32/ai_n53523814/

Chastain, G. (2006). Alcohol, neurotransmitter systems, and behavior. *Journal of General Psychology, 133*(4), 329–335. doi:10.3200/GENP.133.4.329-335

Clapp, P., Bhave, S., & Hoffman, P. L. (2008). How adaptation of the brain to alcohol leads to dependence. *Alcohol Research & Health, 31*(4), 310–349. Retrieved from http://pubs.niaaa.nih.gov/publications/arh314/310-339.htm

Cloninger, C. R., Bohman, M., & Sigvardsson, S. (1981). Inheritance of alcohol abuse: Cross-fostering analysis of adopted men. *Archives of General Psychiatry, 38*(3), 861–868.

Corrigan, P. W., Watson, A. C., & Miller, F. E. (2006). Blame, shame and contamination: The impact of mental illness and drug dependence stigma on family members. *Journal of Family Psychology, 20*(2), 239–246. doi:10.1037/0893-3200.20.2.239

Costa, P. T., Jr., & McCrae, R. R. (1985). *The NEO personality inventory manual.* Odessa, FL: Psychological Assessment Resources.

Crabb, A. C., & Linton, J. M. (2007). A qualitative study of recovering and nonrecovering substance abuse counselors' belief systems. *Journal of Addictions & Offender Counseling, 28*, 4–20. Retrieved from http://goliath.ecnext.com/coms2/gi_0199-10248099/A-qualitative-study-of-recovering.html

Davis, V. E., & Walsh, M. J. (1970). Alcohol, amines, and alkaloids: A possible biochemical basis for alcohol addiction. *Science, 167*(3920), 1005–1007. Retrieved from http://www.jstor.org/stable/1728240

Demetrovics, Z. (2009). Co-morbidity of drug addiction: An analysis of epidemiological data and possible etiological models. *Addiction Research and Theory, 17*(4), 420–431. doi:10.1080/16066350802601324

Desrivières, S., Pronko, S., Lourdusamy, A., Duccia, G., Hoffman, P. L., Wodarz, N. . . . Tabakoff, B. (2011). Sex-specific role for adenylyl cyclase type 7 in alcohol dependence. *Biological Psychiatry, 69*(11), 1100–1108. Retrieved from http://www.ncbi.nlm.nih.gov/pmc/articles/PMC3094753/?tool=pubmed

Dick, D. M., & Agrawal, A. (2008). The genetics of alcohol and other drug dependence. *Alcohol Research & Health, 31*(2), 111–118. Retrieved from http://www.niaaa.nih.gov

Doweiko, H. (2011). *Concepts of chemical dependency* (8th ed.). Pacific Grove, CA: Brooks/Cole.

Duff, C. (2007). Towards a theory of drug use contests: Space, embodiment and practice. *Addiction Research and Theory, 15*(5), 503–519. doi:10.1080/16066350601165448

Eliason, M. J., & Amodia, D. S. (2007). An integral approach to drug craving. *Addiction Research and Theory, 15*(4), 343–364. doi:10.1080/16066350701 500627

Eskapa, R. (2008). *The cure for alcoholism: Drink your way sober without willpower, abstinence or discomfort.* Dallas, TX: BenBella Books. Retrieved from http://www.benbellabooks.com/

Faulkner, C. A., & Faulkner, S. S. (2009). *Research methods for social workers: A practice-based approach* (p. 9). Chicago: Lyceum Books. Retrieved from http://lyceumbooks.com/default2.htm

Feil, J., & Hasking, P. (2008). The relationship between personality, coping strategies and alcohol use. *Addiction Research and Theory, 16*(5), 526–537. doi:10.1080/16066350802025714

Foroud, T., Edenberg, H. J., & Crabbe, J. C. (2010). Genetic research: Who is at risk for alcoholism? *Alcohol Research & Health, 33*(1/2), 64–75. Retrieved from http://www.niaaa.nih.gov

Fox, H. C., Bergquist, K. L., Hong, K. I., & Sinha, R. (2007). Stress-induced and alcohol cue-induced craving in recently abstinent alcohol dependent individuals. *Alcoholism, Clinical, and Experimental Research, 31*(3), 395–403. doi:10.1111/j.1530-0277.2006.00320.x

Gelernter, J., & Kranzler, H. R., (2009). Genetics of alcohol dependence. *Human Genetics, 126,* 91–99. doi:10.1007/s00439-009-0701-2

Goldman, D., Oroszi, G., & Ducci, F. (2006). The genetics of addiction: Uncovering the genes. *Focus, American Psychiatric Association, 4,* 401–415. doi:10.1038/nrg1635

Gourley, M. (2004). A subcultural study of recreational ecstasy use. *Journal of Sociology, 40*(1), 59–73. doi:10.1177/1440783304040453

Graham, M. D., Young, R. A., Valach, L., & Wood, R. A. (2008). Addiction as a complex social process: An action theoretical perspective. *Addiction Research and Theory, 16*(2), 121–133. doi:10.1080/16066350701794543

Harakeh, Z., Scholte, R. H. J., de Vries, H., & Engels, R. C. M. E. (2006). Association between personality and adolescent smoking. *Addictive Behaviors, 31,* 232–245. doi:10.1016/j.addbeh.2005.05.003

Hasin, D., Samet, S., Nunes, E., Meydan, J., Matseoane, K., & Waxman, R. (2006). Diagnosis of comorbid psychiatric disorders on substance users assessed with the psychiatric research interview for substance and mental disorders for DSM-IV. *American Journal of Psychiatry, 163,* 689–696. doi: 10.1176/appi.ajp.163.4.689

Hayatbakhsh, M. R., Mamun, A. A., Najim, J. M., O'Callihan, M. J., Bor, W., & Alati, R. (2008). Early childhood predictors of early substance use and substance use disorders: Prospective study. *The Austrailian and New Zealand Journal of Psychiatry, 42*(8), 720–731. doi:10.1080/00048670802206346

Hopwood, C. J., Morey, L. C., Skodol, A. E., Stout, R. L., Yen, S., Ansell, E. B. . . . McGlashan, T. H. (2007). Five-factor model personality traits associated with alcohol-related diagnosis in a clinical sample. *Journal of Studies on Alcohol and Drugs, 68*(3), 455–461. Retrieved from http://goliath.ecnext.com/coms2/gi_0199-7139245/Five-factor-model-personality-traits.html

Humensky, J. L. (2010). Are adolescents with high socioeconomic status more likely to engage in alcohol and illicit drug use in early adulthood? *Substance Abuse Treatment, Prevention, and Policy, 5,* 19–29. doi:10.1186/1747-597x-5-19

Husak, D. N. (2004). The moral relevance of addiction. *Substance Use and Misuse, 39*(3), 399–436. doi:10.1081/JA-120029984

Hyman, S. E. (2007). Addiction: A disease of learning and memory. *Focus, 5,* 220–228. doi:10.1176/appi.ajp.162.8.1414

Jackson, K. F., & LeCroy, C. W. (2009). The influence of race and ethnicity on substance use and negative activity involvement among monoracial and multiracial adolescents of the Southwest.

Journal of Drug Education, 39(2), 195–210. Retrieved from http://www.ncbi.nlm.nih.gov/pubmed/19999705

Jacob, T., Blonigen, D. M., Koenig, L. B., Wachsmuth, W., & Price, R. K. (2010). Course of alcohol dependence among Vietnam combat veterans and nonveteran controls. *Journal of Studies on Alcohol and Drugs, 71*(5), 629–639. Retrieved from http://www.jsad.com/jsad/article/Course_of_Alcohol_Dependence_Among_Vietnam_Combat_Veterans_and_Nonveteran_C/4484.html

Jacob T., Bucholz, K. K., Sartor, C. E., Howell, D. N., & Wood, P. K. (2005). Drinking trajectories form adolescence to the mid-forties among alcohol-dependent males. *Journal of Studies on Alcohol, 66,* 745–755. Retrieved from http://www.highbeam.com/doc/1G1-138998481.html

Jacob T., Koenig, L. B., Howell, D. N., Wood, P. K., & Haber, J. R. (2009). Drinking trajectories from adolescence to the fifties among alcohol-dependent men. *Journal of Studies on Alcohol and Drugs, 70,* 859–869. Retrieved from http://www.highbeam.com/doc/1G1-213956598.html

Jacob, T., Seilhamer, R. A., Bargiel, K., & Howell, D. N. (2006). Reliability of lifetime drinking history among alcohol dependent men. *Psychology- of Addictive Behaviors, 20,* 333–337. doi:10.1037/0893-164X.20.3.333

Jedynak, J. P., Uslaner, J. M., Esteban, J. A., & Robinson, T. E. (2007). Methamphetamine-induced structural plasticity in the dorsal striatum. *European Journal of Neuroscience, 25*(3), 847–853. doi:10.1111/j.1460-9568.2007.05316.x

Jellinek, E. M. (1946). Phases in the drinking history of alcoholics: Analysis of a survey conducted by the official organ of alcoholics anonymous. *Quarterly Journal of Studies on Alcohol, 7,* 1–88. Retrieved from http://jama.ama-assn.org/content/134/3/321.5.full.pdf+html

Jellinek, E. M. (1960). *The disease concept of alcoholism.* New Haven, CT: Hillhouse Press.

Johnston, L. D., O'Malley, P. M., Bachman, J. G., & Schulenberg, J. E. (2011). *Monitoring the Future-national results on adolescent drug use: Overview of key findings, 2010.* Ann Arbor: Institute for Social Research, University of Michigan. Retrieved from http://monitoringthefuture.org/

Kalivas, P. W., & O'Brien, C. (2008). Drug addiction as a pathology of staged neuroplasticity. *Neuropsychopharmacology, 33,* 166–180. doi:10.1038/sj.npp.1301564

Kelly, J. F., Magill, M., & Stout, R. L. (2009). How do people recover from alcohol dependence? A systematic review of the research on mechanisms of behavior change in alcoholics anonymous. *Addiction Research and Theory, 17*(3), 236–259. doi:10.1080/16066350902770458

Kendler, K. S., Prescott, C. A., Myers, J., & Neale, M. C. (2003). The structure of genetic and environmental risk factors for common psychiatric and substance use disorders in men and women. *Archives of General Psychiatry, 60,* 929–937. doi:10.1001/archpsyc.60.9.929

Keyes, K. M., Grant, B. E., & Hasin, D. S. (2008). Evidence for a closing gender gap in alcohol use, abuse, and dependence in the United States population. *Drug and Alcohol Dependence, 93,* 21–29. doi:10.1016/j.drugalcdep.2007.08.017

King, S. M., Keyes, M., Malone, S. M., Elkins, I., Legrand, L. N., Iacono, W. G., & McGrue, M. (2009). Parental alcohol dependence and the transmission of adolescent behavioral disinhibition: A study of adoptive and non-adoptive families. *Addiction, 104*(4), 578–586. doi: 10.1111/j.1360-0443.2008.02469.x

Klaw, E., Horst, D., & Humphreys, K. (2006). Inquirers, triers, and buyers of an alcohol harm reduction self-help organization. *Addiction Research and Theory, 14*(5), 527–535. doi:10.1080/16066350500537580

Kornør, H., & Nordvik, H. (2007). Five-factor model personality traits in opioid dependence. *BMC Psychiatry, 7,* 37–43. doi: 10.1186/1471-244x-7-37

Krueger, R. F., Hicks, B. M., Patrick, C. J., Carlson, S. R., Iacono, W. G., & McGue, M. (2002). Etiologic connection among substance dependence, antisocial behavior, and personality: Modeling the externalizing spectrum. *Journal of Abnormal Psychology, 111*(3), 411–424. doi:10.1037//0021- 843x.111.3.411

Larkin, M., Wood, R. T. A., & Griffiths, M. D. (2006). Towards addiction as relationship. *Addiction Research & Theory, 13,* 245–258. doi:10.1080/16066350500151747

Le Moal, M., & Koob, G. (2007). Drug Addiction: Pathways to the disease and pathophysiological perspectives. *European Neuropsychopharmacology, 17*(6–7), 377–393. doi:10.16/j.euroneuro.2006.10.006

Littlefield, A. K., Sher, K. J., & Wood, P. K. (2009). Is "maturing out" of problematic alcohol involvement related to personality change? *Journal of Abnormal Psychology, 118,* 360–374. doi:10.1037/a0015125

Luo, X., Kranzler, H. R., Zuo, L., Wang, S., & Gelernter, J. (2007). Personality traits of agreeableness and extraversion are associated with ADH4 variation. *Biological Psychiatry, 61*(5), 599–608. doi:10.1016/j.biopsych.2006.05.017

Lynskey, M. T., Nelson, E. C., Neuman, R. J., Bucholz, K. K., Madden, P. A., Knopik, V. S. . . . Heath, A. C. (2005). Limitations of DSM-IV operationalizations of alcohol abuse and dependence in a sample of Australian twins. *Twin Research and Human Genetics, 8*(6), 574–584. doi:10.1375/183242705774860178

Maultsby, Jr., M. C., & Wirga, M. (1998). Behavior therapy. In Friedman, H., Schwarzer, R., Cohen Silver, R., Spiegel, D., Adler, N., Parke R., & Peterson, C. (Eds.), *Encyclopedia of Mental Health* (pp. 221–234). San Diego, CA: Academic Press. Retrieved from http://www.arcobem.com/-publications/Beh-Tx.htm

Moore, S., Montaine-Jaime, L., Carr, L., & Ehlers, C. (2007). Variations in alcohol metabolizing enzymes in people of East-Indian and African descent from Trinidad and Tobago. *Alcohol Research & Health, 30*(1), 18–21. Retrieved from http://www.niaaa.nih.gov

Moos, R. (2007). Theory-based processes that promote the remission of substance use disorders. *Clinical Psychology Review, 27*(5), 537–551. doi:10.1016/j.cpr.2006.12.006

Moss, H. B., Chen, M. C., & Yi, H. (2007). Subtypes of alcohol dependence in a nationally representative sample. *Drug and Alcohol Dependence, 9*(2–3), 149–158. doi:10.1016/j.drugalcdep.2007.05.016

National Institute on Alcohol Abuse and Alcoholism. (1995). *Alcohol alert, No. 30*, PH 359. Bethesda, MD. Retrieved from http://pubs.niaaa.nih.gov/publications/aa30.htm

National Institute on Alcohol Abuse and Alcoholism. (2005). Module 10-H-Ethnicity, Culture and Alcohol, Participant handout. *NIAAA: Social Work Education for the Prevention and Treatment of Alcohol Use Disorders. Updated March 2005.* Retrieved from http://pubs.niaaa.nih.gov/publications/Social/Module10HEthnicity&Culture/Module10H.html

National Prohibition Act of 1919, Pub. L. No. 66-66, 41 Stat. 305 (1919). Retrieved from http://www.gpoaccess.gov/constitution/pdf/con029.pdf

Nelson, A., & Killcross, S. (2006). Amphetamine exposure enhances habit formation. *The Journal of Neuroscience, 26*(14), 3805–3812. doi:10.1523/JNEUROSCI.4305-05.2006

Nurnberger, Jr., J. I., & Bierut, L. J. (2007). Seeking the connections: Alcoholism and our genes. *Scientific American, 296*(4), 46–53. doi:10.1038/scientificamerican0407-46

Ohlms, D. L. (1983). *The disease concept of alcoholism.* Belleville, IL: Gary Whiteaker Co.

Park, S., Kim, H., & Kim, H. (2009). Relationships between parental alcohol abuse and social support, peer substance abuse risk and social support, and substance abuse risk among South Korean adolescents. *Family Therapy, 36*(1), 50–62. Retrieved from http://www.olc.edu/~jolson/socialwork/OnlineLibrary/Park,%202009,%20Relationshipsbetween%20parentalalcohol%20aubuseandsocialsupport

Patock-Peckham, J. A., & Morgan-Lopez, A. A. (2009). Meditational links among parenting styles, perceptions of parental confidence, self-esteem, and depression on alcohol-related problems in emerging adults. *Journal of Studies of Alcohol and Drugs, 70*(2), 215–226. Retrieved from http://www.ncbi.nlm.nih.gov/pmc/articles/PMC2653607/

Peele, S. (2004). 7 tools to beat addiction. New York: Three Rivers Press. Retrieved from http://www.peele.net/7tools/

Philibert, R. A., Gunter, T. D., Beach, S. R., Brody, G. H., Hollenbeck, N., Andersen, A., & Adams, W. (2009). Role of GABRA2 on risk for alcohol, nicotine, and cannabis dependence in Iowa adoption studies. *Psychiatric Genetics, 19*(2), 91–98. doi:10.1097/YPG.0b013e3283208026

Pietrzykowski, A. Z., & Treistman, S. N. (2008). The molecular basis of tolerance. *Alcohol Research & Health, 31*(4). Retrieved from http://www.niaaa.nih.gov

Porrino, L. J., Lyons, D., Smith, H. R., Daunais, J. B., & Nader, M. A. (2004). Cocaine self-administration produces a progressive involvement of limbic, association, and sensorimotor striatal domains. *Journal of Neuroscience, 24*(14), 3554–3562. doi:10.1523/JNEUROSCI.5578-03.2004

Prentiss, C. (2005). *The alcoholism and addiction cure: A holistic approach to total recovery.* Malibu, CA: Power Press. Retrieved from http://www.powerpresspublishing.com/

Prescott, C. A., Sullivan, P. F., Kuo, P-H., Webb, B. T., Vittum, J., Patterson, D. G. . . . Kendler, K. S. (2006). Genomewide linkage study in the Irish affected sib pair study of alcohol dependence: Evidence for a susceptibility region for symptoms of alcohol dependence on chromosome 4. *Molecular Psychiatry, 11*, 603–611. doi:10.1038/sj.mp.4001811

Prescott, C. A., Sullivan, P. F., Myers, J. M., Patterson, D. G., Devitt, M., Halberstadt, L. J. . . . Kendler, K. S. (2005). The Irish affected sib pair study of alcohol dependence: Study methodology and validation of diagnosis by interview and family history. *Alcoholism: Clinical & Experimental Research, 29*(3), 417–429. doi:10.1097/01.ALC.0000156085.50418.07

Quertemont, E., & Didone, V. (2006). Role of acetaldehyde in mediating the pharmacological and behavioral effects of alcohol. *Alcohol Research & Health, 29*(4), 258–265. Retrieved from http://pubs.niaaa.nih.gov/publications/arh294/258-265.htm

Riley, B. P., Kalsi, G., Kuo, P-H., Vladimirov, V., Thiselton, D. L., & Kendler, K. S. (2006). Alcohol dependence is associated with the ZNF699 gene, a human locus related to drosophila hangover, in the Irish affected sib pair study of alcohol dependence (IASPSAD) sample. *Molecular Psychiatry, 11*, 1025–1031. doi:10.1038/sj.mp.4001891

Room, R. (2005). Stigma, social inequality and alcohol and drug use. *Drug and Alcohol Review, 24*(2), 143–155. doi:10.1080/09595230500102434

Saatcioglu, O., Erim, R., & Cakmak, D. (2006). Role of family in alcohol and substance abuse. *Psychiatry and Clinical Neurosciences, 60*, 125–132.

Schlaepfer, I. R., Hoft, N. R., & Ehringer, M. A. (2008). The genetic components of alcohol and nicotine co-addiction: From genes to behavior. *Current Drug Abuse Review, 1*(2), 124–134. Retrieved from http://www.ncbi.nlm.nih.gov/pmc/articles/PMC2600802/

Scholz, H., Franz, M., & Heberlein, U. (2005). The *"hangover" gene defines a stress pathway required for ethanol tolerance development* [letter]. *Nature, 436*(7052), 845–847. doi: 10.1038/nature03864

Scholz, H., Ramond, J., Singh, C. M., & Heberlein, L. (2000). Functional ethanol tolerance in *Drosophila. Neuron, 28*(1), 261–271. Retrieved from http://www.ncbi.nlm.nih.gov/pubmed/11086999

Schuckit, M., Smith, T., & Danko, G. (2007). A comparison of factors associated with substance-induced versus independent depressions. *Journal of Studies of Alcohol and Drugs, 68*(6), 805–812. Retrieved from http://goliath.ecnext.com/coms2/gi_0199-7172676/A-comparison-of-factors-associated.html

Scott, D., & Taylor, R. (2007). Health related effects of genetic variations of alcohol metabolizing enzymes in African Americans. *Alcohol Research & Health, 30*(1), 18–21. http://www.niaaa.nih.gov

Sher, K. J., Dick, D. M., Crabbe, J. C., Hutchison, K. E., O'Malley, S. S., & Heath, A. C. (2010). Consilient research approaches in studying gene x environment interactions in alcohol research. *Addiction Biology, 15*, 2000–2016. Retrieved from http://www.ncbi.nlm.nih.gov/pubmed/20148780

Sigvardsson, S., Bohman, M., & Cloninger, C. R. (1996). Replication of the Stockholm Adoption Study of alcoholism: Confirmatory cross-fostering analysis. *Archives of General Psychiatry, 53*(8), 681–687.

Sinha, R., Fox, H., Hong, K. A., Bergquist, K., Bhagwagar, Z., & Siedlarz, K. M. (2009). Enhanced negative emotion and alcohol craving, and altered physiological responses following stress and cue exposure in alcohol dependent individuals. *Neuropsychopharmaclology, 34*(5), 1198–1208. doi:10.1038/npp.2008.78

Sjoquist, B., Perdahl, E., & Winblad, B. (1983). The effect of alcoholism on salsolinol and biogenic amines in human brain. *Drug and Alcohol Dependence, 12*(1), 15–23. Retrieved from http://www.ncbi.nlm.nih.gov/pubmed/6196169?dopt=Abstract

Substance Abuse and Mental Health Services Administration, Office of Applied Studies. (2007a). *The NSDUH report: Illicit drug use, by race/ethnicity, in metropolitan and non-metropolitan counties: 2004 and 2005.* Rockville, MD. Retrieved from http://store.samhsa.gov/product/NSDUH07-0621

Substance Abuse and Mental Health Services Administration, Office of Applied Studies. (2007b). *The NSDUH report: Substance use and substance disorders among American Indians and Alaska natives [In Brief].* Rockville, MD. Retrieved from http://www.oas.samhsa.gov/2k7/AmIndians/AmIndians.htm

Terracciano, A., Löckenhoff, C. E., Crum, R. M., Bienvenu, J. O., & Costa, Jr., P. T. (2008). Five-factor model personality profiles of drug users. *BMC Psychiatry, 8*, 22–32. doi:10.1186/1471-244X-8-22

Tu, A. W., Ratner, P. A., & Johnson, J. L. (2008). Gender differences in the correlates of adolescents' cannabis use. *Substance Use and Misuse, 43*(10), 1438–1463. doi:10.1080/10826080802238140

Urberg, K., Goldstein, M. S., & Toro, P. A. (2005). Supportive relationships as a moderator of the effects of parent and peer drinking on adolescent drinking. *Journal of Research on Adolescence, 15*, 1–19. doi:10.1111/j.1532-7795.2005.00084.x

U.S. Department of Health and Human Services. (2008). Alcohol: A women's health issue. *National Institutes of Health: The Office of Research on Women's Health. Revised 2008.* Retrieved from http://pubs.niaaa.nih.gov/publications/brochurewomen/women.htm

van der Zwaluw, C. S., & Engels, R. C. (2009). Gene environment interactions and alcohol use and dependence: Current status and future challenges. *Addiction, 104*, 907–914. doi:10.1111/j.1360-0443.2009.02563.x

Veal, M. L., & Ross, L. T. (2006). Gender, alcohol consumption, and parental monitoring. *The Journal of Psychology, 140*(1), 41–53. doi:10.3200/JRLP.140.1.41-52

Vengeliene, V., Bilbao, A., Molander, A., & Spanagel, R. (2008). Neuropharmacology of alcohol addiction. *British Journal of Pharmacology, 154*, 299–315. doi:10.1038/bjp.2008.30

Weiss, F. (2005). Neurobiology of craving, conditioned reward and relapse. *Current Opinion in Pharmacology, 5*(1), 9–19. doi:10.1016/j.coph.2004.11.001

West, R. (2006). *Theory of Addiction.* Oxford, UK: Blackwell. http://www.blackwellpublishing.com/

White, H. R., McMorris, B. J., Catalano, R. F., Fleming, C. B., Haggerty, K. P., & Abbot, R. D. (2006). Increases in alcohol and marijuana use during the transition out of high school into emerging adulthood: The effects of leaving home, going to college, and high school protective factors. *Journal of Studies on Alcohol, 67*, 810–822. Retrieved from http://www.ncbi.nlm.nih.gov/pmc/articles/PMC2314672/

White, W. (2009). Long-term strategies to reduce the stigma attached to addiction, treatment, and recovery within the City of Philadelphia (with particular reference to medication-assisted treatment/recovery). Philadelphia: Department of Behavioral Health and Mental Retardation Services. Retrieved from http://www.facesandvoicesofrecovery.org/pdf/White/StigmaMedicationTreatment.pdf

White, W. L., Evans, A. C., & Lamb, R. (2009). Reducing addiction-related social stigma. *Counselor, 10*(6), 52–58. Retrieved from http://www.williamwhitepapers.com/pr/2009ReducingSocialStigma.pdf

Windle, M., & Scheidt, D. M. (2004). Alcoholic subtypes: are two sufficient? *Addiction, 99*, 1508–1519. doi: 10.1111/j.1360-0443.2004.00878.x

Yin, H. H. (2008). From actions to habits: Neuroadaptations leading to dependence. *Alcohol Research & Health, 31*(4), 340–344. Retrieved from http://goliath.ecnext.com/coms2/gi_0199-10624756/From-actions-to-habits-neuroadaptations.html

Yin, H. H., & Knowlton, B. J. (2005). Addiction and learning. In R. W. Weirs & A. W. Stacy (Eds.), *Handbook of implicit cognition and addiction* (pp. 167–183). Thousand Oaks, CA: Sage. Retrieved from http://www.sagepub.com

Yin, H. H., Park, B. S., Adermark, L., & Lovinger, D. M. (2007). Ethanol reverses the direction of long-term synaptic plasticity in the dorsomedial striatum. *European Journal of Neuroscience, 25*, 3226–3232. doi:10.1111/j.1460-9568.2007.05606.x

Young, R. A., Valach, L., & Domene, J. F. (2005). The action-project method in counseling psychology. *Journal of Counseling Psychology, 52*, 215–223. doi:10.1037/0022-0167.52.2.215

Chapter 5

American Psychiatric Association. (2010). DSM-5: The future of psychiatric diagnosis. Retrieved from http://www.dsm5.org

American Society of Addiction Medicine. (2007). American Society of Addiction Medicine (ASAM) publishes Second Edition—Revised of Patient Placement Criteria (ASAM PPC-2R). Chevy Chase, MD: Author. Retrieved from http://198.65.155.172/PatientPlacementCriteria.html

Coombs, R. H., & Howatt, W. A. (2005). *The addiction counselor's desk reference.* Hoboken, NJ: Wiley.

Doweiko, H. E. (2011). *Concepts of chemical dependency* (8th ed.). Belmont, CA: Brooks/Cole.

Hart, C. L., & Ksir, C. (2011). *Drugs, society & human behavior* (14th ed.). New York: McGraw Hill.

Kinney, J. (2006). *Loosening the grip: A handbook of alcohol information* (8th ed.). New York: McGraw-Hill.

Lewis, J. A., Dana, R. Q., & Blevins, G. A. (2011). *Substance abuse counseling: An individual approach* (4th ed.). Belmont, CA: Brooks/Cole.

Miller, Franklin G. (2007). SASSI-3 User's Guide: A Quick Reference for Administration and Scoring. Bloomington: Baugh Enterprises.

Myers, P. L., & Salt, N. R. (2007). *Becoming an addictions counselor: A comprehensive text.* Boston: Jones and Bartlett.

Nace, E. P., & Tinsley, J. A. (2007). *Patients with substance abuse problems: Effective identification, diagnosis, and treatment.* New York: W. W. Norton.

National Institute on Alcohol Abuse and Alcoholism. (2003). *Assessing alcohol problems: A guide for clinicians and researchers* (2nd ed.). National Institute of Health: Bethesda, MD.

National Institute on Drug Abuse. (2009). *Principles of drug addiction treatment: A research-based guide* (2nd ed.). National Institutes of Health, U.S. Department of Health and Human Services.

Prochaska, J. O., & DiClemente, C. C. (1983). Stages and process of self-change of smoking; toward an integrative model of change. *Journal of Consulting and Clinical Psychology, 51*(3), 390–395.

Shepard, D. S., Strickler, G. K., McAuliffe, W. E., Beaston-Blaakman, A., Rahman, M., & Anderson, T. E. (2005). Unmet need for substance abuse treatment of adults in Massachusetts. *Administration and Policy in Mental Health, 32*(4), 403–426.

Substance Abuse and Mental Health Services Administration. (2009). *Brief strategic family therapy.* National Registry of Evidence-based Program and Pracices. Retrieved from http://nrepp.samhsa.gov/programfulldetails.asp?PROGRAM_ID=157

Chapter 6

About the army substance abuse program. (2005). Retrieved from http://www.armystudyguide.com

Agnew, R., Mathews, S. K., Bucher, J., Welcher, A. N., & Keyes, C. (2008). Socioeconomic status, economic problems, and delinquency. *Youth & Services, 40*(2), 159–181.

Baron, M., Erlenbusch, B., Moran, C. F., O'Conner, K., Rice, K., & Rodriguez, J. (2008). *Best practices manual for discharge planning: Mental health & substance abuse facilities, hospitals, foster care, prisons and jails.* Los Angeles Coalition to End Hunger & Homelessness.

Bell, M. L., Padget, A., Kelley-Baker, T., & Rider, R. (2007). Can first and second grade students benefit from an alcohol use prevention program? *Journal of Child & Adolescent Substance Abuse, 16*(3), 89–107.

Center for Substance Abuse Treatment. (2009). *Detoxification and substance abuse treatment training manual.* HHS Publication No. (SMA) 094331. Rockville, MD: Substance Abuse and Mental Health Services Administration.

Derry, J. (2009). *The Minnesota model of addiction treatment – What is it, what works, and what's next?* Self improvement: addictions. Retrieved from http://EzineArticles.com/?expert=John_Derry

Dombeck, M. (2005). *Group and individual therapy formats for alcohol and substance abuse.* Retrieved from MentalHelp.net: www.mentalhelp.net/poc/

Doweiko, H. E. (2011). *Concepts of chemical dependency* (8th ed.). Belmont, CA: Brooks/Cole.

Fisher, G. L., & Roget, N. A. (2009). *Encyclopedia of substance abuse prevention, treatment, and recovery.* California: Sage.

Grohsman, B. (2009). *In drug treatment centers: Drug treatment.* Retrieved from http://www.treatment-centers.net/drug-treatment.html

Hoover, E. (2008). For MADD, the legal drinking age is not up for debate. *Chronicle of Higher Education, 55*(11), 1.

Humphreys, K., & Wing, S. (2004). Self-help organizations for alcohol and drug problems: Toward evidence-based practice and policy. *Journal of Substance Abuse Treatment, 26,* 151–158.

Johnston, L. D., O'Malley, P. M., Bachman, J. G., & Schulenberg, J. E. (2010). *Monitoring the future: National results on adolescent drug use. Overview of key findings, 2009.* NIH Publication No. 10-7583.

Laban, R. L. (1997). *Chemical dependency treatment planning handbook.* Springfield, IL: Thomas.

Marsh, J. C., Cao, D., & Shin, H. C. (2009). Closing the need-service gap: Gender differences in matching services to client needs in comprehensive substance abuse treatment. *Social Work Research, 33*(3), 183–192.

Moore, G. F., Rothwell, R., and Segrott, J. (2010). An exploratory study of the relationship between parental attitudes and behavior and young people's consumption of alcohol. Substance Abuse Treatment, Prevention, and Policy, 5(6),1–14.

National Institute on Drug Abuse. (2010). *NIDA info facts: High school and youth trends approaches.* Retrieved from NIDA website: http://www.nida.nih.gov/pdf/infofacts/HSYouthTrends09.pdf

O'Conner, E. E., Dearing, E., & Collins, B. A. (2011). Teacher-Child relationship and behavior problem trajectories in elementary school. *American Educational Research Journal, 48*(1), 120–162.

Owen, P. (2000). Minnesota model: Description of counseling approach. In J. J. Boren, L. S. Onken, & K. M. Carroll (Eds.), *Approaches to drug abuse counseling* (NIH Publication No. 00-4151, pp. 117–125). Bethesda, MD: National Institutes of Health.

Perkinson, R. R., & Jongsma, A. E. (2009). *The addiction treatment planner (Practice Planners).* Hoboken, NJ: Wiley.

Ruiz, B. S., Stevens, S. J., Fuhriman, J., Bogart, J. G., & Korchmaros, J. D. (2009). A juvenile drug court model in south Arizona: Substance abuse, delinquency, and sexual risk outcomes by gender and race/ethnicity. *Journal of Offender Rehabilitation, 48*(5), 416–438.

RTI International. (2006). *2005 Department of defense survey of health-related behaviors among active duty military personnel.* Research Triangle Park, NC: RTI International. Retrieved from http://www.ha.osd .mil/special_reports/2005_Health_Behaviors_ Survey_1-07.pdf

SE Missouri Community Treatment Center. (2008). *Therapy & rehab services. Partial hospitalization treatment.* Retrieved from http:// therapistunlimited.com/index/Articles/Therapy+ &+Rehab+Services/Partial+hospitalization~day+ treatment

Stinchfield, R., & Owen, P. (1998). Hazelden's model of treatment and its outcome. *Addictive Behaviors, 23*(5), 669–683.

Timko, C., Billow, R., & DeBenedetti, A. (2006). Determinants of 12-step group affiliation and moderators of the affiliation-abstinence relationship. *Drug Alcohol Dependence, 28:83*(2), 111–121.

Troubled teen 101 – Help for troubled teen issues. (2009). *Components of effective programs.* Retrieved from http://www.troubledteen101.com/ articles22.html

Volkow, N.D. (2009). *Substance abuse among troops, veterans, and their families.* National Institute on Drug Abuse, *22*(5). Retrieved from http://www.nida .nih.gov/nida_notes/nnvol22n5/dirrepvol22n5 .html

Ybrandt, H. (2010). Risky alcohol use, peer and family relationships and legal involvement in adolescents with antisocial problems. *Journal of Drug Education, 40*(3), 245–264.

Chapter 7

Bandura, A. (1994). Self-efficacy. In V. S. Ramachaudram (Ed.), *Encyclopedia of human behavior, 4* (pp. 71–81). New York: Academic Press.

Bandura, A., & Schunk, D. A. (1981). Cultivating competence, self-efficacy, and intrinsic interest through proximal self-motivation. *Journal of Personality and Social Psychology, 41*(3), 586–598.

Beaumont, S. L. (2009). Identity processing and personal wisdom: An information-oriented identity style predicts self-actualization and self-transcendence. *Identity: An International Journal of Theory, 9,* 95–115.

Beck, A. T., & Weishaar, M. E. (2005). Cognitive therapy. In R. J. Corsini & D. Wedding (Eds.), *Current psychotherapies* (7th ed.). Belmont, CA: Brooks/Cole.

Brewer, J., Sinha, R., Chen, J., Michalsen, R., Babuscio, T., . . . Rounsaville, B. J. (2009). Mindfulness training and stress reactivity in substance abuse: Results from a randomized controlled stage I pilot study. *Substance Abuse, 30*(4), 306–317.

Brooks, F., & McHenry, B. (2009). *A contemporary approach to substance abuse and addiction counseling.* Alexandria, VA: American Counseling Association.

Carroll, K., & Onken, L. S. (2007). Behavioral therapies for drug abuse. *Focus: The Journal of Lifelong Learning in Psychiatry, 5*(2), 240–248.

Ciccocioppo, R., Economidou, D., Rimondini, R., Sommer, W., Massi, M., & Heilig, M. (2007). Buprenorphine reduces alcohol drinking through activation of the nociception/Orphanin FQ – NOP receptor system. *Biological Psychiatry, 61*(1), 4–12.

Courbasson, C. M., & Nishikaway, Y. (2010). Cognitive behavioral group therapy for patients with co-existing social anxiety disorder and substance use disorders: A pilot study. *Cognitive Therapy and Research, 34,* 82–91.

DeFulio, A., Donlin, W. D., Wong, C. J., & Silverman, K. (2009). Employment-based abstinence reinforcement as a maintenance intervention for the treatment of cocaine dependence: A randomized controlled trial. *Addiction, 104,* 1530–1538.

Des Jarlais, D. C., McKnight, C., Goldblatt, C., & Purchase, D. (2009). Doing harm reduction better: Syringe exchange in the United States. *Society for the Study of Addiction, 104,* 1441–1446.

DiClemente, C. C. (2006). *Addiction and change: How addictions develop and addicted people recover.* New York: Guilford.

Doweiko, H. F. (2011). *Concepts of chemical dependency* (7th ed.). Pacific Grove, CA: Brooks/Cole.

Duff, C. T., & Bedi, R. P. (2010). Counselor behaviors that predict therapeutic alliance: From the client's perspective. *Counseling Psychology Quarterly, 23*(1), 91–110.

Ekendahl, M. (2007). Will and skill–An exploratory study of substance abusers' attitudes toward lifestyle change. *European Addiction Research, 13,* 148–155.

Fareed, A., Vayalapalli, S., Casarella, J., Amar, R., & Drexler, K. (2010). Heroin anticraving medications: A systematic review. *American Journal of Drug & Alcohol Abuse, 36*(6), 332–341.

Fields, D., & Roman S. (2010). Total quality management and performance in substance abuse treatment centers. *Health Services Research, 45,* 6 Part 1, 1630–1650.

Finch, J. W., Kamien, J., & Amass, L. (2007). Two-year experience with buprenorphine-naloxone (suboxone) for maintenance treatment of opioid dependence within a private practice setting. *Journal of Addiction Medicine, 1*(2), 104–110.

Gossop, M., & Carroll, K. M. (2006). Disulfiram, cocaine, and alcohol: Two outcomes for the price of one? *Alcohol and Alcoholism, 41*(2), 119–120.

Greene, L., & Burke, G. (2007). Beyond self-actualization. *Journal of Health and Human Services Administration, Fall,* 116–127.

Harm Reduction Coalition, http://harmreduction.org

Hathaway, A. D., Callaghan, R. C., Macdonald, S., & Erickson, P. G. (2009). Cannabis dependence as a primary drug use-related problem: The case for harm reduction–oriented treatment options. *Substance Use and Misuse, 44,* 990–1008.

Kabat-Zinn, J. (2005). *Coming to our senses.* New York: Hyperion.

Krampe, H., & Ehrenreich, H. (2010). Supervised disulfiram as adjunct to psychotherapy in alcoholism treatment. *Current Pharmaceutical Design, 16*(19), 2076–2090.

Lewis, J. A., Dana, R. W., & Blevins, G. A. (2010). *Substance abuse counseling: An individual approach* (4th ed.). Pacific Grove, CA: Brooks/Cole.

Marlatt, G. A. (1998). Highlights of harm reduction: A personal report from the First National Harm Reduction Conference in the United States. In G. A. Marlatt (Ed.), *Harm reduction* (pp. 3–29). New York: Guilford.

Maslow, A. H. (1968). *Toward psychology of being* (2nd ed.). Princeton, NJ: Van Nostrand Reinhold.

Mason, S. J., Deane, F. P., Kelly, P. J., & Crowe, T. R. (2009). Do spirituality and religiosity help in the management of cravings in substance abuse treatment? *Substance Use & Misuse, 44,* 1926–1940.

Mason, B. J., Goodman, A. M., Chabac, S., & Lehert, P. (2006). Effect of oral acamprosate on abstinence in patients with alcohol dependence in a double-blind, placebo controlled trial: The role of patient motivation. *Journal of Psychiatric Research, 40*(5), 383–393.

Miller, W. R., & Rollnick, S. (2009). Ten things that motivational interviewing is not. *Behavioral and Cognitive Psychotherapy, 37,* 1.

Moos, R. H. (2008). Active ingredients of substance use focused self-help groups. *Addiction, 103,* 387–396.

Morley, K. C., Teeson, M., Reid, S. C., Sannibale, C., Thomsom, C., Phung, N., . . . Haber, P. (2006). Naltrexone versus acamprosate in the treatment of alcohol dependence: A multi-centre, randomized double-blind, placebo controlled trial. *Addiction, 101*(10), 1451–1462.

Moss-King, D. (2009). *Unresolved grief and loss issues related to heroin recovery. Grief and loss issues in heroin recovery.* Germany: VDM Verlag Dr. Müller.

Moyers, T. B., Martin, T., Houck, J. M., Christopher, P. J., & Tonigan, J. (2009). From in-session behaviors to drinking outcomes: A causal chain for motivational interviewing. *Journal of Consulting and Clinical Psychology, 77,* 1113–1124.

Mudunkotuwe, J., Arnone, D., & Abou-Saleh, M. T. (2006). Pharmacological treatments of alcohol dependence. *Arab Journal of Psychiatry, 17*(1), 52–65.

National Institute on Drug Abuse. (2009). *Treatment approaches for drug addiction.* Washington, DC: Author.

O'Connell, O. (2009). Introducing mindfulness as an adjunct treatment in an established residential drug and alcohol facility. *The Humanistic Psychologist, 37,* 178–191.

Orman, J. S., & Keating, G. M. (2009). Spotlight on buprenorphine/naloxone in the treatment of opioid dependence. *CNS Drugs, 23*(10), 899–902.

Patra, J., Gilksman, L., Fischer, B., Newton-Taylor, B., Belenko, S., Ferrari, M., . . . Rehm, J. (2010). Factors associated with treatment compliance and its effects on retention among participants in a court mandated treatment program. *Contemporary Drug Problems, 37,* 289–313.

Redko, C., Rapp, R. C., & Carlson. R. G. (2007). Pathways of substance users linking (or not) with treatment. *Journal of Drug Issues. Summer 37*(3), 597–617.

Rogers, C. R. (1977). *Carl Rogers on personal power.* New York: Delacorte Press.

Rothenberg, L. (1988). The ethics of intervention. *Alcoholism & Addiction, 9*(1), 22–24.

Senbanjo, R., Wolff, K., Marshall, J., & Strang, J. (2009). Persistence of heroin use despite methadone treatment: Poor coping self-efficacy predicts continued heroin use. *Drug and Alcohol Review, 28,* 608–615.

Shearer, J. (2007). Psychosocial approaches to psychostimulant dependence: A systematic review. *Journal of Substance Abuse Treatment, 32*(1), 41–52.

Smith, D. E., Lee, D. R., & Davidson, L. D. (2010). Health care equality and parity for treatment of addictive disease. *Journal of Psychoactive Drugs, 41*(2), 121–126.

Suh, J. J., Pettinati, H. M., Kampman, K. M., & O'Brien, C. (2006). The status of disulfiram: A half century later. *Journal of Clinical Psychopharmacology, 26*(3), 290–302.

Vader, A. M., Walters, S. T., Houck, J. M., Prabhu, G. C., & Field, C. A. (2010). The language of motivational interviewing and feedback: Counselor language, client language, and client drinking outcomes. *Psychology of Addictive Behaviors, 24*(2), 190–197.

Walker, M. A. (2009). Program characteristics and the length of time clients are in substance abuse treatment. *Journal of Behavioral Health Services and Research, 36*(3), 330–342.

Wesson, D. R., & Smith, D. E. (2010). Buprenorphine in the treatment of opiate dependence. *Journal of Psychoactive Drugs, 42*(2), 161–175.

West, S. (2008). The utilization of vocational rehabilitation services in substance abuse treatment facilities in the U.S. *Journal of Vocational Rehabilitation, 29*(2), 71–75.

Chapter 8

Agazarian, Y. M. (1997). *Systems-centered therapy for groups.* New York: Guilford.

Alcoholics Anonymous World Services. (2002). *Twelve steps and twelve traditions.* Center City, MN: Hazelden.

Alcoholics Anonymous World Services. (2007). *Alcoholics Anonymous: The big book online* (4th ed.). Retrieved from http://www.aa.org/bigbookonline/

Alexander, F., & French, T. M. (1946). *Psychoanalytic therapy: Principles and application.* New York: Ronald.

American Group Psychotherapy Association. (n.d.). Certification. Retrieved from http://www.agpa.org/stdnt/certreq.html

Amrhein, P. C., Miller, W. R., Yahne, C. E., Palmer, M., & Fulcher, L. (2003). Client commitment language during Motivational Interviewing predicts drug use outcomes. *Journal of Consulting and Clinical Psychology, 71,* 862–878. doi: 10.1037/022-006X.71.5.862

Anton, R. F., O'Malley, S. S., Ciraulo, D. A., Cisler, R. A., Couper, D., Donovan, D. M., et al. (2006). Combined pharmacotherapies and behavioral interventions for alcohol dependence: The COMBINE study: A randomized controlled trial. *Journal of the American Medical Association, 295,* 2003–2017. doi: 10.1001/jama.295.17.2003

APA Presidential Task Force on Evidence-Based Practice. (2006). Evidence-based practice in psychology. *American Psychologist, 61,* 271–285. doi: 10.1037/0003-066x.61.4.271

Bandura, A. (1999). Social cognitive theory of personality. In L. A. Pervin & O. A. John (Eds.), *Handbook of personality: Theory and research* (2nd ed., pp. 154–196). New York: Guilford.

Bernard, H. S. (2000). The future of training and credentialing in group psychotherapy. *Group, 24,* 167–175. doi: 10.1023/A:1007531932047

Betty Ford Center. (n.d.). Welcome to alumni services. Retrieved from http://www.bettyfordcenter.org/alumni/

Bloom, S. (1997). *Creating sanctuary: Toward an evolution of sane societies.* New York: Routledge.

Bogart, C. J., & Pearce, C. E. (2003). "Thirteenth stepping": Why Alcoholics Anonymous is not always a safe place for women. *Journal of Addictions Nursing, 14,* 43–47. doi: 10.1080/10884600305373

Bogenschultz, M. P., Tonigan, J. S., & Miller, W. R. (2006). Examining the effects of alcoholism typology and AA attendance on self-efficacy as a mechanism of change. *Journal of Studies on Alcohol, 67,* 562–567.

Bowen, M. (1974). Alcoholism as viewed through the family systems theory and family psychotherapy. *Annals of the New York Academy of Science, 233,* 115–122. doi: 10.1111/j.1749-6632.1974.tb40288.x

Breslin, C., Li, S., Sdao-Jarvie, K., Tupker, E., & Ittig-Deland, V. (2002). Brief treatment for young substance abusers: A pilot study in an addiction treatment setting. *Psychology of Addictive Behaviors, 7,* 10–16. doi: 10.1037/0893-164x.16.1.10

Brocato, J., & Wagner, E. F. (2008). Predictors of retention in an alternative-to-prison substance abuse treatment program. *Criminal Justice and Behavior, 3*(5), 99–119. doi: 10.1177/0093854807309429

Burke, B. L., Arkowitz, H., & Menchola, M. (2003). The efficacy of Motivational Interviewing: A meta-analysis of controlled clinical trials. *Journal of Consulting and Clinical Psychology, 71,* 843–861. doi: 10.1037/0022-006x.71.5.843

Byrne, M., Edmundson, R., & Rankin, E. D. (2005). Symptom reduction and enhancement of psychosocial functioning utilizing a relational group treatment program for dependent/codependent population. *Alcoholism Treatment Quarterly, 23,* 69–84. doi: 10.1300/J020v23n04_05

Cardoso, E. S., Pruett, S. R., Chan, F., & Tansey, T. N. (2006). Substance abuse assessment and treatment: The current training and practice of APA Division 22 members. *Rehabilitation Psychology, 51,* 175–178. doi: 10.1037/0090-5550.51.2.175

Carnes, P. (1993). *A gentle path through the twelve steps.* Center City, MN: Hazelden.

Center for Substance Abuse Prevention. (March 2005). SAMHSA model programs: Effective substance abuse and mental health programs for every community. Retrieved from http://www.modelprograms.samhsa.gov/template_cf.cfm?page-model_list

Center for Substance Abuse Treatment. (2005). *Substance abuse treatment for persons with co-occurring disorders.* Treatment Improvement Protocol (TIP) Series 42. DHHS Publication No. (SMA) 05-3922. Rockville, MD: Substance Abuse and Mental Health Services Administration.

Chan, J. G. (2003). An examination of family involved approaches to alcoholism treatment. *The Family Journal: Counseling and Therapy for Couples and Families, 11,* 129–138. doi: 10.1177/1066480702250149

Chi, F. W., & Weisner, C. M. (2008). Nine-year psychiatric trajectories and substance use outcomes: An application of the group-based modeling approach. *Evaluation Review, 32,* 39–58. doi: 10.1177/0193841X07307317

Coche, J., & Coche, E. (1990). *Couples group psychotherapy: A clinical practice model.* New York: Brunner/Mazel.

Cohen, L. R., & Hien, D. A. (2006). Treatment outcomes for women with substance abuse and PTSD who have experienced complex trauma. *Psychiatric Services, 57,* 100–106. doi: 10.1176/appi.ps.57.1.100

Connors, J. V., & Caple, R. B. (2005). A review of group systems theory. *Journal for Specialists in Group Work, 30,* 93–110. doi: 10.1080/01933920590925940

Corey, G. (2004). *Theory and practice of group counseling* (6th ed.). Belmont, CA: Brooks/Cole-Thomson.

Corley, M. D., & Schneider, J. P. (2002). *Disclosing secrets: When, to whom, and how much to reveal.* Wickenburg, AZ: Gentle Path.

Dayton, T. (2000). *Trauma and addiction: Ending the cycle of pain through emotional literacy.* Deerfield Beach, FL: Health Communications.

deRuiter, W., & Faulkner, G. (2006). Tobacco harm reduction strategies: The case for physical activity. *Nicotine & Tobacco Research, 8,* 157–168. doi: 10.1080/14622200500494823

D'Sylva, F., Graffam, J., Hardcastle, L., & Shinkfield, A. (2010). Analysis of the Stages of Change Model of Drug and Alcohol Treatment Readiness Among Prisoners. International Journal of Offender Therapy and Comparative Criminology, doi: 10.1177/0306624X10392531

Dishion, T., McCord, J., & Poulin, F. (1999). When interventions harm: Peer groups and problem behavior. *American Psychologist, 54,* 755–764. doi: 10.1037/0003-066X.54.9.755

Dishion, T. J., & Stormshak, E. A. (2007). *Intervening in children's lives: An ecological, family-centered approach to mental health care.* Washington, DC: American Psychological Association.

Dodd, M. H. (1997). Social model of recovery: Origin, early features, changes, and future. *Journal of Psychoactive Drugs, 29,* 133–139.

Dunn, C., DeRoo, L., & Rivara, F. P. (2001). The use of brief interventions adapted from Motivational Interviewing across behavioral domains: A systematic review. *Addiction, 96,* 1725–1742. doi: 10.1080/09652140120089481

Dykeman, C., & Appleton, V. E. (2002). Group counseling: The efficacy of group work. In D. Capuzzi & D. R. Gross (Eds.), *Introduction to group counseling* (3rd ed., pp. 119–153). Denver, CO: Love.

Evans, K., & Sullivan, J. M. (1995). *Treating addicted survivors of trauma.* New York: Guilford.

Fayne, M., & Silvan, M. (1999). Treatment issues in the group psychotherapy of addicted physicians. *Psychiatric Quarterly, 70,* 123–135.

Firestone, R. W., Firestone, L. A., & Catlett, J. (2006). *Sex and love in intimate relationships.* Washington, DC: American Psychological Association.

Fossum, M. A., & Mason, M. J. (1986). *Facing shame: Families in recovery.* New York: Norton.

Fox, R. (1962). Group psychotherapy with alcoholics. *International Journal of Group Psycho-therapy, 12,* 56–63.

Framo, J. L. (1992). *Family-of-origin therapy: An intergenerational approach.* New York: Brunner/Mazel.

Free, M. L. (1999). *Cognitive therapy in groups: Guidelines and resources.* New York: Wiley.

Freud, S. (1966). *The ego and mechanisms of defense.* New York: International Universities Press.

Freyer, J., Tonigan, J. S., Keller, S., Rumph, H. J., John, U., & Hapke, U. (2005). Readiness for change and readiness for help-seeking: A composite assessment of client motivation. *Alcohol & Alcoholism, 40,* 540–544. doi: 10.1093alcalc/agh195

Fry, C. L., Cvetovski, S., & Cameron, J. (2006). The place of supervised injecting facilities within harm reduction: Evidence, ethics and policy. *Addiction, 101,* 465–467. doi: 10.1111/j.1360-0443.2006.01386.x

Futterman, R., Lorente, M., & Silverman, S. W. (2005). Beyond harm reduction: A new model of substance abuse treatment further integrating psychological techniques. *Journal of Psychotherapy Integration, 15,* 3–18. doi: 10.1037/1053-0479.15.1.3

Galanter, M. (2006). Spirituality and addiction: A research and clinical perspective. *American Journal on Addictions, 15,* 286–292. doi: 10.1080/10550490600754325

Goldman, D., Oroszi, G., O'Malley, S., & Anton, R. (2005). COMBINE genetics study: The pharmacogenetics of alcoholism treatment response: Genes and mechanisms. *Journal of Studies on Alcoholism, 66,* 56–64.

Gondolf, E. W. (2008). Program completion in specialized batterer counseling for African-American men. *Journal of Interpersonal Violence, 23,* 94–116. doi: 10.1177/0886260507307912

Gorski, T. T. (1993, March/April). Relapse prevention: A state of the art overview. *Addiction & Recovery,* 25–27.

Gottman, J. M. (1999). *The marriage clinic: A scientifically based marital therapy.* New York: Norton.

Guajardo, H. S., Bagladi, V. L., & Kushner, D. L. (2004). Integrative psychotherapy in addictive disorders. *Journal of Psychotherapy Integration, 14,* 290–306. doi: 10.1037/1053-0479.14.3.290

Hadley, J. A., Holloway, E. L., & Mallinckrodt, B. (1993). Common aspects of object relations and self-representations in offspring from disparate dysfunctional families. *Journal of Counseling Psychology, 40,* 348–356. doi: 10.1037/0022-0167.40.3.348

Heather, N. (2006). Controlled drinking, harm reduction and their roles in response to alcohol-related problems. *Addiction Research and Theory, 14,* 7–18. doi: 10.1080/16066350500489170

Hoag, M. J., & Burlingame, G. M. (1997). Evaluating the effectiveness of child and adolescent group treatment: A meta-analytic review. *Journal of Clinical Child Psychology, 26,* 234–246. doi: 10.1207/s15374424jccp2603_2

Horner, A. J. (1991). *Psychoanalytic object relations theory.* Northvale, NJ: Aronson.

Howard, K. I., Kopta, S. M., Krause, M. S., & Orlinsky, D. E. (1986). The dose-effect relationship in psychotherapy. *American Psychologist, 41,* 159–164. doi: 10.1037/0003-066X.41.2.159

Humphreys, K. (2003). A research based analysis of the Moderation Management controversy. *Psychiatric Services, 54,* 621–622. doi: 10.1176/appi.ps.54.5.621

Humphreys, K. (2006). The trials of Alcoholics Anonymous. *Addiction, 101,* 617–618. doi: 10.1111/j.1360-0443.2006.01447.x

Jellinek, E. M. (1950). Phases of alcohol addiction. *Quarterly Journal of Studies on Alcohol, 11,* 199–204.

Johnson, J. E., Burlingame, G. M., Olsen, J. A., Davies, D. R., & Gleave, R. L. (2005). Group climate, cohesion, alliance, and empathy in group psychotherapy: Multilevel structural equation models. *Journal of Counseling Psychology, 52,* 310–321. doi: 10.1037/0022-0167.52.3.310

Kadden, R. M. (2001). Behavioral and cognitive-behavioral treatments for alcoholism: Research opportunities. *Addictive Behaviors, 26,* 489–507. doi: 10.1016/S0306-4603(00)00139-8

Kaduvettoor, A., O'Shaughnessy, T., Mori, Y., Beverly III, C., Weatherford, R. D., & Ladany, N. (2009), Helpful and hindering multicultural events in group supervision: Climate and multicultural competence. *The Counseling Psychologist, 37,* 786–820. doi: 10.1177/0011000009333984

Karno, M. P., & Longabaugh, R. (2005). Less directiveness by therapists improves drinking outcomes of reactant clients in alcoholism treatment. *Journal of Consulting and Clinical Psychology, 73,* 262–267. doi: 10.1037/0022-006X.73.2.262

Kaufman, E. (1994). *Psychotherapy of addicted persons.* New York: Guilford.

Kosters, M., Burlingame, G. M., Nachtigall, C., & Strauss, B. (2006). A meta-analytic review of the effectiveness of inpatient group psychotherapy. *Group Dynamics: Theory, Research, and Practice, 10,* 146–163. doi: 10.1037/1089-2699.10.2.146

Kotler, L. A., Boudreau, G. S., & Devlin, M. J. (2003). Emerging psychotherapies for eating disorders. *Journal of Psychiatric Practice, 9,* 431–441. doi: 10.1097/00131746-200311000-00006

Kulic, K. R., Horne, A. M., & Dagley, J. C. (2004). A comprehensive review of prevention groups for children and adolescents. *Group Dynamics: Theory, Research, and Practice, 8,* 139–151. doi: 10.1037/1089-2699.8.2.139

Levesque, D. A., Velicer, W. F., Castle, P. H., & Greene, R. N. (2008). Resistance among domestic violence offenders: Measurement development and initial validation. *Violence Against Women, 14,* 158–184. doi: 10.1177/1077801207312397

Litt, M. D., Kadden, R. M., Cooney, N. L., & Kabela, E. (2003). Coping skills and treatment outcomes in cognitive-behavioral and inter-actional group therapy for alcoholism. *Journal of Consulting and Clinical Psychology, 71,* 118–128.

Little, J. (2006). Harm reduction therapy groups: Engaging drinkers and drug users in a process of change. *Journal of Groups in Addiction & Recovery, 1*(1), 69–93. doi: 10.1300/J384v01n01_05

Little, J., Hodari, K., Lavender, J., & Berg, A. (2008). Come as you are: Harm reduction drop-in groups for multi-diagnosed drug users. *Journal of Groups in Addiction & Recovery, 3*(3–4), 161–192. doi: 10.1080/15560350802424845

Magoon, M. E., Gupta, R., & Derevensky, J. (2005). Juvenile delinquency and adolescent gambling: Implications for the juvenile justice system. *Criminal Justice and Behavior, 32,* 690–713. doi: 10.1177/0093854805279948

Marlatt, G. A., & Donovan, D. M. (2005). *Relapse prevention: Maintenance strategies in the treatment of addictive behaviors* (2nd ed.). New York: Guilford.

Marlatt, G. A., & Gordon, J. (Eds.). (1985). *Relapse prevention: A self-control strategy for the maintenance of behavior change.* New York: Guilford.

Marlatt, G. A., & Witkiewitz, K. (2002). Harm reduction approaches to alcohol use: Health promotion, prevention, and treatment. *Addictive Behaviors, 27,* 867–886. doi: 10.1016/S0306-4603(02)00294-0

Marmarosh, C., Holtz, A., & Schottenbauer, M. (2005). Group cohesiveness, group-derived collective self-esteem, group-derived hope, and the well-being of group therapy members. *Group Dynamics: Theory, Research, and Practice, 9,* 32–44. doi: 10.1037/1089-2699.9.1.32

Martin, C. R., & Bonner, A. B. (2005). Towards an integrated clinical psychobiology of alcoholism. *Current Psychiatry Reviews, 1,* 303–312. doi: 10.2174/157340005774575136

Masterman, P. W., & Kelly, A. B. (2003). Reaching adolescents who drink harmfully: Fitting intervention to developmental reality. *Journal of Substance Abuse Treatment, 24,* 347–355. doi: 10.1016/S0740-5472(03)00047-3

Masters, W. H., & Johnson, V. E. (1970). *Human sexual inadequacy.* Boston: Little, Brown.

McCluskey, U. (2002). The dynamics of attachment and systems-centered group psychotherapy. *Group Dynamics: Theory, Research, and Practice, 6,* 131–142. doi: 10.1037/1089-2699.6.2.131

McKay, J. R., & Weiss, R. V. (2001). A review of temporal effects and outcome predictors in substance abuse treatment studies with long-term follow-ups. *Evaluation Research, 25,* 113–161.

McNair, L. D. (2005). Top 10 recommendations for treating comorbid addictive behaviors in African Americans. *Behavior Therapy, 28,* 116–118.

McVinney, L. D. (2006). Harm reduction, crystal methamphetamine, and gay men. *Journal of Gay & Lesbian Psychotherapy, 10,* 159–169. doi: 10.1300/J236v10n03_15

Michael, K. D., Curtin, L., Kirkley, D. E., Jones, D. L., & Harris, R. (2006). Group-based motivational interviewing for alcohol use among college students: An exploratory study. *Professional Psychology: Research and Practice, 37,* 629–634. doi: 10.1037/0735-7028.37.6.629

Miller, S. D., Duncan, B. L., & Hubble, M. A. (1997). *Escape from Babel: Toward a unifying language for psychotherapy practice.* New York: Norton.

Miller, W. R. (1995). Increasing motivation for change. In R. K. Hester & W. R. Miller (Eds.), *Handbook of alcoholism treatment approaches* (2nd ed., pp. 89–104). Boston: Allyn & Bacon.

Miller, W. R., & Rollnick, S. (2002). *Motivational Interviewing: Preparing people for change* (2nd ed.). New York: Guilford.

Monras, M., & Gual, A. (2000). Attrition in group therapy with alcoholics: A survival analysis. *Drug and Alcohol Review, 19,* 55–63. doi: 10.1080/09595230096156

Moos, R. H., & Moos, B. S. (2006a). Participation in treatment and Alcoholics Anonymous: A 16-year follow-up of initially untreated individuals. *Journal of Clinical Psychology, 62,* 735–750. doi: 10.1002/jclp.20259

Moos, R. H., & Moos, B. S. (2006b). Rates and predictors of relapse after natural and treated remission from alcohol use disorders. *Addiction, 101,* 212–222. doi: 10.1111/j.1360-0443.2006.01310.x

Moos, R. H., & Moos, B. S. (2006c). Treated and untreated individuals with alcohol use disorders:

Rates and predictors of remission and relapse. *International Journal of Clinical and Health Psychology, 6,* 513–526.

Morgan-Lopez, A. A., & Fals-Stewart, W. (2006). Analytic complexities associated with group therapy in substance abuse treatment research: Problems, recommendations, and future directions. *Experimental and Clinical Psychopharmacology, 14,* 265–273. doi: 10.1037/1064-1297.14.2.265

Najavits, L. M. (2002). *Seeking safety: A treatment manual for PTSD and substance abuse.* New York: Guilford.

Najavits, L. M. (2003). Seeking safety: A new psychotherapy for posttraumatic stress disorder and substance use disorder. In P. Quimette & P. J. Brown (Eds.), *Trauma and substance abuse: Causes, consequences, and treatment of comorbid disorders* (pp. 147–169). Washington, DC: American Psychological Association.

Najavits L. M. (2009). Psychotherapies for trauma and substance abuse in women: Review and policy implications. *Trauma, Violence, & Abuse, 10,* 290–298. doi: 10.1177/1524838009334455

National Institute on Drug Abuse. (2000). *Principles of effective treatment* (NIH No. 00-4180). Washington, DC: National Institutes of Health. [Available from http://www.drugabuse.gov/PDF/PODAT/PODAT .pdf]

O'Leary-Tevyaw, T., & Monti, P. M. (2004). Motivational enhancement and other brief interventions for adolescent substance abuse: Foundations, applications, and evaluations. *Addiction, 99,* 63–75. doi: 10.1111/j.1360-0443.2004.00855.x

Pines, M. (1999). Forgotten pictures: The unwritten history of the therapeutic community movement. *Therapeutic Communities: International Journal for Therapeutic and Supportive Organizations, 20,* 23–42.

Prochaska, J. O. (2008). Decision making in the transtheoretical model of behavior change. *Medical Decision Making,* Nov–Dec, 845–849. doi: 10.1177/0272989X08327068

Prochaska, J. O., DiClemente, C. C., & Norcross, J. C. (1992). In search of how people change: Applications to addictive behaviors. *American Psychologist, 47,* 1102–1114. doi: 10.1037/0003-066X.47.9.1102

Prochaska, J. O., & Norcross, J. C. (2001). Stages of change. *Psychotherapy, 38,* 443–448. doi: 10.1037/0033-3204.38.4.443

Quintero, G. A., Lilliott, E., & Willging, C. (2007). Substance abuse treatment provider views of "culture": Implications for behavioral health care

in rural settings. *Qualitative Health Research, 17,* 1256–1267. doi: 10.1177/1049732307307757

Rush, B. R., Dennis, M. L., Scott, C. K., Castel, S., & Funk, R. R. (2008). The interaction of co-occurring mental disorders and recovery management checkups on substance abuse treatment participation and recovery. *Evaluation Review, 32,* 7–38. doi: 10.1177/0193841X07307532

Sachs, K. S. (2003). Treating alcoholism as a disorder of the self: Insights from Alcoholics Anonymous and Masterson. *Alcoholism Treatment Quarterly, 21,* 75–85. doi: 10.1300/J020v21n02_05

Sampl, S., & Kadden, R. (2001). *Motivational enhancement therapy and cognitive behavioral therapy for adolescent cannabis users: 5 sessions, Cannabis youth treatment (CYT) series, Volume 1.* Rockville, MD: Substance Abuse and Mental Health Services Administration.

Schein, E. H. (1961). *Coercive persuasion.* New York: Norton.

Schmidt, E. (1996). Rational recovery: Finding an alternative for addiction treatment. *Alcoholism Treatment Quarterly, 14,* 47–57. doi: 10.1300/J020V14N04_03

Schnarch, D. M. (1991). *Constructing the sexual crucible: An integration of sexual and marital therapy.* New York: Norton.

Siegal, H. A., & Inciardi, J. A. (1995). A brief history of alcohol. In J. Inciardi & K. McElrath (Eds.), *The American drug scene: An anthology* (pp. 45–49). Los Angeles: Roxbury.

Sobell, M. B., & Sobell, L. C. (1973). Individualized behavior therapy for alcoholics. *Behavior Therapy, 4,* 49–72. doi: 10.1016/S0005-7894(73)80074-7

Sobell, M. B., & Sobell, L. C. (2006). Obstacles to the adoption of low risk drinking goals in the treatment of alcohol problems in the United States: A commentary. *Addiction Research and Theory, 14,* 19–24. doi: 10.1080/16066350500489212

Southern, S. (2003). *The tie that binds: Relapse prevention through shame reduction and trauma resolution.* Hattiesburg, MS: Center for Relational Therapy.

Soyez, V., & Broekaert, E. (2005). Therapeutic communities, family therapy, and humanistic psychology: History and current examples. *Journal of Humanistic Psychology, 45,* 302–332. doi: 10.1177/0022167805277105

Stein, L. A. R., Colby, S. M., Barnett, N. P., Monti, P. M., Golembeske, C., Lebeau-Craven, R., & Miranda, R. (2006). Enhancing substance abuse treatment engagement in incarcerated adolescents. *Psychological Services, 3,* 25–34. doi: 10.1037/1541-1559.3.1.0

Stenius, V. M. K., & Veysey, B. M. (2005). "It's the little things": Women, trauma, and strategies for healing. *Journal of Interpersonal Violence, 20,* 1155–1174. doi: 10.1177/0886260505278533

Sternberg, R. J., & Barnes, M. L. (Eds.). (1988). *The psychology of love.* New Haven, CT: Yale University Press.

Suire, J. G., & Bothwell, R. K. (2006). The psychosocial benefits of Alcoholics Anonymous. *The American Journal on Addictions, 15,* 252–255. doi: 10.1080/10550490600626622

Tait, R. J., & Hulse, G. K. (2003). A systematic review of the effectiveness of brief interventions with substance using adolescents by type of drug. *Drug and Alcohol Review, 22,* 337–346. doi: 10.1080/0959523031000154481

Tantillo, M. (2006). A relational approach to eating disorders multifamily therapy group: Moving from difference and disconnection to mutual connection. *Families, Systems & Health, 24,* 82–102. doi: 10.1037/1091-7527.24.1.82

Thorngren, J. M., Christensen, T. M., & Kleist, D. M. (1998). Multiple-family group treatment: The underexplored therapy. *The Family Journal: Counseling and Therapy for Couples and Families, 6,* 125–131. doi: 10.1177/1066480798062008

Timko, C., DeBenedetti, A., & Billow, R. (2006). Intensive referral to 12-step self-help groups and 6-month substance use disorder outcomes. *Addiction, 101,* 678–688. doi: 10.1111/j.1360-0443.2006.01391.x

Toneatto, T. (2005). Cognitive versus behavioral treatment of concurrent alcohol dependence and agoraphobia: A pilot study. *Addictive Behaviors, 30,* 115–125. doi: 10.1016/j.addbeh.2004.04.017

Toneatto, T., & Ladoceur, R. (2003). Treatment of pathological gambling: A critical review of the literature. *Psychology of Addictive Behaviors, 17,* 284–292. doi: 10.1037/0893-164X.17.4.284

Trimpey, J. (1996). *Rational Recovery: The new cure for substance addiction.* New York: Simon & Schuster.

Turner, B. W., Bingham, J. E., & Andrasik, F. (2000). Short-term community-based treatment for sexual offenders: Enhancing effectiveness. *Sexual Addiction & Compulsivity, 7,* 211–223. doi: 10.1080/10720160008400219

Ullman, S. E., & Townsend, S. M. (2007). Barriers to working with sexual assault survivors: A qualitative study of rape crisis center

workers. *Violence Against Women, 13*(4), 412–443. doi: 10.1177/1077801207299191

Valliant, G. E. (2005). Alcoholics Anonymous: cult or cure? *Australian and New Zealand Journal of Psychiatry, 39,* 431–436. doi: 10.1111/j.1440-1614.2005.01600.x

Vannicelli, M. (1989). *Group psychotherapy with adult children of alcoholics.* New York: Guilford.

Vannicelli, M. (1992). *Removing the roadblocks: Group psychotherapy with substance abusers and family members.* New York: Guilford.

Velasquez, M. M., Stephens, N. S., & Ingersoll, K. (2006). Motivational Interviewing in groups. *Journal of Groups in Addiction & Recovery, 1*(1), 27–50. doi: 10.1300/J384v01n01_03

von Bertalanffy, L. (1968). *General systems theory: Foundations, development, applications.* New York: Braziller.

Washton, A. M. (1992). Structured outpatient group therapy with alcohol and substance abusers. In J. H. Lowenson, P. Ruiz, B. Milman, & J. G. Langrod (Eds.), *Substance abuse: A comprehensive textbook* (pp. 508–519). Baltimore: Williams and Wilkins.

Webb, C., Scudder, M., Kaminer, Y., & Kadden, R. (2002). *The motivational enhancement therapy and cognitive behavioral therapy supplement: 7 sessions of cognitive behavioral therapy for adolescent cannabis users, Cannabis youth treatment (CYT) series, Volume 2.* Rockville, MD: Substance Abuse and Mental Health Services Administration.

Weegman, M. (2004). Alcoholics Anonymous: A group-analytic view of fellowship organizations. *Group Analysis, 37,* 243–258. doi: 10.1177/0533316404041276

Weiss, R. D., Jaffe, W. B., de Menil, V. P., & Cogley, C. B. (2004). Group therapy for substance use disorders: What do we know? *Harvard Review of Psychiatry, 12,* 339–350. doi: 10.1080/10673220490905723

WGBH Educational Foundation. (2000). Treatment & education vs. prohibition & punishment. Transcript of symposium panel discussion held October 4, 2000 at Georgetown University Law Center. Retrieved from http://www.pbs.org/wgbh/pages/frontline/shows/drugs/symposium/panel1.html

Winnicott, D. W. (1965). *The maturational process and the facilitating environment.* New York: International Universities Press.

Winters, J., Fals-Stewart, W., O'Farrell, T. J., Birchler, G. R., & Kelley, M. L. (2002). Behavioral couples therapy for female substance-abusing patients:

Effects on substance use and relationship adjustment. *Journal of Consulting and Clinical Psychology, 70,* 344–355. doi: 10.1037/0022-006X.70.2.344

Witkiewitz, K. A., & Marlatt, G. A. (2007). (Eds). *Therapist's guide to evidence-based relapse prevention: Practical resources for the mental health professional.* San Diego, CA: Elsevier.

Women's Christian Temperance Union. (n.d.). Early history. Retrieved from http://www.wctu.org/earlyhistory.html

Wong, Y. I., Park, J. M., & Nemon, H. (2006). Homeless service delivery in the context of continuum of care. *Administration in Social Work, 30,* 67–94. doi: 10.1300/J147v30n01_05

Wormith, J. S., Althouse, R., Simpson, M., Reitzel, L. R., Fagan, T. J., & Morgan, R. D. (2007). The rehabilitation and reintegration of offenders: The current landscape and some future directors for correctional psychology. *Criminal Justice and Behavior, 34,* 879–892. doi: 10.1177/0093854807301552

Yalom, I. D. (2005). *The theory and practice of group psychotherapy* (5th ed.). New York: Basic Books.

Young, S. E., Rhee, S. H., Stallings, M. C., Corley, R. P., & Hewitt, J. K. (2006). Genetic and environmental vulnerabilities underlying adolescent substance use and problem use: General or specific? *Behavior Genetics, 36,* 603–615. doi: 10.1007/s10519-006-9066-7

Zane, N., Sue, S., Chang, J., Huang, L., Huang, J., Lowe, S., . . . Lee, E. (2005). Beyond ethnic match: Effects of client–therapist cognitive match in problem perception, coping orientation, and therapy goals on treatment outcomes. *Journal of Community Psychology, 33,* 569–585. doi: 10.1002/jcop.20067

Chapter 9

Ackerman, R. J. (1983). *Children of alcoholics: A guide book for educators, therapists, and parents.* Holmes Beach, FL: Learning Publications.

Adler, A. (1927). *The practice and theory of individual psychology.* New York: Harcourt Brace.

Administration on Children, Youth and Families. (2006). *Child maltreatment 2004.* Washington, DC: U.S. Government Printing Office. Retrieved from http://www.acf.hhs.gov/programs/cb/pubs/cm04/chaptertwo.htm#screen

Ahmed, K. (2006). Data analysis of the interstate Treatment Outcomes and Performance Pilot Project (TOPPS-II) data set from the 16 TOPPS II primary data States. These data were analyzed by Dr. Kazi Ahmed of Johnson, Bassin, & Shaw under contract to the Center for Substance Abuse Treatment on January 29, 2006. Unpublished data. Retrieved from http://www.ncsacw.samhsa.gov/files/Extent_People_Involvement_Factsheet.pdf

Anda, R. F., Dong, M. X., Brown, D. W., Felitti, F. V. J., Giles, W. H., & Perry, G. S. (2009). The relationship of adverse childhood experiences to a history of premature death of family members. *BMC Public Health, 9* (article 106).

Bateson, B. (1971). *Steps toward an ecology of the mind.* New York: Ballantine.

Bertalanffy, L. von (1968). *General systems theory: Foundation, development, applications.* New York: Braziller.

Black, C. (1981). *It will never happen to me.* Denver, CO: MAC.

Bowen, M. (1974). Alcoholism as viewed through the family systems theory and family psychotherapy. *Annals of the New York Academy of Science, 233,* 115–122.

Bowen, M. (1976). Theory in the practice of psychotherapy. In P. J. Guerin, Jr. (Ed.), *Family therapy: Theory and practice.* New York: Gardner.

Capretto, N. A. (2007, April 26). *Addiction: A family disease.* Paper presented at the Ruth Fox Course for Physicians, 38th Medical-Scientific Conference of the American Society for Addiction Medicine, Miami, FL.

Collins, W. A., Maccoby, E. E., Steinberg, L., Hetherington, E. M., & Bornstein, M. (2000). The case for nature and nurture. *American Psychologist, 55*(2), 218–232. doi: 10.1037//0003.066X.55.2.218037//0

Cranford, J. A., Floyd, F. J., Schulenberg, J. E., & Zucker, R. A. (2011). Husbands' and wives' alcohol use disorders and marital interactions as longitudinal predictors of marital adjustment. *Journal of Abnormal Psychology, 120*(1), 210–222.

Craig, R. J. (2004). *Counseling the alcohol and drug dependent client.* New York: Allyn & Bacon. doi: 10.1037//0003-066X.55.2.218OI: 10.1037//0003-066X.55.2.218

Doweiko, H. F. (2011). *Concepts of chemical dependence* (8th ed.). Pacific Grove, CA: Brooks/Cole.

Felitti, V. J. (2004). *The origins of addictions: Evidence from the Adverse Childhood Experience Study.* Retrieved from http://www.acestudy.org/docs/OriginsofAddiction.pdf

Gallup Organization. (2005, April 5). *Drug use still among Americans' top worries.* Retrieved from http://www.gallup.com/poll/15520/Drug-Use-Still-Among-Americans-Top-Worries.aspx

Gladding, S. (2011). *Family therapy: History, theory, and practice* (5th ed.). Upper Saddle River, NJ: Merrill/Prentice-Hall.

Goldenberg, I., & Goldenberg, H. (2010). *Family therapy: An overview* (7th ed.). Pacific Grove, CA: Brooks/Cole.

Gorski, T. T. (1992). Diagnosing codependence. *Addiction and Recovery, 12*(7), 14–16.

Greenfield, S. F. (2007). *Alcohol use and abuse*. Cambridge, MA: Harvard Health Publications.

Guo, Q. M., Zakhari, S. D. Commentary: Systems biology and its relevance to alcohol research. *Alcohol Research & Health* 31(1): 5–11, 2008. http://pubs.niaaa.nih.gov/publications/arh311/5-11.htm

Jackson, D. D. (1960). *The etiology of schizophrenia*. New York: Basic Books.

Jaffe, J. H., & Anthony, J. C. (2005). Substance-related disorder: Introduction and overview. In B. J. Sadock & V. S. Sadock (Eds.), *Comprehensive textbook of psychiatry* (8th ed.). New York: Lippincott, Williams & Wilkins.

Jellinek, E. M. (1960). *The disease concept of alcoholism*. New Brunswick, NJ: Millhouse.

Johnson, J. L. (2004). *Fundamentals of substance abuse practice*. Belmont, CA: Brooks/Cole.

Kaufman, E. (1985). Family therapy in the treatment of alcoholism. In T. E. Bratter & G. G. Forrest (Eds.), *Alcoholism and substance abuse* (pp. 376–397). New York: Free Press.

Kaufman, E., & Kaufman, P. (1992). From psychodynamic to structural to integrated family treatment of chemical dependency. In E. Kaufman & P. Kaufman (Eds.), *Family therapy of drug and alcohol abuse* (pp. 34–45). Boston: Allyn & Bacon.

Kumper, K. L., & Summerhays, J. K. (2006). Prevention approaches to enhance resilience among high-risk youth: Comments on the papers of Dishion & Connell and Greenberg. *Annals of the New York Academy of Sciences, 1094*(1), 151–163.

Lapham, S. (2004/2005). *Screening and brief intervention in the criminal justice system, 28*(2). Washington, DC: National Institute of Alcohol Abuse and Alcoholism.

Lawson, A., & Lawson, G. (2004). *Alcoholism and the family: A guide to treatment and prevention*. Gaithersburg, MD: Aspen.

Leonard, K. E., & Hornish, G. G. (2008). Predictors of heavy drinking and drinking problems over the first 4 years of marriage. *Psychology of Addictive Behaviors, 22*(1). doi: 10.1037/0893-164X.22.1.25

Lewis, J. A., Dana, R. Q., & Blevins, G. A. (2011). Substance abuse counseling. Belmont, CA: Brooks/Cole.

Liddle, H. A. (2002). *Multidimensional family therapy treatment (MDFT) for adolescent cannabis users: CYT series, volume 5*. (BKD388) Rockville, MD: CSAT, SAMHSA.

Ling, W., Rawson, R., & Shoptaw, S. (2006). Management of methamphetamine abuse and dependence. *Current Psychiatry Reports, 8*(5), 335–354.

Lowe, R. N. (1982). Adlerian/Dreikursian family counseling. In M. A. Horne & M. M. Ohlsen (Eds.), *Family counseling and therapy* (pp. 329–359). Itasca, IL: Peacock.

McCauley, J., Kern, D. E., Kolodner, S. D., Dill, L., Schroeder, A. F., DeChant, H. K., . . . Derogatis, L. R. (2004). The "battering syndrome": Prevalence and clinical characteristics of domestic violence in primary care internal medicine practices. *Annuals of Internal Medicine, 123*(10), 737–746.

McCrady, B. S. (2006). Family and other close relationships. In W. R. Miller & K. M Carroll (Eds.), *Rethinking substance abuse: What science shows and what we should do about it* (pp. 166–181). New York: Guilford.

McCrady, B. S., Epstein, E. E., & Kahler, C. W. (2004). Alcoholics Anonymous and relapse prevention as maintenance strategies after conjoint behavioral alcohol treatment for men: 18-month outcomes. *Journal of Consulting and Clinical Psychology, 72*(5), 870–878.

McCrady, B. S., Epstein, E. E., Cook, S., Jensen, N. K., & Hildebrandt, T. (2009). A randomized trial of individual and couple behavioral alcohol treatment for women. *Journal of Consulting and Clinical Psychology, 77*(2), 243–256.

McNeece, C. A., & DiNitto, D. M. (2005). *Chemical dependency: A systems approach*. Boston: Allyn & Bacon.

Merriam-Webster Online Dictionary. Retrieved from http://www.merriam-webster.com/dictionary/system

Miller, T. R., Levy, D. T., & Cox, K. L. (2006). The costs of alcohol and drug-related crime. *Prevention Science* (publication of the Pacific Institute for Research and Evaluation). http://www.pire.org/detail2.asp?core=26368&cms=1790

Minuchen, S. (1974). *Families and family therapy*. Cambridge, MA: Harvard University Press.

Minuchen, S. (1992). Constructing a therapeutic reality. In E. Kaufman & P. Kaufman (Eds.), *Family therapy of drug and alcohol abuse* (pp. 1–14). Boston: Allyn & Bacon.

Napier, A. Y., & Whitaker, C. A. (1988). *The family crucible*. New York: Harper & Row.

National Alliance on Mental Illness. (2011). Retrieved from http://www.nami.org/Content/ContentGroups/Helpline1/Dual_Diagnosis_Substance_Abuse_and_Mental_Illness.htm

Nichols, M. P. (2009). *Family therapy: Concepts and methods* (9th ed.). Boston: Allyn & Bacon.

O'Connor, J., & McDermott, I. (1997). *The art of systems thinking*. London: Thorsons.

O'Farrell, T. J., Fals-Stewart, W., Murphy, M., & Murphy, C. M. (2003). Partner violence before and after individually based alcohol treatment for male alcoholic patients. *Journal of Consulting and Clinical Psychology, 71*(1), 92–101.

Parekh, R. (2006). *Adolescent substance use and abuse.* Paper presented at the Treating Addictions workshop, sponsored by the Department of Psychiatry of the Cambridge Hospital, Boston, MA.

Parrott, D. J., & Giancola, P. R. (2006). The effect of past-year heavy drinking on alcohol-related aggression. *Journal of Studies on Alcohol, 67,* 122–130.

Powers, M. B., Vedel, E., & Emmelkamp, P. M. G. (2008). Behavioral couples therapy (BCT) for alcohol and drug use disorders: A meta-analysis. *Clinical Psychology Review, 28*(6), 952–962.

Satir, V. (1967). *Conjoint family therapy*. Palo Alto, CA: Science and Behavior Books.

Shipway, L. (2004). *Domestic violence: A handbook for health care professionals*. London: Routledge.

Steinglass, P. (1980). A life history model of the alcoholic family. *Journal of the American Medical Association, 254,* 2614–2617.

U.S. Department of Health and Human Services. (2006). *Preliminary estimates from the 2004 National Household Survey on Drug Use and Health*. Washington, DC: U.S. Department of Health and Human Services, Substance Abuse and Mental Health Services Administration.

Zhou, Q., King, K. M., & Chassin, L. (2009). The roles of familial alcoholism and adolescent family harmony in young adult substance dependence disorders: Mediated and moderated relations. In G. A. Marlatt & K. Witkiewitz (Eds.), *Addictive behaviors* (pp. 259–287). Washington, DC: American Psychological Association.

Chapter 10

Akins, S., Smith, C. L., & Mosher, C. (2010). Pathways to adult alcohol abuse across racial/ethnic groups: An application of general strain and social learning theories. *Journal of Drug Issues, 40*(2), 321–351. Retrieved from EBSCO*host*.

Alcoholics Anonymous. (2010). *AA fact file*. Retrieved from http://www.aa.org/pdf/products/m-24_aafactfile.pdf

An-Pyng, S. (2007). Relapse among substance-abusing women: Components and processes. *Substance Use & Misuse, 42*(1), 1–21. doi:10.1080/10826080601094082

Association for Spiritual, Ethical, and Religious Values in Counseling. (n.d.). *Spirituality: A white paper*. Retrieved from http://www.angelfire.com/nj/counseling/Whitepaper1.htm

Atkins, R. G., & Hawdon, J. E. (2007). Religiosity and participation in mutual-aid support groups for addiction. *Journal of Substance Abuse Treatment, 33*(3), 321–331. doi:10.1016/j.jsat.2007.07.001

Baker, T. B., Piper, M. E., McCarthy, D. E., Majaskie, M. R., & Fiore, M. C. (2004). Addiction motivation reformulated: An effective processing model of negative reinforcement. *Psychological Review, 111,* 33–51.

Bandura, A. (1969). *Principles of behavior modification*. New York: Holt, Rinehart, & Winston.

Bandura, A. (1977). Reflections on self-efficacy. *Advances in Behavioral Research and Therapy, 1,* 237–269.

Barry, D., & Petry, N. M. (2009). Cognitive behavioral treatments for substance use disorders. In P. M. Miller (Ed.), *Evidence-based addiction treatment* (pp. 159–174). New York: Academic Press.

Curry, S., Marlatt, G. A., & Gordon, J. R. (1987). Abstinence violation effect: Validation of an attributional construct with smoking cessation. *Journal of Counseling and Clinical Psychology, 55,* 147–149.

Davidson, L., Andres-Hyman, R., Bedregal, L., Tondora, J., Fry, J., & Kirk Jr., T. A. (2008). From "Double Trouble" to "Dual Recovery": Integrating models of recovery in addiction and mental health. *Journal of Dual Diagnosis, 4*(3), 273–290. doi:10.1080/15504260802072396

DiClemente, C. (2007). Mechanisms, determinants and processes of change in the modification of drinking behavior. *Alcoholism: Clinical & Experimental Research, 31*(S3), 13s–20s. doi:10.1111/j.1530-0277.2007.00489.x

Doweiko, H. F. (2011). *Concepts of chemical dependency* (6th ed.). Pacific Grove, CA: Brooks/Cole.

Fernández-Montalvo, J., López-Goñi, J., Illescas, C., Landa, N., & Lorea, I. (2007). Relapse precipitants in addictions: Results in a therapeutic community. *Journal of Addictive Diseases*, *26*(4), 55–61. doi:10. I 300/J069v26ti04 07

Ferrer, R., Amico, K. K., Bryan, A., Fisher, W., Cornman, D., Kiene, S., & Fisher, J. (2009). Accuracy of the stages of change algorithm: Sexual risk reported in the maintenance stage of change. *Prevention Science*, *10*(1), 13–21. doi:10.1007/s11121-008-0108-7

Forcehimes, A. A., & Tonigan, J. S. (2008). Self-efficacy as a factor in abstinence from alcohol/other drug abuse: A meta-analysis. *Alcoholism Treatment Quarterly*, *26*(4), 480–489. doi:10.1080/07347320802347145

Ford, J. A. (2009). Nonmedical prescription drug use among adolescents: The influence of bonds to family and school. *Youth & Society*, *40*(3), 336–352. doi: 10.1177/0044118X08316345

Fox, H., Bergquist, K., Hong, K., & Sinha, R. (2007). Stress-induced and alcohol cue-induced craving in recently abstinent alcohol-dependent individuals. *Alcoholism: Clinical & Experimental Research*, *31*(3), 395–403. doi:10.1111/j.1530-0277.2006.00320.x

Freyer-Adam, J., Coder, B., Ottersbach, C., Tonigan, J., Rumpf, H., John, U., & Hapke, U. (2009). The performance of two motivation measures and outcome after alcohol detoxification. *Alcohol & Alcoholism*, *44*(1), 77–83. doi:10.1093/alcalc/agn088

Galanter, M. (2006). Spirituality and addiction: A research and clinical perspective. *American Journal on Addictions*, *15*(4), 286–292. doi:10.1080/10550490600754325

Gallant, M., Egelko, S., & Edwards, H. (1993). Rational Recovery: Alternative to AA for addiction? *American Journal of Drug and Alcohol Abuse*, *19*, 499–510.

Gorski, T. T. (1990). The CENAPS model of relapse prevention: Basic principles and procedure. *Journal of Psychoactive Drugs*, *22*, 125–133.

Gorski, T. T. (2007). *The Gorski-CENAPS model for recovery and relapse prevention*. Independence, MO: Herald House/Independence Press.

Gorski, T. T., & Miller, M. M. (1986). *Staying sober: Guide to relapse prevention*. Independence, MO: Herald House.

Gossop, M., Stewart, D., & Marsden, J. (2008). Attendance at Narcotics Anonymous and Alcoholics Anonymous meetings, frequency of attendance and substance use outcomes after residential treatment for drug dependence: A 5-year follow-up study. *Addiction*, *103*(1), 119–125. doi:10.1111/j.1360-0443.2007.02050.x

Hagedorn, W., & Moorhead, H. (2010). The God-Shaped Hole: Addictive disorders and the search for perfection. *Counseling & Values*, *55*(1), 63–78. Retrieved from Academic Search Complete database.

Hayaki, J., Anderson, B. J., & Stein, M. D. (2008). Drug use expectancies among nonabstinent community cocaine users. *Drug and Alcohol Dependence*, *94*, 109–115. doi:10.1016/j.drugalcdep.2007.10.013

Horsfall, J., Cleary, M., Hunt, G. E., & Walter, G. (2009). Psychosocial treatments for people with co-occurring severe mental illnesses and substance use disorders (dual diagnosis): A review of empirical evidence. *Harvard Review of Psychiatry*, *17*(1), 24–34. doi:10.1080/10673220902724599

Horton-Parker, R. J., & Fawcett, R. C. (2010). *Spirituality in counseling and psychotherapy: The Face-Spirit model*. Denver: Love.

Hyde, J. J., Hankins, M. M., Deale, A. A., & Marteau, T. M. (2008). Interventions to increase self-efficacy in the context of addiction behaviours: A systematic literature review. *Journal of Health Psychology*, *13*(5), 607–623. doi:10.1177/1359105308090933

Jellinek, E. M. (1960). *The disease concept of alcoholism*. New Brunswick, NJ: Millhouse.

Kelly, J. F., Kahler, C. W., & Humphreys, K. (2010). Assessing why substance use disorder patients drop out from or refuse to attend 12-step mutual-help groups: The "REASONS" questionnaire. *Addiction Research & Theory*, *18*(3), 316–325. doi:10.3109/16066350903254775

Kinney, J. (2009). *Loosening the grip: A handbook of alcohol information*. New York: McGraw-Hill.

Krampe, H., Stawicki, S., Ribbe, K., Wagner, T., Bartels, C., Kroener-Herwig, B., & Ehrenreich, H. (2008). Development of an outcome prediction measure for alcoholism therapy by multimodal monitoring of treatment processes. *Journal of Psychiatric Research*, *43*(1), 30–47. doi:10.1016/j.jpsychires.2008.01.007

Laudet, A. B. (2008). The impact of Alcoholics Anonymous on other substance abuse-related twelve-step programs. In M. Galanter and L. A. Kaskutas (Eds.), *Recent developments in alcoholism, Vol. 18, Research on Alcoholics Anonymous and spirituality in addiction recovery* (pp. 71–89). Totowa, NJ: Humana Press.

Litt, M. D., Kadden, R. M., Cooney, N. L., & Kabela, E. (2003). Coping skills and treatment outcomes in cognitive-behavioral and interactional group therapy for alcoholism. *Journal of Counseling and Clinical Psychology, 71,* 118–128.

Magura, S. (2008). Effectiveness of dual focus mutual aid for co-occurring substance use and mental health disorders: A review and synthesis of the "Double Trouble" in Recovery evaluation. *Substance Use & Misuse, 43*(12/13), 1904–1926. doi:10.1080/10826080802297005

Marlatt, G. A. (1985a). Cognitive assessment and intervention procedures for relapse prevention. In G. A. Marlatt & J. Gordon (Eds.), *Relapse prevention: A self-control strategy for the maintenance of behavior change* (pp. 201–209). New York: Guilford.

Marlatt, G. A. (1985b). Lifestyle modification. In G. A. Marlatt & J. Gordon (Eds.), *Relapse prevention: A self-control strategy for the maintenance of behavior change* (pp. 280–350). New York: Guilford.

Marlatt, G. A., & Gordon, J. (Eds.). (1985). *Relapse prevention: A self-control strategy for the maintenance of behavior change.* New York: Guilford.

Marlatt, G. A., & Witkiewitz, K. (2005). Relapse prevention for alcohol and drug problems. In G. A. Marlatt & D. M. Donovan (Eds.), *Relapse prevention: Maintenance strategies in the treatment of addictive behaviors* (pp. 1–44). New York: Guilford.

Merriam-Webster *Online Dictionary.* (2011). Retrieved from http://www.m-w.com/dictionary/relapse

Meyer, C., Ulbricht, S., Baumeister, S. E., Schumann, A., Rüge, J., Bischof, G., . . . John, U. (2008). Proactive interventions for smoking cessation in general medical practice: A quasi-randomized controlled trial to examine the efficacy of computer-tailored letters and physician-delivered brief advice. *Addiction, 103*(2), 294–304. doi:10.1111/j.1360-0443.2007.02031.x

Miller, W. R., & Rollnick, S. (2009). Ten things that motivational interviewing is not. *Behavioural Psychotherapy, 37,* 120–140. doi:10.1017/S1352465809005128

Moderation Management. (2011). Retrieved from http://www.moderation.org/readings.shtml

Moos, R. H., Moos, B. S., & Timko, C. (2006). Gender, treatment and self-help in remission from alcohol use disorders. *Clinical Medicine & Research, 4*(3), 163–174. Retrieved from EBSCO*host.*

National Institute on Alcohol Abuse and Alcoholism. (2004). *The 12-Month Prevalence and Trends in DSM–IV Alcohol Abuse and Dependence.* Retrieved from http://pubs.niaaa.nih.gov/publications/arh29-2/79-93.htm

Oei, T., Hasking, P., & Phillips, L. (2007). A comparison of general self-efficacy and drinking refusal self-efficacy in predicting drinking behavior. *American Journal of Drug & Alcohol Abuse, 33*(6), 833–841. doi:10.1080/00952990701653818

Preston, P. (2006). Marijuana use as a coping response to psychological strain: Racial, ethnic, and gender differences among young adults. *Deviant Behavior, 27*(4), 397–421. doi:10.1080/01639620600721353

Prochaska, J. O., DiClemente, C. C., & Norcross, J. C. (1992). In search of how people change. *American Psychologist, 47*(9), 1102–1114. Retrieved from EBSCO*host.*

Prochaska, J. O., Evers, K. E., Prochaska, J. M., Van Marter, D., & Johnson, J. L. (2007). Efficacy and effectiveness trials: Examples from smoking cessation and bullying prevention. *Journal of Health Psychology, 12*(1), 170–178. doi:10.1177/1359105307071751

Roffman, R. A., & Stephens, R. S. (2005). Relapse prevention for cannabis abuse and dependence. In G. A. Marlatt & D. M. Donovan (Eds.), *Relapse prevention: Maintenance strategies in the treatment of addictive behaviors* (pp. 179–207). New York: Guilford.

Ruiz, P., Strain, E. C., & Langrod, J. G. (2007). *The substance abuse handbook.* Philadelphia: Lippincott Williams & Wilkins.

Schmidt, E. A., Carns, A., & Chandler, C. (2001). Assessing the efficacy of rational recovery in the treatment of alcohol/drug dependency. *Alcoholism Treatment Quarterly, 19*(1), 97–106. doi: 0.1300/J020v19n01_07

Senbanjo, R., Wolff, K., Marshall, E., & Strang, J. (2009). Persistence of heroin use despite methadone treatment: Poor coping self-efficacy predicts continued heroin use. *Drug & Alcohol Review, 28*(6), 608–615. doi:10.1111/j.1465-3362.2009.00064.x

Shaffer, H. J., & LaPlante, D. A. (2005). Treatment of gambling disorders. In G. A. Marlatt & D. M. Donovan (Eds.), *Relapse prevention: Maintenance strategies in the treatment of addictive behaviors* (pp. 276–332). New York: Guilford.

Slaymaker, V. J., & Sheehan, T. (2008). The impact of AA on professional treatment. In M. Galanter & L. A. Kaskutas (Eds.), *Recent developments in alcoholism, Vol. 18, Research on Alcoholics Anonymous and spirituality in addiction recovery* (pp. 59–70). Totowa, NJ: Humana Press.

Slesnick, N., & Prestopnik, J. L. (2009). Comparison of family therapy outcome with alcohol abusing runaway adolescents. *Journal of Marital and Family Therapy, 35*(3), 255–277. doi: 10.1111/j.1752-0606.2009.00121.x

SOS Meetings. (2011). Retrieved from http://www.sossobriety.org/meetings/

The SOS Story. (2011). Retrieved from http://www.sossobriety.org/james%20christopher.htm

Thakker, J., & Ward, T. (2010). Relapse prevention: A critique and proposed reconceptualisation. *Behaviour Change, 27*(3), 154–175. doi:10.1375/bech.27.3.154

Tonigan, J. S. (2008). Alcoholics Anonymous outcomes and benefits. In M. Galanter & L. A. Kaskutas (Eds.), *Recent developments in alcoholism, Vol. 18, Research on Alcoholics Anonymous and spirituality in addiction recovery* (pp. 59–70). Totowa, NJ: Humana Press.

Trimpey, J. (1996). *Rational Recovery: The new cure for substance addiction.* New York: Simon & Schuster.

Wahab, S. (2010). Motivational interviewing and social work practice. In K. van Wormer & B. A. Thyer (Eds.), *Evidence-based practice in the field of substance abuse* (pp. 197–210). Los Angeles: Sage.

Wanberg, K. W., & Milkman, H. B. (2008). *Criminal conduct and substance abuse treatment: Strategies for self-improvement and change.* Los Angeles: Sage.

Ward, T., & Stewart, C. A. (2003). The treatment of sex offenders: Risk management and good lives. *Professional Psychology: Research and Practice, 34,* 353–360. doi: 10.1037/0735-7028.34.4.353

White, W. L., & Kurtz, E. (2008). Twelve defining moments in the history of Alcoholics Anonymous. In M. Galanter & L. A. Kaskutas (Eds.), *Recent developments in alcoholism, Vol. 18, Research on Alcoholics Anonymous and spirituality in addiction recovery* (pp. 37–57). Totowa, NJ: Humana Press.

Witkiewitz, K., & Marlatt, G. A. (2004). Relapse prevention for alcohol and drug problems: That was Zen, this is Tao. *American Psychologist, 59*(4), 224–235. doi: 10.1037/0003-066X.59.4.224

Witkiewitz, K., & Marlatt, G. A. (2006). Overview of harm reduction for alcohol problems. *The International Journal of Drug Policy, 17*(4), 285–294. doi:10.1016/j.drugpo.2006.03.005

Witkiewitz, K., & Marlatt, G. (2007). Modeling the complexity of post-treatment drinking: It's a rocky road to relapse. *Clinical Psychology Review, 27*(6), 724–738. doi:10.1016/j.cpr.2007.01.002

Witkiewitz, K., Marlatt, G., & Walker, D. (2005). Mindfulness-based relapse prevention for alcohol and substance use disorders. *Journal of Cognitive Psychotherapy, 19*(3), 211–228. Retrieved from EBSCO*host.*

Zackon, F. N. (1988). Relapse and "re-joyment": Observations and reflections. In D. C. Daley (Ed.), *Relapse: Conceptual, research and clinical perspectives* (pp. 67–78). New York: Hayworth.

Chapter 11

Agrawal, A. (2005). *Patterns of use: Initiation to treatment.* SAMHSA's National Survey on Drug Use and Health. Rockville, MD: SAMHSA.

Americans with Disabilities Act of 1990. (1991). Pub. L. No. 101-336, 2, 104 Stat. 328.

Bartels, S. J., Blow, F. C., Brockmann, L. M., & Van Citters, A. D. (2005). *Substance abuse and mental health among older Americans: The state of the knowledge and future directions.* Rockville, MD: SAMHSA.

Bishop, M. (2007). Quality of life and psychosocial adaptation to chronic illness and acquired disability: A conceptual and theoretical synthesis. In A. E. Dell Orto & P. W. Power (Eds.), *The psychological and social impact of illness and disability* (pp. 230–248). New York: Springer.

Blank, K. (2009). Older adults & substance use: New data highlight concerns. *SAMHSA Newsletter, volume 17, number 1.*

Brady, T. M., & Ashley, O. S. (Eds.). (2005). *Women in substance abuse treatment: Results from the Alcohol and Drug Services Study (ADSS).* DHHS Pub. No. (SMA) 04-3968, Analytic Series A-26. Rockville, MD: Substance Abuse and Mental Health Services Administration, Office of Applied Studies.

Brooks, M. K. (2009). Legal issues for programs treating LGBT clients. In *Center for Substance Abuse Treatment: A provider's introduction to substance abuse treatment for lesbian, gay, bisexual, and transgender individuals* (pp. 61–67). HHS Pub. No. (SMA) 09-4104. Rockville, MD: Department of Health and Human Services.

Cabaj, R. P., & Smith, M. (2009). Overview of treatment approaches, modalities, and issues of accessibility in the continuum of care. In *Center for Substance Abuse Treatment: A provider's introduction to substance abuse treatment for lesbian, gay, bisexual, and transgender individuals* (pp. 61–67). HHS Pub. No. (SMA) 09-4104. Rockville, MD: Department of Health and Human Services.

Califano, J. A. (2007). Foreward. In P. Tolan, J. Szapocznik, & S. Sambrano (Eds.), *Preventing youth substance abuse: Science-based programs for children and adolescents* (pp. 159–181). Washington, DC: American Psychological Association.

Capuzzi, D., & Gross, D. R. (2005). *Introduction to the counseling profession* (4th ed.). New York: Pearson Education.

Cass, V. C. (1979). Homosexual identity formation: A theoretical model. *Journal of Homosexuality, 4,* 219–235.

Cass, V. C. (1984). Homosexual identity formation: Testing a theoretical model. *Journal of Sex Research, 20,* 143–167.

Center for Substance Abuse Treatment (CSAT). (2005). *Tip 51: Physiological effects of alcohol, drugs, and tobacco on women.* Rockville, MD: Department of Health and Human Services.

Center for Substance Abuse Treatment (CSAT). (2009). *A provider's introduction to substance abuse treatment for lesbian, gay, bisexual, and transgender individuals.* HHS Pub. No. (SMA) 09-4104. Rockville, MD: Department of Health and Human Services.

Didenko, E., & Pankratz, N. (2007). Substance use: Pathways to homelessness? Or a way of adapting to street life? *Visions: BC's Mental Health and Addictions Journal, 4,* 9–10.

Dunn, M. G., & Mezzich, A. C. (2007). Development in childhood and adolescence: Implications for prevention research and practice. In P. Tolan, J. Szapocznik, & S. Sambrano (Eds.), *Preventing youth substance abuse: Science-based programs for children and adolescents* (pp. 21–40). Washington, DC: American Psychological Association.

Gans, J., Falco, M., Schackman, B. R., & Winters, K. C. (2010). An in-depth survey of the screening and assessment practices in highly regarded adolescent substance abuse treatment programs. *Journal of Child & Adolescent Substance Abuse, 19,* 33–47.

Gay and Lesbian Medical Association, (GLMA). (2010). *Healthy people 2010 companion document for lesbian, gay, bisexual, and transgender health.* San Francisco: Gay and Lesbian Medical Association.

Gender Research in the National Institutes on Drug Abuse National Treatment Clinical Trials Network: A Summary of Findings. (2011). *American Journal of Drug and Alcohol Abuse, 37*(5), 301–312.

Gfroerer, J., Penne, M., Pemberton, M., & Folsom, R. (2003). Substance abuse treatment needed among older adults in 2020: The impact of the aging baby-boom cohort. *Drug and Alcohol Dependence, 69*(2), 127–135.

Healthy People 2010: Lesbian, Gay, Bisexual, Transgender Health. San Francisco: Gay and Lesbian Medical Association.

Johnson, G., & Chamberlin, C. (2008). Homelessness and substance abuse: Which comes first? *Australian Social Work, 61,* 342–356.

Johnston, L. D., O'Malley, P. M., Bachman, J. G., & Schulenberg, J. E. (2005). *Monitoring the future national results on adolescent drug use: Overview of key findings, 2001* (NIH Publication No. 02-5105). Bethesda, MD: National Institute on Drug Abuse.

Kinney, J. (2009). *Loosening the grip: A handbook of alcohol information.* Boston: McGraw-Hill.

Korper, S. P., & Raskin, I. E. (2008). The impact of substance use and abuse by the elderly: The next 20 to 30 years. Rockville, MD: Substance Abuse and Mental Health Services Administration, Office of Applied Studies.

Kumpfer, K. L., Alvarado, R., Tait, C., & Whiteside, H. O. (2007). The strengthening families program: An evidenced based, multicultural family skills training program. In P. Tolan, J. Szapocznik, & S. Sambrano (Eds.), *Preventing youth substance abuse: Science-based programs for children and adolescents* (pp. 159–181). Washington, DC: American Psychological Association.

Lanzetta, B. J. (2005). *Radical wisdom: A feminist mystical theology.* Minneapolis: Fortress Press.

Lee, H. S., & Petersen, S. R. (2009). Demarginalizing the marginalized in substance abuse treatment: Stories of homeless, active substance abusers in an urban harm reduction based drop-in center. *Addiction Research and Theory, 17,* 622–636.

Livneh, H., & Antonak, R. F. (2007). Psychological adaptation to chronic illness and disability: A primer for counselors. In A. E. Dell Orto & P. W. Power (Eds.), *The psychological and social impact of illness and disability* (pp. 125–144). New York: Springer.

McCabe, P. T. (2009). Families of origin and families of choice. In *Center for Substance Abuse Treatment: A provider's introduction to substance abuse treatment for lesbian, gay, bisexual, and transgender individuals* (pp. 61–67). HHS Pub. No. (SMA) 09-4104. Rockville, MD: Department of Health and Human Services.

McCabe, S. E., Bostwick, W. B., Hughes, T. L., West, B. T., & Boyd, C. J. (2010). The relationship between discrimination and substance use disorder among lesbian, gay, and bisexual adults in the United States. *American Journal of Public Health, 100,* 1946–1952.

McNally, E. B. (2009). The coming out process for lesbians and gay men. In *Center for Substance Abuse Treatment: A provider's introduction to substance abuse treatment for lesbian, gay, bisexual, and transgender individuals* (pp. 61–67). HHS Pub. No. (SMA) 09-4104. Rockville, MD: Department of Health and Human Services.

McWhirter, J. J., McWhirter, B. T., McWhirter, E. II., & McWhirter, R. J. (2007). *At risk youth: A comprehensive response for counselors, teachers, psychologists, and human service professionals.* Belmont, CA: Thomson Brooks/Cole.

National Alliance to End Homelessness. (2011). Snapshot of homelessness. Retrieved from http://www.endhomelessness.org/section/about_homelessness/snapshot_of_homeless

National Center on Family Homelessness. (2009). *America's youngest outcasts: State report card on child homelessness.* Newton, MA.

National Coalition for the Homeless (2006). Addiction disorders and homelessness. NCH Fact Sheet #6. Washington, DC.

National Coalition for the Homeless. (2009). *Substance abuse and homelessness.* Washington, DC.

National Coalition for the Homeless. (2010). *Hate crimes against the homeless: America's growing tide of violence.* Washington, DC.

National Institute on Drug Abuse. (2007a). *Preventing drug use among children and adolescents: A research based guide.* NIH Pub. No. 04-4212 (B). Rockville, MD: National Clearinghouse for Alcohol and Drug Information.

National Institute on Drug Abuse. (2007b). Message from the director: Women's health week. Bethesda, MD: U.S. Department of Health and Human Services.

National Institute on Drug Abuse. (2010). *Monitoring the future survey: Overview of findings 2009.* Bethesda, MD: U.S. Department of Health and Human Services.

National Law Center. (2010). *Homeless and poverty in America.* Washington, DC.

Office on Disability (2010). Substance abuse and disabililty. Washington, DC: U.S. Department of Health & Human Services.

Partnership for a Drug-Free America. (2009). *Partnership attitude tracking study (PATS).* Princeton, NJ: Robert Wood Johnson Foundation.

Putnam, M. L. (2007). Crisis intervention with adolescents with learning disabilities. In J. Carlson & J. Lewis (Eds.), *Counseling the adolescent: Individual, family, and school interventions* (pp. 61–104). Denver: Love.

Rawson, R. A., & McCann, M. J. (n.d.). The matrix model of intensive outpatient treatment: A guideline developed for the behavioral health recovery management project. The Behavioral Health Recovery Management Project: Los Angeles, CA.

Reivich, K. (2010, Mar/Apr). Building resilience in youth: The Penn resiliency program. *National Association of School Psychologists, Communique.*

Sankar-Gomes, A., & Malley, J. (2006). *Assessing school climate with the Beck/Basic quality school survey: A survey of the Plainville School District.* Unpublished manuscript, Department of Counseling & Family Therapy, Central Connecticut State University, New Britain, Connecticut.

Shillington, A. M., Lehman, S., Clapp, L., Hovell, M. F., Sipan, C., & Blumberg, E. J. (2005). Parental monitoring: Can it continue to be protective among high-risk adolescents? *Journal of Child & Adolescent Substance Abuse, 15,* 1–15.

Smart, J. (2009). *Disability, society, and the individual.* Austin, TX: Pro-ed.

Stevens, S. (2006, January). *Women and substance abuse: A gendered perspective.* Paper presented at the Fifth Annual Women's Mental Health Symposium, Tucson, AZ.

Stevens, S. J., Andrade, R. A. C., & Ruiz, B. S. (2009). Women and substance abuse: Gender, age, and cultural considerations. *Journal of Ethnicity in Substance Abuse, 8,* 341–358.

Substance Abuse and Mental Health Services Administration. (2006a). *Prevention of alcohol misuse for older adults.* Rockville, MD: Older Americans Technical Assistance Center.

Substance Abuse and Mental Health Services Administration. (2006b). *Results from the 2005 National Survey on Drug Use and Health: National findings.* DHHS Pub. No. (SMA) 06-4194, NSDUH Series H-30. Rockville, MD: Office of Applied Studies. Retrieved from www.oas.samhsa.gov

Substance Abuse and Mental Health Services Administration. (2009). *Results from the 2008 national survey on drug use and health: National findings.* HHS Pub. No. (SMA) 09-4434, NSDUH Series H-36. Rockville, MD: Substance Abuse and Mental Health Services Administration, Office of Applied Studies.

Substance Abuse and Mental Health Services Administration. (2011). Results from the 2010 National Survey on Drug Use and Health: Summary of

National Findings, NSDUH Series H-41, HHS Pub. No. (SMA) 11-4658. Rockville, MD.

Substance abuse treatment for disabled persons. (2006). *Counselor, 7,* 62–66.

Sussman, S., Skara, S., & Ames, S. L. (2008). Substance abuse among adolescents. *Substance Use & Misuse, 43,* 1802–1828.

Szapocznik, J., Tolan, P., Sambrano, S., & Schwartz, S. J. (2007). Preventing youth substance abuse: An overview. In P. Tolan, J. Szapocznik, & S. Sambrano (Eds.), *Preventing youth substance abuse: Science-based programs for children and adolescents* (pp. 3–17). Washington, DC: American Psychological Association.

United States Conference of Mayors. (2008). Hunger and homelessness survey: A status report on hunger and homelessness in America's cities. Retrieved from http://www.usmayors.org/uscm/home.asp

U.S. Bureau of the Census. (2008). *Population profile of the United States.* Washington, DC: U.S. Government Printing Office.

U.S. Department of Health and Human Services. (2005, September). *National summit on recovery: Conference report.* Rockville, MD: SAMHSA/CSAT. Retrieved from http://pfr.samhsa.gov/docs/Summit-Rpt.pdf

West, S. L., Graham, C. W., & Cifu, D. X. (2009). Prevalence of persons with disabilities in alcohol/other drug treatment in the United States. *Alcoholism Treatment Quarterly, 27,* 242–252.

West, S. L., Luck, R. S., & Capps, C. F. (2007). Physical inaccessibility negatively impacts the treatment participation of persons with disabilities. *Addictive Behaviors, 32,* 1494–1497.

White, W. L., & Kilbourne, J. (2006). American women and addiction: A cultural double bind. *Counselor, 7,* 46–50.

Winkel, B. (2011). Autism and Substance Abuse. Treatment Solutions Network. Retrieved from www.treatmentsolutionsnetwork.com/blog/

Chapter 12

Abe-Kim, J., Takeuchi, D. T., Hong, S., Zane, N., Sue, S., Spencer, M. S., & Alegria, M. (2007). Use of mental health-related services among immigrant and US-born Asian Americans: Results from the National Latino and Asian American study. *American Journal of Public Health, 97*(1), 91–98. doi:10.2105/AJPH.2006.098541

Alarcon, R. D., & Ruiz, P. (2010). Hispanic Americans. In P. Ruiz & A. Primm (Eds.), *Disparities in psychiatric care: Clinical and cross-cultural perspectives* (pp. 30–39). Baltimore, MD: Lippincott Williams and Wilkens.

Alvarez, A. N., Juang, L., & Liang, C. T. H. (2006). Asian Americans and racism: When bad things happen to "Model Minorities." *Cultural Diversity and Ethnic Minority Psychology, 12,* 477–492.

Banks, J., & McGee Banks, C. (Eds). (2010). *Multicultural education: Issues and perspectives* (4th ed.). New York: Wiley.

Bell-Tolliver, L., Burgess, R., & Brock, L. J. (2009). African American therapists working with African American families: An exploration of the strengths perspective in therapy. *Journal of Marital and Family Therapy, 35*(3), 293–307.

Blume, A. W., & Escobedo, C. J. (2005). Best practices for substance abuse treatment among American Indians and Alaskan Natives: Review and critique. In E. H. Hawkins & R. D. Walker (Eds), *Best practices in behavioral health services for American Indian and Alaskan Natives* (Draft). Portland, OR: One Sky National Resource Center for American Indian and Alaskan Native Substance Abuse Prevention and Treatment Services.

Centers for Disease Control and Prevention. (2009). *Health United States, 2008.* Table 61. Retrieved from http://www.cdc.gov/nchs/data/hus/hus08.pdf

Centers for Disease Control and Prevention. (2011). *CDC Health Disparities and Inequalities Report United States, 2011. MMWR, 60* (Suppl). Retrieved from http://www.cdc.gov/mmwr/pdf/other/su6001.pdf

Chang, T., & Subramaniam, P. R. (2008). Asian and Pacific Islander American men's help-seeking: Cultural values and beliefs, gender roles, and racial stereotypes. *International Journal of Men's Health, 7*(2), 121–136.

Chen, S. X., & Mak, W. S. (2008). Seeking professional help: Etiology of beliefs about mental illness across cultures. *Journal of Counseling Psychology, 55*(4), 442–450.

Chen, W. W. (2006). Drug abuse prvention research for Asian and Pacific Islander Americans. In Z. Sloboda & W. J. Bukowski (Eds), *Handbook of drug prevention: Theory, science and practice.* Social Research, Part V (pp. 411–426). San Francisco: Jossey-Bass.

Chou, R. S., & Feagin, J. R. (2008). *The myth of the model minority: Asian Americans facing racism.* St. Paul, MN: Paradigm Publishing.

Cleveland, J., Feinberg, M. E., & Greenberg, M. T. (2010). Protective families in hi-and-low risk environments: Implications for adolescent substance use. *Journal of Youth Adolescence, 39,* 114–126. doi: 10.1007/s10964-009-9395-y

Constantine, M. G., & Sue, D. W. (2007). Perceptions of racial microaggressions among Black supervisees in cross-racial dyads. *Journal of Counseling Psychology, 54,* 142–153.

Costello, D. M., Swendsen, J., Rose, J. S., & Dierker, L. C. (2008). Risk and protective factors associated with trajectories of depressed mood from adolescence to early adulthood. *Journal of Consulting and Clinical Psychology, 76*(2), 173–183.

de Arellano, M. A., & Danielson, C. K. (2005). *Culturally-modified trauma-focused treatment (CM-TFT). Treatment manual.* Charleston, SC: National Crime Victims Research & Treatment Center, Medical University of South Carolina.

Edlin, G., & Golanty, E. (2010). *Health and wellness. Achievement gap.* Retrieved from Sudbury, MA: Jones and Bartlett.

Education Week and Harvard Graduate School of Education. (2001, May). http://www.edweek.org/ew/issues/achievement-gap/

Falk, D. E., & Hiller-Sturmhöfel, S. (2006). *An epidemiological analysis of co-occurring alcohol and tobacco use disorders: Findings from the National Epidemiological survey on alcohol and related conditions.* National Institute on Alcohol Abuse and Alcoholism.

Furman, R., Negi, N. J., Iwamoto, D. K., Rowan, D., Shukraft, A., & Gragg, J. (2009). Social work practice with Latinos: Key issues for social workers. *Social Work, 54*(2), 167–174.

Garza, Y., & Watts, R. E. (2010). Filial therapy and Hispanic values: Common ground for culturally sensitive helping. *Journal of Counseling and Development, 88,* 108–113.

Goffman, E. (1963). *Stigma: Notes on the management of a spoiled identity.* Upper Saddle River, NJ: Prentice Hall.

Guofang, L., & Wang, L. (2008). *Model minority myth revisited.* Charlotte, NC: Information Age.

Hall, E. T. (1984). *The dance of life: The other dimension of time.* Anchor Books: New York.

Hardaway, C. R., & McLoyd, V. C. (2009). Escaping poverty and securing middle class status: How race and SES shape mobility for African Americans during transition to adulthood. *Journal of Youth and Adolescence, 38,* 242–256.

Hawkins, E. H., & Walker, R. D. (Eds.). (2005). *Best practices in behavioral health services for American Indian and Alaskan Natives* (Draft). Portland, OR: One Sky National Resource Center for American Indian and Alaskan Native Substance Abuse Prevention and Treatment Services.

Indian Health Service. (2006). *Trends in Indian health.* Washington, DC: U.S. Department of Health and Human Services, Public Health Service.

Juthani, N. V., & Mishra, A. S. (2009). Asian Americans and their families: Focus on acculturation stressors. In Y. C. Rho, F. G. Lu, & K. M. Sanders (Eds,), *Handbook of mental health and acculturation in Asian American families* (pp. 179–193). New York: Human Press.

Karch, D. L., Dahlberg, L. L., & Patel, N. M. (2007). *Surveillance for Violent Deaths—National Violent Death Reporting System, 16 States, 2007.* Centers for Disease Control and Prevention. Retrieved from http://www.cdc.gov/mmwr/preview/mmwrhtml/ss5904a1.htm

Kochanek, K. D., Xu, J., Murphy, S. L., Miniño, A. M., & Kung, H. C. (2011, March). *National Vital Statistics Report, 59*(4). U.S. Department of Health and Human Services. DHHS Publication No. (PHS) 2011-1120.

Kyomugisha, F. G. (2006). HIV, African American women are high risk in heterosexual relationships. *Journal of African American Studies, 10*(2), 38–50.

Le, C.N. (2011). *"14 important statistics about Asian Americans" Asian-nation: The landscape of Asian America.* Retrieved from http://www.asian-nation.org/14-statistics.shtml

Le, T. N. (2009). Acculturation factors and substance abuse use among Asian American youth. *The Journal for Primary Research, 30*(3–4), 453–473.

Lewis-Fernandez, R., Das, A. K., Alfonso, C., Weisman, M. M., & Olfson, M. (2005). Depression in U.S. Hispanics: Diagnostic and management considerations in family practice. *Journal of the American Board of Family Medicine, 18*(4), 282–296.

Martinez, C. R. (2006). Effects of differential family acculturation on Latino adolescent substance use. *Family Relations, 55,* 306–317.

McLoyd, V. C., Hill, N., & Dodge, K. A. (Eds.). (2005). Ecological and cultural diversity in African American family life. *In African American family life: Ecological and cultural diversity.* New York: Guilford.

Morning Edition. (2008, May). *American Indian boarding schools haunt many.* National Public Radio. Retrieved from http://www.npr.org/templates/story/story.php?storyId=16516865

Mosher, C. J., & Akins, S. (2007). Drugs and drug use: *The control of consciousness alteration.* Thousand Oaks, CA: Sage Publishing.

National Institute on Drug Abuse (NIDA) (2011). NIDA News: Research training opportunities for young investigators. Retrieved from www.drugabuse .gov/researchtraining/traininghome/html

Palmer, R. T., Davis, R. J., Moore, J. L., & Hilton, A. A. (2010). A nation at risk: Increasing college participation persistence among African American males to stimulate U.S. global perspectives. *Journal of African American Males in Education, 1*(2), 105–124.

Pamber, A. (2010, February). High school graduates low where most American Indian and Alaskan Natives live. *Diverse Issues in Higher Education.* Retrieved from http://diverseeducation.com/article/ 13555

Peregoy, J. J., & Gloria, A. M. (2007). Applying multicultural guidelines to American Indian/Alaskan Native populations. In M. G. Constantine (Ed.), *Clinical practice with people of color: A guide to becoming clinically competent* (pp. 61–94). New York: Columbia University Press.

Pew Hispanic Center. (2011). *Hispanics account for more than half of the nation's growth in the past decade.* Pew Research Center. Retrieved from http:// pewhispanic.org/reports/report.php?ReportID=140

Pollard, D. T. (2011). *Blackout: Black unemployment rate rises as overall rate falls.* Retrieved from http://pollardpost.blogspot.com/2011/04/ blackout-black-unemployment-rate-rises.html

Ponterato, J. G., Casas, M. J., Suzuki, L., & Alexander, C. M. (Eds.). (2009). *Handbook of multicultural counseling.* Thousand Oaks, CA: Sage.

Raphel, S. (2008). Eye on Washington kinship care and the situation for grandparents. *Journal of Child and Adolescent Psychiatric Nursing, 21*(2), 118–120.

Richardson, T. Q., Bethea, A. R., Hayling, C. C., & Williamson-Taylor, C. (2009). African Amercian and Afro-Caribbean identity development: Theory and practice implications. In J. G. Ponterato, M. J. Casas, L. Suzuki, & C. M. Alexander (Eds.), *Handbook of multicultural counseling* (pp. 227–240). Thousand Oaks, CA: Sage.

Robertson, T. (2007, October). Alcohol exposure affects generations on Indian reservatoins. Minnesota Public Radio. Retrieved from http://minnesota.publicradio.org/display/web/2007/10/17/ indianfasd

Rosario-Sim, M. G., & O'Connell, K. A. (2009). Depression and language acculturation correlate with smoking among older Asian American adolescents in New York City. *Public Health Nursing, 26,* 532–542. doi: 10.1111/j.1525-1446.2009.00811.x

Saint-Jean, G., Martinez, C. A., & Crandall, L. A. (2008). Psychosocial mediators of the impact of acculturation on adolescent substance abuse. *Journal of Immigrant and Minority Health, 10*(2), 187–195. doi: 10.1007/s10903-007-9060-z

Smith-Adock, S., Daniels, M. H., Lee, S. M., Villaba, J. A., & Arce, N. (2006). Culturally responsive school counseling for Hispanic/Latino students and families: The need for bilingual school counselors. *Professional School Counseling, 10,* 92–101.

Spillane, N. S., & Smith, G. T. (2010). Individual differences in problem drinking among tribal members from one First Nation community. *Alcoholism: Clinical and Experimental Research, 34,* 1985–1992. doi: 10.1111/j.1530-0277.2010.01288.x

Substance Abuse and Mental Health Services Administration. (2010). *Results from the 2009 National Survey on Drug Use and Health: Volume I. Summary of National Findings* (Office of Applied Studies, NSDUH Series H-38A, HHS Publication No. SMA 10-4586 Findings). Rockville, MD.

Sue, D. W., & Sue, D. (2007, 4th). *Counseling the culturally different: Theory and practice.* New York: Wiley.

Suicide Prevention Action Network USA. (2011). *Suicide among Asian Americans/Pacific Islanders.* Retrieved from http://www.sprc .org/library/asian.pi.facts.pdf

Thomas, L. R. (2005). Journeys of the Circle Project, Seattle Indian Health Board; Addictive Behaviors Research Center, Department of Psychology, University of Washington, Seattle.

Trimble, J. E. (2010a). Counseling research with ethnocultural populations. In J. Ponterotto, J. M. Casasas, L. Suzuki, & C. M. Alexander (Eds.), *Handbook of multicultural counseling* (pp. 147–160). Thousand Oaks, CA: Sage.

Trimble, J. E. (2010b). The virtues of cultural resonance, competence and relational collaboration with Native American Indian communities: A synthesis of counseling and psychotherapy literature. *The Counseling Psychologist, 38,* 243–256.

Trinh, N., Rho, Y. C., Lu, F. G., & Sanders, K. M. (Eds.). (2009). *Handbook of mental health and acculturation in Asian American Families.* Springer, NY, NY: Human Press.

U.S. Census Bureau. (2006). *2006 American Community Survey*. Retrieved from http://factfinder.census.gov/homes/staff/main

U.S. Census Bureau. (2010). *Statistical abstract: Population*. Washington, DC: U.S. Bureau of Census. Retrieved from http://www.census.gov/compendia/statab/cats/population.html

U.S. Census Bureau. (2011). *Facts for features: African American history month*. Retrieved from census.gov/newsroom/releases/archives/facts-for-features-special-editions/cb11ff-01.html

U.S. Department of Health and Human Services, Office of Health Service Policy. (2007). *Data on health and well-being of American Indians, Alaskan Natives, and other Native Americans data catalog* (HHS Contract: 233-02-0087). Retrieved from http://aspe.hha.gov/hsp/06/catolog-AI-N-NA/

U.S. Department of Health and Human Services (HHS). (2011). Testimony of Eric Broderick. Retrieved from www.hhs.gov/asi/testify/2009/09/t20090910a.html

U.S. Department of Justice, Bureau of Justice Statistics. (2011). *Criminal victimization in the United States, 2008 statistical tables* (NCJ 231173). Retrieved from http://bjs.ojp.usdoj.gov/content/pub/pdf/cvus0805.pdf

Williams, J. (2011). *Racial disparities in the criminal justice system*. North Carolina Bar Association. Retrieved from http://criminaljustice.ncbar.org/newsletters/criminaljusticefeb11/racialdisparities.aspx

Witko, T. M. (Ed.). (2006). *Mental Health care for urban Indians: Clinical insights from Native practitioners*. Washington DC: American Psychological Association.

Chapter 13

Botvin, G. J., & Griffin, K. W. (2007). School-based programs to prevent alcohol, tobacco, and other drug use. *International Review of Psychiatry, 19*(6), 607–615. doi:10.1080/09540260701797753

Botvin Life Skills Training. (n.d.). *Frequently asked questions*. Retrieved from http://www.lifeskillstraining.com/faq.php

Capuzzi, D., & Stauffer, M. D. (2012). *Foundations of addictions counseling* (2nd ed.). Upper Saddle River, NJ: Pearson Education.

Council for Accreditation of Counseling and Related Educational Programs. (2010). *2009 standards*. Retrieved from http://www.cacrep.org/template/index.cfm

Drug Abuse Resistance Education (D.A.R.E.). (2006). *A longitudinal evaluation of the new curricula for the D.A.R.E. middle (7th grade) and high school (9th grade) programs: Take charge of your life—four year progress report*. Inglewood, CA: Author. Retrieved from http://www.dare.com/home/about_dare.asp

Dusenbury L., Brannigan, R., Hansen, W. B., Walsh, J., & Falco, M. (2005). Quality of implementation: Developing measures crucial to understanding the diffusion of preventive interventions. *Health Education Research, 20*(3), 308–313. doi:10.1093/her/cyg134

Griffin, K. W., Botvin, G. J., & Nichols, T. R. (2006). Effects of a school-based drug abuse prevention program for adolescents on HIV risk behavior in young adulthood. *Prevention Science, 7*(1), 103–112. doi:10.1007/s11121-006-0025-6.

Miller, G. (2010). *Learning the language of addiction counseling*. Hoboken, NJ: Wiley.

National Center on Addiction and Substance Abuse at Columbia University (CASA). (2006). *Program demonstration*. Retrieved from http://www.casacolumbia.org/absolutenm/templates/AboutCASA.aspx?articleid=203&zoneid=26

National Center on Addiction and Substance Abuse at Columbia University (CASA). (2007). *CASASTART overview*. Retrieved from http://casastart.org/files/folders/guides/entry8.aspx

National Center on Addiction and Substance Abuse at Columbia University (CASA). (2010). *CASASTART—About us*. Retrieved from http://casastart.org/

National Health Promotion Associates. (2010). *Botvin Life Skills Training*. Retrieved from http://www.lifeskillstraining.com

National Institute on Drug Abuse (NIDA). (1984). *Drug abuse and drug abuse research*. DHHS Pub. No. (ADM) 85-1372. Washington, DC: Department of Health and Human Services.

Okamoto, S. K., LeCroy, C. W., Tann, S. S., Rayle, A. D., Kulis, S., Dustman, P., & Berceli, D. (2006). The implications of ecologically based assessment for primary prevention with indigenous youth populations. *The Journal of Primary Preventions, 27*(2), 155–170. doi:10.1007/s10935-005-0016-6

Pan, W., & Bai, H. (2009). A multivariate approach to a meta-analytic review of the effectiveness of the D.A.R.E. program. *International Journal of Environmental Research and Public Health, 6*, 267–277. doi: 10.2290/ijer[h6010267

Payne, A. A., Gottfredson, D. C., & Gottfredson, G. D. (2006). School predictors of the intensity of implementation of school-based prevention programs: Results from a national study. *Prevention Science, 7*(2), 225–237. doi:10.1007/s11121-006-0029-2

RAND Corporation. (2005). *Promising Practices Network on children, families and communities: About PPN*. Santa Monica, CA: Author. Retrieved from http://www.promisingpractices.net/about_ppn.asp

Redmond, C., Spoth, R. L., Shin, C., Schainker, L. M., Greenberg, M. T., & Frienberg, M. (2009). Long term protective factor outcomes of evidence-based interventions implemented by community teams through community-university partnership. *Primary Prevention, 30*, 513–530. doi:10.1007/s10935-009-0189-5

Roe, S., & Becker, J. (2005). Drug prevention with vulnerable young people: A review. *Drugs: Education, Prevention, and Policy, 12*(2), 85–99. doi:10.1080/0968763042000322639

Rosenbaum, D. P. (2007). Just say no to D.A.R.E. *Criminology and Public Policy, 6*(4), 815–824. doi:10.1111/j.1745-9133.2007.00474.x

Saxe, L., Kadushin, C., Tighe, E., Beveridge, A. A., Livert, A., Brodsky, A., & Rindskopf, D. (2006). Community-based prevention programs in the war on drugs: Findings from the "Fighting Back" demonstration. *Journal of Drug Issues, 36*(2), 263–293.

Spoth, R. L., Clair, S., Shin, C., & Redmond, C. (2006). Long-term effects of universal preventive interventions on methamphetamine use among adolescents. *Archives of Pediatric & Adolescent Medicine, 160*, 876–882. doi:10.1001/archpedi.160.9.876

Spoth, R. L., Randall, G. K., Trudeau, L., Shin, C., & Redmond, C. (2008). Substance use outcomes 5½ years past baseline for partnership-based, family-school preventive interventions. *Drug and Alcohol Dependence, 96*, 57–68. doi:10.1016/j.drugalcdep.2008.01.023

Substance Abuse and Mental Health Services Administration (SAMHSA). (2010). *SAMHSA's national registry of evidence-based programs and practices.* Retrieved from http://nrepp.samhsa.gov

U.S. Department of Education. (2007). *Office of safe and drug-free schools.* Retrieved from http://www2.ed.gov/about/offices/list/osdfs/index.html

U.S. Department of Health and Human Services, Centers for Disease Control and Prevention. (2009). Youth risk behavior surveillance—United States, 2009. *Morbidity and Mortality Weekly Report, 59*(SS-5). (ISSN: 1546-0738). Retrieved from http://www.cdc.gov/mmwr/pdf/ss/ss5905.pdf

Van Wormer, K., & Davis, D. R. (2008). *Addiction treatment: A strengths perspective* (2nd ed.). Belmont, CA: Brooks/Cole.

VanderWaal, C. J., Powell, L. M., Terry-McElrath, Y. M., Bao, Y., & Flay, B. R. (2005). Community and school drug prevention strategy prevalence: Differential effects by setting and substance. *The Journal of Primary Prevention, 26*(4), 299–320. doi:10.1007/s10935-005-5390-6

Wang, M. Q., Matthew, R. F., Bellamy, N., & James, S. (2005). A structural model of substance use pathways among minority youth. *American Journal of Health Behavior, 29*(6), 531–541.

INDEX